SYMPHONIES
& OTHER
ORCHESTRAL WORKS
Selections from Essays in Musical Analysis

SYMPHONIES
& OTHER
ORCHESTRAL WORKS
Selections from Essays in Musical Analysis

DONALD FRANCIS TOVEY

DOVER PUBLICATIONS, INC.
Mineola, New York

Bibliographical Note

This Dover edition, first published in 2015, is an unabridged republication of *Symphonies and Other Orchestral Works: Essays in Musical Analysis,* originally published by Oxford University Press, London, in 1981.

Library of Congress Cataloging-in-Publication Data

Tovey, Donald Francis, 1875–1940.
  Symphonies and other orchestral works : selections from essays in musical analysis / Donald Francis Tovey.
    p. cm.
  "This Dover edition, first published in 2015, is an unabridged republication of Symphonies and Other Orchestral Works: Essays in Musical Analysis, originally published by Oxford University Press, London, in 1981."
  ISBN-13: 978-0-486-78452-6
  ISBN-10: 0-486-78452-5
  1. Symphonies—Analysis, appreciation. 2. Orchestral music—Analysis, appreciation. I. Title.

MT125.T69 2015
784.2015—dc23

2014025107

Manufactured in the United States by Courier Corporation
78452501   2015
www.doverpublications.com

CONTENTS

Introduction   1

J. S. BACH

Overture in C major, for orchestra   21
Orchestral suite in D major, No. 3   24
Overture in B minor for flute and strings   27
Prelude to Church Cantata No. 29, *Wir danken Dir, Gott*   29

C. P. E. BACH

Symphony in D major   31

BEETHOVEN

Symphony in C major, No. 1, Op. 21   36
Symphony in D major, No. 2, Op. 36   40
Symphony in E flat major (Sinfonia Eroica), No. 3, Op. 55   44
Symphony in B flat major, No. 4, Op. 60   49
Symphony in C minor, No. 5, Op. 67   53
Symphony in F major (Sinfonia Pastorale), No. 6, Op. 68   59
Symphony in A major, No. 7, Op. 92   72
Symphony in F major, No. 8, Op. 93   76
Symphony in D minor, No. 9, Op. 125. Its place in musical art   83
Overtures *Leonora*, Nos. 2 and 3   128
Overture *Leonora*, No. 1   140
Overture *Fidelio*   141
Overture *Coriolan*, Op. 62   143
Overture *Egmont*, Op. 84   145
Overture for the name-day of Kaiser·Franz, Op. 114   147
Overture *Zur Weihe des Hauses*, Op. 124   150

BERLIOZ

Symphonie Fantastique, Op. 14   164
Harold in Italy, symphony with viola obbligato, Op. 16   171
Overture *King Lear*   179
Overture *Le Corsair*   183
Overture *Béatrice et Bénédict*   186

BRAHMS

Symphony in C minor, No. 1, Op. 68   188
Symphony in D major, No. 2, Op. 73   199
Symphony in F major, No. 3, Op. 90   211
Symphony in E minor, No. 4, Op. 98   219
Serenade in D major, Op. 11 (for orchestra)   227
Serenade in A major, Op. 16 (for small orchestra)   235
Variations for orchestra on a theme by Haydn, Op. 56a   242
Akademische Festouvertüre, Op. 80   245
Tragic Overture, Op. 81   247
A further note on Brahms's *Tragic Overture* (Op. 81)   250

BRUCKNER

Romantic symphony in E flat major, No. 4   253
Symphony in A major, No. 6   263

DVOŘÁK

Symphony in D major, No. 1 [now No. 6], Op. 60   268
Symphony in D minor, No. 2 [now No. 7], Op. 70   273
Symphony in F major, No. 3 [now No. 5], Op. 76   280
Symphony in E minor, [now No. 9], Op. 95 (from the New World)   285
Symphonic variations on an original theme, Op. 78   290
Scherzo Capriccioso, Op. 66   293

ELGAR

Symphony in E flat, No. 2, Op. 63   297
Falstaff, symphonic study, Op. 68   304
Variations for orchestra, Op. 36   317
Overture *Cockaigne*, Op. 40   320
Concert overture, *In the South* (Alassio), Op. 50   322
Introduction and allegro for strings (quartet and orchestra), Op. 47   326

FRANCK

Symphony in D minor   329

HAYDN

Haydn the inaccessible   337
Symphony in G major, No. 88 (Letter 'V')   339
Symphony in G, No. 92 (Oxford)   342
Symphony in G major, No. 94 (Salomon, No. 5) (Surprise)   346
Symphony in C minor, No. 95 (Salomon, No. 9)   348

Symphony in B flat No. 98 (Salomon, No. 8)   349
Symphony in E flat, No. 99 (Salomon, No. 10)   355
Symphony in G major, No. 100 (Salomon, No. 11) (Military) 358
Symphony in D major, No. 101 (London, No. 11) (The
   Clock)   361
Symphony in B flat, No. 102 (Salomon, No. 12)   363
Symphony in E flat, No. 103 (Salomon, No. 1) (With the
   Drum Roll)   369
Symphony in D major, No. 104 (Salomon, No. 2)   373

GUSTAV HOLST

Ballet from *The Perfect Fool*, Op. 39   376
Fugal overture for orchestra   377

MAHLER

Symphony in G major, No. 4   379

MENDELSSOHN

Italian Symphony in A major, Op. 90   389
Overture *Melusine*   394
Overture *The Hebrides*   398
Overture *Calm Sea and Prosperous Voyage*   401
Overture *Ruy Blas*   402
Overture *A Midsummer-Night's Dream*   405
Incidental music to *A Midsummer-Night's Dream*   410
Scherzo in G minor for orchestra   417

MOZART

Serenade in D major, K. 250 (Haffner Serenade)   420
Symphony in D major, K. 297 (Paris Symphony)   424
Symphony in C major, K. 338   429
Symphony in C major, No. 36, K. 425 (Linz Symphony)   431
Note on Mozart's last three symphonies   434
Symphony in E flat, No. 39, K. 543   435
Symphony in G minor, No. 40, K. 550   439
Symphony in C major, No. 41, K. 551   443
Overture *Der Schauspieldirektor*   446
Overture *Le Nozze di Figaro*   447
Overture *Die Zauberflöte*   448
Overture *La Clemenza di Tito*   450
Overture *Così Fan Tutte*   451
Orchestral Dances   452
Masonic Dirge (K. 477)   453

SCHUBERT

Obiter Dicta
Symphony in B flat, No. 5 [now No. 7]   454
Symphony in C major, No. 7 [now No. 9]   456
Unfinished Symphony in B minor [now No. 8]   458
Entr'acte in B minor and Ballet in G major from *Rosamunde*   464
    468

SCHUMANN

Symphony in B flat major, No. 1, Op. 38   469
Symphony in E flat major, No. 3, Op. 97   477
Symphony in D minor, No. 4, Op. 120   480
Overture, Scherzo, and Finale, Op. 52   486
Overture to Byron's *Manfred*, Op. 115   489

SIBELIUS

Symphony in C major, No. 3, Op. 52   492
Symphony in E flat major, No. 5, Op. 82   496
Symphony in C major, No. 7, Op. 105   500
Tapiola, symphonic poem for full orchestra, Op. 112   503

SMETANA

Overture *The Bartered Bride*   506

RICHARD STRAUSS

Tone-Poem *Don Juan*, Op. 20   507

TCHAIKOVSKY

Symphony in E minor, No. 5, Op. 64   512
Pathetic Symphony in B minor, No. 6, Op. 74   519

VAUGHAN WILLIAMS

Pastoral Symphony   524
Overture *The Wasps*   529

WAGNER

Overture *Der Fliegende Holländer*   531
A *Faust* Overture   533
Prelude to Act III of *Tannhäuser* (Tannhäuser's Pilgrimage),
    in the original version   538
Introduction to *Tristan and Isolde*   540
Prelude to *The Master-Singers*   542
Siegfried Idyll   544
The Venusberg music (*Tannhäuser*)   548

WEBER

Overture *The Ruler of the Spirits*   550
Overture *Der Freischütz*   552
Overture *Euryanthe*   554
Overture *Oberon*   557

To

ROBERT CALVERLEY TREVELYAN

Dear Poet

These volumes must be dedicated to you. The dedication is the only part of them that has not profited by your suggestions as to grammar, syntax, punctuation, spelling, logical form, discoverable meaning, and such other negative decencies of prose as may be attained by a writer concerned only with music.

You have added much to your labours by your meticulous care not to interfere with anything that could charitably be construed as a feature of my style. The scholiast will (alas!) find these pages as unenlightened by Trevelyanese as he will find your poems free from any tendency to sink into musical analysis.

Now that I have profited by your help, my nobler instincts impel me to beg you not to give to the correction of other people's prose too much of the time that the Muses (at least five of them, for Terpsichore controls song as well as dance—I have just looked her up in Enc. Brit.) *intend you to devote to your own poetry. That is the claim which the General Reader has upon you. But to him I commend your example in that you have enabled (if not know-*

ingly permitted) me to advertise that these volumes have been read with unremitting attention by one who has not learnt musical notation, plays no instrument, and has not been heard by close friends of a quarter of a century to sing even in his bath.

Yours while these habits endure,

DONALD FRANCIS TOVEY

INTRODUCTION

THESE essays are programme notes written for the concert room. The reader will know better than to expect from such things a complete system of criticism. The duty of the writer of programme notes is that of counsel for the defence. If the defects of the works analysed are too notorious to be ignored, he must find what can be said in favour of keeping the work in the concert repertoire. A series of essays produced under such conditions cannot have a good cumulative effect. The writer cannot even vary his optimism by praising the work in hand at the expense of something he dislikes; that procedure often irritates the reader and may become extremely inconvenient when the writer has to change his point of view. (*Vide* Ruskin, *passim*.)

The present series of essays is then certainly not designed for continuous reading. Nor, on the other hand, can it pass for a work of reference. Here again its range is limited. Programme notes need not be confined to what can be digested in the concert-room, but they cannot take the form of a work of research. I have not, in fact, made any researches beyond occasionally verifying my quotations, where they are not better unverified.

The reader of these volumes will not find that works of equal importance always receive equivalent treatment, nor will he find any system in the selection of works. Some of the analyses, e.g. that on the Eroica Symphony, were written on occasions where there was no opportunity for musical quotations, which accordingly have been added afterwards, though the letterpress has not been expanded. Others again, such as the essays on the Ninth Symphony and the B minor Mass, were published some time before the concerts for which they were written, and have accordingly taken advantage of the opportunity for a fuller treatment of their subjects.

The essay on the Ninth Symphony has been reprinted several times, and I have accordingly thought fit to supplement it by a radically different kind of analysis,* the sort of précis-writing, which, as a result of my early experience as a pupil of Sir Hubert Parry, I expect from students of musical form. Its method underlies most of what I have written in these volumes, and I have used it elsewhere in my *Companion to the Art of Fugue* (Oxford University Press) and in my *Companion to Beethoven's Pianoforte Sonatas* (Assoc. Board of R.A.M. and R.C.M.). If such précis-writing constituted the whole of the contents of the present volumes, they would certainly amount to a work of reference; but I have no intention of producing such a work. It would defeat the object

* Not reprinted in this volume.

I have in view in including my précis of the Ninth Symphony: the object of inducing lovers of music to get at the bare musical facts by doing such précis-writing themselves; and so, by their own efforts and such other guidance as they can obtain, learning what is knowable about music as music, instead of indulging in abstruse fancies which can never be matters of knowledge.

The necessary optimism of these essays, monotonous though it be, is at all events honest. The programmes were those of my own concerts, where I had no reason to produce any music I disliked. No doubt my prejudices will appear in spite of my most diplomatic efforts. It will be evident that I do not like certain kinds of oiliness and slickness, however admirable the technique with which they are often associated. But nevertheless, like Sir Charles Stanford, I simply cannot help producing *Le Rouet d'Omphale* and *Phaëton*; 'they are so damned clever'. On the other hand, I do not consider clumsiness and other results of a defective technique as inherently noble. But my views as to musical form are unorthodox in some matters; and I am quite certain that the musical orthodoxy of my young days had no means whatever of knowing how far such composers as Schubert and Dvořák were right or wrong in their 'heavenly lengths'. I was not brought up in that orthodoxy. Parry's method of analysis taught me that no piece of music can be understood from *a priori* generalizations as to form, but that all music must be followed phrase by phrase as a process in time. It is very unlikely that this principle has been essentially violated in these volumes.

Few technical terms are used here, and those few are not used consistently. In my *Companion to Beethoven's Pianoforte Sonatas* I have discarded the term 'second subject', which has worked such havoc in our notions of sonata form and sonata themes. There is no prescribed number of subjects to a movement in sonata form; and the only correct description of what theorists mean by the 'second subjects' of such movements is 'second group', which has the merit of not necessarily implying themes at all. But these essays would need a thorough recasting before I could achieve a consistent substitution of the term 'second group' for 'second subject' throughout the volumes; and the use of the old-fashioned term has not been allowed to vitiate the analysis.

With the exception of the précis of the Ninth Symphony, none of these essays assumes any more technical knowledge than is likely to be picked up in the ordinary course of concert-going by a listener who can read the musical quotations or recognize them when played. But even the simplest musical terminology is in a very unscientific state in all languages, and the legal profession itself is not richer than music in terms that have a meaning in ordinary language widely different from their technical meaning. Accordingly I add here an explanation of the terms that are used in a musical sense in these volumes. A musical dictionary will hardly serve the reader's purpose, for my terms are apt to bear a Pickwickian sense as well.

Key, key relations, and tonality. 'Key' is a term primarily applicable to the music of the eighteenth and nineteenth centuries, and to such later music as has not revolted from what the term implies. When it is possible to say that a piece or passage of music is in a certain key, the statement is aesthetically equivalent to saying that the perspective of a picture is related to a certain vanishing-point. 'Tonality' is the art or system of such key perspective; and 'key relations' are facts concerning areas of the whole composition which are large enough to have a key of their own. Statements about the character of a key in itself are of interest mainly to psychologists, and the psychologist is at the mercy of a large mass of nonsense and malobservation thrust upon him by obsolescent musical theories. The true interest in the character of a key taken by itself is of the same order as that of number-forms and colours—the various ways in which people visualize the letters of the alphabet and the Arabic numerals. Beethoven thought B minor a 'black' key; I find it a rather light brown. Beethoven said that the key of A flat was 'barbarous'; yet he used it often, and almost always in a particularly amiable lyric vein. The strongest subjective fancy as to the character of a key in itself is annihilated by the slightest contact with other associations or with actuality. Most of Beethoven's work in the key of A flat is in the character that key assumes in relation to C minor. If you know enough about keys to name them at all you can hardly escape relating them to C. Key relations are among the most powerful and accurate means of expression in music. The reader who wishes to test these essays by closer technical inquiry will find the facts on which I rely in two publications: my article on 'Harmony' in the fourteenth edition of the *Encyclopaedia Britannica*, and my Introduction to the *Companion to Beethoven's Pianoforte Sonatas*.

I will attempt to summarize the theory in more popular style here, at some loss to cogency and accuracy. Readers who play any instrument will have encountered the names of keys and the dogmas of theorists often enough to welcome any chance of relief from a load of traditional mystification. Other readers may skim lightly over what may or may not convey a meaning to them. I cannot be sure how far the facts of tonality can become as vivid to the listener who does not know the names of keys as they are to musicians. The difficulty of describing them is no ground for doubt as to their value for the layman. It is not the difficulty of describing red to the colour-blind: it is the difficulty of describing red to anybody; you can only point to red things and hope that other people see them as you do. It is even more like trying to describe the taste of a peach; and, as a person with no pretensions to an expert palate, I doubt whether my most thorough researches in tonality can approach the august indefinables and incommunicables of the expert wine-taster.

The *tonic* is the horizon, or vanishing-point, of any piece of music that can be said to have the harmonic perspective which we call key. There are two modes of key, major and minor. The reader may rest satisfied with his familiar experience of these modes; the scientific definition of familiar sensations may prevent those who can follow it from talking nonsense, but does not make the sensations more vivid. Let us therefore keep this discussion on the plane of descriptive analogy. The kind of tonality which we are now discussing is not that of mere melody, but is the result of a long history of harmony, or rather counterpoint: that is to say, the combination of several simultaneous melodies. The chords produced at each moment of such a combination will differ in their acoustic and physiological effects. If the listener takes no interest in the sequence of events, his estimate of each chord will have purely physiological and acoustic criteria; all chords that irritate the ear by their acoustic 'beats' will be classed as discords, and the absence of beats will be the only criterion of concord. This primitive criterion survives to the present day in the terms 'perfect' and 'imperfect' concords, though for the last four centuries the naïve Western listener would find the bareness of a music confined to perfect concords harsh to a degree hardly surpassable by constant discord. The art of counterpoint took some five centuries to evolve into maturity; and the criteria of its Golden Age, the sixteenth century, differ so widely from those of the eighteenth and later centuries that it is inconvenient to base our theory of tonality on their foundation. Palestrina's modes are not quite what we call keys, though musicians are beginning to realize that a study of them is essential to a correct view of tonality. They are like paintings in which the draughtsmanship of figures and details is often impressively solid, but the horizon is different for each item.

Note, however, throughout this argument, that there is a radical difference between pictorial perspective and musical tonality. Perspective is a science which exists whether art chooses to use it or not; whereas tonality is wholly the product of musical art. This makes it all the more remarkable that classical tonality, including that of the musical primitives, should by its purely artistic coherence have dominated classical music almost as long as perspective has dominated Western painting. Musical theorists can hardly be blamed for the wish to found a system of classical harmony on an acoustic basis equivalent to the scientific basis of perspective. It is a hopeless task; and the failure of all such attempts may serve to convince us that the foundations of an art can never be identical with those of a science, however much works of art may use material which is capable of scientific analysis. But the truth about a work of art cannot be contrary to scientific truth. The facts of musical harmony cannot contradict the facts of acoustics, though the terms concord and discord soon show themselves to have acquired musical implications which pure acoustics can give no means of knowing. Optical perspective is a comparatively simple region of science, concerned with sensations which we have learnt to regard as immediate, but which are in reality quite interesting intellectual habits. And such a compound of immediate sensations with intellectual analysis already amounts to an aesthetic pleasure. The modern painter who refuses to let his art be dominated by optical science may find in the history of music moral support for his revolt. The atonal composer may get into trouble when, finding his atonal resources lacking in contrast, he tries to effect a harmonious relation between the twentieth century and the sixteenth. The difficulty lies in the nature of his art, not in any external nature; and the painter who finds that he must be careful how he mixes a scientific with an unscientific perspective is probably in no essentially different position from the modern composer.

Whatever reservations may be necessary in comparing tonality with perspective, I can find no other analogy equally clear or equally trustworthy, and I shall continue to use it without scruple.

The *dominant* of a scale is its fifth note reckoned upwards from the tonic, as G from C. With harmonized music, its chord is normally major, even when the mode of the key is minor. This major chord is the normal penultimate chord of a full close. Consequently, if a major triad has not been previously established as a tonic, you cannot harp very long upon it without arousing a suspicion that it is really a dominant to the key a fifth below—a suspicion which becomes certainty when a seventh is added to the chord. Hence the almost proverbial importance of the 'dominant seventh'. The dominant governs the tonic as a transitive verb governs its object. 'Dominant preparation' is a convenient term for the process of arousing expectancy by harping upon the dominant of a key; and one of the most important lessons that students of music, whether scholars or composers, need to learn is that which will teach them to recognize when a major key is really a key and when it is only a dominant. On this point most text-books are uninformative, and many widely accepted commentaries definitely unsound. The analogy of perspective may be made to give further light on tonality if we leave the art of painting and bring in the elements of time and movement which are so essential to music. A picture with more than one vanishing point is out of drawing as a whole; but in real life the vanishing point moves with the movements of the spectator. Most compositions in classical tonality end in the key in which they began; this being the obvious way to secure unity and finality in that category. But they often visit other keys, and this not merely by the way but in such a fashion as to carry the listener's tonal sense away from the original tonic and establish a new tonic with a complete set of relations of its own. The harmonic perspective is not that of a 'primitive' painting in which different objects, each solidly drawn in itself, have different horizons; it is that of a space in which we ourselves move from object to object. On this analogy you may call the tonic the listener's point of view and the dominant the vanishing point. This gives a good idea of the effect of harping on the dominant as a means of fixing the position of an expected tonic.

In these essays the term 'dominant' sometimes means the dominant of a key, and sometimes an established key on a tonic which is the dominant of the main tonic. Latterly I have found the terms 'home dominant' and 'home tonic' useful for showing when I am referring to the main key of the work or movement.

The 'subdominant' is usually described as the note or chord below the dominant. Historically and harmonically, the correct notion is that of the fifth below the tonic, as F downwards from C; and the illuminating term would be 'anti-dominant'. As a foreign key, it is the key to which the home-tonic is dominant; and beginners in composition are apt, like some seventeenth-century pioneers of tonality, to upset their tonic by a top-heavy subdominant introduced too early in a short piece. The effect of the subdominant is inevitably the opposite to that of the dominant. Stepping on to or into the dominant is an active measure like walking towards the vanishing point; subsiding into the subdominant indicates recession and repose. When the tonic is minor, the change of key to the subdominant means changing the home-tonic chord from minor to major, with an effect necessarily pathetic, since the bright major chord instantly shows itself as an illusion, being no tonic, but the threshold of a darker minor key. The subdominant has a solemn effect as penultimate chord in 'plagal cadences'. In all probability it was the Lost Chord which the weary and uneasy organist failed to find again after stumbling upon the Sound of a Great Amen. One chord does not make a cadence any more than one syllable makes an Amen; and perhaps the organist often played the Lost Chord in the wrong context without recognizing it again.

As a technical term in music, the word 'modulation' means change of key, and is used in these essays in no other sense. From your home tonic you can modulate easily to five directly related keys. The direct relation between two keys consists in the fact that the tonic triad of the one is among the triads of the others. This definition is carefully worded so as to avoid troublesome details in reckoning from a minor tonic. By way of summarizing a troublesome grammatical affair in a simple, comprehensive, and concrete illustration I give here the series of direct relations of C major and C minor, with their particular names above and their generic names and numeral symbols below.

* i.e. mediant between tonic and *lower* subdominant.

It will be seen that with A minor as home tonic the table of relations to a minor tonic is that of the relations to a major tonic read backwards. Probably this is why the terms 'relative minor' and 'relative major' are applied to (vi) and (♭III) respectively. Both terms are misleading; these relations are no more direct than the others.

Major and minor keys on the same tonic are identical in spite of their vivid emotional contrast; that is to say, a composition in C minor has not ended in another key if it ends in C major. The brightening to the major mode is a fact that strikes literally home, and is thus far more powerful than any change of key. Compositions beginning in a major key and ending in its tonic minor are more rare and represent some unusual emotional conflict.

Bach normally moves within the range of these direct key-relations. When he goes outside them, his purpose is always to astonish or mystify, except in a few cases of unnoticed drift a little beyond and back again. And he never fails in his purpose of astonishing, because all his extraordinary modulations go at once to the extremes of the harmonic universe, avoiding the regions which later music has annexed to the scheme of key-relations. These regions Haydn, Mozart, and Beethoven extended so enormously that many theorists have jumped to the conclusion that all keys are equally related and that Bach's miracles are miracles no longer. This is the negation of all harmonic sensibility. It is a hasty reaction from old orthodoxies which regarded unrelated keys as forbidden, and recognized none but direct relations.

The wider key-relations used by Haydn, Mozart, and Beethoven were first exploited by Domenico Scarlatti as paradoxes. To Haydn they were true mysteries; and the dark ones, but not the bright ones, make an almost systematic feature in some of Mozart's procedures. When we come to Beethoven we find the whole range of key-relationships expressible in musical notation rationally mapped out, with an exact knowledge of each degree of remoteness and each possibility of relation. The governing principle of the extension is based simply upon accepting the fact that major and minor keys on the same tonic are identical, so that the modes of either member of a pair of keys may be changed and the resulting pair still accepted as related. There is also a group of relations which I sometimes call Neapolitan, consisting of the flat super-tonic and its converse, the sharp seventh, which are derived from an intensification of the minor mode. There are many complicated details in the aesthetics and technique of these wider relations, and I have treated of them in the works and articles mentioned above. For the present purpose the reader should understand that when I talk of key-relations as remote, dark, or bright, I am describing not subjective impressions but facts. I cannot promise always to have used the word 'key-relation' instead of 'key', but if I say that A flat is a dark key or E major a bright key I mean dark or bright according to the direction from which the key is approached. If a composer chooses to make a brilliant modulation from C to A flat, or a gloomy modulation from C to the bright key of E, then there is an element of conflict (imaginative or unimaginative) between his manner and his matter. If he modulates from C major to D major in such a manner that the D major does not explain itself away as a mere dominant of the dominant, then he has either achieved a stupendous stroke of genius, like that of Beethoven in a famous passage in the Eroica Symphony, or he has shown that this juxtaposition of keys means no more to him than similar accidents in the key-sequence of dances in a ball-room.

Music-lovers should not load their consciences with alarming ideas as to what great composers expect of the listener in recognizing key-relations. It is one thing to recognize what is addressed to the ear, but quite another matter to recognize the causes of weakness in a structure. This is where these programme notes are debarred from giving help, except in cases so weak that counsel for the defence can only plead 'confession and avoidance'. But the reader may be glad to know that great composers quite consistently refrain from basing definite effects of key-relations on the assumption that the ear will recognize them otherwise than in juxtaposition or, if at a distance, by collateral evidence. By far the most important effect of tonality at a distance is that of returning to the home tonic. Not only can I recall no case where the importance of recognizing this does not coincide with the return of matter that is already associated with the tonic, or expected to appear in it; but I find that in every case where no such aid is given to the listener there is a definite aesthetic value in the fact that we do not recognize the tonic immediately. Of course, if a composition returns to the tonic without any purpose at all, it is simply wasting its opportunities, and its key-relations will neither surprise nor interest. But the reader may safely disregard any criticism or theory which assumes that the ear assigns definite values to two tonics as being connected through the medium of a third tonic, or as perceptible across intervening matter without some element of recapitulation.[1]

Often the purport of a modulation is to obliterate the sense of key-relationship. This is most typically effected by 'enharmonic' modulations, where a chord changes its intonation by a minute interval lost in the compromise of the pianoforte's 12-semitone octave, but expressible by voices and stringed instruments; as when the diminished 7th C♯ E G B♭ is changed to, D♭ F♭ G B♭ and so swings from the dominant of D minor to that of A♭ minor. The mastery of the composer determines whether the effect is that of a bad pun or a sublime mystery: the listener needs no theoretic knowledge to experience the proper degree of surprise in each case. Though the actual change of intonation is lost in the tempered scale the ear has no more difficulty in appreciating it than in appreciating puns.

Art-Forms. Some technicalities are defined as they arise in each essay; and in volumes so little calculated for continuous reading I have not avoided repetition. But the reader may find it convenient to have the terms of sonata form defined here once for all.

In the first place, the classical use of the word 'sonata' implies a group of pieces called movements. It will, I hope, be always clear from the context when I am using the word 'movement' in its English sense, whether extended metaphorically or not, and when

---

[1] It would be ungracious not to acknowledge the service the tonic-solfa system has done in awakening the sense of local tonality in the young and the musical laity; but if it can inculcate any larger grasp of tonality, I have been unfortunate in the examples I have seen of its treatment of keys and key-relations.

I mean a member of a sonata. By some curious accident, the word 'sonata' is not applied to compositions for more than two instruments. This has tiresome results. In *Grove's Dictionary of Music and Musicians*, Parry felt so bound by the usages of language that his article on 'Sonata Form' was actually cramped by a conscientious objection to quote from any of the larger works which display sonata forms in a normal full size. He was able to refer to Brahms's Quintet in F minor because the composer, in arranging it for two pianofortes, was able to call it a sonata. In these essays it is assumed that the trios, quartets, quintets, &c., of composers from Haydn onwards are sonatas, and that a symphony is a sonata for orchestra.

A 'concerto' is a sonata for one or more solo instruments in concert, contest, or contrast with an orchestra.

The normal movements of a full-size sonata are four, viz. an important and more or less dramatic first movement in a form hereafter to be summarized; a slow movement, which may take any form ranging from lyric forms to that of the first movement; a minuet or scherzo, representing to some extent the forms of dance music in contrast to the more lyric style of slow movements; and a finale, generally lively, often in the same form as the first movement, but typically in rondo form.

The normal form of a first movement has earned the title 'sonata form' *par excellence*. Its evolution can be easily traced as originating in the so-called 'binary form' of a certain kind of melody. Melodies that consist of more than one phrase naturally fall into two classes: that in which the first phrase is complete, and that in which it is incomplete. If the first phrase is complete, it, or the end of it, may also be used as the end of the whole melody; with the result that the middle portion tends to become detached from the first phrase, if not also from the last. Hence, the shape of such melodies may often be summarized as A B A. This is what is commonly meant by 'ternary form'. Melodies in binary form are supposed to fall into only two parts because, the first part being incomplete, the middle portion does not stand out so distinctly. Now these terms, 'binary' and 'ternary', not only miss the essential grounds of classification, but are thoroughly misleading in all that they imply. The essential distinction is that between a form in which the first member is complete in itself and a form in which the first member is incomplete. Musical experience shows that if the melody, or form, is small enough to make the repetition of its portions desirable, the division always falls into two, and never into three. One of the best-known ternary melodies in classical music is that of the slow movement of the Kreutzer Sonata. Nothing could be clearer than its division into a complete 8-bar strain A, an 11-bar middle portion B, mainly in the dominant, and a complete da capo of strain A. But it is worth while trying the experiment of repeating these three strains in the order A A B B A A, so as to see how impossible it is to regard the whole structure as divisible otherwise than into A, BA. The experience of this test would justify us in concluding that all melodic forms are binary. On the other hand, Sir Henry Hadow in his primer on *Sonata Form* found himself driven by the facts of form on a larger scale of developed movements to conclude that sonata form was essentially ternary: that is to say, that its main divisions of exposition, development, and recapitulation were comparable rather with the A B A form than with anything that could reasonably be called binary.

But his difficulties are forced on him not by a system of mere cross-classification, but by an irrelevant terminology. For one thing, any musical terminology must be wrong if it assumes a map-like or space-like view of music instead of a time-like view. Whether a composition is divisible into three or four sections is a fact that can be ascertained only when we have heard the whole, and even then it is not the kind of fact that 'vibrates in the memory'. But it is a vital and immediately impressive event in time that the first clearly marked division of a piece of music should impress the listener as complete in itself or incomplete. Obviously, the kinds of form in which the first section is incomplete will tend to be more highly organized than those in which it is complete. To take an extreme case, if in your A B A form the B is as complete as the A, the total form is a mere symmetrical arrangement of detachable objects, like a picture with a vase of flowers to the right and another vase of flowers to the left of it. Such a case is the classical scheme of minuet, trio, and minuet da capo. On the other hand, when the first member of a musical form is incomplete, it creates a strong presumption that the rest will be more or less highly organized. The most highly organized of all musical forms is that of the first movement of a sonata in the miscalled 'binary' form. Externally, its mature examples are not easily distinguishable from its earlier evolutionary types as shown in the dance forms of suites; and inextricable confusion will result if we try to follow the orthodox lines according to which the distinction depends on the number of themes. I regret that in all but the latest of these essays I have used the current English terms 'first subject' and 'second subject' for the materials of sonata-form movements. In my *Companion to Beethoven's Pianoforte Sonatas* I have introduced the unobjectionable terms 'first group' and 'second group', which commit the analyst to no propositions as to themes or subjects. You may find dance movements by Bach with several beautifully distinct themes and full-sized first movements by Haydn with only one, but you will find no movement by Bach with the essentials of sonata style and hardly even an early first movement by Haydn without signs of them. The typical features of sonata form are these: the 'exposition', which contains a first group which asserts the tonic key, and a second group which not only asserts, but firmly establishes, another key, usually the dominant if the tonic was major, and the mediant major or dominant minor if the tonic was minor; a section of 'development' which treats the materials of the exposition discursively, wandering through various keys; a 'recapitulation' of the whole exposition giving both groups in the home tonic, and, if this recapitulation does not give an effect of finality, a coda or peroration. By firmly establishing another key, we understand some process which causes the original tonic as it were to sink below the horizon. In Bach the tonic cannot thus sink out of sight unless in some series of remote modulations, the object of which is to startle and bewilder. From most points in movements by Bach or Handel it would be possible to drop back into the tonic without much ado; and the establishment of a key did not become a dramatic, or even important, event until Haydn and Mozart brought to maturity the style that could make it so.

There are no rules as to the number of themes the exposition of a sonata movement may contain; nor, indeed, is it worth while to define what we mean by a 'theme', still less what we mean by a 'subject'. One theme may be derived from another in all sorts of ways, and a group of a few notes may be detachable as a 'figure', and shared by several otherwise contrasted themes. The sonata form, even on the largest scale, retains so much of the primitive character of the melodic form in which it originated that huge movements, like the first movement of the Eroica Symphony and the first movement of Brahms's Second Symphony, can afford to repeat the exposition.

These repetitions sometimes present a curious problem in musical aesthetics. In their total effect they undoubtedly become recognized by the ear as mere encores, even though, as in Brahms's Second Symphony, the composer has effected them by a specially beautiful joint. In suite movements and early sonatas the custom was for both parts to be repeated; and the second repeat survives in certain quite late and important works of Beethoven, where one object is the effect produced by the special joint that sinks back to the beginning of the development, and the other is the effect upon the coda. In modern performances there is a natural tendency to sweep away all these repeats. In many cases this is justified and would not be objected to by the composer. But we must not overlook the cases in which the composer has vividly imagined the moment at which the repeat begins. Nor must we consider the whole question settled if we lose nothing obviously thrilling by omitting the repeat. The objections to which repeats are most liable are: first, that they make the work too long; and secondly, that 'we don't want to be told the same thing twice over'. The question of length is partly a question of programme making. Spacious works notorious for their repeat marks, such as Beethoven's last three trios and the Quartet in E minor, op. 59, no. 2, are all the better for being placed in programmes where there is room for them to be displayed in full. The dramatic point of their repeats will prove surprising if we are given a chance of appreciating it. The objection that we don't want to be told the same thing twice is based on a radical misapprehension of the nature of music. It obviously does not apply to symmetrical repetition, which has the same kind of function in music as it has in architecture. But the repeats we are here discussing are not symmetries. They are peculiar to an art that moves in time, and their nearest analogy in architecture would be opportunities, more or less charmingly contrived by a guide, for going over part of a building twice. To enjoy this you must of course be in the best mood for enjoying every feature of the work. The practical musician is seldom able to consult his palate and digestion in these matters, and he is naturally most dyspeptic with the best-known works.

After the exposition comes the 'development'. As its name implies, its function is to develop the resources already in hand. Not only will it tend to avoid the tonic and the complementary key already established, but it will be apt to range widely over many keys, establishing none until the time comes for the recapitulation. Many illustrations of the processes of development will be found in these essays. The essential idea of sonata development is the break-up of the themes as originally phrased, and the rebuilding and recombining of their figures into sentences and sequences of a different kind. There are no rules for the conduct of a development, but of course it is possible to say that such-and-such a procedure more or less enhances or reduces the energy of a development. Thus, Schubert is apt to weaken and lengthen his expositions by processes of discursive development where Beethoven would have had a crowd of terse new themes; while, on the other hand, Schubert's developments are apt indeed to develop some feature of one of his themes, but by turning it into a long lyric process which is repeated symmetrically. Dvořák is apt to be dangerously discursive at any point of his exposition, and frequently loses his way before he has begun his second group, while his developments often merely harp upon a single figure with a persistence not much more energetic or cumulative than that of the Dormouse that continued to say 'twinkle, twinkle' in its sleep. But none of these matters can be settled by rule of thumb. If a short development contains an entirely new theme, the whole tends to become a detached episode, though the enormous development of the Eroica Symphony contrives to introduce a new lyric melody in two places in the course of executing its own energetic voyage round the harmonic world. On the other hand, if you find that the development of some mature work by Mozart or Beethoven consists almost wholly of an irresponsible episode, you have no reason to suppose that the composer has made a mistake.

After the development comes the recapitulation', which consists, as its name implies, of a restatement of the material of the exposition. Both groups are restated, and it is more important to restate the second group fully than the first, for the restatement of the second group will not be in the complementary key, but, with rare exceptions, in the home tonic. Three points in the recapitulation present dramatic possibilities. Those of the return to the opening are obvious. Then there is the process by which the original complementary key of the second group was established. Some alteration must evidently happen here if the second group is to appear in the tonic. Lastly, there is the end of the exposition, which now will have either to end the whole movement satisfactorily with its own momentum, or to lead into the 'coda', or peroration.

For the construction of the coda there are many possibilities and no rules but common sense. Clearly, if the coda departs from the home tonic, it must spend a due proportion of its later energies in re-establishing it.

If the form of a first movement is applied to a slow movement, the composer must not lose sight of the fact, frequently pointed out in these essays, that in music 'slowness' means 'bigness'. If the orthodox reader is inclined to be shocked at me for describing the slow movement of Beethoven's D major Trio, op. 70, no. 1, as in full sonata form, when the portion which I describe as its development is only 8 bars long, I can justify myself by pointing out that those 8 bars contain two distinct lines of development passing through several different keys, and that, as measured by metronome, they come to a considerably greater length than the unquestionably orthodox development of the finale. So long as the reader finds a consistent meaning in my use of terms, he need not worry about musical terminology. I am concerned only to convey clear impressions of musical facts without adding a new terminology to the confusions of an old one. In spite of the limitations of a slow tempo, Beethoven has several times achieved a sonata-form slow movement with quite a long development. One example is the slow movement of the Quartet, op. 59, no. 1, where Beethoven has actually found room for an independent episode, and others are the slow movements of the Second and Sixth Symphonies, fairly fully analysed in the present volume. If the composer wishes to get a sonata-like breadth of effect in a smaller space, there is always the possibility of a movement consisting of exposition, recapitulation, and (*ad libitum*) coda, without development at all. On the other hand, there are many varieties of the A B A form; and a slow movement may economize space and yet attain a high degree of development by making B an elaborate and discursive affair. Or the whole movement may be predominantly lyric, with A as one tune and B as another.

Next in importance to the sonata form is the 'rondo', which is typical of finales. As its name implies, it consists essentially of a melody that comes round again and again after contrasted episodes. In its early forms, as in the suites of Couperin and Bach, it shows its derivation from the *rondeau* of the sixteenth-century French poets. Orlando di Lasso set many such poems to music which faithfully reflects the poetic form. Couperin, again, shows the identity between the poetic and the musical form by calling the episodes of his rondos 'couplets'. In the rondos of sonatas the main theme is usually more than a single strain; though Beethoven in his early works (up to the Quartet, op. 18, no. 4) took over from Haydn a development of the older kind of rondo in which the main theme is a single epigram and the episodes are highly sectional, with a final accumulation of coda-episodes in the tonic. Mozart developed to its fullest extent the type of rondo which is usually ascribed to Beethoven. In this the main theme is a complete tune, possibly 'binary' or 'ternary', and evidently designed for recurrence rather than for development. The first episode behaves like the second group of a sonata-form movement, being recapitulated in the home tonic at the penultimate stage of the rondo. The second episode may be a new tune-like structure fixed in another key, or it may be a process of development on material new or old. It is obvious that, if the first return of the main theme has been curtailed and made to lead quickly to an elaborate development, the line which distinguishes such a rondo from a first movement will become so faint that disputes as to classification will be inconclusive. The only important criterion is that of style. Mozart is not particular. If a movement begins with a square-cut tune, he may call it a rondo, even when it has exactly the repeat marks and shape of a first movement; and for some obscure reason it is seldom that a movement will be labelled as a rondo unless it happens to be a finale.

The full-sized scheme of a sonata includes a movement which

does not normally admit of development at all, but is typically a dance movement, consisting of two complete members arranged in the form A B A; as minuet, trio, and minuet da capo. Why the minuet alone of the suite dances should have been taken over into the sonata scheme nobody knows. Perhaps it was eminently fitted to survive in the early stages of the sonata style by being lively enough to contrast with the slow movement and not so lively as to foreshadow the finale. In Haydn's hands it became surprisingly energetic, and developed to considerable length without losing its character as a dance movement. When Beethoven expanded it into the scherzo, he took pains and pleasure in preserving and enhancing that character. Only twice, and that in early works, did he enlarge the minuet by giving it a second trio. His notion of the way to expand the form is at once more dramatic and more pre-servative of its character as a dance. It consists in going twice round the alternation of scherzo and trio, with no variation except perhaps a damping-down to pianissimo at the second or third recurrence of the scherzo. The listener is caught up in the un-ceasing round and is extricated only by some drastic intervention when the trio seems about to recur a third time. Of all Beethoven's repeats, these most arouse the impatience of modern performers and critics. But they are among the most vividly imagined subtle-ties of Beethoven's invention, and music-lovers are well advised who keep their musical digestions in a fit state to enjoy them.

The scheme of a sonata admits among the four movements, either in the position of the slow movement or finale, two other forms which are radically different from those of a movement of development. 'Variations' are restatements of a theme complete in itself, and a set of variations is fairly often to be met with as a sonata movement. In that position, its range, and more especially its depth, are limited by the fact that the sonata style trains the ear to recognize themes by their melody, whereas the deeper type of variation is often not concerned with the melody at all. In any case, variations are not developments of the theme. To develop a theme is practically to break up and re-arrange its figures into different structures. To make a variation in the classical sense of the word is to take the whole structure of a theme and build a similar structure with a different exterior. The proper effect of a set of variations is cumulative. The theme may or may not be recognized by the listener, though in the sonata style melodic resemblance will not long be absent; but, whether the theme be recognized or not, its momentum will become powerful through all changes of tempo and emotion. The composer's main difficulty will be to stop this momentum or bring it to a climax in a natural and conclusive way. Post-classical variations depend upon a much more superficial view of the theme, and they take no account of this factor of momentum at all. Recent criticism shows a mistaken idea as to what the listener is expected to hear in a classical set of variations. Such variations may depend on the composer's profoundest insight into the form of his theme, but this is to the ear what the painter's or sculptor's knowledge of anatomy is to the eye. Without it the figure becomes a sack stuffed with straw and the variations lose their momentum.

More rarely than variations, but still often enough to need description at this point, the 'fugue' may figure as a sonata movement. If 'discussion' were equivalent to 'development' in the dramatic sense, a fugue might be said to be all development, but in fact it is neither more nor less amenable to the sonata idea of development than a prolonged argument on the stage is to the development of a drama. The first fact to realize about fugue is that it is a medium, like blank verse, not a thing, like a rondo. You should not think of 'fugues' but of passages or pieces written 'in fugue'. A piece written entirely in fugue is 'a fugue', and the rules for its composition are many, vexatious, and largely the result of malobservation and of early nineteenth-century Italian generalizations that meticulously exclude Bach. The essentials of fugue consist in the discussion of a compact melodic idea by a definite number of voices. The melodic idea is called the subject; the number of voices is definite in this respect, that the voices employed in the discussion are supposed to be self-sufficient, and that any further accompaniment is outside the scheme. 'Fugato' is the term used for passages in fugue. A fugue normally begins with a single voice announcing the subject, though 'double fugues' may begin with two voices and two subjects. A second voice announces the answer, which is a reproduction of the subject *in* or *on* the dominant. The distinction between *in* and *on* is important; and being *on* the dominant has the obvious aesthetic advantage of not involving a stiff change of key to and fro as the subject enters in the successive voices. An answer *on* the dominant usually avoids being *in* the dominant by slightly altering the subject in certain ways vexatious to codify and analyse, but very satisfactory to the ear when properly achieved without pedantry. Far be it from me to vex any reader with grammatical minutiae, but the essential principle of the so-called tonal answer is a self-evident musical fact of which you can convince yourself by striking in succession the notes G C (upward or downward) and noticing the effect of answering them by C G instead of by D G. The 'tonal' answer is a reflection at an angle; the exact, or 'real', answer is a mere transposition. But it is absurd to found upon this feature a solemn distinction between real fugues and tonal fugues. especially as the rules for producing a tonal answer happen as often as not to give an exact transposition.

The 'countersubject' is normally the matter with which the voice that announced the subject accompanies the answer, if that matter is preserved on later occasions; and in the same way the first voice may proceed to a second countersubject when the third voice enters. But the term is also used for new subjects introduced at later stages of a fugue. Such a new subject, if stated by itself and vividly contrasted with the main subject, will produce a brilliant effect when, as is probably its purpose, it afterwards enters into combination with it.

The term 'episode' is used for those portions of a fugue during which the complete subject is not being heard. It thus has a wholly different sense from its use in sonata forms and rondos. Generally speaking, the devices of fugue, though argumentative, are entirely unlike those of the sonata style and contribute nothing except contrast to the idea of sonata development.

'Augmentation' is the delivery of a subject or countersubject in consistently slower notes; 'diminution' the delivery in quicker notes.

The term 'inversion' has two meanings: first, inversion in double counterpoint, a device essential to polyphonic music if the bass is to have its fair share of subjects and countersubjects. A combination of themes is said to be in 'double', 'triple', &c., counterpoint, when each theme is equally capable of being a bass to the others. This implies transposition by octaves, and therefore double counterpoint is normally said to be at the octave. But sometimes a combination of themes can be so designed that one of them will bear transposition by some other interval, and this will produce a quite new set of harmonies. Some fairly vivid illustrations of these facts appear in the present essays, and my *Companion to Bach's Art of Fugue* illustrates fully from that work the aesthetic purpose of these matters. 'Inversion' has another sense: the melodic sense of the reversal of every interval in a melody, replacing each upward movement by an equal downward movement, and vice versa.

A 'stretto' is the overlapping of the subject with one or more answers. The term should not be applied to mere sketchy allusions to the first figure of the subject, such as might occur in any episode, but only to episodes where the subject and answers survive more or less completely in each voice.

Other technical terms will be found defined in the glossary provided in the Index-volume.

In conclusion, I once more beg to reassert my first article of musical faith: that, while the listener must not expect to hear the whole contents of a piece of music at once, nothing concerns him that will not ultimately reach his ear either as a directly audible fact or as a cumulative satisfaction in things of which the hidden foundations are well and truly laid. Whatever the defects of these essays, they do not contain speculative and fanciful thematic derivations which exist only to the eye, nor do they rest on theories which imply a *coup d'œil* view of music. I have myself often been fascinated by the theory that classical music, like classical sculpture, measures its proportions in 'golden sections', that is to say, that unequal divisions follow the law that the smaller part is to the larger as the larger is to the whole. Possible illustrations of this are innumerable; there is one by no means hackneyed quartet of Haydn (op. 50, no. 5 in F) where the first movement falls into golden sections in every way, from point to point, and backwards and forwards, with one of Haydn's characteristic silent bars falling beautifully into place. Yet I have become sceptical; there are so many ways of taking your sections that I doubt whether any musical composition can avoid golden ones somewhere. And I see no means of allowing for 'who time gambols withal, who time trots withal, who time gallops withal, and who he stands still withal.'

I should retain more interest in such speculations if the deeper researches in them did not so often show an inability to recognize the most obvious musical facts. Such inability is far more serious than any failure to recognize subtleties. The obvious musical facts, when they are facts at all, lead of their own accord to the profoundest subtleties; and it is my hope that the lines of analysis indicated in these volumes may lead in the right direction.

BACH

OVERTURE IN C MAJOR, FOR ORCHESTRA

1 (*Grave: leading to Allegro*). 2 *Courante*. 3 *Gavotte I and II*. 4 *Forlane*. 5 *Menuet I and II*. 6 *Bourrée I and II*. 7 *Passepied I and II*.

Of Bach's four orchestral overtures, or suites, the first, in C major, is perhaps the most witty. Comparisons in respect of absolute beauty are impertinent. Masterpieces of art should never be compared, except as to technicalities and historical matters. When a work of art has attained perfection, it is a form of infinity; and with infinities no process of addition, subtraction, or other arithmetical operation has the slightest relevance.

The C major Overture is scored for the ordinary string band and a trio consisting of two oboes and a bassoon. To these resources we must add the continuo, the harpsichord, or pianoforte in the hands of a player whose task is to fill in the harmonies from a figured bass. The string harmony of the C major Suite lies unusually well for euphony without the aid of the continuo; but this does not mean that a discreet background of keyboard harmony is not an immense improvement, or rather a restoration of the true character of Bach's orchestration. The cold and tubby resonance of Bach's and Handel's string-writing, as left unfilled by the background which these masters deemed essential, is really a modern invention, and the pious opinion that it represents chastity and severity is as the hardness of the Greek G or gamma in the Ἔλγιν marbles.

Where a large string band is used, Bach's trio of oboes and bassoon needs reinforcing. It does not matter what reed instruments we take for the purpose; clarinets will do just as well as oboes, if we cannot afford or obtain the overwhelming number of oboes to which Handel was accustomed. Nobody at the present day knows exactly what twelve Handelian oboes would sound like, and Handel himself was more accustomed to twenty. Anyhow, the resemblance to ordinary oboe-tone would be far remoter than the mixture of clarinets and oboes which I propose to use in the tuttis for purposes of balance. The trio passages, which are especially marked 'trio' by Bach, should, of course, be played by three soloists, who may well be given ample time to breathe during the tuttis.

The title 'overture' applies properly to the first number in this suite, and means, of course, an overture on Lully's French model, beginning with a *grave* (in this case rather more flowing and less

jerky than the traditional type) and leading to a lively fugato movement. Here is the theme of the fugue:

and the quick movement, which is developed at considerable
length, is very clearly articulated by its natural division between
the tuttis and the trio passages for the three wind instruments. The
grave returns at the end by way of climax.

If this were the overture to an opera, the curtain would rise upon
a ballet. Hence the suite of dances which follows; and hence, con-
versely, the custom of prefacing such suites by a French overture.
The first dance is a French courante, scored for the tutti throughout.

I quote the whole first part of this in order to show two points, one
of which does not in this case reach the ear at all unless the continuo player brings it out. Although the time is 3/2, the last note
of the first part is written as if it were 6/4. This is a faint trace of
the fact that the French courante is really in an old kind of triple
time, in which the rhythms of twice three and thrice two are mixed
in a manner which always appears at the cadences and often causes
confusion elsewhere. It is not generally realized that our clear-cut
notions of triple time, such as the rhythm of waltzes and minuets,
are of no great antiquity. Occasional groups of three beats are as
frequent in Palestrina as metrical feet of three syllables in verse;
but not one per cent. of any sixteenth-century master's work is
written ostensibly in triple time, and those in which the triple
time-signature is used are extraordinarily remote from our ideas
of any such rhythm. The other reason why I quote the whole
first strain of this courante is that Bach opens the second strain by
giving the whole of these eight bars a step higher. This is the first
example of a kind of wit peculiarly characteristic of this suite and
of the Flute Suite in B minor.

The next dance is a pair of gavottes, of which the first is scored
for the tutti.

The second (alternating) gavotte is scored for the wind trio, but is accompanied by trumpet flourishes on all the violins and violas.

The next dance is a forlane, or forlana, which, I learn from *Grove's Dictionary*, is a favourite lilt with Venetian gondoliers. It is scored for tutti with a running accompaniment of the second violins and violas. The bass supports the harmony with a somewhat derisive approval, until towards the end it is carried away with the other dancers. Perhaps it represents the strokes of the gondolier's pole.

Then there are a pair of minuets, the first scored for tutti—

and the second, a tune of beautiful gravity, scored for the strings in a quiet low position.

Then follows a pair of bourrées. The first is a tutti—

and the second is for the wind trio, and is the only section of the suite in the minor mode.

The suite ends with a pair of passepieds. Of these I quote only the second, because it consists of the whole melody of the first assigned to the violins and violas in unison an octave below its

original pitch, with the wind group (not necessarily in solo trio)
playing a flowing counterpoint.

Ex. 10.

ORCHESTRAL SUITE IN D MAJOR, NO. 3

1 *Ouverture: Grave, leading to Allegro.* 2 *Air.* 3 *Gavotte I and II.*
4 *Bourrée.* 5 *Gigue.*

Bach's own title for his orchestral suites is 'Ouverture'. They are,
in fact, French Overtures, which earn the title Suite or Partita
inasmuch as they consist of an overture proper followed by a suite
of dances.

Immensely as Bach transfigured every art form that he used, he
left its essential character more clearly defined than it had ever been
before; and in the French Overtures of Bach we can see, even more
vividly than in their models, the appropriate music of the solemn
introduction in iambic marching rhythm as the nobility and gentry
enter to take their seats; the lively movement paying perfunctory
homage to the art of fugue, but really more concerned to give the
concertino an opportunity for showing off individual players; and,
with the rise of the curtain, a display of the *corps de ballet* before
the (less?) serious business of the drama begins.

In none of Bach's orchestral overtures are the suite movements anything like as numerous as those in the Suites and Partitas for clavier and for solo violin and violoncello. In the present case, there is no allemande, no courante, and no sarabande; that is to say, with the exception of the gigue, the staple dance-movements of the suite are absent, and only the 'Galanterien', which we may call the movable feasts, are represented.

The orchestra consists of strings, two oboes, three trumpets, and kettle-drums. The first and second trumpets are Bach's usual 'clarino' parts, such as my unregenerate soul loves, though some fastidious modern ears, trained to the most drastic contemporary discords, find them too shrill.

In the solemn introduction of the overture, the iambic dotted rhythm is at first buried in the inner parts, being overlaid by another figure in the main melody—

This quotation displays the treatment by inversion of the overlying figure (a) and the close canonic presentation of the iambic figure (b).

Throughout the introduction the oboes are in unison with the first violins; and the trumpets, after punctuating the first two bars with chords, mark the iambic figure (b) during those bars in which the music is in the tonic.

The vivace, indicated by Bach's archaic French instruction in the first violin part, 'viste', begins with a solid fugato, of which I quote the subject and its three countersubjects as we hear them all together at the bass entry.

Of the three countersubjects, the last and topmost one with its ringing monotone is by no means the least effective. The working out of this fugue-material is given to the full orchestra, with the

oboes in unison with the strings, and with punctuating parts for
the trumpets, except where the first trumpet can, by a *tour de force*,
produce the main theme. Immediately after this event, the theme
enters in the basses and is brought in a few bars to a full close. Here
follow what may be called the solo episodes of the movement.
There is no reason for segregating a solo quartet from the rest of
the strings, but there is no doubt that the following theme is in the
character of a solo; and it is confined to the first violins.

Ex. 3.

It retains its character when the second violin and viola proceed
to combine the main theme (Ex. 2) with it, in a passage which occurs
twice in the movement, and which is distinguished by the independence of the oboes, who contribute an exquisite series of
slow suspensions over the throbbing rhythm of the trumpets.

The materials now accumulated revolve twice in their cycle, and
close into a resumption of the opening *Grave*.

The second movement is Bach's famous Air *not* on the G string.
At my concerts it will be heard as Bach wrote it, in its original D
major as an angelic soprano strain, and not in C major as a display
of contralto depths. The last time I heard this Air I did expect,
since it occurred in a performance of the whole Suite, that I should
for once in my life hear it as Bach wrote it. Unfortunately the
conductor had discovered that it makes a beautiful oboe solo. It
does, and it was beautifully played, but this does not alter the fact
that what Bach wrote is incomparably more beautiful than any
such arrangement. Early eighteenth-century string scoring suffers
in modern presentation if it is attempted without an adequate
rendering of the continuo part on a harpsichord or (with all respect
to other scholars, preferably) a pianoforte. But, except in a very
few notes, this Air happens to be more independent of the continuo
than most things in Bach's orchestration; and when the continuo
correctly fills up the very few hollow moments, the result is one of
the classical touchstones of string orchestration. As for Wilhelmj's
discovery that the melody sounds magnificent a ninth lower on the
fourth string, we need not doubt that Bach would have thought
this quite interesting. But imagination boggles at the idea of Bach's
reception of Wilhelmj's piety in leaving the inner parts undisturbed
and in crassly ungrammatical relation to the melody in its new
position; and it is no very simple task to correct the four or five
gross blunders that have thus been foisted upon Bach in one of the
most impressive examples of his purest style. Recently, a conductor who combines in the highest degree his own sense of humour

with a reverence for the classics has managed to extract a useful lesson even from Wilhelmj's devastating derangement. Weingartner allows a full string orchestra to play this Air in C major on the G string, but avoids all grammatical blunders by leaving out the inner parts altogether! The result demonstrates, as nothing else could, the amazing power of Bach's harmony as tested by Brahms's method of criticism. Brahms, when asked his opinion of a new composition, was accustomed to place his hand over everything except the top and the bottom of the score, saying: 'Now let's see what your melody and bass come to: all the rest is trimmings.'

I am not likely to forget the impression Weingartner's demonstration of this Air made upon me, and I shall not scruple to repeat it on some occasion when I am not doing the whole Suite. Otherwise, I can only devoutly wish that everybody who insists on playing this Air on the G string will have the goodness also to play it with one finger: the result can add but little to the sloppiness of the popular arrangement.

The Gavotte is again one of Bach's best known tunes, both in its first and its second sections. It may be as well to point out the witty inversion of the opening figure in the course of the first gavotte—

The scoring of both gavottes is again as in the tuttis of the overture; namely, the oboes are in unison with the violins, and the trumpets partly double the theme and partly punctuate.

The same scoring prevails in the bourrée and is disguised in the final gigue only by the fact that the trumpets transfer the actual theme to the topmost octave and so mask the tone of oboes and strings below. Thus in the whole overture the notes of the 'solo' episode in the vivace have been the only passages in which the oboes have had an independent part.

OVERTURE IN B MINOR FOR FLUTE AND STRINGS

1 OVERTURE (*Grave, Allegro, Lentement*). 2 *Rondeau* (*Gavotte*).
3 *Sarabande*. 4 *Bourrée I, II*. 5 *Polonaise, Double*.
6 *Minuet*. 7 *Badinerie*.

The term Overture applies formally to the long first movement of a suite of this type, and means a design such as Lulli established as the orthodox introduction to an opera. A grave movement in slow but jerky iambic rhythms—

Ex. 1.

leads to a fugato, allegro—

Ex. 2.

in which the orchestral fugue passages alternate with florid solos. In the present instance Bach follows the procedure of resuming the slow iambic movement at the end, but ingeniously transforms it to triple time.

Now follows a suite of dances. The first is a gavotte in rhythm, and in form a *rondeau en couplets*, which, on this small scale, corresponds obviously and almost exactly to the rondeau in verse.

Ex. 3.

Next we have a solemn sarabande, with the bass following the melody in canon.

Ex. 4.

A lively bourrée (note the obstinate bass)—

Ex. 5.

alternates with a second bourrée in which the flute has something of its own to say.

Ex. 6.

The polonaise is a more gentle and indolent affair than the brilliant things which go by that name in the nineteenth century.

Ex. 7.

Its *double* consists of a florid counterpoint by the flute while the basses play the original tune.

Bach's minuets are short, sturdy little tunes, neither runaway like Haydn's nor stately like the dance in *Don Giovanni*.

Ex. 8.

The finale is called by Bach a *Badinerie*, and in it the flute and violins play in a humorous disguised unison throughout.

Ex. 9.

PRELUDE TO CHURCH CANTATA NO. 29, 'WIR DANKEN DIR, GOTT', FOR ORGAN AND ORCHESTRA

This is the prelude to one of Bach's Rathswahl Cantatas, written for the Sunday service at the time of the municipal elections at Leipzig in 1731.

Violinists and their audiences will at once recognize that we have here in D major a glorification of the prelude to the E major Partita for unaccompanied violin.

There are several modern arrangements of this prelude. The objection to them is not merely the general objection to such things on principle; it is that the arrangers have for the most part shown no knowledge of Bach's own solution of their problem, although the cantata containing it was published by the Bach-Gesellschaft as long ago as 1860. Arrangers who show so little curiosity as to Bach's own methods are not likely to show much grasp of the technical problems of translating 'into the round' a composition originally not only flat but consisting of pure line. It is indeed an extraordinary *tour de force* to find an independent bass for a thing that is already its own bass. Only the fact that most of this prelude consists of arpeggios makes the *tour de force* possible at all. If the movement really were pure line-drawing, like most of these violin solos, its own bass, being also its melody, would not bear doubling, and any other bass would be either stupid or ungrammatical. Even in this prelude there are several places where an arranger can go wrong, and the opportunities have not been neglected. Yet one of my earliest recollections is that of a performance in the 'eighties by Lady Hallé of this prelude in its original key with an orchestral accompaniment of which I distinctly remember the comments of Bach's trumpets, represented delicately by flutes. That is to say, I remember the glorious details of these flutes; and the fact that many years later I recognized them in the trumpets of Bach's score makes me almost certain that Sir Charles Hallé, with characteristic honesty and modesty, produced Bach's own version retransposed to the original key and replacing the organ by the original violin.

Bach's arrangement achieves the miracle of being necessary in every detail though the original was already perfect. In essentials what he has done has been to write a new prelude for orchestra, which combines with the original violin prelude as arranged for the organ, and throws it into high relief by radical contrasts of rhythm. This new orchestral prelude consists mainly of staccato chords distributed antiphonally among the groups of orchestral instruments. Sustained chords now and then strike a deeper and more solemn note, and flourishes of trumpets mark a livelier rhythm, to which the strings add rapid descending scales. Towards the end the livelier rhythm ♩ ♫ ♫♫ | ♩ pervades the whole orchestra, including the drums, and thus becomes a definite theme. Otherwise the form consists merely in the symmetrical balance of long sequences of harmony establishing first the tonic and then the other related keys in a natural order, working round to the tonic again with recognizable repetitions of long sections. One thing only is needed to hold the scheme together, and that is supplied by the perpetual motion of the original prelude, the outlines of which coincide with such details as the occasional descending scales of the strings, while the first two bars (and no others in the whole original prelude) give rise to the livelier rhythmic figure of the orchestra. The efforts of later arrangers are all very much cleverer, and, like a well-known make of safety-match, harmless to those employed in the manufacture.

The cantata 'Wir danken dir, Gott' then proceeds to a chorus which afterwards became (to the same words in Latin) the 'Gratias' of the B minor Mass. But the prelude is an equally appropriate introduction to the mighty double chorus 'Nun ist das Heil', which is published as No. 50 of the Cantatas in the Bach-Gesellschaft edition, but consists of a single chorus, which may or may not be part of a larger work.

CARL PHILIPP EMANUEL BACH

SYMPHONY IN D MAJOR

1 *Allego di molto, leading to* 2 *Largo, leading to* 3 *Presto.*

The symphonies of Philipp Emanuel Bach beautifully display the gradual emancipation of the orchestra from its slave-state dependence on the continuo. The emancipation was not the philanthropic process of emancipating slaves. It was the still nobler and more austere problem of teaching the orchestra, including the most aristocratic solo instruments, to serve themselves. To the second volume of *The Heritage of Music* (Oxford University Press) I contributed an essay on Gluck in which I have tried to show that Gluck's reform of opera—that is to say, the whole problem of making music dramatic, instead of merely architectural and decorative—was but one aspect of a radical revolution in the whole art of music. Social philosophers may consider whether there is not in political, as well as in artistic, history a negative aspect of such revolutions that is more evident to contemporaries than the positive aspect. Certainly, one of the greatest pioneers and emancipators in the musical revolution of the eighteenth century was loudest in his complaints that the art of accompanying from a continuo had declined. His symphonies profess to rely upon a pianoforte, with chords indicated by a figured bass, to fill up hollow places in the written score. Philipp Emanuel Bach tells us that this is always necessary, that the pianoforte is better for the purpose than the harpsichord (an opinion which I am delighted to find that Dr. Schweitzer emphatically endorses in the case of John Sebastian's works), and that, even in open-air performances where you cannot hear the keyboard instrument at all, its use greatly improves the general quality of tone. But, if we want an excuse for the neglect of continuo playing which so alarmed Philipp Emanuel Bach, we need seek no farther than the remarkable efficiency of his own orchestration without any such supplement. He is himself obliged to tell the continuo player to rest for pages together, and the only passages where he can indicate any figuring at all are simple and massive outbursts of full harmony. The continuo part is manifestly obsolescent in the very works in which it is most carefully prescribed.

Nevertheless, I was greatly relieved when I found in an edition of this symphony older than the current reprints that there was a genuine continuo instead of the mid-nineteenth century additional accompaniments which I suspected as being such in the ordinarily available score. I was also amused to find that my conjectures were right as to certain places where the Leipzigers of the 'fifties or 'sixties had found Philipp Emanuel's style not quite literal enough to be accepted as correct. Their minds had not advanced from the use of explicit simile to that of metaphor, pure or mixed; and I found my suspicions well grounded that the symphony has been carefully amended on the lines of the great Shakespeare scholar who restored its manifest original common sense to the sentiment of the Duke who could find (according to the true reading) 'sermons in books, stones in the running brooks'. Another thing which the mid-nineteenth century Leipziger abhorred was abrupt endings, and my head swells with the pride with which I verified my guess that the end of Philipp Emanuel's finale had been amended in the style of one of Barry Pain's sententious domestic tyrants, who observed that 'the inevitable consequences then happened, as they so often do'.

Philipp Emanuel Bach is, as all the world knows, the link between the polyphonic style and forms of his father and those of

Haydn and Mozart. On this assumption nothing should be easier
than to distinguish between those aspects of his art which reflect
the past and those which 'coldly predict the style of the future';
and if you happen to quote from an edition of his sonatas by Bülow
you can easily find excellent illustrations of both tendencies where-
ever Bülow has been pleased to put in something of his own. Even
without Bülow's 'splendid emendacity', the history of music is
enormously simplified if we do not drag in dates. The trouble
begins when we find that Philipp Emanuel Bach was writing in
a well-developed style of his own at the time when his father
produced the B minor Mass, and that his last set of sonatas was
produced in the year of Mozart's *Don Giovanni*. The present
symphony was, as far as I can make out, composed in 1780, and is
thus a year later than Mozart's epoch-making Paris Symphony.
In style and form it has not the remotest resemblance either to his
father's work or to the styles of Mozart and Haydn. Unlike the
pianoforte works, it is not really on sonata lines at all, except in
certain superficial matters. In relation to contemporary music, it
is in line with Gluck's overtures, and it shares with them a doubtful collateral ancestry with the early concerto grosso. Probably
Sammartini's style may be among its origins. At all events, we
have the negative evidence that Haydn was very much annoyed
with people who saw in his work the influence of Sammartini, who
he said was 'a dauber', and who, as I have pointed out in the
above-mentioned essay on Gluck, was for that very reason a most
useful pioneer in the art of splashing the colours of stage scenery
out of a pail.

Philipp Emanuel Bach's Symphony in D has the right of a
mature work of art to exist on its own merits. Its historical origins
have needed this amount of explanation, because without them the
listener is sure to approach the work under preconceptions equally
historical in appearance, but entirely misleading as to its character.

* Here a disastrous explanatory chord is inserted by the Leipzig editors.

Ex. 2.

The first movement consists of masses of material alternating
more or less on concerto grosso lines and connected by an all-
pervading rhythmic figure. Of the two groups, one is for strings
and the other for wind. They alternate in a scheme not unlike that
of Gluck's *Iphigénie en Aulide* (without the introduction), and
have, in virtue of a certain amount of recapitulation, the same
resemblance to sonata form. The second group contains a definite
new theme.

Ex. 3.

At the end of the movement there is a surprising modulation to
the dominant of E flat, with a moment of dramatic recitative.
Philipp Emanuel Bach's works are often distinguished by some
such fantastic event, but his dramatic or recitative-like gestures,
while beautiful in themselves, are precisely what deprives the
incidents of any importance as an addition to the resources of
music. Not many years after this symphony, Haydn put the slow
movement of his greatest pianoforte sonata into the key a semitone
above that of the first movement; but you will not find Haydn
explaining away his paradox by saying 'Then a strange thing happened'. He is not telling fairy tales, but is establishing facts which
permanently enlarge the range of music. Far be it from us to say
that Philipp Emanuel Bach is mistaken in leaving his harmonic
miracle in the state of a fairy-tale surprise. The *Arabian Nights*
would not be improved, either as a work of art, or as a study in
anthropology, by any explanation of the Magic Carpet as an intelligent anticipation of the aeroplane.

Philipp Emanuel Bach's little miracle leads to a delightful slow
tune scored for divided violas and basses doubled by two flutes

a couple of octaves higher. Bach explicitly leaves this essentially modern or Haydnesque orchestral effect without help from the continuo. Certainly, nothing better illustrates how inevitable was the doom of that excellent institution. It has, in fact, already attained the state indicated by Barry Pain's hero; the inevitable consequences are beginning to happen often, and the Bread-and-butter-fly has already perished for lack of weak tea with cream in it.

Bach's delicious tune rouses itself to begin a second part, which has the energy to modulate in rising sequences. Such energy is dangerous. The original D major breaks through the unguarded harmonic frontiers, and the symphony ends with a brilliant little jig in binary form.

Some ten or a dozen years after this symphony Haydn produced his ninety-eighth symphony in London and galvanized the gentleman 'at the pianoforte' into life by a brilliant figure near the end of the finale, pencilled into the score, probably during rehearsal. That gentleman ought already to have long been obsolete, but Spohr found him still in possession in London years after Mendelssohn had persuaded the Philharmonic Orchestra to play under the guidance of his baton. Thus slowly did we bid farewell to the continuo generations after we had lost all idea of what it meant.

BEETHOVEN

FIRST SYMPHONY IN C MAJOR, OP. 21

1 *Adagio molto, leading to* 2 *Allegro con brio.* 3 *Andante cantabile con moto*
4 MENUETTO: *Allegro molto, e vivace.* 5 *Adagio, leading to*
6 *Allegro molto e vivace.*

Beethoven's first symphony, produced in 1800, is a fitting farewell
to the eighteenth century. It has more of the true nineteenth-
century Beethoven in its depths than he allows to appear upon the
surface. Its style is that of the Comedy of Manners, as translated
by Mozart into the music of his operas and of his most light-
hearted works of symphonic and chamber music. The fact that it
is comedy from beginning to end is prophetic of changes in music
no less profound than those which the French Revolution brought
about in the social organism. But Beethoven was the most conservative of revolutionists; a Revolutionist without the R; and in his
first symphony he shows, as has often been remarked, a characteristic caution in handling sonata form for the first time with a full
orchestra. But the caution which seems so obvious to us was not
noticed by his contemporary critics. We may leave out of account
the oft-quoted fact that several Viennese musicians objected to his
beginning his introduction with chords foreign to the key; such
objectors were pedants miserably behind the culture not only of
their own time but of the previous generation. They were the kind
of pedants who are not even classicists, and whose grammatical
knowledge is based upon no known language. Carl Philipp
Emanuel Bach, who, much more than his father, was at that time
regarded as a founder of modern music by persons who considered
the lately deceased Mozart a dangerous person, had gone very much
farther in this matter of opening in a foreign key than Beethoven
ever went in the whole course of his career. Where the contemporary critics showed intelligent observation was in marking,
though with mild censure, the fact that Beethoven's first symphony is written so heavily for the wind band that it seems almost
more like a 'Harmoniemusik' than a proper orchestral piece. This
observation was technically correct. Beethoven had at that time
a young composer's interest in wind instruments, which he handled
with a mastery stimulated by the wind-band ('Harmonie') masterpieces of Mozart. His handling of the strings was not less masterly,
though his interest in their possibilities developed mightily in later
works.

The position then is this: that in his first symphony Beethoven
overwhelmed his listeners with a scoring for the full wind band

almost as highly developed as it was ever destined to be (except that he did not as yet appreciate the possibilities of the clarinet as an instrument for the foreground). The scale of the work as a whole gave no scope for an equivalent development of the strings. Even to-day there is an appreciable difficulty in accommodating the wind band of Beethoven's first symphony to a small body of strings, and consequently an agreeable absence of the difficulties of balance which have become notorious in the performance of classical symphonies by large orchestras without double wind.

The introduction, made famous by pedantic contemporary objections to its mixed tonality, has in later times been sharply criticized by so great a Beethoven worshipper as Sir George Grove for its ineffectual scoring. With all respect to that pioneer of English musical culture, such a criticism is evidently traceable to the effect of pianoforte arrangements, which often suggest that a chord which is loud for the individual players of the orchestra is meant to be as loud as a full orchestral passage. When two pianists play these *forte-piano* chords in a duet, they naturally make as much noise as they can get out of their instrument. This sets up an impression in early life which many conductors and critics fail to get rid of. Hence the complaint that the pizzicato chords of the strings are feeble, a complaint that assumes that it is their business to be forcible.

I am delighted to find myself anticipated by Mr. Vaclav Talich in the view that the opening is mysterious and groping, and that the first grand note of triumph is sounded when the dominant is reached.

For the rest, a list of the principal themes will cover the ground of the work, leaving but little need for comment.

The first theme of the allegro con brio is a quietly energetic, business-like proposition, moving in sequences from tonic to supertonic, and thence rising through subdominant to dominant.

It is the opening of a formal rather than of a big work. If you wish to see the same proposition in a loftier style, look at Beethoven's C major String Quintet, where the same harmonic plan is executed in a single eight-bar phrase.

The transition-theme needs no quotation. Not only is it extremely formal, but, instead of establishing the key of the 'second subject' (G major) by getting on to its dominant, it is contented with the old practical joke, which Mozart uses only in his earlier or lighter works, the joke of taking the mere dominant *chord* (here the chord of G) as equivalent to the dominant *key*, and starting in that key with no more ado.

Ex. 3.
Oboe.   Flute.

It is solemn impertinence to suppose that there is anything early or primitive in Beethoven's technique in this symphony. In at least twenty works in sonata form he had already been successful in a range of bold experiments far exceeding that covered by Haydn and Mozart: and it now interested him to write a small and comic sonata for orchestra. After Ex. 3 he strikes a deeper note; and the passage in which that theme descends into dark regions around its minor mode, while an oboe sings plaintively above, is prophetic of the future Beethoven in proportion as it is inspired by Mozart. Several other themes ensue. The development is terse and masterly, and the coda is more brilliant and massive than Mozart's style would have admitted.

The slow movement begins, like its more enterprising twin-brother, the andante of the C minor String Quartet, op. 18, No. 4, with a kittenish theme treated like a fugue.

Ex. 4.

Here again, as in the first movement (and *not* as in the C minor Quartet), the second subject follows with no further transition than a taking of the old dominant chord for the new dominant key.

Ex. 5.

Two other themes follow; the second being notable for its under-lying drum-rhythm. Beethoven got the idea of using C and G drums in this F major movement from Mozart's wonderful Linz Symphony.

Dr. Ernest Walker has well observed that the minuet is a really great Beethoven scherzo, larger than any in the sonatas, trios, and quartets before the opus fifties, and far more important than that of the Second Symphony. I quote the profound modulations which lead back to the theme in the middle of the second part.

Ex. 6.

The trio, with its throbbing wind-band chords and mysterious violin runs, is, like so many of Beethoven's early minuets and trios prophetic of Schumann's most intimate epigrammatic sentiments. But, as Schumann rouses himself from romantic dreams to ostenta-tiously prosaic aphorisms, so Beethoven rouses himself to a brilliant forte before returning to the so-called minuet.

The finale begins with a Haydnesque joke; the violins letting out a scale as a cat from a bag.

Ex. 7.

The theme thus released puts its first rhythmic stress after the scale, as shown by my figures under the bars. It has a second strain, on fresh material.

Ex. 8.

The transition takes the trouble to reach the real dominant of the new key. The second subject begins with the following theme.

and, after a syncopated cadence-theme, concludes with a development of the scale figure.

The course of the movement is normal, though brilliantly organized, until the coda in which an absurd little march enters, as if everybody must know who it is.

As it, like every conceivable theme, can be accompanied by a scale, the Organic Unity of the Whole is vindicated as surely as there is a B in Both.

SECOND SYMPHONY IN D MAJOR, OP. 36

1 *Adagio molto, leading to* 2 *Allegro con brio.* 3 *Larghetto.*
4 SCHERZO, *Allegro.* 5 *Allegro molto.*

The works that produce the most traceable effects in the subsequent history of an art are not always those which come to be regarded as epoch-making. The epoch-making works are, more often than not, merely shocking to just those contemporaries best qualified to appreciate them; and by the time they become acceptable they are accepted as inimitable. Even their general types of form are chronicled in history as the 'inventor's' contribution to the progress of his art, only to be the more conspicuously avoided by later artists. Thus Beethoven 'invented' the scherzo; and no art-form has been laid down more precisely and even rigorously than that of his dozen most typical examples. Yet the scherzos of Schubert, Schumann, Mendelssohn, and Brahms differ as widely from Beethoven's, and from each other, as Beethoven's differ from Mozart's minuets. The nearest approach to a use of Beethoven's model is to be found where we least expect it, in the grim and almost macabre scherzos of Chopin.

Far otherwise is it with certain works which immediately impressed contemporaries as marking a startling advance in the art without a disconcerting change in its language. Beethoven's Second Symphony was evidently larger and more brilliant than any that had been heard up to 1801; and people who could understand the three great symphonies that Mozart had poured out in the six weeks between the end of June and the 10th of August 1788, would find Beethoven's language less abstruse, though the brilliance and breadth of his design and the dramatic vigour of his style were so exciting that it was thought advisable to warn young persons against so 'subversive' (*sittenverderblich*) a work. What the effect of such warnings might be is a bootless inquiry; but Beethoven's Second Symphony and his next opus, the Concerto in C minor (op. 37), have produced a greater number of definite echoes from later composers than any other of his works before the Ninth Symphony. And the echoes are by no means confined to imitative or classicist efforts: they are to be found in things like Schubert's Grand Duo and Schumann's Fourth Symphony, works written at high noontide of their composers' powers and quite unrestrained in the urgency of important new developments. Indeed, Beethoven's Second Symphony itself seems almost classicist in the neighbourhood of such works as his profoundly dramatic Sonata in D minor, op. 31, no. 2; while we can go back as far as the C minor Trio, op. 1, no. 3, and find Beethoven already both as mature and as *sittenverderblich* in style and matter.

The Second Symphony begins with a grand introduction, more in Haydn's manner than in Mozart's. It is Haydn's way to begin his introduction, after a good *coup d'archet*, with a broad melody fit for an independent slow movement, and to proceed from this to romantic modulations. Mozart, on the rare occasions when he writes a big introduction, builds it with introductory types of phrase throughout. Beethoven here makes the best of both methods; and the climax of his romantic modulations, instead of ending in one of Haydn's pauses in an attitude of surprise, leads to a fine quiet ('dominant-pedal') approach, in Mozart's grandest style, that finally runs without break into the allegro. Contemporaries were probably the last to feel, as we feel, the 'influence' of Haydn and Mozart in all this; for this is in all respects the real thing, and Beethoven was the only survivor of Haydn and Mozart who could do it.

The main theme of the first movement—

Ex. 1.

has often been quoted thus far as an example of complacent formalism; but if you get to the end of the paragraph you will not accept that view. The sentence fills eighteen bars (overlapping into the next sentence), and takes shape, not as a formal sequence, but as an expanding melody by no means easily foreseen in its course or stiff in its proportions.

The main theme of the second subject—

Ex. 2.

has a certain almost military brilliance, which is in keeping with the fact that nobody wrote more formidably spirited marches than Beethoven.

Towards the end of the exposition, the semiquaver figure (*a*) of the 'complacently formal' first theme (Ex. 1) gives rise to one of Beethoven's most *sittenverderblich* dramatic incidents.

The whole course of the movement is normal, but its brilliance and energy were quite unprecedented in orchestral music at the time; nor could Beethoven himself have surpassed the choral grandeur of the climax of his coda until he had revolutionized the language of music. The choral quality comes from 'The Heavens are telling' in Haydn's *Creation*.

The larghetto is one of the most luxurious slow movements in the world; and there is small wonder that the discursive Schubert ran away with large slices of it in his Grand Duo (see Ex. 6). Beethoven begins with a leisurely tune in two strains, of which Ex. 3 shows the first figures.

Ex. 3.

Both strains are repeated; the repetitions being almost the only passages in this symphony in which the clarinets emerge from an archaic state of servitude. To many a musical child, or child in musical matters, this movement has brought about the first awakening to a sense of beauty in music. A binary melody with repeats is a bulky affair to work into sonata form in a slow tempo; and so, in spite of the direction *larghetto*, the tempo is not really very slow. Beethoven later on arranged this symphony as a pianoforte trio (astonishingly badly too); and it is significant that he added to the slow movement the direction *quasi andante*.

The music flows along with a reckless opulence of themes. In the second subject three are well worth quoting; the opening theme—

Ex. 4.

for the sake of its influence on the jaunty second subject of the finale of Schumann's Fourth Symphony; its continuation—

Ex. 5.

on account of its dramatic urgency in the most lofty vein of Italian *opera seria*; and its debonair cadence theme—

Ex. 6.

which so completely captivated Schubert in his Grand Duo.

In spite of all this luxury the movement achieves its career in perfect form, and at no unreasonable length.

The tiny scherzo—

Ex. 7.

is not as large as Haydn's later minuets, but is typical Beethoven of any period, early or late: that is to say, he would not have been ashamed to write a movement on similar lines even in his last quartets. But when we come to the trio there is a notable contrast between the young man of 1802 playing with children, and the seer of 1824 revealing intimations of immortality. (Compare the trio of the scherzo of the Ninth Symphony.)

Ex. 8.

Brahms, in his Serenade, op. 11, exercised himself in small classical forms by an amusing combination of the scherzos of Beethoven's Septet and Second Symphony.

With the finale we find ourselves unquestionably in Beethoven's 'second period'. It is a rondo on a powerfully humorous theme as original as any that Beethoven invented.

The transition-theme, with its almost ecclesiastical tone, strikes a grand note of contrast which will be very useful in the coda.

Just before the second subject a figure requires quotation—

as being afterwards put to dramatic use in effecting the returns to the main theme.

The second subject expands in more leisurely rhythms.

The coda is pure Beethoven in full power.

THIRD SYMPHONY IN E FLAT MAJOR (SINFONIA EROICA), OP. 55

1 *Allegro con brio.* 2 *Marcia Funebre: Adagio assai.* 3 SCHERZO: *Allegro vivace.* 4 FINALE: *Allegro molto.*

Every one knows the story of how Beethoven's admiration for Napoleon inspired this symphony, and how the news of Napoleon's coronation infuriated Beethoven almost to the point of destroying the finished work. A copy with an autograph title-page is in the musical archives of Vienna; and where Bonaparte's name once stood, a ragged hole attests the truth of the story.

Much comment has been wasted on the position of the funeral march, and on the scherzo and finale which follow it. One very useful treatise on composition actually cites the Eroica Symphony as an example of the way in which the sonata form loads the composer with inappropriate additions to his programme. Such criticism has two aspects, the literary, which concerns the programme, and the musical, which concerns the form. In order to be literary, it is not necessary to be unmusical. Beethoven does not think a symphony a reasonable vehicle for a chronological biography of Napoleon; but he does think it the best possible way of expressing his feelings about heroes and hero-worship. Death must be faced by heroes and hero-worshippers, and if what heroes know about it is of any value to mankind, they may as well tell us of their knowledge while they are alive. And the mere courage of battle is not enough; it is the stricken nations whose sorrow must be faced. Afterwards the world revives, ready to nourish more heroes for happier times.

I. *Allegro con brio.* After two strong introductory chords the violoncellos state the principal theme. It is simply the notes of a common chord swinging backwards and forwards in a quietly energetic rhythm. Then, as the violins enter with a palpitating high note, the harmony becomes clouded, soon however to resolve in sunshine. Whatever you may enjoy or miss in the Eroica Symphony, remember this cloud: it leads eventually to one of the most astonishing and subtle dramatic strokes in all music.

Long afterwards, when the vast 'second subject' has displayed its procession of themes, beginning with one which, though of cardinal importance, has escaped the notice of analysts—

and when the still more vast development has twice introduced an entirely new lyric passage—

we are waiting on the threshold of the original key in breathless suspense for the return of the first theme. At last the suspense becomes too much for one of the horns, who, while the echoes of the dominant chord are still whispering, softly gives out the tonic chord of the theme. The orchestra instantly awakens and settles down to recapitulate the opening. (Let us hope that the days are past when any one could doubt the sanity of Beethoven's genius in that famous collision of shadowy harmonies; but even Bülow corrected the passage into exactly the sort of lopsided platitude that creeps into a classical text through the mediation of a 'gloss'.) Soon the theme reaches the little cloud that we noticed in the beginning. The cloud 'resolves' in a new direction, and the sun comes out in one of the two keys whose only characteristic is that of complete contradiction to the tonic which has been regained after all that suspense.

Ex. 4.

The other contradictory key follows, by way of restoring the balance; and then the main key proves strong enough to stand the shock, and the design finishes its normal course and expands freely in its huge peroration.

The other surprises and strokes of genius in this movement may safely be left to speak for themselves; with the exception of the last of all, which, together with the unobtrusive but cardinally important theme it concerns (Ex. 2), has singularly contrived to escape the notice of all the best-known commentators, including even Weingartner. It need not escape the notice of any listener, for it is marked by a sudden and impressive lull at the very height of the final climax.

II. *Marcia Funebre.* The great length of the funeral march results mainly from the size of its principal theme. This is a broad melody in two portions, each of which is given out by the strings and repeated (in the first case with a close in a new key) by the wind. This takes time; and in addition there is a series of afterthoughts

which brings this main theme to a close on a scale almost large
enough for a complete movement. Yet Beethoven's purpose is
to work out the whole in rondo form; that is to say, a form in
which the main theme recurs like a choral refrain alternating with
at least two contrasted episodes. It is obvious that such a purpose
can here be carried out only by a miracle of concentration and
terseness; but such miracles are Beethoven's normal form of
action, and this funeral march broadens in its flow as it develops.
The first episode is a regular trio in the major mode, beginning in
consolation and twice bursting into triumph. Then the light fails
and the mournful main theme returns. Its energy cannot carry it
even through its first phrase; and the second episode breaks in.
It is a solemn double fugue which Weingartner has well called
Aeschylean.

Ex. 5.

This comes to a climax and ends with a solemn slow close in the
dominant. Upon this a fragment of the main theme rises upwards
with a sigh which is suddenly answered by a roar from the depths,
and an upheaval fit for a setting of the *Dies Irae*. 'Never' (says
Weingartner) 'has a fearful catastrophe been described with simpler
means.' The tumult subsides in the weeping of a *lacrimosa dies*,
and through the sound of weeping the entire theme of the march
is heard in both its portions and with its whole series of afterthoughts. These close in a change of harmony; and then some
moments are measured only as it were by the slow swing of
a pendulum. Above this enters at last, in a distant key, the
beginning of a new message of consolation, but it dies away and
the movement concludes with a final utterance of the main theme,
its rhythms and accents utterly broken with grief.

III. This scherzo is the first in which Beethoven fully attained
Haydn's desire to replace the minuet by something on a scale
comparable to the rest of a great symphony. Its characteristics
are unmistakable, and we need only mention the long, subdued
whispering of the opening, blazing out so suddenly into a fortissimo;
the trio with its three horns, whose classical imperfections of technique Beethoven has exploited to poetic ends, which the perfectly
equipped modern player has to rediscover by careful research; and
the mysterious coda with its menacing drums.

IV. The finale is in a form which was unique when it appeared,
and has remained unique ever since. This has given rise to a widespread notion that it is formless or incoherent. It is neither; and its

life, which is its form, does not depend upon a label. The best way to understand it is not to think of the important earlier pianoforte *Variations and Fugue on a theme from Prometheus*, on which its material is based, but simply to identify its material under three headings, a Bass, a Tune, and a Fugue. But first there is a short and fiery introduction which asserts a foreign key. It abruptly corrects this as if it had found it to be a mistake. Then the Bass is solemnly given by the strings, pizzicato, and echoed by the wind. Its first part happens to make a grotesque but presentable theme, and many a later composer has owed Beethoven a grudge for thus indelibly stamping his name on one of the most unavoidable basses a simple melody can have. But the second part is quite absurd, and we can almost see Beethoven laughing at our mystified faces as it digs us in the ribs. However the whole Bass proceeds to put on clothes, of a respectable contrapuntal cut; and by the time we are almost ready to believe its pretensions, the Tune comes sailing over it in full radiance and we think no more of the Bass, though it faithfully performs its duty as such. The vision of dry bones is accomplished.

Ex. 6.

So far Beethoven's design has been exactly that of his *Introduzione col basso del tema* in the *Prometheus* variations; but now, instead of making variations, he leads in a few argumentative steps to a new key and then proceeds to the Fugue. The subject of the Fugue comes from the Bass, and is worked up to a vigorous climax which suddenly breaks off into a rich double variation (i.e. a variation in which the repeats are themselves varied) of the Tune in a remote key. In the second part of this variation the flute is very brilliant, and the orchestra repeats the part with rough energy, leading to a high-spirited episode in a dance-rhythm, with the first four notes of the Bass sturdily marking time throughout. After this the first part of the Tune reappears and soon leads to a resumption of the Fugue with new features—inversion of its subject; combination with part of the Tune in a new accentuation, &c. The Fugue, which is here throughout in the main key, now comes to a grand climax ending with an anticipatory pause. Then, like the opening of the gates of Paradise, the Tune enters slowly (*poco andante*) in a glorious double variation, the richness of which has led some analysts to think that much of its material is gratuitously new, whereas in fact the slightness of the second part of the Tune is expressly designed to give scope for the utmost freedom in variations. Then (as in the parallel finale to the pianoforte variations, though with incomparably more solemn pomp) there is a tremendous fortissimo variation with the Tune in the bass. The original Bass had finally disappeared with the last Fugue.

After this climax all is coda, and one of the most profound codas Beethoven ever wrote. With a passing hint at a new variation, the music modulates with some passion through a distant key to a point where it suddenly melts into a mood we have not found before in the whole symphony. It is the mood of that mysterious and true humour that is not far from tears; and without it the greatest of heroes is but a demigod with powers alien to humanity and therefore less than divine. Here, just upon the close of his heroic symphony, Beethoven holds us for the last time in suspense, until the orchestra blazes out in a larger version of the fiery introduction and brings the work to its triumphant end.

FOURTH SYMPHONY IN B♭ MAJOR, OP. 60

1 *Adagio, leading to* 2 *Allegro vivace.* 3 *Adagio.* 4 *Allegro vivace.*
5 *Allegro ma non troppo.*

As in later years Beethoven followed his gigantic Seventh Symphony by the terse and unshadowed comedy of his Eighth, so he followed his Eroica Symphony (the longest of all his works except the Ninth) by a symphony the proportions and scope of which are, except for three powerful passages, almost within the range of Mozart and Haydn. Yet the exceptional passages are in no way 'out of the picture'; and the contemporary critics who accused Beethoven's Fourth Symphony of every fault a symphony could have, would have had more difficulty than we in picking them out. The solemn introduction, which excited Weber's derision for its few notes spread over five minutes; the dramatic hush and crescendo leading to the recapitulation in the first movement; the astonishing middle episode of the slow movement, and the double alternating repetition of scherzo and trio; these are the features we recognize as peculiarly Beethovenish in this work. To contemporaries they were mere additional eccentricities in a work in which the whole style, being Beethoven's, was notoriously extravagant; and the chances are that if the work had been produced under the name of Mozart or Haydn, the outstanding features would not have been noticed at all, and the work would have been sleepily accepted as a master-piece at once. As it was, people listened whether they liked it or not.

The Fourth Symphony is perhaps the work in which Beethoven first fully reveals his mastery of movement. He had already shown his command of a vastly wider range of musical possibilities than that of Mozart or Haydn. And he had shown no lack of ease and power in the handling of his new resources. But now he shows that these resources can be handled in such a way that Mozart's own freedom of movement reappears as one of the most striking qualities of the whole. The sky-dome vastness of the dark intro-duction is evident at the outset; but it is first fully understood in the daylight of the opening of the allegro; for which reason I give the connecting passage.

Ex. 1.

Note how the new quick tempo asserts itself with the muscular strength of real bodily movement. Ordinary writers of Italian opera buffa, and some ambitious modern composers, would think they were asserting the quick tempo if they began the allegro with the pianissimo passage (with figure (*b*) in the bassoons) which follows the tutti counterstatement of the present theme, and which, put where Beethoven puts it, has the settled vital energy of a top that has 'gone to sleep'. The 'spin' of the whole movement, tremendous as it is, depends entirely on the variety, the contrasts, and the order of themes and sequences, varying in length from odd fractions of bars (e.g. the exciting three-minim staccato sequence early in the second subject) to the 32-bar and even longer processes in the development. This statement may seem self-evident; but, of all the arts that have been lost since 'classical' times, this art of movement is the most characteristic, the most universally necessary, and the most immediately successful in its results. A composer who could keep up the spin, as Beethoven keeps it up in the most ordinary levels of his Fourth Symphony, would have no difficulty in tackling the most powerful inspirations when they occurred to him.

The second subject begins with a conversation between the bassoon, the oboe, and the flute, which leads to the 3-minim sequence I mentioned above, and to a number of other themes, ending with a syncopated cadence-theme which gathers up a thread started in the transition between first and second subject.

The development keeps up the spin by moving on lines far broader than any yet indicated by the exposition. The delightful cantabile added as a counterpoint to the entries (in various keys) of the main theme, is one of the salient features. Nearly half the whole development is occupied by the wonderful hovering on the threshold of the remote key of B natural major in order to return therefrom to the tonic B flat, by a process resembling, more subtly and on a higher plane, the return in the first movement of the Waldstein Sonata (written about a year earlier). The recapitulation is quite normal, and the coda is no longer than one of Mozart's usual final expansions.

The slow movement is a full-sized rondo, a form which is extremely spacious when worked out in a slow tempo. I need only quote its main theme, with the stroke of genius achieved in the all-pervading rhythmic figure of its introductory bar—

Ex. 2.

and the opening of its first episode or second subject, a still more subtle melody—

Ex. 3.

The main theme returns in a florid variation; and the middle episode, which follows, is one of the most imaginative passages anywhere in Beethoven. From its mysterious end arises the return of the main theme in its varied form, this time in the flute; whereupon follows a regular recapitulation, including the transition and the second-subject episode (Ex. 3). The coda consists of a final allusion to the main theme, dispersing itself mysteriously over the orchestra, till the drums make an end by recalling the opening stroke of genius.

For the scherzo no quotations are needed: the double repetition of scherzo and trio makes everything as clear as any dance, in spite of the numerous rhythmic whims. The final repetition of the scherzo is abridged (in other cases Beethoven prefers to make full repetition aggressively the point of the joke). Never have three short bars contained more meaning than the coda in which the two horns blow the whole movement away.

The finale represents Beethoven's full maturity in that subtlest of all disguises, his discovery of the true inwardness of Mozart and Haydn; a discovery inaccessible to him whenever, as in a few early works (notably the Septet), he seemed or tried to imitate them, but possible as soon as he obtained full freedom in handling his own resources. Everything is present in this unsurpassably adroit and playful finale; and it is all pure Beethoven, even when, by drawing out its opening theme into quavers with pauses, it borrows an old joke of Haydn's, the excellence of which lies in its badness. Lamb would have understood it—in spite of the Essay on Ears.

I quote the main themes of the first subject—

and of the second—

To do justice to the boldness and power that underly all the grace and humour of this finale, it would be necessary to go into details. It is a study for a lifetime; but, once begun, it is in many ways more directly useful to the artist than the study of things the power of which is allowed to appear on the surface. Those who think the finale of the Fourth Symphony 'too light' will never get nearer than Spohr (if as near) towards a right understanding of the Fifth, however much they may admire it.

FIFTH SYMPHONY IN C MINOR, OP. 67

1 *Allegro con brio.* 2 *Andante con moto.* 3 *Allegro, leading to*
4 *Allegro, ending with* 5 *Presto.*

This work shares with Beethoven's Seventh Symphony the distinction of being not only among the most popular but also among the least misunderstood of musical classics. It has not failed to inspire 'roaring cataracts of nonsense' from commentators, but the nonsense has, for the most part, been confined to technical matters of little concern to the naive (or ideal) listener; though one heresy I shall discuss here, since on it depends one's whole view of the difference between real composition and mere manufacture. Another immensely lucky fact conducive to the popular appreciation of this symphony is that the famous phrase (made still more famous by Robert Louis Stevenson in *The Ebb Tide*)—the phrase which describes the theme of the first movement as 'destiny knocking at the door'—is no mere figment of a commentator, but is Beethoven's very own words. Mistakes and misreadings in this mighty work have been as frequent as anywhere; the very band-parts issued under the auspices of the 'critical' edition have some scandalously stupid editorial alterations; but not even the notorious old trick of changing the first three quavers into crotchets has been able to make any headway against the overwhelming power and clearness of the whole.

Some good, however, may be done by denouncing the heresy which preaches that 'the whole first movement is built up of the initial figure of four notes'. It is well worth refuting, for it has led to most of the worst features of that kind of academic music which goes furthest to justify the use of the word 'academic' as a term of vulgar abuse. No great music has ever been built from an initial figure of four notes. As I have said elsewhere, you might as well say that every piece of music is built from an initial figure of *one* note. You may profitably say that the highest living creatures have begun from the single nucleated cell. But no ultra-microscope has yet unravelled the complexities of the single living cell; nor, if the spectroscope is to be believed, are we yet very fully informed of the complexities of a single atom of iron: and it is quite absurd to suppose that the evolution of a piece of music can proceed from 'a simple figure of four notes' on lines in the least resembling those of nature. As far as I know, Weingartner is the first writer who has pointed out the truth that the first movement of the C minor symphony is really remarkable for the length of its sentences; that the first sentences, instead of being 'built up' from a single figure, *break up* into other sentences of even greater variety and breadth; and that the composer who first really 'built up' symphonic movements out of short figures was not Beethoven but Schumann, whose handling of the larger forms became sectional, diffuse, and yet stiff for this very reason.

Obviously the same argument applies to the whole theory of Wagnerian *Leitmotif*. Wagner attained full mastery over the broadest sweep of sequence that music has yet achieved. This alone suffices to refute the orthodox Wagnerian belief that his music is 'built up' from the scraps of theme to which it can be reduced by its dramatic associations, and by the general possibility of articulating big phrases into small figures.

In the first fine careless rapture of Wagnerian analysis it was discovered that the 'four taps', with which 'destiny knocks at the door' in the first movement, recur elsewhere; once (quite accidentally, though in an impressive passage) in the slow movement, and very prominently in the second theme of that dream of terror which we technically call the scherzo (Ex. 4). This profound discovery was supposed to reveal an unsuspected unity in the work; but it does not seem to have been carried far enough. It conclusively proves that the Sonata Appassionata, the G major Pianoforte Concerto, the third movement of the Quartet, op. 74, and, with the final consummation of a fifth tap, the Violin Concerto, all belong to the C minor Symphony; for the same rhythmic figure pervades them too. The simple truth is that Beethoven could not do without just such purely rhythmic figures at this stage of his art. It was absolutely necessary that every inner part in his texture should assert its own life; but at the same time it was equally necessary that it should not cause constant or rapid changes of harmony by doing so. Figures that can identify a theme while remaining on one note are the natural response to these requirements. In his later works Beethoven used more and more polyphony in Bach's sense; and rhythmic figures no longer pressed into the foreground of his invention, though he could still use them when he wanted them. It is astonishing how many of Beethoven's themes can be recognized by their bare rhythm without quoting any melody at all.

Here are some specimens, not including those mentioned above:

In selecting the following illustrations for the C minor Symphony I have been guided mainly by the purpose of counteracting the effects of the 'short figure' heresy, and secondly, by the chance of removing by numerals a misconception which is likely to arise from the notation of long sentences in such very short bars. Thus Ex. 1 evidently comprises only the first half of a big sentence. (The crotchet tails and the small added notes show the pathetic new light in which it appears at the very end of the movement.)

Ex. 1.

Ex. 2, which gives the opening of the second subject, shows first the way in which the famous rhythmic figure (*a*) pervades the whole movement, and secondly, with the aid of my numerals, the scansion of the four-bar rhythm.

Ex. 2.

From the second and third bars of this quotation (marked 1 and 2 in the rhythmic periods) are derived, first, the famous diminuendo of chords in dialogue between strings and wind near the end of the development, and secondly, the furious opening of the coda, one of the most powerful tuttis ever written, and written with incredibly few notes for its weight. Of the recapitulation two observations may here be made: first, that, as Weingartner points out, the pathetic cadenza for the oboe at the end of Ex. 1 is the outcome of a melodic line which it has been tracing for the last sixteen bars; and secondly, that it is really a mistaken reverence for Beethoven which puts up with the comic bassoon instead of horns when we have Ex. 2 in C major. Beethoven had not time to change the horns from E flat; but now that the modern horn has all the notes that were missing in Beethoven's day, there is no reason why his spirit should continue to put up with an unmitigated nuisance, even if we are sure that he put up with it in a mood of Shakespearian humour. The continuation of the passage has a bitter note that was not in the original statement.

The andante I have left without illustration. Shakespeare's women have the same courage, the same beauty of goodness, and the same humour. In form the movement is unique, if dimly suggested by Haydn's special form of variations on two alternating themes. But here the themes are of quite peculiar types. Violas and 'cellos (it is curious that Beethoven never uses orchestral 'cellos for melody without doubling them by violas) state the first theme in a single broad phrase, the end of which the higher instruments echo and carry on into a series of echoing afterthoughts. Then the second theme begins, very simply, pauses on a wistful note, and suddenly bursts into a blaze of triumph in a remote key, C major, the tonic of the whole symphony. The triumph dies away into a passage of profound mystery and pathos, which leads back to the key of the movement (A flat). The first theme now returns varied in notes twice as rapid as the time-beats (the kind of variation which in the eighteenth century would be called a double). A clarinet holds a sustained note above, with a boldness which led early critics to suspect a blunder. (Dvořák did not think so when he reproduced it in the slow movement of his first symphony.) Again the second theme follows, likewise with a quicker accompaniment, and leads to its blaze of triumph, which again dies out in the recognition that its day is not yet come. A second double of the first theme follows in due course, but, instead of getting beyond the first phrase, is given three times, the last time forte, leading to a climax and a pause. Then there is an astonishing series of meditations and adventures, on which the second theme breaks with its full note of triumph. The reaction from this (in one of those profound passages which early critics found quite ridiculous because they listened with ears attuned to the proportions of a Mozart symphony) leads to an exquisite treatment of the first theme smiling through tears in the minor mode. Then, after more meditative delay, it comes fortissimo, for the

first and only time, on the full orchestra. Note the imitation by
the wood-wind, if you can hear it through the far from evenly-
balanced scoring. This time the echoing afterthoughts follow;
and nothing in music is bolder and more convincing than the
profusion with which these afterthoughts give rise to others, until
the whole movement is rounded off in perfect proportions which
at no point have revealed to us what they are going to be until the
last note has been heard.

The third movement I will not describe seriatim; but there
is one piece of information which is very interesting historically,
and which commentators, including Sir George Grove, have failed
to make as clear as it might be. My quotations are again furnished
with numerals which show where the pulses of four-bar rhythm
begin. The movement has often been scanned wrongly from
beginning to end, and the writer in *Grove's Dictionary* who cites
the trio as an unacknowledged case of three-bar rhythm has
blundered straight into the trap.

Now it is well known that in the early editions there were two
superfluous bars where the first theme (Ex. 3) returns after the trio.
The second and third full bars (marked 1 and 2 in my rhythmic
numbers) were written twice, at first legato as in Ex. 3, and then
in crotchets with rests, as they ought to be after the trio. Beethoven
wrote to his publishers to correct the redundancy; but it still
remained upheld as a stroke of genius forty years after his death.

How did it originate? The answer is that this movement was,
until after its first performance, meant to be of the same form as
the scherzos of the Fourth, Sixth, and Seventh Symphonies (compare also the Pianoforte Trios, op. 70, no. 2, and op. 97, and the
String Quartets, op. 59, no. 2, opp. 74, 95, and 132)—that is to say,

the whole movement, trio and all, was to be given twice; and the breathless pianissimo da capo was to be the third presentation of the main theme. The redundant bars were for the *prima volta*, and they led back to bar four of Ex. 3 (here marked 3 in my rhythmic periods). The double-bar and $ that must have stood there at the time would have had the effect of making it impossible to misread the rhythm; and Beethoven had actually chosen this point for marking his repeat, though it forced him to write out those two bars which afterwards became redundant when the repeat was abandoned. That it was abandoned shows how Beethoven's own special form of the round-and-round scherzo, alternating twice over with its trio, had to yield to the terrific impressiveness of the emotions created by these themes. Probably the long repeat proved detrimental, not to the great darkness that leads to the finale (nothing could weaken that), but to the reappearance of the 'scherzo' in the development of the finale.

In the finale trombones appear for the first time in symphonic music. I quote a part of the first theme in order to show that it is again a case of a magnificently long sentence, weighted with repetitions even more powerful than those of the first movement, inasmuch as they are not sequential repetitions, but plain reiterations on the same position in the scale.

Ex. 6.

The main theme of the second subject (Ex. 7) I quote in order to point out that the minims in the 'cellos form an important figure (*c*) turned to powerful account in the development.

Ex. 7.

The final theme of the second subject (Ex. 8) is destined to be worked up in the presto coda.

Ex. 8.

&c.

Spohr, who thought the theme of the first movement scrappy and undignified, and the whole finale an orgy of vulgar noise, admitted that the reappearance of the 'scherzo' in the middle of the finale was a stroke of genius for which the rest of the work might be forgiven. It is indeed a stroke of genius. Spohr liked it because it was interesting as a feature of form. He evidently disbelieved or disapproved of anything that could be said about emotional values in this symphony, and so he can hardly have realized where the genius really lay in the stroke. Let us remember that the 'scherzo' had a tremendous emotional value, and then consider how it is to be reintroduced into the sustained triumph of the finale. Any one would think that there were only two ways of working the problem: first, to reproduce the mood just as it was. Of course this is impossible. We cannot forget that the terror is passed. Secondly then, could we recover the mood by elaborating the details? This would betray itself as fictitious. If you cannot recover the sensations you felt during an earthquake, it is not much use telling as your own experience things about it that you could not possibly have known at the time. We can easily see, now that Beethoven has shown us, that his is the one true solution which confirms the truth of the former terror and the security of the present triumph; but no lesser artist could have found it. Beethoven recalls the third movement as a memory which we know for a fact but can no longer understand: there is now a note of self-pity, for which we had no leisure when the terror was upon our souls: the depth and the darkness are alike absent, and in the dry light of day we cannot remember our fears of the unknown. And so the triumph resumes its progress and enlarges its range until it reaches its appointed end.

SIXTH SYMPHONY IN F MAJOR (SINFONIA PASTORALE),
OP. 68

1 *Awakening of happy feelings on getting out into the country. (Allegro ma non troppo.)*
2 *By the brook side. (Andante molto mosso.)*
3 *Merry gathering of the country folk. (Allegro), leading to*
4 *Thunderstorm. (Allegro), leading to*
5 *Shepherd's Song: Happy and thankful feelings after the storm. (Allegretto.)*

The first and the last word of common sense about programme music in general was said by Beethoven on this symphony in particular. He said it was 'the expression of feelings rather than painting'. This has not prevented the usual 'roaring cataract of nonsense' from descending upon this intensely musical work and swamping it in volumes of literature; sometimes praising Beethoven for his intelligent anticipation of the true functions of music as a purely illustrative art, but more often blaming him for leading music into so dangerous a bypath by sacrificing musical form to the demands of his external musical programme. The passage which has given most offence in this symphony is the representation of the cuckoo, the nightingale, and the quail at the end of the slow movement. That passage is a master-stroke of pure musical form. It differs from a dozen earlier examples in Beethoven's works (and about a hundred' in Haydn's) only in one essential respect, that it is by far the ripest in style; and in one unessential respect, that persons who can tell the difference between the birdcalls of cuckoos, quails, and nightingales can recognize something rather like them here. But for this unessential detail the passage would never have been supposed to be abnormal at all. No treatise on musical form enters into enough detail to make its analysis of this passage distinguishable from its errors of observation. As for the thunderstorm, it is a monumental introduction, dramatically cutting short a very typical Beethoven scherzo, and leading equally dramatically into a serene and spacious rondo. The only unusual thing about it is that it is in a quick tempo, whereas most introductions are slow. The kind of objection that is raised against the thunderstorm is the assertion that 'the thunder comes first and the lightning afterwards'; as if anybody were quite sure that he had seen the first flash which preceded the first loud thunderclap. Authorities on scoring have remarked that the use of the piccolo in this movement does not show that instrument at its best, since sustained notes are not highly characteristic of it. In other words, a real thunderstorm would be an expensive and inefficient substitute for the piccolo. Beethoven, then, should have used the piccolo to imitate, not the whistling of the wind, which it does exceedingly well, but the more characteristic whistle of the railway guard. Let us be quite fair, then, and call it the bos'n's whistle, which might be in place in a storm; but then let us remember that this is not a storm at sea, but a thunderstorm that has interrupted something like a dance round the maypole, and which, far from being a danger, gives rise to 'happy and thankful feelings' afterwards. In the whole symphony there is not a note of which the musical value would be altered if cuckoos and nightingales, and country folk, and thunder and lightning, and the ˌhowling and whistling of the wind, were things that had never been named by man, either in connexion with music or with anything else. Whether we have words for common objects and events of the

countryside, or whether we have no words, there are feelings
evoked by these objects in proportion to our intelligent suscepti-
bility; and the great master of any language, whether that language
be music, painting, sculpture, architecture, or speech, can invoke
the deepest part of these feelings in his own terms. And his art will
always remain pure as long as he holds to Beethoven's dictum;
which may be philosophically re-translated 'more the expression
of feelings than the illustration of things'.

There is one more mare's-nest over which we may stumble at the
very beginning of this symphony. It has been alleged that large
tracts of it are transcribed from Rhenish folk-songs. It would take
too long to investigate this matter thoroughly; but it will all eventually come to this, that the symphony is a composition in large
and diversely coherent paragraphs, and that when Beethoven is
writing under the inspiration of country life, he uses appropriate
types of melody.

We have then to deal with a perfect classical symphony. Like
every one of Beethoven's symphonies, some forty of Haydn's, and
at least seven outstanding ones of Mozart's, this symphony contains
features that are not to be found in any other. Otherwise it would
not be a classic. But Beethoven has told us, with certain very
broad particulars (themselves more like universals), that this
symphony expresses his love of country life. If it does not express
ours, so much the worse for us.

The first movement opens at once with a quiet melody full of
lively figures.

The harmonization throughout the first movement, the scherzo,
and the finale, is of a rustic simplicity, asserting, with primitive
directness, the tonic, dominant, and subdominant of whatever key
it is in. There are very few definite drone-bass effects, but the possibility of them is never far off, and each figure of each theme is apt
to be piled up in a long series of bird-song repetitions. Much time
has been wasted in identifying other birds than those Beethoven has
mentioned in that famous place in the slow movement. Schindler,
a solemn Boswell without the genius, who used to inscribe 'Ami
de Beethoven' on his visiting-card, bored Beethoven so fearfully
with silly questions that Beethoven generally put him off with

answers of the same quality. These answers have been faithfully
transmitted to posterity. And so Beethoven's 'yellow-hammer'
comes down to us as a bird with a compass of two octaves
consisting of the arpeggio of G major; and it is a regrettable
anachronism that has prevented the Jub-Jub bird and the Orient
Calf from the Land of Tute from helping Beethoven to satisfy
Schindler's curiosity. The real meaning of these bird-song repetitions is not that they represent birds in particular, but that birds
themselves repeat their songs continually when they are happy and
have nothing else to do. The Pastoral Symphony has the enormous
strength of some one who knows how to relax. The strength and
the relaxation are at their highest point in the slow movement, as
we shall see when we come to it; but they are already gigantic in the
first movement, which is in no respect but externals less powerful
than that of the C minor Symphony. Nothing could be easier to
follow, and yet nothing could be more unexpected than its course.
The transition, in which the first figure (*a*) of Ex. 1 is built up into
phrases punctuated by subdued chuckles in the wood-wind, leads
in three indolent strides to a second subject which slowly stretches
itself out over tonic and dominant as a sort of three-part round.

The cadence-theme of the second subject also needs quotation
for the sake of a delicious variation of it in the coda.

The development sets out in the subdominant, B flat, and
therein proceeds slowly to pile up a long passage out of bird-song
repetitions of figure (*b*). An immense stretch of the chord of B flat
is followed by a still bigger stretch of the bright chord of D major
with a slow crescendo to a fortissimo. This dies away, and the last
two notes of the figure (*b*) are broken off in a comic dialogue
between the bassoon and the violins. Then the first theme is given
out again in G, and here again figure (*b*) is piled up into an immense

crescendo. This time the change of harmony is in the opposite direction, from G to E, with the same climax and the same decline. A third time the theme starts in A major, and is now allowed to proceed to its second phrase, figure (*d*). This is then developed fluently in broad steps, moving simply through D and G minor to the dominant of F, where a fortissimo climax leads with exquisite warmth to the return of the first subject in the tonic. The beginning of this recapitulation is expanded and adorned by beautiful new counterpoints in the first violin. Otherwise the recapitulation is quite regular, an imperceptible change of harmony being all that is required for the transition. The coda is grafted on to the recapitulation by proceeding for a few bars as at the beginning of the development. This brings us to the subdominant, B flat, in which key the first theme bursts out forte, but is instantly checked and gives place to a delightful dance-like variation of the cadence-theme (Ex. 3) in smooth triplets. It moves round to the tonic and there again bursts out forte and is developed to a broad climax. From this a slow diminuendo leads to a terse and lively phrase built out of figure (*b*), a very different kind of treatment from that which it had in the development; and then a clarinet turns figure (*c*) into a brilliant dance. When this has died away, the first three bars of Ex. 1 float upwards into the air as lazily and as imperturbably as a cloud. Suddenly the movement rouses itself, for everything must have an end, even if the last chords are as soft as the opening.

I once said that the slow movement is one of the most powerful things in music, and the statement can be proved by merely drawing up the facts as to its form. The form is that of a fully developed first movement. To achieve this in a slow tempo always implies extraordinary concentration and terseness of design; for the slow tempo, which inexperienced composers are apt to regard as having no effect upon the number of notes that take place in a given time, is much more rightly conceived as large than as slow. Take a great slow movement, and write it out in such a notation as will make it correspond in real time-values to the notes of a great quick movement; and you will be surprised to find how much in actual time the mere first theme of the slow movement would cover of the whole exposition of the quick movement. Any slow movement in full sonata form is, then, a very big thing. But a slow movement in full sonata form which at every point asserts its deliberate intention to be lazy and to say whatever occurs to it twice in succession, and which in so doing never loses flow and never falls out of proportion, such a slow movement is as strong as an Atlantic liner that could bear taking out of water and supporting on its two ends. The brook goes on for ever; the importance of

that fact lies in its effect upon the poetic mind of the listener bask-
ing in the sun on its banks. The representation of its flow with the
aid of two muted solo violoncellos is a stroke of genius that will
always seem modern. The broken character of the first bars of the
overlying theme, settling down in the later bars to an enthusiastic
sustained melody—

is a perfect explanation of the poet's mood, as shown by the natural
way in which his thoughts and utterances gradually take shape.
The murmur of the brook becomes more continuous (in other
words the accompaniment is broken into semiquavers) throughout the rest of the movement; not because it has changed in itself,
but because the poet is no longer attending to it. The whole
first phrase is repeated, and there are bird-song trills above it.
Now comes a new theme in which, as with other themes in this
symphony, there is the tendency for various instruments to come
in one after another in the fashion of a round.

In its formal aspect this theme might be guessed to be the transition-theme; and if the highest ideal of form were that everything
should turn out exactly as one expects, it would be the duty of
this theme to effect the transition. By so doing it would achieve
a comparatively low kind of efficiency. But its higher duty is
to express the mood of the poet accurately. Transition-themes
belong to something a little nearer town. This theme is going to
close quietly in the tonic; and if we are going to move to any other
place on the banks of this brook, we will do so quite contentedly
without any theme in particular. The music gathers itself up in
quiet broken phrases and starts the first theme again. It follows
the course of the brook (which is never tired) into the dominant, and
there with all requisite deliberation and breadth prepares for the
second subject. This begins with a sort of tonic-and-dominant
theme not unlike that of the first movement (Ex. 2). Beethoven
intends no allusion, any more than he does in the similar case of
the second subject of the finale. These themes have come to be
of the same type, because the moods and situations are the same.
But in each case the theme takes a different course. Here its richly.

melodious fourth bar drifts into a new phrase starting on a remote
chord—

Ex. 6.

&c.

and repeating itself again and again as one instrument crowds in
upon another. It comes to a massive cadence of which the final
trill is dying away into dreamland; but it is so beautiful, and the
sunlight has shifted through the trees to such new purpose, that
we must look at the scene again. This time the cadence is still
broader and the colouring is slightly grotesque, as if the poet were
laughing at his own laziness, but it is all too beautiful not to be
serious. Below the trill Ex. 5 re-enters and is answered by an increasing chorus of other voices. A fine account of the slow movement
of the Pastoral Symphony has been written by the eminent composer
Hans Pfitzner, in a pamphlet dealing with the whole theory of
absolute music and programme music. I gratefully borrow from
him the notion that this particular theme, with its constant recurrences at cardinal points of the structure, closely corresponds to the
kind of mood in which one would say to oneself on a sleepy summer's
day by Beethoven's brook, 'How beautiful!' The perpetual motion
of the brook is now outlined in a short cadence subject which dies
away gradually. And now comes the most subtle master-stroke of
all; a feature far more abnormal than the passage in the coda representing the songs of the three birds. It is time for the development
to begin, and of course it should begin by discussing one of the
extant themes. But just as we saw that Ex. 5 was too deeply satisfied
with the beauty of the moment to set about any such business
as a transition-theme, so we find that here there is no hurry to
begin the development. Having had the effrontery to give his
second subject twice over, Beethoven has here the yet more sublime
effrontery to start a new theme. It is another of these simple tonic-
and-dominant affairs, the laziest of them all.

Ex. 7.

And Beethoven has no intention of following it up. It has the
energy to move in its own stride into the brilliant key of G major,

and now the development is ready to begin. The first theme (Ex. 4) comes out on the oboe with several new accessories in the accompaniment, including poor Schindler's giraffe-throated yellow-hammer, and a slow descending arpeggio in the violins. Weingartner advises that this last detail should not be brought out, as it makes the scoring too thick. I am unable to agree with him. It seems to me that the thing to keep in the background is the incessant rippling of the brook, which by this time cannot fail to be recognized, however slightly it is touched in; whereas this new detail is systematically elaborated throughout the development and recapitulation as an integral part of the scheme, and is by no means easy to hear. The continuation of the theme is quite new and moves broadly to a cadence with a trill. Below the trill comes Ex. 5 and moves ecstatically to E flat, the key of the subdominant and of shade. Here the whole process is repeated with new scoring and with the new accessory details still further enriched. The modulation which led from G to E flat is now begun in another direction, and leads from E flat to G flat. (Precisely the same plan, with the same inexact correspondence, but with keys of the opposite colour, was to be found in the development of the first movement.) The deep shadow of this remote key of G flat becomes still deeper as C flat, which, changing enharmonically to B natural, swoops round to our original key B flat. At the outset of this wonderful passage the theme was that of the first subject with the murmur of the brook becoming articulately melodious in the clarinet and the bassoon. At the moment when the melody gathers itself up into a sustained phrase and makes its enharmonic modulation, there comes a phenomenon full of deep meaning. From this point nothing is left of the melody but sustained notes and bird-song trills; the whole of the rest of the return to the main key is harmonic and rhythmic. In this as everywhere else the movement remains true to type, a perfect expression of happiness in relaxation.

In its own due proportions the passage brings back the recapitulation. This time the theme reaches its climax of rich scoring, the flute having the melody, the quick arpeggios of poor Schindler's yellow-hammer being multiplied by three instruments in three different parts of the bar, and the slow descending arpeggios being similarly distributed among horns, clarinets, and the second flute. Thus the air is full of tiny sounds which no one can tell to be less vast and distant than the stars of the Milky Way. Beethoven does not give the first subject a restatement now, but passes on in two bars to the second subject. This he preserves in full, repetitions and all. It has never been heard in the development, and to shorten it would be to violate the mood of the composition. And now after the cadence-theme comes the final consummation. There is a crescendo, but the melody is again drawn out into notes more sustained than any articulate phrase. Suddenly for a moment all is silent; we have no ears even for the untiring brook, and through the silence comes the voice of the nightingale, the quaint rhythmic pipe of the quail, and the syllabic yet impersonal signal of the cuckoo. This trio is answered by the motto of the whole movement, figure (*a*) from Ex. 4; and much nonsense might have been spared about this passage if the superior persons who regard it as violation of the absoluteness of music had taken the trouble to notice that the three birds make with this motto a perfectly normal four-bar phrase. Even if the whole passage were a new irregular theme, it would still be a closer structure than, say, the last bars of the slow movement of the D minor Pianoforte Sonata, op. 31, no. 2, or of the whole last pages of the slow movements of the Violin Sonatas in F major, op. 24, and in C minor, op. 30, no. 1. In fact it may safely be said that this coda is a perfect example of the form which Beethoven had only just contrived to suggest rather too broadly and with rather insufficient means in that page in the C minor Violin Sonata. Once more the three birds are heard and answered by the poet; and with his motto-theme a short dialogue of wind instruments brings this gigantic movement to its beautiful close.

The scherzo may claim to be programme music inasmuch as its programme implies all that is most typical of the strictest form of a Beethoven scherzo. Like its parent form the minuet, the scherzo originates aesthetically in the general notion of dance music, and in the specific notion of two dance melodies alternating with each other. And when out of the minuet, which had already in Haydn's hands utterly transcended its original limits, Beethoven developed his own gigantic type of scherzo, far from obliterating the typical dance character of the form, he emphasized it to the utmost. He did not in his most typical examples allow the themes to become so developed as to give the movement a character of dramatic progress; on the contrary he insisted that, however large his scherzo and his trio might be in themselves, the listener should thoroughly realize that they were two dances that were going to alternate not once but twice, and but for the intervention of some rather drastic closure even thrice. Since Beethoven's time, the doctrine has arisen that the purpose of music is to convey information; so that what has been said clearly once need not be repeated to listeners of ordinary intelligence. On the same principle we may as well demolish any part of a building which symmetrically repeats any other part. Experience soon convinced Beethoven of the necessity of writing out the repeats of his typical scherzos in full, as performers will be more afraid to cut out whole written pages than to disobey a mere repeat-mark. But this has not protected his scherzos from serious damage to their typical character; and nowadays it is not preventing damage to much more dramatic structures. The whole question depends upon whether architectural and formal motives or dramatic impulses and processes preponderate. In discussing the C minor Symphony (which Beethoven produced at the same time as the Pastoral) I have pointed out that there too the scherzo had originally been made to alternate twice with the trio; and that, in consequence of traces of the long repeat-mark being left in the score and parts, commentators were for many years puzzled by two superfluous bars at the return to the first theme. Beethoven had seen during the rehearsal for the first performance that the dramatic power of the scherzo of the C minor Symphony was far too intense for any such insistence on its dance-form. But here in the Pastoral Symphony it would be a crime not to let Beethoven's rustics have their dance out before the thunderstorm intervenes. The whole movement is thoroughly in character. It has Beethoven's full wealth of contrasted themes, beginning with a couple in the brightly opposed keys of F and D major.

Ex. 8.

The trio begins, not, as some commentators would have it, with the change to 2/4 time (there is a double bar there simply because the change of time demands it), but with the following delightful theme:

Ex. 9.

Sir Henry Hadow has wittily commentated upon the rustic bass notes supplied by the second bassoon who is 'never quite sure how many of them to put in'. I respectfully submit that the point is rather that the bassoon knows this so well that he is a little too proud of the fact. The realism is comic, but it is in keeping with the dazzling brightness of the poet's holiday in the country, where the commonest things are enjoyed as if they had never been seen

before. To say that the Pastoral Symphony is animated by the
spirit of folk-music is to show an enthusiasm for folk-music. But
any one who says that the three themes we have hitherto quoted
are actual folk-songs is talking obvious nonsense: those rhythms
and key relationships do not exist outside classical symphonies.
A real, or at least a possible folk-dance asserts itself boisterously
in 2/4 time as follows:

Ex. 10.

And now we have an instance of the clear characterization of every
instrument which Beethoven uses in this symphony. Nothing is
more familiar, or more often troublesome in the performance of
classical works, than the primitive set of glaring notes to which the
trumpets of classical days were confined. It is to be presumed that
good players and good conductors did not allow the trumpets to
run wild with their fragmentary signals and their frequent inability
to provide suitable notes for rapid changes of harmony. Modern
conductors and modern trumpet-players are constantly moderating
the force of the trumpets in a classical tutti; but to think this
moderation a purely modern refinement is to make rather hasty
assumptions as to the stupidity of musicians in Beethoven's
time. Now, however, at this point in the Pastoral Symphony,
the trumpet in its most primitive state enters for the first time.
In all the previous five symphonies trumpets and drums were
present from the outset, and were in no sense kept in reserve for
special effects. In this trio the trumpets are active in the dance;
they enter as personalities, and when they mark time on the notes
of the chord of C, they crown the festivity. Their last note dies
away romantically and leads back to the repetition of both scherzo
and trio. When the scherzo comes back for the third time it is
shortened, its conclusion being given presto; when suddenly there
is a murmur of distant thunder and large raindrops fall.

This is what Beethoven obviously tells us by the titles of his
movements. What he achieves is something much higher; it is
a physical shock of terror, which is far more thrilling when all
that is at stake is the prospect of getting one's clothes wet than
when there is any real human danger. Soon the thunderstorm
bursts; and the thunder is very simply and efficiently represented
by the entry of the drums, which are used in this symphony for no
other purpose. The rumbling passages of the 'cellos and double-
basses are generally cited as Beethoven's representation of thunder,
but they are only a part of it; they give, not the roll and the clap
of thunder, but a peculiar shuffling sound that pervades the air

during a thunderstorm, and is not accounted for by the rain. The modulations of this thunderstorm are musically superb. Current arrangements for pianoforte duet give a number of unauthorized indications as to what represents hail and what represents wind and all the other incidents of the thunderstorm. Some of these are fairly obvious, and none of them can affect the musical value of the piece. The storm moves in grand steps to its climax. This is marked by the entry of the trombones (only two of them instead of the normal group of three), and it would be best appreciated, both in its realism and in its ideal grandeur, by the listener who notices that the trombones fall into a slow articulate fragment of melody. Then the storm dies away, until with the last distant mutterings of the thunder the oboes give a long slow fragment of bright sustained melody on the dominant of F. This has been aptly compared with a rainbow. Sir George Grove has noted that in Beethoven's sketches this rainbow was itself derived by gradual transformation of the quaver figure of the raindrops with which the storm begins. The real moral of this is that Beethoven found it easy thus to arrive at this passage in a sketch, but did not imagine, as so many theorists nowadays would teach, that any such process constitutes 'logical development' when it comes to getting the real composition into shape.

And so we come to the 'Thanksgiving after the Storm'. It begins on the dominant with a kind of yodel on a pastoral pipe, which settles down into the following peaceful rondo theme:

Ex. 11.

In accordance with the expression of utter leisure which dominates this symphony, the theme is given three times, the second time an octave lower, and the third time another octave lower on the full orchestra, the trumpets and trombones joining in with solemn glow. From the last two notes of this theme arises an important transition theme—

Ex. 12.

which leads to a short second subject of much the same type as that in the first movement. Like most of Beethoven's rondo second

subjects, this comes to no definite end, but makes a point of leading
back as quickly as possible to the rondo theme, drifting back
through its yodelling introduction. The rondo theme with new
details of scoring seems as if it was again going to be given more
than once, but the repetition drifts towards the subdominant and
leads to a middle episode, where a new theme comes with all the
manner of being about to settle down to a broad cantabile.

But its very enthusiasm is too much for its strength. It modulates
ruminatingly to the comparatively distant key of D flat, where it
cannot resist the temptation of slipping back to C major as dominant of F, and anticipating a return to the rondo theme. A new
semiquaver counterpoint here requires quotation.

This passage soon leads back to the tonic, and again the yodelling
above the new semiquaver figure leads into the main theme. This
is now given in a brilliant variation, a semiquaver version on the
top, a pizzicato version below. Then it is repeated with the semiquavers in the middle and the pizzicato version both above and
below at different parts of the bar. Then for the third time the full
orchestra has it, with semiquavers in the 'cellos and pizzicato version
in the horns (which need doubling to make it audible). The transition follows, and is easily made to lead to the second subject in the
tonic.

So far the movement has been short and terse, in spite of the
spacious effect of those repetitions of its main theme. But now
comes one of Beethoven's broadest codas. In this the theme is
worked out first in a somewhat round-like scheme with new counterpoints, leading to a grand solemn tutti, glorious as the fields
refreshed by the rain. Suddenly this subsides into the passage
which led to the round-like development of the main theme. Again
we have this round-like development, but this time in the semiquaver variation; and now the tutti rises to a solemn height and
descends slowly to a not less solemn but very quiet song of thanksgiving on the figure of the main theme. At last the movement is
dying away on the continuation shown in Ex. 14, with the yodel
figure on a muted horn, an effect employed nowhere else by
Beethoven. This is abruptly cut short by the final chords.

SEVENTH SYMPHONY IN A MAJOR, OP. 92

1 *Poco sostenuto, leading to* 2 *Vivace.* 3 *Allegretto.* 4 *Presto.*
5 *Allegro con brio.*

Beethoven's Seventh and Eighth Symphonies, written in 1812, were, like his Fifth and Sixth some four years earlier, produced almost as twins. He was vaguely meditating a third companion of which he knew this much, that it was to be in D minor. After some ten years the Ninth Symphony did take shape in that key.

The Seventh Symphony has been called the romantic symphony; rightly in so far as romance is a term which, like humour, every self-respecting person claims to understand, while no two people understand it in the same way. There is no 'programme' to the Seventh Symphony, and no reason why we should not call it heroic (which is one aspect of romance) except that Beethoven himself has bespoken that title elsewhere. The symphony is so overwhelmingly convincing and so obviously untranslatable, that it has for many generations been treated quite reasonably as a piece of music, instead of as an excuse for discussing the French Revolution. Berlioz, it is true, talked sad nonsense about the vivace being a *Ronde des paysans*. But that was a long time ago; and though, as W. E. Henley pointed out, Berlioz is very good reading, we need not go to him for information about anything but his own state of mind as he would like us to conceive it. Nobody now sees anything 'rustic' in the main theme of the vivace, and though it would be quite easy and even profitable to devote a voluminous analysis to the subtleties and profundities of this one of Beethoven's greatest works, there is no popular heresy or pitfall for the listeners of to-day. Probably of all Beethoven's works the Fifth and Seventh symphonies are at present the best understood both in detail and as wholes. This does not make either of them the less exacting for orchestras and conductors; the scoring is exceedingly full of pitfalls, though the deaf composer's imagination never fails in the essentials of his miraculous inventions.

The introduction is in itself a movement of considerable development, containing two fully-formed themes. The first I quote in combination with its sequel and accessory, the scale figure here given in small notes.

Ex. 1.

The second alternates with it twice, in a pair of remote keys (C and

F). Here again I give with it in small notes the accessory rhythmic figure which eventually leads, in one of Beethoven's most famous (and, when it was new, most notorious) passages, to the vivace.

Ex. 2.

That famous passage gives rise to the dactylic rhythmic figure which pervades almost every bar of the vivace, much as the four taps of 'Destiny at the door' pervade the first movement of the Fifth Symphony.

Ex. 3.

The letters by which I mark the figures of the first subject may help any one curious in such matters to trace the many and various derived themes to their origin. But it must not be forgotten that the individual character of a derived theme is a fact of perhaps greater importance than its derivation, interesting and natural though that may be. Indeed, it is possible to hear too much about the way in which a whole work is based 'on the one idea embodied in its first four notes'; and some day an analyst may arise who will administer a drastic cure by persuading people to swallow the soul-stirring doctrine that every piece of music whatever is based on the one idea embodied in a figure of one single note.

The beginning of the second subject, like that in the Eroica Symphony, has often eluded the commentators, in spite of its containing one of the most important figures (d) in the movement. The only difficulty in finding it comes from the habit of searching for something that looks different on paper, instead of listening for the point at which harmony and phrasing settle firmly in the new key.

Most of the development is derived, often very surprisingly, from the figures of the first theme. One of its most original features is the kind of round with which it opens. I cannot resist the temptation of quoting the passage compendiously in the notation in which rounds and catches are usually written.

Soon afterwards the figure (*d*) from the second subject (Ex. 4) plays a considerable part. It also reappears in the final climax of the coda, after the mighty *crescendo* which arose from that grand sustained note which frightened young Weber into declaring that Beethoven was 'ripe for the madhouse'.

At its first performance the slow movement was an instant success, and was encored, a thing which slow movements very rarely experience. Its popularity grew at the expense not only of the rest of this symphony, but of other works; and concert-directors used at one time to insert it into the Eighth Symphony to make that brightest of comedies 'go down'!

A fairly good clue to the tempo of this most impressive and solemn of allegrettos is given by the fact that Beethoven afterwards thought he ought to have called it andante. This sometimes leads, like all corrections, to the opposite extreme; one must always hold the two facts of the published thought and the afterthought together. Beethoven could never have called it allegretto if he had not thought it a little too fast for an ordinary andante. Neither quotations nor descriptions seem necessary here.

For the scherzo I quote the principal theme, not as it occurs at the fiery outset, but as it slips in quietly half-way through the second part. I do this partly for the sake of the new counter-theme in the bassoons, which grows enormously; and partly to display the inversion of rhythm which makes this scherzo one of Beethoven's most incalculable movements. The subsequent crescendo seems a bar short, but really brings the theme back into step.

The trio will always remain as marvellous as ever, though we may not be able to remember a time when we did not know it by heart.

The finale is and remains unapproached in music as a triumph of Bacchic fury. I can attempt nothing here by way of description; and my quotations can do no more than show the first part of the first theme, with the figures duly lettered for those who will promise not to be too curious about their development—

its second part, for the sake of an important figure (*d*) in the bass, which in the development is fiercely brandished on the surface—

the transition theme (*e*), which is rather difficult to catch at first, as the scoring is not favourable to it, but which is destined to make an immense climax in the coda—

Ex. 9.

and the beginning of the second subject, in an unusual key soon afterwards varied with romantic modulations in an exciting crescendo.

Ex. 10.

One of the profoundest characteristics in this symphony is the fact that when the time comes for recapitulating these romantic modulations, while the general framework of the passage remains unchanged, the modulations are quite different. Schubert alone of Beethoven's younger contemporaries understood what this means to the life of the classical forms. Brahms understood it also, and thus was able to make those forms live after nearly half a century of pseudo-classicism had driven most of the active-minded musicians into revolt. These points may be called technicalities; and they are, no doubt, symptoms rather than causes. But they have their meaning after the music is finished and the memory tries to recapture some of its vibrations.

EIGHTH SYMPHONY IN F MAJOR, OP. 93

1 *Allegro con brio.* 2 *Allegretto.* 3 *Tempo di menuetto.* 4 *Allegro.*

When an artist is great enough to produce a number of works widely differing in character, there is nothing he enjoys so much as the strongest possible contrasts between two successive works. And nothing is more likely to annoy his contemporaries. When the hero of Mr. Arnold Bennett's *Great Adventure* burst on an astonished Royal Academy with a huge picture of a policeman, he ought, by all the etiquette of pictorial boom, to have painted policemen for the rest of his life. But he never painted a policeman again.

Beethoven's Seventh Symphony was too big for its time. But its slow movement was an instant and sensational success. To the indignation of the critics and the public the Eighth Symphony turned out too small. They had pestered Beethoven all his life with exhortations to learn from Mozart and Haydn, those unapproachable masters of true beauty and proportion. And now he was incapable of imitating Haydn and Mozart; but he was also no longer to be bound by any sense of the mere novelty or range of an idea or form apart from its intrinsic character. And so he produced in the allegretto of his Eighth Symphony a movement which would have earned from both Mozart and Haydn the hearty wish that they had written it themselves, so full is it of all that made them feel happy, and so free from anything that could disturb their artistic habits. And then the public did not like it! A demand grew up for performances of this rather trivial Eighth Symphony with the wonderful allegretto of the Seventh, released from its monstrous surroundings, and put where it could redeem an otherwise unworthy work from oblivion. This raises the question, what on earth Beethoven's contemporaries could after all have seen in their favourite allegretto of the Seventh Symphony; a question perhaps to be answered by the dismal person who at that time made a pot of money by turning it into a male-voice part-song entitled *Chorus of Monks*.

Beethoven took the matter with grim good-nature; and when told that the Eighth Symphony was less of a success than the Seventh, said, 'That's because it's so much better'. This is neither a matter-of-fact judgement nor wholly ironical; what it expresses is the unique sense of power which fires a man when he finds himself fit for a delicate task just after he has triumphed in a colossal one. In the finale of the Eighth Symphony this sense of power causes the work to stretch itself, with a glorious effect not unlike that which must have been produced by Lablache, when the sightseer knocked at his door instead of at General Tom Thumb's. Lablache's magnificent voice was all the grander for the colossal figure from which its tones proceeded; he was nearer seven than six foot high. But he answered to the name of the General, and drawing himself up majestically, explained, 'Voyons donc, monsieur! quand je suis chez moi je me mets à mon aise!'

The first movement, though by no means a dwarf, begins with a pocket-size theme. The first three phrases, with their opening in forte, their answer in piano, and their chorus-like forte confirmation of that answer, at once mark out the scale to be small and the action lively.

Ex. 1.

But the next theme promptly shows that, like Haydn, Beethoven does not depend on the mere scale of his work to give a sense of boundless freedom. The sky is always on the same scale, whatever the size of your garden.

Ex. 2.

The leisurely giant strides of this theme bring about the most
singular of all Beethoven's transitions to a second subject. There is
a pause after four insistent staccato chords on a harmony which,
though simple enough in itself, is of curiously doubtful import
here. I cannot recall any other passage in classical or modern music
in which, if the composer had abandoned his work at that point,
it would be so impossible to guess how to continue it.

The dubious harmony had indicated a sombre unrelated key on
the wrong side of the subdominant, as far as it indicated anything.
It now resolves, with a chuckle, into one of the brightest keys that
can be brought into relation with the tonic at all; and in this key the
second subject begins with an exquisitely graceful tune, which I do
not quote. A cloud comes over it at its sixth bar; and it finishes its
first sentence by explaining that it didn't mean to turn up in such
a gaudy key, and will, if you will kindly overlook that indiscretion,
continue in the orthodox dominant. It does so; blushes again over-
come it at the sixth bar; melodramatic mystification ensues; but if
any one has been pretending to be shocked, the incident is closed in
shouts of laughter. From the remaining group of themes I quote an
important pair, first a short fortissimo answered by a long cantabile—

Ex. 3.

of which figures (d) and (e) are destined to give great power and
breadth to the coda of the whole movement; and secondly the
blustering wind-up which leads, first back to the beginning, and
afterwards on to the development, where, in conjunction with
Ex. 1, it plays a great role.

Ex. 4.

The development storms along through broadly designed modulations in an unbroken course towards a grand climax, over which the
recapitulation sails with the first subject (Ex. 1) in the bass. It is
not easy to make out the tune with all the noontide glare beating
down over it; but Beethoven leaves us with no grievance on that
account, for the wood-wind restate it in the most good-natured
way in the world. Then the basses take it up again, crescendo, and
proceed with Ex. 2, which the violins imitate in an ingenious
variation. Here again the theme eventually rises to the surface; the
ambiguous modulation takes a different turn; and the second
subject, determined not to offend with remote keys again, now
enters in the too humble key of the subdominant. This is easily put
right, and the rest of the recapitulation is quite regular.

The coda, plunging into a soft remote key, begins by holding a
conspirator's discussion of figure (b) of Ex. 1, which soon flares up
into a triumphant insistence on the whole theme. At the first performance of the symphony this climax was immediately followed
by the comic quiet ending; but Beethoven speedily recognized
that, though that is the right ending, his coda was inadequate and
more suggestive of an imitation of Haydn and Mozart than of a
new classic bringing their spirits back to an emancipated world.
With complete success Beethoven inserted the new expansion of
the second phrase of Ex. 3, which gives his peroration its characteristic power and breadth.

For the allegretto I should need at least five quotations if the
listener demanded a correct account of its themes. This statement
of fact sufficiently indicates the concentration and variety that
go to the clear and unaffected presentation of this Marjorie
Fleming of symphonic movements. A man must possess wisdom,
a healing touch, and have been young for a very long time, before
he can describe children of this kind; which shows how much less
the sad distractions of the artists' biography can tell us of him
than almost any one of his works. Beethoven's life was a tragedy,
and he lived in constant and often undignified discomfort; but
the damper musical biographers ought to be shoo'd off the premises
by the allegretto of the Eighth Symphony. Its last bars would do
that very well; but perhaps they more nearly express Marjorie's
mature conclusion that 'the most Devilish thing is Five times
Seven'. (Four times Six and Six times Eight are Beethoven's
propositions.)

This was not the first time that one of Beethoven's slow movements had refused to be slow enough; consequently, as in the
Sonata in E flat, op. 31, no. 3, instead of a lively scherzo we
have a minuet in the old dignified slow tempo. It is a curious
instance of the complete ignorance shown by Beethoven's con-

temporaries concerning the very classics they professed to revere at
Beethoven's expense, that till as late as Mendelssohn's last years
and Wagner's manhood this minuet was taken like a German waltz,
though the trio must have been a mere scramble at any such pace.
Wagner accuses Mendelssohn of acquiescing in this tradition; but
it is clear from his own account of what Mendelssohn said to him,
that Mendelssohn was good-naturedly trying to keep two tiresome
people's tempers for them; a routined conductor's, whom he had
done his best to persuade, and Wagner's, who was waving his red
flag and would recognize no improvement short of the mark.

I quote the theme of the minuet in order to call attention to the
extremely close work developed from the short figures (*a*), (*b*), and
(*c*), into which the flowing melody divides itself. No fugue of Bach
is more complex than the treatment of these figures in what sounds
like a smooth and old-world flow of gallant tune.

Ex. 5.

The trio I quote for the sake of an interesting point in which it is
not difficult to carry out Beethoven's final intentions.

Ex. 6.

On the stave I give the rhythm of the third bar as Beethoven first
wrote it, making it rhyme with the others. Below the stave I give
the alteration which is now in the score. Beethoven regretted it,
and called it 'that tiresome little witticism' (*das kleine pikante
Zuviel*). So he wished to restore the original reading, which is
difficult for us now to view as he did. Still, we would gladly obey
him: but the brilliant violoncello accompaniment fits only the
second reading; and so it must be altered, if it is not to make a bad
pair of octaves with the other. Beethoven was no pedant in such
matters, but here he would certainly draw the line.

The finale is one of Beethoven's most gigantic creations. Yet
its peculiar form results, with perfect artistic fitness, from the fact

that it begins by executing a complete sonata form on a scale no larger than that of the first movement. It has a witty rondo-like first subject with a stumbling-block in its last note.

Then follows a leisurely transition-theme. Elephants, says Kipling, move from place to place at various rates of speed; if you want an elephant to overtake an express train you cannot hurry him—but he will overtake the train.

This, as the quotation shows, leads to a serenely melodious second subject beginning in the dark remote key of A flat, but soon brightening, with a slow smile, into the orthodox dominant, with another theme to follow and lead to a climax. Then there is a rondo-like return to the first subject, swimming out at the eighth bar (see Ex. 7) into a short but vigorous development, based on figure (c) of the theme. This development, having reached a key that has not the remotest suggestion of tonic about it, effects the funniest return in all music, parent of all the bassoon jokes in the Sullivan operas, and poetic with the mystery of the drums.

Upon which the recapitulation sails in and follows a perfectly regular course (the A flat of the second subject now becoming D flat, and so leading to the tonic) until the point is reached where the first theme returned. This point is now the subdominant; and there is some hesitation, whereat the basses, with figure (*b*), show annoyance. What is to be done about it?

With all its originality and wealth, there has so far been no puzzling or abnormal feature in the movement, with one glaring exception. What on earth did that irrelevant roaring C sharp mean at the end of Ex. 7? Thereby hangs a tail, videlicet, a coda that is nearly as long as the whole body of the movement. My pun is not more violent than Beethoven's harmonic or enharmonic jokes on this point. The coda begins quietly on an obviously huge scale, with a new figure (unquoted) stealthily stalking in minims beneath figure (*a*), and rising in a slow crescendo to a climax, upon which the idea of Ex. 9 brings back the main theme. This reaches that C sharp; and now it suddenly appears that Beethoven has held that note in reserve, wherewith to batter at the door of some immensely distant key. Out bursts the theme, then, in F sharp minor. Can we ever find a way home again? Well, E sharp (or F natural) is the leading note of this new key, and upon E sharp the trumpets pounce, and hammer away at it until they have thoroughly convinced the orchestra that they mean it for the tonic. When this is settled, in sails the radiant second subject again. Now Ganymede is all very well; but the original cup-bearer of the gods is Hephaestus, who is lame, and grimy with his metallurgy in the bowels of the earth. However, he will not be ousted; and so the basses sing the theme too. Straightway unquenchable laughter arises among the blessed gods as they look at him bestirring himself about the house. The laughter has all the vaults of heaven wherein to disperse itself, and to gather again into the last long series of joyous shouts, which, after all its surprises, brings the symphony to its end as punctually as planets complete their orbits.

NINTH SYMPHONY IN D MINOR, OP. 125
—ITS PLACE IN MUSICAL ART

It is well known that Beethoven had in his earliest period the ambition to set Schiller's 'Ode to Joy'. This project had in itself nothing to do with the idea of a choral symphony. At the time he was sketching his Seventh and Eighth Symphonies, he had already made up his mind that the next symphony should be in D minor, though he did not jot down any themes for it. This project again had nothing to do with Schiller's 'Ode'. Years later, after the Choral Symphony had been produced, Beethoven, no doubt in a moment of depression, said to some friends that the choral finale was a mistake, and that perhaps he might some day write an instrumental finale. This, in fact, had been his first intention, and the early sketches of the Ninth Symphony give the theme of the finale of the great A minor Quartet in D minor as the finale of the symphony. Beethoven had not hitherto written much choral music; and the study of that stagnant backwater of musical history, the choral art as practised by composers for the church and the stage in Vienna at the beginning of the nineteenth century, does not reveal the existence of anything like a 'good school' in this branch of composition. Nobody cares for the choral works of Beethoven's contemporaries, and so the extravagant compass Beethoven assigns to his voices looks like some enormous violence of Beethoven's genius; whereas it is but little worse than the habits of contemporaries of his who were under no excitement whatever. Other difficulties more enormous and less effective in Beethoven's choral writing arise from the fact that his two great choral works, the Ninth Symphony and the Mass in D, are for him, morally speaking, early works in this art. The Mass in D is longer than the whole of the Ninth Symphony, and is choral from beginning to end; yet, enormously difficult as is the Mass, the finale of the Choral Symphony is more exhausting in twenty minutes than the whole Mass in an hour and a quarter.

Beethoven was only fifty-seven when he died of a complication of disorders aggravated by a neglected chill. Constitutionally, in spite of his deafness and the moodiness it naturally engendered, he was on the whole a healthier and stronger man than, say, Samuel Johnson; and there is nothing but accident that deprived the art of music of a fourth period in Beethoven's development, which should have been distinguished by a body of choral work fully equal in power and perfection to the symphonies and string quartets.[1]

The arguments which would persuade us that the chorale finale of the Ninth Symphony is the outcome of a discontent with instrumental music are by this time discredited. Wagner committed some indiscretions on these lines, but they were too obviously grist to the official Wagnerian mill to survive in a musical civilization which recognizes Wagner as one among the greatest composers instead of putting him into a category which excludes all the rest of music. On the other hand, those arguments are equally futile which would persuade us that the choral finale was a 'mistake', because of some fundamental fallacy in the introduction of voices and words into a symphony. Contemporary performances, and contemporary judgements of the work, gave Beethoven abundant cause for moments of depression. At Aachen not only did the choral parts not arrive in time for performance, but the conductor, Beethoven's favourite pupil Ries, had to make large cuts in the slow movement simply because the orchestra could not master its difficulties. The only way to understand, not only the choral finale, but the other three movements of the symphony, is to attend strictly to the music from its own point of view as Beethoven wrote it; and not to be distracted by what he may have said about it when he was thinking of writing something else. We have no right to dismiss it as a mistake until we have thoroughly followed its meaning, whether we like it or not. The more we study it, from whatever point of view, the more obvious do its real mistakes become; and the more obvious they become, the more readily, and even impatiently, will the music-lover with a sense of proportion dismiss them from his mind as trivial accidents. The question as to the 'legitimacy' of bringing voices and words into a symphony is an exploded unreality. Professor Andrew Bradley, without saying a word about music, exploded it for all time when, in his inaugural lecture in the Chair of Poetry at Oxford in 1901, he discussed 'Poetry for Poetry's sake', and showed the fundamental fallacy in theories of artistic 'absoluteness', viz. the fallacy of separating form from matter at all. In the case of a choral symphony the essential facts are these; first, that all instruments and all harmonic and contrapuntal arts imitate, on the one hand, voices,

[1] This view has been hotly challenged by critics who urge, as a fatal objection to it, that Beethoven shows no appreciation of the beauty of the unaccompanied chorus. Such critics must extend their objection to the whole of classical choral music between the death of Palestrina and the maturity of Brahms. Bach, Handel, Mozart, and Haydn wrote not a line of unaccompanied choral music, unless you count canons scribbled on menu cards. Bach's so-called 'unaccompanied' motets all require instrumental support.

and on the other hand, dance rhythms or pulse rhythms: secondly, and consequently, the voice is the most natural as well as the most perfect of instruments as far as it goes; so that its introduction into instrumental music arrests the attention as nothing else will ever do, and hence must not be admitted without the intention of putting it permanently in the foreground: thirdly, that the introduction of the voice normally means the introduction of words, since that is how the human race uses its voice: and lastly, that it follows from this that the music must concern itself (conventionally or realistically or how you please) with the fit expression of the sense of the words. The correct application of Professor Andrew Bradley's philosophy (a classical statement of the case which, though not addressed to musicians, every musician should know) will show that there is no inherent impossibility in thus reconciling the claims of absolute music with those of the intelligent and intelligible setting of words. There is no part of Beethoven's Choral Symphony which does not become clearer to us when we assume that the choral finale is right; and there is hardly a point that does not become difficult and obscure as soon as we fall into the habit which assumes that the choral finale is wrong. I am not arguing that it is necessary to prove that it or any other work of art is perfect. That is never necessary, and most people would rashly say that it is never possible. All that is required is a point of view which assumes that Beethoven is not an inattentive artist who cannot keep his own plan in mind, until we have clear evidence to the contrary. If Beethoven were a Berlioz, a Bruckner, or a Mahler, we should find him out all the sooner by assuming that he is nothing of the kind. Hot-headed enthusiasts for these three composers fail to realize the gravity of their inconsistencies, because they assume that Beethoven was no better. The criticism which discovers the inconsistencies starts by assuming that these composers are as consistent as Beethoven. They break down under the test; but the critic who has applied it admires them more than the blind enthusiasts, because he sees more in the art of music wherever he finds it.

If a great work of art could be made responsible for all subsequent failures to imitate it, then Beethoven might have had cause for doubting whether the opening of his Ninth Symphony was worth the risk. It is a privilege of the greatest works of art that they can, if they will, reveal something gigantic in their scale, their range, and their proportions at the very first glimpse or moment. This power is quite independent of the possibility that other works may be larger; it is primarily a matter of proportion, and the actual size enters into the question only when the work of art is brought by some unavoidable accident into relation with the actual size of the spectator. Thus Macaulay once shrewdly observed that the size of the Great Pyramid was essential to its sublimity, 'for what could be more vile than a pyramid thirty feet high?' And thus the faithful reproduction of the noblest proportions will not give sublimity to an architectural model that you can put under a glass case. The truth is that in architecture the size of the human frame is one of the terms, perhaps the principal term, of the art. In pictures this is not so, or rather it is so with a more elastic relativity: you can give any proportions you like to your pictures by introducing human figures or other known objects on whatever scale you please. Music has, like architecture, a fixed element to deal with, the subtlest and most implacable of all. It is no use comparing the dimensions of music for a few instruments with those of music for vast masses: the string quartets of Beethoven are in the most important of all their dimensions fully as large as the symphonies. It is no use saying that the string quartet is a pencil drawing, and the symphony an oil painting or a fresco: pencil drawings are not executed on the scale of frescoes. It is no use saying that the string quartet is monochrome, while the symphony has all the tone colours of the orchestra: people who seriously talk of string-quartet style as monochromatic are probably tone-deaf, and certainly incapable of recognizing anything short of the grossest contrasts in orchestral music. Yet there is what you may call a dimensional difference between a string quartet and an orchestra; and the difference is hardly greater in volume of tone than in range of tone colour. These differences, again, cannot fail to have some effect on the architecture of the works designed for few or for many instruments, but such effects on the designs are not less subtle than profound; and the composer himself is so far from recognizing them until his plans are matured that, as we have already seen, Beethoven for a long time thought that what eventually became the finale of his A minor Quartet was to be the finale of the Ninth Symphony.

The all-pervading, constant element in musical designs is time. Beethoven's chamber music (extending the term so as to include everything from one to eight instruments) is for the most part on the same time-scale as his symphonies. That scale was from the outset so large that his First Symphony, a masterly little comedy, shows him taking the precaution to design his first independent orchestral work on a smaller scale than much that he had already written for solo instruments. But while it was obvious from the outset that his compositions were on the largest known scale, it only gradually became evident that that scale was growing beyond all precedent. Beethoven himself did not avow this fact until he recommended that the Eroica Symphony, being longer than usual, should be placed nearer the beginning than the end of the concert.[1] And the Eroica does not from the outset promise to be larger than the Second Symphony, nor indeed in its first sketches did it show any signs of being so large. Contemporary critics throughout Beethoven's career were continually deceived about the scale of his designs, or they would not so constantly have considered Beethoven inferior to Mozart in power of construction. With the rarest exceptions they always listened to a work of Beethoven in the expectation that its proportions would be those of a work of Mozart; and the mere measurement of the actual length of the work as a whole would not suffice to correct that assumption, for several very perfect works of Mozart may be found which are considerably longer than some characteristic great works of Beethoven. The enlargement of the time-scale is not a matter of total length; it is a matter of contrasts in movement. Mozart's aesthetic system does not admit of such broad expanses side by side with such abrupt and explosive actions as are perfectly natural in Beethoven's art. The first signs of intelligence in this matter came from those contemporary critics of Beethoven who had the sense to be bewildered by many things which are now accepted inattentively. Two of Weber's notorious gibes will clear up the matter once for all. He regarded the introduction to the Fourth Symphony as a monstrous and empty attempt to spread some four or five notes over a quarter of an hour. This shows that he had a sense of something new in Beethoven's time-scale. The other case was that of the sustained note five octaves deep towards the end of the first movement of the Seventh Symphony; a feature which he declared showed that Beethoven was now ripe for the madhouse. This shows that he perceived something unprecedented in Beethoven's scale of tone. Now the scale of tone is a very much more difficult matter to discuss than the scale of time, and I must be content, for the present, to leave all statements about it in the form of dogmatic assertion. It naturally is more easily measured in orchestral works than in works where there is less volume of tone to deal with; but again, as with the time elements, it is not a question of the actual volume, but of the range of contrast. In Beethoven's string quartets it is not less manifest than in his orchestra. In short, just as it is possible in the very first notes of a work to convey to the listener the conviction that this is going to be something on a large scale of time, so is it possible, however small the instrumental means employed, to arouse in the listener a confident expectation of an extraordinary depth and range of tone.

[1] His notion of 'nearer the beginning than the end' was 'after, perhaps, an overture, an aria, and a concerto'. When he produced his next symphony, the Fourth, he preceded it with the First, the Second, and the Eroica. Four hours was short for a concert in those days.

The opening of the Ninth Symphony is an immediate revelation of Beethoven's full power in both of these ways. Of all passages in a work of art, the first subject of the first movement of Beethoven's Ninth Symphony has had the deepest and widest influence on later music. Even with an ordinary instrumental finale, the Ninth Symphony would have remained the most gigantic instrumental work extant; its gigantic proportions are only the more wonderful from the fact that the forms are still the purest outcome of the sonata style. The choral finale itself is perfect in form. We must insist on this, because vast masses of idle criticism are still nowadays directed against the Ninth Symphony and others of Beethoven's later works in point of form; and these criticisms rest upon uncultured and unclassical text-book criteria as to musical form; mere statements of the average procedure warranted to produce tolerable effect if carefully carried out. We shall never make head or tail of the Ninth Symphony until we treat it as a law unto itself. That is the very treatment under which Berlioz and Bruckner break down; and it is also the treatment under which a Mozart symphony proves itself to be a living individual, though he wrote so many other symphonies externally similar in form.

The opening of the Ninth Symphony is, then, obviously gigantic. It is gigantic in relation to the sonata style of which it is still a perfect specimen. But its gigantic quality is so obvious in itself that it has been the actual and individual inspiring source of almost all the vast stream of modern music that has departed from the sonata style altogether. The normal opening for a sonata movement is a good, clear, pregnant theme. Whatever happens before the statement of such a theme is evidently introductory, and the introduction is generally so separable that it is in an obviously different tempo, whether or not it does itself consist largely of something broadly melodious. But it would hardly do to call the opening of the Ninth Symphony an introduction: it is impossible to imagine anything that more definitely plunges us into the midst of things. No later composer has escaped its influence. Nearly all modern music not on sonata lines, and a great deal that is on sonata lines, assumes that the best way to indicate a large scale of design is to begin with some mysteriously attractive humming sounds, from which rhythmic fragments gradually detach themselves and combine to build up a climax. When the climax is a mighty theme in unison for the whole orchestra, and the key is D minor, the resemblance to Beethoven's Ninth Symphony becomes almost absurd. And this is actually the case in Bruckner's third and ninth symphonies; while he hardly knows how to begin a first movement or finale without a long tremolo. It is no exaggeration to say that the typical opening of a modern orchestral work has become as thoroughly conventionalized on these lines as any tonic-and-dominant sonata formula of the eighteenth century. There is no objection to this, so long as the composer can draw the rest of his work to scale. Only through lifelong mastery of the sonata style could such an opening be continued in anything resembling sonata form; and the crushing objection to the forms of Berlioz and Bruckner is not their departure from sonata principles, but their desperate recourse to them in just the most irrelevant particulars. Another set of difficulties arises when the composer continues such an opening without relying upon sonata forms. The orthodox reproach that is levelled against 'symphonic poems' is that of form-lessness: it is generally a foolish reproach because it is based on some foolish text-book notion of form as the average classical procedure. The real trouble with an unsuccessful symphonic poem is generally that it either fails to maintain the scale set up by its ninth-symphony type of opening, or makes an even more radical failure to come to a definite beginning on any scale at all; as, for instance, in the extreme case of Liszt's *Ce qu'on entend sur la montagne*. This work consists of an introduction to an intro-duction to a connecting link to another introduction to a rhapsodic interlude, leading to a free development of the third introduction, leading to a series of still more introductory developments of the previous introduction, leading to a solemn slow theme (which, after these twenty minutes, no mortal power will persuade any listener to regard as a real beginning), and so eventually leading backwards to the original mysterious opening by way of conclusion.

The whole difference between Wagner and such interesting but unconvincing pioneers is that Wagner, when he abandoned the sonata time-scale, thoroughly mastered his own new proportions. He talked partisan nonsense about Beethoven's attitude to 'abso-lute' musical forms, but he made no mistakes in maturing his own musical style; and the fact that his medium was music-drama must not mislead us into denying the validity of his mature sense of musical form as a factor in the purely instrumental music of later times.

This opening of the Ninth Symphony has, then, been a radiating point for all subsequent experiments for enlarging the time-scale of music; and the simplest way to learn its lessons is to set our mind free to expect to find in the Ninth Symphony the broadest and most spacious processes side by side with the tersest and most sharply contrasted statements and actions. There are listeners (indeed their complaint is one of the intellectual fashions of the day) to whom it is a cause of nervous irritability that the Ninth Symphony is recognized by orthodoxy as the most sublime musical composi-tion known. Orthodoxy happens to be perfectly right here, and

for the same reason that it is right about Handel's *Messiah*, and
Bach's *Matthew Passion* and Mass in B minor. These things do
not rest upon fashion: they rest upon the solid fact that these works
deal truthfully with sublime subjects. As a modern poet has
remarked, 'All is not false that's taught at public schools'; and if
there are large numbers of contemporary music lovers who are
in heated revolt against the aesthetics of Beethoven's music, that
is a nervous condition which concerns nobody but themselves.[1]
There will always be still larger numbers of music lovers who
have not yet heard anything like as much classical music as they
wish to hear. It is just as well that they should realize that there
is nothing more than an irritated condition of nerves behind the
talk that still goes on about the need of a revolt against Beethoven.
No artist of such a range as Beethoven has ever set up a tyranny
from which revolt is possible. We hear a great deal about the way
in which English Music was 'crushed by the ponderous genius of
Handel'. It was crushed by nothing of the sort; it was crushed
simply by the fact that the rank and fashion of English music
patrons would for centuries listen only to Italian singers and
Italian composers. Handel's methods were Italian, and he
benefited accordingly. The real objection that is felt against
Beethoven's aesthetics is the eternal dread felt by the artist of
genre in the presence of the sublime. Modern British music has
derived much stimulus from highly specialized *genres* of French
music, and these *genres* do not aim at the sublime. They thus do
not blend well with the Ninth Symphony, though they are conspicuously free from the false sublime that would blend infinitely
worse.

We have seen that there are two factors which cause the impression of the enormous size in the opening of the Ninth Symphony.
The one factor, that of proportion in time, we have already dealt
with, and on that head all that remains is to explain how the actual
length of the opening is not exceptional. Indeed, the whole first
movement, as Sir George Grove has pointed out, is, though the
greatest of Beethoven's compositions in this form, by no means
the longest. And this does not mean that it is more terse than
longer movements such as the first movement of the Eroica
Symphony. Those longer movements are not diffuse; but the
compression of Beethoven's later style is balanced by a still wider
power of expansion. What happens is that, as we have already

[1] The quaintest manifestations of the revolt were those of the writers
who at the centenary of Beethoven's death told us that the 'humanism' of
Beethoven's slow movements was antiquated. From time to time the
Superman *may* seem to be as fashionable as all that: but nevertheless he
does not exist as yet.

pointed out, the range of contrasts in phrase-length is greater; and the result is that more space is gained by compression than will ever be filled up by expansion. Sir George Grove pointed out how, already as soon as the first mysterious sounds begin to make their crescendo, the rhythmic fragments are compressed and hurried. So much, then, for the rhythmic side of this opening.

The rest of its enormous effect is the result of the scale of tone. And here again the Ninth Symphony, like the Fifth and the *Leonora* Overtures, teaches us that there is for the massive treatment of the orchestra a criterion which many modern orchestral composers have entirely forgotten. Orchestral music since Beethoven has undergone its greatest developments chiefly at the hands of composers who contemplated music from the standpoint of the theatre. It is true that Liszt wrote nothing for the theatre, and that Berlioz's operas were brilliant failures; but the fact remains that nearly everything that marks an advance in nineteenth-century orchestral technique since Beethoven is an advance in essentially dramatic orchestration; and this in the narrow sense, that the characteristic orchestral discoveries would be even more useful in an opera than in a purely symphonic work. Finally, it is universally admitted, even by partisans, that Liszt and Berlioz did not often achieve complete mastery of their art problems, and that if we are to find a style for the post-Beethoven orchestra which we can always confidently expect to say what it means and mean what it says, we must turn to the later music-dramas of Wagner. It is no more necessary to prove that these are perfect works of art than to prove the perfection of ethics, theology, science, and sentiment throughout *Paradise Lost*. But you can, on the whole, find mastery wherever you look in the later works of Wagner, just as you can in Milton, without taking any precaution to select specially inspired passages; whereas with Liszt and Berlioz you will find mastery about as sporadically as you will find it in Walt Whitman. Wagner is, in short, the most authoritative classic of the orchestral technique of the age after Beethoven; and Wagner's life's work is for the stage.

Now there are two far-reaching consequences of this that we must take into account before we adopt Wagner as a criterion for the symphonic orchestra. The composer for the stage (like the composer of symphonic poems on the basis of Liszt and Berlioz) is constantly occupied by illustrating something outside the music. This *may* tend to limit his capacity for inventing sounds which do not obviously illustrate something external; and it *must* limit his opportunities for developing such sounds. The purely symphonic composer has no use for illustrative sounds unless they are also useful to a purely musical design; and as soon as they are so useful, their imitative aspect ceases to attract notice. There is a very large class of orchestral procedure which is thus common to the symphonic orchestra and the stage; and so long as music confined itself to Mozart's range of expression the distinction between symphonic and dramatic orchestration remained a subtlety. In music of his period you might perhaps be able to distinguish between first-rate and second-rate mastery of the orchestra in this way, that with second-rate composers the dramatic orchestral devices lacked musical point, while the musical devices lacked dramatic point. But the divergence of interests did not as yet amount to this, that a composer could write symphonic orchestration which would be impossible in stage music. All that had happened was that much which was tolerable or even effective on the stage, would be too thin and commonplace for the symphonic orchestra. The mature works of Wagner are far too highly organized in all respects for this to be crudely manifest; but it is self-evident that the orchestration of Wagnerian opera contains much that is not only out of place but inadequate for symphonic writing. And practically this is a more important truth to the modern composer than the converse truth, that the mastery of a symphonic style for full modern orchestra is in itself no qualification for the handling of operatic orchestration. There are far more composers who can write a good modern opera than there are composers of good modern symphonies.

But the subtle aesthetic distinction between the dramatic and symphonic in orchestration is not more important than the very much simpler practical fact which determines the opera-writer's orchestral outlook. Nine-tenths of the opera-writer's orchestration is designed for the accompanying of voices. It does not matter whether, like Wagner, he puts all his invention into the orchestra and gets the voice to declaim through the orchestral design as it best can, or whether, like Mozart, he puts his primary invention into the voice. Whatever he does, he knows that the voice must be heard somehow; and his orchestral climaxes are severely restricted to situations in which there is either no solo singing, or the voices are able actually to interrupt the full orchestra, and so to convey an ingenious illusion of dominating the storm when all the time the orchestra gives way to the singer with the readiest tact. The imagination of the public and of students is impressed by the extent to which Wagner enlarged the orchestra; and Wagner is one of the greatest composers in the handling of massive orchestration; but massive orchestration seems such a simple thing, and the immense majority of Wagner's interesting orchestral devices are so closely associated with the singer on the stage (even where they are not actually accompanying the voice) that very few critics and students pay much attention to Wagner's handling of an orchestral tutti. Hence there arises a conception of the modern orchestra as an organization which on the one hand can make an alarmingly loud noise, and on the other hand can indulge in astounding complexities of musical spider-lines. The attempts of ordinary go-ahead composers to handle the tutti of a modern orchestra with no technique at all, or perhaps with a humdrum military bandmaster's technique, can hardly fail to produce a noisy impression; 'noisiness' being a popular term for bad balance of tone. The position, then, with commonplace exploitations of the modern orchestra is that the tuttis are apt to be scored with no technique to speak of, and that the rest of the writing, though often very interesting and clever, is unwittingly based upon a conception which reduces itself to the art of accompanying a voice. Again and again the inner history of an ambitious piece of contemporary orchestration has been that it was scored in some complicated and interesting way; and that, after the usual disheartening experiences of inadequate rehearsals, the composer has found that the full passages had better be expressed in the old scrubbing-brush of tremolo, with the theme entrusted to the trumpet as the only person capable of carrying it through.

The real method for scoring a tutti will be found in Wagner, in Richard Strauss, and Elgar, and a very few other composers since Beethoven; and it will be found to be in all essentials surprisingly like Beethoven's method. Now the clue to the whole orchestration of the Ninth Symphony is to be found in the statement of I forget what French authority that the whole work, or at all events a great part of it, is one grand tutti. This must not be taken to mean that it is full of useless doublings, or that it does not contain numberless passages in which single instruments weave delicate threads. What it does mean is that the composition is for a whole orchestra employed for its own sake, and that no part of its aesthetic system is concerned with the accompaniment of anything else—until, of course, the voices enter in the finale. And there we find proof of how curiously irrelevant that present-day style of criticism is which patronizes Beethoven for having 'attempted' in the Ninth Symphony an orchestration which only the resources of Wagner could have enabled him to carry out successfully. No such criticism can tackle the choral part of the symphony at all; for, whatever may be said against Beethoven's choral writing (and choral technique is no strong feature in modern musical progress), Beethoven is completely at his ease in *accompanying* the voice. There is, in fact, very little trouble with the orchestration of the choral finale; nor is there much difficulty in getting the slow movement to sound clear, although there is a prevalent and very gross misunderstanding of a certain horn passage therein, which we will discuss in its place. The whole set of difficulties of the orchestration of the Ninth

Symphony is confined to the first movement and to one famous theme in the scherzo. Wagner adjusted these matters easily; Weingartner adjusts them more accurately: with a large orchestra such as that of Dresden, with 150 players and triple wind (six flutes, six oboes, and so on), the adjustment becomes purely the business of the conductor, and of some one's marking the extra wind parts according to his directions.[1] The first movement of the Ninth Symphony is no doubt the most troublesome of all Beethoven's scores; but no virtuoso has ever written a work for the pianoforte which does not, in proportion to its size, throw far more responsibility upon the player for adjusting its balance of tone.

The first thing, then, to realize about the Ninth Symphony is that it is a work for the orchestral tutti; and that nine-tenths of the patronizing criticism that is nowadays directed against it is based on a judgement that is frankly incapable of following any genuine orchestral tutti whatever. If your ear is accustomed entirely to the pianoforte, the clearest organ-playing in the world will be a chaos of echoes to you. If you know nothing but music for the full orchestra, your first impressions of the finest string quartet will consist mainly of squeak and scrape. And if your only conception of the orchestra is fundamentally operatic, it is no use to argue that Beethoven's symphonies are so often performed that you have nothing to learn from them; a cathedral choir-boy may have sung in the church services every day, and yet have escaped understanding the English of the Bible and Prayer Book. I have noticed that any truly symphonic orchestration sounds to me, for the moment, impenetrably thick after I have got my ears into focus for operatic or otherwise illustrative modern orchestration. Of course the impression is only momentary, because I know by experience that such impressions are mere physiological effects of contrast; the mind learns its accommodations just as the eye or the ear. But it will not learn its accommodations if it is told that there is no moon because the first step out of a brilliantly lighted room seems to be a step into pitch darkness.

ANALYSIS

1 *Allegro ma non troppo, un poco maestoso.*
2 SCHERZO: *Molto vivace* alternating with *Presto.*
3 *Adagio molto e cantabile* alternating with *Andante moderato.*

---

[1] It has been objected that all bad scoring can be defended and rectified on these lines. This is not so. Errors of calculation are not defects of imagination. Beethoven's imagination never fails; and there is no master of modern instrumentation who could trust himself to publish fewer miscalculated passages than Beethoven, if he were, like Beethoven, deprived of the opportunity for correcting his scoring at rehearsals.

4 FINALE: *Presto* alternating with quotations from previous movements, and leading to *Allegro assai*; leading to recapitulation
of *Presto* with a Baritone solo followed by the Choral Finale,
which consists of variations and developments of the theme of
the *Allegro assai* as follows:

Allegro assai: theme and two variations (quartet and chorus),
Allegro assai vivace alla marcia: variation with tenor solo and
male chorus; fugal episode; variation with full chorus.

Andante maestoso: new theme with full chorus.

Allegro energico, sempre ben marcato: double fugue on the two
themes.

Allegro ma non tanto (with changes of tempo) leading to *Prestissimo*: coda with quartet and chorus.

FIRST MOVEMENT

When we compare the opening of the Ninth Symphony with
many of those imitations of it that have almost become a normal
procedure in later music, two characteristic features reveal themselves. First that, as has already been indicated, Beethoven
achieves his evidences of gigantic size in a passage which is, as a
matter of fact, not very long; and secondly that this moderate
length is filled with clearly marked gradations, which succeed one
another more rapidly as the intensity increases. It is interesting to
see how few composers have ever by any refinement of technique
and apparatus mastered the natural aesthetics of climax as shown
in any of Beethoven's crescendos and most simply of all in this
opening. External details have been echoed by later composers
with excellent though sometimes obviously borrowed effect.
Bruckner's Ninth Symphony even gets in Beethoven's characteristic anticipation of the tonic chord on an outlying bassoon under
the dominant chord before the full orchestra bursts in with the
mighty unison theme.

Ex. 1.

But such resemblances are fatal; there is only one ninth-symphony
opening, and that is Beethoven's. If anybody else could get
those proportions right, he would arrive at Beethoven's Ninth
Symphony and not his own. If his own is going to be different
enough to justify its existence, it will not adopt, long after its
harmonies have moved into all manner of foreign keys and emotional tones, a characteristic external detail the whole point of
which was that the harmony had not yet begun to move at all.
And the real sublimity of Beethoven's conception has not yet fully
appeared with the entry of the mighty unison theme in the tonic

after this mysterious crescendo on the dominant (mysterious, by the way, because, as the harmony was nothing but bare fifths and octaves, that characteristic anticipation by the bassoon was the first indication that it was not the tonic chord of either A major or A minor). This opening is indeed gigantic, but its full power begins to manifest itself in the fact that it is not unwieldy. The mighty unison theme leads to a variety of short melodic and harmonic sequences, no two phrases being of easily predictable length; and it comes to a kind of full close very characteristic of Beethoven's latest work, a close in which the tonic chord has been arrived at without the intervention of the dominant as a penulti-mate. And so the theme, as Weingartner says, disappears into the ground like some Afrit vanishing in a column of smoke. And now we find ourselves on the tonic, with the same mysterious bare fifth quivering and growing until it pervades the whole orchestra. Immediately before the climax the bass changes the harmony, this time in the unexpected direction of B flat; and in this key the unison theme bursts out again, soon to make its way back to the dominant chord, where another new and terse theme appears.

Ex. 2.

This new theme leads, by a movement of its last three notes down-ward in a very few further steps, to the famous pathetic introduc-tion to the second subject; a passage which attracted the eager attention of the musical symbolists who surrounded Liszt, on account of its superficial and entirely accidental resemblance to the theme of the *Ode to Joy*.

Ex. 3.

It cannot be too often or too strongly urged that no such thematic resemblances are of the slightest importance unless the composer himself establishes the connexion on the spot by the most unmis-takable formal methods.[1] We shall find plenty of such methods in the Ninth Symphony and in any late work of Beethoven; which will conclusively prove that what is said about Beethoven's revolu-tionary tendencies in musical form is, for the most part, nonsense which it would be a mistaken courtesy to treat as anything but

[1] Strange to say, no English musician has been more strongly bitten by the Lisztian view than Stanford, who always upheld Liszt as the awful example of lack of musical logic; in spite of the fact that Liszt was a fanatic pioneer of music on a single leitmotif.

ignorance. Here it will suffice to say that Beethoven's forms become more and more precise in his later works; and that if thereby they become less and less like each other, this is what anybody who understands the nature of artistic forms as compared to living forms ought to expect. I am obliged to leave these general statements dogmatic where I am dealing with only one work; if proof is required I am ready for it with any work and any part of a work in Beethoven's third period; no very large field of survey, comprising, as it does, only thirteen works in sonata form, and not half a dozen other important compositions.

The second subject, at which we have now arrived, consists of a large number of different themes grouped into paragraphs of every imaginable size and shape. Of these I quote five: the consolatory opening cantabile divided between wind instruments of contrasted tone—

the stormy figure of scales in contrary motion—

the energetic theme with its contrast between sharp rhythm and cantabile, leading to the famous modulation into a distant key (flat supertonic)—

which in its turn leads to the most flowing and elaborate paragraph in this exposition where all is so flowing and rich; and so to the complicated and expressive dialogue between wind and strings (a difficult passage where Wagner's and Weingartner's suggestions are valuable in the interests of clearness)—

and the final triumphant tutti on the tonic chord of B flat—

which ends the exposition and collapses dramatically onto the dominant of D and back to the cloudy opening.

In discussing the first subject we saw the advantage of terseness in the very act of establishing an impression of immense size, for we noted that Beethoven was enabled thereby to give two great waves rising from mystery to their sublime crash. It might be argued that these two great waves are perhaps not so enormous as the longer passages often achieved by later composers, where it is inconceivable that the passage should be given twice over in its entirety. Very well then; Beethoven can do this greater type of passage also. The mysterious opening is now going to develop; it remains intensely quiet without crescendo, its periods marked by a distant boom of drums and flashes of red light from the trumpets, an extraordinarily solemn resource in the primitive classical treatment of these instruments already well known to Mozart and often used by him with sublime effect. The novelty in the present instance consists in the very low pitch of the trumpets. The harmonies drift through a major chord to the subdominant. The passage still remains intensely quiet, but in the subdominant the articulate main theme gathers shape in dialogue between the wind instruments. Suddenly on a fierce discord the energetic rhythmic figure of Ex. 8 bursts out on the full orchestra. The following plaintive treatment of figure (b) then makes, with the addition of four closing chords, a six-bar phrase.

This closes into G minor, and the dialogue on figure (a) is resumed. Now it leads to C minor, and again Ex. 8 intervenes on the full

orchestra and yields to the six-bar phrase. This time the last two
bars are repeated with a crescendo, and the orchestra plunges into a
vigorous triple fugue with figure (*b*) (Ex. 1) for its main subject
and a pair of admirably clear and contrasted counterpoints. This
drifts with the grandest and simplest breadth straight through
from C minor to G minor, D minor, and so to A minor. On
reaching this key its energy abates until it subsides into a famous
and exquisitely plaintive passage, which Sir George Grove was fond
of quoting as an example of Beethoven's peculiar use of the word
cantabile. Grove indicates that Beethoven applies the term rather
specially to passages of a simplicity which makes them liable to be
overlooked. To this we may add that as long as Beethoven refrains
from using the German language he can hardly find any word that
will give the player the chance of putting what the Germans call
Innigkeit into his rendering. Beethoven does not want to prescribe
what he calls *intissimo sentimento* here: his best chance of getting
what he wants is to tell the player to sing, and as the passage is too
quiet to lend itself to obvious swellings of tone, the mere action
of getting a singing quality into its calm will go far to express its
inwardness.[1]

This A minor cantabile develops itself almost happily in its own
touching way (notice, for example, the place where the whole mass
of wood-wind gathers itself together in a staccato crescendo).
Suddenly, with childlike pathos the main theme of the second
subject (Ex. 4) appears. The basses take it up in F major, and in
that consolatory key the dialogue on figure (*b*) is resumed. Nothing
indicates that the situation is going to change in any near future.
The development has in fact been on fully as large a scale as the
rest of the movement, but the present passage has every appearance
of being in the middle of its flow. If Beethoven had left the movement unfinished here, no mortal could have made a better guess
at the sequel than that somehow or other Beethoven would climb
to another climax, and from it build a passage of anticipation of
return which should surpass in length and excitement any of the
famous returns he had achieved before; such as the return to the
tonic in the Eroica Symphony, or the return three times anticipated
in the first movement of the First Rasoumovsky Quartet. It would,

[1] I know of no more crushing evidence of racial incompatibility of
temper than is furnished by Debussy's beautiful arrangement of Schumann's pedal pianoforte studies. The French composer shows all his
exquisite sensibility for pianoforte tone and his scrupulous scholarship in
every note of these arrangements, yet where Schumann writes *innig*
Debussy translates it *très expressif*, which is as flatly the opposite term as
any two languages could supply between them. This leaves open the
question whether Debussy has not after all correctly interpreted Schumann's sentiments, which hardly reach Beethoven's *Innigkeit*.

however, be difficult to know exactly what a long and exciting preparation of a return is to prepare for in this case; for the opening of the Ninth Symphony is itself a long and exciting passage of preparation. There are people who talk *a priori* nonsense about the sonata forms, as if these forms were stereotyped moulds into which you shovel your music in the hope that it may set there like a jelly. The real facts of sonata form seem complicated only because we have to describe them in purely musical terms, just as the facts of pictorial forms would seem enormously complicated if we had to describe them in geometrical terms. In reality such a fact of sonata form as this matter of 'return to the tonic for the first subject', is the barest definition of the capacity of the music to make us expect to return to anything whatever.

Beethoven's conduct of this great development has so far contrived the course of events as to make us feel thoroughly in the swing of an almost happy conversational episode, when suddenly, with a change of harmony, four abrupt bars carry us roughly into the tonic major, and the whole development is at once a thing of the past, a tale that is told.

This return to the recapitulation is utterly unlike any other in Beethoven's works; and we shall always find that in these cardinal features of form, no two works of Beethoven are really alike. In this matter of return to the first subject Beethoven achieved every conceivable gradation, from famous record-breaking lengths of anticipation to not less record-breaking abruptness; nor did he neglect the possibilities of bringing about the return with all Mozart's quiet formal beauty and symmetry. The present catastrophic return now reveals fresh evidence of the gigantic size of the opening. Hitherto we have known the opening as a pianissimo, and only the subtlety of Beethoven's feeling for tone has enabled us to feel that it was vast in sound as well as in spaciousness. Now we are brought into the midst of it, and instead of a distant nebula we see the heavens on fire. There is something very terrible about this triumphant major tonic, and it is almost a relief when it turns into the minor as the orchestra crashes into the main theme, no longer in unison, but with a bass rising in answer to the fall of the melody. Each phrase given out by the strings is now echoed by the wood-wind (it is ridiculous to complain of Beethoven's orchestration here, when the whole difficulty of such passages might easily be remedied by simply doubling and trebling certain of the wind parts—a purely financial question). The whole first subject is thus on the one hand amplified by this dialogue treatment, while on the other it is mightily compressed by being gathered up in one single storm from the outset of its introduction down to its abrupt subsidence into the consolatory preparation for the second subject.

From this point the recapitulation follows bar for bar the course of the exposition, but there are new details of far-reaching significance. There is an interesting historic process in the expression of pathos in sonata form. The first great master in whose hands sonata forms became definitely dramatic is Haydn. When Haydn writes a sonata movement in the minor mode, his second subject will certainly be in the relative major key. What will happen to it in the recapitulation? If the work is of Haydn's maturity and the character of the movement is blustering and impetuous, Haydn's sunny temperament is almost certain to impel him to recapitulate his second subject in the major, and so to end with childlike happiness. Not so Mozart, who rises to his highest pathos by translating the second subject from the relative major to the tonic minor, and translating it by no means literally, but in every way heightening the pathos in both harmony and melody. Beethoven has further resources at his command, and his practice in such a case depends upon his power to design a coda equal in importance to the whole development of a movement. Accordingly, if Beethoven chooses to recapitulate the whole of his second subject in the tonic major, this does not commit him to a happy ending; on the contrary it is, for him, a powerful expression of tragic irony. Nowhere since Greek tragedy do we so forcibly feel the pathos of the messenger who comes with what has the appearance of good news but which really brings about the catastrophe, as when we have in a tragic work of Beethoven the comfort of the recapitulation of the second subject in the tonic major. In the Ninth Symphony, however, Beethoven has achieved a yet more powerful pathos; he can get both major and minor wherever he pleases. For six bars the second subject proceeds happily in the major, and then, sorrowfully repeating the fifth and sixth bars in the minor, continues in minor, with the exception of the pleading second phrase of Ex. 6. The wonderful modulation to the flat supertonic in this passage looks much simpler as a modulation from D minor to E flat than it did when it was written as a modulation from B flat, not to C flat, but to B natural. Gevaert and other eminent writers on music have argued from this that it actually sounds less remarkable here; but with all respect I submit that they are misled by appearances. The modulation was, in the first instance as in the second, a simple modulation to the flat supertonic; and if Beethoven chose in the first instance to spell it in an extraordinary fashion, that is no reason for playing it out of tune. Classical and modern music from the time of Mozart onwards is constantly offering us passages in which the notation is enharmonic while the sense is diatonic. On the other hand, many real enharmonic changes are not visible in the notation at all. The real difficulty here between the first and the second passages is that in the first instance the whole context is in a major key, whereas now in the recapitulation we are in the minor tonic, and so to this extent it is true that the modulation to the flat supertonic is less remote. On the other hand it is more pathetic, and Beethoven contrives to heighten the pathos by a subtle change in the position of the loud figure. From the following crescendo onwards, all the rest of the recapitulation is in the minor, including the once triumphant energetic close (Ex. 8).

What is going to happen next? Put this into technical language, and ask how Beethoven is going to begin his coda. The superior person who assumes that everything is silly as soon as it can be designated by a technical term will hereupon quote the gentleman who asked the painter where he was going to put his brown tree. But this is not a true parallel to our question. A fair parallel would be, what are you going to put in the middle distance on the left-hand side of your picture? or what form of dome, tower, or spire are you going to have in the middle of your cathedral roof? These technical terms for the sonata forms describe no more than the points of the compass, and there is no more resemblance between the standard examples of even the most particularized of these forms than there is between them and works in totally different forms. If we once more imagine that the movement be left unfinished at this point, we should find it just as difficult to guess the next event as we did at the end of the development. The coda of the first movement of the Eroica Symphony began with an astounding and mysterious modulation which carried it off into distant keys. Other codas of Beethoven begin as if to lead into the development again in the same way as the close of the exposition did; others bring the main theme or some other theme out in a great climax; others settle down at once to a comfortable tonic-and-dominant swinging passage on some important figure. Nearly every great coda will contain some such passage as its most natural means of expressing finality in the action of the piece. I suppose that if we did not know how Beethoven's coda was to begin here, our first guess would be some dramatic stroke of genius. Bruckner's most enthusiastic admirers are the first to deplore the fatal ease with which their master strikes his dramatic stroke whenever his huge creations try to lift their acreage of limbs without muscles to work them   One of the reasons why the first movement of the Ninth Symphony dwarfs every other first movement, long or short, that has been written before or since, is that, more evidently than in other compositions, it shows that no member of its organization is so large as to lose freedom in its function as part of a larger whole. The whole, when it has been heard, proves greater than the sum of its parts. In works of art which take time instead of space, it is inevitable that the highest organization should be concentrated towards the beginning; thus the first movement of a great classical work is normally the most highly organized. What has just been said of the first movement of the Ninth Symphony is true of every other mature work of Beethoven. It is only more easily seen here, and more profitably pointed out, because of the enormous influence this particular movement has had upon later music dealing with totally different forms. The technicalities or points of the compass of sonata form are merely relative; the principles of form are universal. As every part of the Ninth Symphony presents us with a constantly increasing impression of greatness in due proportion to a whole which is still greater than the sum of its parts, so does this movement stand towards the rest of the symphony. It matters not that the other movements are all simpler in organization; or rather, it is necessary that they should be. The simplicity means increase of breadth, and it is so organized that the mind is always fully occupied with the right actions and reactions.

And now for Beethoven's coda. We have just heard the end of the exposition, an emphatic close to one of the most flowing and elaborate paragraphs ever written in music or words. And instead of any abrupt modulation, Beethoven quietly and in a gentle vein of melancholy continues a flowing dialogue with the figures of the mighty first subject (Ex. 1), as if mysterious introductions and stormy outbursts were but old ancestral memories. The form of the dialogue is that which arose out of the mysterious introduction at the beginning of the development, but the tone-colour is not mysterious now; it is a grey noonday. Gradually and without change of key, the dialogue rises in an impassioned crescendo and bursts into a storm paragraph developing Ex. 5, which is followed up by a sequence based on Ex. 8. Suddenly the whole mass of strings stands hushed and overawed while the horns, softly in the full major tonic, are heard developing figure (b) of the main theme. This moment of distant happiness has never been surpassed for tragic irony. It is very characteristic of Beethoven, and many parallel passages can be found, besides what has been adduced above as to his habit of finding room for the major tonic in recapitulations where his main key was minor. Here it is evident that his translating most of his second subject into the minor was done as much for the sake of throwing this passage into relief as for its own pathos at the moment. Soon the whole mass of strings takes the theme up in four octaves, while isolated wood-wind instruments give out the semiquaver countersubject of the big fugue passage in the development. The strings carry on their quaver figure in a menacing crescendo. Neither in numbers nor in tone do the wood-wind make the slightest effort to be heard

through this crescendo; but as Weingartner points out, there is
something peculiarly fascinating in the very effect of their dis-
appearance behind this rising granite mass of sound, and their
quiet emergence again as the mass subsides. No sooner has it
subsided than Ex. 5 bursts out again with the utmost passion. (In
the score the entry of the first violin of this theme shows a capricious
change of octave which looks exactly like an accidental omission of
the *ottava* sign[1]; it is always corrected accordingly in performance,
perhaps rightly. Other cases of the kind are frequent throughout the
symphony, but are sometimes much more difficult to deal with, as
Beethoven purposely made capricious changes of octave a feature
of his later style.) This passage suddenly ends with the pathetic
ritardando phrase (Ex. 9) which preceded the triple fugue passage
in the development. It now leads to the final tragic passion. We
have noted that a great symphonic coda is pretty sure to contain
a passage that swings from tonic to dominant on some important
figure. One such passage we had when those horns entered so
suddenly in the tonic major. We now have the most famous of all
tonic-and-dominant passages, in the minor; the famous dramatic
muttering in semitones of the whole mass of strings, beginning with
the basses and rising until it is five octaves deep in the violins. Next
to the opening of the symphony this passage has been more imitated
by ambitious later composers than any other in music, classical or
modern. As Beethoven has it, the universal quality in it is its
normal truth of emotional tone and musical form; its unique
quality is that the melody that is sung above it is to all intents and
purposes quite new.

Ex. 10.

Of course the rhythm in dotted notes vaguely recalls the figure of
the opening, which is more clearly alluded to by the trumpets and
drums; but the fact remains that Beethoven here shows himself
capable (as he has done elsewhere though never in a movement
on so colossal a scale) of introducing at the very last moment
a theme that has never been heard before. The procedure is perfectly logical. This melodic expression is external and emotional;
the logic is no more to be looked for in melodic connexions of
figure here than it is to be relied upon where such connexions
are abundant. Like all musical logic, it lies in the proportions of

---

[1] The autograph, and the corrected MS. sent to the publishers, and
every other authentic document, are in absolute agreement on this and
almost every other disconcerting detail!

the rhythms and paragraphs. And so it is the most natural thing in the world that the paragraph should finally burst into the mighty unison of the main theme, and thus end the tragedy abruptly, yet in the fullness of time, with its own most pregnant motto.

SCHERZO

After tragedy comes the satiric drama. The next movement is, as Sir George Grove remarks, at once the greatest and the longest of Beethoven's scherzos. The chord of D minor is thrown at us by the strings in a rhythmic figure which pervades the whole; the drums tuned in octaves supply the minor third of the chord, and it is only as the work proceeds that we realize how this grotesque introduction makes an eight-bar phrase.

EX. 11.

Then the strings begin a very regular five-part fugue on the following subject, the wood-wind marking the first of every bar—

EX. 12.

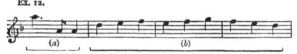

until almost the whole orchestra is mysteriously alive and busy. Soon there is a short crescendo, and the theme bursts out in a tutti. Suddenly the key swings round towards C major, the flat seventh (a relationship, by the way, which Beethoven had only once before brought into prominence, and that in one of his most mysterious imaginations, the ghostly slow movement of the D major trio, op. 70, no. 1). On the dominant of this key there is an exquisitely harmonious passage of preparation, after which nothing less than a broad second subject bursts out in the wood-wind which the strings furiously accompany with the octave figure.

EX. 13.

With Beethoven's scoring the theme cannot be heard with less than double wind; and even triple wind would be better (as at Dresden, for instance, where there are six flutes and six oboes, &c.), for they can divide the parts among themselves according to their importance. For less well-endowed orchestras the measures indicated by Wagner and Weingartner are absolutely necessary. They have this disadvantage that the horns, to which Beethoven could not give the melody because of their imperfect scale, now have the effect of throwing the weight of tone into the lower octaves. The trouble about all difficulties of balance with Beethoven is that his feeling for tone-colour is invariably poetical and Beethovenish, while the obvious ways of getting correct balance are apt to produce tone which is neither.

So far the scherzo, including its grotesque opening, has proceeded in clear four-bar periods. Beethoven's scherzos, however, will never permanently settle down to the spin of a sleeping top: before the swing of the rhythm can cease to stimulate us it will be enlivened by some momentary change of period. Here in the first lull we have a six-bar period.

Ex. 14.

The wood-wind echo its last four bars, and then the exposition is brought to a tonic-and-dominant end in an even number of two-bar phrases with a new figure.

Ex. 15.

The initial figure now moves down a series of thirds in a harmonious pianissimo dialogue between strings and wind. Having thus reached a D minor chord it stops abruptly, and the exposition is repeated from the beginning of the fugue theme. After the repeat the development begins by carrying on the dialogue in descending steps of thirds which are so managed as to lead crescendo through an enormous range of key until the dialogue ends angrily on the dominant of E minor, a key entirely alien to D minor. And now comes the famous passage in three-bar rhythm, *ritmo di tre battute*, which has drawn the attention of commentators to this scherzo as containing an interesting rhythmic effect presumably not to be found elsewhere. The truth is that this passage differs from incidents such as that quoted (Ex. 14) only in being extended over a wide region systematically enough for the special mention of three-bar periods to save trouble in construing it. It is carried out in great simplicity and breadth through E minor and A minor.

Suddenly the drums burst in with their figure on **F**, and the whole passage continues perfectly happily in F major. The entry of the drums has often been described as throwing the three-bar periods out again. It does nothing of the kind; it goes on making three-bar periods, giving figure (*a*), while the wind continue with figure (*b*). The key shifts in a leisurely way round to D minor. Now that we are in the tonic again, suddenly without the slightest break the rhythm relapses into four-bar periods, various instruments taking the theme up bar by bar.

Ex. 16.

The harmony drifts towards E flat (the flat supertonic), on the dominant of which the drums and horns mysteriously build up figure (*a*) into a chord. At last there is a crescendo, the chord suddenly changes to D minor, and the whole orchestra bursts out with the main theme in a tutti which stands for a recapitulation of the first subject. The key changes to B flat, where we have the harmonious transition passage. Again two odd bars are inserted bringing the passage on to the dominant of D; it is now expanded, with suggestions of the minor mode; and the second subject then bursts out, at first in D major; but from the ninth bar onwards it is translated into D minor. Otherwise this recapitulation is quite regular. The dialogue on figure (*a*) leads back to the development which is marked to be repeated, an injunction not often followed in these days of hustle. Afterwards this dialogue leads very simply to a short imitative coda. The tempo is hurried until the octave figure is compressed into duple time as follows—

Ex. 17.

And here a great confusion has arisen from the history of a certain change in Beethoven's way of writing the ensuing trio. The autograph shows that the bars of the trio were originally half their present length, and that the time was 2/4. With this notation it would have been impossible to conduct the trio too fast; and it is quite certain, from the very nature of the connecting passage, that Beethoven's intention is that two crotchets of the trio should correspond roughly to three (that is, one bar) of the scherzo. I say roughly, because a stringendo has intervened, and if the half-bar corresponds too exactly to the original tempo the effect will be heavy and stiff. Beethoven has given metronome marks throughout the symphony, and they have been much studied; with the general effect of confirming Beethoven's own recorded dissatisfaction with efforts so to fix the tempi. They do serve, however, to prove what tempo corresponds to what other tempo; and in general they prove *relative* tempi. Unfortunately, through the aid perhaps of a misprint, the trio, now that the notation is changed, still has a metronome mark indicating that its bars correspond to the bars of the scherzo; with the result that for the best part of a century violent efforts were made to take it twice as fast as it has any business to go. There is no possible doubt of Beethoven's real intentions; and the best tradition has no more been misled by the metronome mark than scholars would be misled by the reading *mumpsimus* instead of *sumpsimus*.[1]

The trio thus violently brought into being out of the stretto of the scherzo, proceeds with heavenly happiness on the following combination of themes.

Ex. 18.

The upper melody is as old as the art of music. Beethoven had already written something very like the whole combination, bass and all, long ago in the trio of the scherzo of his Second Symphony. Moreover, in some of the earlier sketches for the Ninth Symphony he reverts very nearly to the exact terms of this passage in the Second Symphony. The difference between the mature final idea and

---

[1] After this analysis was in the press, Sir Charles Stanford wrote to *The Times* (March 4th, 1922) conclusively proving, by a photograph of the page in question in the original edition, that the original metronome mark was for a minim and not a semibreve.

these earlier versions is that the final conception makes a point of its simplicity. The idea in the Second Symphony is childlike only in so far as it is without affectation and without introspection. A child-prodigy like Mozart or Mendelssohn might have invented it quite spontaneously as regards infant mental activity, but without any more understanding than is employed in the child's special faculty of mimicry. In the Ninth Symphony the meaning is very different: this naïve self-repetition with delicate differences (see the notes marked *) that carry more weight than they seem aware of; this swarm of fresh themes all ending in full closes; this piling up of the primitive little theme into a climax of mere tonic-and-dominant and merely square rhythms, but of grandiose proportions: all this is true of the child as seen by the poet who recognizes that the outward semblance belies the soul's immensity.

If Beethoven had read Wordsworth he would never have forgiven him for speaking of 'fading into the light of common day'. Nowhere is Beethoven's power more characteristically shown than when his ordinary daylight bursts in upon the trailing clouds of glory; as the mere formal da capo of the scherzo bursts in when the climax of the trio dies romantically away.

If this scherzo had been on a less gigantic scale, Beethoven would unquestionably have done as he did with his earlier great scherzos, and caused the alternating cycle of scherzo and trio to go at least twice round; that is to say, the scherzo would again lead to the trio, the trio would again be given in full, the scherzo would come round yet again and show every sign of again drifting into the trio, whereupon some drastic stroke would cut the process short. This double recurrence is possible only where the main body of the scherzo is worked out on a scale not greatly transcending what we may call the melodic forms, at least in its first strain. We have seen that the present scherzo, quite apart from the trio, is a fully differentiated and developed sonata movement; and the miracle therein is that it has never lost the whirling uniform dance-movement character essential to the classical scherzo. Amid all the variety of Beethoven's works you will always thus find each individual movement true to type. The minuet had already come to be regarded by Haydn and many of his contemporary critics as too slight an art-form longer to retain its place in the growing scheme of classical symphonies. Haydn's own minuets tend more and more to foreshadow the Beethoven scherzo, while Mozart's minuets never show what we may call the scherzo temperament; yet Mozart's are sometimes capable in their own calm way of being quite as big as the other movements of the work to which they belong. The most significant thing about the Beethoven scherzo is that it becomes worthy of its position in Beethoven's most gigantic works, not by abandoning the dance character, but by emphasizing it. There are people who apply to music certain eighteenth-century methods of criticising poetry; methods which simply measure the amount of information that would be conveyed if the art in question were reduced to prose. To such critics the double repetitions of Beethoven's scherzos are an idiotic mystery. Why should Beethoven say the same thing three times over in the same words? Why should dancers dance three times round the same ball-room? That depends upon the size of the ball-room, not upon the interest of its decorations. The size of the scherzo of the Ninth Symphony makes double repetitions out of the question; but an adequate expression of the characteristic perpetual circle is attained when for the second time the scherzo leads into the trio, and the first phrase (Ex. 18) starts on its course surrounded in a blaze from the whole orchestra, breaks off abruptly, and is closured by the two bars which have just led to it for the second time.

ADAGIO

In the slow movement Beethoven explores melody to its inmost depths. All musical form is melody 'writ large'; but there are forms in which the composition is felt not primarily as a single whole but as a series or colony of identical melodic schemes. The obvious case of this is the form of a theme with variations. The external form of the whole set of variations can tell us little about the composition except the number of variations, and the points, if any, at which they cease to confine themselves within the bounds of the theme. We are forced from the outset to attend to the emotional and other contrasts produced by their grouping; so that the analysis of a set of variations becomes instantly and automatically an analysis of style. The primitive simplicity of the external quasi-collective organism leaves us with nothing else to understand except the structure of the theme. Now when a great set of variations exists as a composition by itself, there is full scope for the variations to explore many aspects of the theme beyond the melody. Some of the greatest works in variation form have been based on themes of which melody was by far the least significant aspect. In these cases, at least the phrase rhythm of the theme will be found to be specially distinctive, so that its identity may be recognized in a totally different melody with totally different harmonies and totally different metric rhythm. In fact, this condition of things, which Sir Hubert Parry called rhythmic variation, is the highest type of independent variation form. If the phrase rhythm is not strong enough to support entirely new harmonies and melodies, then the harmonic scheme must be strong enough to support new melodies: the phrase rhythm, strong or weak, is prior to everything else, and cannot be altered without dissolving the sense of variation form. (Most modern sets of variations do thus dissolve the classical conception of the form, and compensate for the loss by retaining the melody far more constantly than Beethoven and Brahms think worth while.)

Now all this may seem a digression, inasmuch as the variations in the Ninth Symphony, both in the slow movement and the choral finale, are purely melodic. But it is worth while drawing attention to the fundamental importance of phrase rhythm in all classical variations; because until this is grasped the vaguest ideas are apt to prevail as to the value of purely melodic variations; and cases have been known where composers have introduced most interesting variations into works in sonata form, and wondered why procedures perfectly justifiable in an independent variation work somehow did not prove satisfactory in the sonata environment. We must not lose grasp of the principle that all sonata form works through external melody. It follows from this that variations must stick to the melody of their theme if they are to form part of a sonata scheme. It is also certain that a variation which is faithful to the melody is also faithful to the phrase rhythm. It is not good criticism to dismiss with contempt a merely ornamental variation as a poor thing; it is a simple thing, but it is also safe. If it is stupid, that is because the composer has a bad style. In the hands of the great composers the ornamental variation reaches the sublime just because of its utter simplicity and dependence upon the melody of the theme. In other words, the theme is pre-eminently sublime, and the variations are its glory. Some of the critics who have sneered at melodic variations should be more careful to make sure that they can recognize them.[1] I have seen more than one of the strictest of Beethoven's late slow movements in variation form described as 'a group of detached episodes with no discoverable connexion' by writers who are very full of 'the progress that has been made in the variation form since Beethoven's time'. And this is not a matter of speculative opinion; speaking generally I may say that no statement is made in any analysis of mine which the reader cannot verify for himself by following it in the score.

The slow movement of the Ninth Symphony is a set of variations on two alternating themes; at least, we could say so, if the second theme had more than one variation. On strict formal principles it does not matter whether the theme is actually varied at all so long as it is repeated: for instance, most of the slow movement of Beet-

---

[1] I have often been told that all good musicians deplore the disgraceful poverty of the first vocal variations in the choral finale. This does not represent a very advanced professional point of view. Good musicians do not estimate variations only as models for a student's exercises.

hoven's Seventh Symphony is aesthetically a set of variations, though the very essence of its variations is the cumulative effect of their repeating the same combination of melodies with no change except growing fullness of orchestration. In the Ninth Symphony Beethoven carries to its highest development a scheme for which he has given us only one exact counterpart, the Lydian Hymn of Thanks in the A minor Quartet; though he had written two earlier variation movements depending upon a pair of alternating themes, the slow movement of the Fifth Symphony, and the first allegretto which does duty for slow movement of the great E flat Trio, op. 70, no. 2. For all purposes except that of the antiquarian, it was Haydn who invented the idea of making variations on two alternating themes. Whichever theme was in the major, the other is in the minor; both themes are complete binary melodies with repeats, and the first impression on the listener is that the second theme is a contrasting episode like the trio of a minuet. Then the first theme returns, perhaps unvaried in its first strain, which however is repeated with ornamental variation, the rest of the theme continuing in the varied state. Then, just as Beethoven's most characteristic scherzos go twice through their cycle of repeating their trio, Haydn goes on to a variation of his second theme, and his scheme often goes far enough to include a third variation of the second theme, before the fourth variation of the first expands into a coda. Beethoven in his great E flat Trio adopts Haydn's form exactly, with the mock-tragic difference that, his first theme being in the major, he makes his coda end in pathetic childish wrath with a development of the minor theme. In the Fifth Symphony the two themes grow one out of the other in a more subtle way than Haydn's; and the second theme, though starting in the tonic, makes its point in the famous triumphant outburst in a bright foreign key. This is the only recorded sign of preparation for the bold and subtle art-form invented by Beethoven in his slow movements of the Ninth Symphony and the A minor Quartet. In these cases the two alternating themes are in brilliantly contrasted keys and tempi. In the Ninth Symphony the formal effect is enriched by the fact that the second theme is, on its second reappearance, in another contrasted key, so to speak twin, but not identical twin, with its first key. The scheme is as follows:

(1) First theme B flat major, 4/4.
(2) Second theme (*andante moderato*) D major, 3/4.
(3) Variation of first theme in tonic.
(4) Second theme in G major almost unvaried except for new scoring. As B major led back to B flat, so G major leads back to E flat as if to resume the first theme therein. This involves

(5) a modulating episode which will be described in due course
The episode leads suddenly back to the tonic where

(6) a complete second variation is given. At the point where
the second theme should appear, the change of harmony
which led back to it is replaced by a modulation to the
sub-dominant, such as is typical of the last phase of a
design that is to end quietly.

(7) The rest of the movement is coda, and the strong backbone
of the most complicated parts of this coda consists of
repetitions of melodic figures of the first theme, as will be
shown in our musical illustrations.

Now let us look at the themes. I need not quote the two bars of
introduction, famous as they are for their profound pathos. I write
the melody on one stave, numbering its phrases; and on the upper
stave I write the echoes of each phrase given out by the wood-wind

Ex. 19.

It will be seen that at first these echoes punctuate a melody that without them would be in symmetrical square phrases; but at last the wind instruments tend to develop something independently complete out of them, and end by taking over the climax of the main melody itself. They hesitate however at its close, and, while so hesitating, faint in the bright light of a change to a remote key.[1] The second theme is a single strain swinging along with glorious tenderness and warmth in its new key and rhythm.

Ex. 20.

The small notes in the musical illustration indicate the fragmentary counterpoint which enhances the effect of its immediate repetition. Its last bar is echoed with a change of harmony which plunges us back into the rich shadows of the main theme. Nowhere is the art of florid ornament more consummate than in the first violin part of the two complete variations in this slow movement. I say the first violin part, because the point of these variations is that, while the melody is given in Beethoven's finest florid ornament, the echoes of the wood-wind remain unvaried. If we had been given the theme, echoes and all, as the subject for a work in variation form, we might have felt at a loss to see what sort of variation could be made of it. To preserve the echoes as an unvaried background is a stroke of genius self-evident only because Beethoven has accomplished it. (He could not have accomplished it at once; for the first sketches of the theme show that at one time he seriously thought of making the wind instruments repeat regular whole sections instead of fragmentary echoes.) Now when the wood-wind take over the climax of the theme they still keep their part unvaried; and the

[1] I was not prepared, when I wrote this essay, to find that the slow movement of the Ninth Symphony was so out of fashion that an eminent critic could ask, apropos of this change, 'Where is the skill in abandoning your idea as soon as you have stated it?' To which the only fit answer is to ask, 'Where is the sense in supposing that the "idea" has been completely expressed before the first change of key or time that catches the eye by its appearance on paper?' People whose attention is not roused by that first modulation must be tone-deaf: people who don't see the point of its leading to an analogous but different key next time can have no memory. People who have noted it clearly both times will be wondering what will happen when the music approaches it for the third time; and when they hear the grand burst into the subdominant, they will have heard the complete statement of Beethoven's 'idea'. If critics are then going to argue that an idea cannot thus be spread over ten minutes, they must abandon any claim to understand Wagner, who spreads them over four whole evenings.

great change of harmony leads without effort to G major instead of D major. The melody of the second theme is not varied, but the scoring is now bright instead of deep, and the counterpoint added by the first violins is lighter. At the end, the change of harmony leads to E flat, and the clarinets give out the first two bars of the main theme unvaried. This is taken up by a horn, the clarinets giving a syncopated counterpoint. The slow figure of the theme descends into the depths and the key shifts to C flat major. The syncopated counterpoint is now given to the horn, the notes in this distant key being such as the player on the ordinary horn of Beethoven's time could produce only as closed notes by skilful use of his hand in the bell of the instrument. These notes are all very muffled and mysterious; they are not easy to produce in this way, and they therefore occurred so rarely in orchestral music that conductors used to need some experience and decision to protect themselves and Beethoven against the round assertion of the average player that the passage was impossible. It was, indeed, extremely difficult, but Berlioz (in the chapter which Strauss declares, in editing the *Grand Traité d'instrumentation*, to be of merely historic interest) quotes the very bar that culminates the difficulty, and demonstrates that it is skilfully written for the hand-horn. Now it has been discovered that Beethoven gave all these passages in this movement to the fourth horn, because he knew a fourth-horn player who possessed a pioneer two-valved specimen of the ventil-horn! The moral is not that we ought to play these passages with a boastful confidence to show that modern instruments make them child's-play, but that we ought to admire the sense of style and practical wisdom with which Beethoven uses the pioneer new instrument in the way best calculated to graft its resources on to the old stock.

The whole character of the passage is profoundly reflective, tender, and remote. Its dying fall seems about to be echoed; but instead of an echo the tone becomes rich and full, and the harmony brightens into a full daylight of the tonic. The second and last variation bursts in with the richest ornament achieved in music since Bach; and now we may appreciate fully the deep simplicity of Beethoven's most elaborate conceptions, inasmuch as throughout this variation the wood-wind have the theme without ornament except in so far as it is adapted to the prevailing triplet rhythm. The violins are silent while the wind instruments finish each phrase with its unadorned echo. In due course the point is reached where the wood-wind are dwelling upon the final cadence before breaking into one or other of the distant keys in which the second theme appeared. Instead of the exquisite soft foreign chord, there is now a sudden resolute modulation to the subdominant and an outburst

of solemn triumph in which the trumpets enter for the first time.
The drums also have their first forte; the drum-part being elsewhere throughout this movement remarkable for mysterious, soft
rhythmic figures. The solemn outburst of triumph yields to a
pleading development of the first two notes of the theme without
ornament.

Ex. 21.

Mark well its four distinct entries within two bars, and note that the
calm continuation in the tonic with what has the freshness of a new
melody is simply an ornamental version of figure (*a*). As it proceeds, listen to the bass and you will find that the whole first phrase
of the theme is moving upwards two bars at a time, each pair of
bars being repeated.

Ex. 22.

Again the solemn triumph bursts out on the subdominant. Now
see what becomes of the two bars of modulating sequence on
figure (*a*). The magnificent plunge into the sombre key of D flat,
with the four bars in which its consequences are worked out—these
are the magnified version of those last two bars of Ex. 21, twice as
slow and with richer harmonic detail.

Ex. 23.

They lead back to the new version of figure (*a*), which now continues happily, echoed bar by bar, with another new figure (note the dialogue between the drums and the basses).

Ex. 24.

Cantabile.

Drums.

Then the second phrase of the theme is taken up and treated in the same way; at first two bars at a time, then its last bar alone, until it expands into a final broad melodious climax. At last nothing is left but the solemn rhythmic figure of the drums and the basses, the dying sigh of the clarinets, and the throbbing of the strings, from which last arises one final majestic crescendo. And hereupon the movement, like most of Beethoven's late slow movements, closes with subtle allusions to figures of the principal melody, in such a way as to fill the last bar with articulate musical speech up to its last quarter.

FINALE

The great problem for Beethoven in the composition of the Ninth Symphony was obviously that of providing a motive for the appearance of the chorus. The general scheme of the whole symphony as a setting for Schiller's 'Ode to Joy' is simple and satisfactory enough. The first movement gives us the tragedy of life. The second movement gives us the reaction from tragedy to a humour that cannot be purely joyful, except in a childhood which is itself pathetic when contemplated from that distance of time at which alone it can be appreciated. The slow movement is beauty of an order too sublime for a world of action; it has no action, and its motion is that of the stars in their courses—concerning which, however, Beethoven has surprising things to tell us later on. But it is a fundamental principle in Beethoven's art that triumph is to be won in the light of common day. Only twice in all his works (Sonatas, opp. 109 and 111) has Beethoven allowed the conclusion of the whole matter to rest in a slow movement of this type—a paradise like that of Dante, in which the only action and the only movement are the ascent from Heaven to higher Heaven as measured by the enhanced glory in Beatrice's eyes.

Now we shall find that this account of the first three movements of the Ninth Symphony is Beethoven's own; and the Ninth Symphony is not the first work in which he had attempted something of the kind, a search for a theme on which the mind could rest as a final solution of typical human doubts and difficulties. The Fantasia, op. 77, adumbrates a search for happiness through a storm of conflicting emotions and humours: so bold is the sketch and so violent the contrasts during the conflict, that the work is hardly to be understood except in the light of the Ninth Symphony. Again in the Choral Fantasia a solo pianoforte executes a massive and cloudy introduction (which at the first performance Beethoven extemporized); the orchestra enters group by group, exchanging rhetorical questions with the pianoforte; and then the pianoforte settles down to a placid melody not unlike a childish foreshadowing of the great choral melody in the Ninth Symphony; a set of variations ensues which passes through various tempi and keys with developing episodes; until a dramatic crisis is reached, giving rise to further questions which are answered by the entry of voices, bringing the matter to a conclusion with a short ode in praise of music.

In the Ninth Symphony Beethoven's plan is to remind us of the first three movements just as they have been described above; and to reject them one by one as failing to attain the joy in which he believes. After all three have been rejected, a new theme is to appear, and that theme shall be hailed and sung as the Hymn of Joy. Beethoven's first idea was that a baritone should express all this process in words, from the outset, in an impassioned recitative. The orchestra was to start with a confused din expressing terror and violence; the singer was to rebuke it; whereupon the orchestra was to give out the opening of the first three movements, after each of which the singer was to point out why it was not to the purpose; until, on the appearance of the new theme, the singer was to accept it with triumph and set it to Schiller's Ode. Beethoven sketched all the recitatives with the necessary words, very sensibly making no effort to achieve a literary style in such a sketch, but writing the flattest prose to indicate what was going on. In any case it would have been a mistake to aim at poetic diction when *ex hypothesi* not only is the poem not yet begun, but the music of it has not been found. Plain prose is absolutely necessary to this scheme, if such a recitative is to be sung at all; that being so, Beethoven soon saw that he had better commit himself to the smallest amount of plain prose that could possibly suffice. Moreover, words without metre may be prose, but music without metre is recitative; and recitative, especially in a symphony, is by all historic association either the most lofty symbolism, or it is pretentious rubbish. Away, then, with these paragraphs of amateur prose attempting to describe emotions which only music can express. Let the basses of the orchestra seem on the point of articulate speech with their passionate recitative. Everything is there without words; nor could any words do justice to the pathos with which the recitative, after furiously rejecting the tragic solemnity of the first movement, seems to hope wistfully for something better, only to be stung into indignation by the playful theme of the scherzo. At the appearance of the slow movement the pathos touches perhaps the greatest height ever attained in recitative; fully as great as Bach and Handel achieved in accompanied recitative with voice and with Bible words. A few wind instruments give a halo of mysteriously luminous harmony above the basses so long as these remain softened. Then for a moment the passion breaks out again in despair; and now comes the new theme.

Ex. 25.

At once the situation is changed; the recitative of the orchestral basses greets the new theme with exultation. The wind-band closes the recitative with the old conventional final chords, and instantly the basses take up the theme and give it out in full. (It is customary to make an impressive pause before this definite entry of the theme; but Beethoven's notation of the final chords of the recitative is against this reading. There is no meaning in his putting the last chord at the end of a triple-time bar, unless it is to have the special rhythmic effect of leading straight into the next bar. It may be argued that this effect is not convincing; but whether it convinces us or not, it is thoroughly characteristic of Beethoven's later style and, like all such features, is the only possible alternative to an effect which, if convincing, is also the kind of commonplace Beethoven studiously avoids.)

Here now is the great theme which is to carry the stanzas Beethoven has collected from Schiller's 'Ode to Joy'. The melody is in two parts, of which the second is always repeated.

Ex. 26.

When the basses have given out the whole melody unharmonized, with its repeat, the violas in unison with the violoncellos go through it again in a higher octave also with the repeat. The double-basses have a melodious counterpoint, forming with the melody a very interesting two-part harmonic framework, to which the first bassoon adds an inner part melting occasionally into unison with the melody in a very subtle way.[1] The first violins enter in the soprano octave, and the theme is now in transparent widespread four-part harmony, to which the interior bassoon adds a more symphonic colour by doubling the melody at every odd pair of bars (see bars 3–4, 7–8, &c.). With the repeat there is now a crescendo: then the theme bursts out in the full wind-band, the trumpets blazing at high pitch with the melody, which is so simple that they can play every note of it in spite of the imperfect scale the trumpet had in Beethoven's time. (And yet such is Beethoven's delicate feeling that in one place in the eleventh bar he avoids a note which the trumpet has already played, because at this moment it is so harmonized as to suggest something beyond the natural character of the instrument.)

After the repeat the last four notes (*a*) of the theme are taken up and turned into a neat codetta, which henceforth becomes an integral part of the theme as treated in future variations.

Ex. 27.

I give it here as it occurs in the choral statements.

This codetta is developed in energetic sequences, rising to a climax in which fine detail is crowded together in short phrases such as we find in the most elaborate paragraphs in the first movement or in Beethoven's latest sonatas and quartets. A quite new phrase with a ritardando now appears, sounding a reflective note

---

[1] The second bassoon should play with the double-basses.

After this analysis was printed Sir Charles Stanford wrote to me, 'There is no question that the 2nd bassoon is *col Basso* in the Finale of the Ninth Symphony. It is in the autograph; it is written in *by himself* in the copy made for the King of Prussia in Berlin (I've seen it); and in the copy he sent to the Philharmonic of London (ditto) he always writes it thus / / / (I think) for about 30 bars'.

The autograph, now published in facsimile, is perfectly clear. How, then, did Beethoven's intentions come to be so contradicted in the first edition? It happened thus. In the fair copy revised by Beethoven and sent to the publishers, the contra-fagotto had no separate stave, but was indicated as playing *col. fag. 2do*. Beethoven suddenly saw a disastrous possibility at this point, and, forgetting about the second bassoon, scrawled 'contra-fagotto tacet', adding rests to make sure.

which becomes mysterious in a change to an extremely remote key (*poco adagio*).

Ex. 28.

This is brushed cheerfully aside; but the doubt which it suggested receives tragic justification in the renewal of the panic of the introduction, which bursts out with greater violence than ever.

And now comes the revelation. The human voice is heard, summing up the beginning and the end of those instrumental recitatives. Beethoven's one piece of verbal prose is, after all, as fine as any master of style could make it. The situation demands a careful abstention from any diction that encroaches on poetry. Critics may cavil at the word *angenehm*, which the dictionary tells us means 'agreeable' or 'pleasant': but a German ear would be accustomed to it as a Biblical word without losing its familiar prosaic sense. Beethoven says 'Oh, friends, not these sounds; but let us attune our voices more acceptably and more joyfully'.[1]

The wood-wind give their first foreshadowing of the theme, the singer cries 'Freude' and is answered by the chorus basses; and then the singer gives out the great theme as a setting of the first stanza of Schiller's Ode. The repeat of the second half is given by the chorus in octaves without the sopranos, and then the orchestra concludes with the codetta.

> Praise to Joy, the god-descended[2]
> Daughter of Elysium,
> Ray of mirth and rapture blended,
> Goddess, to thy shrine we come.
> By thy magic is united
> What stern Custom parted wide:
> All mankind are brothers plighted
> Where thy gentle wings abide.

The next stanza is given by the vocal quartet, and the second part of it repeated by the full chorus in four-part harmony, the orchestra again concluding with the codetta.

> Ye to whom the boon is measured,
> Friend to be to faithful friend,
> Who a wife has won and treasured,
> To our strain your voices lend.

[1] Bülow wickedly used the phrase by way of prelude on the pianoforte when he had to play immediately after a dismally bad singer.

[2] Lady Macfarren's translation is reprinted here in revised version by permission of Novello & Co.

Yea, if any hold in keeping
Only one heart all his own,
Let him join us, or else weeping,
Steal from out our midst, unknown.

The third stanza is given in an ornamental variation by the quartet
(probably the most difficult passage ever written for voices).

Draughts of joy, from cup o'erflowing
Bounteous Nature freely gives,
Grace to just and unjust showing,
Blessing ev'rything that lives.
Wine she gave to us and kisses,
Loyal friend on life's steep road:
E'en the worm can feel life's blisses,
And the Seraph dwells with God.

Again the full chorus repeats the second part with the utmost
triumph, and this time the codetta is accompanied by massive
vocal harmonies dwelling upon the last line—'und der Cherub
steht vor Gott'. This is expanded with a modulation which
suddenly plunges to the dominant of a darker key, B flat.

The blaze of glory vanishes. The solemn silence is broken by
grotesque sounds in the depths of darkness. These sounds gather
into rhythm, and take shape as the melody transformed into a
military march, mysteriously distant, and filling a vast harmonic
interval between deep bass and its shrill treble. Ruskin has finely
described the Grotesque Ideal as a veil covering the terror of
things too sublime for human understanding; and that is unquestionably one of Beethoven's reasons for this treatment of the
stanza in which the poet exhorts mankind to run their course as
joyfully as the stars in the heavens.

But there was another motive which impelled Beethoven towards
the Grotesque Ideal here. He had dismissed all illusions about
Napoleon as soon as Napoleon made himself Emperor, but he had
not dismissed the poet's ideals of war and victory. No artist,
certainly no musician, has more forcibly sounded the true note of
military music than Beethoven. He did not often write or wish to
write a military march, but whenever he did, he struck with un-
erring accuracy the formidable note which should underlie the
strains which are to inspire those who march to them. Nowhere
has the terror of war been so simply and so adequately presented
as in the *Dona nobis pacem* of the Mass in D. Beethoven indulges
in no silly realism (we may ignore his pot-boiler, the Battle Symphony): he tells us no details about war; but he unfailingly gives
the note of terror wherever war is symbolized. In this light we
must read the military character of his setting of Schiller's stanza

about the stars in their courses. Thomas Hardy has said of the facts of astronomy that when we come to such dimensions the sublime ceases and ghastliness begins. Beethoven is not afraid of the depths of the starry spaces—not more afraid than he was of Napoleon's armies; and so it is his military note that he sounds when Schiller compares heroes with the stars in their courses.

> Glad as suns His will sent flying
> Through the vast abyss of space,
> Brothers, run your joyous race,
> Hero-like to conquest flying.

A solo tenor declaims the stanza triumphantly, but in broken phrases which seem to stagger dizzily across the rhythms of the variation. A male-voice chorus joins in on the repetition of the second part, which is concluded with the codetta. Then the orchestra breaks into a double fugue, of which the first subject is derived from the original melody, and the second subject from its transformation into march rhythm.

Ex. 29. (2) (1)

This double fugue is worked out with great energy, passing through various keys, and aiming at the dominant of B, on which there is a mighty unison climax. As this dies away, three notes of the main melody appear softly in B major, then again in B minor. The bass drops from B to A in an impressive way which we shall recognize again later—

Ex. 30. 3 bars. 3 bars.

and then the full chorus bursts out with the first stanza of the poem set to the unvaried original theme, while the whole string band accompanies with a running bass in the triplet rhythm. After the repeat the orchestra begins the codetta but breaks off abruptly at its second bar. A mighty new theme appears, sung by the tenors

and basses and supported by the bass trombone, the first entry of
the trombone since the scherzo. This is the song of the universal
brotherhood of man, well-placed in harmonious reaction from that
military note associated with the stars in their courses.

The sopranos take up the new theme; and then the basses answer
with another and yet more solemn note, 'Brothers above the starry
vault there surely dwells a loving Father'. This, again, is repeated
in full harmony by all the voices. To strike these solemn notes is
only too easy for a small artist; but great artists, when they strike
them, do as Beethoven does; they show by instinct, not by antiquarian knowledge, that these are the oldest harmonies in the
world. Beethoven had opportunities for understanding the church
modes as used by Palestrina; he was not as completely cut off from
them by temperament and training as was, for instance, Mendelssohn. On the other hand, he had nothing like the scholarship in
such matters shown in modern times by Sir Charles Stanford and
Mr. Gustav Holst. Yet here, as in the 'Incarnatus' of the Mass
in D and in the Lydian slow movement of the A minor Quartet,
he shows exactly the Palestrina instinct for the expression of awe,
mystery, and infinity, in terms of pure concord and subtle inter-
mixture of key.

And now comes the stupendous claim that Joy is meant to raise
us from our prostrate awe to the starry heights where the Godhead
dwells. I give a literal translation, as here the printed English
versions fail:[1]

> Ye millions, why fall prostrate?
> Dost thou, oh World, feel the presence of the Creator?
> Seek Him beyond the starry vault!
> Above the stars He surely dwells.

This is the central thought of the Ninth Symphony, and it also
underlies Beethoven's whole treatment of the liturgical text of his
Mass in D, where we have, throughout the Gloria, the Credo, and

---

[1] Lady Macfarren's translation, though skilfully designed for singing,
here reverses Schiller's and Beethoven's conception, the point of which
is *not* to fall prostrate, but to rise from prostration and look upwards to
the Father above the starry vault.

the Sanctus, three conceptions continually emphasized; first the divine glory; secondly, and always in immediate contrast, the awe-struck prostration of mankind; and thirdly the human divinity of Christ ('Qui propter nos homines'; 'et homo factus est').

As in the Mass in D so here in the Ninth Symphony, the thought of divine glory overawes at first, only to inspire action. The chorus breaks into a torrential double fugue on the two main themes, the invocation to Joy, and the appeal to the brotherhood of mankind.

Ex. 32.

This fugue (the standard example of Beethoven's extreme demands on the voices, justified in this instance by convincing effect) rises to its notorious climax in which the sopranos hold a high A for twelve bars. After this terrific outburst there is an abrupt plunge into the deepest prostration, from which again mankind raises itself in contemplation of the Father above the starry vault. And now, before the final climax, comes that full revelation of Beethoven's range which is seldom absent from his greatest works; the note which only the greatest poets can master, and which lesser artists avoid because it offends their pride. The main theme has been given several complete variations for the orchestra and for the voices; it has been developed in episodes and interludes; the second theme has been stated; and the two themes have been combined in a double fugue. Now comes the coda. And the note of the coda is the purest happiness of childhood; nothing like it had been sounded in music since Mozart's *Magic Flute*; and if we are shocked at the notion of comparing Beethoven's endless round-canon (Ex. 33) with the happiness of Papageno and Papagena, why, then the poet and the composer may twit us with our slavery to fashion which sternly separates what the magic of joy reunites! Beethoven regards this childlike note as the very consummation of joy in *Gloria Dei Patris*. There is only one way to understand an artist of Beethoven's range, and that is to assume that he means what he says and that he has ample experience of the best way to say it.

It is not necessary to assume that he is infallible; but it is quite idle to compare his range of style with something narrower, and to rule out as in bad taste whatever exceeds those limits. It is strange but true also of other artists besides Beethoven that the very points which give most offence to superior persons are just those in which the great artist most whole-heartedly echoes his predecessors. Not only does the round just quoted recall Papageno and Papagena, but when it suddenly drops into a slow tempo (*poco adagio*) as Papageno and Papagena did, it rises to one of Mozart's most characteristic forms of medial cadence.

Indeed we confidently expect the notes I have put in brackets; but here the round intervenes again, gathering itself up as before into the full chorus; and so leading again to the *poco adagio*. And then a miracle happens. The solo voices enter in a bright new key, B major, and turn the Mozartian medial cadence into a wonderful florid cadenza that expands grandly and ends on the heights in this distant region. It is the same region to which, after the military variation of the stars in their courses, the energetic instrumental fugue led; and now the same thing happens that happened then (Ex. 30), but in a much more subtle and simple form. The key of B major becomes minor, and while its upper notes are still being held, the bass drops down to A. It is as if the four solo voices had ascended into the heavens, and had then expressed by their change of harmony the link between heaven and earth. The orchestra at first hesitating but with growing confidence, repeats the message (that is to say, this mysterious step in the bass)—

and in a moment the whole mass of singers and voices is ablaze with the wildest outburst of joy. In all this final fury, with the big drum, cymbals, and triangle marking time with frenzied persistence, Beethoven maintains his Greek simplicity and subtlety of proportion. It is only in externals that the music seems to break all bounds; the substance and form are as exactly measured as the most statuesque coda of any string quartet, and most of all in that supreme stroke of genius, the sudden drop into a slow triple time (*maestoso*) with a lyric turn of melody, on the words 'Daughter of Elysium'.

In this solemn tempo the chorus finishes, and then the orchestra rushes headlong to the end. Even here there is no waste of energy, no chaos nor anything perfunctory. The very last bars are a final uprush of melody which happens to be quite new and might easily have been an important theme.

OVERTURES TO 'LEONORA', NOS. 2 AND 3

THE OPERATIC PRELUDE AND THE PERFECT TONE-POEM

It is a commonplace of criticism to say that the opera *Fidelio* proves Beethoven's ignorance of the theatre; and throughout the second half of the nineteenth century there was overwhelming temptation to those musicians who admitted no dramatic music except Wagner's, to explain away the embarrassing fact that *Fidelio* invariably makes a deep impression in spite of the many obscurities of its libretto and the difficulties of the music. An adequate account of *Fidelio* (or as it was first called, *Leonora*), and its place in Beethoven's art was not to be expected so long as the musical world was divided between Wagnerian martyrs and persons with a conscientious objection to all forms of opera. As for myself, I have been diagnosed as a case of paralysis of mind by an eminent critic who happened to see some notes of mine indicating that *Fidelio* is after all quite a good opera. It certainly is a horribly embarrassing phenomenon for exclusive Wagnerians, and it is an even worse stumbling-block to those abstract-minded musicians who object to all recognition of the rhetorical force of purely instrumental music.

Some writers have even gone so far as to deny that Beethoven's style is dramatic at all; maintaining this position by pointing out that if certain passages in *Fidelio* are dramatic, they are not more dramatic than similar passages in the pianoforte sonatas, string quartets, and symphonies. Such writers are to this extent in sympathy with Beethoven, that they are making the very mistakes that Beethoven made in his first version of his opera. But unfortunately they make them on the assumption that dramatic expression in instrumental music is more reserved and less intense than that of music for the stage. Now we shall never understand the aesthetics of opera (nor even of instrumental music) until we realize that dramatic expression on the stage is merely more immediately effective, and that it is in the interests of intensity and concentration that 'absolute music' demands conditions untrammelled by the stage. If we once fix our attention upon the right illustrations, this ceases even to appear paradoxical. Few things in opera are more effective, for instance, than the short passage at the beginning of *Don Giovanni* where the Commendatore is

killed. Is the passage too highly pitched in rhetoric for a symphony? Would it, if introduced into a symphony of Mozart or
Beethoven, throw the rest of the work into the shade or seem
exaggerated in tone? On the contrary, the passage is precisely
the sort of thing Mozart wrote in his symphonies at the age
of twelve, where it sounds as dry and without atmosphere as the
corresponding thing in slabs of scene-painting would look if
transported from the stage to the walls of an academy exhibition.
The real objection to theatrical art when it is removed from the
theatre is always that it is sketchy and bald. The tremolos that
have such a fine gruesome effect in the incantation scene in *Der
Freischütz* sound ridiculous when Weber introduces them into a
piece of chamber music. When Beethoven attacked, somewhat
late in life for a first opera, the problems presented to him by
Fidelio, he encountered a most unlucky combination of circumstances and influences, which his own dramatic instincts served only
to aggravate. He was too much in revolt against the eighteenth
century to appreciate a comedy of manners. This unfortunately
meant that the one supreme master of opera from whom he could
have learned exactly what he needed was the one whose libretti
most scandalized him. If only Mozart had lived to come, as Beethoven did, under the influence of Cherubini, and to take up the
romantic style which was arising in French opera, then Beethoven
might have profited by Mozart's experience.

As it was, the only master from whom Beethoven could learn to
set the kind of drama that appealed to him, was Cherubini. With all
his mastery and nobility of style, Cherubini lacked precisely that
quality of dramatic movement which Mozart had both by instinct
and experience, and which Beethoven had already acquired in instrumental music to an extent altogether transcending the possibilities of theatrical music. The strange and touching result was
that Beethoven impetuously threw himself at Cherubini's feet,
explicitly and personally acknowledging him as his master; a
compliment which poor Cherubini could return only by complaining that Beethoven's music made him sneeze. Cherubini's
masterpiece, *Les deux Journées*, or *The Water-Carrier*, was based
on a tale of a heroic woman, who in a series of thrilling adventures
rescues her husband from death as a political prisoner. The author
of the libretto had written at least two more libretti on much the
same theme. One of these, *Helène* (containing the idea of a
trumpet-signal behind the stage as *deus ex machina*), was composed by Méhul; while *Fidelio, ou L'amour conjugal*, was the
subject which attracted Beethoven. Here the heroism of the
woman and the tragic plight of the prisoner are on a far greater scale
than in the other two stories. There were two things, however,

which Beethoven did not know. One was that Mozart would never accept a libretto until the librettist had shown himself thoroughly reasonable in threshing out every problem of musical importance to the composer. The other was that the whole French school of opera, of which the Italian Cherubini was by far the greatest master, had long ago completely abandoned (if it had ever seriously tackled) the problem of reconciling musical and dramatic movement, so that all French libretti of that period were designed accordingly. Mozart seems constitutionally incapable of deficiencies in movement. Beethoven is no less incapable of leaving a problem of movement unsolved, though his first sketches may get into difficulties. When he came to compose *Fidelio*, he threw his whole energy into a story the climax of which was highly dramatic and impressive; but it took him nine years, from 1805 to 1814, to find out that the first part of the libretto was designed like a vaudeville, full of absurdities which Mozart would never have allowed to stand. When *Leonora* was first produced the critics complained that words and passages were repeated far too often. It is a touching proof of Beethoven's docility that he, with every natural disposition towards terse dramatic expression, should have been misled by taking Cherubini as his model in this obvious and avoidable defect. In the final version of *Fidelio*, as produced in 1814, Beethoven secured the services of a more experienced craftsman to revise the libretto; and the result was at last a fairly coherent and consistent work of art, though there are still some obscurities left in the first act, particularly in the complete lack of motive for the music to interrupt the dialogue where it does, or for the dialogue to interrupt the music.

But the most impressive result of Beethoven's nine years of meditation on the subject of this opera that had cost him so much thought, is the fact that the *Leonora* overtures, which had been inspired by the heroic climax of the last act, proved to be too great for use in connexion with the opera at all.

Indeed, it is difficult to see how Beethoven ever brought himself down to the love affairs of the jailer's daughter as an opening to his first act, after such a tremendous prelude as the *Leonora* overture was, even in its first version. The first version is of course that known as *No. 2*. *Leonora No. 1* is the latest of the three overtures of that name, and is on entirely different material. Being the smallest, it is by far the most suitable for connexion with any but the final version of *Fidelio*, for which Beethoven in 1814 composed the one entirely suitable prelude. The overture to *Fidelio* in E major, dramatic, brilliant, terse, and with an indication of some formidable force in the background, is in just the right tone to indicate that there is something serious behind the pretty comedy of Jaquino and Marzellina on which the curtain rises. In fact, by 1814 Beethoven had learnt the musical values of the stage. In 1805 he had his instincts, which were undoubtedly theatrical as well as dramatic; but not even the endless vexations of the production of his opera could enlighten him as to their true cause, and in 1806 very little of the extensive revision which he gave to the work was better than mutilation and makeshift. Not until the libretto was severely taken in hand by an expert in 1814 was it possible for Beethoven to get to the root of the matter, where the composition was remediable at all. In the meantime the one thing that really profited by the revision of 1806 was the overture; but it profited in a fatal way, which raised it to one of the greatest instrumental compositions in existence, and at the same time ensured that it should absolutely kill the first act. This is how Weingartner comes to find that *Leonora No. 2* is an eminently successful dramatic introduction, while *Leonora No. 3* is a great concert-piece. It is not because *No. 3* is less dramatic than *No. 2*. The trouble with *Leonora No. 3* is that, like all great instrumental music from Haydn onwards, it is about ten times as dramatic as anything that could possibly be put on the stage. Here again we must discriminate.

Sir George Grove got into extraordinary difficulties in connecting *Leonora No. 3* with the subject of *Fidelio* at all, probably for no other reason than that he was so deeply impressed by it as a piece of instrumental music. Unfortunately he tried to give his reasons, and gave some of the worst the mind of man could devise. He argued that the subject of the rescue of a prisoner from a petty country jail was too small for so wonderful a composition, and that the least one could think of was the sufferings of a beleaguered city. Grove must have understood music and life better than to believe in this argument himself. If there is one thing certain about art and life, it is that the heroic acts or sufferings of the individual are as big as the mind can hold, and that the horrors and heroisms of a besieged city are not emotionally cumulative. Beethoven found the heroic devotion of Leonora, the faithful wife, a more inspiring subject than any romantic story of young love, or any general catastrophe of war. He knew as much as most civilians about war, and if in those Napoleonic times a subject had been brought to his attention which (like the siege of Weibertreu)[1] implied the heroic devotion of a thousand faithful wives, he would still have seen that the sublimest artistic treatment of that subject would consist in taking a single case.

---

[1] Weibertreu is the town where the conqueror allowed the women to go free with such property as they could carry on their backs. So they carried their husbands. Classical poetry prefers the single parallel case of Aeneas and Anchises.

Let us now compare the two great *Leonora* overtures on this basis, that both are inspired by a theme which Beethoven rightly considered sublime, and that they are not related as a sketch and a finished product, but that the earlier is definitely a theatrical prelude, while the later is, though Beethoven did not at first realize the fact, an ideal piece of instrumental music. Otherwise we shall get into a hopeless tangle if we regard the alterations in *Leonora No. 3* as of the nature of criticisms of *No. 2*.

Introduction. The first alteration is in the first bars, which in the earlier version begin with what Grove, in his Irish vein, called a 'false start'.

That is to say, the figure (*a*) is given separately in *No. 2* before being embodied in the long descending scale. But the listener who has never heard any of the *Leonora* overtures before, must be gifted with a spirit of prophecy if he takes that very emphatic opening of *No. 2* for a 'false start'. When Beethoven wrote *No. 2* he must have meant (*a*) as a definite figure and the long scale as a development of it. And when we inquire into the meaning of this figure (*a*) we find that it foreshadows Florestan's aria, which, after a mysterious modulation to the distant key of B minor, enters in A flat, the key in which it is to appear in the opera when Florestan sings memories of his wife and his 'fight for truth' that brought him to die in chains and darkness.

As the quotation shows, the two overtures differ in the details of this melody; and they also differ from not less than three other different versions which Beethoven made for Florestan's aria.

The omission of the first three notes of *Leonora No. 2* of course obliterates the reference to figure (*a*), and is highly significant as showing how little Beethoven relies on thematic connexions as a means of construction.

The continuation of Florestan's theme is a wonderful series of remote modulations on figure (*a*). The first six bars are in *No. 3* compressed from the vast but regular eight bars of the earlier version. The next five bars, where (*a*) appears in the bassoons and basses, with light triplets in dialogue between violins and flute, are compressed from ten bars of a much more elaborate and exciting passage in *No. 2*, leading in both cases to a tremendous crash of the full orchestra on the chord of A flat, while the violins rush up and down in gigantic scales. In the earlier version this crash is repeated (with a change of harmony) after a bar's silence, and in this slow time such a silence is surprisingly long. Beethoven then follows the second crash by fortissimo short chords, each at a bar's distance. But in *Leonora No. 3* he does not wish his introduction to be so gigantic or even so impressive. He approves of his earlier material, but prefers to state it in a less startling way. It is enough for him that the new version should cover the same ground as the old in key and phrase, without indulging in effects that leave no room for growth to unexpected climaxes later on. So he has only one great crash in A flat, and fills up the gaps between the short fortissimo chords by quavers on the woodwind.

Then follows a passage on the dominant of C as a preparation for the allegro. In *No. 3* it is five bars long, and is founded on a phrase (*b*) that forms the staple of the earlier part of the development in the allegro. The corresponding passage in *Leonora No. 2* was fourteen bars long, and, though closely resembling this in character and outline, was not sufficiently definite to be made the subject of allusions later on. Lastly, Beethoven alters into something much more normal the amazingly impressive notes which in *No. 2* led to the allegro with dark mysterious colouring:

Altogether his revision of his introduction is not pleasing to that habit of mind which studies works of art from one fine point to the next, and neglects to consider them as wholes.

Allegro. The opening of the allegro, up to the end of the second subject, is substantially the same in both versions, except that Beethoven skips four bars wherever he can. In the *crescendo* that continues the theme, Beethoven leaves out four bars at the beginning, in order to put in a fortissimo delay of four bars just where we expect the climax. Then, as the full orchestra takes up the theme, Beethoven takes the opportunity of keeping up the fortissimo more continuously in *No. 3* than in *No. 2.* Example 4, which in *No. 2* interrupts the tutti by its appearance *piano* on the 'cellos, is in *No. 3* given by the full orchestra.

In the passage that follows in *No. 3* he allows *pianos* and *fortes*
to alternate rapidly, instead of the fortissimo of *No. 2*. And it is
important to note that he uses triplet tremolo quavers in the first
version throughout his tuttis, thereby showing that he was thinking
of a slower tempo than that which is obviously right in *Leonora
No. 3*. This difference of tempo is of the utmost importance in
performance; and throughout *Leonora No. 2* we need to remember
that Beethoven knew nothing about *No. 3* until he came to write it.

The passage leading to E major for the second subject is much
shortened, and much louder and less mysterious, in the later than
in the earlier version; and the second subject itself is re-scored
beyond recognition by the eye, though to the ear it is much the
same in both overtures. It begins with a transformation of
Florestan's aria, with wonderful remote modulations—

and though the scoring of *No. 3* is much easier and simpler than in
No. 2, the later version will be seen to divide the melody between
instruments on different planes. The sequences and subsidiary
themes that follow grow at once to a fortissimo in the earlier
version, but in *No. 3* they are given intensely, quietly, and
mysteriously, only at the last moment coming to a fortissimo as
they approach the great syncopated scale-theme, suggested, no
doubt, by (*a*).

The quotation shows how the wood instruments in *No. 3* are following the syncopated theme on the beat, a feature which is not found in *No. 2*. Moreover, *No. 3* disposes of the theme in eight formal bars, whereas *No. 2* continues discursively for seventeen. *No. 3* ends its exposition with a little cadence theme of two bars in which the horns are answered by the full orchestra, and this is followed by a descending sequence for the violins alone, which leads quietly without a break into the development, the change to the minor mode being one of the well-known romantic moments in *No. 3*. All this is very different from *No. 2*, which has substantially the same two-bar cadence theme in quite different scoring, but continues in a triumphant forte, ending in a sustained note followed by a remote modulation, that marks off the development from the exposition by a typical *coup de théâtre*.

At this point *Leonora No. 3* takes leave of *Leonora No. 2*, and has no more in common with it (except the idea of the trumpet-call behind the scene) till we come to the coda. We may still, however, find it profitable to contrast the two versions, as the differences are as unexpected as ever. The mind that lives indolently on fine passages and special effects will find even more to regret here than in the revision of the introduction. The development of *Leonora No. 2* begins, as we have said, by a *coup de théâtre* which plunges us into F major. From this point Florestan's aria is carried on in rising sequences alternating with plaintive dialogues on figure (*d*) until the key of D major is reached. Here the whole first theme, as at the opening of the allegro, bursts out in the violoncellos, leading to G major. (This use of the dominant in the course of the development has a very happy effect; how happy Beethoven himself did not realize until at quite a different point in *No. 3* he raised it to a sublime level.) At the present stage (in *No. 2*) the violoncello continues with Ex. 5, which is taken up by the wood-wind; and now follows a series of mysterious and remote modulations, mostly pianissimo, with an intensely characteristic episodic figure in the bass and wood-wind, and a sustained level of lofty inspiration that entitles it to a place among Beethoven's grandest conceptions.

Ex. 7.
(c)

In *Leonora No. 3* Beethoven, with a self-denial almost unparalleled

in art, writes as if all this had never existed. He founds all the
earlier part of the development on a very large and simple sequence
of great orchestral crashes of single chords sustained for four bars,
alternating with quiet plaintive eight-bar phrases, founded on
figure (*b*) of the introduction (see Ex. 3), combined with (*c*) of
the first subject. To this combination is added, as we proceed, a
development of figure (*d*) like that already mentioned in *No. 2*.

Ex. 8.

Five long steps of this process lead, with a short crescendo, to
a stormy tutti in which figure (*c*) of the main theme is imitated
between violins and basses in rising sequence. In twenty bars this
leads, with a rush of ascending scales, to a pause on B flat; and a
trumpet-call is heard behind the stage. In *Leonora No. 2* the storm
breaks out quite suddenly after a much longer and almost entirely
pianissimo development, and it is worked up for forty-four bars
before closing with the trumpet-call, which is more florid and in
the key of E flat; a not very remote key, and less startling than
B flat, which is of all possible keys the most opposed to C major.

We are now about to learn Beethoven's motives for his stern
rejection of all the finest features of *Leonora No. 2*. The young
author who was advised to strike out all his finest passages would
hardly have had that advice given him if they had been as fine
as those Beethoven rejected. Beethoven's motives are not those
that prompted that advice; he has struck out his finest passages
because he needs room to develop something finer. The fact is
that *Leonora No. 2* is too gigantic up to the present point to be
worked out within the reasonable limits of an orchestral piece in
classical style at all. After the trumpet-call Beethoven makes no
attempt to treat the rest of it on the same scale, but simply brings
in Florestan's aria in C major in its original form (*adagio*, 3/4), and,
without attempting any such thing as a recapitulation of the first
and second subjects of the allegro, goes straight on to a coda,
which we will compare in due course with its vastly larger version
in *Leonora No. 3*. Continuing now with *No. 3*, we have, in the
surprising key of B flat, the trumpet-call of the watchman on

the tower, warning the scoundrel Pizarro that the Minister has
arrived to investigate his unlawful detention of his own private
enemies in the state prison of which he is governor; and that
therefore it is too late for him to put Florestan and his heroic
wife out of the way. The flutes and clarinets sing the melody
which accompanies Florestan's and Leonora's breathless exclama-
tion: 'Ach! du bist gerettet! Grosser Gott!' (There is no trace of
this passage in *No. 2*, though the material for it was already present
in the opera.)

Ex. 9.

(I number the bars in fours, so as to indicate the rhythm. Some
analysts identify the first four notes with (*c*) of the main theme.
I cannot believe in distant thematic references that contradict the
rhythmic sense; and even when external evidence shows that they
have some foundation, the lesson of the first bars of the introduction is surely that these things are often of no importance in the
composer's own mind.)

The trumpet-call is given again (a little louder, according to the
direction in the opera); and the song of thanks re-enters in the
remote key of G flat, leading very slowly and quietly to G major.
We are now beginning to learn a lesson in proportion. Beethoven
has, by his compressions and alterations, gained a hundred bars,
or nearly a third of the bulk up to the trumpet-call. *Leonora No. 3*
reaches that point in 236 bars as against the 335 of *Leonora No. 2*.
He has thus left room to grow; and so he continues his development at leisure, with a sunshiny passage in which the flute and
bassoon give in G major the substance of the tutti that followed
the first subject, from which Ex. 5 was quoted. This is the
sublime and unexpected use of the dominant to which I referred
in connexion with the development of *Leonora No. 2*. Suddenly
all is still, except for the strings climbing upwards with figure
(*c*). Then there is a perfectly unadorned rising slow chromatic
scale in octaves, leading with immense deliberation to the above-
mentioned tutti (omitting Ex. 5), fortissimo in the tonic as
at first. This does duty for the recapitulation of the first subject,
and leads at once to the second, which is given in full, with no
alteration except the necessary transposition to the tonic. The
syncopated scale theme (Ex. 8) leads straight to the coda, which
begins with Florestan's aria once more, as in the second subject.

This corresponds roughly with the adagio that followed the trumpet-call in *Leonora No. 2*; but the gain in not changing the tempo is immense, and the passage is much expanded so as to keep us long in suspense.

Again we may note that the alteration obliterates the original connexion between the last notes of the Florestan figure and the sequence of scales with which the peroration begins. The idea in *No. 2* is to turn the last notes of the theme into a staccato scale passage, capable of making an effective short crescendo in the original allegro tempo, so as to lead quickly to a brilliant final presto. The idea in *No. 3* is that of a whirlwind of sound, presto from the beginning, twice as long as the earlier passage, and relying upon its intrinsically exciting quality of sound in a way which makes any question of its derivation merely pedantic. The logic of the excitement is rather to be sought in the enormous breadth of the coda to which it leads. In *No. 2* the first theme bursts out presto in a diminution. This is to say, that besides being presto, it is also rhythmically twice as fast, with quavers for crotchets. In *No. 3* there is no doubt that this would not do, though after the first two bars the framework is for some time the same in both overtures, the scoring being brighter and less bustling in detail in *No. 3*. Soon we come to the syncopated scale theme (Ex. 7). *No. 3* first gives it for eight bars pianissimo instead of being part of an unvaried fortissimo as in the early version. It gains still greater breadth in *No. 3* from the fact that it is now for the first time prolonged, whereas in *No. 2* it was already as long when it first occurred at the end of the second subject.

The tremendous passage that follows in *No. 3*, leading through
another and even more deliberate slow chromatic scale to a really
terrific climax on a chord of the *minor* ninth, is entirely new and
makes the rejected grandeurs of *No. 2* fade into insignificance.
This is the very point at which the coda of *No. 2* ceases to aim
higher than an interesting theatrical finish. *No. 3*, the grandest
overture ever written, then returns to the joyful reiteration of the
figure of its main theme, and ends in the utmost height of triumph.

OVERTURE, 'LEONORA', NO. I

Beethoven's opera was first produced under the title *Leonora* in
1805, with the overture now known as *Leonora No. 2*. In 1806 it
was produced again, with alterations that were little better than
mutilations, except in the case of the overture, which was expanded
into the tremendous symphonic poem known as *Leonora No. 3*.
In 1807 a project was mooted for producing the opera at Prague.
This came to nothing, but it was probably the cause of Beethoven
writing *Leonora No. 1*, which clearly shows that he had already
discovered that the former mighty works annihilated the first act
of the opera, which begins quietly with apparently trivial matters,
and only very gradually prepares for the tense and heroic drama
of the last act. Seven years later, when the opera was thoroughly
overhauled and largely rewritten as *Fidelio*, Beethoven abandoned
the *Leonora* themes altogether in the new overture, with which
he at last achieved the perfect introduction to his first act.

Leonora No. 1 thus represents an interesting middle stage in
Beethoven's treatment of the *Fidelio* problem. It also shows
amusing signs of the irritation which the whole business of the
opera had caused him in 1805 and 1806. When performers were
careless in any respect, Beethoven was apt to give them a severe
lesson by writing something calculated to betray their weaknesses.
The singer of the part of the villain Pizzaro was conceited, so
Beethoven asked him if he could sing the following passage at
sight—

Ex. :.

Bald krüm - met sich der Wurm,   bald krüm - met sich der Wurm!

Of course, it seemed perfectly easy; but when Pizzaro found that
he had to sing it against the following figure in the whole orchestra—

Ex. 2.

then the worm *did* begin to squirm!

The orchestration of *Leonora No. 1* is full of similar disciplinary measures, though none quite so atrocious. For the rest, it is an admirable opera-overture, with a broad and quiet introduction containing several distinct ideas: an energetic and terse allegro—

Ex. 3.

with a second group expressive of anxiety and suspense—

Ex. 4.

and with an extensive meditation on Florestan's aria in the dungeon, to replace the development of the overture and to foreshadow the central situation in the opera.

Ex. 5.

OVERTURE TO 'FIDELIO'

Of all the new parts of *Fidelio* none deserves greater reverence than its overture. The mere act of renouncing that mightiest of all overtures, *Leonora No. 3*, is enough to inspire awe. Beethoven was obviously right; *Leonora No. 3*, even in its earlier version (*Leonora No. 2*), referred entirely to the climax of the story in the last act, and was utterly destructive to the effect of the first act. The only chance for the first act of the opera lies in its conveying the impression of a harmless human love-tangle proceeding between certain good-natured young people connected with the jailer of a fortress governed by the villain. Grim forces are thus manifest in the surroundings, together with a growing sense of mystery about one of the persons in the love-tangle—Fidelio, the disguised wife of the unnamed prisoner, who is rescued by her heroism, when she has helped to dig his grave in the dungeon where he has lain in darkness for two years. A music that reveals Leonora's full

heroic stature (like the overture *Leonora No. 3*) simply annihilates
the first act. In the *Fidelio* overture Beethoven achieves what the
first act requires. A formidable power, neither good nor bad except
as it is directed, pervades the whole movement, and in the introduction alternates with a quiet pleading utterance—

Ex. 1.

which is soon lost in the darkness of Florestan's dungeon, until,
after the drums have entered with slow footsteps, it emerges and
leads into the active daylight of the allegro.

Ex. 2.

This is worked out in sonata form with a terseness and boldness
which is more akin to Beethoven's 'third period' than is commonly
realized. The 'second subject' is in the dominant, as usual, and
contains several short new themes, of which I quote the first—

Ex. 3.

in order that the listener may more readily note a remarkable
feature of form in this overture which occurs in the recapitulation.

The development is short and quiet, the drums bringing back
the main theme dramatically. In the recapitulation an unexpected
turn of harmony brings the 'second subject' (Ex. 3) into the dark
remote key of C major, in which the trumpets, hitherto confined to
repeating a single note on the only chords which admitted it, come
into their own and dominate mightily. Then at last, with a return
to the key of E, the trombones blaze out as the full orchestra breaks
into Ex. 1. The ensuing adagio passage is adorned with a graceful
new triplet figure, and soon bursts into a brilliant final presto.

Throughout the overture the scoring is of Beethoven's most subtle and, at the same time, powerful order; and in its form great issues, dramatic and musical, often hang upon a single bar.

OVERTURE TO 'CORIOLAN', OP. 62

It does not greatly matter that the *Coriolanus* for which this overture was written is not Shakespeare's, nor a translation or adaptation of Shakespeare's, but an independent German play, by Collin. That poet was a contemporary of Beethoven. His plays fill some dozen volumes and, if his *Coriolan* be a typical example, show him to be a master of smooth verse, determined to allow nothing to happen on the stage that can be described in narrative, and to let no consideration of action or movement prevent each character from uttering all the noblest sentiments that the occasion and person inspire. From Collin's play Beethoven derives the vacillating development and the abrupt final collapse of this overture. Collin's Coriolanus finds excuses for delaying the attack upon Rome until the moment at which he can effectively commit suicide. Both plot and denouement are eminently un-Shakespearian; but even Collin, as well as Beethoven, had read Shakespeare, who breaks through like Nature in Beethoven's music. Wagner then, in that analysis of this overture which is one of his finest and most attractive prose works, did well to ignore everything but Shakespeare and Beethoven. No doubt all unauthorized attempts to name descriptive details in 'programme music' will rouse the healthy opposition of those who want to give or withhold names themselves; yet if ever one piece of music could correspond to one dramatic scene, Wagner was right in describing Beethoven's overture as a musical counterpart to the turning-point in Shakespeare's *Coriolanus*, the scene in the Volscian camp before the gates of Rome (Act v, sc. iii). Here, after every political embassy has been dismissed with the annihilating contempt of the banished conqueror, whose figure, as Wagner says, is presented to us with the first notes of the music—

Ex. 1.

there come to him ambassadors against whom his pride struggle in vain.

Ex. 2.

Thence follow restless doubts and delays:

Ex. 3.

Wagner rises to heights of original poetic power in his profoundly true description of the vicissitudes of agonized pleading [Ex. 3], and the fierce pride that breaks the hero, body and soul, before it yields. Wagner's analysis cannot be shortened without injury; but the gist of it may here be indicated in Shakespeare's own words. In the concert-room Beethoven will say the rest, and readers and listeners may perhaps then do the better justice to Shakespeare when they read *Coriolanus*, or at least this scene of the fifth act, at home. Most of us will agree with Wagner, that music has comparatively little to do with politics, human as these may be in the hands of Shakespeare; and in any case it is a mistake to suppose that a single piece of music, especially so terse a movement as the *Coriolanus* overture, could represent the various aspects of a whole play. Even in Beethoven's own opera, *Fidelio*, he at first wrote an overture which referred exclusively to the stirring events of the last act; and when, in his final revision of the opera, he realized that the gigantic tone-poem we know as the overture *Leonora No. 3* totally eclipsed the quiet opening scenes, he based the present overture to *Fidelio* entirely upon the moods and suggestions of the first act.

Here, then, is the beginning of Shakespeare's analysis of Beethoven's *Coriolanus*—

ACT V, SC. iii.

COR.   Fresh embassies and suits,
   Nor from the state, nor private friends, hereafter
   Will I lend ear to. [*Shout within.*] Ha! what shout is this?
   Shall I be tempted to infringe my vow
   In the same time 'tis made? I will not.
(*Enter, in mourning habits,* VIRGILIA, VOLUMNIA, *leading young* MARCIUS,
              VALERIA, *and Attendants.*)
   My wife comes foremost; then the honour'd mould
   Wherein this trunk was fram'd, and in her hand

The grandchild to her blood. But out, affection!
All bond and privilege of nature, break!
Let it be virtuous to be obstinate.
What is that curtsy worth? or those doves' eyes,
Which can make gods forsworn? I melt, and am not
Of stronger earth than others. My mother bows;
As if Olympus to a molehill should
In supplication nod; and my young boy
Hath an aspect of intercession, which
Great nature cries 'Deny not'. Let the Volsces
Plough Rome, and harrow Italy; I'll never
Be such a gosling to obey instinct, but stand
As if a man were author of himself
And knew no other kin.

And this is the end—
                              (*Holding* VOLUMNIA *by the hand, silent.*)
                              O, mother, mother!
What have you done? Behold! the heavens do ope,
The gods look down, and this unnatural scene
They laugh at. O, my mother! mother! O!
You have won a happy victory to Rome;
But, for your son, believe it, O! believe it,
Most dangerously you have with him prevail'd,
If not most mortal to him.

OVERTURE TO 'EGMONT', OP. 84

1 *Sostenuto ma non troppo, leading to* 2 *Allegro, leading to*
3 *Allegro con brio.*

One of the problems that haunts the lover of the rarer products of
theatre-music is how to do justice to Beethoven's *Egmont* and
Mendelssohn's *Midsummer-Night's Dream*, when Goethe's play is
unknown outside Goethe's and Beethoven's country, and is even
there kept on the stage-repertoire avowedly because of the music;
while the theatre-goers of Shakespeare's country have for centuries
frustrated the best efforts of theatre-musicians by maintaining a
rooted belief that theatre-music is divinely ordained to be the
worst music that money can be stinted upon. Even opera-goers
have hardly learned to wait for such things as the last chord of the
first act of *Tristan and Isolde*, a wonderful chord for trumpets
behind the scene, long known in the British Islands only to readers
of the score. Yet opera-goers are in a fair way to become as musical
as concert-goers; and some day play-goers may treat fine incidental
music to Shakespeare not less respectfully than we now treat
Wagner.

The overture to *Egmont* is theatre-music. Like the overture to *Coriolanus*, it does not deal with the whole play, though I am unable to find (as Wagner found in *Coriolanus*) any one scene which covers the ground of the whole overture. But a comparison is possible. Wagner was right in saying that while the political themes of Shakespeare's *Coriolanus* were not musical, Beethoven found inspiration in the conflict of the hero with the not less heroic mother and wife, who vanquish his pride. With *Egmont* the balance is reversed. Clärchen is, indeed, a figure of eminently musical pathos, both in her heroic temper and her incapacity to move mountains by it; and if Goethe could have done for her what Turgenev did for the sparrow that died of heroic rage in the successful effort to frighten a big dog away from her helpless young, then Beethoven could have given more development to the feminine note in this overture. What Beethoven can do for it he does with noble poetic power in the second subject of the allegro, where fierce reminiscences of the introduction alternate with pleading notes, and yield to a glorious remote modulation.

Ex. 1.

For the rest, Goethe has not achieved his best with the Clärchen-Egmont-Brackenburg affair. What inspires Beethoven's overture is not the rather sketchy individual characters of the play, but just that political aspect that can furnish so little of musical import in *Coriolanus*. The scene of the drama is in Brussels; and the deliverance of the Netherlands was a more inspiring theme than the persons of Goethe's play. History tells us that when Egmont was on the scaffold Alva took the precaution to drown his farewell speech in the fanfares of a military band. Whether Goethe is alluding to this fact, I cannot say; but it is a fine irony of poetic justice that Duke Alva's fanfares have come down to us as the Symphony of Victory with which Beethoven, following Goethe's behest, sends Egmont to his death. This symphony ends the overture as well as the play; and its meaning is fully explained in the last scene. To Egmont, asleep in prison, appears a vision of Freedom, with the face and form of Clärchen. She shows him that his death will achieve freedom for the Provinces. She acknowledges him victor, and offers him a crown of laurel. She holds it hovering over his head. A distant drum is heard, and at its first faintest sound the vision disappears. The sound grows louder. Egmont awakes; daylight is glimmering in the prison. Egmont feels in vain for the crown—

'The wreath has vanished! Fair vision, the light of day hath banished thee! Yes, it was they; they were become one, the two sweetest joys of my heart. Divine Freedom borrowed the form of my love: ... She came to me with blood-stained feet, the swaying folds of her garment stained with blood. It was my blood and the blood of many a noble. No, it was not shed in vain. March on, brave nation! The goddess of Victory leads you! And as the sea breaks through your dykes, so break, so tear down the tyrant's rampart and whelm the drowning tyranny away from the ground it arrogates to itself!' (The drums approach.) 'Hark! Hark! How often this sound called me to march in freedom to the field of battle and victory! How blithely my comrades trod the path of danger and glory! I, too, march from this dungeon to an honourable death: I die for the Freedom for which I lived and fought, and for which I suffer in sacrifice.' (The background is filled with Alva's soldiers.) 'Yes, bring them together! Close your ranks, you scare me not. I am used to stand spear against spear, and, surrounded by menacing death, to feel with redoubled pulse the courage of life.' (Drums.) 'Thy enemies encompass thee on every side! Swords flash: Friends, raise your courage! Behind you are your parents, wives, children! And *these*' (pointing to Alva's guards) 'are driven by the empty word of their ruler, not by their own spirit. Guard your possessions! And to save all that you hold most dear, fall joyfully, as I give you the example.'

Ex. 2.

OVERTURE FOR THE NAME-DAY OF KAISER FRANZ, OP. 114

This work does not deserve to be neglected; and when it is 'revived', it should be so played that it can be heard. As far as custom can be imputed to such rare events as its performance, it is customarily played far too fast. Weingartner has remarked that, whereas he takes the finale of Beethoven's Seventh Symphony at an unusually moderate pace, he is constantly told, sometimes in praise and sometimes in blame, that nobody else has ever taken it so terrifically fast. Things will always sound fast when every rhythmic unit bristles with detail. But if we increase the pace until the rhythmic units become a hum, the listener will sleep like a top.

The *Namensfeier* overture is a short and energetic work consisting of a majestic introduction and a bustling *allegro quasi
vivace*. (Note the precautionary *quasi*.) The majesty of the introduction and the sledge-hammer power of climax in the allegro
bring this work into spiritual alliance with the mighty *Weihe des
Hauses*, op. 124. Eight years passed between the two works;
Namensfeier being written in 1814, the year of the revival (and
revision) of the opera *Fidelio*, and *Weihe des Hauses* being written
in 1822. The themes of *Namensfeier* are almost in the nature of
short formulas designed to display vivid contrasts of colour and
phrase-rhythm without attracting attention to themselves. There
is nothing perfunctory in the work: like the overture to *Fidelio*
(a work of the same date) it is microscopically perfect in detail.
Romantic, however, it does not claim to be, except in so far as
there is romance in the impulse of a crowd of loyal subjects to
greet their sovereign in his progress through the streets of his
capital. Beethoven's tremendous sense of movement was still under
the impulse of his Seventh Symphony, and his interest in imperial
Name-days was official rather than personal. The crowd interested
him more; and after the maestoso introduction has worked its
pair of themes (a phrase in loud rhythmic chords and a broad
cantabile tune) into a spacious exordium, the rest of the overture
suggests an excited and joyful rumour, beginning in whispers and
adding information gathered from many different quarters, until
the glad news is confirmed and the populace rush together from
all sides. No definite 'programme' can be or need be erected
from this basis, but such is the mood of the allegro, which is in
very terse sonata form with many abrupt little themes, a short
development, and a coda which is by far the largest section of the
whole work.

An interesting point in the history of the first theme—

Ex. 1.

is that the repeated quaver figure (*b*) was first thought of as a
crotchet-and-quaver figure identical with (*a*). Nottebohm is probably right in thinking that Beethoven changed it because he did
not like to use in this overture a figure so prominent in the scherzo
of the Seventh Symphony which he had just produced.

The transition to the second group of themes is effected by
the old Italian practical joke of treating the mere home-dominant
chord as if it were the dominant key.

Ex. 2.

But in the recapitulation Beethoven sheds a new light on the old joke by taking it literally. Instead of admitting that those chords were merely *on* the dominant he substitutes tonic chords, with the air of correcting the former mistake.

Ex. 3.

It is strange, but a fact, that this drastically simple stroke in connexion with one of the most hackneyed of structural devices is quite unique.

Less unique but more romantic is the following impressive detail in the scoring of another short and simple phrase. The phrase is stated three times, with a sustained inner dominant throughout. The first statement is on violin and violas in octaves, and it closes into a repetition by flute, clarinet, and bassoon in three octaves. An oboe and horn sustain the dominant throughout. Against this, during the second statement, the strings add a seventh, three octaves deep, with a crescendo and an excited uprush.

Ex. 4.

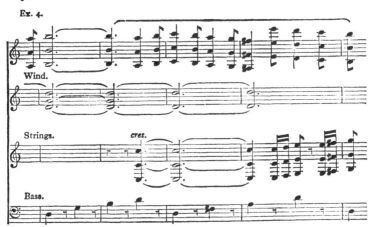

The overture is full of such typical traits of Beethoven's style. Another great moment is the sudden hush and unexpected move to the subdominant just at the moment of returning to the recapitulation from Ex. 1. The many incidents which thus fleet by almost

too rapidly for the ear, make this overture one of Beethoven's
most difficult orchestral works. It does not sound difficult; and
if its points are missed either by performers or listeners, no disaster
is felt, except by those who have had leisure to study the work.
It is an eminently 'practical' work, that does not, like the *Fidelio*
overture or the Fourth Symphony, court disaster by risky passages.
A perfunctory performance can do no worse than make it sound
like a perfunctory composition. But if we compare it with a really
perfunctory work like the *König Stephan* overture, the difference
will soon appear. The harder you work at *König Stephan*, the slighter
it becomes; and slight without the engaging frivolity of the *Ruinen
von Athen*, but with the insolence of a master who really can't be
bothered with such official functions. Beethoven was under no
illusions about these patriotic *Festspiele*. The eminent critic,
Rochlitz, devoted one or more articles in his musical journal to
rebuking Beethoven for becoming increasingly stagey in these
works. Beethoven's legitimate defence might have been that as
Kotzebüe's *Ruinen von Athen* and *König Stephan* were the flimsiest
of stage spectacles, staginess was the only quality admissible in
their music. Instead of this reflection he scrawled upon the margin
of his copy of Rochlitz's journal some unprintable remarks as to
the relative value of Rochlitz's highest thoughts and his own *pièces
d'occasion*. But he implied that his own opinion of these pieces
was much severer than Rochlitz's. And the *Namensfeier* overture
is not among these pieces, for though its opus number (114) is
earlier than that of *König Stephan* (Op. 117), it was written three
years later. And the sketches show great care.

OVERTURE: ZUR WEIHE DES HAUSES, OP. 124

This overture, written to inaugurate a new theatre in Vienna, is
unique in form. It consists of a solemn slow march, followed by
a passage of squarely rhythmic fanfares for trumpets, through
which bassoons may be faintly heard in a sound suggestive of
hurrying footsteps; then there is the tread of some concourse not
less excited, but more certain of its goal; a moment of solemn calm;
silence, and the first faint stirring of a movement impelled from some

vast distance by a mighty rushing wind, which then seizes us in the career of a great orchestral fugue, rising from climax to climax in a world which is beyond that of action or drama because all that has been done and suffered is now accomplished and proved not in vain.

The above paragraph has been the only account I have hitherto given of the *Weihe des Hauses* Overture. I retain it because its conciseness is more immediately effective than a point-to-point analysis in putting before the listener the sublime combination of energy and immobility which characterizes this overture. But I cannot leave without further illustration one of Beethoven's grandest and least understood works, especially as its forms and procedures have never been anticipated or imitated either by Beethoven or anybody else.

An instinct, which the event proves to be well grounded, has prevented me from attempting an extended analysis on the numerous occasions on which I have performed this work; for a more indescribable piece of music I have never yet encountered: Even précis-writing gives but little help, for none of the incidents can be summed up in technical terms. Beethoven's fugues have always been considered such debatable ground that for many amateurs and critics the mere statement that the allegro of this overture is a fugue suffices to bar all further inquiry. But this prejudice is now a little old-fashioned. Fugues are coming into their own; and in this overture it is probably the introduction which most takes listeners, conductors, and critics by surprise. Beethoven has never written anything that is quite so unlike everything else. This would cause no difficulty if the unusual features were obviously strokes of genius. But they are mostly formulas; only we have never met them elsewhere.

The first four bars consist of introductory chords.

If we compare these with the introductory chords of two of Beethoven's most cautious early works, his first symphony, and his first overture, that of *Prometheus*, we find that those early works begin with a stroke of genius, which did in fact shock the contemporary critics.

Ex. 1 b.
Prometheus Overture.

It is the same stroke of genius in both cases, and is far more powerful in the relatively unimportant *Prometheus* Overture than in the
symphony. The *Prometheus* Overture anticipates the *Weihe des
Hauses* in the tone and scoring of the solemn tune which follows
the introductory chords. But the first four bars of the *Weihe des
Hauses* Overture are plain tonics, dominants, and subdominants,
with no systematic interest in the bass. Their purpose is, of course,
to define the key, but they also have the more important purpose
of measuring out the rhythm, from the broad end foremost. They
stimulate the listener to do what he should always do with music,
to listen from point to point and allow each musical fact to enter the
mind without letting gratified anticipation degenerate into information received. Thus, it is not until the third bar that we can know
that the long intervals of silence are not unmeasured pauses. During
the third bar the intervals are halved, and in the fourth bar the
quarter beats and the rhythm of the trumpets have set us in step with
a slow march. Elementary as all this may seem, it has surprisingly
few parallels in other music. Mozart separated the opening chords
of the *Zauberflöte* Overture by unmeasured pauses; but Beethoven
is here contriving his chords so that in the course of the third bar we
discover not only what the rhythm is but that it has been in swing
from the beginning. For this purpose it is essential that the opening
chords should not be monotonous. If they were mere reiterations we
should in the retrospect feel as if the rhythm had begun before the
music. On the other hand, it is equally important that they should
not contain a stroke of genius, nor, as in the *Prometheus* Overture,
a systematic feature such as a bass descending by steps. Lastly, there
must be no air of mystery about them. I have not seen any sketches
of this overture; but Beethoven's sketches often show elsewhere
(as in those for the Eroica Symphony) that these architectural for-
malities give him endless trouble. It is worth while seeing what
happens when they go wrong or lack necessity, as in the following
Awful Example from the adagio of Spohr's ninth concerto, where
the rhythmic angularities of slow 6/8 time are as unsuited to this
kind of solemn exposition as limericks for a tragic chorus.

Ex. 1 c.

Beethoven follows his chords by a big tune, given out first by soft winds and then by the whole orchestra. It is full of harmonic subtleties, such as the sudden bare octaves at the end of its first clause.

The trombones, though intimately associated with the trumpets, have a symbolical meaning of their own, for they are confined to the introductory chords and to the echoing of each cadence in this great tune in both its soft and its loud statements. When the loud statement is finished the echo-cadence of the trombones marks their final exit from the overture. Then (un poco più vivace) the trumpets erect a series of typical flourishes into a symmetrical theme of two 4-bar sections, each repeated, the rest of the orchestra marking the time in big tonic and dominant chords. At the repetition of the first section, it is the bassoons which supply what I have above described as the sound of hurrying feet. This gives occasion to remark that there is no doubt that the overture was calculated for performance with at least double wind. Financial restrictions do not often allow me to give it fair play in this matter in my concerts; but in the course of many performances my astonishment has steadily grown at the ease with which its fine details may be made to penetrate even with single wind, in a work written at a time when Beethoven's deafness already made him quite unable to test his orchestration in matters of balance. With this trumpet theme, however, the 'hurrying footsteps' certainly need four bassoons to make them audible, unless the trumpets and drums are weakened below Beethoven's manifest intention. Beethoven probably quite understood that even a Handelian proportion of bassoons would not make these runs more than a background effect. The suspicion that there is any miscalculation here seems to be quite out of the question, although I must admit that in the previous loud scoring of the big tune the bassoons have been given some independent quaver movement which I see no prospect of ever making more audible than the independent low flutes of Haydn's tuttis.

The opening chords I have shown to be unusual in spite of their commonplace appearance. The big tune is obviously impressive, and its restatement with full orchestra deepens its impressiveness.

But this fanfare-theme, with its square repeats and its eccentric scoring, throws the orthodox Beethoven-lover completely out of his step. Nevertheless, I find myself enjoying it as a convincing item in one of Beethoven's greatest inspirations, and it certainly throws into high relief the more dramatic passage that follows. The close of the fanfare-theme has been echoed; and the horns, relapsing into slower time, fix the echo on to the dominant. Now throughout this overture the dominant is kept, so to speak, out of office. The main modulation of the big opening tune was to the mediant, E minor; and this re-echo of the last fanfare is the first moment in which the dominant is emphasized. It is now promptly treated as a key, G major, but that key will never be established until we hear its own dominant, and this Beethoven does not allow.

Musical philologists may enjoy the suggestion that in what follows Beethoven has a mild attack of the Rossini fever which about this time was devastating Vienna, inciting Schubert to write overtures in parody of the Italian style, and putting Weber's nose the more out of joint because he confessed that he was himself 'beginning to like this rubbish'. The suggestion is my own, and all I beg is that it should not be taken as a criticism, for I have the greatest horror of the imbecilities which these philological discoveries generate when they are applied without sense of the composition as a whole. Rossini himself, if not the Rossinians, may have intended some dramatic thrill in the tramp-tramp-tramp of his favourite accompaniment of monotonous staccato chords, though I find the earlier and Mozartean Cimarosa already using it with the vulgarest inanity in the overture to a tragic opera. To Beethoven it is evidently, when taken in the right tempo, an intensely dramatic thing, whether he got it from Rossini or invented it himself. Here it accompanies a fugato at the octave on a staccato theme, which for all its fugal treatment is almost as Rossinian as the accompaniment. A bassoon and the violoncellos bring the fugato into the home tonic, and soon afterwards all the strings take it up, massed four octaves deep on the dominant, which is now maintained as a long pedal-point. The strings rise in cross-rhythmed sequences to a climax where the Beethoven lover may find himself on more familiar ground. Yet both the climax and the decline from it are as unique as everything else in this work, and are typical of its drastic severity. The sure way to misunderstand the whole work is to regard its features as deviations from Beethoven's style. The most Beethovenish thing about it is the composer's grasp of the fact that a deviation *into* Beethoven's normal style would be a fatal lapse. Nobody but Beethoven could have written a line of it, for nobody but Beethoven could have maintained its style consistently. If I were less afraid of the musical philologists

I should say that it realizes what Beethoven saw in his beloved
Cherubini; the sublimity which that unresponsive master always
intended but missed because he lacked that which could cast out
his fear.

A sudden diminuendo leads to a passage of the most halcyon
calm, of which the first faint stirrings give rise to a lyric turn of
melody which moves into the key of the dominant and almost
comes to a close therein. The first faint stirrings might be by
Cherubini, but are much more sublime in a music that does not
consist wholly of inhibitions; the lyric turn is pure Beethoven.

But, as the quotation shows, the cadence is interrupted. Harmonically the interruption is a drastic example of the subtleties with
which this overture is full; for the quite unaccented first note of
the following short upward runs disclaims any intention to bear
the strain of resolving the previous leading note. The sweet concession to lyric melody has simply been disavowed by a moment of
silence, followed by the first stirrings of a pentecostal wind. Notice
again the extreme simplicity and originality of the crescendo and
stringendo that lead from the introduction to the fugue. The
stringendo is no exception to the rule that Beethoven does not
accelerate his pace except in approaching the last section of a
finale, for, as my short summary has indicated, the essence of this
whole composition is finality.

With all its audacious simplicity, this uprush is ingeniously
calculated to avoid accent on the previously emphasized dominant;
and just before the tempo has reached allegro con brio the lower
octaves have deviated and ended on the tonic, leaving the violins
alone to find their way into the first note of the double fugue (Ex. 4).
I have some reason to believe that the thrice three quaver chords (e)
♪♪♪ ⌐ ♪♪♪ ⌐ | ♪♪♪ ⌐ that accompany figures (c) and (d)
are a Masonic symbol, like the *Dreimaliger Akkord* in Mozart's
Zauberflöte. The structure of the subjects would in any case enable
Beethoven to preserve these chords as thrice three more often than

to repeat them indefinitely or to cut them short; so they may be an accidental feature. But I doubt whether anything is accidental in this very solemn *Weihe*; and there are several places where the thrice three is preserved without being associated with the subjects.

Ex. 4:

The two subjects are duly answered in the dominant; and the third entry, giving the first subject to the bass and the second to the treble, returns to the tonic. Another entry follows in the dominant, with the first subject in the violins and the second in the basses. All this has been delivered apparently with full strength, but Beethoven is able to make still more powerful fifth and sixth entries by giving one subject to the united winds and the other to the strings.

The sixth entry shows that the fugue has passed beyond the stage of exposition, for the first subject is now definitely in G major by its own right, instead of entering as a tonal answer to C. By this time it ought to be clear why the dominant has not hitherto been more definitely asserted as a key. The swing from tonic to dominant is so essential a part of the exposition of a fugue that, if the subject is long enough to make it a matter of alternating keys instead of non-committal chords, there is no sense in treating the dominant as an important centre of contrast. I have used the term 'exposition' rather loosely here, for the exposition of a fugue means the initial portion which brings in all the voices one by one; and Bach and Handel realized, as well-meaning arrangers of their works have not, that it is folly to conceive an orchestral fugue, or any orchestral music, as written for a definite number of parts. The notion of a four-part fugue for orchestra is, despite the pious efforts of arrangers, nonsense; and neither Bach nor Handel ever perpetrated any such thing. For them, as for the pioneer monodists and the modern orchestrator, the orchestra consists of a top, a bottom, and a *tertium quid* to hold them together. Any third or fourth part will belong aesthetically to the top, however independent its behaviour. Bach and Handel differ from the later masters of the orchestra only in the fact that they shelved the whole problem of the *tertium quid* (in other words, of orchestral domestic service) by relegating it to the continuo, the gentleman at the harpsichord who filled in the background from a figured bass, or the organist who could provide a background when the orchestra was adequate and drown the orchestra when it was not.

The counterpoint of this overture gives neither Beethoven nor the listener the slightest difficulty, its whole material being contained in its classically simple and formal combination of fugue-subjects. When Beethoven's polyphony deals with themes that are less conformable to old fugue-types, the harshness of his counterpoint becomes open to criticism, though not to disrespect. Apart from this, objections to Beethoven's fugues are based mainly on the widespread notion that all fugues since Bach are bound to be hybrid and pedantic. The dangers implied by the word 'hybrid' are precisely those into which Beethoven is least likely to fall. If students need a warning against them, the safest advice is to take the forms of Beethoven's fugues as models if they can ascertain them. The difficulties of Beethoven's counterpoint in general are quite another matter. Therein he is obviously no model for students, and the main mistake of his critics has been in supposing that the highest art lies only in the safest models. But the idea that Beethoven's fugues are concerned either to propitiate or to annoy the academic musician is worthy of the proverbial backwoods millionaire who urbanely took leave of the Professor of Latin in the words: 'And now I will leave you to the study of your irregular verbs.'

Let us return to the study of Beethoven's irregular fugues. So far we have had six entries of the pair of subjects, and the sixth entry, by being definitely *in* the dominant instead of *on* it, has begun to make us feel that the fugue has passed beyond the stage of exposition. Accordingly, events now begin to move more rapidly, and this is where the difficulties of fugue-writing begin. The difficulties are not matters of counterpoint, but of composition. The first question is: does the composer intend the whole piece to be a fugue? Or (as in Mozart's *Zauberflöte* Overture and the finale of Beethoven's C major Quartet, op. 59, no. 3) has he merely stated his first theme in the form of a fugue exposition? Many critics, and even some composers, see red at the sight of a fugue exposition, for the same reason that Byron saw red at the mention of Horace. Yet Horace was a most gentlemanly writer, and the only difference between a fugue exposition and other ways of stating a theme is that the fugue exposition takes up more room than most ways of stating a theme, and has a decidedly argumentative effect. In the sonata forms there is neither more nor less difficulty in passing from such argument to action than there is in drama. The difficulty begins when you determine *not* to abandon the argumentative fugue style. This is partly inherent in the nature of the orchestra. When Bach and Handel begin an orchestral movement with a fugue exposition, they soon take to alternating the fugue with matter in the style of a concerto. Really the problem of an overture so consistently fugal as the *Weihe des Hauses* is essentially new. The orchestral aspect of it Beethoven has mastered in his stride. Here, as in all his fugues, the themes are at once contrapuntal, rhetorical, and magnificently instrumental. Their distribution in the orchestra is entirely unhampered by irrelevant notions of choral style with a definite number of voices. Beethoven knows very well how far anything is to be gained by applying such notions to keyboard music, and in the fugue of the Sonata, op. 106, he is justifiably proud of the fact that the *alcune licenze* consist in so few departures from three-part writing. But such questions of licence are mere grammatical trivialities compared to the difficulties and dangers that arise at the point when Beethoven's instrumental fugues have irrevocably committed themselves to continue beyond the stage of exposition. Quite apart from 'real' part-writing, the scoring, whether it be for pianoforte alone, for string quartet, or full orchestra, is inseparably associated with a dramatic style. This in itself is not incompatible with maintaining the fugal argument style. It merely enhances the elements of drama proper to all rhetoric. The trouble is that it is also inveterately associated with sonata-like methods of phrasing, of modulation, and of establishing keys. And here we have Beethoven at the height of his powers taking up the problems of fugue, when he has already summed up and transcended the whole experience of Haydn and Mozart in the totally opposite system and habits of the sonata style.

Consider the matter for a moment in the light of the things which Beethoven must not do. The most obvious Don't is that which every student has to learn: he must not make sectional full-closes. Like most Don'ts, this rule is much more accurate and helpful when it is turned into a Do. Anybody can avoid full-closes by simply not having enough meaning to distinguish a grammatical subject from a predicate: your music and your philosophy will sound learned enough if nobody can make head or tail of them. The true advice is to think as clearly as you can from one full-close to the next, and to undermine your full-closes after you have drafted and arranged your propositions. Much the most serious difficulty for fugue-writing in Beethoven's style is that you must not prepare and establish your keys in the sonata fashion. Your home tonic must be like the horses of the Red and White Knights in *Alice Through the Looking-Glass*: however wide the range of modulation, the tonic must allow the fugue to get off it and on again as if it were a table. There is thus no scope for a dramatic return to the tonic, and the necessary architectural preponderance of the home tonic at the end must be, as with Bach and Handel, unaided by any such interest. Similarly, anything like the process of firmly establishing other keys will tend to be associated with a dropping-away from fugue-writing. In plenty of classical fugues some such licence has proved a welcome diversion; but the strictest fugue-writing in the world could not digest such a process as harping on the dominant of a new key by way of establishing that key.

Let us see how Beethoven modulates now that his fugue is in full swing. His sixth entry having been definitely in the dominant, he annuls the effect of that key by passing quickly through the tonic into the subdominant; and at the same time he indicates a nuance which is one of the most impressive characteristics of his fugues, and significantly related to their whole aesthetic system. The all-pervading fortissimo quickly subsides into a whispering piano. Just as the tonic is not allowed to assert the 'here and now' aspect of the music with undue pride, so the dynamics of the sound have a way of receding abruptly into illimitable space, and of bursting upon us in full strength, not as dramatic surprises, but as thunders and lightnings too unconcerned with our little temporalities to warn us to get out of their way. Beethoven, having now retired into the subdominant, takes occasion to show us that this fugue is not concerned with contrapuntal paraphernalia in themselves. Stretto, the overlapping of subject and answer, is a device usually explained to students as an effective and ingenious means of producing climaxes in the later stages of a fugue. The orthodox teaching on this point goes so far as to assume that it is the main means of climax and a positive necessity, so that a rule is laid down that 'every fugue subject must be capable of at least one harmonious and effective stretto'. Of this doctrine it is enough to say that it wipes out thirty of the fugues in Bach's Forty-Eight, besides at least seven in the *Kunst der Fuge*. Where Bach does use stretti his habit is to bring them on at an early stage of his fugue, and only in a minority of cases does he rely upon them as a means of climax. Beethoven knew his Bach well enough to give little weight to the already orthodox doctrine that the stretto is necessarily a method of climax; and he takes early opportunity deliberately to minimize its effect by making this first soft passage begin with a perfunctory indication of a stretto in the subdominant before the full-sized subject enters. The first subject is then allowed to complete itself in F major, the second having lost emphasis by being disguised in tremolo. Then figures (*c*) and (*d*) move easily through related keys back through the tonic to the unexpectedly bright region of A major, where in another adumbration of stretto Beethoven perfunctorily inverts the first figure of the main theme. The momentary gleam of A major is the first excursion beyond the key-relationships of Bach and Handel. It is a mere natural addition to the harmonic vocabulary, but its effect is as accurately calculated as every other subtlety in this extraordinary composition.

The impression of stretto now becomes more serious, though the device remains rigorously debarred from dealing with complete themes. But the following sequence—

shows a strong drift towards E minor, and on the dominant of this key there is enough pause with a short crescendo to produce a moment's feeling of sonata-like preparation, as if the key had some dramatic meaning. It has, and the meaning exactly shows how far such plotting and preparation are admissible as a means of reconciling the fugue style with that of the symphonic orchestra.

The pair of subjects now bursts out in the full orchestra in E minor and leads to a magnificent dispute between E minor and the home tonic of which the following is the outline (Ex. 6). I do not know a finer stroke of genius in musical architecture and accurate delimitation of style. The key (E minor, the mediant) is that of the only modulation in the big tune of the introduction (Ex. 1). That is its precise dramatic meaning; it has a just perceptible association with a memorable melody. Not with any event that could have interrupted the flow of that melody or made its tonic vanish below the horizon. Had the dominant, or any major key, such as the bright A major which we have already heard, been chosen either in that tune or in this place, the magnificent effrontery of Ex. 6 would have been impossible, with its obstinate attempt of the home tonic chord to overbalance the key of E minor and its contemptuous yielding to the E minor cadence at the last crotchet.

Ex. 6.

Moreover, any major key, related or remote, would here have had the wrong kind of dramatic importance. Thus emphasized, it would have definitely looked forward to actions and excursions in sonata style. And such things have already long ceased to be possible to this music. Beethoven is still as free to abandon polyphony as Bach is to let his orchestral fugues drop into concerto passages; and he does at this point need to mark that the fugue has reached its middle stage and closed an epoch in its course. Accordingly, Beethoven allows himself a drop into sonata style in its most inactive phase, that of a tonic and dominant winding-up process, which, beginning by playing with figure (c), answers the paradoxical effrontery of Ex. 6 with the more drastic effrontery of ordinary tonic and dominant chords ending with unisons on the tonic.

Upon this mundane conclusion fugal wisdom suddenly descends as from the heavens, and the chord of E minor changes in Beethoven's most characteristic way into that of the home tonic, each descending interval being an allusion to figure (a).

Ex. 7.

The fugue is resumed pianissimo, the second subject being still more disguised with semiquaver ornament. The entries are crowded closer together with a more serious effect of stretto. Suddenly the sequences begin to rise instead of falling—

and in four bars of crescendo the full orchestra is ablaze over a dominant pedal, figure (*a, b*) of the theme swinging to and fro in the middle part, while the rhythmic figure which I believe to be Masonic assists as accompaniment. The Beethoven-lover is now on more familiar ground. For, while the sonata-like dramatic treatment of keys, themes, returns, and recapitulations is inadmissible to an orchestral fugue, sonata-like methods of emphasizing the home tonic in the coda will, however unknown to Bach and Handel, always be welcome as soon as the fugue has reached its final stages. And now, with no physical conditions to fatigue us, we can enjoy climbing the last stages of a mountain with a series of surprises at discovering again and again that there is yet another stretch before the summit. With all its symphonic resources, this coda never lapses into a merely symphonic style. It never implies that the return to the home tonic has been a return from a long journey. The first deceptive cadence, without dropping into a Handelian idiom, uses Handel's device of being an ordinary full-close played very slowly.

As will be seen, this close is interrupted by Bach's characteristic flattened seventh on the tonic, which brings us into the subdominant regions associated with plagal cadences. Beethoven, having rounded off into a brisk four bars the phrase begun in Ex. 9, proceeds to repeat it, and the repetition drifts mysteriously into dark modulations, climbing up through the flat supertonic. These dark modulations are the accurately timed counterpoise to the momentary flash of A major which occurred early in the fugue. The home tonic is again reached in a two-bar crescendo, and we again have an ordinary tonic and dominant swing on figure (*c*) with the Masonic rhythm. We have often heard it descend in sequences, but it is a new thing to have it brought to a cadence on the last beat of the bar. By means of this behaviour, it leads to a quite new four-

bar phrase as unexpected as the little notch in the last ridge of the
Matterhorn which Edward Whymper feared might block his way
at the last moment, but which turned out to be an easy change of
slope when he came to it.

And so figure (c) begins climbing again, this time on a tonic pedal.
Suddenly, on the fourth beat of the bar, the subdominant appears
in its grandest solemnity, and the main theme is given a new
epigrammatic turn as a two-bar phrase repeated and leading once
more to the tonic. Then the whole first theme is given in the tonic,
and its close is insisted upon in a new way, on the tonic without
the dominant, until a passage of scales with strings and wind in
antiphony seems to be leading us towards the summit. But again
there is an obstacle. At first the sudden dark intervening A flat
seems to be merely alternating with the tonic, but on repetition it
becomes a serious dark modulation.

When this has yielded, nothing interferes with the final tonic and
dominant cadential climaxes, which Beethoven keeps spinning with
all his astronomical momentum. He knows a good deal about the
music of the spheres, and is not afraid in his Ninth Symphony to

make the stars march to the Turkish music of big drum, cymbals, and triangle, and the singing of a tenor whose rollicking and broken rhythms suggest that, at all events for humanity, the sublime spectacle is almost too intoxicating. Whatever the difficulties of the *Weihe des Hauses* Overture, it does not shock decorum; but, though it does not use the big drum, it agrees with the Ninth Symphony that the stars in their courses do not thump on tubs.

BERLIOZ

'SYMPHONIE FANTASTIQUE', OP. 14

1 REVÉRIES, PASSIONS. *Largo, leading to Allegro agitato e appassionato assai.* 2 UN BAL. *Valse. Allegro non troppo.* 3 SCÈNE AUX CHAMPS. *Adagio.* 4 MARCHE AU SUPPLICE. *Allegretto non troppo.* 5 SONGE D'UNE NUIT DE SABBAT. *Larghetto, leading to Allegro.*

Boiling oil awaits me for my irreverent treatment of Berlioz in the fourth volume of these Essays. Nevertheless, I claim to see a great deal more than his out-and-out admirers see in Berlioz, for they give me no sufficient evidence that they see enough in the art of music to measure anything so important as Berlioz's actual musical achievement. I have been blamed for 'repeating exploded fallacies' when I say that his musical technique is amateurish compared with that of his prose. My own literary claims are entirely amateurish, and I accept the judgement of such an acknowledged master of literature as W. E. Henley when he hails Berlioz as a fellow craftsman in prose. My judgement of Berlioz's technique is not based on the exploded fallacies of the musical critics of his day. Matthew Arnold thought that an institution such as the Académie Française was a safeguard against the weedy growth of *jugements saugrenus* and of projects that ought never to have been undertaken. Unfortunately French musical academicism is responsible for almost all that is most *saugrenu* in French music; and when it rises above that, it achieves the kind of perky slickness which deprives me of the last remains of my sense of fair play. So far, then, my sympathies are entirely with Berlioz. But I refuse to be bound by a statute of limitations which licenses me to tell brutal truths about the amateurishness of Gluck because he died in 1787, and forbids me to criticize Berlioz because he died in 1869 and is about to be canonized at his centenary. The canonizers (including the cleverest of all French academicians, Saint-Saëns) seem almost to wish to institute Berlioz's harmonic weaknesses into doctrines for the future.

But these weaknesses coincide suspiciously nearly with the commonest mistakes of a student with a defective ear for counterpoint. Schumann, the first and on the whole the most broadly and deeply sympathetic of Berlioz's early champions, pointed out that whenever Berlioz makes what seems manifestly a mistake every attempt to correct it substitutes for something characteristic something impossibly banal. I have never yet found a mistake in a student's composition of which this is not true. In a work of imagination every mistake (other than mere clerical errors or oversights) represents either a confusion of thought or an essentially impossible project. Hence any correction of it means abandoning at least half the thought or the whole essence of the project. Technical training consists mainly in the modest attempt to teach students to recognize and tackle the possibilities. One of the standard riddles of my class-room runs as follows:

Q. What is it which we all wish to learn from the Great Masters, and why can we never learn it?

A. How to get out of a hole: because they never get into one.

There is not sufficient reason for believing that the most promising student is the one who never gets into a hole; but there is still less reason for supposing that every student who spends all his time getting into holes is a Berlioz. It has been suggested that it was a pity Cherubini did not grant Berlioz's wish for the professorship of harmony. Cherubini's own academicism was bad enough in all conscience; but a traditional academic tyranny would be freedom itself compared with that of a composer who proclaimed a crusade against appoggiaturas (which is like proclaiming a crusade against all figures of speech), and who professed an utter detestation of all sixteenth-century polyphony, all Bach, all polyphonic organ music, and, in fact, everything that he would not have written himself. Berlioz's most violent aversion was Wagner. Whatever may be said of his harmonic theories, they were anything but advanced.

Grammatical rules can be very silly; perhaps sillier in music than in literature, because in spoken languages they are demonstrable questions of usage, whereas in music they are questions of sound, and hence of taste. It is possible that a split infinitive may be less illiterate than the only circumlocution that can be devised to avoid it; and it is possible that an incorrect doubled leading-note may not 'tickle like cake-crumbs in bed'. But the least pedantic of critics will agree with Mr. Punch that the English infinitive was racked beyond human endurance by the sonnet which began

To with the lark and with the sun arise—

And so perhaps it is as well that Berlioz gave warning in the very first two bars of the *Symphonie Fantastique* that he did not feel doubled leading-notes as the Real Princess in the fairy-tale felt the pea under a mountain of bed-clothes.

The *Symphonie Fantastique* has the advantage, rare in Berlioz's greater works, of illustrating a programme of his own invention. We are thus not vexed by the effort to trace any evidence of his attention to Shakespeare (as in *Roméo et Juliet, avec le dénouement de Garrick*) or to Byron, as in *Harold en Italie*, which consists exclusively of scenes not described by Byron: nor need we speculate, as in the case of his *Grande Messe des Morts* and *Te Deum*, about his attitude to religion, or about any other things which he had the statesmanship to keep to himself.

Here is his own account of the *Symphonie Fantastique*, interspersed with the few musical quotations and supplementary remarks necessary or provocative.

NOTICE

The following programme should be distributed among the audience whenever the *Symphonie Fantastique* is performed dramatically, that is to say, followed by the Monodrama of *Lélio*, which ends it and completes the *Épisode de la vie d'un artiste*. In that case the orchestra is invisible and placed on the stage of a theatre with lowered curtain.

Nothing will induce me to expose Berlioz by any such scheme, nor will I discount, by any description of *Lélio*, the effect the *Symphonie Fantastique* ought to produce. There are good things in *Lélio*, but its scheme is supremely absurd and its final fantasia on Shakespeare's *Tempest* is beyond redemption by the canonizers of Berlioz.

When the Symphony is played alone in a concert this arrangement is unnecessary: indeed, even the distribution of the programme is not absolutely essential so long as the titles of the five movements are set forth; for the author hopes that the Symphony can provide its own musical interest independently of any dramatic intention.

A very just claim, sometimes ignored by the canonizers of Berlioz. Nevertheless, his 'programme' is here a very considerable help to the understanding of his music, and no analysis, nor any score, however miniature, should omit it.

PROGRAMME OF THE SYMPHONY

A young musician of morbid sensibility and ardent imagination is in love, and has poisoned himself with opium in a fit of desperation. Not having taken a lethal dose, he falls into a long sleep in which he has the strangest dreams, wherein his feelings, sentiments, and memories are translated by his sick brain into musical ideas and figures. The beloved woman herself has become a melody which he finds and hears everywhere as an *Idée fixe*.

First Movement. Reveries, Passions.

First he remembers the uneasiness of mind, the aimless passions, the baseless depressions and elations which he felt—

Ex. 1.

[In C minor. Later, at the same pitch, harmonized in E flat.]

before he saw the object of his adoration—

Ex. 2.

The *Idée fixe*.

then the volcanic love which she instantly inspired in him, his delirious agonies, his jealous rages, his recovered love, his consolations of religion.

Ex. 2 gives the whole of the *Idée fixe*. Other details and phases are easily followed without too meticulous an attention to the 'programme'. The quiet end represents the consolations of religion, by several kinds of 'amen' chords.

Second Movement. A Ball.

He meets his beloved at a ball in the midst of the tumult of a brilliant festival.

The *Idée fixe* enters as a middle episode, and reappears as a lingering farewell in a quiet passage in the coda.

Third Movement. Pastoral Scene.

On a summer evening in the country he hears two shepherds [presumably a lad and a lass] playing a *Ranz des Vaches* in dialogue.

This pastoral duet, the place, the gentle sound of wind in the trees, a few recently conceived grounds of hope, all tend to give a new calm to his heart and a brighter colour to his thoughts.

But She [the *Idée fixe*] appears again. His heart misses a beat; he is troubled by grievous forebodings. What if she should deceive him? . . .

One of the shepherds resumes his simple lay; the other does not answer. The sun sets. Distant thunder. Solitude. Silence.

Fourth Movement. March to Execution.

He dreams that he has killed his beloved; that he is condemned to death, and led to the place of execution. The procession moves to a march, now gloomy and wild—

Ex. 7.

—now brilliant and grand—

Ex. 8.

during which the dull sound of heavy footsteps follows abruptly upon the noisiest outbursts.

Berlioz's prize modulation, which he implores the orchestral players not to 'correct', is the following juxtaposition of the chords of D flat and G minor.

Ex. 9.

At last the *Idée fixe* reappears for a moment, as a last thought of love, cut short by the stroke of death.

Fifth Movement. Dream of a Witches' Sabbath.

[Elsewhere described by Berlioz as the dream of a cut-off head.]
He finds himself in a Witches' Sabbath, in the midst of a frightful crowd of ghosts, sorcerers, and all manner of monsters assisting at his entombment. Weird noises, groans, bursts of laughter, distant cries echoed by others. The Beloved Melody enters again, but it has lost its noble modesty; it has become a vulgar dance-tune, trivial and grotesque. SHE has come to the Witches' Sabbath.

The *Idée fixe* on an E flat clarinet (or broomstick).

Ex. 10.

&c. through the
whole extent of Ex. 2.

Roars of joy at her arrival. She joins in the devilish orgies. Funeral bells, parody of the Dies Irae [one of the grandest of all plain-chants].

Ex. 11.
Dies Irae.

repeated in quicker notes until it becomes a jig.

Round-dance of the witches.

La Ronde du Sabbat et la *Dies Irae* ensemble.

And so Berlioz, for all his hatred of what the academic musicians taught him, really lets himself go and best displays his freedom as a composer when he is building up long rounds as in the *Scène aux champs* (Ex. 5) and fugues, as upon Ex. 12, which swings along splendidly; and his proudest climaxes are wholesale combinations which he naïvely advertises as such. He is big enough to stand our poking a little fun at him; and I am sorry if the out-and-out Berliozians are not.

'HAROLD IN ITALY', SYMPHONY WITH VIOLA OBBLIGATO, OP. 16

1. *Harold in the Mountains. Scenes of melancholy, happiness, and joy.*
2. *March of Pilgrims singing their evening prayer.*
3. *Serenade of a mountain-dweller in the Abbruzzi to his mistress.*
4. *Orgy of Brigands. Memories of past scenes.*

There are excellent reasons for reading *Childe Harold's Pilgrimage*. But among them I cannot find any that concern Berlioz and this symphony, except for the jejune value of the discovery that no definite elements of Byron's poem have penetrated the impregnable fortress of Berlioz's encyclopaedic inattention. Many picturesque things are described in famous stanzas in *Childe Harold*; but nothing remotely resembling Berlioz's Pilgrims' March, nor his serenade in the Abbruzzi. As to the brigands, Byron has described the varieties of costume in a crowd of mixed nationality consisting undoubtedly of potential brigands; but the passage is not in the Italian cantos, and Berlioz tells us that his work concerns Harold in Italy. On the other hand there is no trace in Berlioz's music of any of the famous passages in *Childe Harold*. No doubt 'there was a sound of revelry by night' in the Orgy of Brigands, but the Duchess of Richmond's ball was not an orgy of brigands, nor was it interrupted by a march of pilgrims singing their evening prayer. Nor is there anything to correspond to an invocation of the ocean, except a multitude of grammatical solecisms equivalent to Byron's 'there let him lay'.

There, then, let Berlioz lie; the whitest liar since Cyrano de Bergerac. (This sentence is a completely Berliozian enharmonic modulation.) There is a river in Monmouth and a river in Macedon; there is a B in Byron and a B in Berlioz; and as Byron stood upon the Bridge of Sighs and stood in the Coliseum, and in this and that historic or picturesque spot, to meditate on history, politics, and family affairs, so the viola solo delivers its *idée fixe* unchanged and unadorned, while Berlioz does whatever occurs to him to do with his orchestra. There is nothing Byronic about that *idée fixe*. It did not occur to him in connexion with Byron. It comes in fully ripe glory of instrumentation, exactly as in the *Harold* Symphony, except that it is for a cor anglais an octave higher than its position in the viola, in a work described by Berlioz as an early indiscretion which he burnt, an overture to *Rob Roy*. In Berlioz's vocabulary 'burnt' means carefully preserved, so that an admiring posterity can discover evidence of the truth of Oscar Wilde's assertion that a true artist lives in a series of masterpieces in which no progress whatever can be discerned. The Overture to

Rob Roy turned up early in this century, and proved to be quite a presentable and engaging work. Mendelssohn declared that what he found so Philistine about Berlioz was that 'with all his efforts to go stark mad he never once succeeds'. From its own standpoint the criticism was neither unfriendly nor untrue; a large part of Berlioz's charm consists in his earnest aspirations to achieve the glamour of a desperate wickedness against the background of his inveterate and easily shockable respectability. Poor Byron had Lady Byron for his background, Berlioz had to content himself with his master Cherubini. Master and pupil deserved each other: you have only to read Cherubini's treatise on counterpoint to see the psychological origin of all revolutions; and you have only to read Berlioz's own account of his diplomatic triumphs over Cherubini to see how low human nature can sink, when an ill-bred younger artist gets his chance of scoring off a disappointed old one.

On the whole, Berlioz's imaginary wickednesses are more amiable than the virtues, real or imaginary, for which he professes admiration. He is as adventurous as Jules Verne, who never went farther from his native Amiens than Paris, and spoke no language but French, though he sent Mr. Phileas Fogg of the London Reform Club round the world in eighty days, and a small company of Franco-Algerians, Russians, and other nationalities round the solar system on a fragment of a comet in eighteen months. And Berlioz is quite as innocent as Jules Verne, though he also succeeds when he is as macabre as Poe. Perhaps only the profounder Verne-scholars are aware that Jules Verne also made an essay in the macabre, in his story of Maître Zacharius the clockmaker, whose soul went into his clocks and watches, until it came to a bad end in his masterpiece which, designed to display pious texts every hour, suddenly took to displaying horrid blasphemies, till at midnight it burst with a thunderclap, while the soul of its author went Elsewhere. There are some quite good Berliozian touches in the Verneal innocence, and I am strongly inclined to trace the resemblances between Harold in Italy and Hector Servadac on the comet Gallia.

But—and this is a very big but—Berlioz, whose genius for instrumentation has always been acknowledged, also had a genius for composition. Two causes have prevented the recognition of this: first, that he notoriously failed to learn anything his masters tried to teach him; and, secondly, that almost everything they tried to teach him was wrong. The musical authorities of Paris in the first quarter of the nineteenth century had been the Latin contemporaries of the supreme Viennese classics of instrumental music. These classics were as foreign to them as Berlioz's adored Shakespeare (with or without *la dénouement de Garrick*); yet the Parisian ideas of musical form were supposed to have advanced with the times; and Berlioz undoubtedly thought that the expositions of the first allegros in his *Fantastique* and *Harold* Symphonies were symphonic expositions in the style established by Mozart and Haydn and developed by Beethoven. To us such an idea seems ridiculous; it is like constructing the first act of a drama round the incident of the loss of an umbrella which turns out to have no connexion with the plot; and we naturally blame Berlioz for so obviously deficient a sense of form. But, in the first place, did his teachers know better? Cherubini had a very good sense of form; he was profoundly moved by Haydn and Mozart, nor did Beethoven fail to influence him more than he liked to admit to himself. But his treatment of the Viennese forms results only by a precarious series of flukes in anything that can be judged by the same criteria; and in some of his best movements, such as the overture to *Anacreon*, the form has no resemblance to that of any other classic, ancient or contemporary. We had better ascertain what Cherubini thought about form before we decide whether Berlioz thought like-wise, otherwise, rightly, or wrongly. In the second place, we shall be driven to recognize that his genius for composition is independent of any external shapes. His sonata expositions are quite flat and do not establish their 'complementary key'. Then why call them sonata expositions? They are very clear, entertaining, and all the better for the repeats which Berlioz prescribes. He cannot 'develop' a theme; he can only submit it to a process aptly described by Dannreuther as 'rabbeting'. But this process leads to excellent climaxes, whatever it may be called. And what about Berlioz's codas? Ah, there his natural element coincides with the classical form; he is a born perorator, and everything leads up to his perora-tions. But notice that everything does genuinely lead up to them; he does not perorate upon a vacuum. He cannot argue; he cannot meditate: he has at least this in common with Byron that 'sobald er reflektirt ist er ein Kind'. But he can sum up and pile on the agony or the exultation; he can also begin at a real beginning. I am not quite certain about his middle. Just as his harmony is, like even his divinest instrumentation, all top and bottom, so there is a certain hollowness about his forms, apart from the fact that they are in any case totally different from (and infinitely better than) anything they profess to be. From the two typical defects of bad highbrow music Berlioz is absolutely free: he never writes a piece consisting of introductions to introductions; and he never writes a piece consisting, like the Intermezzo (and most of the rest) of *Cavalleria*, entirely of impassioned ends. His hollowness may be said, in Hibernian metaphor, to lie on the surface; inwardly all is as true as if Mr. Gulliver had spoken it.

Perhaps the most gloriously nonsensical fact about the *Harold*

Symphony is that its viola solo is the result of the work having been commissioned by Paganini, who is said to have played it at the first performance in 1834.[1] Anything less like a concerto has never been conceived: the part has its difficulties of endurance, tone-production, and conception, but is about as suited for the display of a virtuoso's powers as a bath-chair for a world's speed-record.

You have now (if I have had the honour of your undivided attention thus far) read as close an analysis of the 'programme' of the *Harold* Symphony as the tangential velocity of Berlioz's mind permits the sympathetic analyst to achieve; and all that remains is to quote the themes.

I. *Harold aux Montagnes.*

Introduction.—A melancholy double fugue or round, typical of Berlioz's broadest openings, arises from the depths (Exx. 1 and 2)—

and leads to a minor version, announced by the wood-wind, of the main theme (Rob-Roy-Servadac-Harold-Byron-Berlioz), which soon afterwards enters more dramatically in the major on Paganini's viola.

---

[1] Both Berlioz and Paganini drew the line somewhere. Paganini refused to play the work but persisted in paying for it.

This entry is admirably timed. The theme is accompanied by a harp and two clarinets in thirds. From Berlioz's treatise on instrumentation we learn that, in the language of Hollywood, soft cantabile clarinets in thirds 'register' chastity; and, thanks to Berlioz, the works of Marie Antoinette's favourite composer Sacchini now survive for us solely in a couple of such thirds with which that master accompanied the downcasting of Eriphyle's eyes on receiving a proposal. Thus surrounded by the virtue which sultans revere so highly as to delegate it to their potential or actual wives, Harold surveys the scene. His delightful theme, after a meditative continuation harmonized in the style of 'there let him lay', is soon restated in a most gorgeous orchestration in which the winds echo the strings at the distance of one beat. I have purposely quoted almost the whole theme, and shall quote equally largely from others, to bring out the fact, insufficiently appreciated even by some who have glorified Berlioz at the expense of Beethoven, that Berlioz is eminently a master of the long melodic paragraph. The resemblance of this tune to the main theme of the Vivace of Beethoven's Seventh Symphony has often been noted, and it is a very curious and by no means superficial fact. The two themes are related as widely contrasted variations of the same idea, and the resemblance covers the whole first eight bars.

After the glorious restatement has died away, an allegro begins with a group of lively figures upon which Harold-Rob-Roy-Hector-&c., intervenes with palpitations that lead to a crisis in the full orchestra. Then the viola, after spelling out the first five notes gradually, announces the following cheerful melody:

Ex. 4.

Allegro.

Restatements of this in dialogue with the full orchestra are suddenly interrupted by a new theme in an unexpected key.

Ex. 5.

Proceeding conversationally from thence to D major, where it is developed and echoed by the wind with displaced rhythm, this does duty for the second group of what Berlioz undoubtedly took for a sonata exposition. He accordingly repeats the whole from Ex. 4, and then proceeds to a development leading to a free recapitulation that gradually merges into a coda at least twice the length of all the rest of the movement. It flows magnificently, and reintroduces Harold himself in a kind of fugue, started very impressively by the double basses and taken up in gradually quicker vibration by the other parts.

II. *Marche de Pèlerins.*

After some mysterious chords the song of the approaching pilgrims is heard.

Ex. 6.

It is punctuated by muttered prayers—

Ex. 7.

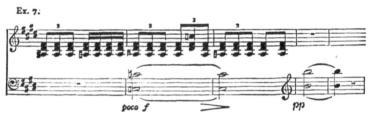

which are accompanied by the sounds of two bells that impart strange modulations to the harmony at every phrase.

After four phrases on the lines of Ex. 6, the melody descends to the bass, and Harold, with his slow theme, contemplates the approaching pilgrims. They continue to approach for no less than twelve phrases in all. Then a more solemn hymn (canto religioso) is heard high in the air—

Ex. 8.

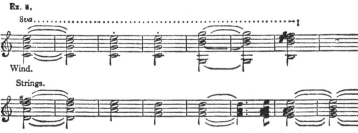

while the footsteps of the pilgrims retreat in unbroken march, represented by pizzicato basses. The viola accompanies with mysteriously rustling arpeggios, *sul ponticello*, no longer representing Harold, but some angelic or natural phenomenon. The first theme, Ex. 6, returns in its own E major, punctuated by Ex. 7. At last the bell-notes of Ex. 7 and the retreating footsteps are almost all that is heard in a die-away of fantastic length and originality.

III. *Sérénade d'un Montagnard des Abruzzi.*

After some lively pipings over a drone-bass—

Ex. 9.

a cor anglais begins the vocal substance of the serenade in a tempo twice as slow.

Ex. 10.

Soon Harold appears and contemplates the scene benignantly, while the serenade proceeds independently. His sympathies are roused to more lively utterance as the vocal serenade reaches its end. Then the introductory pipings are resumed. Their lively rhythm is then combined with the slower rhythm of the serenade, now played by the viola, while the Harold theme hovers in bell-like tones (harp-harmonics and flute) above, until all dies away.

IV. *Orgie de Brigands. Souvenirs de scènes précédentes.*

Beethoven, in the introduction to the choral part of his Ninth Symphony, may have suggested to Berlioz the notion of the *souvenirs de scènes précédentes*; but Berlioz's execution of this design is his own. With admirable sense he begins at once, allegro frenetico, with his brigands, stating their theme shortly. It 'registers' franticness and frightfulness in the cross-rhythms of its last four bars.

Ex. 11.

The memory of the melancholy part of the introduction (Exx. 1 and 2) arises. 'We'll none of that!' say the brigands. The pilgrims' march (Ex. 6) rouses a less immediate but more uneasy opposition. The serenade (Ex. 10) is fiercely suppressed; but the memory of Harold's own past happiness (Allegro, Ex. 4) is not so easily ousted. And, whatever may have induced Harold to enrol himself among the brigands, it is a moment of genuine pathos as well as of genuine music when he parts with his very identity in the last broken reminiscences of the main theme (Ex. 3), now heard faintly in those chaste clarinets, echoed with sobs, and dying away slowly at the beginning of its fourth bar. Sardonic laughter is heard, growing to exultant cries; and the orgy starts in full vigour. You will learn most about Berlioz's brigands from *Lélio*, his sequel to the *Symphonie Fantastique*. According to *Lélio* they are, in their boisterous way, very gallant to ladies—

Ex. 12.

whom they invite to drink from cups made of the skulls of their lovers. The following passage may possibly show how the raw material of these utensils is obtained; at all events it is eminently suggestive of bright deaths quivering at victims' throats, of streams of gore, and of round objects rolling on the ground.

Ex. 13.

Pathetic pleas for mercy are also heard—

and are received, we regret to say, with fiendish laughter.

Berlioz traverses this mass of material twice. Then a very short passage of development leads to the beginning of a recapitulation of Ex. 12 in the tonic major. Suddenly it is interrupted. With palpitating heart Harold listens to the chant of the pilgrims; no mere reminiscence this time, but the real sound in the distance. This breaks his heart; he can endure life no longer; he drinks poison and leaves the brigands to finish their orgy without him.

OVERTURE TO 'KING LEAR'

One of the largest and most curious subjects in musical aesthetics is the capacity of music to illustrate things outside music. The most difficult question in this subject is the capacity of the composer to attend to the thing he purports to illustrate. In the case of Berlioz the problem is simple; for his capacity for attending to anything but the most immediate melodic, orchestral, and rhetorical impulses is nil; and as for accepting his own statements about anything in his life or his works, you would be far wiser to hang a dog on the evidence of Benvenuto Cellini (Berlioz's own ideal), supported by Captain Lemuel Gulliver and Cyrano de Bergerac. In one way, and one only, Berlioz was perfectly truthful; he is a noble example of aesthetic sincerity. What he tells us of his enthusiasms and hatreds may be taken as the bare truth without exaggeration or softening. Every other statement that he makes should be regarded as possibly an unscrupulous invention in support of his prejudices. He saw no harm in saying that at the first performance of his *Grande Messe des Morts* he averted disaster by taking up the baton when Habeneck laid it down at a critical moment to take a pinch of snuff. Many years after this story had made Habeneck infamous throughout Europe, Berlioz coolly confessed that he had told it simply because it was *ben trovato*. Probably there is just as much truth in the wonderful tale of passion which he tells us was the origin of his *King Lear*

Overture. According to that tale the inspiration came during or after a crisis of jealousy in one of his love-affairs, when he rushed off on a journey with the purpose of murdering his beloved. According to the title of the work, you ought to read Shakespeare's *King Lear* to find out the meaning of the music. But no one who has any independent power of following Shakespeare as drama and Berlioz as music will waste five minutes over the attempt to connect Berlioz's *King Lear* with Shakespeare's. He may go so far as to agree with Richard Strauss that the startling shrill pizzicato chord at the chief climax of the work suggests something snapping in the mad king's brain; but that detail is not to be found in Shakespeare, nor has Berlioz left that (or any) explanation of it. Again, nobody need quarrel with the suggestion that the beautiful melody for the oboe in the introduction is worthy of Cordelia; but it is quite another question whether, if Cordelia could ever have expressed herself so freely and attractively, the tragedy would have happened at all. Again, what elements or persons in the play are we to connect with the second subject of the allegro (Ex. 3 and its continuations)? Surely not Cordelia; if the melody in the introduction might perhaps claim to sound the depths of Cordelia's heart and show us the tenderness her father could not find in her sincerity, *this* kind of melody wears its heart on its sleeve. And no one who knows Berlioz's ideas of the beautiful will dare to suggest that these themes are meant to show the specious 'tender-hefted nature' of Regan or Goneril; though it would on that theory be easy to explain the furious transformation of Ex. 3 (just before 'something snaps', according to Richard Strauss's interpretation) as the unmasking of their true character. Berlioz, however, we may be sure, intended these melodies to be types of pure beauty. There is no other feminine element in the play, and I would like to see the faces of Kent and Edgar if they were confronted with Ex. 3 and its continuation as the expression of their devotion and sympathy. Even in externals, such as Berlioz most enjoyed to handle realistically, you will not be able to fit this work to *King Lear*. Where are the thunderstorms? The

drum-figure ♪♪♪♪♪♪ in the introduction is very impressive;

but it is everything else that thunder is not: it is rhythmic, it ends with a crack which does not reverberate, and it is invariable. Berlioz never meant it for thunder: when he wants thunder he can get it with highly poetic and accurate observation of the facts, as in his *Scène aux Champs*.

In short, we shall only misunderstand Berlioz's *King Lear* Overture so long as we try to connect it with Shakespeare's Lear at all.

What Berlioz has achieved is exactly what he has attempted: a magnificent piece of orchestral rhetoric in tragic style, inspired neither by particular passages in literature nor by particular events in Berlioz's life, but by much the same impulses that lead him to tell effective tales of himself, of his friends, and of enemies, whether under the guise of memoirs or of the brilliant and witty fiction of his *Soirées d'orchestre*. Above all, he is inspired by the orchestra itself. You have only to dip into his *Traité d'Instrumentation* to see that even as a prose-writer (in which capacity he is more adroit than as a musician) the mere tone of an orchestral instrument inspires him, much as Nature inspires Ruskin, with vivid powers of description and characterization. Indeed, Ruskin and Berlioz have enough in common to make an imaginary conversation between them full of comic possibilities: Ruskin would disapprove horrifically of all Berlioz's tastes and artistic methods; and yet the two men have the same burning proselytizing sincerity and the same lack of suspicion that a wider knowledge might change their opinion of much that was distasteful to them at the moment. The oddest part of it is that Berlioz, whose sublimest music is constantly at the mercy of a total lack of sense of the ridiculous, is full of humour as a prose-writer, and would make glorious fun of Ruskin in our imaginary conversation, which, if properly conducted, ought to leave them excellent friends cheerfully convinced of each other's perdition. This one point, that Berlioz is a master of humour in prose and notoriously without sense of humour in music, ought to convince us of the hopelessness of looking to external subject-matter as a guide to music, even where the music is given an external title by the composer. If the music does achieve a real connexion, it will illustrate the subject; but you will get nothing out of the expectation that the subject will illustrate it. The music can express moods, just as nature can inspire moods. And sometimes these moods may fit certain dramatic situations, so that nature or music may seem to sympathize. Not less often the artist uses the power of nature or music to cast on the dramatic situation the light of tragic irony; the heavens are as brass above us, and the beautiful melody refuses to change when the happiness it first sang has turned to sorrow.

And sometimes the composer has written a piece of tragic music and hastily named it after the most powerful tragedy he has read, without troubling to make any real illustration of the subject. As for the story Berlioz told about the origin of this overture in a murderous fit of jealousy, if that was true why did he not call it *Othello*?

No; let us frankly call this overture the Tragedy of the Speaking Basses, of the Plea of the Oboe, and of the Fury of the Orchestra;

and let us be content, in the admirable phrase of Sir Henry Hadow, to speak of an 'angry sunset' without troubling ourselves about the cause of the anger.

The overture begins, then, with one of the finest extant examples of the 'speaking bass' since the recitatives in the Ninth Symphony.

Ex. 1.

These noble and indignant sentences of the basses are repeated softly by muted violins. After two pairs of phrases, each pair thus repeated in its entirety, the strings thrum a naïve triplet accompaniment in pizzicato repeated notes below a melody for the oboe which I need not quote. It is one of those inspirations, frequent in Berlioz, which makes you feel that the instrument which plays it is the most natural thing in the world, and that you have never heard it before.

This melody is taken up by a soft chorus of wind instruments with an admirable florid counterpoint for the first violin (Berlioz has no troubles as a contrapuntist so long as he is inspired by the tones of an orchestra); and then there is a rich and simple modulation to E flat, where the brass instruments softly sing the whole melody for its third time, gorgeously accompanied by the whole orchestra. After this the storm breaks; but, as I pointed out above, it is not a thunderstorm, whatever else it may be. It consists of a recapitulation of the Speaking Basses, accompanied by the full orchestra and punctuated by the impressive drum-figure quoted above. After the last of the four phrases, two echoing chords bring the introduction to an abrupt end, and the allegro bursts out with one of Berlioz's characteristic violently agitated themes, the straggling phrases of which are, however, held together by an excellent opening figure (a).

Ex. 2.

The course of the movement is simple and quite easy to follow, though there are several more themes than are quoted here. The second subject begins with another glorification of the oboe, this time bringing out a far more impassioned aspect of its pathos.

Ex. 3.

The main points to watch for in the rest of the overture are the first return of the Speaking Basses; the recapitulation, quite formal and regular, of the first and second subjects (Ex. 2 and 3, &c.); the second and greatest return of the Speaking Basses (by way of beginning the coda); and lastly the transformation of Ex. 3 into an outburst of rage for the full orchestra, culminating in that wonderful pizzicato chord which suggests to Strauss that something has snapped in King Lear's brain.

One of the most remarkable things about this unmistakably tragic work is that not only is it written in a major key, but its first four bars are the only important theme that can be construed in the minor mode at all.

OVERTURE, 'LE CORSAIR'

Berlioz has been officially pronounced by himself and others to be an inveterate writer of programme music. Every instrumental piece paints a picture, and every picture tells a story; and the greatest story-teller is Berlioz himself. When we turn to the alleged sources of his inspiration, the educational value in his propaganda is revealed as a stimulus to the study of literature for literature's sake. We need not trouble to assume that Berlioz's *Corsair* can be any other than Byron's. Byron is out of fashion nowadays, and I seldom read poetry, because I find that poetry must be read aloud, and that I cannot long continue to read aloud in a room whence all but I have fled. Berlioz has now twice induced me to read works of Byron—viz. *Childe Harold's Pilgrimage* and *The Corsair*—which otherwise I might have failed to read; and I can proudly claim now to have read them for their own sake, since the light they throw upon Berlioz's music is nil. Byron's Corsair is, of course, Byron himself, mythically wicked, sinister, and diabolically noble. Berlioz himself is a Brocken spectre masquerading as Byron upon a cloud-scape of abstract orchestration which is for him the one solid reality among the illusions of what Kipling has somewhere described as the child that has hit its head against the bad, wicked table. Gigantic as the Brocken spectre is, Berlioz himself is greater than Byron. He is not, perhaps, as great as Cervantes, but he is as great as Don Quixote. Only very silly people will take him seriously, but they are not as silly as the people who don't.

The Overture to *Le Corsair* is as salt a sea-piece as has ever been written. Wagner, we are told, was a good enough sailor to derive inspiration by experience for his Overture to *The Flying Dutchman*. Turner, we are told, lashed himself to the mast of a fishing vessel in order to make sketches at sea during a storm. I believe Berlioz tells some similar story about himself. If not, he ought to have done so. The duty of the analysis writer will have been done if these hints will project the imagination of the audience into the composite mind of Berlioz-Wagner-Turner-Byron lashed to the broken mast of a fishing vessel foundering in a gale while we listen in comfort to this saline music. Of the parting of Conrad and Medora, Francis Jeffrey has said: 'We do not know anything in poetry more beautiful or touching than this picture'; and my childhood memories are dominated by an engraving of this subject in which the figures of Conrad and Medora are hardly noticeable in a vast Elysian landscape by John Martin, in whose heyday Turner was as invisible as Wagner in the glare of Meyerbeer, but whose more favourite subjects were the destruction of towered cities by the letter Z descending from lurid skies. There can be little doubt that the slow theme in A flat near the beginning of Berlioz's Overture is inspired by the parting of Conrad and Medora. It 'registers' feminine chastity and tenderness, in much the same universal formulas as the first feminine theme in Berlioz's *Roméo et Juliette*.

Ex. 1.
Adagio sostenuto.

Sea breezes and sea foam are suggested to me and other naïve listeners by the impetuous opening, which I do not quote. I cannot identify anything else in the overture with any special features in Byron's *Corsair*. Byron has one other feminine character, Gulnare, chief jewel of the Harem of the Pacha Seyd, from whose fetters she heroically rescues the captive Conrad, whose constancy to his Medora is confirmed by his horror at discovering that Gulnare has slain her detestable lord and master as part of the procedure of his rescue. His own countless murders in the sacred cause

of piracy write no wrinkle on his azure brow. Eventually he finds
his Medora dead and her castle in ruins. I cannot trace any of
these events in Berlioz's entirely brilliant overture, and have not
the slightest idea of what Byronic subjects, other than generalized
brilliance, are represented by the main theme into which the
breezy elements settle.

Eminent critics (the epithet is as essential as 'indefatigable' to
secretaries) are warned against imputing to deficiency of ensemble
Berlioz's discovery that this theme, like any theme that will kindly
stay long enough on one arpeggio, goes into canon at one beat's
distance. Like most of his latest works, such as the *Harold* Symphony, the *Corsair* Overture was revised from things drafted in his
Conservatoire days, when human nature revolted against the crass
stupidity of his counterpoint masters, and at the same time
snatched at every opportunity of displaying the canonic accom-
plishments they purported to teach. Ex. 2 eventually appears
jauntily in the dominant as a soprano melody. But I cannot find
any feminine element to correspond to the heroic Gulnare. Perhaps she shocked Berlioz even more than she shocked the pirate
and Byron.

The processes that may be academically described as development are dominated by Ex. 1, thus giving the pirate credit for his
constancy to Medora. But, on the whole, it is dangerous to accuse
Berlioz of attention to his programme.

I do not know why *Le Corsair* is not more often played. To me
it is one of Berlioz's most attractive works. Like all of them, it
arouses my irreverence, and my fiercest resentment against any
one who dares to say a word against it. Berlioz must have been
even more than usually proud of the harmonic originality of his
final cadence—

and here he commands the complete sympathy of any one who can
appreciate good harmony.

OVERTURE, 'BÉATRICE ET BÉNÉDICT'

Berlioz's *Béatrice et Bénédict* consists of *Much Ado about Nothing* without the Ado.

Hero and Claudio are the serious lovers; and they both display a decorous melancholy without being troubled by the Don John plot. This is to the advantage of Claudio, of whom Berlioz lets us know nothing worse than that he is a lovesick hero returned safely from a singularly bloodless war. As for Hero, somebody has got to be serious, to give the opera a chance for slow tempi. The main concern of the opera is the cat-and-dog bickerings of Beatrice and Benedick (it would be pedantry to expect a Parisian, to say nothing of a Gascon, to distinguish between Benedick and Bénédict, when no Parisian ever got nearer to the name of Franz Liszt than 'Monsieur Lits'), and the sudden conversion of the two into lovers when certain minor characters arrange that they shall overhear conversations about the evidently true state of their affections.

As this does not give enough material for a two-act opera, Berlioz has not only a number of Sicilian dances and choruses as *divertissements*, but introduces a *maestro*, of the appropriate name of Somarone, who in honour of Claudio and Hero rehearses an asinine epithalamium in a form which Berlioz's training at the Paris Conservatoire led him to believe was a possible parody of a sixteenth-century madrigal. Maestro Somarone, finding that the composition lacks unction as it stands, sketches with masterly rapidity an extra oboe obbligato which worms and warbles its way through the final performance with the intended comic effect. The text of the madrigal begins appropriately with *Mourez, tendres époux*, which causes the dear old Duke to inquire why the happy couple should die just yet. He is duly informed that this is an expression characteristic of the higher orders of poetry, and the public is informed in an aside that His Highness is a Philistine and a bourgeois.

Berlioz, having thus spent twenty minutes in venting his nasty temper on the subject of all that he had been taught at the Paris Conservatoire by poor old curmudgeon Cherubini, and incidentally in revealing that master's dismal lack of genuine sixteenth-century culture, is free to devote the rest of his opera to very pretty music, of which the overture is an excellent example. It has three contrasted themes, of which the first is stated in triple time in what proves to be an introduction.

Ex. 1.

Allegro scherzando.

The exposition of this is interrupted by an excerpt from the aria in which Béatrice finds herself in love.

Ex. 2.

Then the main movement of the overture begins. It is in compact sonata form with Ex. 1 turned into allabreve time as its main theme, a brassy transition-theme—

Ex. 3.

and a short second group in the dominant consisting chiefly of a theme in minims—

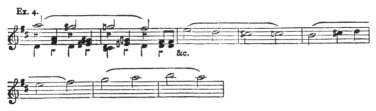

Ex. 4.

which I am not able to associate with anything particular in the opera, though there are passages more or less resembling it.

I do not know why this Overture is not more often played; nor, indeed, why the whole opera is not better known. Perhaps it is because Berlioz, like Liszt, took pains to give himself a reputation as a devil-worshipper. Most of his contemporaries had already come to think that the main purposes of a Black Mass were those of sensational fiction; but it was long before they came to realize that the writers of sensational fiction are for the most part the most respectable and amiable of persons. *Dulce est desipere in loco*, and the Overture to *Béatrice et Bénédict* is excellent fooling, and neither more nor less scholarly than the fooling of the persons it describes.

BRAHMS

SYMPHONY IN C MINOR, NO. 1, OP. 68

1 *Un poco sostenuto, leading to* 2 *Allegro.* 3 *Andante sostenuto.*
4 *Un poco Allegretto e grazioso.* 5 FINALE: *Adagio—Più
Andante.* 6 *Allegro non troppo, ma con brio.*

(These notes were written for the London concerts of the Meiningen
Orchestra, 1902.)

Though this is Brahms's first symphony, it is by no means his first
published orchestral work in symphonic form. His two early
Serenades, opp. 11 and 16, are, like the great orchestral serenades
of Mozart, symphonies in every sense of the word, differing from
those known by the more dignified name not so much in form and
length as in style. There is an exuberance of simple pleasure in
all representative works of the serenade type, that finds expression
in a larger number of movements than is usual in a symphony; so
that Brahms may be said to have had, so far as technical experience
goes, more than two symphonies behind him by the time that he
attacked that which is known as his first. We should also add the
great D minor Pianoforte Concerto, op. 15, bearing in mind that
the artistic problems of the concerto form are even more difficult
to solve in a truly classical spirit than those of the symphony.
When we finish the list with the extremely brilliant and highly
organized Variations on a theme of Haydn, op. 56 a, and take into
account the orchestral element in those wonderful choral works—
the *Deutsches Requiem*, the *Triumphlied*, *Rinaldo*, and the *Schick-
salslied*—we shall come to the conclusion that there is at least
as much experience of orchestral writing behind Brahms's first
symphony as there was behind Beethoven's third.

At the same time there is no doubt that Brahms moved with all
Beethoven's caution in the matter. He kept the first three movements by him for ten years before attacking the finale; and there
were probably many alterations meanwhile. Frau Schumann's
letters and diary show, for instance, that the first movement
originally had no introduction; so that its first phrase (Ex. 4) was
the most abruptly dramatic opening ever attempted. It may well
have taken ten years of a great man's experience to work out the
grand transition from the immense tragedy of the first movement
and the deep pathos of the andante, to the triumph of the finale.
That triumph, nevertheless, was inevitable, for in the first movement the tragedy was already completed and done with; and the
rest of the work is concerned with those larger issues which make
tragedies beautiful. It is the special privilege of the classical forms
of instrumental music that they can thus bring within the compass
of a single work something more than a tragedy; a work that ends

in triumph, not because the world has been stopped in its course in order to spare our feelings, but because our feelings are carried through and beyond the tragedy to something higher.

Among many striking parallels between Brahms and Beethoven may be mentioned the way in which their greatest orchestral works are grouped in pairs. Just as Beethoven's C minor Symphony appeared at the same time as the *Pastorale*, so Brahms's First and Second Symphonies appeared within a year of each other. Again, Beethoven's Seventh and Eighth Symphonies are a pair; the one 'important', though not tragic, and the other unquestionably comic. The parallel may even be pushed as far as to include the contrast between the works in each pair. Brahms's C minor Symphony is, like Beethoven's in the same key, a powerfully emotional work with an exceptionally dramatic transition to a triumphant finale. And his D major Symphony is, like Beethoven's *Pastorale*, full of happiness and sunshine, in every way sharply contrasted with its predecessor. Here, however, the analogy ends, for while Beethoven's Pastoral Symphony is decidedly of smaller range of feeling and in an intentionally lighter style than its companion, Brahms's D major Symphony is, if anything, on a larger scale than his C minor. It is, measured by the clock, the longest of his four symphonies, and its first movement is one of the few perfectly constructed examples than can be compared in length to that of Beethoven's Eroica.

INTRODUCTION

Brahms's tragedy has a solemn introduction, a very rare thing in his work. There are only two cases, with a possible third, in his earlier works, viz. the finale of the very early Sonata, op. 2, the finale of the Pianoforte Quintet, and possibly the short movement entitled *Rückblick*, in the Sonata, op. 5—though this might more appropriately be considered as just the reverse of an introduction.

The present introduction is a gigantic procession of cloudy figures, destined to take shape as the themes of the first movement.

Ex. 1.

Ex. 2.
(b)

Ex. 3.
(c)

ALLEGRO

The great clouds drift slowly away as the plaintive wailing of an oboe rises and falls, losing itself among the other instruments; and when the last anticipating chord has died down the allegro begins stormily. Its first four bars consist of figure (*a*) with a pendant (*d*).

Ex. 4.

after which the impassioned principal theme of the movement appears. This consists of a melody derived from Ex. 3, with Ex. 4 as bass, and containing an important new figure (*e*).

Ex. 5.

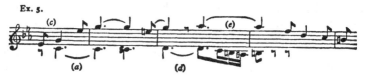

Then Ex. 2 appears in the following form—

Ex. 6.

and is continued stormily with very rich modulations till it settles down in the tonic. The main theme (Ex. 6) is now developed, with figures (*a, d*) in the bass inverted thus—

Ex. 7.

to the accompaniment of a very Beethovenish rhythm ♪ ♫ | ♩

Soon a climax is reached, and the key changes to the dominant of E flat (relative major, the usual key for the second subject in minor movements). Here follows a very beautiful passage of preparation for the second subject; a pathetic diminuendo, beginning angrily with figure (*e*) and softening (while passing quickly through very remote keys) to tones of profound tenderness and pity; till at last the second subject itself enters.

The beginning of this contrasts all the more vividly with the
first subject by being constructed from the same figures. Here it
is (*a*) that is in the treble, and (*c*) in the bass.

Ex. 8.

The pathetic continuation on the oboe gives rise to a new
figure—

Ex. 9.

in dialogue with other wind instruments; and (after a lovely
transition through C flat) the colouring darkens, and there are
ominous gaps in the rhythm and minor harmonies. Then the
storm breaks. A new theme in E flat minor bursts out from the
broken phrases; its bass is in the inversion of the main theme and
its rhythm is closely allied to the rhythmic figure heard before the
transition began.

Ex. 10.

This is repeated with change of position, the new theme in the
bass and the inverted first theme above; and then a stormy cadence
theme, accompanied by figure (*f*) in the horns, brings the first part
of the movement to a close. Figure (*c*), inverted as in Ex. 10 and
divided between wind and strings, then leads, in the first instance
to the usual repeat of the whole exposition from the beginning of

the movement, and, after the repeat, to the development, with a plunge into the remote key of B major.

In this key the first theme appears in canon between basses and violins, in a grand fortissimo. This suddenly gives place to a mysterious pianissimo in which the theme is treated in long drawn notes ('augmentation') and divided between bassoon and basses thus—

Ex. 11.

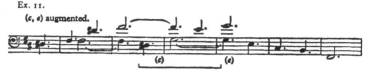

This modulates rapidly and mysteriously, till the dominant of F minor is reached and we hear the ominous broken phrases that led to the storm towards the end of the second subject. Then figure (g) from Ex. 10 appears in conjunction with a new figure that has no traceable connexion with the material of the first part.

Ex. 12.

This new figure, so casually introduced, throws into splendid relief the close thematic treatment of the movement. It is worked out by itself for several steps of a broad modulating sequence that leads to the dominant of C (our principal key) with bold major chords—a masterly example of that power of tragic irony which Brahms has grasped as no other composer since Beethoven. (Observe the grand effect of the deep notes of the contra-fagotto, the double-bass of the wind-band.) The episode, with (a) appearing in the bass, subsides into a long dominant pedal preparing for the return of the first subject. This passage of preparation is probably the longest and most intense that has ever been produced in this part of a first movement: at all events, it is a matter of five closely printed lines of music, breathlessly exciting from the moment of its quiet beginning in the clouds to its end, delayed at the last moment by the entry of the theme in an utterly unexpected and remote key. The whole passage is constructed from figure (a), with the rhythm (g) ♪♪. ♪ perpetually echoing between bass and drums.

From the reappearance of the first theme, quickly moving from the unexpected B minor into its right key, the recapitulation is perfectly regular. A single change of harmony brings the long transition passage into the tonic, and the second subject, with its pathetic beginning and its impassioned end, is not altered at all.

The coda grows naturally out of that stormy end, with a diminuendo; and the initial figure (*a*), turned into a song of sorrow by the wind instruments, closes the movement in almost the slow tempo of the introduction, while the drums and basses throb with the rhythm ♫♫ ♪—and at last figure (*c*) arises in a mighty sigh that tells that the tragedy is finished.

ANDANTE SOSTENUTO

The slow movement is in a very distant key, E major, like the slow movements of Beethoven's C minor Concerto, and Brahms's C minor Pianoforte Quartet. It is as close in its texture as the first movement, but does not need so many separate quotations, since the only themes that recur are all given out in the course of what appears to be a single melody. This melody begins with a beautiful four-bar phrase which one would expect to be continued in equally quiet and regular strains; but, as will be seen, the continuation is impassioned and expansive. Sir George Grove in his analysis of this symphony tells us that the passage which thus breaks into the quiet melody was an afterthought, added after the symphony had been performed in public. If so, the whole movement must have been different in design, for in its present form this passage plays a most important part in the structure of the last three pages.

The melody falls into two parts.

Ex. 13.

The passionate digression dies away in another important figure—

which is combined (in the bass) with (*b*). With hardly any break the second part follows.

Ex. 14.

When this has come to a close the strings introduce a series of
declamatory phrases, beginning thus—

Ex. 15.

and leading to C sharp minor, where the oboe has a plaintive florid
solo, which will attract attention without needing quotation here.
Experienced listeners will observe that its sighing syncopated accompaniment on the strings describes figure (*a*) in shadowy outline,
and that when the clarinet takes up the oboe's song this outline is
inverted. A moment later the song is taken up by the basses, and
figure (*b*) appears in the accompaniment quite distinctly. The episode now comes to a climax; but after a short outburst of passion the
music dies away in broken phrases, and a return to the original key
is effected by a singularly rich and terse rising sequence in dialogue
between strings and wind. The principal theme then reappears in
the wind instruments, with a gorgeous new accompaniment in the
strings, marked by the first entry of trumpets and drums. But a
surprise awaits us as soon as we reach the digression that follows
on the opening phrase. Instead of passing through the chord of
C, it goes straight to the dominant with a strangely bright effect,
and is much expanded before it falls to its close in that key. Then
the second part appears in its old position, but with fresh effect
after this new turn of harmony. Apart from that, it is given to a
solo violin in the octave above the wind instruments; and the
thrill of this new and yet familiar tone-colour crowns the pathos
of the whole.

A coda, bringing this second part into a tonic and subdominant
position, and giving somewhat more florid passages to the solo
violin, brings the movement to an end, with a gentle suggestion
of the passage that led to the central episode. The last phrase
of all is a touching utterance from the solo violin, founded on
figure (*c*).

UN POCO ALLEGRETTO

In the place of a scherzo we find one of those terse and highly
organized movements which are so short that contemporary
criticism frequently fails to see that they are on a symphonic scale
at all. With something like the familiarity that we should presumably have with the works of Beethoven, impressions change;
and we realize that five minutes, a small orchestra, and quiet
climaxes may suffice for a very large movement indeed. It is
always important to discount the first impression that such movements make of being small and fragmentary. The following line

gives us the whole first theme, its inversion (exact and complete), and part of the second theme in the dominant.

Ex. 16.

When the second theme has come to a close, both are repeated (listen to the delightful by-play of the clarinet); but the close in the dominant now leads to F minor, where the clarinet introduces a new and rather agitated melody, of which some is new while the rest is derived from (*a*). This soon returns to A flat and is merged into an accompaniment to the first theme, which, however, breaks off after its first phrase, leading with three notes (*c*) to the trio thus—

Ex. 17.

This trio, in B major, is a lively, well-developed complete section in the usual two parts, with the usual repeats, of which the first is varied by a change to a darker key. It makes a considerable crescendo towards the end, where its theme is given to the trumpets with brilliant effect. After the trio the first section, as usual, reappears; but this time it takes a different course, with important effect on the whole design. Not only has the first theme a delightful new continuation in place of the original inversion, but the second theme is brought into the tonic and expanded so as to lead to a short coda, up in the clouds, with the theme of the trio; thus rounding off the movement in short time while setting in balance far more themes and subordinate episodes than scherzos and trios usually have.

The finale is prefaced by the most dramatic introduction that has been heard since that to the finale of Beethoven's Ninth Symphony; and the allegro resembles Beethoven's finale in one of those enormously broad, square, and simple tunes that will always seem to form a family with striking resemblances. If the resemblance were confined to generalities, no sensible person would worry about it; but there is here a certain provocative element.

INTRODUCTION

Brahms's introduction to his finale brings all the future materials forth in a magnificent cloudy procession, as in the introduction to the first movement, but on a larger scale and with far more of human terror and expectation.

Ex. 18.

This first group of figures is repeated in different keys, giving place suddenly to a new group.

Ex. 19.

This quickly flares up to a climax; there is a moment's darkness and terror, and then day breaks. There is no more tragedy. The mode of the principal key changes to major for the last time in this symphony as the solemn trombones utter their first notes, and the horns give out a grand melody that peals through the tremolo of muted violins like deep bells among glowing clouds. (When this symphony was first performed at Cambridge, this passage excited special comment from its resemblance to Dr. Crotch's well-known clock-chimes. These chimes are, foolishly enough, alleged by Crotch himself to be derived from a figure in Handel's 'I know that my Redeemer liveth'.)

Ex. 20.

The melody is then repeated by the flute, and followed by a second part beginning with a wonderfully solemn phrase that should be carefully noted, as it will be heard only once more, in a most impressive context.

Ex. 21.

Example 20 is resumed in an intensified form, and brought to a half-close with a pause.

FINALE

Then the finale begins with the famous melody that has been compared with that in the Ninth Symphony, only because it is the solitary one among hundreds of the same type that is great enough to suggest the resemblance.

Ex. 22.

Allegro non troppo ma con brio.

Its first figure will be seen to be identical with (*b*) of the introduction. In the second part of the tune the resemblance to the Ninth Symphony becomes obvious, but it is precisely at that point that the essential meaning and harmony are most original. The resemblance is, in fact, of the nature of a pointed allusion. And this obviously gives some trouble to listeners who can notice it. The melody is great enough to stand on its own merits; and our attention is distracted if we notice that its most complex phrase alludes to a simple figure in an older classic. So let us forget this allusion. After the great tune has been fully stated, it is developed animato, with diminution and new figures, leading to a transition theme—

Ex. 23.

derived (with use of inversion) from Ex. 19, as subsequent developments show. This is brought to a climax, at the height of which the bell-theme (Ex. 20) enters leading to the dominant.

The second subject begins, playfully at first, with a long theme on a basso ostinato consisting of the first bass notes (*a*) of the introduction.

Ex. 24.

Then follows a subsidiary in the minor, epigrammatic in style and treatment. This leads to E minor (note the bustling diminution), where we have the following version of Ex. 19 (*e*) from the introduction.

Ex. 25.

This is worked out with high spirits, and brings the second subject to a blustering close in the new key, E minor. The great tune of the first subject then reappears at once, as if the movement were, in spite of its elaboration, to be a rondo. Brahms, however, has a grander design, which shall give the tune its full repetition once for all in this place, while at the same time providing all the interest of more dignified forms. The tune leads to E flat, from whence it begins to modulate, alternating with (*c*) of Ex. 18 from the introduction (a dramatic surprise). Suddenly the animato transition that led to the second subject bursts in and leads to a grand development, treating the scale-figure (*d*) in rich counterpoint and broad sequences, with every variety of tone and colouring, in combination with a diminution of (*b*).

Ex. 26.

A tremendous climax is reached, and we are surprised at the following apparently new figure which staggers as if under a falling sky.

Ex. 27.

But we suddenly realize with a thrill that it is a transformation of the 'bell-theme', which returns in all its grandeur and leads quietly into the second subject in the tonic.

The recapitulation of the second subject is exact, except for the simple change of harmony needed to bring the high-spirited subsidiary themes into the same key as the playful opening.

The coda begins with a grand series of remote modulations with figure (*b*) looming large in the deep bass. The time quickens until we reach a *presto* with a new combination of the figures of the great first tune.

Ex. 28.

Suddenly, at the height of the jubilation, the most solemn note in the whole symphony is struck in the second and final appearance of that grand phrase from the introduction Ex. 21. A new version of Ex. 25 brings us to the end, with the repeated figure of Ex. 28.

SYMPHONY IN D MAJOR, NO. 2, OP. 73

1 *Allegro non troppo*. 2 *Adagio non troppo*. 3 *Allegretto grazioso*
(*quasi Andantino*). 4 *Allegro con spirito*.

Brahms's Second Symphony appeared so soon after his First, that the contrast between the two became a convenient topic for critics. Comedy will always tend to be more popular than tragedy; and critics will often exact too heavy a discount accordingly. On the whole Brahms's Second Symphony was well received. It was obviously on quite as large a scale as his first, and its brightness was a relief to a public that had no means of knowing that Brahms's symphonies were going to differ more from each other than Bruckner's. The slow movement was a stumbling-block; but probably, if it had been less difficult, Brahms would have encountered more opposition on the ground that his Second Symphony was less important than his First. Bruckner was far from anything like popular success; but he already represented the official Wagnerian view of symphonic art. According to that view it was vulgar to begin a symphony with anything so trivial as a tune; and in this matter Brahms's Second Symphony was a most dangerous indiscretion. I give, with some alterations, the analysis I wrote for the London Meiningen Concerts in 1902.

ALLEGRO NON TROPPO

It begins quietly with a broad theme for horns and wood-wind, punctuated by a very important figure in the basses.

The continuation of this broadens out into a mysterious passage, in which the violins enter quietly and expand figure (*a*) into a strange sequence that falls slowly as the tone-colour darkens; till the solemn trombones enter with quiet minor chords and rolling drums, while a few instruments utter figure (*a*) like a plaintive question. The question is soon answered as the music closes in the major, and figure (*a*) becomes a new theme (*e*).

The solemn, quiet, pastoral character of the opening, with its mysteriously romantic continuation, thus gives place to a mood of daylight activity that speedily works to a climax. Figure (*a*), with (*b*) diminished (i.e. in shorter notes), is vigorously developed by the full orchestra (except the trombones, which for the rest of the exposition are reserved for a single crash). This short tutti leads to a diminished version of (*a*) which, in conjunction with (*b*) diminished, becomes a playful sequence—

and this, after modulating rapidly, leads through some sustained chromatic chords to the second subject. This begins with a large cantabile melody in F sharp minor (accompanied by (*b*) diminished).

Like all classical composers, Brahms here, as at the beginning, disturbs the complacency of his contemporaries by continuing his melody on an unexpectedly large scale. There are fully twenty bars of it before we reach a counter-statement, and the counter-statement pursues a different course, leading to the dominant, A major, the normal key for the second subject. To this key the whole remainder of the exposition is accordingly confined with a strictness that preserves the balance after the foreign key of No. 4 and the rich modulations that followed it. The group of short and independent themes that are now given in A major may be described without quotation, as they do not occur in other contexts. First there is an energetic theme in dotted quavers, repeating at cross accents its short phrases that leap over two octaves. Then follows a still more lively theme (partly derived from a new diminution of (*a*) in quavers and semiquavers), also very terse, and grouped in sequences across the rhythm of the bars.

This culminates in the single crash of trombones referred to above; and now follows a great expanse of impressive sequence in dialogue between basses and violins with an energetic syncopated rhythm in the inner parts—

Twenty bars of this lead through a stirring climax to a sudden *piano*; and Ex. 4 reappears in A major with a gay triplet accompaniment for the flute. After eight bars this is given in an expanded counter-statement with beautiful modulations and changed parts, the wind instruments having the melody and the violins a new triplet accompaniment. The close is expanded in a sequence that leads neatly in the first instance to the repeat of the exposition from the beginning, and in the second instance to the development, which begins in F major with Ex. 1. Figure (*c*) becomes expanded into—

Ex. 5.

This is treated in modulating sequences (the basses imitating the upper parts) until C minor is reached. Figure (*d*) (see last four bars of No. 1) is now treated in regular fugue, with several new figures for counter-subjects unnecessary to quote here. As the excitement grows and the steps become quicker, the trombones give a note of warning, and then enter with figure (*a*) in angry dialogue and harsh dissonance. The magnificent series of modulations that ensues leads (with the diminished version of (*a*) as in Ex. 3, but fortissimo) to a grand climax. **Figure (*b*) is thundered out by the trombones,** giving place to Ex. 2 and another new sequence of (*a*), which seems to rise plaintively from the darkness as the harmony reaches a dominant pedal on A, anticipating the return to the principal key. The harmony brightens, and figure (*b*) crashes out once more on the full orchestra, gradually approaching the harmony of D major. Suddenly the trumpets have it in that harmony, quite softly, while figure (*a*) is heard augmented (in notes of double length) in the violins and basses. A few more bars lead us to the recapitulation of the first subject in the original key. Again the trombones have figure (*a*), greatly augmented.

Ex. 6.

It will be seen that Ex. 1 is now combined with the transition theme Ex. 2, and that the alternate phrases ((*d*), with its answer in the next eight bars) are richly accompanied with a flow of quavers. The strange expansion, that followed in the exposition and led to that romantic passage with trombones and drums, now modulates in rising semitones and leads, with intense, quiet and only a brief reference to its former sequel, almost directly to the second subject.

This is recapitulated bar for bar as in the exposition, but all the scoring and accompaniments of the quiet parts are entirely changed. The first great cantabile (now given in B minor) has a fresh accompaniment in dialogue between strings and wind. The continuation, leading to D, is exactly transcribed, and there is no alteration in the vigorous tutti themes that follow, except that the drums are able to aid the trombones in the crash that begins the grand broad expanse in the middle of this section. In the brilliant *piano* close where the cantabile (Ex. 4) reappears, the whole grouping of instruments is changed, the strings having the parts originally given to the wind, and vice versa. The close is diverted into the beginning of the coda. The wood-winds make a crescendo with figure (*b*), as at the climax of the development. Figure (*c*) is given in an expanded form by the trumpets, and is developed by the horn in a deeply expressive solo. Figure (*e*) may be heard floating through the accompaniment meanwhile. Then we settle down in a delightful

easy-going passage in which figures (*a*) and (*b*) are transformed into
the following tune:

Ex. 7.

In tempo ma più tranquillo.

This leads to an equally leisurely passage, in which the diminution
of (*a*) and (*b*), as in Ex. 3, is built into square eight-bar phrases with
other versions of (*a*). As this proceeds playfully the solemn bright
tones of high trumpets bring in figure (*b*) softly; and this wonderful
movement astonishes us, after its immense variety of material and
power of development, by ending with as quiet a glow as that with
which it began.

ADAGIO NON TROPPO

That solemnity which gave life and reality to the sunny pastoral
character of the quiet parts of the first movement, rises to the surface as the dominating characteristic in the slow movement. The
opening melody was considered very obscure by contemporary
critics, who saw nothing remarkable in the slow movement of
Mozart's G minor Quintet. They thought that what they did
not expect could not be right: but instead of listening to Mozart,
they assumed that he always wrote in eight-bar rhythm, and so
did not notice that he often deals with rhythms that expand as
irregularly as those of the slow movement of Brahms's Second
Symphony. It is never the complexity of Brahms that makes him
difficult for us; it is simply his originality. And this slow movement is intensely original. Its complexities are easily disposed of
by quoting its four principal themes.

Ex. 8.

Adagio non troppo.

This opening melody modulates to D major, and is then given by
the violins in a counter-statement, which however breaks off at the
fourth bar. Figure (*c*) is taken up by the horn as the subject of a
fugue, and answered by the oboes—

Ex. 9.

with austerely grotesque tone-colour, until the basses enter in the
subdominant. The modulations deepen, till, with the solemn
trombones to give warmth to the tone, figure (*b*) appears in the
dominant and rises to a climax. Then we fall into a lighter vein.
In the dominant, with a change to 12/8 time, appears a graceful
syncopated theme, contrasting with what went before, as a second
subject might contrast with a first.

Ex. 10.

This is built into a four-square structure, of which the end is left
open, so as to lead to another quiet and naive theme—

Ex. 11.

which we naturally expect to remain in its key and round off this
section formally. A child may say the word which makes history;
and so this unpretending theme startles us by moving, with a rapid
crescendo, into distant keys, and blazing out in a stormy fugato
with a counter-subject in flowing semiquavers. A few rolls of
drums and some short trombone chords punctuate the stages of
this powerful development. Then, as Ex. 11 subsides into broken
phrases of three notes, while weird moans are heard in the brass
instruments, the strings come soaring above with the first phrase
of the first theme in G major ((*a*) of Ex. 8). This is interrupted
by a bar of agitated crescendo. Once more we hear that weird
moaning in the trombones, with the fragments of Ex. 11 in the
wood-wind. Again the first theme (*a*) appears, this time in the
oboe, in E major. Then, in three amazing chromatic steps,
the violins, clarinets, and flutes, in succession, bring the theme

round in one quiet bar and a half, through A minor and B flat, into B major.

The whole first theme now returns varied in triplets.

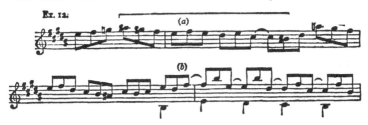

The continuation, after the ninth bar, is put in a new (subdominant) position, and is, in compensation for this change, otherwise unvaried, except in tone-colour. It leads to a reference to the first fugato (Ex. 9), which makes a rapid crescendo. Then the full orchestra with the stately tread of trombones and drums bursts out in a grand florid sequence on figure (b).

Then we have Ex. 11 in the strings, imitated by the wood-wind and accompanied by rolling drums. The music dies down; figure (a) returns in the highest region of wood-wind, and the violins carry it through falling sequences while the drums beat the triplet rhythm of Ex. 11.

The clarinet dies away with the last low notes of the sequence, and the grand song closes with a bright, soft chord for the whole orchestra, except the trombones, which are always reserved for dramatic effects.

ALLEGRETTO

The scherzo is one of Brahms's best-known movements. Like many well-known things, it is not always remembered in its full variety and range, or we should hear less of its being 'too small for its place in a big symphony'. The answer is that in the first place the symphony would be much less great if it did not contain surprising contrasts of proportion and mood, and that in the second place the scherzo is larger than it looks. It is scored for small orchestra, without drums or any brass but three of the horns, and begins with a simple melody on the oboe, with a luxurious pizzicato accompaniment in the violoncellos.

Ex. 14.

Allegretto grazioso (quasi Andantino).

The second part of this tune grows out of the last two notes of the first. The Beethoven-Schubert alternations between major and minor as the theme draws to a close are the foundation of a surprise at the end of the movement.

Suddenly the time changes to 2/4 with bars as short as the 3/4 beats. The theme changes also, but only in pretence.

Ex. 15.

Presto ma non assai ($\downarrow = \downarrow$).

Our delightful first melody cannot escape recognition so easily. Perhaps when it springs up merrily in a freely inverted form it may call itself a new theme—

Ex. 16.

but it soon returns to its other transformation (Ex. 15). However, when we hear this rhythm | ♩. ♪ | ♩. ♪ | ♩ | in the wood-wind, recalling the original 3/4 slow time through the rapid tripping quavers of the presto, we feel that we are returning to something which has never been really out of sight; and so Brahms not only harmonizes the original theme (Ex. 14) differently, but confines himself to its first four bars and turns figure (*a*) into the following basso ostinato—

Ex. 17.

which is repeated, crescendo, for eleven bars, while the wind instruments make loud comments in phrases of their own. This dies away in an unexpectedly solemn little close in E major; and then, with delicious effrontery, the strings run, with the triplet figure of Ex. 17, to A major. This is the most unorthodox possible key for an important point in the structure of a movement in G. Here we have a new version of Ex. 16 in 3/8 time.

Ex. 18.

This soon leads to C major, where, allowing for the new rhythm, matters proceed as they did on the first appearance of Ex. 14. But the preparations for the return of the original theme are modified, and it calmly returns in the remote key of F sharp major, on the strings, who now retain it to the end. Its second clause (figure (b)) is given in B major, with a peculiarly happy turn that brings us easily into a position where the second part can follow in the original key. From this point there is no further change till we come to those alternations between major and minor at the close. Here a new figure appears in all the upper strings, giving rise to a beautiful bit of free inverted imitation in the wind—

Ex. 19.

thus adding an unexpected warmth of tone to the graceful movement, before the oboes and other wind instruments bring it to an end with its first figure, crowned by a quiet cadence in the strings.

FINALE

The finale, though it has an even greater number of richly developed themes, does not need as much illustration as the first and second movements, except for one subtle passage in the middle. The first theme is a flowing melody, of which the first figure (a) is used as an accompaniment in any number of different contexts, while the second (b) forms a basso ostinato to the rest of the theme, as the following extract indicates.

Ex. 20.
Allegro con spirito.

A subsidiary appears in the dominant.

Ex. 21.

The subsequent developments are quite easy to follow, though Brahms maintains his inexhaustible variety of proportion and his wealth of subsidiary figures. Among these we may note the following version of Ex. 21, augmented by being broken up—

Ex. 22.

as it occurs some way on in the tutti that crashes with Haydnesque high spirits into the ruminating continuation of the first theme. Then comes a dramatic event. The clarinet suddenly swells out, above the bustle of the orchestra, with the utmost vehemence in an impassioned passage in F major. This is taken up by other instruments and expanded more quietly in A major, the orthodox dominant in which the second subject enters with the following broad melody.

Ex. 23.

Accompanied by figure (b).

This also has a number of subsidiaries that need not be quoted. The most important of these is a new derivative of (a), that leads to some extremely brilliant scale passages for wind with pizzicato strings, which I quote here for a reason that will appear later.

Ex. 24.

After some stirring syncopated chords, we have a short, lively, snapping cadence-subject, that quickly calms down and leads playfully back to the first theme in the tonic. This finale is undoubtedly the great-grandson of that of Haydn's last London Symphony (no. 104), where we find in just the same part of the movement a very similar series of whirling scales in terms of an earlier orchestral language, followed by a snapping cadence-subject in terms nearly as modern as Brahms's. Unlike Tennyson, Brahms, who to the last years of his life used to puzzle the superior person by studying the quartets of Haydn, was glad to acknowledge such ancestry, which has no more to do with plagiarism than originality has to do with freedom from the restrictions of good sense and taste. When this symphony was plundered in its turn by a friend, Brahms met the composer's apologies with words to this effect: 'One of the stupidest topics of the noodles is plagiarism. Your theme is one of your freshest and most attractive ideas; the thing it resembles in my symphony is a mere accidental accessory.'

With the development of this finale we come to the most profound passage in the symphony. At first events are normal, though the treatment is very ingenious. The first theme, Ex. 20, leaves the tonic at the fourth bar, the last notes of which are taken up and passed through various keys in rapid dialogue, till the dominant of F sharp minor is reached. Then the theme (*a*, *b*) is freely inverted, the result being treated and diminished in quaint combinations.

Ex. 25.

The close, in C sharp minor, is followed by the bursting in of Ex. 21, forte, followed by its other version, Ex. 22, in B minor. This is worked to a climax, which is marked by the entry of the trombones for the first time since the slow movement. (In all Brahms's orchestral works the listener will find it interesting to watch the trombones or, where they are not used, the trumpets and drums, or other instruments useful in a climax. No composer, not even Beethoven himself, is more careful than Brahms to organize his resources with power in reserve.)

Now we come to the quintessence of Brahms. The main group (*a*, *b*) is transformed into an apparently new idea.

Ex. 26.

(Like all things that Brahms marks *tranquillo*, this passage has a peculiar atmosphere of tenderness and mystery, not unlike that which characterizes all passages marked *cantabile* in Beethoven.)

A change to B flat minor brings back Ex. 21 plaintively in the oboe; but we at once return to F sharp, and this new transformation, Ex. 22, modulates (*sempre più tranquillo*) through A and C, with increasing breadth and calm. Again Ex. 21 appears; but this time it is in solemn augmentation given out softly by the trombones, while the violins fall slowly with a legato tremolo. The original key is reached in darkness, and the cold unison of the first theme meets us like the grey daylight on a western cloud-bank opposite the sunrise.

The recapitulation is regular, except that Brahms with quiet humour inverts the subsidiary (Ex. 21) bodily, with all its accompaniments, and shortens the big tutti, varying its scoring and making it plunge straight into the second subject. This is given in the tonic with no alteration whatever; broad melody, subsidiaries, whirling scales, and Haydn's snapping cadence-figure which rushes immediately into the coda. This begins in the minor with a new version of the second subject on the trombones, which have rested since their solemn words in the development, but have now come to stay and sanction the glorious triumph that is to follow.

Ex. 27.

This transformation, beginning in darkness, becomes jubilant and bright, and gives way suddenly to an exciting combination of the figure of the second subject (Ex. 23) with that of the mysterious tranquillo development (Ex. 26).

Ex. 28.

Then the initial figures (a, b) are worked up in a tremendous dialogue between strings and trombones. The music broadens enormously, and at what appears to be the height of the climax we are startled by the appearance in the full orchestra of the whirling scale-figure (Ex. 24), punctuated by silent half-bars that take our breath away. Nor is this the crowning point of the movement. The main figure (d) of the second subject is turned into a flourish of trumpets on their highest notes. And perhaps the sustained blast of the trombones, during the penultimate staccato chords of the rest of the orchestra, is the most surprising effect of all in a coda which is among the most brilliant climaxes in symphonic music since Beethoven.

SYMPHONY IN F MAJOR, NO. 3, OP. 90

1 *Allegro con brio.* 2 *Poco Allegretto.* 3 *Andante.* 4 *Allegro.*

Of Brahms's four symphonies, the third is the shortest and, in externals, the most romantic and picturesque; yet it is, next to the Double Concerto and the D minor Pianoforte Concerto, perhaps the most neglected of his orchestral works.   It is also technically by far the most difficult, the difficulties being mainly matters of rhythm, phrasing, and tone.   These are unsuited to an age of hustle; but they are not to be dismissed as 'bad scoring'.   It is much easier to practise works in which all the difficulty contributes rather to the production of special effects than to musical ideas.   There is certainly no reason why the music, as music, should not be among the most popular that Brahms ever wrote: and this was certainly the impression which the work made upon me when I first heard it thirty years ago.   I give here with slight alterations the analysis I wrote for the Meiningen Orchestra, when it played in London in 1902.

The symphony begins with three notes (*a*), which pervade the whole movement and even recur in the finale.

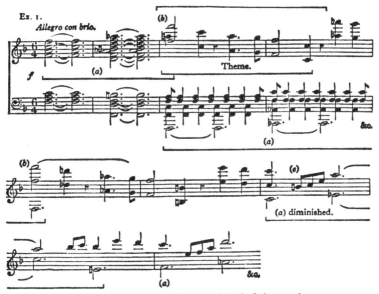

This closes in a quiet subsidiary, with bright and warm tone-colouring.

Figure (a) bursting out in the bass, answered by the violins, leads in a thrilling modulation to D flat, where Ex. 2 reappears. Precisely the same process leads, more gently but with yet more brilliant tone-colour, to A major, in which somewhat remote key, after a little quiet preparation, the second subject begins with a most graceful pastoral theme in 9/4 time.

Ex. 3.

This has a second part beginning thus:

Ex. 4.

The violins take up figure (d) freely inverted and, with a return to 6/4 time, figure (a) appears in a new form.

Ex. 5.

This leads, crescendo, to the cadence theme in A minor, partly derived from Ex. 5. Note (a) diminished in the inner parts.

Ex. 6.
8ves above and below.

(a) diminished.

The whole wind band takes this up fortissimo, and the exposition ends stormily in the minor, and is then repeated, as usual, from the beginning. After the repeat the violins continue their last (syncopated) chords in sequences that quickly modulate to C sharp minor, where the development begins with an angry transformation of the gentle pastoral second subject (Ex. 3), its rhythm expanded so as to fit the 6/4 bars in pairs, thus:

Ex. 7.

The second part of the tune (Ex. 4) is then worked up in inverted canon through various keys—

and the excitement calms down, till we are startled by an intensely serious passage in E flat, of all keys the most remote both from the tonic and from the other keys we have dwelt in. The horn gives out figure (a) like the beginning of a sustained melody, while the deep notes of the contra-fagotto make the tone-colour darker than anything we have expected to hear. The passage ends, più sostenuto, in profound night, while figure (b) appears in many octaves, from the deepest possible notes of the contra-fagotto to the violins descending from their upper register. From this darkness and this distant key, E flat minor, we cannot conceive any near prospect of returning to F; yet the three great opening chords—(a) of Ex. 1—harmonized in a yet bolder way, burst forth with all the sudden splendour of a tropical sunrise, and we find ourselves in the full swing of the recapitulation before we have recovered breath. The transition-theme (Ex. 2) is so turned as to lead straight to D major, where the second subject (Ex. 3) appears in ordinary course. The repetition of its first phrase is omitted, and a slight change in its second part brings Ex. 5 into F major. So far, this shifting of keys in the course of the subject is just what Beethoven does in most cases where the second subject was in a remote key in the exposition; but Brahms, for reasons which appear in the coda, does not let his recapitulation remain in the tonic, but shifts it once more back to D minor, before Ex. 6 appears. The result is that, when Ex. 6 rises to a storm, as at the end of the first part, it is able to lead back to the first subject at the beginning of the coda with all the effect of another return to the tonic. The first theme is now given with greater force than ever, and (a) in the bass is in quite a new and surprising position (C, E flat, C) as a kind of dominant pedal. Figure (c) and the remaining figures of the theme are considerably developed; and the splendid outburst is followed by the inevitable quiet glow of a sunset, as the two main figures (a) and (b) rise and fall through the sustained final chords.

The slow movement, with its manner of pastoral plainness, is really one of the most solemn things Brahms ever wrote. Its first theme is a dialogue between clarinets and the lower strings, beginning thus:

The continuation will explain itself, but the end of the theme must be quoted for future reference.

The sequel, in which the first figures (*a*, *b*) are varied in semi-quavers and made to modulate to the dominant, crescendo, needs no quotation. The mysterious passage in which figure (*b*) is treated in dialogue between basses and violins should be noted; and the wistful melody that follows in the dominant like a second subject, is a thing to be taken more seriously than first impressions indicate.

In the lovely continuation the quiet quaver figure of the violins and its equally naïve inversion must speak for themselves; but it is necessary to quote the extraordinary series of harmonies that bring this section to a close.

This is immediately followed by an ornamental development of the first theme in the violoncellos, with triplets in the violins. I give the gist of the variation here:

Passing through B major and other keys, with sequences of figure
(*b*) in its original form with the new accompaniments, this comes
to a climax as the bass reaches the tonic C and holds it as a pedal.
The trombones enter, for the first time in the movement, and hold
sustained chords, while figure (*a*) is passed from one wind instrument to another, and the strings keep up a flow of semiquavers
derived from the transition variation that followed the original
statement of the first theme. At last the theme itself returns
calmly with this flowing accompaniment and several delightful
details of ornament. It is given in full, and towards the end the
flow of the accompaniment slackens. The last notes—(*d*), Ex. 10
—give rise to a broad crescendo passage—

Ex. 14.

that dies away into the wonderful harmonies of Ex. 12, transposed
to the tonic. Then some quiet descending sequences on the first
theme over a tonic pedal, while the violoncellos and basses repeat
the rhythmic figure (*e*) of Ex. 12—

bring this movement to a quiet end, with chords that sound great
depths of solemn beauty. Humperdinck did not escape them at the
end of the prelude to *Hänsel und Gretel*.

The delightful poco allegretto is so easy to follow that I need
only quote the beginnings of the theme of its first section and the
two contrasted themes of its trio.

Ex. 15.

This melody, instead of being worked out in binary form like a
minuet, has a middle section in the tonic major (of all poetical and
surprising things) with a delightful return through A minor to the
first theme.

The trio is in A flat, and contains two themes—

Ex. 16.

and Ex. 17, which, though contrasted, is derived from the last
notes of its partner.

The da capo of the main section is complete and exact as to material,
but the scoring, which was astonishingly rich the first time, is
entirely changed, and new groups of the small orchestra come
forward with the melody. A single line, developed from the strange
chord that led to the trio, makes the coda of the movement.

The finale is very dramatic and terse; and it needs either a close
analysis or none at all. The listener will do well to be prepared
for short themes, violent changes of mood, and romantic depth
and power. Joachim, who fully agreed with Brahms in disliking
unauthorized literary interpretations of music, could not resist
the temptation of comparing this finale to the story of Hero and
Leander. Brahms said nothing, but did not snub him. The
opening theme is dark and quiet.

Figures (c) and (d) should not escape notice. A counter-statement
follows, shedding weird light on the theme by prolonging some of
its notes, and putting (c) in the bass with (d) above. Then the key
changes, and we have an exceedingly solemn theme of a strange
rhythmic character, with trombones and contra-fagotto.

To Sir Edward Elgar I owe the remark that this is the tragic out
come of the wistful theme in the middle of the slow movement
(Ex. 11).

Suddenly the first theme bursts out angrily in a transformed
version.

Ex. 20.
a, b, simplified.

This leads stormily to C minor, where a new figure appears.

Ex. 21.
(f)

The first notes of this (f) make a bass to the second subject, which begins victoriously in C major.

Ex. 22.

This, however, does not remain in triumph throughout. It leads to a climax in the minor, where several new themes and figures appear; among others a remarkable moment in the extreme distance of B minor, with figure (a) in the wind instruments. I quote the cadence-figure, which is necessary for future reference.

Ex. 23.

Figure (a) in various strange positions (e.g. pizzicato, augmented in the stringed instruments) leads angrily back to the first theme in the tonic. This is not given quite as at the outset; figure (c) is augmented, and the counter-statement is expanded, not in the original way, but by a new development of the fourth bar of the theme. This leads to a mysterious passage, with (d) augmented in combination with a broken version of (a, b) in A flat minor.

Ex. 24.

Suddenly this is taken up by the whole orchestra forte, except the trombones, which, however, soon thunder out the solemn rhythmic theme (Ex. 19) with a new accompaniment of whirling triplets.

This proceeds in sublime modulations till F major is reached, and then we find ourselves in the midst of the recapitulation, for the angry transformation of (*a*, *b*), Ex. 20, appears suddenly in F minor. It gives place to new variants of the theme, and develops figure (*c*) rapidly, leading to the transition-figure Ex. 21, and so to the recapitulation of the second subject in the tonic with no alteration at all till we reach the cadence-figure, Ex. 23, which we are now surprised to hear in combination with the first theme.

Ex. 25.

The short dialogue on (*a*), that led to the return from second subject to first, now leads to the extremely remote key of B minor, where the coda begins mysteriously with a new version of the first theme on muted violas.

Ex. 26.

This soon leads back to F minor, and the wood-wind give us the original counter-statement, with its prolongations of notes here and there, its rich harmony, and its semiquaver accompaniment of violins, now muted. Suddenly the mode becomes major, and the theme, augmented, becomes an eight-bar phrase.

Ex. 27.

Here we recognize the initial figure of the first movement. Before this is further developed we have a most beautiful passage in which the rhythmic theme, that was so wistful in Ex. 11, so sombre in Ex. 19, and so tremendous in the development, expresses a happiness and calm that only increases its solemnity. It is like the end of Brahms's First Violin Sonata with something tragic behind it. Then the initial figure of the first movement reappears in combination with that of the finale; and the violins are heard floating down with the melody—Ex. 1, figure (*b*)—with which the symphony began so vigorously, and which ends it with the romantic, quiet glow that we have now learnt to regard as its destined result.

Ex. 28.

&c.

SYMPHONY IN E MINOR, NO. 4, OP. 98

1 Allegro non troppo. 2 Allegro giocoso. 3 Andante moderato.
4 Allegro energico e passionato.

This symphony is one of the rarest things in classical music, a symphony which ends tragically. In drama a tragedy tells a story which a happy ending would weaken and falsify: in the music of the sonata forms this is not so. In so far as the first movement maintains a tragic note, it may be said to tell its tragic story from beginning to end, and the other movements are free to provide the most refreshing emotional reactions from it. Brahms, in his Fourth Symphony and a few other great sonata works (notably the Pianoforte Quintet and the Third Pianoforte Quartet), has done what Beethoven did only three times in all his works; he has given us a tragic finale. This finale is unique in form among all symphonic movements, and the form is by no means the scholastic display which contemporary criticism has imagined it to be, but a very powerful expression of a great dramatic truth. The first movement acts its tragedy with unsurpassable variety of expression and power of climax. The slow movement, heroic though in pastoral style and ballad measures, has also an eventful tale to tell. The third movement, functionally the scherzo, has all the features of such a blend of sonata form and rondo as is common in finales; yet with all its bacchanalian energy it is evidently no finale. It is not in the main key, and its extreme terseness, while increasing its energy, destroys what finality it might otherwise have had. After three movements so full of dramatic incident, what finale is possible? And how will the tragic note regain the domination after the triumph of the third movement?

The very reason why the finale of Brahms's Fourth Symphony was such a stumbling-block to contemporary critics is the answer to these questions. It is a passacaglia; that is to say, a set of variations in moderately slow triple time on a theme, or ground, consisting of a single 8-bar phrase. As this is one of the most ancient of musical forms and, as such, is taught to young students at school, popular criticism assumes that, like the Ablative Absolute, it must

be something extremely learned and difficult. Common sense would
rather indicate that an ancient form that can be taught in schools
must be something simple enough for primitive artists to produce
and clear enough for schoolboys to understand. Brahms chose the
form of variations on a ground for this finale, because dramatic
activity (always on the ebb in finales, alike in drama and music, no
matter what surprises effect the dénouement) was fully exploited
in the other three movements. He desired a finale that was free to
express tragic emotion without being encumbered by the logical
and chronological necessities of the more dramatic sonata forms.
The climax of the first movement is as great as ten minutes of
crowded drama could make it; but the full tide of emotion that
it implies can be revealed only in a finale in which the attention is
directed to little else but emotional contrasts and climaxes. All
successful sonata finales, whether tragic or not, gain their emotional freedom by some simplification of this kind; and Brahms's
ground-bass ranks with Beethoven's fugues as an extreme case of
this law. It is the same law that makes rondo form preferable for
finales, and that makes the phrasing of a sonata-form finale plainer
than that of a first movement. (See, for example, the finales
of Beethoven's Sonata Appassionata, and the Fourth, Fifth, and
Seventh Symphonies.)

From the large procession of themes on which Brahms's first
movement is organized I make three quotations, marking with
letters and brackets those figures which are built up into fresh
ideas in later developments.

No one experienced in great music could fail to see that the long,
quiet opening sentence is the beginning of a great and tragic work.

Ex. 1.

Its close is overlapped by a counter-statement in which the first phrase is divided antiphonally between the violins, while the echo of the wood-wind is transferred to the basses (in another part of the scale), and the wood-wind weave a beautiful tissue of new polyphony. At the ninth bar of this counter-statement, with the entry of figure (*b*), the harmony takes a new direction and moves towards the dominant, B minor, where, after a climax, an impassioned transition theme appears. This I do not quote, except for the spirited triplet figure (*d*), which ends it, and, as will be seen, plunges into the broad violoncello melody that begins the second subject.

The sequel rises through heroism (figure (*d*)) to radiant happiness in a procession of themes which economy forbids me to quote. Then comes a cloud of mystery—

from which the triplet theme (*d*) emerges triumphant, and works up the exposition of this movement to an exultant climax, the final glory of which is its unexpected sweet and gentle close that leads back to E minor and the first theme (Ex. 1).

With this resumption of the first theme the development begins. As in the first counter-statement of Ex. 1, so here the ninth bar sees a change in the trend of the harmony, and we are moved to a more remote key. Figure (*b*) becomes more agitated, and forms the accompaniment to a new variation of the theme in G minor.

Again at the ninth bar the same change of harmony carries it to the
extreme distance of B flat minor. From this point the theme, in its
new variation, is carried through a passage of energetic action in
which various orchestral groups answer each other, gaining and
yielding ground in rapid sword-play, until a close is about to be
reached in the very key in which the exposition had ended. Here,
however, the theme of figure (d) (from Ex. 2) intervenes, no longer
with its original bold spirit, but in hushed mystery. Then, through
the solemn clouds of Ex. 3, figure (f), the wood-wind utter plaintive fragments of the first theme (a) and its variation, rising through
distant keys in slow chromatic steps, till we reach the very threshold
of our tonic. And here again the theme of figure (d) appears
mysteriously. But it suddenly blazes into passion, and, plunging
again into distant keys, leads to a solemnly heroic close in G sharp
minor. This close, and the fierce passage that leads to it, will be
heard again at the catastrophe of the tragedy.

Now follows a new and very rich variation of the first theme.
As usual the ninth bar, with figure (b), brings a change of harmony, and the figure is passed from voice to voice in a series of
wistful modulations, drifting steadily towards the tonic, E minor,
in a long decrescendo. At last, in slow and solemn semibreves,
we hear the first notes of Ex. 1. The great cloud-figure of Ex. 3 (f)
separates the first two steps of the theme, with all the majesty
of the Norns prophesying the twilight of the Gods. The
rest of the theme is taken up from its fifth bar as if nothing had
happened.

We are now in the full swing of a perfectly regular recapitulation.
A slight change of harmony brings the impassioned transition
theme (ending with Ex. 2) into the tonic, and the whole second
subject with its radiant procession of themes follows in due course.
Only when we approach the triumphant close there is a sudden
catastrophic change of harmony, and we are confronted with a
fiercer version of the sudden outburst of heroic passion which
startled us in the middle of the mysterious part of the development.
This time the climax is evidently going to be greater. Suddenly the
cloud-figure (f) becomes a whirlwind, and the first theme bursts
out fortissimo in the basses, answered by the violins. It is worked
up in its entirety, together with the transition-theme (the unquoted
part) and the whirlwind-figure, into a peroration which, from its
inception to its final grim 'Amen', bears comparison with the
greatest climaxes in classical music, not excluding Beethoven. And
Brahms does not even use trombones for it.

With a heroic call from the horns in a unison, which suggests C
major while emphasizing the tonic note, the andante lifts us from
the world of our tragedy to some ancestral region of legend, the

unforgotten source of the hero's pride. The long and straightforward tune which begins with Ex. 4—

Ex. 4.

is scored with delicious varieties of the blending of sustained tone
with the pizzicato of strings. For all its ballad-like simplicity there
are signs of drama in its structure, and we are not surprised when
the strings' take up the bow with the clear intention of breaking
away from rigid stanzas and leading into the larger flow of a developed sonata movement. Soon the dominant is reached; and an
energetic triplet figure prepares the way for the second subject
which, as Ex. 5 shows, builds its broad melody on an 'augmentation' of it.

Ex. 5.

(b)   &c.   Second Subject.

The continuation seems as if it was going to lead to a crowd of
accessory themes, but it very soon shows signs of drifting back to
the tonic. The drift is slow, and its apparent indecision leads to one
of the most beautiful modulations Brahms or any man ever wrote.
By this modulation the main theme is brought back in the tonic,
with gorgeous new scoring. At the point where it showed signs of
dramatic freedom, there now arises an energetic passage of polyphonic development. This leads to a powerful climax with the
triplet figure of Ex. 5; which subsides quite suddenly, and then
the second subject sails grandly in, with sumptuous harmony
of divided strings. It is being repeated in soaring triumph, when
suddenly it melts into tenderness; a shadow comes over the harmony, and wistful questions from the clarinet and oboe bring
back the close of the first theme with an added sweetness. On its
last note the horns burst out with their opening call, and the conflict between the keys of C and E, implied at the outset, now
appears in full harmony as that solemn splendour which Palestrina
would have recognized as the Phrygian mode, used by him where
doubts and fears are given full expression in order to be convicted
of ignorance by the voice from the whirlwind (e.g. the Motet and
Mass *O magnum mysterium*).

Within six or seven minutes Brahms's third movement, perhaps
the greatest scherzo since Beethoven, accomplishes a form which
you may call either a sonata-rondo or a first movement, according

to the importance you give to the fact that the first six bars of its
theme—

return just between the short second subject—

and the quite fully organized and widely modulating development.
The shortness of the whole movement used to blind critics to its
bigness of design; and at one time people thought it clever to say
that the second subject (Ex. 7) was too slight, a criticism which
would have condemned nearly every second subject in Beethoven's biggest rondos and sonata-form finales, as, no doubt, in
Beethoven's day it did. A slender childish figure for a second
subject is of the very essence of this phase of Brahms's drama; and
nothing can be more quaintly original (or, in the sequel, more
powerful) than the way in which the counter-statement of this
innocent tune is reduced to a staccato outline, as indicated by the
small notes in Ex. 7.

What it throws into higher relief is the tiger-like energy and
spring of the whole movement. Some idea of the terseness and
swiftness of the action may be gained by noting that my first quotation (Ex. 6) contains three complete and sharply contrasted themes.
All three have important variations, one of which I have tried to
indicate by extra tails, while the others I have not space to quote.
The third (c), with its abrupt plunge into E flat, produces two
of the most powerful strokes in the movement; first by means of
the fact that the anxious, mysterious, questioning close of the
development is answered by it, and not by the first theme, as at the
beginning of the recapitulation; and secondly by its triumphant
outburst on the trumpets, for the first and only time in the tonic,
C major, at the end of the movement.

A piccolo, a contra-fagotto, and a triangle contribute with grotesque poetic aptness to the bacchanalian fury of this movement. It is now thought correct to be shocked at Brahms's abuse of the triangle in the only three movements in which he has admitted it to the orchestra. We are told that the triangle is an instrument of the highest poetic power when used for one single stroke in a whole opera, as shown by the wonderful flash of sunlight at the end of the second act of *Siegfried*, and the one note of the triangle in the Vorspiel to *Meistersinger*. The statistics of these miracles are not quite accurately given by the critics, who would forbid Bacchants and processions the free use of triangles and cymbals. After its first entry in the *Meistersinger* Vorspiel Wagner's triangle is almost as shamelessly processional as Brahms's; and there is no restraint on it when Siegfried is forging his sword. Brahms was acutely sensitive to the effect of tones that arrest attention by being on a different plane from that of the normal orchestra. But he may see fit to arrest attention by such tones without thereby becoming obliged to submit to the economics of a music-drama in which the 'effects' have to be distributed over several hours. In fact we know that Brahms occasionally preferred that certain obvious effects should, if used at all, get over their 'effective' shock at once. Thus he projected, but never executed, an orchestral and choral setting of the ballad *Edward*, and proposed that the harps should be prominent at the very beginning 'so that they don't go and make an effect' (*nicht etwa Effekt machen*).

So far, then, this symphony has shown us life and action. These are what its heroism fights for; but the hero is not fighting for his own happiness. He is to die fighting. After what I have said as to the meaning of Brahms's choice of the passacaglia form, little remains but to give the theme—

Ex. 8.

and to catalogue the variations. The listener need not worry as to whether he can trace the theme in the variations. If and where he can, that is well; but beauty is skin-deep, though it does need bones to keep it in shape.

The theme, stated, with trombones, in harmonies too remarkable to be intended to bear repetition, descends angrily with rolling drums and pizzicato chords into the depths of the orchestra (Var. 1), while plaintive melodies crowd above in the wood-wind (Var. 2), rising to a bold reassertion of the theme (Var. 3). Then the violins take up the bow with a striding declamatory melody (Var. 4, theme in bass), which becomes more flowing and is agitated by a lively cross-rhythm in the wood-wind (Vars. 5 and 6). A sharply rhythmic variation follows (Var. 7), and leads to a pair of stormy variations in semiquavers and triplet semiquavers (Vars. 8 and 9). Plaintively the storm subsides into a pathetic dialogue of beautiful sustained harmonies between the violas and the wood-wind (Var. 10). The same harmonies underlie the April sunshine of the next variation (11), and then the time changes to 3/2, twice as slow— which with triple time always produces a momentary sense of cross-rhythm.

Now we have perhaps the most pathetic flute passage since Gluck's wonderful adagio in the Elysian scene of *Orfeo* (Var. 12). The theme, which had been in the bass since Var. 4, is now in the outlines of the melody and the inner parts of the harmony. (I mention this merely as a safeguard against the temptation some listeners feel to hunt for it.) With the next variation (13) the major mode quietly appears, in a pathetic dialogue between clarinet, oboe, and flute. The cadence of this is reproduced in the two next variations (14, 15), which bring the trombones forward with the most pathetic and solemn passage in the whole symphony. When this has died wistfully away on an inconclusive chord, the original theme sternly reappears in the wind-band, to be fiercely cut across by the indignant strings (Var. 16). Then there is a dramatically agitated variation (17), followed by a sonorously determined one (18), which leads to a pair of staccato variations increasing in energy and movement (19, 20). The next (Var. 21) is the most volcanic outburst of all. Suddenly it gives way to a panic-struck and hushed staccato in which Var. 22 hurries by. With Var. 23 the staccato triplets recover courage and strength, working easily up to a climax. This climax is of powerful and unexpected effect, for it gives a sense of big design to the whole movement by making the next two variations (24, 25) reproduce in a blazing *fortissimo* the substance of the first two, while the 26th variation gives in an awe-struck *piano* what the third variation had given boldly. Now two specially graceful variations (27, 28) relieve the tension. Then in the next variation (29) we notice a quiet series of falling thirds which may remind some listeners of the theme of the first movement. I doubt, however, whether this was Brahms's intention, and the doubt does not worry me. At all events this sequence of thirds, taken up energetically in the 30th and last regular variation, seems dramatically to set the ground-bass reeling and staggering to its end, for the rhythm expands and there is an ominous ritardando. Then the theme bursts out with new harmonies in quicker time. Hesitating at the fifth bar, the ground-theme suddenly finds that its second half (bars 5-8) is capable of executing a grand series of modulations (very apposite

after all this confinement to one key), if the bass imitates the treble
at two bars' distance a semitone higher. With this resource, a compressed version of the ground in crotchets, and a pathetic new
derivative therefrom, one of the greatest orchestral works since
Beethoven storms to its tragic close.

SERENADE IN D MAJOR, FOR ORCHESTRA, OP. 11

1 *Allegro molto.* 2 SCHERZO *and* TRIO. *Allegro non troppo.* 3 *Adagio non
troppo.* 4 MENUETTO *I and II.* 5 SCHERZO. *Allegro.* 6 RONDO. *Allegro.*

Brahms's First Serenade is an epoch-making work in a sense that is
little realized. It sins against the first and most ephemeral canon
of modern criticism, the canon which inculcates the artist's duty
to assert his originality in terms so exclusively related to this
week's news as to become unintelligible by the week after next.
The Second Serenade, in A major, op. 16, is a much more acceptable work in an age where the nature and duty of originality are thus
misconceived; but it could not have been written, or at all events
could not have achieved its consistently subtle and intimate style,
without the experience gained in the First Serenade. And the First
Serenade is by no means the kind of school exercise that some critics
have taken it to be. In any age when questions of musical style
are understood like other questions of scholarship, Brahms will be
admired for the wit of the homage he pays to Beethoven's Septet,
Second Symphony, and F major Violin Sonata, in the second
scherzo of this serenade. At present we have hardly yet emerged
from the days when it could be supposed that Brahms did not know
his classics too well to be in doubt as to when and why he was
alluding to them. We now, at all events, know enough of the musical
history of the nineteenth century to realize that Brahms was effecting
a renascence of classical principles. Such a renascence is no matter
of putting new wine into old bottles; the forms are not imposed
upon the material from outside, but they are principles of growth
from within, just as they were in classical times. The modern
environment reacts upon them because they are alive, and this
reaction may be identified by critics as a mixture of styles. But
the critic has not emerged far from the stage of the raw student
if he mistakes the humours of Brahms's First Serenade for the prim-
nesses of an academic exercise. The naïve listener is much more
likely to see the point. It does not depend upon his being able to
give chapter and verse for the influence of Beethoven's early
scherzos; on the contrary, such a capacity is a mere hindrance to
enjoyment, until it has become so ingrained as to produce no more
than an automatic internal chuckle. The real point lies in the
intrinsic quality of the ideas, and in the natural yet surprising

effect of the juxtaposition of childlike themes with adventurous developments.

A very good game may be played between music lovers, if one person quotes the beginning of a piece and the others see how soon they can recognize it. With experienced musicians it is surprising how often the piece can be identified by its first chord, even when this seems quite commonplace. An advanced variety of this game is to ignore as far as possible previous knowledge, and to carry the quotation further, until it is possible to say that the music is of extraordinary quality. When the quality is of the highest order, it is possible to infer from it that the composer who has got thus far will not fail to carry out a great design. We cannot, of course, predict that his great design will have no inequalities; that Wotan's grievances will not put more of Schopenhauer into the second act of *Walküre* than the drama will bear; that Handel will always take the trouble to write his own works, or that, taking that trouble, he will not leave an unconscionably large margin for extemporization. But it is always interesting to fix the attention upon the way in which the quality of the music asserts itself; to see whether a beautiful opening is going to show something more than a gift for epigram; and (to come to the most interesting and difficult cases) to note the point after which a purely formal open-ing, having shown that its composer is a master in a good school, proceeds to prove that it is the shrine of the Olympian Zeus.

The opening of Brahms's First Serenade is an excellent exercise for beginners in this critical game. The drone-bass is one of the richer sounds of the classical orchestra, and already shows that Brahms was well advised in turning the serenade into an orchestral composition instead of leaving it in the state in which it was first performed as a nonet for strings and wind. Above this pastoral drone-bass a horn plays a pastoral theme.

Ex. 1.

(As with a similar theme in the finale, this is how Haydn would have used the horn in his last symphony if he could have trusted the horn-players of London in 1795. But as they were by no means the virtuoso horn-players of Esterhaz, they ventured upon their theme only under the shelter of a full orchestral tutti, leaving it to the violins in quieter passages.) Brahms shifts his drone-bass

to the dominant, and the theme is transferred to the clarinet. It
seems in no hurry; but suddenly the bass shifts to G. The transition is not beyond the bounds of classic wit, but it is abrupt
beyond the immediate expectation of the opening; and the next
step down to F sharp defines the scope of the wit, and shows that
the range of harmony and tonality is that of the later and not of
the earlier nineteenth century. The process reaches a climax which
shows that the work is to be on a large scale. How large we do
not yet know, but the proportions are already noble, and show a
freedom that ought to have convicted of error those critics who
explained Brahms as an imitator of Schumann. But they were preoccupied with the discovery that the opening theme, like most of
the themes in Mozart's Jupiter Symphony, was lacking in originality.

This climax is marked by a new theme on the dominant of B
minor.

Its continuation leads to a tutti counter-statement of Ex. 1,
glorified by Beethovenish high trumpets and modulating to the
dominant, from which the bass takes a new turn, passing through
F sharp minor and C sharp minor, to return from that remote
region abruptly to the tonic. Here Ex. 2 appears, and for the
moment we have an impression of a structure frequent in the first
works of Brahms's maturity, very large in its immediate impression,
but needing all Brahms's caution to prevent it from forming a completeness of its own that may prove destructive to the completeness
of the whole. Here that danger is averted, inasmuch as Ex. 2 now
proves to be not on the tonic at all, but to be running down the
dominant seventh of the key of A, thus presenting the old classical
feature known as 'dominant preparation' in a very drastic form.
Not less bold is the way in which the last two notes are turned
into the accompaniment to the main theme of the second group.
Theme and accompaniment are alike the quintessence of Brahms.

No one before Brahms had attempted musical sentences of such range; and Brahms alone developed a means of continuing them without stiffness or obscurity. Two short cadence-themes complete the exposition. The first is repeated with an expansion by echoes in a manner first invented by Brahms. The second—

Ex. 4:

is also repeated, and expanded by development. In its expanded counter-statement it is combined with a derivative of Ex. 3 in the bass. The exposition is repeated, and the repeat should be observed as an essential feature of the style. In spite of the great breadth of the design it is not inordinately long, and the tempo is exceptionally quick for Brahms.

The development begins by discussing Ex. 4, which leads to the remote key of C sharp minor. Here a new derivative of Ex. 1 appears. It is another kind of transformation invented by Brahms, and having the value of a spontaneous new idea.

Ex. 5:

Another novel transformation in double counterpoint bursts out hilariously in D flat (C sharp) major, and afterwards with reversed scoring in B flat—

Ex. 6:

alternating with another version combined with the figure of Ex. 3.

Then the untransformed first theme (as in Ex. 1) appears in the full orchestra in G, and is broadly developed, especially as to its second figure (*b*), modulating widely and quickly till it reaches a climax in D minor, a key which, being the home tonic, subsides on to the home dominant. On this, a long passage of preparation, punctuated by the rhythmic figure ♩ | ♩ ♩ | ○ , slowly leads to the return of Ex. 1 in the tonic, with sunset glow from the subdominant. In this key the clarinet continues the recapitulation, which is easily brought into its normal course, comprising everything from Ex. 2 to Ex. 4 in the tonic. The coda is grafted into Ex. 4 without break. Beginning in triumph it dies away in one of the wittiest pianissimo exits since Haydn.

The first scherzo is an important movement with typically Brahmsish themes, of which the opening—

Ex. 7.

Sempre piano.

afterwards goes into close canon. It flows into another idea, as the quotation shows; and later on it gives rise to a more lyric phrase.

Ex. 8.

cres.

mf

The trio is a little quicker, and consists of a broad, symmetrical melody—

Ex. 9.

&c.

lounging in 8-bar periods over a bass that had been set swinging by the last two notes of the scherzo. The repeats of both parts are written out in full, the winds and strings having exchanged parts.

In the slow movement Brahms writes in full sonata form with
second group, a big development, a full recapitulation, and a large
coda. He never did this again; in all his later slow movements, if
he approaches to sonata form in some features, he shortens it in
some others. Yet the present movement is not inordinately long:
the only question is whether *adagio* is not a misleading tempo-
mark for it, even with the qualification *non troppo*. Certainly there
is no part of it that would not be obviously ruined by dragging,
and the details are perfectly consistent with a flowing tempo
throughout. The listener, not taking the trouble to observe that
the conductor is beating quavers, will certainly think the first
theme very broad, with its shadowy turtle-dove crooning—

Ex. 10.

and its sequel not less broad, with its brighter colour and imitative dialogue.

Ex. 11.

Brahms alternates this pair in a miniature binary scheme which
saves itself from premature completeness by expanding and closing
into a new transition-theme.

Ex. 12.

This owes much of its inspiration and quality of tone to the brook
in Beethoven's Pastoral Symphony; and it flows into a wide river,
passing through a remote key into a peaceful lake. Here, in the
dominant, reached through a remote key, we have the main theme
of a big second group.

Ex. 13.

This, also a paragraph of grand breadth, leads to another
big imitative theme in Brahms's most majestic and personal
style.

The exposition closes with a short cadence-group in counterpoint over the main figure of his theme. A spacious development
concerns itself first with Ex. 14; then with a peaceful rumination
on Ex. 13. This leads to the remote key of B major, really C flat.
And in this key the main theme, Ex. 10, enters in full, followed
after a moment's hesitation by Ex. 11. Before this reaches its first
close, it discovers that the home tonic is not so remote after all,
and so the counter-statement of both themes follows at home,
Ex. 11 being now richly varied. Its end gives rise to a debate which
eventually leads to the transition-theme Ex. 12, now flowing in
home channels. Ex. 13 sails upon it triumphantly, and the rest
of the recapitulation follows without further change. A quiet
coda alludes to the treatment of Ex. 14 towards the end of the
development.

The tiny pair of minuets (scored practically for the instruments
of the nonet which was the original form of this serenade) has
always been a popular orchestral trifle. In its rightful place it will
be still better appreciated. The second scherzo needs no quotation.
The more risky (*sittenverderblich*) features of the scherzo of Beethoven's Septet and Second Symphony have been bowdlerized in the
main body; and the trio of the scherzo of Beethoven's F major
Violin Sonata has been kept in order by Brahms's wind-band, led
by the horns.

The final rondo is on a grand scale, with a big rondo theme in
three strains of the usual A B A form for such members.

Ex. 16.

The epigrammatic twist in the 3rd and 4th bars of Ex. 16 is characteristic of many other simple-seeming utterances in this dangerous
work. Still more dangerous is the theme of the first episode or
second group. Its point is not that, like all possible horn-themes,
it reminds us of the first movement, but that where it seems to
repeat itself the repetition is at a different rhythmic place. This
makes a zeugma or syllepsis of the form typified by 'the lady left
in tears and a sedan chair'. Further, it consists of two themes in
double counterpoint.

Ex. 17.

The second episode develops the two themes of Ex. 17 independently, beginning in an unexpected key thus—

Ex. 18.

A short circuit is made, eliminating a third entry of the rondo
theme and leading to a recapitulation of the first episode, in which
the themes of Ex. 17 are interchanged in position and the triplet
theme varied in semiquavers.

Ex. 19.

After this the expected return of the main theme is, for a few surprising bars, in the minor. But it soon brightens to major, and a magnificent coda broadens out in triumph, introducing several further transformations, and trailing clouds of glory to the end.

SERENADE IN A MAJOR FOR SMALL ORCHESTRA, OP. 16

1 *Allegro moderato*. 2 SCHERZO. *Vivace*. 3 *Adagio non troppo*. 4 *Quasi Menuetto*. 5 RONDO. *Allegro*.

Brahms wrote his first serenade in 1858, and his second, the present work, in 1859. The instrumental serenade of Mozart and Haydn is, at its largest, a symphony in cheerful style with a large number of movements, sometimes including a kind of intercalary concerto which counts as a separate work. Thus Mozart's Haffner Serenade has, besides a second minuet among its five symphonic movements, three large movements in concerto style with a solo violin; and his next largest serenade ('with the post-horn') has a concertante of two movements for a group of solo wind instruments. Not all serenades are so large; many contain no highly developed movements. A divertimento is supposed to be a serenade for a few solo instruments not constituting an orchestra; but the distinction is not clearly maintained. Mozart gives the name of serenade to his three largest works for wind instruments alone, though one of them is in perfectly regular form and was simply called a quintet when he arranged it as a string quintet. There is no accepted name for a piece for thirteen instruments; and perhaps Mozart had not heard of the word 'octet' as a current term, so this may account for his calling his C minor Octet a serenade.

Brahms's First Serenade, in D major, op. 11, was first written as a nonet, and accordingly called a divertimento. But it was immediately recast for 'grosses Orchester'. The term 'full orchestra' implies the use of trumpets and drums; trombones are not necessary for the title; but without trumpets and drums the orchestra ranks as 'small'. The D major Serenade contains much that is quintessentially Brahms, and also much that is ostentatiously reminiscent of early Beethoven—the Beethoven of the Septet. Every age has its own central criterion of art; and each later age sees how its predecessor's criterion was misleading. In the eighteenth century our central criterion was correctness. We are emerging from an age in which the central criterion is originality, a much less fruitful concept. Correctness may be wrongly defined and wrongly valued; but it will always refer to ascertainable things, and the mistakes in its use will be witnesses available for cross-examination as to the truth. Originality is a concept which everybody can apply without control, while nobody can judge of it unless he knows every possible antecedent of the work he is criticizing. After a century it becomes unrecognizable: unless the power of extended composition is shown, there is not an expert living who can tell Handel from Buononcini by ear; and the contemporary poet was quite right in summing up the Handel-Buononcini controversy in the lines—

> Strange that such difference there should be
> 'Twixt Tweedledum and Tweedledee.

Permanent values depend on more ascertainable things than the question, who told the truth first. The artist's conviction of the truth is not to be weakened by such a question; the poet can call the sky blue, or even rhyme 'dove' with 'love', if these details are the right things in the right place. The quality of the style line by line, and the power to organize the work as a whole, these things will remain, though 'tea' cease to rhyme with 'obey', and though the embargo be removed that forbids the poet of to-day to apply the epithet 'blooming' to his mistress's cheek. Meanwhile it is extremely doubtful whether any valuable criticism, or any artistic principle whatever, has been pronounced by people who take originality for their criterion. They do not even make significant mistakes: they fail to touch permanent values at any point; and their judgements will be merely unintelligible a generation hence. But this useless criterion still dominates us to such an extent that a performance of Brahms's First Serenade is a risky undertaking for a conductor who cares for the fashion of to-day. I have produced it; and shall produce it again if and when I dare. But there is no danger in producing the Second Serenade. It ranks high among Brahms's works for mellowness of style, and for the number of peculiar features in whole and in detail. It was coldly received in Germany, but had extraordinary success at its first performances in England, which took place before Brahms's symphonies had come into existence. Since then it has dropped out of the ordinary concert repertory, being quite as difficult as the symphonies, and very quiet and intimate in style.

The 'small orchestra' has a full complement of wood-wind and two horns, but no violins. At the beginning of the nineteenth century Méhul wrote a rather beautiful opera, *Uthal*, on an Ossianic subject; and, in order to obtain an atmosphere of Northern mystery and fog, used no violins. Musical historians usually tell us that the result was monotonous, and that Grétry cried 'Five francs for an E string!' But they omit to mention that the opera was only in one act. It is, in fact, not much longer than Brahms's Second Serenade. Brahms is hardly likely, at the age of 26, to have read *Uthal*, though Joachim produced it many years later in Berlin. If the sound of violas as leaders came to Brahms from any source but his own imagination, he may have heard it in the second act of *Tannhäuser*, during the ascetic praises of love which exasperate Tannhäuser into revealing his mortal sin. But Brahms's intention in this Serenade differs from that of all previous examples of the absence of violins. As in *Uthal*, the tone of the violas is dark and veiled, and has its own value accordingly; but its main purpose is to throw the wind into high relief. Thus the Serenade is a work mainly for wind instruments, which are treated with the utmost fullness and variety of tone, while they are at the same time relieved from the burden of supplying their own background. Brahms took great pains over this work and set great store by opportunities for an adequate performance. Composed in 1859, it was twice revised, first in 1860, to what extent I do not know, and again in 1875. The revision of 1875 concerns only a few details of scoring.

The first movement, in normal sonata form, begins with a pair of contrasted themes, of which the first—

Ex. 1.

establishes the tonic, and leads to the second—

Ex. 2.

which emphasizes the dominant chord with minor colouring. A counter-statement shifts Ex. 1 into the subdominant, and brings Ex. 2 on to the dominant of the dominant key, which key it establishes fully, leading to a second group containing two new themes. The first of these, swaying indolently over a dance-rhythm—

Ex. 3.

is one of those long paragraphs in which Brahms, from his very first works onwards, showed an inventiveness and mastery that amounted to new resources in musical architecture. The second is a quiet cadence-theme, still accompanied by the same dance-rhythm.

Ex. 4.

The development, starting with the eight bars of Ex. 1, as if to repeat the exposition, works Ex. 2 into an imbroglio which modulates widely and comes to a climax in F. This dies down with a sudden drop into D flat, where Ex. 1 is resumed and combined in new ways with Ex. 2. The first two notes (a) of Ex. 1 become accelerated into an oscillation, first in crotchets, then in triplets, which settles down as a steady accompaniment. Again we have covered a wide range of key, from which an oboe brings us back with a long-drawn strain which lands us on a tonic pedal. This pedal is on our home-tonic—though we may not at first be sure of the fact. But it is a great moment when we first reach it as the beginning of a dialogue—

Ex. 5.

that lasts for no less than twenty-six bars, and then, by drifting into the recapitulation, reveals to us that we have been at home all this time.

The recapitulation is quite regular. The coda begins with Ex. 1 in F major on the strings, with a beautiful new counterpoint on the oboe. In the course of a very expressive dialogue the bass drifts downwards. The climax of emotion brings us back to the home tonic, and the bass thence descends in terms of Ex. 3, while figure (a) makes slow cadences in dialogue until the movement dies away.

A tiny little scherzo displays great energy with cross-rhythmed epigrams in the key of C.

Ex. 6.

Its main rhythmic figure underlies the quieter but not less epigrammatic trio.

The slow movement, though not long, is one of the most elaborate things Brahms ever wrote. Its main section moves on a ground bass—

which, like those in some of Bach's slow movements, from time to time changes its key. After eight rotations have brought us to a full close in C major, an episode begins with dramatic modulations.

These modulations lead to the extremely remote key of A flat, on the dominant of which a horn bursts out surprisingly with a passionately triumphant urgency.

Two new themes follow in tonic positions. The first—

includes in its paragraph an inversion of the ground-bass figure.

The second I do not quote. It is given out by the clarinet and answered by the basses, and its close finishes the central episode.

The ground-bass reappears in C minor as a fugue-subject, answered in syncopated inversion and developed closely in modulating sequences. After a climax, the first of its original counterpoints (unquoted) appears in the horn, and is carried up through three steps of modulating sequence which bring us to the home tonic, where the original counterpoint is delivered in the manner of a return to the opening. At first, however, the ground-bass is 'diminished' to a quaver figure of accompaniment in the violas. But it soon resumes its original shape, and the movement is rounded off by the recurrence, in the home tonic with subdominant colour, of the counterpoint which had led to the close in C before the episode.

The *Quasi Menuetto*, in D major, brings the mellow mood of the whole serenade to its full ripeness.

The initial figure (*a*) of the main theme—

set at a different harmonic angle, underlies the whole of the mysterious and plaintive trio.

In the final rondo the mood changes to one of child-like high spirits. It is the childlike quality that keeps the rollicking details in touch with the thoughtfulness of the rest. The triplet figure (*c*) of the main theme—

is pure merry-go-round; but it is the merry-go-round as enjoyed by the child, not as exposed by the realist. A transition-theme in imitative dialogue—

leads to the main theme of the first episode, which is more reflective in its Mendelssohnian way. (Brahms saw no reason to suppose that Mendelssohn's idioms were inherently bad.)

It is elusive in its rhythm, sometimes, as here at the outset, dating its period before its first note, and sometimes making its first note an anacrusis to the rest, so that the first clause is three bars instead of four. (A still more complex rhythmic quibble characterizes the first episode of the finale of the D major Serenade, in a theme which has often been accused of being quite unoriginal.) A feature of the second episode is the augmentation of the rollicking main theme into a quiet ruminating passage in D major.

A piccolo is added to the orchestra of this finale, and is used with a recklessness about which Brahms does not seem to have felt squeamish, since he left it in evidence after two careful revisions at intervals of fifteen years. Presumably his standard of performance was high, and piccolos were not supposed to squeal without restraint, even if their parts were marked like those of less democratic instruments.

VARIATIONS FOR ORCHESTRA ON A THEME BY HAYDN, OP. 56*a*

The theme of this work comes from an unpublished Divertimento by Haydn for wind-band. The theme is inscribed *Corale
St. Antonii*, a fact which tells us nothing, but which has led that
otherwise attractively enthusiastic and well-informed biographer,
Kalbeck, to read into Brahms's variations a musical description of
the temptation of St. Anthony. Brahms did not live to see this
outrage on one of his most serenely beautiful monuments to the
joy of sanity. But if intimacy with a diamond so true and so
rough as Brahms could not scarify the nonsense out of his accredited
biographer, we can at least give an independent listening to the
music. It is quite as imaginative as any masterpiece that ever dealt
with St. Anthony's trials; but whatever the temptations it deals with
they never endangered the soul or the reason of saint or sinner.

It is difficult to describe in words the shape of a beautiful
vase or building; but nobody would think worse of the object
because the description is necessarily statistical and dry. Now it so
happens that, apart from what instinct can give, by far the best
way to obtain definite musical insight into the variations of
Beethoven and Brahms is to grasp the form and proportions of
their themes. Form and proportion are dull things to describe,
but in music they produce such important subjects of instinctive
enjoyment as tunefulness and swing. And in such sets of
variations as Beethoven and Brahms delighted in, the swing of
the theme, as conveyed in its rhythmic form, is all-important.
The tunefulness is important in another and somewhat paradoxical way. If the theme happens (as in the present case) to be
a specially beautiful melody, well and good; but mere embroidery
of the most beautiful melody will soon become more tiresome than
any number of plain repetitions, if the melody has no such 'swing'
as repetition or variation may enhance. On the other hand, the
most grotesque bare bass may make an ideal theme for variations,
when the composer has Beethoven's grasp of form; as we may see
in the finale of the Eroica Symphony. And one effect of this grasp
of form is to set the 'tunefulness' free in the variations; there is no
more need for them to keep on reminding us of the original melodic
surface of the theme, than there is for birds of paradise to remind
us of crows because the anatomist knows that that is what they are.

The listener need not try to recognize Haydn's melody throughout Brahms's variations: he will have no difficulty in doing so
wherever Brahms wishes; and an elaborate analysis would show
something like a nervous system of melodic connexions. But the
best way to enjoy these is to become familiar with the whole work.
To begin with the finishing touches is not the best way to enjoy the

whole. In music, as in all art that moves in time, the listener should fix his attention on some element that pervades the whole, not upon some guess as to the course of events. In a set of classical variations the all-pervading element is the shape of the whole theme. How its external details may be treated is a matter of decoration and wit. The promise of life is not there, but in the Vision of Dry Bones.

No musical quotations are needed here beyond Haydn's theme, the bones of which I give completely, as follows:

Ex. 1.

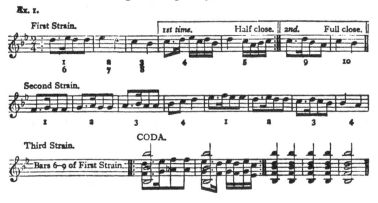

Like a bell the solemn last five notes of this coda toll from beginning to end throughout the first variation (poco più animato). This does not mean that the real order of events in the theme is altered, it simply shows that the surface-melody is now completely free to discuss in any order whatever topics are suggested by Haydn's theme, or added to it by the variations; meanwhile, in each variation you will still be borne irresistibly along by the same peculiar momentum of the three strains: the first, of five bars ending in a half-close repeated with the substitution of a full-close; second, of four rising bars answered by four falling bars ending on a half-close; the third, of the last half of the first strain closing into a coda consisting of twice two bars and the five tolling chords. This description is as dry as the description of the Spenserian stanza, but the forms themselves are among the loveliest resources in music and poetry.

The second variation (più vivace, in the minor mode) discusses the details of the first with some temper; the third variation (con moto) is peaceful and flowing.

With the fourth variation (andante con moto; 3/8 time, in the minor), we have a pair of new melodies, melancholy, simple, and smooth. No one would guess that their combination is of an order of counterpoint which, at the beginning of the second strain, reaches to a development which the severest scholastic theorists

have declared to be unattainable. It *is* unattainable by conscious
calculation; but in great art these things happen, and the art is at
no pains to conceal them—on the contrary, it owes its apparent
simplicity to the fact that they are effective where less highly
organized processes would be awkward. The fifth and sixth
variations (vivace 6/8, and vivace 2/4) are brilliant from the outset
of the fifth to the rousing close of the sixth. The seventh variation
(grazioso 6/8) is the crowning point of new melody and new
lusciousness. Those who play this work in what is better called
its co-equal form rather than its arrangement for two pianofortes,
will know more of its gorgeous wealth of detail than any one
orchestral performance will ever bring out; but it is characteristic
of all classical polyphony, as we may see in the Eroica and Jupiter
Symphonies, that while no two performances will bring out the
same set of details, no performance need sound obscure or incomplete. Nature herself has more details than one aspect of
light reveals in a scene, but the scene may be complete in any
aspect.

The eighth variation (presto non troppo 3/4) is again in the
minor, and strikes the only dark and mysterious note in the work.
When it has hurried by in whispering awe, we hear the first five
bars of Haydn's theme as a solemn ground-bass harmonized in
ecclesiastical style; and in this charmed five-bar circle the finale
(andante ₵) moves—

Ex. 2.

through various phases of triumph and meditation, until suddenly
(as in Schumann's first symphony) the sound of a triangle and the
stirring of busy life throughout the orchestra remind us of 'the
spring-time, the only pretty ring-time'. Then the charmed circle
expands into the full sweep of Haydn's third strain, and the
glorious tune crowns everything until the last bell-strokes toll high
and deep.

AKADEMISCHE FESTOUVERTÜRE, OP. 80

A student-song intimately associated with beer-mugs—

leads to mysterious stratagems and spoils—

until with the dawn of major harmony the mischief shows itself to
be unadulterated high spirits with the promise of dignity when
occasion shall demand it.

For the moment, however, dignity is not encouraged; the strutting
theme is turned into mock-mystery again, and the first theme is
resumed. But now it dies away into real solemnity; and the spirit
of Alma Mater is manifested in the old student-song, *Wir haben
gebauet ein stattliches Haus.*

And out of this the high spirits of youth arise in their full athletic
dignity in the following triumphant derivative of the mysterious
first theme, which builds itself into the phrases of the solemn song.

Though the time-signature is changed from 2/2 to 4/4 there is no decided change of tempo; Brahms's intention is merely that the accents should be heavier and more frequent.

The first figure of this derivative then settles down to calm activity and modulates with dignity to the bright key of E major, where another old student-song swings in with an aristocratic energy and grace imparted to it by Brahms's invention of holding its top note in a higher octave while the tune continues below.

Ex. 6.

This, which we may call the second subject, drifts towards G major, where, with the aid of the Great Bassoon Joke, the song *Was kommt dort von der Höh'* inaugurates the harmless ragging of the guileless freshman.

Ex. 7.

The tune is allowed to continue for one odd bar, when it is run away with by other instruments. Soon the fat is in the fire. Conciliatory strains nevertheless indicate that all is essentially peace—

Ex. 8.

followed by

but the ribald song, like the cheerfulness of Dr. Johnson's friend Edwards,[1] breaks into the philosophy and leads to a catastrophic irruption of Ex. 2 in full fury. From this point the overture recapitulates everything in the tonic, dealing freely and tempestuously with Exs. 2, 3, 4, and 5. This recapitulation makes a great mock-mystification of its dealings with the claims of Ex. 3 to self-respect, and it does not repeat the solemn entry of Ex. 4. The second subject (Ex. 6) is given in C major, unaltered except that its modulations are not allowed to drift away. The Great Bassoon Joke is omitted as a thing that cannot work a second time; so the peaceful phrases of Ex. 8 now have no mockery behind them, though, as before, cheerfulness breaks in. This time it leads to a tune which every audience presumably knows, and so with a solemn full orchestration of *Gaudeamus igitur* the overture ends.

---

[1] Edwards has broken into these essays already some five times, and will break in again. The reader has been warned that these volumes are not designed for continuous reading.

TRAGIC OVERTURE, OP. 81

For one reason and another, the popular musical judgements of the last thirty or forty years seem often to show less grasp of the nature of tragedy than might be expected where the fine arts are taken seriously. It is to be hoped that the day is not distant when it will be thought strange that so thorough a musician as Weingartner should endorse the once widespread doubt whether Brahms's Tragic Overture deserves its name, and when Tchaikovsky shall be duly applauded for his wisdom in calling his last symphony *pathetic*, though it was at first universally acclaimed as tragic.

Without troubling to go as far back as Aristotle, we may safely say that if there is any use in the special term 'tragedy', the term implies something more sublime than pathos. When we try to define this sublime element, we instantly run counter to a large current of prejudice, which every age has regarded as its own modern unconventionality, though it belongs to the childhood of every human mind. This prejudice impels us to talk of the classic dignity and reserve of a truly tragic work of art when we wish to do it justice, and to talk of classical (or even of 'academic') coldness when we are out of temper with it. The truth would seem to be that the word 'reserve' already indicates far too negative a view of the whole matter. It is not academic coldness that makes Shakespeare close the tragedy of *Hamlet* in the triumph of Fortinbras; nor is it warmth of feeling that makes Garrick bring down the curtain on the moment of Hamlet's death. Shakespeare is far from despising the interests of the actor; he writes well for his instruments; but they are not going to prevent him from giving us the one final proof that the Hamlet whom we have been privileged to see in self-confessed weakness was not a successful actor-manager, but a man whose foes knew him for a soldier who as king would have 'proved right royally'.

Impressions of formality, and even of anti-climax, whether in music or in tragedy, are often by no means frigid in their ultimate results. We have been taken into an idealized world, and before we leave it we are made to understand that what we have been shown in it was really true. We have not been regaled by a mere feast of effects with 'no dull moments, and the best reserved for the end'; still less have we had a story told us by a narrator who stands outside and points the moral or tells us what to admire. The story, the music, the art, each is made to convince us of its own reality, and the means by which it so convinces us are not merely those which rouse our emotion, but also those which show that we were justly moved. True art gives us more than the artist's word for his capacity to understand or believe in his own sentiments.

Brahms's Tragic Overture is certainly not written at the dictation of any one tragedy, either in literature or in his own experience; and any tragic characters of which it may remind us can be safely regarded only as our own illustrations of its meaning. On this understanding, we may legitimately compare Brahms's energetic but severely formal conclusion with Shakespeare's Fortinbras, not as a course of events, but as an aesthetic fact; and there is no harm in comparing the mysterious and pathetic development (molto più moderato, in the middle of the work) with the Fool in *King Lear*, or perhaps with some frightened child, the burden of whose. grief is not 'what will become of me?' but 'what ought I to be doing?'

The order of events in this overture is as follows. After two powerful chords which embody one of the principal figures of the themes, a noble subject is stated by the strings, rising swiftly to an uprush of energy, and followed by a counter-statement in the full orchestra.

(All groups of notes bracketed under a letter, as [a], [b], are separately used in new developments and derivatives of the main themes.)

Ex. 1.

A procession of energetic and terse new themes follows, including one that has an important formal function, playing, as it were, the part of Fortinbras.

Ex. 2.

Soon there is a dramatic crescendo, in which the basses, giving a fragment (*b*) of the first theme in a rising series of questions, are passionately answered by the wind-instruments (*c*). This culminates in a decisive close to the first subject, a close which will eventually prove to be at the root of the whole tragedy.

Ex. 3.

Then comes a sustained passage beginning in utter dejection, the broken utterances of an isolated oboe being sternly answered by the horns. The oboe nevertheless rises into the upper light while the clouds darken below. We are now in an extremely remote major key; and through the solemn darkness a message of peace comes from the trombones while the glow brightens above.

Ex. 4.

And so we reach what is commonly called the second subject. This begins with an aspiring melody, full of passion and comfort.

Ex. 5.

It rises to a magnificent climax of pride, and ends defiantly with some of the terse sequels of the first subject, notably Ex. 2. Then we return to the opening: the powerful short chords and the first theme (Ex. 1). The continuation of this, however, turns into a passage of solemn mystery, and leads to the long più moderato (already described), which has the musical function of the development, and the dramatic function of throwing an unexpectedly pathetic light on those traits of the first theme which have hitherto been liveliest.

Ex. 6.

Upon this descends, in muted violins, the solemn message of peace which we have once before heard from the trombones (Ex. 4). It is now in the tonic major instead of in a remote key. The impassioned second subject (Ex. 5) follows, in accordance with principles of form which are no scholastic conventions to hamper an inspired composer, but are to this music what the laws of human probability are to the dramatist. The proud climax and defiant close of the second subject are a natural preparation for the coda, which gathers up the remaining threads of the story in a catastrophe clearly represented by the solemn emphasis with which the trombones bring in the 'decisive close to the first subject' (Ex. 3). As the trombones have played so personal a part throughout the work, Brahms is not going to degrade them to the conventional function of adding more volume of tone to the last chords. Hence they are silent in the conclusion, where the most formal of the energetic accessory themes (Ex. 2) shows us the poet's conviction that tragedy is more deeply pathetic in daylight than in limelight.

A FURTHER NOTE ON BRAHMS'S TRAGIC OVERTURE (OP. 81)

It is some time since Brahms has definitely come into his own and escaped from the dangerous championship of the anti-Wagnerian Brahmsian, as well as from the helpless fulminations of the people whose only approach to music is through the theatre and literature. But certain features of Brahms's style still seem to lie beyond the range of current criticism. In recent judgements of the Tragic Overture, I cannot trace the slightest progress in intelligence since the days when it was a new work. My analysis of it, as issued by me at Reid Concerts, and as now published by the Oxford University

Press (see above), began with a discussion of the meaning of tragedy in music and literature. This was rash. I was as helpless as Huckleberry Finn arguing with Jim the nigger. Cats have a right to talk like cats; but Frenchmen, being men, ought to talk like other people. And so Brahms ought to write Russian music. Let's begin again on a clean slate.

Ex. 1.

The main difficulty in appreciating Brahms's right to call this greatest of his orchestral movements tragic seems to me to lie in current ignorance of the meaning of his language. In Ex. 1, the two figures marked (*e*) and (*f*) are the real stumbling-blocks to most critics and many conductors. They are lively figures, and the treatment of fig. (*e*) in the *più moderato* development is child-like. In *Coriolanus*, the boy Marcus makes us laugh at one of the tensest moments of the drama. We have enough faith in Shakespeare to believe that this is not an oversight, and we do not insist upon having the boy represented with a Roman nose as developed as that of his father. Current notions of tragic values in music are less advanced.

The other unappreciated aspect of Brahms's style concerns his most characteristic ruminating passages: such things as the development of the finale of the Second Symphony, and almost the whole of the finale of the C minor Pianoforte Quartet. There was a time when, under the guidance of John Hullah, Bach was regarded as a monumental composer with a style entirely devoid of expression, but 'unique', as Hullah said, 'like the Pyramids, in the quality of being satisfactory'. Many of us can recollect with affection some dutiful and venerable music-lover who, at the prospect of listening to Bach, would say 'Yes, Bach is so SATISFACTORY' before closing her eyes. It is an unfortunate fact that Brahms's profoundest ruminating developments and episodes are inevitably woven in a close contrapuntal texture which is very interesting to analyse and very much like the most elaborate textures of Bach. Experience has taught me simply to withhold the analysis of such passages altogether so long as the view prevails that all such things are inherently pedantic. It is, of course, foolish to suppose ingenuity to be more than a practical necessity for the construction of such passages. But it is worse than childish to suppose that the necessary ingenuity is a sign of pedantry.

This prejudice has now attained such a vogue that it has become worse than the silliness of the listener and critic who can understand music only in terms of literary and pictorial illustration. All good musicians hate the practice of illustrating purely instrumental music by other objects, and we musicians have even acquired an habitual resentment against any tendency to lay stress upon the musical illustration of words, even when the words or dramatic actions are essential to the very existence of the music. I have often protested against the habit of digesting Beethoven with the aid of a diet of Carlyle's *French Revolution* relieved by doses of *The Scarlet Pimpernel*; but there comes a point when the persistent decrying of such a work as Brahms's Tragic Overture must be met by propaganda more popular than an attempt to explain pure music to people who greatly prefer it impure. I find that the middle part of the overture is considered unintelligibly dry, and that many conductors have grave doubts as to whether Brahms can possibly have meant it to be taken twice as slow as the rest. Perhaps listeners so prejudiced may get some idea of what I take to be Brahms's intention if they will remind themselves of the character of Grizel in *Sentimental Tommy*, with particular reference to the passages where she is described as persistently prying upon the laying-out of a corpse because she knows that her outcast mother, the 'painted lady', is dying, and that she herself had better practise betimes a task in which she does not wish for the help of the scornful. I had not read *Sentimental Tommy* when I had the good fortune to get my first impressions of the Tragic Overture from a perfect performance under Steinbach at Meiningen in 1899; but I was then deeply impressed by the mysterious purposefulness of its quiet development and the overpowering pathos of its musical consequences in the recapitulation. Joachim had all the absolute musician's horror of gratuitous literary illustration, but Brahms did not snub him for comparing the finale of the Third Symphony with the story of Hero and Leander; and I do not think, if I had been able to show Brahms this passage in *Sentimental Tommy*, that he would have snubbed me. I had forgotten all about it when I wrote of the frightened child whose thought was 'what ought I to do?'

BRUCKNER

ROMANTIC SYMPHONY IN E FLAT MAJOR, NO. 4

1 *Ruhig bewegt.* 2 *Andante.* 3 SCHERZO. *Bewegt: with* TRIO: *Gemächlich.* 4 FINALE. *Mässig bewegt, alternating with a tempo twice as slow.*

Of the childlike rustic person that Anton Bruckner was apart from his music there are anecdotes without number and without form. They should be told where his music is understood. In these British Islands Bruckner has not yet come into his own; and we had better concentrate upon his music for the present. Bruckner was a helpless person in worldly and social matters; a pious Roman Catholic humbly obedient to his priest, and at ease neither in Zion nor in the apartments the Emperor of Austria assigned to him in his palace in Vienna. But the musical party politicians who honoured Wagner with their patronage felt that *das Allkunstwerk* of Bayreuth lacked a writer of symphonies. And they found their desideratum in Bruckner, whose third symphony was dedicated to Wagner, and whose symphonies always began with Rheingold harmonic breadths and ended with Götterdämmerung climaxes.

Meanwhile Brahms was working out his own salvation, in ways that no Wagnerian could understand. For Brahms the aesthetic system of Bayreuth was the affair of one composer whose style had only a special relation to the whole art of music. To be a Wagnerian symphonist was no more an ambition of Brahms than to be an agnostic pope or a breeder of St. Bernard dachshunds. The devout Brucknerite, regarding Bruckner's 'pyramidal' and 'lapidary' structures as the result of the mating of Beethoven's Ninth Symphony with *Götterdämmerung*, thought Brahms's ideas ridiculously small. (I must specifically say *Beethoven's* Ninth Symphony, for Bruckner's ninth is *also* in D minor, and *also* begins with a tremolo from which rhythmic fragments build themselves up into a mighty unison.)

The 'Brahminen', on the other hand, if they troubled to express a printable opinion, could fairly say that size does not become proportion until it is differentiated; and that Bruckner's proportions were not masterly. And in this matter the Brahminen had the advantage that they knew what they were talking about; whereas the Wagnerians evidently did not. As far as the composers were concerned, we need not expect a fair judgement from either of them. Brahms was never satisfied with less than complete mastery in his own work, and destroyed fully half of what he wrote.

How then should he, who seemed to his friends to be too severe
with himself, trouble to see the merits of a style not only more
foreign to him than Wagner's, but obviously clumsy in matters
where Wagner was masterly? Bruckner, on the other hand, had
none of Brahms's capacity for overcoming all initial social disadvantages; he impressed people as, apart from his music, a rather
cringing and puzzle-headed man whc had neither education nor
the desire for it. He tipped Richter a thaler for conducting the
Romantic Symphony, and displayed excited concern at a public
banquet when he received a telegram from a practical joker telling
him that the Bulgarians had chosen him for their king, and were
clamouring for his presence. The carrying out of his vast symphonic conceptions was quite enough occupation for him, without
the burden of understanding other kinds of art which interested
persons who were anything but kind to him.

What the two masters thought or said of each other is no more
evidence than 'what the soldier said'. It ought to be treated as
private conversation. But Hanslick, who constituted himself the
official leader of the Brahminen, saw in Bruckner fair game.
Wagner gave Hanslick only too lenient a treatment when he im-
mortalized him in Beckmesser, named Hans Lich in the first sketch
of the poem of *Meistersinger*. Beckmesser at all events knew the
rules he so humbly adored. I have read Hanslick's collected works
patiently without discovering either in his patronage of Brahms or
in his attacks on Wagner, Verdi, Bruckner, the early works of
Beethoven, Palestrina's *Stabat Mater*, or any other work a little off
the average Viennese concert-goer's track in 1880, any knowledge
of anything whatever. The general and musical culture shown in
Hanslick's writings represents one of the unlovelier forms of para-
sitism; that which, having the wealth to collect *objets d'art* and the
birth and education to talk amusingly, does not itself attempt a
stroke of artistic work, does not dream of revising a first impression,
experiences the fine arts entirely as the pleasures of a gentleman,
and then pronounces judgement as if the expression of its opinion
were a benefit and a duty to society.

All marked individuality in the fine arts can be seen from an
angle from which it seems that 'this will never do'. It is Bruckner's
misfortune that his work is put forward by himself so as to present
to us the angle of its relation to sonata form. That very relation
is a mistake: but if we are to condemn all art that contains a mistaken principle, I am not sure that *Paradise Lost* is less mistaken
than these symphonies of the old Austrian organist who dedicated
his last symphony *An meinen lieben Gott*.

Defects of form are not a justifiable ground for criticism from
listeners who profess to enjoy the bleeding chunks of butcher's

meat chopped from Wagner's operas and served up on Wagner nights as *Waldweben* and *Walkürenritt*. If you want Wagnerian concert-music other than the few complete overtures and the Siegfried Idyll, why not try Bruckner? It is interesting and gratifying to know that Bruckner, who made a great impression in London and Paris by his wonderful extemporizations on the organ, told Nawrátil that in England his music was really understood. This was in the 'seventies or 'eighties, and I fear that he over-estimated our general culture of music other than that of the organ. His own orchestration reveals a state of musical culture very much wider than anything to be found in British music of the 'seventies. His orchestration is often said to be influenced by the organ. But that is because it often sounds like an organ. And it could not sound thus unless it were completely free from the mistakes of the organ-loft composer. The scores bristle (as Weingartner says) with abnormalities; but the quintessence of orchestral quality is manifest in every line. Nothing is more astonishing than the way in which *naïvetés* that look on paper (and sound on the pianoforte) as if they really 'will never do', become augustly romantic in the orchestra if their execution is not hurried. We must clear our minds of other wrong points of view than mere prejudices if we are to understand Bruckner. It is not mere prejudice that judges Wordsworth an unequal poet, or Sir Charles Grandison an imperfect specimen of the ideal gentleman. These judgements are relevant. But such truisms should not be allowed to delay us in the more important business of finding what Wordsworth and Richardson really achieved.

At the present day Bruckner's Romantic Symphony ranks in Germany and Austria as a 'best-seller' item in the orchestral repertoire; being now probably more popular than Tchaikovsky's Pathetic Symphony, which is beginning to show signs of wear. Such signs, we may be sure, Bruckner will never show; his defects are obvious on a first hearing, not as obscurities that may become clear with further knowledge, but as things that must be lived down as soon as possible. No other defects will appear; this art has no tricks. Listen to it humbly; not with the humility with which you would hope to learn music from Bach, Beethoven, and Brahms, but with the humility you would feel if you overheard a simple old soul talking to a child about sacred things. The greater masters inspire that humility too: Bruckner's helplessness is not in itself a virtue. But to despise it is to miss the main lesson of the masters, without Brahms's excuse that he was one of those masters and a severer critic of his own work than of anybody else's.

At no time ought it to have been possible not to recognize that the opening of the Romantic Symphony is a thing of extraordinary beauty and depth.

Ex. 1.

The counter-statement of this theme shows ample capacity to carry it out through modulations worthy of its solemnity. The mood is that of Schubert's *Du bist die Ruh'*. Two influences outweighed the recognized spell which Wagner exercised on Bruckner. Schubert is always ready to help Bruckner whenever Wagner will permit; and Bruckner never forgets the High Altar of his Catholic Church.

Though this opening is both broader and more four-square than any sonata-opening conceived by the classics, it is by no means impossible to follow up on an adequate scale. As with Schubert's finest openings, so here there is no evidence that this is a quick movement at all, until the first tutti bursts out.

Ex. 2.

Then for a while the action moves with classical energy. The orthodox critic has no right to complain of a shock to his habits of thought until he is confronted, not with an innovation, but with a stiff archaic pause on the dominant of B flat, the most conventional key that can be chosen for the second group of material. The stiffness is not accounted for by the fact that that group here begins in D flat instead; such evasions are as old as Cherubini's Overture to *Faniska*. And when Bruckner begins his second group and catechizes children with it in four-bar sequences ranging easily round the harmonic world, no wonder our musical Francis Jeffreys said (and in London continue to say) 'This will never do!' But this will have to do; for we are at the parting of the ways; and Bruckner has no theoretic labels with which to disguise his simplicity.

The main leitmotiv (yes, that is the magic word) of the large complex (another magic word) that now follows consists of the large-headed notes in Ex. 3.

Ex. 3.

The accompanying figures are just as distinct, and it is only in the light of later developments that we have reason to select figure (c) as the most important. If such phrases were obviously Wagnerian leitmotiv, that is to say, figures detached from an evidently larger whole, whether or not identifiable with poetic or dramatic elements, nobody at this time of day would have any difficulty in understanding the enormous process that now follows. The trouble is that Bruckner's mind moves no faster than in four-bar steps of moderate alla breve time. These steps the mind of the alert listener accustomed to classical symphonies takes for whole themes. We then wonder at their shortness of breath, and we marvel at the effrontery of the Brucknerite who claims that Bruckner is 'lapidary', 'pyramidal', and a master before whom Brahms dwindles to the proportions of an insect. The Brucknerite is wrong about Brahms, but he is right about Bruckner, whose four-bar phrases should be regarded as atoms, or at most as molecules. Nor should we be surprised that such giant molecules build themselves up into very simple forms; for art is not biology. We are dealing here with matters in which size is essential. Macaulay, who is only once recorded to have recognized a tune, and who certainly never heard of Bruckner, summed up the whole aesthetics of the pyramidal style by putting the simple question, 'What could be more vile than a pyramid thirty feet high?' Bruckner's following up of Ex. 3 is the right size. The opening of the symphony was huge from the sonata point of view, but not so huge as to show us that Ex. 3 is not meant for a whole statement. The storm that bursts in upon that childlike garrulity works its way, in terms of Ex. 2, with a grandeur that convinces us that the opening of the symphony is, in relation to the whole, no more than a normal passage of lyric leisure. Twice the storm dies down and mounts again. At last, upon a solemn summons from the brass, the key of B flat (the orthodox dominant) is triumphantly asserted: and in that key the accessory figures of Ex. 3 (without figure (c)) bring the exposition to a conclusion which has a very dramatic dying fall. With all its discursiveness, the movement has undoubtedly so far devoted itself, as Bruckner intends, to the business of exposition; and what follows is unquestionably a development, which the discursiveness has by no means forestalled. We must not expect Bruckner to move quickly. First the strings, putting on sordines, seem to be trying plaintively to lead back to the tonic, the wind giving hints of figure (*a*). But the brass rises from the home dominant to an alien dominant, on which a clarinet and flute, with plaintive diminutions of the last chromatic string figure, lead to a spacious development of Ex. 1 in combination with Ex. 2, both figures finding echoes in every region of the orchestra. In vast modulating sequences the development proceeds, alternating from quiet to climax on Schubertian lines easy to follow and enjoy. Bruckner's scores are full of echo-effects which look grotesquely crude on paper, but are so euphonious that almost the only word for them is 'comfortable'. At last we hear figure (*c*) from Ex. 3 in a solemn augmentation. With deep emotion this leads to the recapitulation.

Few things in orchestration are more impressive than the new depth of Ex. 1, in octaves, with a flowing figure in muted violins surrounding it as with clouds of incense. And the classical critic does not know his own favourite art-forms if he fails to acknowledge the mastery with which Bruckner composes the rest of his recapitulation and grafts on it one of his grandest codas. In this first movement there is no helplessness; though, as we have seen, there is a considerable difficulty in adjusting oneself to Bruckner's time-scale when his action really begins (at Ex. 3).

The defence of Bruckner, still necessary in this country, would defeat itself by attempting to claim that there is nothing helpless about the slow movement of the Romantic Symphony. In general, Bruckner's slow movements have been the first things that the classical critic has learnt to approach properly. Bruckner's tempo is always really slow, whatever its rate of vibration, and in the avowedly slow movement he meets the sonata style on its own ground. The plan of his adagios consists of a broad main theme, and an episode that occurs twice, each return of the main theme displaying more movement in the accompaniment and rising at the last return to a grand climax, followed by a solemn and pathetic die-away coda. The official view derives this scheme from the slow movement of Beethoven's Ninth Symphony; mistakenly, for Bruckner never has anything to do with the variation form. The slow movement of the Eroica Symphony would be nearer the mark if its two episodes were not different; and the allegretto of Beethoven's F minor Quartet would be nearest of all. Bruckner's difficulty, this time a real inherent dilemma, in even his most perfect slow movements is, first, that his natural inability to vary the size of his phrases is aggravated by the slow tempo, and

secondly, that the most effective means of relief is denied him by
his conscientious objection to write anything so trivial and un-
Wagnerian as a symmetrical tune. Consequently his all-important
contrasting episode is as slow as his vast main theme. The result
is curious: the thing that is oftenest repeated and always expanded,
the vast main theme, is welcomed whenever it returns; while, as
Johnson would have said, 'the attention retires' from even a single
return of the episode. In the Sixth Symphony Bruckner triumphed
over this difficulty, and even steeled himself to cut out a beautiful
passage to secure fine proportions. But in the Romantic Symphony
the difficulty is almost schematically exhibited by the structure of
the episode, which consists of no less than seven phrases, all ending
in full closes or half-closes, all four bars long except the last but
one, which is six bars, and all given to the viola with a severely
simple accompaniment of pizzicato chords in slow-march time.
There may, for all I know, be Brucknerites who consider this the
finest thing in the symphony; and it so obviously 'will never do'
that to criticize it on Jeffrey's lines will 'do' still less. However, the
Brucknerites have the sense to apologize for the *Brucknersche
Längen*—by which they mean *longeurs*, not that length which is
essential to the size. I believe this is a case in point; and the above
account goes some way towards its defence as a not unreasonable
effort to deal with a genuine problem.

Here is Bruckner's main theme, of which figure (c) underlies
important later developments—

And here is Sir Charles Grandison's oak-panelled room.

Ex. 5.

The final climax and coda are deeply pathetic.

The scherzo is one of Bruckner's most brilliant movements. It begins with one of his usual *Walkürenritt* scherzo openings—

Ex. 6.

continues with a more reflective theme—

Ex. 7.

and rises to Bruckner's invariable scherzo-fanfare on the dominant as the end of an exposition. The development begins in mystery, according to type, and is pensive throughout, till the exciting moment of return to the recapitulation, which ends with the invariable fanfare.

But the trio violates every Bruckner precedent by being quite frankly a tune; a slow and comfortably pinguid *Ländler*, too rustic to be called Viennese.

Ex. 8.

The da capo of the scherzo violates Bruckner's precedents in another way by taking an extremely effective short cut from the first stage of the exposition to the beginning of the development, the sudden hush being highly dramatic.

With the finale the first thing to realize is that, whatever Bruckner chooses to call it, it is really a slow movement, with all the positive qualities thereof. No Bruckner finale ever purports to 'go', nor does it attempt to sum up the whole symphony like the last act of a drama, though Bruckner's habit of reducing all his themes to terms of the common-chord and piling them up in his last bars goes far to create that impression. In the Romantic Symphony this is particularly easy, as the characteristic dip of (*a*) in Ex. 1 is present in the main themes of the slow movement and scherzo. But the listener's attention is better employed on the new themes of the finale. So long as we do not expect speed, we shall have no difficulty in following their progress through climax, reaction, combination, and final piling up.

First, then, there is the main theme; main, though delivered like an introduction. It is a single figure, (*a*), rising by tones and speeding up as it rises.

The rhythm of the scherzo (Ex. 6) is heard as the figure (*a*) begins to spin across the beats. Finally (*a*) becomes one of Bruckner's grandest ninth-symphony unison themes.

A new figure (*c*) arising from this is heard first merely as a mode of vibration—

but it becomes important hereafter. At last this first section of the movement comes to a grand tonic close in which the horns may be heard recalling Ex. 1.

After a pause an entirely new group of themes begins: at first solemn—

then as garrulous as Chaucer.

Ex. 13.

(I forbear to quote the next two bars lest the enemy blaspheme.)
The garrulity increases, but with it the romance.

Ex. 14.

Other quotations are unnecessary, except for the characteristic
inversion of (*a*), with which a section we may call the development
begins.

Ex. 15.

This initiates a crescendo that leads to a solemn delivery of
Ex. 13 by the brass. On paper it looks like an augmentation; but
this is an optical illusion as the tempo is twice as fast.

In the last resort, the form of this movement is the same kind
of three-decker arrangement as that of Brucker's slow movements,
and to distinguish recapitulation from development is merely to
use long words. The penultimate stage follows, a most impressive
calm after a storm upon Ex. 10, with a wonderful augmentation of
Ex. 11. Then Ex. 10, in a remote key, with mysterious throbbing
accompaniment, is inverted thus—

Ex. 16.

Muted violins ask elvish questions as to (*b*); and the rhythm of
the scherzo-theme (Ex. 6) hovers timidly in the background. Then
there is an exciting crescendo towards—No; the key of D minor
intervenes, and we have a free recapitulation of the complex of
Exs. 12-14. Then at last introduced by a combination of Exs. 13
and 10, the final climax builds itself up on the lines of Ex. 9.

SYMPHONY IN A MAJOR, NO. 6

1 *Maestoso.* 2 *Adagio* (*Sehr feierlich*). 3 SCHERZO (3/4 *Ruhig bewegt*): *with Trio in slow 4/8 time.* 4 FINALE, *Bewegt, doch nicht zu schnell.*

If we clear our minds, not only of prejudice but of wrong points of view, and treat Bruckner's Sixth Symphony as a kind of music we have never heard before, I have no doubt that its high quality will strike us at every moment. In the slow movement I can see no difficulty. The one redundant passage has been, though reluctantly, excised by Bruckner himself, and the excision leaves us with a perfectly balanced movement in classical form and of a high order of solemn beauty.

The alarming technical difficulty of the first movement is probably the reason why this is the most neglected of Bruckner's symphonies. It begins, not with Bruckner's usual tremolo and chord theme, but with a lively rhythmic figure below which a theme of dark tonality stirs, Leviathan-like, in the bass.

Leviathan moves towards brighter harmonies. Soft horns, trumpets, and clarinets rise with livelier figures. A counter-statement for full orchestra now follows, and dies away in the direction of a new key.

The 'second subject' enters in slower time and with triplet rhythms.

Bruckner's paragraphs are simple in form, seldom if ever deviating from four-bar or eight-bar phrases; but their inner details and harmonies are very rich. The present example is perhaps the most complex in all Bruckner's works. An inner figure in sevenths, in its second four bars, leads to much quiet rumination. In thirteen four-bar phrases this train of thought pursues its course, raising

several new melodic issues by the way. At last a powerful tutti
bursts out and leads through grand Wagner-Bruckner crescendos
and diminuendos to a quiet close in E major, glowing as in
solemn evening sunshine. The accompaniment-figure that arises
from this leads to the development, which slowly drifts into other
keys.

Then it sails out in full swing with one of Bruckner's character
istic free inversions of the main theme.

The enemy blasphemes when the devout Brucknerite exclaims
at the wonderful contrapuntal mastery of these devices. Technically they are remarkable only for their *naïveté*; the genius of them
lies in the fact that they sound thoroughly romantic. (Another
curious and very effective feature is that they are always accompanied by echoes, which are always imperfect, and always scored
for weaker instruments just on the border-line of audibility.) At last
the livelier figures join in, also freely inverted. The music rolls on
in its four-bar swing till the full orchestra thunders out the main
theme in the remote key of E flat. (Note the half-heard echoes
throughout.) From this it gradually swings back to the tonic
A major, and so initiates the recapitulation. The livelier phrases
die away; and the counter-statement is not only soft but beautifully
decorated by figures in the oboe and flute, floating like clouds
of incense in such Services of the Church as are never far from
Bruckner's thoughts.

The recapitulation of the 'second subject' alters its key-system,
starting in F sharp minor, and shortens it by twelve bars. The
tutti outburst now begins *piano* and leads into the coda by a dramatic
return to the tonic. The whole coda is one of the greatest passages
Bruckner ever wrote; and Wagner might have been content to sign
it. The first theme mounts slowly in Bruckner's favourite simultaneous direct-inverted combination, passing from key to key
beneath a tumultuous surface sparkling like the Homeric seas. The
trumpets join in a long-drawn cantabile, swelling and diminishing;
until at last the rhythmic figure of the opening is heard, and the
theme comes together in a fanfare.

The slow movement begins with a solemn theme—

to which, in the sequel, the oboe adds a pathetic counterpoint. Bruckner seldom if ever allows a theme to take shape as a lyric tune: his fundamental notion is always that of a Wagnerian leitmotiv of some four bars; and if he generally answers this stiffly by another four bars, this is only because he is building up an enormously larger whole, such as the 52 bars beginning with Ex. 2. This is, in fact, what Brucknerites mean by his 'lapidary' style. Here, however, as in the slow movements of his seventh and eighth symphonies, the slow tempo inspires him to a mastery of the big and supple paragraph such as Brahms would have been compelled to praise. The sequel of Ex. 5 does not proceed with another four bars, but with two, which are repeated in rising sequence and developed to a grand climax, after which there is no final close until, in the 24th bar of the whole, the music closes into the remote key of E. Here a 'second subject' gives us another beautiful example of quintessential Bruckner.

Listen to it with reverence; for the composer meant what he said, and he is speaking of sacred things. The music again expands enormously, and moves to a climax in C major. From this there is a slow decline till, at length, a solemn strain is heard, as of a funeral march in C minor combined with A flat.

From this the music drifts into a spacious development, based at first on the figures of Ex. 5 with the bass transferred to the treble. Then the theme is inverted and imitated, as follows—

Ex. 8.

with a wealth of new melody above it. At last it returns in the tonic with its counterpoint in the oboe and with a triplet accompaniment in growing agitation. A grand crescendo covers the whole expanse of the original first paragraph, and subsides into the recapitulation of the 'second subject' in the tonic. Reluctantly, perhaps on Bruckner's part, certainly on mine, the orthodox recapitulation which he wrote in full, with rich new details, is shortened at the composer's suggestion, and we proceed at once to Ex. 7 in F minor. The movement as a whole gains a perfection of emotional sequence by this excision, which still leaves us with adequate allusion to Ex. 6 in the exquisitely poised long-drawn coda. That allusion, moreover, has itself a power that it would have lost after a complete recapitulation.

Bruckner's scherzos are usually something like paraphrases of the *Walkürenritt* with trios consisting of quiet house-music or Church music. In the Sixth Symphony the scherzo is slower than usual and has, as Nawrátil says, a touch of *Walpurgisnacht* in its mood.

Ex. 9.

&c.

The trio is one of Bruckner's richest and most original inspirations. Strange pizzicato chords and rhythms introduce the three horns of Beethoven's Eroica Symphony into the *Urwald* of Wagner. The violins pronounce a solemn blessing in their cadences.

Ex. 10.

Horns.

The finale is full of tragedy, though at last it ends in triumph. You must not expect Bruckner to make a finale 'go' like a classical finale. He is in no greater hurry at the end of a symphony than at the beginning; and though his finales all begin with ample energy, the first change of key and theme brings about a mood of argument and meditation which will not be bothered with by people who want to catch the last train home. The finale of the Sixth Symphony is not long; and Bruckner has himself excised the one dangerous place towards the end.

It opens with a tragic theme in the Phrygian mode—

Ex. 11.

which leads to a tutti, marked by one of Bruckner's favourite figures (here marked (*x*)), which pervades the *non confundar* of his *Te Deum* and the slow movement (in memory of Wagner) of his Seventh Symphony.

Ex. 12.

After a tremendous climax this subsides into the most naïve of all Bruckner's 'second subjects'—

Ex. 13.

The lower figure receives the inevitable inversion during the leisurely progress of this childlike argument all round the harmonic and orchestral universe. (Bruckner must have suffered agonies from conductors who waded through these ruminations in march-tempo and such intonation as occurred to the average sight-reader.) At last it mounts to its Wagnerian climax, and so drifts into the development. This is set in motion by a new wistful figure—

Ex. 14.

which associates itself with the other themes and becomes lively on its own account. The main theme returns in a slower tempo (4/4) and, after a further discussion of Ex. 14, is inverted in F major as bass to a consolatory melody in the style (but not the actual shape) of Ex. 6. This inversion gives rise to some discussion, till the brass intervenes with Ex. 12 and carries things to a grand climax, reaching the tonic, A, and thereafter subsiding into a free recapitulation of the 'second subject' (Ex. 13).

This is cut short by a coda which intervenes with Ex. 14. The rhythm of Ex. 1 may also be heard in the crescendo which follows. Wisely cutting out a page of pianissimo interruption in a foreign key, Bruckner concludes with Ex. 12, on to which he triumphantly grafts the figures of the beginning of the symphony (Ex. 1).

DVOŘÁK

SYMPHONY IN D MAJOR, NO. 1 [NOW NO. 6], OP. 60

1 *Allegro non tanto.* 2 *Adagio.* 3 SCHERZO, *or Furiant (a Bohemian dance). Presto.* 4 FINALE. *Allegro con spirito.*

If Dvořák's first three symphonies were of the nature of 'early indiscretions', we might acquiesce in the fate that has for the best part of a generation deprived the public of any wider knowledge of this great master of the orchestra than is given by over-familiarity with the 'New World' Symphony and the *Carnaval* Overture. It is no disparagement of these brilliant and delightful works to say that they are popular for other than their finest features, and that Dvořák has written greater music. When Brahms and Joachim brought him to the notice of a world he did not know how to tackle, his genius was as naïve as Haydn's; and naïve it remained to the end. Unfortunately it often failed to retain that sublimity which inspired its best moments, and which Haydn never lost; that sublimity which is utterly independent of the size or range of the artist's subject; which trails clouds of glory not only with the outlook of the child but with the solemnity of the kitten running after its tail. With a loud instructive voice the world informed Dvořák that his genius was naïve; and a certain rustic craftiness, harmless perhaps in some earlier civilization, perverted his *naïveté* thenceforth. He tried to do as he thought the world bid him, and the world was the first to grumble when he wrote an oratorio expressly to suit what he understood to be the English taste. Unhappy as this result was, it was perhaps better, because more obviously unsuccessful, than the result of that most dangerous of all affectations, the affectation of qualities one actually happens to possess in abundance. Dvořák is not the only artist who injured his own originality and power by strenuously obeying the insistent clamour of the world that he should 'let himself go and be himself'. A naïve man affecting to be naïve will not often produce works like the 'New World' Symphony, which, if it has been allowed to oust its greater predecessors from their rights, is at all events full of fine things; but he will be apt to write himself down with bad and curiously ignorant imitations of his own style. Contrast this calamity with the wiser artist's fear of his own worldly successes. The Kreutzer Sonata is not Beethoven's greatest work; though no sensible musician has anything to say against it: but Beethoven would have gone rapidly downhill if he had allowed himself to increase in such easy breadth and brilliance without deepening, enlarging, and concentrating his whole range of musical thought.

Dvořák's First Symphony shows him at the height of his power. It is by no means the work of a young man; its opus number is true to the facts, and shows that Dvořák, like Brahms, had waited long and experienced much before venturing on the publication of a symphony. Yet the very first line presents us with those intimations of immortality that make the child sublime.

Ex. 1.

No man of the world would take this theme so seriously as to make a symphony of it, or, taking it seriously, would get so excited over it as to swell out from pianissimo to a forte at the first top note. But Dvořák knows what he is talking about, and the world has not yet made him self-conscious. To the child the silver-paper stars of the Christmas tree are really sublime: that is to say, no poet can fill his own mind more entirely with the sublimity of the real starry heavens. All depends on the singleness, the fullness, and the purity of the emotion; and in works of art, also on the skill to convey it truly. In this symphony Dvořák moves with great mastery and freedom; the scale and proportions are throughout noble, and if the procedure is often, like Schubert's, unorthodox and risky, it is in this case remarkably successful.

No one can wish to disillusionize Dvořák when his first theme, after the intervention of an energetic auxiliary, comes out *grandioso* on the full orchestra. There is no illusion about it; the grandeur is not that of particular styles or particular themes, it is that of life itself; and when that grandeur is present art has little leisure for even the most solemn questions of taste, except in so far as the power to appreciate life is itself the one genuine matter of taste.

Dvořák's second subject is reached, as usual with him, by a curiously long and discursive transition, one of the themes of which must be quoted.

Ex. 2.

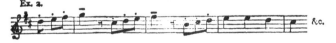

The second subject itself contains two great themes—

Ex. 3.

Ex. 4.

of which the second is very prominent in later developments.

The exposition is repeated, the return being brought about by a characteristically long passage, which accordingly makes it out of the question to 'cut the repeat'. Fortunately there is no temptation to do so, as the movement is by no means of unwieldy length.

The development begins with one of the most imaginative passages Dvořák ever wrote. No listener can fail to be impressed with its long-sustained chords, from the depths of which fragments of the first theme arise until the basses put them together in a dramatically mysterious sequence, which suddenly breaks off with a masterly and terse working up of the energetic auxiliary themes, including Ex. 2 and others unrepresented in my quotations. The whole development has all the ease and clearness of Dvořák's methods, with none of the flat reiterations that disfigure his weaker works: and I need not further describe its course, beyond calling attention to the dramatic stroke which leads to the return of the first subject. This stroke is easily recognized by the way in which at the climax of a full orchestral storm (based on Ex. 2) the strings are suddenly left alone, and after coming to an abrupt stop, proceed to stalk in stiff indignant crotchets to a remote chord, from whence the full orchestra plunges grandly into the main key.

The recapitulation of both first and second subjects (Exs. 1, 2, and 3) is regular, including all the accessories and the elaborate transition-passages. The climax of the second subject, however, is not allowed to subside as before, but leads immediately to a brilliant coda in which Ex. 4 is combined in free fugue with Ex. 2. This combination leads inevitably to the dramatic stroke that ended the development, and that now recurs to bring about the final triumph of the first theme, which dies away ecstatically in the height of its glory, and seems about to end in a quiet dream when suddenly **Ex. 4** (once the quietest theme of all) rouses the movement to its real end, abruptly and in full daylight.

It is a sad mystery how the man who had once written so highly organized a movement, could ever have lost the power.

The slow movement is not difficult to follow, but I know few pieces that improve more upon acquaintance. It has in perfection an artistic quality which Dvořák elsewhere unfortunately allowed to degenerate into a defect, the quality of a meandering improvisation on a recurring theme, the episodes being of the nature of ruminating digressions rather than of contrasts. This is a subtle achievement, and if Dvořák could have either left the slow movement of his First Symphony as his one example, or produced several others as perfect, we should be in no danger of missing the point of a design as peculiar as that of the slow movement of Beethoven's C minor Symphony, or as many designs of Haydn's which elude classification. At all events this movement will not fail to make its point if we dismiss from our minds any preconception that its ruminating modulations are intended to lead to something new, or that its one dramatic storm (at the beginning of the second episode) is an incident of more than fairy-tale solidity. That storm leads back to the main theme in one of Dvořák's most imaginative passages; and the whole function of all the episodes and developments in the movement is to present the most interesting possible appearance of leading back to a melody which we have really never left. Here is that melody:

The figure marked (*a*) more or less pervades the whole movement from its introductory bars (Dvořák seldom begins a slow movement without a charmingly wavering introduction) to its shy close. There is something very touching in the way the coda seems to pay homage to that supreme utterance, the end of the slow movement of Beethoven's Ninth Symphony; before which Dvořák's innocent drum figure ♪♫♫ seems to dance as the clown in the legend danced his devotions before the altar of the Virgin, to the scandal of the monks who surprised him there.

The scherzo or *Furiant* needs no quotation: nor is much wisdom to be gained from the information that the *Furiant* is a Bohemian dance. I yield to no one in my respect for folk-music and for the experts who have the tact and sympathy which alone can collect and appreciate it; but it has been noticed that the people who are loudest in saying that the *Dumky* and the *Furiant* are new and

national art-forms are very apt to collect the Hunting-chorus in
Der Freischütz as a folk-song from the whistling of a country milk-
boy. Dvořák writes a lively scherzo with a picturesque trio in
perfectly normal form; and some listeners may be chiefly amused
by the village merry-go-round humours of the piccolo in the trio,
while others may be more impressed by the poetic quality of the
long-drawn phrases of the rest of the trio (very chracteristic of
Dvořák and exceedingly unlike any possible folk-music) with its
fine contrast to the high spirits of the scherzo.

For the finale we need at least four quotations; one for the first
theme—

one for an important little figure—

and two for the second subject, the one designed for the tripping-
up of the Superior Person—

and the other designed for a grand climax in the coda.

The development arises mainly from Ex. 7 and from the second
bar of Ex. 8, which has the oddest ways of detaching itself from
its frivolous surroundings and producing powerfully romantic
passages.

In the brilliant presto coda, the onset of which may be recognized
by the dramatic stroke where the violins are left to do a volplane by
themselves, the listener should not fail to notice the happy effect
of breaking up the first theme (Ex. 6) into this rhythm.

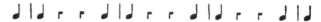

Altogether the finale, far from being, as too often with Dvořák, the
weak point, is a magnificent crown to this noble work, and is
admirably endowed with that quality that is rarest of all in post-
classical finales, the power of movement. Rapid tempo and accelera-
tion of pace can do nothing if the phrases themselves lack variety
and energy in their proportions. It is pitiful to see the *sempre più
presto* of many ambitious finales (including some of Dvořák's)
struggling vainly to make headway against the growing sluggish-
ness of their phrases. In his first symphony, however, as in a considerable volume of other neglected works, Dvořák had the classical
secret of movement, which is not a power that can be obtained at
the expense of higher qualities, for it is one of the highest.

SYMPHONY IN D MINOR, NO. 2, [NOW NO. 7], OP. 70

1 *Allegro maestoso.* 2 *Poco Adagio.* 3 SCHERZO: *Vivace*
4 FINALE: *Allegro.*

I have no hesitation in setting Dvořák's Second Symphony along
with the C major Symphony of Schubert and the four symphonies of Brahms, as among the greatest and purest examples in
this art-form since Beethoven. There should be no difficulty at
this time of day in recognizing its greatness. It has none of the
weaknesses of form which so often spoil Dvořák's best work, except
for a certain stiffness of movement in the finale, a stiffness which is
not beyond concealing by means of such freedom of tempo as
the composer would certainly approve. There were three obstacles
to the appreciation of this symphony when it was published in
1885. First, it is powerfully tragic. Secondly, the orthodox
critics and the average musician were, as always with new works,
very anxious to prove that they were right and the composer
was wrong, whenever the composer produced a long sentence
which could not easily be phrased at sight. And this naïve and
irresponsible Dvořák, when he is at the height of his power,
happens to be a great master of the long meandering sentence
that ramifies into countless afterthoughts. The great sentences that
the unspoiled Dvořák was allowed to write, remain; and such
examples as the continuation of the second subject in the first
movement of this symphony (following Ex. 5 of our quotations)
and the trio of the scherzo (Ex. 12) would, if they were alone
preserved as fragments of nineteenth-century music, prove to
a future civilization that Dvořák was a great composer. To the
immediate contemporaries they proved that they were not easy to
remember; and, as Hans Sachs says, 'That annoys our old folks.'
The third obstacle to the understanding of this symphony is
intellectually trivial, but practically the most serious of all. The

general effect of its climaxes is somewhat shrill. Dvořák was at once recognized as a great master of the orchestra. Prout, in both of his treatises on instrumentation, always quotes him as 'the greatest living master of scoring'. And there is no page of Dvořák's orchestration which does not instantly carry conviction as eminently brilliant and orchestral. Yet his scores are almost as full of difficult problems of balance as Beethoven's, and he is anything but a correct and disciplined writer. Now if a work is loosely constructed, many a point which the scoring tends to obscure may be left in obscurity without much damage to the listener's enjoyment. The trouble comes when the composition tells such a well-constructed story that the listener cannot afford to lose a sentence. These great works of the middle of Dvořák's career demand and repay the study one expects to give to the most difficult classical masterpieces; but the composer has acquired the reputation of being masterly only in a few popular works of a somewhat lower order. It is time that this injustice should be rectified.

The first movement begins with the following sombre but energetic theme.

Ex. 1.

The delicate rhythmic contrast between the two figures marked (a) and (b) is of great importance in the whole scheme, and is typical of all that makes highly organized work more difficult to perform than the most elaborate technique of external effect.

From figure (a) arises an impassioned phrase.

Ex. 2.

In dramatic dialogue this passes on to a new figure with (a) in the bass.

Ex. 3.

This comes quickly to a climax, and closes into a new theme—

Ex. 4.

which is taken up vigorously by several voices, and suddenly
softens into a gentle dialogue between a horn and an oboe in a
remote key; but the passion instantly breaks out again, and the
rhythmic figure (*b*), in angry dialogue between the strings and the
wind, returns through a wide range of harmony to the main key,
D minor. And now the first theme blazes out on the full orchestra.
(It is not very easy to hear it through the high tremolo of the
strings.) Figure (*b*) brings about a fine dramatic stroke as masterly
in execution as in conception, and leads through a wistful transition
passage of rich harmonic interest to the second subject. This
begins with a broad melody—

Ex. 5.

the continuation of which I have already referred to as one of
Dvořák's greatest musical paragraphs. After this has risen to its
impassioned climax, we notice through its long-drawn close
plaintive fragments of the first theme, Ex. 1. After a moment's
hesitation this theme emerges energetically, and the exposition is
brought to a full orchestral climax with a magnificent combination
of Exs. 1, 3, and 5. Just as it seems to be settling to a close, it
plunges suddenly on to the dominant of D as if to return to the
key of the opening. But the harmony moves far away into other
regions, and the development sets out in B minor with a pathetic
dialogue on the second subject, alternating with passionate outbursts of the first. It is impossible to over-praise the mastery and
tragic power with which this shortest of all Dvořák's developments
swiftly fetches its compass through distant keys to a recapitulation
in which the first subject is represented only by its outbursts on
the full orchestra immediately before the transition. There is the
true inwardness of musical form and dramatic power in all this.
The themes, the climaxes, the emotional contrasts are related to
each other as character is related to fate. A new turn given to the
harmony brings the transition into the right direction to lead to
the second subject in D major. Dvořák gives us its glorious main

paragraph in full, as is essential to the enjoyment of it; but when it comes to a close, and the fragments of the first theme appear, the full tragic power of the movement becomes revealed. The climax does not lead to triumph; on the contrary, the figure of Ex. 3 arises in the brass instruments like some stroke of fate, and brings the movement to a crisis of the utmost power, towards the end of which we can just catch a glimpse of one more of the themes which were so energetic in the exposition, Ex. 4. From this climax there is a still more impressive and sudden decline; and the first movement dies away in the dark mood of the opening, with the full pathos of that theme now made manifest.

The slow movement begins with one of Dvořák's finest melodies.

Ex. 6.

When the clarinet has completed its melody in two strains, the strings enter and the full orchestra surprises us within the next two bars by crowning the melody with a grand tonic chord. From this emerges a more impassioned and less naïve sequel to the tune—

Ex. 7.

which leads to one of the profoundest passages in any symphony since Beethoven.

Ex 8,

The nearest approach to this in mood and orchestration might perhaps be found in the loftiest and most characteristic moments of the symphonies of Bruckner, but it is something strange and unique in music to find an idea characteristic of that sincere but maladroit composer carried out with perfect mastery and terseness. This wonderful passage leads to another new theme in which a horn and a clarinet play the parts of a rustic Tristan and Isolde to a crowd of sympathetic orchestral witnesses.

Ex. 9.

This seems to be dying away, but it suddenly mounts to a climax in which the first notes of the main theme, Ex. 6, are heard in the brass, closing, however, into a stormy new theme in the minor. The storm dies away into D flat major, from which key a passionate dialogue sets out with several new themes which I need not quote. The modulations are rich, the orchestration is clear and varied, and the rhythms are impulsive. The return to the main key is, like every cardinal point in the forms of this symphony, a stroke of genius. Its power as such is enhanced by the fact that Dvořák does not return to the first theme, Ex. 6, but to its continuation, Ex. 7. Very few composers since Mozart have appreciated the force of a return which is made to the middle of a subject instead of to its beginning; and it is a tragic puzzle how a composer who had achieved such mastery throughout this work could ever lose it or cease to exercise it. The mysterious Bruckner-like passage follows, and leads to a much greater climax. The music seems to be dying away finally; yet we are waiting for something. At last it comes. It is the original first theme, this time upon an oboe instead of a clarinet. The oboe seems to reveal the inwardness of the melody; yet the clarinet also has its say in a final dialogue, in which the phrases are echoed on the still softer flute. Towards the end we are also shown the inwardness of that grandiose tonic chord which intervened between Exs. 6 and 7. In a new and more emotional context we have something like it started by a roll of the drums, as the wind instruments rise to one last melodious climax.

All Dvořák's scherzos are effective, but not all of them are as distinguished as the scherzo of his second symphony. Any composer who has a lively recollection of the dance-rhythms of his own province, and who is the possessor of a Czechoslovak language in which to give them names which are neither English, German, nor Italian, may easily figure in musical journalese and musical dictionaries as the inventor of a new art-form by writing quite ordinary dance music and calling it a *Furiant* or a *Trepak*. The scherzo of Dvořák's first symphony is an excellent movement, and is called a *Furiant*. The scherzo of the second symphony has no such advantage, but it is a finer movement throughout. The trio I have already mentioned as containing one of Dvořák's most beautiful musical paragraphs. From the scherzo I quote the main theme with its characteristic deux-temps rhythm—

Ex. 10.

and the cadence theme which towards the end of the movement dies away in a very impressive passage before finally flaring out.

Ex. 11.

The splendid main theme of the trio begins as follows—

Ex. 12.

but the quotation can give no idea either of the length of the paragraph, nor of the peculiar mood produced by the incessant rumbling of the basses. On the appearance of a livelier theme—

Ex. 13.

this becomes a gentle rustling on the flutes and violins. With the return of the first paragraph in a quite unexpected key, F major, the ominous rumbling again pervades the air, and at last a rapid crescendo leads to the return of the scherzo, its course shortened in some ways, but expanded emotionally in connexion with its cadence theme, Ex. 11.

The finale is no less rich in themes than the rest of the symphony. At the outset two require quotation, connected with each other by the figure marked (*b*).

Ex. 14.

Ex. 15.

There is no mistaking the tragic effect of the deliberate chorale-like march of the second of the two. In quoting the first I give in small notes the impulsive arpeggio-figure (c), with which it is varied when the wind instruments or the full orchestra take it up forte, as they very soon do, adding various other figures in the course of an agitated dialogue. These other figures become gathered up into new themes, of which the most important is the following.

Ex. 16.

This may be called the transition-theme. Dvořák's transitions, unlike those of Schubert whom he so often resembles in his habits of form, are almost always very discursive and elaborate; and we need not be surprised to find yet another theme assuming importance in later developments.

Ex. 17.

After a stormy discussion of this, the second subject arrives in the shape of a broad triumphant melody in A major.

Ex. 18.

This is brought to a full climax which ends in A minor and dies away into the beginnings of a development on a large scale. There is no difficulty in following its course with the aid of these quotations. Indeed the only trace of inequality in this symphony lies, as I have already suggested, in the fact that the rhythms of this finale are rather uniformly regular, which causes the themes and their alternations to lie side by side rather than to build up into continuous action. Yet there is plenty of drama and plenty of coherence in the scheme; but the task of the conductor is rather to keep the movement flowing than to articulate what is already so clear in the phrasing.

The development takes the themes of the first subject more or less in their original order, and combines them with great resource and vigour; the chief climax being produced by the sudden outburst of the two transition themes, Exs. 16 and 17, with solemn new signals on the trombones and trumpets. When this storm has died away there are further quiet developments on the first theme in various remote keys; from which a rapid crescendo returns to the tonic and brings back the first subject in the full orchestra. From this Dvořák passes rapidly to his recapitulation of the second subject without going through his transition material. This he holds in reserve for the short but powerful coda which is easily grafted on to the end of the second subject. The solemn tone of the close is amply justified by every theme and every note of this great work, which never once falls below the highest plane of tragic music, nor yet contains a line which could have been written by any composer but Dvořák.

SYMPHONY IN F MAJOR, NO. 3 [NOW NO. 5], OP. 76

1 *Allegro ma non troppo.* 2 *Andante con moto, leading to* 3 *Allegro scherzando.* 4 FINALE. *Allegro molto.*

In 1874 and 1875 Dvořák, approaching the middle of his thirties, but still unrecognized either in his own Bohemia or abroad, wrote three symphonies. Later, in 1877, Brahms read some of Dvořák's works, and promptly wrote to Simrock, urging him to make a beginning by publishing the Moravian Duets. The works which then aroused Brahms's interest almost certainly included the symphony in F, which was originally intended to have the opus number 24, but was withheld from publication until after the great works now known as Dvořák's First and Second Symphonies. It was probably considerably improved after this delay. The other two early symphonies have now been published posthumously, and they show conclusively that Dvořák, though not the most self-critical of artists, never intended to revive them, for he has distributed their best passages in other works. The so-called Third Symphony, on the other hand, has preserved its integrity, and, while obviously and even naughtily Dvořáky, is almost as unlike his other works as it is unlike other people's music. Its nearest parallel is a later and much weaker work, the Fourth Symphony in G major, published in England, and showing traces of an effort to meet what the composer took for English musical taste. Foreign musicians have more than once supposed that the popularity of symphonic music is as wide in Great Britain as in their native land; and hence they are apt to include in their contributions to our musical festivals features that are popular only to audiences who are surprised to find that a symphony has four movements. No such audiences exist on the Continent: even the Prussian officer of pre-war caricature left the auditorium when the symphony was due, because 'das Aas hat vier Sätze!' (Translation deleted by censor.)

Dvořák's Third Symphony begins with a theme which the orthodox pedagogue would censure as being founded entirely on a triad, with no other notes until the very end.

Ex. 1.

It is true that the young composer will either find such a theme difficult to develop or fail to see the difficulty; and that to get into the difficulty is more promising than not to see it. Moreover, it is impossible to maintain that this chord-theme and its nearest classical parallel, the theme of Weber's Sonata in A flat, are the openings of orthodox models of form. But they are unquestionably the openings of works that have a right to be taken on their own terms. A revival of Weber's sonatas is by no means out of the question, though their romantic solemnity is almost more out of fashion than their gold-lace brilliance. But Haydn himself is not more unvexed by matters of fashion than the light-hearted, inexhaustibly inventive and discursive Dvořák of the Third Symphony. And fashion itself has never found much difficulty in lionizing rustics.

As to the difficulty of developing a chord-theme, the reason why Dvořák fails to see it is because he never grasped the difference between development and exposition at all. His mind is like the mind of Jean Paul, who complained that 'it is rather inconvenient that everything reminds one of everything else'. For the rest, it matters almost as little whether Dvořák's expositions are expositions as whether Shaw's plays are plays. Not quite as little; for in the days when the question was asked about Shaw's plays, a play 'within the meaning of the act' meant a clockwork story that exacted far more attention than any of Shaw's arguments; whereas musical exposition is really a much more general and less technical matter.

The above essay is very like the exposition of Dvořák's Third Symphony. After that delightful chord-theme, the lightest symphonic opening since Beethoven's Pastoral Symphony, there is a certain amount of discussion; not too much for an exposition, but enough to show that there is no hurry. The chuckling clarinet triplets of the Pastoral Symphony do not fail to make their point

here. Eventually one of Dvořák's *grandioso* themes takes shape.
And when Dvořák says 'grandioso', he means, as I have suggested
in another essay, the grandeur of a Christmas tree.

Ex. 2.

Grandioso.

After some time we find ourselves on the threshold of a bright
foreign key, D major; and in this key a well-contrasted new theme
appears, in the guise of a quite orthodox 'second subject'.

Ex. 3.

But nothing could be less orthodox than the discussion which
follows, and which even returns to the tonic for a while, with such
emphasis as to suggest that the establishment of the new key was
a casual incident. However another accessory figure, by asserting
a much remoter key, saves the whole story from premature mar-
riage-and-living-happily-ever-afterward.

Ex. 4.

The claims of orthodox form being to this extent met, Dvořák,
like Swift at each paragraph in his *Critical Essay on the Faculties
of the Mind*, says 'but, to return from this digression'—and repeats
the exposition.

And, after all this unorthodoxy, the development, the recapitulation, and coda prove the whole movement to be a masterpiece!
The development begins by taking up Ex. 4 in a series of keys that
are new contrasts in the harmonic scheme. Soon all the themes
are discussed in turn. The last to join the argument is Ex. 2,
which leads by poetic dying modulations to a thrilling return to
the main theme in the tonic. After this the recapitulation is for
a while both full and regular. The curious result of its regularity
is that the passage which in the exposition so unscrupulously
returned to the tonic, now inevitably moves far elsewhere. Accordingly there is no further need for Ex. 4, which was active enough
in the development. And so the recapitulation drifts into a peaceful
coda, at the end of which we hear a combination of Ex. 1 on the
surface, with Ex. 3 in the bass.

The first sentence of the prettily plaintive slow movement shows the power of a master of composition not only in its unexpected extra last bar, but in the overlapping of its answer by the violins in a higher octave.

Ex. 5.

Very characteristic of Dvořák is the way in which its opening figure becomes an accompaniment to other statements and to new themes.

Ex. 6.

Brahms's way of stating and using such devices is quite different: they are a feature of his most concentrated style; whereas with Dvořák the manner is that of Lewis Carroll's Dormouse continuing to say 'Twinkle-twinkle' until pinched or put into the tea-pot.

The central episode is a series of broad sequences on a new figure—

Ex. 7.

punctuated by pathetic ejaculations from Ex. 5. It is very picturesque; and with Dvořák, as with Schubert, the step from the picturesque to something serious, if not sublime, is always imminent. Certainly the two climaxes of this slow movement, that which leads to the return and that which constitutes something like a dramatic catastrophe near the end, amply suffice to make the whole movement sound important enough for any symphony. The movement is complete. But after a short pause an epilogue on the dominant of its flat supertonic leads to the scherzo. Simply and apparently naïvely as this link is made, it is one of the many unique master-strokes in this symphony—unique, though many, for they are all different.

Experts in folk-music tell us that Dvořák has enriched the art with two new and national forms, the Furiant and the Dumky.

I must own that I have never been able to tell a Furiant from any
other kind of scherzo that is too fast for a waltz; and that when an
elegiac slow movement suddenly shows an uncontrollable impulse
to dance on its grandmother's grave, I have sometimes been wrong
in supposing that it was a Dumky, since such impulses have been
yielded to by composers who knew of no such excuse. For all I
know, the present scherzo may be a Furiant. While it has none
of the fierceness of the Furiant of the First Symphony, it is not
unlike that of the Pianoforte Quintet in tempo and rhythm. But
Dvořák has given it no special title; possibly because nobody had
told him that it was his duty to prophesy the future glories of
Czechoslovakia.

Here is his Furiantic-corybantic scherzo-theme—

Ex. 8.

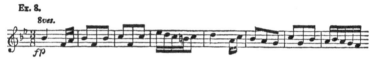

and here is the theme of the quieter trio.

Ex. 9.

(Dvořák's habit of writing *Tempo I* after a mere ritardando is apt
to produce a dangerous misunderstanding here, where *Tempo I*
looks like a return to the tempo of the andante.)

None of the movements of this symphony is very long; but
the habit of beginning discussion before exposition has taken shape
makes the listener feel as if he had come into a theatre during the
third act of the play; and his estimate of the length thus becomes
magnified by an indefinite factor. This is especially true of the
present finale. Beethoven, Schubert, and Brahms are masters of
the possibilities of finales that begin in foreign keys; whether by
way of introduction, or by means of a theme which, beginning and
obstinately returning in a foreign key, swings no less persistently
to the proper key within its own length. Dvořák, however, has
no such concern here. His main theme, beginning in A minor
(which has this point, that it was the key of the slow movement),
is at first little more than such a text for discussion as a fugue-
subject might give.

Ex. 10.

All the figures here indicated by letters are used in various combinations. The proper key, F major, is reached in triumph, after some dramatic discussion. It might as well have been any other key, for all its power to suggest that it is the harmonic centre of the symphony. But, as in the first movement, this unorthodoxy does not matter. A second theme, full of Dvořák's Bohemian-Italian lyric passion, asserts a new key, with a colour not hitherto exploited—

Ex. 11.

and a seraphic passage, in the style of the Gretchen-angelic theme in Wagner's Faust Overture, completes the material. The end of the development is marked by an impressive incident in which a bass clarinet gives out Ex. 10 in expiring tones; after which a crescendo leads to the recapitulation. As the coda approaches, Dvořák shows that he had no reason to worry about establishing F major as the true key of this finale, for he rounds off his whole work by other means altogether. The angelic Faust-Overture chords drift into a clear reminiscence of bars 9–11 of the first movement (see Ex. 1). Soon the other figures of that most original and unmistakable opening reappear; and so, when the themes of the finale gather themselves up for a final climax, we are not surprised to find the first figure of Ex. 1 forming part of the last fanfares.

SYMPHONY IN E MINOR, 'FROM THE NEW WORLD',
NO. 5 [NOW NO. 9], OP. 95

1 *Adagio, leading to* 2 *Allegro molto.* 3 *Largo.* 4 SCHERZO: *Molto Vivace*
5 *Allegro con fuoco.*

This, the most famous of Dvořák's symphonies, has a high place in his art independently of its reputation. Whether the composer has adopted melodies from the negroes, or whether the negroes, finding Dvořák's style congenial, have taken up themes from this symphony and sung *Massa dear* to them, is a matter for historians. Dvořák's phrasing was primitive, Bohemian, and childlike before he went to America. It is primitive, Bohemian, and childlike to punctuate your phrases with chuckles; and the pentatonic scale pervades folk-music from China to Peru. And Abraham Lincoln emancipated the negroes in America The negroes in America are very musical. Last of all, Dvořák had a great success on that continent. This paragraph is my exhaustive *magnum opus* on Racial Characteristics in Music.

Now let us examine Dvořák's fifth symphony. It begins with a very slow introduction, of which the melancholy hesitating opening theme may speak for itself. Ominous dramatic developments include a surging figure which eventually takes shape as the main theme of the first movement.

When the whole orchestra has taken this up, its second figure (*b*) is developed into a transition-passage leading to the 'second subject'. This contains two main themes, one in G minor (Doric, note the F natural)—

and the other, reached after a climax, in G major.

When this bursts out fortissimo in the basses as a climax we notice, what was not so evident in its calm first statement, that its rhythm resembles that of Ex. 1. This is a good reason for obeying Dvořák's direction to repeat the exposition. After that the development, which is occupied mainly by sequences on Ex. 3 treated twice as fast, stands out in higher relief. At first it seems short as well as straightforward, for in a few bold steps it reaches a grand climax with Ex. 1, bursting out in E minor, our tonic. But this proves deceptive, like some of Haydn's forestalled returns; for several more dramatic modulations are needed before this climax can subside far enough for the real recapitulation to begin. When it arrives, it begins in the same scoring as at the outset of the Allegro. But its further course embodies another stroke of genius, for in a few bars it reaches the remote key of G sharp minor, just a semitone higher than the key of the 'second subject'. And in this G-sharp-A-flat key it recapitulates the whole second subject from Ex. 2 to the climax after Ex. 3. But this climax necessarily takes a more dramatic form, for only a vigorous dramatic action can restore our tonic key.

Accordingly the pitch rises from G sharp to A, the main figures of Ex. 1 and Ex. 2 are combined, and E minor is restored in a climax of tragic fury which brings the movement to an end.

Dvořák, like Haydn, Beethoven, Schubert, and Brahms, likes now and then to put his middle movements into remote keys. But, unlike those masters, he is not very willing to allow the remote key to assert itself without explanation. The wonderful opening chords of the slow movement are there simply for the purpose of explaining the connexion between E and D flat (*alias* C sharp). But, as Dvořák is a man of genius, the explanation, like the conjuror's offer to show 'how it is done', is more mysterious than the mystery itself.

Ex. 4.

These glorious harmonies usher in the beautiful negro song which, in its wonderful setting here, has become a glory of Western art.

Ex. 5.

After the dying fall has been echoed, the chords of Ex. 4 in a new position make as if for action, but culminate in the same tonic again. Action is impossible. The melody itself takes a more declining tendency, and dies away into a plaintive episode in the minor. This episode, though highly emotional, has no power of action; like the terror of dreams it remains rooted to the spot, sometimes in agitated rhythms, sometimes held in suspense, but always meandering, always distressed, and always helpless. At last, like fireflies dancing, a strange ghost of the main theme (Ex. 5) appears.

Ex. 6.

It soon fills the orchestra; but terror grows with it, and the figure of the first movement (Ex. 1) bursts out like a menace. This is answered solemnly by the slow first figure of Ex. 5, the whole melody of which then returns, and, fading away into almost nothing, leads to the opening chords (Ex. 4), and so to an end on a ghostly pianissimo chord of four double basses.

The scherzo, after promising to build a triad from the top downwards, in the rhythm ♫ ♩, solemnly arrives at a wrong note. With this wrong note in its chord it proceeds cheerfully with negroid persistence in the reiteration of its main theme (freely canonic; note the discrepancies marked **).

Ex. 7.

A contrasted outpouring in Dvořák's most enthusiastic vein of sentiment—

Ex. 8.

turns out not to be the trio, but a mere interlude in the scherzo. Dvořák thinks that to lead into a trio is a much more serious business. The Ghost of the first movement must be summoned. Then the three notes marked (x) in Ex. 1 may furnish a figure of accompaniment for a trio, which may then proceed cheerfully enough.

Ex. 9.

The finale has powerful themes of its own; first the great melody to which its nine stormy bars of introduction lead;

Ex. 10.

secondly (after transitional accessories) an impassioned 'second subject', punctuated by irreverent negroid chuckles;

Ex. 11.

and thirdly a thoroughly negroid outburst of which the three blind mice at the end become persistent, refusing to run.

Ex. 12.

Other accessories might be quoted, and the 'diminutions' of bars 1–4 of Ex. 10 are very effective. But these materials are not enough for Dvořák. As the development proceeds the themes of the Largo (Ex. 5) and of the scherzo (Ex. 7) intervene. A climax is marked by the appearance of Ex. 1, soon after which a pathetic recapitulation, giving Ex. 10 in a mood of exhaustion, assigns Ex. 11 to the fourth string of the violins, and afterwards to the 'cellos. Then the rowdy theme of Ex. 12 surprises us by assuming a quiet sentimental tone. The horns take it up, after combining it with Ex. 1. Suddenly there is a tragic catastrophe, almost grotesque in its violence. The main theme (Ex. 10), heralded by Ex. 1, bursts out in full fury and leads to a climax in which the chords of Ex. 4 stride over the world like Wagner's Wotan when he rides the storm. After this, fragments of all four movements die away in tragic despair, until cut short by a final storm, with a combination of Ex. 1 and Ex. 10. Even so, the composer is reluctant to close; and the last chord, violently struck, dies away to pianissimo.

SYMPHONIC VARIATIONS ON AN ORIGINAL THEME,
FOR FULL ORCHESTRA, OP. 78

There is evidence in the fine arts for a paradoxical law by which persons notoriously slack and irrelevant in their treatment of matters and forms that are popularly supposed to be 'free', become remarkably shrewd in their handling of forms which are obviously more strict and of specially intellectual interest. There are in music few things more obviously intellectual than the variation form. This does not prevent variations from being, next to the concerto form, the most misunderstood and mishandled form in music, nor does it mean that there are many great sets of variations in existence. If great groups of variations were as numerous as great sonata movements, of course the form would be better understood. Current ideas of the nature of the form have been derived, as in the case of concertos, not from the few masterpieces, but from the enormous majority of plausible works on false lines. But it is wonderful to see how the superb instinct of a naïve genius, such as Schubert or Dvořák, grasps the essentials of this eminently scholarly problem in music, though the patience is lacking which can bring the same concentration of mind to bear upon the apparently more free, but really more complex, problems of other instrumental forms. Neither Schubert nor Dvořák has left many sets of variations; but those which they have produced are, with a few trivial exceptions, perfect. They are also of types peculiar to their composers. In discussing variation works elsewhere, I have ventured to lay down a basis for a strictly scientific classification of the form. The basis of my classification is the teaching of Sir Hubert Parry. Variations may be classified into (a) those which show that the composer knows his theme, and (b) those which show that he does not. Dvořák certainly knows his themes; and indeed he invented a rather peculiar type of theme for variations. At all events, his three outstanding variation-movements, the wonderfully clever finale of the Terzet for violin and viola, the brilliant and poetic finale of the otherwise unsatisfactory Sextet for strings, and the present orchestral work, are all on themes of this peculiar type, which has since been made more familiar to the public in Elgar's Enigma Variations. Instead of relying upon any solid rhythmic or harmonic structure, the composer takes two alternating strains as full of different melodic figures as possible, and states them in the order A, B, A. It will be seen from my quotation—

Ex. 1.

that every pair of bars of this whimsically severe theme contains a
very recognizable melodic figure (like (*a*), (*b*), (*c*), (*d*)); and that the
second strain B groups its new figure (*d*) on steps of a rising scale
reaching to a climax. These melodic facts are solid enough to allow
Dvořák in some of his later variations to break away from the
original rhythmic limits of the theme, and to indulge in considerable
passages of development without seeming to break the backbone
of his variation.

The theme having been stated in harmony of portentous bareness, the first three variations simply clothe it in all sorts of bright
counterpoints.

The 4th variation disguises the first strain of the melody,
although retaining its harmonic outline; but the second strain,
with its rising scale, is easily enough recognized.

The 5th variation has brilliant running figures.

In the 6th variation there are symptoms that the theme is able
to stretch itself, for the first strain begins by taking two bars for
one of the original theme. The second strain, however, moves at
the old pace.

In variation 7 the freedom of rhythm grows as the colouring
becomes more dramatic, and in variation 8 it is possible for the
strings to add a little introduction on a diminished version of
figure (*b*) before the winds enter mysteriously with the theme.

Variation 9 again spreads out the first strain, and, apropos of
the F sharp in its second bar, enriches the harmony throughout
more boldly than hitherto.

Variation 10 is vivace in a springing rhythm.

Variation 11 returns to a meditative tempo, in dialogue with the
lower strings and the wood-wind, the modulations becoming richer
as it proceeds; and it expands into a dreamy cadenza for the violins,
which leads to variation 12 poco andante, a highly expressive
violin solo.

Variation 13 is again lively, and of almost the same length as the
original theme.

Variation 14 (lento) is wrapped in mystery, which is not revealed
until the third strain, where the bassoon shows that the palpitating

harmonies are a beautiful and natural accompaniment to the first strain.

Variation 15, maestoso at the same pace, arises in its wrath, and after an attempt to expostulate gently in the second strain, broadens out into an interlude in which the pace accelerates, until in variation 16 the orchestra storms through the theme at double quick time.

So far the variations have remained in the original duple time. Now a new epoch begins with the scherzo (variation 17). This is a somewhat expanded statement in the tempo of a triple-time scherzo. Beginning quietly enough, it flutters away mysteriously into variation 18, a larghetto, in which we have the original melody in a very unexpected harmonic position. Imagine the theme as quoted above, with no alteration but the presence of two sharps in the signature, the notes remaining the same; and imagine the bass-note of the whole to be A. Thus this whole variation is in D major, a key very contradictory to that of C. It leads straight to the other contradictory key, on the other side, B flat.

In this key variation 19 appears in tempo di valse, with a transformation of the theme so ingenious that I must quote it.

Ex. 2.

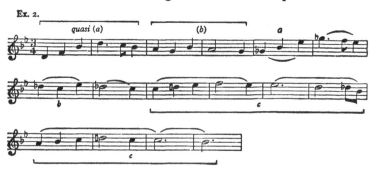

Variations 20 and 21 continue in B flat minor, with livelier transformations.

In variation 22 a horn climbs up from the depths by way of throwing the first strain to the higher wind instruments. The second strain is of the nature of a hilarious pillow-fight between the basses and the full orchestra.

In variation 23, still in B flat minor with the same type of rhythm, the original melody is much more easily recognized, and in variation 24 the orchestra settles solemnly down to a broad and gloomy treatment of the figures in a 12/8 andante. This brings the B flat section to a close.

In variation 25 we find ourselves in the extremely distant key of G flat minor. The outlook is serene, with the peculiar naïve, almost Italian sentiment, which Dvořák commands in his romantic mood.

From G flat (or F sharp) to D major is a natural step, and variation 26 begins in D major with the melody of variation 25 in the bass. It turns plaintively into the minor, and so moves round to C major, where with some wistful questionings it leads to variation 27.

Here, in the original key and in a tempo near to that of the original theme, the figures of the first strain are repeated dryly one at a time by the strings and wind alternating. There is a decrescendo and a ritardando until the violins break away dramatically and bring down the whole string orchestra with a solemn cadential shake, closing into a fugue. This fugue is the finale, allegro maestoso. Dvořák simply takes strain A as his fugue subject, with a shake on the last note but one, and he amuses himself and us by storming along at it with the greatest vigour and any amount of resource. There are quieter passages, and passages which are no more in strict fugue than similar things in Beethoven; but the whole is thoroughly solid and quite easy to follow, until at the end it culminates in what would be a unison statement of its subject if the trumpets and drums did not insist on playing only one note. The tempo is considerably quickened by the time this unison is reached, and after one of Dvořák's grandioso climaxes the work ends più animato in 2/2 time. Why it is not better known passes the comprehension of any one who can recognize good music. Sir Charles Stanford places it *non longo intervallo* after the *Études Symphoniques* of Schumann; and it is so far unlike all other variation-works in existence that it cannot suffer by comparisons.

SCHERZO CAPRICCIOSO, OP. 66

It is surprising that this great and most brilliant orchestral work should ever have fallen into neglect. It is obviously one of Dvořák's most important movements, and in it all his characteristics are summed up with complete strength and mastery. The title describes it admirably. The work is a scherzo worthy of Beethoven: it is also a capriccio worthy of the author of *The Shaving of Shagpat*. It is a masterpiece of form and especially of the imaginative handling of remote key relationships. Finally its humour, ranging from riotous high spirits and mock tragedy to luxurious pathetic sentiment, is as true as its form. There is no great music whose company it need fear.

The aesthetic value of a system of key relationships is not a thing that can be explained in untechnical language; and I must be allowed to leave it as a dogmatic statement that in this piece every harmonic effect and especially every change of key throw into highest relief the contrasts and the perfect balance of the whole composition. Nobody except Schubert was less conscious of any responsibility in these matters than Dvořák, and accordingly both Schubert and Dvořák have produced weak works in which a riot of gay modulations produces no better effect than the modulations in any operatic pot-pourri. But when Schubert and Dvořák are writing with inspiration their imaginative power shows itself nowhere more vividly than in their use of rich and remote contrasts of key. In this they rank with Beethoven, Brahms, and Wagner as masters whose modulations are always true, always prepared so as to carry the utmost weight, never weakened in ultimate result by appearing in response to insufficient need, and never cramped by mannerism or by the discipline of the inadequate theories that have driven so many composers into complete scepticism as to any aesthetic principles whatever in this matter.

Dvořák's Scherzo Capriccioso begins with a theme cheerfully thrown forward by the horns in the key of B flat major.

Ex. 1.

The strings, as we see, are far from convinced that this is the right key. Nevertheless they ruminate about and about its dominant; and a flute answers the theme thereon. Other instruments, however, continue to take a pessimistic view. The first figure (*a*) is tossed up agitatedly on this dominant of B flat, and suddenly, in a short crescendo, the whole orchestra realizes that of course (but why 'of course'?) the right key is D flat. In this key, then, they all burst out with the figures of Ex. 1 in four-bar phrases, *fortissimo* with big drum and cymbals, and *piano* with harp and triangle. Soon it goes in an orthodox manner, though in none too regular a rhythm, to A flat, the dominant of D flat, thus clearly proving that D flat is the real harmonic centre of the composition. (From

B flat the key of A flat would be a direct contradiction.) Now on this dominant the second stage of the design opens, with a note of interrogation.

Ex. 2.

The answer is a miracle. We have been convinced that D flat is our main key to which this note of interrogation demands our return; and now there appears a glorious waltz beginning in G major, the one key that sounds infinitely remote from D flat.

Ex. 3.

In irregularly expanding rhythms this sweeps through four changes of key until it reaches F sharp major, which, could we but recognize our whereabouts after these magic-carpet journeys, is really G flat, the safe and comfortable subdominant of our D flat. Here, at all events, we settle down with a derivative of the main theme.

Ex. 4.

When this has come to its formal close there is a bustling return to the key of—what? Of the opening, B flat major. The orchestra sets about repeating this whole exposition from the beginning. The scepticism as to B flat being the right key is, however, far more pronounced now, and the passages that express doubt are greatly developed and enriched. The establishing of D flat is all the more triumphant, and from this point the repetition is varied only by richer scoring and by a slightly longer and much angrier version of the note of interrogation (Ex. 2). And so we again pass through the glorious sequences of the waltz (Ex. 3) to the cadence-group in the subdominant (Ex. 4). This cadence-group is now allowed to subside slowly into silence. Then in another unexpected key, D major, the trio begins. The system of keys is now complete. The mystery of the effect of these keys, G and D, is that they are unfathomably distant from D flat, but they are in a clear and brilliant relation to B flat, the key of the opening.

The main melody of the trio is one of Dvořák's great passages of
naïve Italian sentiment, given at first to the cor anglais—

and repeated higher with a halo above it. Another theme appears
in B minor, a key equally remote from B flat and D flat.

As the quotation shows, it soon bursts into a forte in F sharp
minor, whence it passes triumphantly to A, where, with trumpet
and trombone signals, it comes to a grandiose close. Then it
solemnly, slowly, and quietly returns to repeat the trio from the
beginning. After the repeat the figures of Ex. 6 are vigorously
developed in combination with those of Ex. 1, which is given in
comic forcible-feeble rage by various small groups of wind instruments. Soon the opening key of B flat is reached. This time there is
no longer any pretence of believing in it; the bass clarinet and the
flute cheerfully blow the theme away into B natural and thence
into G; after which many further developments follow in a steady
progress. Here, for instance, is a combination of Exs. 1, 3, and 6,
with a new counterpoint (Ex. 7).

Before long the key of D flat is reached in triumph and the main theme comes out *grandioso* in a higher position than ever before. It is continued in a regular recapitulation which passes through Ex. 2, in its simple version, to Ex. 3. Here a simple change of harmony makes the waltz-tune lead to Ex. 4 in D flat. The cadence dies away plaintively, mysteriously, and slower and slower. There is now no longer the slightest doubt that D flat is the key of the composition; and the coda begins peacefully swinging the themes of Exs. 1 and 3 on its tonic and dominant. Suddenly the tempo revives; the horns put the theme in the form of a question; the harp seconds them with a cadenza; and then the orchestra builds up an excited stretto, and brings this great movement to a brilliant *presto* end.

ELGAR

SYMPHONY IN E FLAT, NO. 2, OP. 63

1 *Allegro vivace e nobilmente.* 2 *Larghetto.* 3 RONDO: *Presto.*
4 *Moderato e maestoso.*

On the fly-leaf of this work stands the following inscription: 'Dedicated to the Memory of His Late Majesty King Edward VII. This Symphony designed early in 1910 to be a loyal tribute, bears its present dedication with the gracious approval of His Majesty the King. March 16th 1911.'

Besides this, the symphony takes from Shelley its motto:

Rarely, rarely, comest thou,
Spirit of Delight.

The second figure (*b*) of the main theme—

Ex. 1.

may be taken as representing this motto, for it occurs elsewhere than in the first movement, and generally with a wistfulness as if it referred to something no longer, or not yet, present in the impetuous strength displayed here.

Readers who have followed my essay on Elgar's *Falstaff*
(below) may find it interesting to note how much easier is the
analysis of a work of similar calibre that proceeds on the lines
of classical sonata form. This is not because classical forms are
simpler. On the whole they are more complex than those of
Falstaff. Nor are the forms of *Falstaff* non-classical. The only
conception of form that has any truth in it is that according to which
the form represents the natural growth of the matter so intimately
that, in the last resort, form and matter are interchangeable terms.
But it saves an immense amount of trouble in analysis if the matter
happens to grow into forms which have enough family likeness to
those of many other works of art to have produced a number of
technical terms by which they can be named. Thanks to the very
complexity and richness of the forms of a classical symphony, I am
saved the trouble of trying to identify this or that feature, structural
or emotional, of the present work with the glories and sorrows of
the reign of Edward VII. It is perhaps permissible to say that no
one who has met the composer or studied this symphony can
possibly fail to see that it is animated by no mere official imperialism,
but by a deep glow of personal and affectionate loyalty.

The first movement begins at once with its main theme, containing, as I have said before, in figure (*b*), the musical representation of its motto. This is the beginning of a long paragraph which
builds into large sequences a number of other themes, from which
I quote three.

Ex. 2.
Ex. 3.
Ex. 4.

As in the Violin Concerto and other large works of Elgar, the
sequential structure and the shortness of the figures built up therein
are apt to produce an analysis like that of the Wagnerian *motiv*-
hunter, according to which the music would appear lamentably
short of breath and still more lamentably long of procedure. As a
matter of fact, Elgar's paragraphs are big and his action is swift.

I have not quoted all the themes of the first group. The tonic, E flat, stands firm at the outset and the drift towards another key is sudden and decisive. But when that other key appears it proves an iridescent mixture of several keys, remote enough for the home tonic itself to appear foreign in its new surrounding as one of the chords of the main theme in the second group.

Ex. 5.

The orthodox dominant is more nearly concerned in the following accessory theme—

Ex. 6.

and various sequences that arise on the materials of Exs. 5 and 4 tend more and more to establish it.

I leave the double climax, at first brilliant and hereafter solemn, to speak for itself, and I quote only the quiet cadence theme into which the exposition subsides.

Ex. 7.

From this it passes without perceptible break into the development, which begins by alternating the expiring strains of Ex. 7 with a new figure—

Ex. 8.

in a series of remote modulations. These lead to E major, in which remote key the development takes action by using a combination of Exs. 8 and 1 as accompaniment to an important new episodic theme.

Ex. 9.

This falls in sequence, descending by semitones in bold dissonance over a persistent E natural, until at last the E gives way and both figures of the first theme (Ex. 1) appear in C major, associated with a new figure.

Ex. 9 a (compare Ex. 5).

The development is chiefly concerned with these materials, alternating with developments of Exs. 4, 2, and 3.

As soon as the quiet episode dies away, the action becomes rapid; and the last stage of the development, in which the figures (*a*) (*b*) of Ex. 1 reappear, moves swiftly to a grandiose return prepared for by a solemn summons from the horns and trombones. The recapitulation of both groups is regular, though the handling of the mixed tonalities of the second group has a classical subtlety and freedom.

The coda arises naturally from the expiring of the cadence group (Ex. 7) and, without alluding either to Exs. 8 or 9, proceeds to give Ex. 9 *a*, augmented to twice its size, pianissimo in the tonic, after which it builds up a quick crescendo on Ex. 3, and ends with an appeal to the Spirit of Delight (Ex. 1, figure (*b*)).

The slow movement is elegiac, with something of the character of a funeral march. Its first seven bars are an introduction, which I do not quote, on a figure somewhat reminiscent of Ex. 2. It is the main theme—

Ex. 10.

to which this movement chiefly owes its suggestiveness of a funeral march; and that characteristic is perhaps more inherent in the accompaniment than in the melody. (Note the figure (*a*), common to Exs. 1 and 10. With Elgar such points are significant.)

A modulating transition-theme—

Ex. 11.

leads towards F major, and in a tonal region compounded of that key and of A minor, one of the main themes of the middle section appears.

Ex. 12.

Moving in broad lines and with free rhythm, as if Bruckner had become a master of phrasing, this passes through an agitated sequence on a new figure which I do not quote, to a grand and simple climax fully in F major, with another important theme which completes the exposition.

Ex. 13.

This dies away, and Ex. 11 effects a mournful return to C minor and to the main theme, which is given in full with the addition of a beautiful ruminating counterpoint on an oboe. The whole of the sequel is recapitulated in due order, Exs. 12–13 being given in and around E flat.

The coda arises from a dramatic return to the dominant of C, upon which is heard an appeal to the Spirit of Delight (Ex. 1), alternating with Ex. 11, after which the movement expires in a mournful allusion to the first phrase of its main theme (Ex. 10), which closes into another allusion to the unquoted introductory bars.

The scherzo is, as its title shows, in rondo form. A mystery underlies its playful opening theme.

Ex. 14.

The meaning of the portion marked x in this quotation will appear later.

The first episode is in the tonic minor.

Ex. 15.

Considerable development of the figures of the main theme, at first in cross accents and then in combination with a new figure—

Ex. 15 a.

follows before the main theme is allowed to return in full. The
second episode is in an unorthodox key or tonal region, that of the
major supertonic, D.

A wistful introductory figure—

Ex. 16.

is delivered and echoed by several wood-wind instruments, and
afterwards worked into paragraphs together with the swinging
theme of the episode itself.

Ex. 17.

The second return of the main theme is a quiet affair, and the
strings have a tendency to adorn the outline of the group x with a
halo. This halo becomes gradually clearer until, in the key of E
flat, it takes solid shape as the important episodic theme (Ex. 9)
with which the development of the first movement had begun. On
a long tonic pedal this episode now grows to a mighty cantabile,
which eventually passes, via the trombones, into the bass, while the
scherzo-theme just contrives to penetrate the mass of tone above.
As the mass of tone dies away, another origin of the theme, Ex. 8,
becomes audible. It is always an interesting problem in aesthetics
how, when a lively movement has mounted on to a sublime pedestal,
it can come off it again. Elgar's solution of this dangerous problem
is Schumannesque and classical. Without any preaching or tub-
thumping, the music resumes the first episode (Ex. 15) quietly, as
Schumann's Florestan, or any other nice young undergraduate,
might relight his pipe after he had allowed it to go out during an
outburst of enthusiasm. As before, steps towards a return to the
main theme are taken by a development of Ex. 14, with cross
accents; but what is reached is Ex. 15 a in a grand climax without
the semiquaver figure. When this has died away, the rest of the
coda piles itself up in brilliant cross-rhythmed sequences.

The finale seems to be, as the directions for its tempo imply, a comparatively slow movement; but this is rather an illusion of notation, for it is in reality remarkably swift, with an irresistible momentum in the strength of its current. No stronger contrast could be found than that between it and the standard difficulty of the clever composers whose finales and thematic transformations call themselves prestissimo in a vain struggle against the flaccid uniformity of their phrase-lengths.

The finale moves on the lines of a broad sonata form with the following tune as its main theme:

Ex. 18.

A transition theme, starting in the subdominant—

Ex. 19.

leads in massive sequences to a second group consisting of a single new theme in the dominant—

Ex. 20.

closing with a four-bar allusion to Ex. 18. This plunges into a development consisting mainly of a fugue on the figures of Ex. 19 combined with new counterpoint. The tendency of fugues is not to modulate widely. They are arguments rather than actions, or they are actions at law rather than at large. Accordingly the venue of this development remains in the tonal region around D major and B minor, in which latter key the first figure of the main theme (Ex. 18) begins to assert itself obstinately.

A new figure—

brings a persuasively pacifying note into the discussion, and soon combines with larger portions of the main theme. Eventually a return to E flat is effected, and the more or less regular recapitulation of all the material builds itself up into a grand climax and leads to a peaceful coda. From the quiet heights into which it recedes, this coda is dominated by the Spirit of Delight (figure (*b*) of Ex. 1 in very slow tempo) and the symphony ends in solemn calm.

'FALSTAFF', SYMPHONIC STUDY, OP. 68

Since I wrote this analysis the composer kindly gave me permission to correct it by comparison with his own commentary, which appeared in *The Musical Times* of September 1st, 1913, and which, to my shame, I had not read. But my delinquency has its advantages; for it gives rise to a unique opportunity for demonstrating how far a great piece of 'programme music' can be intelligible as pure music and at the same time convey the subject of the composer's illustration to other minds without the use of words. Accordingly I have retained my analysis with all its mistakes, and have corrected it by the composer's analysis in footnotes marked (E). This initial must not be taken to make the composer responsible for the wording of the footnotes; but it implies his authority for their substance. On the whole I am quite satisfied with my success in guessing the composer's literary meaning. Glaring failure about main points would be as unsatisfactory from the composer's point of view as from mine; for my impressions are those of a musician, and not those of a dilettante who might be excused for all manner of blunders in appraising musical values. Where I am wrong I do not see how I could have guessed right, but I have no difficulty in seeing the composer's point when his account corrects me.

Prophecy about the judgement of posterity is as otiose a game in matters of art as in other matters of history. But I have sometimes been compelled to investigate works of art that I should not care to revive; and I have never found in a perishable work anything like the signs of greatness and vitality that abound in Elgar's *Falstaff*. How its musical values can ever diminish I cannot see. To prove the greatness of a work of art is a task as hopeless as it would be tedious; but, like the candidate who failed in geometry, I think I can make the greatness of this one appear highly probable.

Let me begin by 'blowing the expense', and for once giving a tolerably complete list of thematic quotations. With thirty-three musical examples I have to omit any theme or incident that does not recur outside its first context; hence, any theme that appears only or always in continuity with a quoted theme, and any variation that can be described in words or easily recognized on a first hearing. Even so, I could describe several passages more easily with the aid of another six quotations.

This enormous mass of definitely different themes is about equal to that of Beethoven's Eroica or Ninth Symphony; and Elgar's work is one continuous movement, not essentially interrupted by its two intermezzi. It is completely independent of the Lisztian doctrine that all the themes of a symphonic poem should be derivable from a single thematic cell or *U-keim*. The plausibility of that doctrine lies in the fact that a ripe and highly intellectual musical style tends to develop fascinating thematic connexions as a form of wit. The fatal weakness of the doctrine is that such wit does not concern the foundations of musical composition at all, and is not necessarily more logical than a series of puns. Speaking without the composer's correction, I see and hear no musical reason why these thirty-three quotations should prove to have any thematic relations beyond those to which I draw attention. But in the art of composition the work coheres like a diamond. Its clarity is the crystalline artistic simplicity that comes from the enormous pressures of an inexhaustible imagination; not from the weary eliminations of a taste that declines from one boredom to the next. It is not a matter of previously ascertained form; nor is it a matter of literary illustration.

To the task of musical illustration Elgar brings the resources of a mind long ago well and deeply read, and especially replenished for the matter in hand. He is of the classical race of *attentive* artists; his view of his literary subject will be intensely his own, because his mind will be concentrated upon it. Hence his musical illustrations will amount to a close symbolical tissue, like those by which Bach, Mozart, and Beethoven habitually illustrate words when illustration is called for. Nevertheless I do not propose to analyse *Falstaff* from this point of view. I know neither this music nor the two parts of *King Henry the Fourth* well enough to do so; and in the nature of the case the music is (as Mendelssohn urged in a very profound argument on musical illustration) much more definite than words. And it so happens that Shakespeare has not given Sir John to us in a connected narrative at all, but in a series of episodes deftly but by no means closely wrought into an historic pageant, which is another series of episodes with little more coherence than that of popular history. But, strange to say, it is just in the management of such pageantry that the capacity for composition is most severely tested. Elgar's *Falstaff* is as close and inevitable a musical structure as anything since Beethoven; and this cannot be claimed for *Henry the Fourth*. But for *Henry the Fourth*, alike in the aspects of comedy, chronicle, and tragedy, it can be claimed that Shakespeare's power of movement is at its height; in other words, that the art of composition is omnipresent in that general sense which is more vital than any external form. And here Elgar's power is identical with Shakespeare's, and, being subject to none but purely musical conditions that are its own breath of life, it also achieves a perfect external form. One of the essential characteristics of that form **is** the combination of weighty symphonic development with episodic leisure and freedom. I hope to show, as occasion arises, how vividly the composer brings before us, by sheer power of abstract form, the contrast between the irresponsible roisterings of the comedians and the ominous background of dynastic troubles.

But I am not going to look for minute details. The particular illustrations I can at present see are obvious enough. I should not be surprised to learn that there were hundreds more; but the composer has not lost grasp of his music in their pursuit, and you and I certainly will lose grasp of the music if we do not attend exclusively to it. When we know both Elgar's and Shakespeare's Falstaff by heart we may amuse ourselves with Gadshill robberies and the arithmetical progression of rogues in buckram. Till then let us be broadly general over the human characters, and attentively musical about details and forms. (By the way, I take it that *The Merry Wives of Windsor* may be neglected. The composer who wishes to put Falstaff into an opera must use *The Merry Wives of Windsor* as the only possible framework of a plot; but the real Falstaff is not there except in one or two good phrases.) Here is unquestionably the real Falstaff, wallowing, protesting, and formidable in his absurdity.[1]

No doubt it may be possible to find the Shakespearian origin of the following pair of satellite themes; but all I know is that one is perky or quizzical, like any Elizabethan page—

and the other scolding, like some aspects of Mistress Quickly[2] or less respectable persons (overleaf).

---

[1] Not as yet quite absurd but (as Morgann says, writing in 1777) 'in a green old age, mellow, frank, gay, easy, corpulent, loose, unprincipled, and luxurious'. (E.)

[2] Exx. 2 and 3 are among Falstaff's personal themes. 'I am not only witty in myself, but the cause that wit is in others.' (E.)

But the later developments of these themes do not fit any particulars of the kind, and Ex. 2 is no subordinate character in the whole work. A counterstatement gives Ex. 1 in the bass below a cataract of trills into which the scoldings have merged. One of the most significant features of style in this work is the fact that most of the themes will make powerful basses, as already shown at the outset by the fact that Ex. 1 stands without harmony. In this respect Elgar may remind us of Richard Strauss, especially as something like the Straussian *panache* is essential to the character of Falstaff. But, with all respect to Strauss, there is more art in *Falstaff* than in *Ein Heldenleben*. The unaccompanied main theme of *Heldenleben* is great; but the problem of its eventual harmonization is contemptuously evaded, whereas Elgar's harmonization never suggests that it was ever a problem at all, whether it consists of a combination of themes or a mass of impressionist scoring. And every one of Elgar's combinations of themes is a statement of excellent harmony made by the combined melodies. The more modern view regards the technical difficulty of this as a restraint. The wiser view recognizes it as a resource. A student with a dangerous sense of humour once brought to my score-playing class some pages of *Falstaff* as a prepared task. He forestalled my comments by explaining that being pressed for time, he had chosen these pages as a 'soft option' because, though for full orchestra, they consisted entirely of two-part harmony. This satisfies Brahms's test with a vengeance, the test of covering up the middle of the score in order to see what the top and bottom is worth 'without trimmings'.

In the fourth theme of the opening complex we clearly recognize Prince Hal in the mood[1] of that soliloquy when he declares his intention of imitating the sun by allowing himself to be hidden in base contagious clouds in order to be more wondered at when he breaks through them.

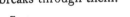

This theme is noble; and the composer would have gone wrong in his musical and dramatic psychology if he had made it otherwise. Breeding will tell, whatever flaws may deface the character. But

[1] In his most courtly and genial mood. The symbol of his stern military character will be found in Ex. 28 of the present essay. (E.)

Elgar withholds his accolade; this theme is *not* marked *nobilmente*,
though that is how it must be played. It is true to the Shakespearian
irony, deeper than the Sophoclean, and perhaps less aware of itself
than the Euripidean; true to the irony which indulges in popular
sentiments with apparent zest until the very groundlings must feel
the approach of shame. Shylock and the glorious sport of Jew-
baiting; Hamlet and the diverting farce of lunacy; Prince Hal, who
owes Falstaff his love, and who has from first to last been stealing
the pleasures of disreputable 'ragging' with the deliberate intention
of pompously and publicly disgracing his poor dupes as soon as he
is crowned; all these things the interpreter of Shakespeare should
give us with the illusory side foremost. The poet's deeper views
may be subversive, but the uneasy censor will discover nothing but
impenetrable popular orthodoxy.

The continuation of Ex. 4 is broadly melodious and based on
different material which I do not quote. Its counterstatement is
followed by a re-entry of Ex. 1 in violas with a sinuous counterpoint
in the 'cellos. Suddenly it turns aside into the remote key of E
minor, where a new theme appears.

Ex. 5.

Except in obvious cases, I do not propose to identify themes with
persons. But we may go so far as to identify bass registers with male
characters. And Ex. 5 lends itself to stratagems and spoils.[1] It is
given time to explain itself in square statements and counter-
statements. Then the perky-and-scolding complex (Exx. 2 and 3)
returns and leads to a grand peroration reviewing all the themes
and unobtrusively introducing a new tottering bass to Falstaff.

Ex. 6.

The peroration ends with a descent of Ex. 1 from the top of the
orchestra to the bass register of the last bars of the theme. These
are reiterated expectantly, with a pause.[2] Now, in a quicker tempo,

---

[1] The rising scale in the latter part of this quotation shows Falstaff as
cajoling and persuasive. (E.)

[2] Thus far Section 1, presenting Falstaff and Prince Henry. (E.)

action begins.¹ Still we have to deal with new themes, and not until the fat is in the fire (as might be Falstaff larding the lean earth at Gadshill) do the new themes combine with the old.

First we have a group of four new figures conspiring together in a single sentence.

Ex. 7.

Ex. 8.

Ex. 9.

Ex. 10.²

These are repeated with a new modulation after a pause. A new theme impinges on them, blown up like a bladder with sighing and grief.³

Ex. 11.

It is given plenty of room to vent its grievance; and then the action begins. Both the figures of Ex. 6 are developed in a fugato in combination with Exx. 1 and 5. This quickly leads to a collapse upon Ex. 7, which is thrice insisted on. Then the figures of Exx. 8 and 9 conclude this exposition.

At the present juncture, whatever events may have been so far represented they issue now in a noble outburst of Falstaffian moral indignation.

¹ Section II. Eastcheap—Gadshill—The Boar's Head, revelry, and sleep. (E.)
² Women, such as the Hostess, Doll Tearsheet, and 'a dozen or fourteen honest gentlewomen'. (E.)
³ Not at all! 'A goodly, portly man, of a cheerful look, a pleasing eye and a most noble carriage.' (E.)

Ex. 12.¹

Harmonized grandly in two-part counterpoint, relieved from austerity by occasional faintly heard inner notes, this theme, like many others in the work, is exposed in the manner of a fugue. There are three entries: soprano, alto, and bass. It is important to realize, as Bradley points out, that Falstaff is no coward, either in fact or in reputation. In battle Sir John Coleville surrendered to him on the strength of his name. The object of Poins in the Gadshill plot was to show him up not as a coward but as a boaster. Poins clearly distinguishes him from his two colleagues thus:

'Well, for two of them, I know them to be as true-bred cowards as ever turned back; and for the third, if he fight longer than he sees reason, I'll forswear arms.'

Honour hath no skill in surgery, and Falstaff will tolerate no humbug but himself. I ask the reader to glance ahead to Ex. 17 for the magnificent combination of Exx. 12 and 11, which here follows in a lower key, less convenient for printing in an economical way. Ex. 11 is then continued in combination with the quaver figure of Ex. 7. With a rapid decrescendo the music recedes into distance, and the conspirators, Exx. 7, 8, 9, now plot in whispers. Falstaff (Ex. 1 broken up in a variation alternately with the figure of Ex. 9) is alert but mystified. Something new and innocent makes its appearance.²

Ex. 13.

But I am afraid that the Prince is also tiptoeing in the neighbourhood with mischievous intent—

Ex. 14.   Outline of Ex. 4.

and though Falstaff in 'diminution' does not seem formidable, I would not trust him with my money.

---

¹ 'I am a rogue if I were not at half sword with a dozen of them two hours together.' (E.)
² A cheerful out-of-door ambling theme. (E.)

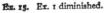

Ex. 15. Ex. 1 diminished.

As this mysterious episode develops, the connexion between Ex. 13 and Ex. 4 becomes more obvious. Ex. 12 persists quietly in its course, with evident effort to maintain its nonchalance. But the surrounding darkness is too much for it, and eventually all themes are lost in a passage consisting of ominous rustlings and whisperings. Prince Hal, in a new variation anticipating Ex. 16, is present; another conspirator (Ex. 5, Falstaff himself?)[1] is groaning in the background. The ominous rustlings are resumed with deeper tone; but they suddenly end in a sportive version of Prince Hal's theme, accompanied by running triplets.

Ex. 16. Variation of Ex. 4.

This is given room to display itself thrice in different keys. Then shrill cries and whistles[2] lead to a fierce fight. Ex. 12, diminished in quavers, hacks its fugal way in A minor with the utmost energy,[3] and soon settles down in E minor to reiterating its first figure with growing emphasis, until it merges into a re-entry of Ex. 10, loud, complaining, and, as before, soon combining grandly with Ex. 11 at its full size, thus—

Ex. 17.

Suddenly this dies away, and Ex. 7, with both its figures, expresses unholy glee in dialogue between various treble instruments. A new theme of syncopated minim chords,

appears softly and timidly above tambourine-sounds of marching steps. At a sudden stand-and-deliver, Ex. 13 reappears, at first with a new full-toned boldness, but it fades out into Ex. 11, plangent as ever, though faint, on muted horns below derisive scales descending in the violins. Falstaff also bestirs himself in diminution (as in Ex. 15), perhaps a little testy under the persistent and monotonous gibes of Ex. 10.

[1] Yes; see note on Ex. 5.
[2] The short struggle for the twice-stolen booty 'got with much ease'. (E.)   [3] The discomfiture of the thieves. (E.)

And now comes one of the most remarkable features in the form of this work. In and around the key of G minor, Ex. 10 occupies no less than fifty-eight bars, thirty-two of which are marked to be repeated.[1] Nothing breaks the monotony of two-bar rhythm, and there are not many breaks in the series of 4-bar or even 8-bar phrases in which the episode runs its course. As with the stiff, antithetic style of Schumann, the interest lies largely in epigrammatic wit. Elgar has temperamentally much in common with Schumann, and at any time in his career he could have made himself as popular as Grieg by abandoning all methods of composition except the rigid mosaic of Schumann's larger works. But such a style ceases to be rigid and becomes a mighty achievement of athletic muscle when it is absorbed into the contrasts of a freely organized work. This episode has, in relation to the rest, exactly the audacity of movement by which Shakespeare carries us through the several scenes in which Prince Hal is wasting unlimited time with his pot-house companions. Among details, notice the combination of Exx. 10 and 5, classically euphonious like all Elgar's counterpoint.

At length Falstaff protests. The solo Falstaff of the orchestra, the bassoon, almost as loud as Coleridge thought it to be, declaims in terms of Ex. 12, *quasi recitativo*. It collapses cynically into Ex. 9, out of which arises a new theme in the chattering staccato of the wood-wind.

Ex. 18.

The composition still maintains its sectional, episodic character while this new theme, together with a complaining, slow chromatic counterpoint, develops into a row. When this has run its course and died away, the former badinage is recapitulated with an effect of insolent regularity, though it is really only epitomized. But it includes Ex. 12 again, although Falstaff's voice, worn out in the singing of anthems, becomes alarmingly wheezy. Soon we hear him sleeping. And though the musical illustration of this is as audible as sleep can be, it reveals, both in itself and in its context, the poetic depth of the whole work. A mere musical illustrator would, even if he failed to show why Falstaff was in hiding behind the arras, certainly have tried to illustrate the exposition of the contents of Falstaff's pockets, and the derision aroused by the famous bill for a ha'porth of bread with an intolerable deal of sack. But the more we study Elgar's Falstaff the clearer does it appear

[1] The 'honest gentlewomen's' theme, now complete and raised to due importance, runs its scherzo-like course. (E.)

that the composer is achieving something lofty, severe, consistent, and far out of the depth of opera or even of drama. He is giving us Falstaff entirely from Falstaff's own point of view. The old rascal is not sentimental; but, as Theobald divined from a corrupt text, ' 'a babbled of green fields' on his death-bed; and Elgar knows that when he slept there was a wistful beauty in his dreams of Jack Falstaff, a boy who could have crept into any alderman's thumb-ring, page to the Duke of Norfolk.

The theme of the 'Dream Interlude' has a purposely indefinite family resemblance to such quizzicalities as Ex. 9; but not even the thread of personality itself can make a solid bridge over the gulf between that dreamland past and the drastic present.[1]

Ex. 19.

Falstaff awakes again to his roistering world.[2] Exx. 2–3 return in full vigour. And now he must play the soldier. I hazard the guess that in the following new complex of themes we may perhaps see Falstaff as recruiting officer, and can agree with his estimate of his mouldy, feeble, warty, and vituline recruits.

Ex. 20.

Ex. 21.[3]

Ex. 22.[4]

Between Ex. 21 and Ex. 22 the contrapuntal combination of Ex. 10 over Ex. 5 intervenes. I know nothing more 'gravity-removing' than the effect of Ex. 22 when it is delivered timidly in musical dumb-crambo by the various thumpers and tinklers known as the 'kitchen' department of the orchestra.

[1] The contrast of 'what might have been'. (E.)
[2] Section III. Falstaff's March—The return through Gloucestershire— The new king—The hurried ride to London. (E.)
[3] A fanfare, once distant, then nearer. (E.)
[4] A fitting accompaniment to the marching gait of the scarecrow army. (E.)

Another theme joins the slouching march and initiates a fugato which gradually develops into a fight (without prejudice to the etymological connexion of fugue and flight).

Ex. 23.[1]

There is also evidence of what Bradley calls 'so ridiculous an object as Falstaff running'. (Combination of Exx. 1 and 6.) But such absurdity, Bradley also implies, is immune, and Falstaff gains credit in battle by frauds which show effrontery rather than cowardice. There are a few more new figures in this battle episode (if such it be), but they do not recur, and the tumult soon dies away. With extraordinary subtlety Ex. 22 becomes a new formal lyric episode, in alternation with Ex. 23.

Ex. 24.[2]

Then, as if the land were once more safe for wayfarers, we renew our acquaintance with Ex. 13, in alternation with a new rustic and reedy motive of laziness.

Ex. 25.

And so we come to Shallow's orchard, where, in another self-contained episode, we listen to tabor and pipe—

Ex. 26.

and indulge in drowsy reminiscences.

Ex. 27.

[1] The March. 'I have foundered nine score and odd posts.' (E.)
[2] As we approach the fields and apple-trees the march assumes a song-like character. (E.)

This interlude comes to a definite end: but the drowsy motive of Ex. 26 would fain continue. It is rudely interrupted by a shrill outburst of violins (another new figure), reintroducing Ex. 8. 'Under which king, Bezonian? Speak or die?' Harry the Fifth's the man; and we shall all be augmented in the new fount of honour. (Ex. 12 by augmentation. No extra marks will be awarded to candidates who detect this point.) Exx. 23 and 22 scurry away post-haste into the distance.

After a pause we find ourselves near Westminster Abbey amid solemn sounds betokening the approach of the coronation procession.[1] A new theme—

Ex. 28.

sounds a note of insistent appeal. As it eventually proves to be Falstaff's last death-bed gesture, I presume that it indicates his passionate belief[2] that the king will be to him the beloved prince glorified. Laughter is in the air—

Ex. 29.

and, in another new theme, Falstaff shares in the glow of affectionate loyalty to the new king.

Ex. 30.

(This immediately combines in counterpoint with Ex. 1.) Another theme may be taken to be at least consistent with cheers and the waving of caps.

Ex. 31.

Poor Falstaff still believes that Henry the Fifth is the light fantastic Hal of Ex. 16. So that brilliant variation is the substance of the

---

[1] Section IV. King Henry V's progress.—The repudiation of Falstaff, and his death.
[2] No. It is the King himself in military character. (E.)

next crescendo, and Falstaff's cheers transform Ex. 31 to its rhythm.

Ex. 32.

The king arrives in all his glory (Ex. 4, *grandioso*, for Elgar still will not say *nobilmente*). The cheers are loud, but there is a barrier between the king and his old friends.

Ex. 33.

Falstaff's heart is fracted and corroborate: the joyful whoop at the end of Ex. 28 becomes a bewildered question, and nothing is left for him but disillusioned memories. The rest is easy for the listener to follow, there are no new themes, and the long tale of old themes is given in the form of reminiscence, not development. Here is the tale: Ex. 28 last figure, Ex. 5; pause; Ex. 28 revived; Exx. 12, 5, 21,[1] 31, 33, subsiding into a mournful decline on the subject of Ex. 28; a faint echo of Ex. 33, then the laughter of Ex. 29 at half pace, transformed as if to falling tears; failing memories of Exx. 7, 1, and 5: a long pause; a breath of sleep-laden wind from Shallow's orchard, Ex. 27, disturbed for a moment by the quizzical accent of Ex. 10, now heard for the last time; it melts into pathos, and Ex. 27 declines farther into an entirely unspoilt memory of the prince whom Falstaff loved (Ex. 4, in full, pianissimo and cantabile); then Ex. 1, failing.[2] Mistress Quickly's account of his death is neither more nor less pathetic than Elgar's; but here, as throughout the work, Elgar is giving us Falstaff's own mind, which is far beyond the comprehension of any other character in the play. We may perhaps recognize Mistress Quickly in a mournful cadence of the clarinet just after the fading out of Ex. 1; but up to the last we cannot be sure that we are spectators: the sudden final rally on Ex. 28, with its bold presentment of the remote key of E minor as penultimate to the last chord, will do equally well for a salute from Falstaff to his estranged king,[3] or as an epitaph in praise of his

[1] It is the furious fanfare of Ex. 21 which marks the King's sentence of banishment. (E.)

[2] The moment of death is marked here by a full chord of C major pianissimo on the brass. (E.)

[3] The King's stern theme thrown curtly across the picture. (E.)

loyalty. He was a soldier, and, with all his humbug, no coward; so let him go to Arthur's bosom with a roll of muffled drums.[1]

It will not surprise me to learn that every one of my parallels between the music and the particulars of Falstaff's doings and surroundings is wrong, except the illustration of his snoring. About such sounds there can be no mistake; snores are snores whether they are produced by double-basses and a contrafagotto or by the nose; and if the composer does not mean them he ought not to produce them. But I have hopes that this analysis may not be misleading as to the musical form and Shakespeare-Elgar psychology of the work as a whole.

VARIATIONS FOR ORCHESTRA, OP. 36

This delightful work, which first revealed to foreign nations that there was more mastery of orchestration, as well as of form, in British music than they were aware of, has been known, with the connivance of its composer, as the 'Enigma Variations'. One part of the enigma is, in a sense, musical, and I confess that I do not know its answer. The 'Enigma', as the theme is called, is said to be a counterpoint to a well-known tune which is not alluded to in the variations. This being so, the 'well-known tune' and the difficulty of guessing what it is are things that do not belong to the music as we have it. At all events I find nothing enigmatic in the composition, and until I do I shall not bother my head with an enigma which concerns no question of mine. Another part of the enigma is personal; and, as such, is the private affair of the composer and those friends of his whom it concerns. To them it is probably no enigma. The variations are 'Dedicated to my friends pictured within', and the evidently delightful people therein pictured are indicated by initials and pseudonyms. If there is one thing that music can clearly illustrate without ceasing to be musical, it is just this kind of character-drawing that is independent of narrative and concrete fact. At the same time if I were a policeman I think I should ask Mr. G. R. S. of variation 11 to produce his dog-licence; the behaviour of those basses paddling, with the theme, after a stick thrown into the pond by the violins, and the subsequent barking of the brass, can hardly be mere coincidence. Even so, the result is quite as musical as if there were no such things in nature. None of these externals detracts from the pure musical beauty and value of a work which has long taken rank as a permanent addition to the classical repertoire. No amount of practice wears it thin, and there is many an ambitious composer

[1] No: the drum roll is shrill; the man of stern reality has triumphed. (E.)

of brilliant and revolutionary reputation who ought to be taken by the scruff of his neck and, orchestrally speaking, washed in its crystal-clear scoring until he learns the meaning of artistic economy and mastery.

The theme, with its two contrasted strains in minor and major, is given in its essentials in the following quotation:

Ex. 1.

The variations, with the partial exception of Var. 10 (Dorabella) and the Romance, Var. 13 (***), are all melodic; that is to say, it is the melody, and not essentially the structure or phrasing, which they reproduce. Where the melody is not recognizable, the composer's object is to give an independent episode, after the manner of Schumann's *Études Symphoniques*. These episodes are placed so as to relieve the melodic variations without breaking the coherence of the whole work.

Var. 1 (C. A. E.) is a beautiful glorification of the theme, which we shall encounter again in the finale. To quote Weber's *Oberon*, 'a gentle ray, a milder beam breaks sweetly on' phrase B of the theme when it is here removed to the softer key of E flat.

Var. 2 (H. D. S.-P.), in quick 3/8 time, begins with a fluttering staccato figure in dialogue with the violins, to which anxious harmonies soon enter wailing in the wind. Then the basses enter with A of the theme. When this is done, the fluttering figures are left behind, soon to vanish into darkness.

Var. 3 (R. B. T.) is a kind of mazurka, in the major mode and in a regular form with repeats. B, suddenly removed to F sharp major, is expanded to a climax from which the basses crawl with grotesque mystery back to the graceful, playful opening.

Var. 4 (W. M. B.), 3/4, in the minor again, storms through the whole theme in a violent temper which the feeble-forcible expostulations of a few frightened wood-winds only exasperate.

Var. 5 (R. P. A.), 12/8 and 4/4, in C minor, takes a gloomy view of A, in the bass with a sombre counterpoint in the violins. The flute runs away with B, which allies itself with a new tripping measure. This, however, does not prevail against the serious outlook, and the variation is dying away sadly, when—

Var. 6, 3/2, C major (Ysobel), who must, in her quiet way, be a perfect hostess, discusses the whole theme in a delightful dialogue, led by a solo viola and shared by all the nicest conversationalists in the orchestra. No tea-cup ever had a more delicate aroma than the last long note of the horn with the viola's last word below it: nor is there any exaggeration in calling the whole episode tone-poetry of an order far too high to be damaged by the lightness of its subject.

Var. 7 (Troyte), with his three drums, is as impossible at afternoon tea as Bernard Shaw's Professor Higgins was in his mother's drawing-room. But Pygmalion is a good fellow for all that.

Var. 8 (W. N.), 6/8, G major, restores peace and comfort with an exquisite epigrammatic neatness and amiability.

Var. 9 (Nimrod), 3/4, E flat, strikes a deeper note. The gay company of the others is not rebuked by it, for no one is hard or silly in this symposium; but the unworldly idealism of this new character is completely at home in its surroundings.

Var. 10 (Dorabella), 3/4, G major, is charming, fluttering, a little plaintive, and so constituted as to float inevitably into the middle of the picture.

Var. 11 (G. R. S.), 2/2, G minor, is the man I have already described as probably the owner of a lively retriever.

Var. 12 (B. G. N.) turns the theme into a melancholy serenade for the 'cellos. It leads to—

Var. 13 (***), Romance, a free episode which is indeed the most romantic thing in the work. The sound of a kettledrum-roll, beaten with side-drum-sticks, and the heaving swell of the violas are suggestive of the sea; and this confirms the rumour that the quotation-marks which the composer puts round the first phrase of the wonderful clarinet solo refer to Mendelssohn's overture, *Calm Sea and Prosperous Voyage*, the main theme of which contains the same familiar figure. To explain this typographical detail, however, is not to explain away the originality and depth of this most impressive passage.

Var. 14 (E. D. U.), the finale, rouses us with the approach of a spirited march. When this has reached the height of its course, there is a sudden dramatic stoppage. The wood-wind ask a question which turns out to be a prominent counterpoint in Var. 1 (C. A. E.). That seraphic and sympathetic being thereupon sails in with all its gentle radiance; and the march (the rhythms of which have accompanied this reappearance) resumes its course and rises to a climax which would be solemn but for its irrepressible tendency to hurry. This tendency increases, while the theme strides over

the two-time bars in triple rhythm and the organ begins to boom
in the background, until at last the great work rushes in semibreves
to its cheerful end.[1] Written at the end of the nineteenth century,
it had an immediate success which was no more than the twentieth
century will deem a bare acknowledgement of its due. A work of
the ripest mastery, it is a glorious beacon to the young composer
in the storm and stress of ideas not newer than its own.

OVERTURE, 'COCKAIGNE', OP. 40

British music is emerging from various forms of darkness before
dawn; and of these forms perhaps the darkest is that which a now
almost too popular psychology calls 'the inferiority complex'.
When, at the turn of the century, Elgar expressed his love of
London in an overture neither more nor less vulgar than Dickens,
the principal impression made on the musical criticism of those
ancient days was one of reverential dread at the audacity of an
English composer who handled the resources of sonata form as
if he had the presumption to understand them. There had been
British symphonic works in sonata form before; but orchestration
had not been our forte, and here was sonata form stated in terms
of consummate orchestration. This was clearly wrong; so clearly
that nobody could say why it was wrong. Hence it followed that
the work must be appallingly clever and complicated.

Even now, nobody can say why it is wrong. I believe some think
it vulgar. Nobody nowadays thinks it complicated. There were
people at the end of last century who thought Albert Chevalier's
songs vulgar; presumably because of their dialect. But vulgarity
in the ordinary (or vulgar) offensive sense lies not in dialects and
not in facts, but in errors of valuation. I cannot find vulgarity
in Elgar's Brass Band as it comes blaring down B flat Street, for
I see no evidence that he intends it to strike a religious note, or
a White Man's Burden note, or any note except the healthy note
of marching in good athletic form on a fine day. The *Cockaigne*
Overture is true to nature, and says its say straightforwardly in
terms of the highest art.

Its first theme, of which I quote only one phrase—

Ex. 1.

---

[1] I am indebted to the original of Var. 8 for information correcting a
rumour that the work was at first planned to end quietly. It had ended
abruptly but not quietly, and the present coda was a necessary expansion.

has a magnificent Cockney accent in that pause on the high **C**. A further sequel anticipates (if my chronology is right) by some years the vogue of the idiom of the Londoner who strongly affirms that he does *not* think.

Ex. 2.

After a full orchestral counterstatement of Ex. 1, a new theme, designated by Elgar's favourite mark, *nobilmente*, sounds a deeper note.

Ex. 3.
Nobilmente.

Rude little street-boys, each conscious of being born with a Lord Mayor's Mace up his back-bone, are apt, in later developments, to whistle it away in irreverent diminution, as the *Lehrbuben* in *Meistersinger* treat the theme of their masters; but at present its dignity is undisturbed.

There are quiet spaces in London, with room for lovers in sunshine and moonshine; and with these the second subject (in E flat) is concerned.

Ex. 4.

But it is also concerned with the irreverent diminishers of Ex. 3, and it has room for a climax based on Ex. 1. Other themes might well deserve quotation as the overture moves quietly to its development, but I have space only for the appearance of the brass band which, after various warnings in distant sounds, bursts round the corner, while all the bells chronicled in 'Oranges and Lemons' ring at random.

Ex. 5.

This conspicuous event is followed by the quietest and most poetic developments in the whole overture, passages as deep as any in all Elgar's works; and when the recapitulation arrives it is expanded with admirable freedom and resource. The brass band returns in C major; and the noble strains of Ex. 3, supported by the organ, lead to a brilliant abrupt end with Ex. 1.

CONCERT OVERTURE, 'IN THE SOUTH' (ALASSIO), OP. 50

I have not been to Alassio, and so I cannot talk of Elgar's special sources of inspiration for this brilliant and sunshiny overture. I only hope that, if I ever do go there, I may not find myself in the position of the old lady who said to Turner that she could not see in sunsets anything like his pictorial representations of them; to which, of course, he replied, 'Don't you wish you could?' If she could, she would not have been able to find words for them; and if ever I can see at places like Alassio what Elgar saw as he saw it, I would much rather write a concert overture about it than an analytical programme.

There is still a suspicion of faintness in praising a work for its orchestration, though the time has perhaps passed since nobility was thought to be inherent in clumsy scoring; but, so long as tastes differ as to a composer's style, there is something to be said for calling the listener's attention to a merit which every competent judge must admit to be supreme, not only in its artistic results, but in its practical efficiency. I shall not easily forget my impression when, on first attacking this overture with considerable fear and expectation of its being as difficult as it is brilliant, I found that it simply carried the orchestra away with it and seemed to play itself at the first rehearsal. On inquiry, I found that one single member of the orchestra was not reading it at sight. This exception, of course, accounted for the whole phenomenon, and I am far from claiming that the rehearsal was such as I should willingly accept in lieu of a performance. But I and my students have never had a more impressive demonstration of the enormous efficiency of Elgar's scoring. In brilliance the nearest approach to it in other modern music is the scoring of Richard Strauss; and Elgar and Strauss have in common a panache which is popularly expressed in both the title and the substance of Elgar's *Pomp and Circumstance* Marches, and mystically expressed in the best parts of Strauss's *Heldenleben*. But the scores of Strauss bristle with technical abnormalities, and he drives through his musical traffic like a road-hog, with a mastery that has merely overawed the police

without reforming the rules of the road. Some think that even
Ein Heldenleben is now wearing too thin to reward the labour of
thirty rehearsals for the purpose of securing accuracy where the
composer merely intends effrontery.

To the Straussian panache Elgar adds the enormous sonority
and cogency of a style which is meticulously pure. This is a matter
of fact, and not of taste. Perhaps the word 'meticulous' may be
misleading, and 'classical' might be a better epithet. But I think
'meticulous' is right. Whether you are carried away by Elgar's
style or whether you dislike it, there is no doubt that it is not the
style of a man who is at ease in himself or in Zion. Neither in
poetry nor in music is the atmosphere of *The Dream of Gerontius*
that of a muscular Christian after Charles Kingsley's heart; and
those for whom Kipling's sixth-form imperialism obliterates his
art will not like *Pomp and Circumstance*. But I should be surprised
if the most nervous of reasonable music-lovers could not enjoy *In
the South*. When it appeared in 1904, any approach to mastery
of instrumental form on the part of a British composer was still
considered dangerous. I cannot remember whether *In the South*
had a better reception than the *Cockaigne* Overture; but it is both
a larger and a simpler work, of which the portion normally devoted
to developments is occupied by two detachable episodes. When
Steinbach conducted it at a concert of English music at Cologne
in, I think, 1906, I was surprised to find that he thought it patchy.
That impression probably arose from these episodes, but I am
sure that it is a superficial impression, perhaps intensified by the
comparative orthodoxy and greater concentration of the other
works played on that occasion. In itself, *Alassio* is by no means a
loose-knit work. It has more unity than the *Enigma* Variations,
and far more coherence than Elgar's First Symphony. Classical
overtures, especially when they are preludes to operas, do not profess to have the concentrated texture of symphonic movements,
and my most beloved overtures of Weber are things of shreds and
patches compared to *Alassio*.

Elgar begins with a group of heroic themes swinging along at
full speed from the outset.

There are more of these than it is necessary to quote, but Ex. 1
shows itself as a counterpoint to all the others. The initial impetus

is strong enough to survive a solemn climax marked by Elgar's favourite direction, *Nobilmente*.

After an apparently casual incident in the decline—

a pair of gentler themes appears in C minor—

and leads to a quiet second group, passionately lyrical, in duple time and the extremely unorthodox key of F major.

Even in the tranquillity of Ex. 8, Ex. 1 intrudes as a counterpoint. Soon Exx. 5 and 6 bring about a gradual revival of energy and carry us into the current of a vigorous development. But this does not last long before we are confronted with a terrifically impressive structure.

I shall be highly pleased with myself if any Roman bridge or viaduct, at Alassio or elsewhere, can make an impression on me that is not mainly dominated by my knowledge of this magnificent passage with its superbly proportioned repetitions, climax, and diminuendo. People differ greatly in the extent to which sounds suggest visual impressions. With me this happens very rarely, but then very intensely; and Ex. 10 gives me the strongest suggestion of a horizontal line of roadway immensely high up, with the piers descending from it into greater and greater depths along a precipitous hill-side.

After the vision has become distant, the progress of development is resumed with a new bustling theme.

Eventually Ex. 1 intervenes, and there is another glimpse of the bridge or viaduct before Ex. 11 is resumed. The incident quoted in Ex. 4 becomes important in an impressive diminuendo, typical of Elgar's most mystic style; and eventually we have what has become known in a separate arrangement as a piece for small orchestra, *Canto Popolare* (*In Moonlight*). As a separate piece it is a very pretty thing, but in its context in this Overture it is as gravely and romantically beautiful as music can be.

Quiet and slow reminiscences of Ex. 1 intervene contrapuntally, and there are warnings of a revival of energy in allusions to Exx. 4 and 5.

The *Canto Popolare* dies away, and in the original key and tempo Ex. 1 returns pianissimo, but with a rapid crescendo which soon brings us into the full swing of a regular recapitulation of everything from Exx. 1 to 8: the F major group from 6 to 7 being, of course, now in the home tonic. From the quiet end of this recapitulation arises Ex. 3, a fourth lower and in the tenderest pianissimo. It swells out and leads to fresh developments of the livelier themes in a noble coda which is one of the best of all Elgar's perorations, its rhetoric entirely unspoilt by tub-thumping, and leaving us with a magnificent impression of punctuality in its end.

INTRODUCTION AND ALLEGRO FOR STRINGS
(QUARTET AND ORCHESTRA), OP. 47

Comparisons of this important work with the concerto grosso of the early eighteenth century are misleading. In its form and texture there is neither the antiquity of Wardour Streete Englisshe nor that of the genuine furniture that may be bought in that street by those who know. It is a piece of modern music, modern in the lasting sense of the term. That is to say, its date, 1905, is no more identifiable in 1937 than it will be in 2005. The kind of concerto form which it embodies is in line with Beethoven and Brahms, and definitely out of line with Handel and Bach. The sound of the strings, in both solo and tutti, will remind us of the older masters, simply because the Concerti Grossi of Handel and his predecessors and the third Brandenburg Concerto of Bach are the only classical works for string orchestra that we ever hear, with the solitary exception of Mozart's toy masterpiece, *Eine Kleine Nachtmusik*. But if it had ever occurred to Beethoven or Brahms to experiment with the problem of concerto form for an orchestra of strings alone, they would have produced something with the essential features of the present work. It is highly probable that, like Elgar, they would have treated the contrast between string quartet and string tutti as rather a matter of fine shades than of the intense dramatic opposition of solo and orchestra that inspired them when the orchestra was full. Also the fitness of the occasion for fugue-writing would not have escaped their notice, nor would they have been slow to take advantage of it.

In the present work, as in others, Elgar's form is his own; and doubtless Beethoven and Brahms would each have achieved a different and unique solution of its special problem. A long classical orchestral ritornello has another function besides that of giving scope to the full orchestra. It presents the main features of the movement in an introductory form. This introduction naturally has a processional character when the ritornello is long; and only something highly dramatic can be justified in curtailing it. Hence nothing could be more appropriate than that, instead of the formal ritornello, the present work should have a grand introduction in which the themes appear at first as fragments in a highly dramatic dialogue between orchestra and quartet; the united forces propounding a sternly majestic question—

to which the quartet adds another in wistful tones—

After the dialogue has made some progress with the discussion the viola is allowed to give full lyric form to a new melody in E flat—

which the quartet and orchestra take up with quiet enthusiasm. Ex. 1 intervenes again dramatically, bringing back the key of G minor. The lyric melody pathetically accepts the decision; but its dying fall, after a long pause, resolves in the cheerful and active daylight with which the allegro now begins.

Nobody could have foreseen what the functions of these themes are now to be. Ex. 2, with its typically Elgaresque quick dactylic figure, becomes the main theme. A new three-bar theme, stated in a lower octave by the quartet and answered by the tutti—

executes a broadly designed transition to the dominant, in which key the second group begins in triumph. The *a-priori* theorist expects it to consist of an enlargement of the lyric melody, Ex. 3. It proves, on the contrary, to consist of a grand tutti on Ex. 1, in terms of the utmost confidence and power, worked out in a brilliant paragraph, the close of which is reached through an allusion to Ex. 4. Suddenly, as the figure of Ex. 1 reverberates above, through and below the last chords, the beginning of the

lyric melody is faintly heard in a tremulous unison of the muted
string quartet—a moment of romantic power worthy to be set by
the Romanza in the *Enigma* Variations. A lively fugue in G minor
has the function of the development-portion of the work. It exercises this function the more efficiently by being completely independent of previous themes. In all genuine concerto styles the
exposition itself is compelled by circumstances to have many
features more typical of development than of exposition; and thus
only by means of episodic matter can the development-portion
maintain a character of its own.

Here is the new fugue-subject—

Ex. 5.

The key-changes of fugues are necessarily drifting rather than
sharply contrasted. In as far as a fugue can be dramatic it is a
debate; and dramatic action will probably stop a debate altogether. Hence Elgar leaves us to discover only when this debate
has reached its climax that we have been at home in the tonic all
the time. (No two works could be less like each other than this
allegro and the finale of Beethoven's Sonata, op. 101, but you will
find exactly the same phenomenon there, as a result of the same
insight into the nature of music.) As the fugue dies away, allusions
to the transition theme (Ex. 4) indicate that the most episodic of
developments can be organically connected with the exposition so
long as there is a B in Both.

A full and regular recapitulation brings symmetry into the
design; but the symmetry extends beyond the allegro and includes
the Introduction; for the lyric melody, Ex. 3, is now neither a far-
off echo nor a gentle strain with a dying fall for the ear of Duke
Orsino, but a solemn triumphal march of full Elgarian pomp.

Throughout the whole work the instrumentation has all Elgar's
subtlety and consummate mastery, shown more obviously by the
limited means here available, though not more perfectly than in
works for full orchestra.

CÉSAR FRANCK

SYMPHONY IN D MINOR

1 *Lento, alternating with Allegro non troppo.* 2 *Allegretto.*
3 *Allegro non troppo.*

Nowadays the only difficulty than can come between the listener
and this great model of clarity and breadth is its misleading resemblances to the forms of older classical music. The resemblance
misled the teaching, but not the practice, of the composer, much
as it misled Bruckner both in teaching and practice. Such is the
nature of most artistic revolutions; the conscientious revolutionaries
survive by what they preserved in spite of themselves, and the
conservatives design motor-cars with a high box-seat for the driver.
But the cars are quite efficient. When we see César Franck twice
alternating his introduction with his allegro, we instantly recognize
the influence of Beethoven's B flat Quartet, op. 130; and so, in
all probability, did Franck himself. But critics have been known
to complain that Franck's first movement drags because of this
expensive procedure. That impression comes only from expecting
something like the pace of the classical sonata from a composer
whose sense of pace, whether he knows it or not, is in process of
becoming Wagnerian. The externals of sonata form, such as the
division into self-contained movements, the balance of keys and
contrast of 'subjects', &c., are surprisingly tolerant of Wagnerian
movement; and César Franck's wonderful improvisatorial style,
often the result of endless labour, makes admirable sense of them.
But it does not make sonata style of them; it produces 'symphonic
poems' whether they call themselves Symphony in D minor, or
Éolides, or *Chasseur maudit*.

In almost every case the form is convincing, and the movement, whether slow or swift, so comfortable as to be discoverable
only by external evidence. The terms of sonata form are convenient in the four first-rate works (the Violin Sonata, Quartet,
Quintet, and Symphony), which imply an acknowledgement of
them; but in his F sharp minor Trio, op. 1, it was already
obvious that the sonata standard of movement was not in Franck's
mental gear.

The symphony begins with a group of three slow themes, of which I quote the first two.

Ex. 1 then piles itself up, harmonized chromatically in three steps of sequence rising in thirds from D minor through F sharp minor and B flat (= A sharp) minor, thus reaching home through an enharmonic circle, and leading straight to the allegro. This begins with the main figure of Ex. 1 worked into a paragraph with new figures—

and coming to a cadence-clause thus—

With a dramatic gesture the key is changed to F minor and there the whole process is repeated note for note from Ex. 1 to Ex. 4. No wonder critics are disappointed who expect anything like the athletic movement of Beethoven's op. 130. Franck's drastic simplicity belongs to quite another view of the universe. At all events, if we prefer to cling to sonata terms, we are now very comfortably landed in the proper key for a Second Subject; and here it is, in orthodox cantabile contrast and thoroughly Franckish in its way of hovering around the mediant.

Ex. 5.

It is not to be hurried; and it culminates punctually in another theme, also pivoted on the mediant and delivered exultantly.

Ex. 6.

This rises to a grand climax that disguises the final cadences of the exposition in gorgeous modulations. These expire slowly, and the theme lingers among pianissimo echoes with pauses. One of Franck's most beautiful strokes of genius is the sudden gleam of D major with which, amid these pauses, the development begins. The D major is the first descent in a key-sequence of thirds, F, D, B = C flat. This brings us to A flat minor in which remote region the themes begin to combine in energetic development. All the figures of Exs. 3, 4, and 6 are soon at work in triple fugue. A new episodic figure, of descending scales over a sustained pedal D, intervenes, and when the bass falls to D flat, leads to the resurrection of Ex. 2, pianissimo in minims approximating (without change of tempo) to the pace of the introduction. A quick change brings this to a crisis and to the next phase of the development. Now, starting in A flat minor, Ex. 4 alternates with a new episodic theme, which, with its bass descending by semitones, has a capacity for wide changes of key.

Ex. 7.

Soon Ex. 2 strides majestically over the slowly descending bass. During its third step it declines into a pianissimo, and its further course is in the bass underlying a series of pathetic efforts to resuscitate Ex. 5. These efforts persist and gain strength; the figure of Ex. 1 surges up in the deepest bass, and so this masterly and lucid development accomplishes its last climax and arrives punctually to the recapitulation.

Nothing tests a composer's sense of form more severely than a recapitulation. Where it is exact, it must not sound mechanical. Where it deviates, it must not demonstrate that the original statement was imperfect or redundant. Wagner's art depends as much on the sensitive handling of extensive recapitulations as any classical sonata; and the recapitulation of the present movement is a perfect example of such handling. To begin with, it completely justifies the rigid architecture of the opening. The main theme of the lento (Ex. 1) is given in a grand sombre fortissimo by the full orchestra, with trumpets answering in canon at the half-bar. The fifth bar is insisted upon and turned aside into B minor, a new and grand modulation upon which the six bars are repeated in that key, the whole twelve thereby forming a complete counterpoise to the exactly opposite D-minor-F-minor pair in the gigantic exposition. Another 4-bar clause, with a sudden pianissimo, suffices to lead into the allegro again. But now we find ourselves in the incalculably remote key of E flat minor. In this kind of surprise, which is often suspected of unorthodoxy, Franck's recapitulations are as classical as in his most exact transcribings. Ex. 3 starts as if it were at home in E flat minor and needs only five bars, interpolated after our quotation, to swing round to G minor, the home subdominant where (on a bass that worries around D) the theme, treated in canon, strides homeward and subsides into Ex. 4 in the home tonic, closing into an exact recapitulation of the whole second group (Exs. 5–6) therein.

The exactness of this recapitulation is entirely welcome to the listener. It includes the first expiring modulations and pauses around Ex. 6. The wonderful gleam of D major at the beginning of the development finds a dark antithesis in a change to B flat at the beginning of the coda. Few writers of symphonies can escape the influence of the awe-inspiring ground-bass at the end of the first movement of Beethoven's Ninth Symphony, especially when they write in D minor. They might as well try to escape the course of nature; and the wise composer will yield and prove his right to deal with such facts in his own way. And so Franck's coda movement combines the figures of Ex. 6 and the upper voice of Ex. 4 in a slow crescendo over the following modulating ground—

Ex. 8.

The movement ends with a grand plagal cadence upon the augmented figure of Ex. 1 in canon between treble and bass in slow tempo.

There is no slow movement: the allegretto has decidedly the

allure of a slow minuet, a dance rather than a lyric. The saintliness of Franck shines nowhere more brightly than where his music is most *mondaine*.

The wisdom of the serpent is foreign to the harmlessness of the dove; and the combination has an exotic glamour all its own. The artistic danger of the combination is that innocence may break through in a disconcerting form of bad taste: the saint does not really know what the world understands by its formulas. And so the exquisite main theme of this middle movement will eventually find itself striding grandly, in its white confirmation dress, over a large area of the finale; and the finale has a mildly sentimental second theme of its own, which of all types of phrase is most vulgarized by being given to red-hot brass, however softly played. I take this opportunity of uttering these criticisms as a sop to Cerberus; they contain all that I have to say against this wonderful and most lovable symphony, and, uttered here, may save some listeners from shocks of a kind that often repel persons of sensitive taste from whole regions of art which they are best qualified to appreciate.

The middle movement is in almost unbroken 8-bar rhythm throughout, and begins with the evident intention of, so to speak, staking out that rhythm in 16 bars with chords of harp and pizzicato strings. These 16 bars contain the harmonies of the two strains of melody which now follow.

A cor anglais delivers the first strain, beginning thus—

Ex. 9.

It is repeated with a counterpoint in the violas. The second strain is on new figures, but similar in its self-repeating epigrammatic style. It needs more tone than a cor anglais can produce, and so it is given to a clarinet and horn in unison. In repetition (with a flute added in an upper octave) it ends unexpectedly in the major. Now comes a very Schumannesque trio.

Ex. 10.

This develops with a temperature just a little high for Schumann, and, before dying down, it has traversed the 8-bar rhythm by two bars. Then Ex. 9 returns in the lowest register of the cor anglais. But many things are to happen before we have a da capo. A pause interrupts at the fourth bar, and the next phrase is turned aside into G minor, where, after another two bars of hesitation, with another pause, we hear a whispering, fluttering, new theme—

Ex. 11.

punctuated by plaintive questions. After more hesitations and pauses this theme takes shape in regular 8-bar phrases. The shape really is a strict variation of the whole main theme in both its strains; but Franck does not let us hear the melody. He is one of the few real masters of the classical variation form; he knows his theme, and his variations can afford to be unrecognizable because they do not forget it.

Immediately upon this variation a second trio follows in E flat; again a Schumannesque warm-hearted creature.

Ex. 12.

The fluttering movement of Ex. 11 has persisted throughout this second trio as an accompaniment. Ex. 11 itself returns in its native G minor. But after eight bars we are delighted with the revelation that it is a counterpoint to the main theme (Ex. 9) with which the cor anglais now sails in. A little free development follows, breaking the rhythm with odd bars and carrying the figures quickly through a wide enharmonic circle until the home tonic is reached. Here the complete da capo of both strains (with Exs. 9 and 11 in combination) sets in without stopping the movement. Its sixteen bars re-establish the tonic firmly enough to admit of a coda which modulates further afield than any other part of the movement. The themes of the two trios, Exs. 10 and 12 are reviewed alternately in B major, and then the first trio swings round to B flat major and concludes the movement in a warm glow of quiet happiness.

The finale is festive, effective, and leisurely. You will miss much if you expect from it the energy of a Beethoven finale; the introductory first six bars ought to suffice as a warning that the ensuing pageantry is not to be hurried. They serve to show the contrast between D major and the key (B flat) of the previous movement. Then the main theme is delivered. Its first three notes are destined to resuscitate Ex. 6 from the first movement later on; but at present the theme exists in its own right. (But cf. Ex. 2, bars 3 and 4.)

Ex. 13.

Its continuation has a figure which lends itself to cumulative effects—

Ex. 14.

and so in due course effects the transition, in a grand crescendo, to B major, in which bright key the Second Group is placed. The main theme of this group is in dialogue between brass and strings.

Ex. 15.

As is not unusual in finales, it is soon rounded off; and the development begins without delay. But at first the development proceeds like a separate episode, belying the promise of modulation by letting the following opening return upon itself.

Ex. 16.

On repeating itself with an additional upper part, it drifts into triplets, which become an accompaniment to the theme of the middle movement (Ex. 9), the beats of which match the half-bars of the finale. Unperturbed, this runs its gentle course, and Ex. 15 returns in B major, high in the violins. It is then given in close canon. The whole eight bars are repeated in G major, and thus the development gradually gets under way, using more of the theme (such as Ex. 14), and moving in shorter sequences through quicker modulations. At the climax, Ex. 15 is developed fortissimo. This phase suddenly ends in a collapse. The next phase begins with a dialogue between Ex. 16 and the main figure of the middle movement (Ex. 9), broken by pauses. When it settles to continuity, it climbs very slowly to a splendid culmination, on which the main theme (Ex. 14) returns in triumph in the home tonic. I have already expressed regret that Franck should expose Ex. 9 to the strain of becoming grandiose; but this event, which now takes the place of the recapitulation, is less regrettable than if any further strain had been put upon Ex. 15, which we do not hear again.

The ensuing coda is magnificent; arising from the close of the second strain of the middle movement it begins with the resurrection of Ex. 6 from the first movement, non troppo dolce, in the dark key of B flat; and then, as the harmony returns to the home tonic, the first theme of all (Ex. 1) slowly piles itself up over another Ninth-Symphony ostinato which modulates in giant strides when it moves at all.

Ex. 17.

The figure of Ex. 6 joins in the process, and proves by juxtaposition (the only possible proof) its kinship with Ex. 13, the theme of the finale. At the end it is Ex. 13 itself which (in a new canon at two bars) is allowed the last word.

Thus the finale maintains its own integrity, and this magnificent coda has none of the weakness of so many works where the ghosts of former movements seemed to be summoned by the composer to eke out his failing resources.

HAYDN THE INACCESSIBLE

Handel and Haydn are, each in a different way, the most unknown of popular classics. What the public hears of Handel represents about one-fiftieth of his works, and that fiftieth is so disguised by modern 'traditions' and by ignorance of eighteenth-century technique that Handel would often have difficulty in recognizing it. But at all events his complete works are published, so that scholars can find out the truth.

Haydn is in better case in so far as it is etiquette to present his music in a fairly authentic way; but otherwise he is in worse case than any other classic, for not one tenth of his work is accessible in print at all. It is a thousand pities that Haydn was not included in the great series of soi-disant critical editions of musical classics which were produced in the 'seventies, and, with all their defects, have at least placed within reach of every respectable musical library a plain ungarbled text of the complete works of Bach, Beethoven, Mozart, Handel, Mendelssohn, Schubert, Schumann, Schütz, Palestrina, Victoria, and Sweelinck—to mention only those undertakings which have been completed. No doubt a critical edition of Haydn begun in 1875 would have been as badly begun and as imperfectly carried out as the rest of the series; but the later volumes would, as usual, have corrected and criticized the earlier, and our knowledge of the most interesting and important chapter in the whole history of music—the early history of the art which Beethoven consummated—would be incomparably clearer than it is at present. Moreover, hundreds of masterpieces would assuredly be brought to light which ought never to have been allowed to be buried. Mendelssohn and Schumann, whose copyrights have hardly yet expired, could well have waited; even Schütz was less important; and as for some of the 'historically interesting' composers whose works have since been produced with remorseless completeness, I confess that I sometimes wonder whether a cultivated interest in them is compatible with a cultivated interest in anything worth hearing.

Early in this century a complete edition of Haydn's works was begun. Unfortunately the great musical scholar to whom it was entrusted began his enormous task at the beginning, by publishing three volumes containing the first forty-one of Haydn's 104 symphonies. If the editor had been a dryasdust all would have been well. But his full powers as a scholar required mature and highly organized music to bring them out, music where textual problems are interesting and can be solved only by artistic insight and knowledge of style. Haydn's maturest style is far from

precise: his early style is of a roughness that removes every vestige
of interest from questions of detail. Pedants raised dull controversies over the first three volumes; the Great War intervened
before the vast gap between Haydn's earliest and mature style
was bridged; and Haydn still remains without the near prospect of
an authoritative text of the works in which he formed his style.

We need hardly be surprised, then, if musical treatises prove to
be rather at sea about most points in Haydn's art and style. He is
rightly acknowledged to be 'the Father of the Symphony'. Accordingly the first edition of Grove's Dictionary of Music and Musicians,
in the perky and up-to-date article on Instrumentation, quotes a
passage from the Surprise Symphony (written somewhere about
the time Mozart died) with patronizing approval as from an 'early
work' of Haydn. He is rightly believed to be on a level with Mozart
as a master of form: but his form is described as 'regular and
symmetrical'. And when you come to look at it, you find not only
that all the rules of form as observed by both Mozart and Beethoven
are frequently violated by Haydn, but that they are so seldom
observed that it would be quite impossible to infer them from his
mature practice at all.

More recent writers have tried to show some recognition of this
by saying that in Haydn's works we see the sonata forms 'in the
making'. This only increases the confusion; for Haydn's most
nearly regular works are his earlier ones, when he wrote on the lines
of J. C. and C. P. E. Bach; whereas his freedom of form becomes
manifest just about the time when he came to know Mozart. The
mutual influence of Haydn and Mozart is one of the best-known
wonders of musical history; and the paradox of it is that while its
effect on Mozart was to concentrate his style and strengthen his
symmetry, the effect on Haydn was to set him free, so that his large
movements became as capricious in their extended course of events
as his minuets had always been in the cast of their phrases. The
orthodox theory of a sonata form with a first subject in the main key
and a second subject in a 'complementary' key will do fairly well
for Mozart and Beethoven as long as we understand by 'subject'
no single theme but a large group of heterogeneous material. And
it is fairly true for Mozart and Beethoven that, after the 'exposition'
of these two groups, there will be a 'development' which develops
whatever it chooses from these themes by grouping their fragments
into changing combinations in various shifting keys; and that,
with a return to the main key, there will be a 'recapitulation' which
recapitulates the first and second subject, both in the tonic; while
whatever then remains to be said, will be said as a 'coda'.

But with most of the mature works of Haydn this account
simply will not do. Here follows a perfunctory analysis of eleven of

Haydn's last thirteen symphonies (Nos. 92–104). Précis writing, such as I have given of Beethoven's Ninth Symphony, would, though unreadable except as a dictionary is readable with a Greek play, compel the student to see that no two such symphonies are alike. There is no such monotony in them as there is in my enforced reiterations that Haydn is not conforming to a scheme based on what Hummel, Spohr, and Clementi could make of him and Mozart in generalizations imitable by docile students. But, as I am only too thankful that there are any such students to write for, I must consider their needs and enforce my reiterations.

SYMPHONY IN G MAJOR 'LETTER V'

CHRONOLOGICAL LIST, NO. 88

1 *Adagio, leading to Allegro.* 2 *Largo.* 3 MENUETTO. *Allegretto.* 4 FINALE. *Allegro con spirito.*

Haydn's own catalogue of his works numbers this as his 88th symphony, and so places its probable date as 1786, the year of the Paris Symphonies and five years before the first of the London Symphonies. The quality of Haydn's inventiveness is nowhere higher and its economy nowhere more remarkable than in this work. To judge a piece of music by its themes is never wise, and the habit of so judging rests on the mistakes of assuming that all musical ideas are expressed in that single category of musical articulation to which the word 'theme' belongs. A work of which the identifiable themes are conspicuously beautiful may be like this exquisite little symphony of Haydn's, or like Beethoven's great B flat Trio, or like any work whatever by Spohr. In Spohr case the beauty of the themes is the reason why the works exist: their treatment is the same in all cases. But with Haydn, as with Beethoven, Mozart, Bach, and Handel, the themes are not really more separable from their treatment (or, in other words, are not more the sole repository of the ideas) when they are conspicuously beautiful than when they appear to consist only of tags. The themes of Mozart's G minor Symphony are for the most part highly original and pregnant in themselves. In the so-called Jupiter Symphony the only theme that is not common property is that of a little *aria buffa* ('Voi siete un po' tondo, mio caro Pompeo') borrowed for use and rich development in the first movement. But a critic who should say that Mozart's invention was drying up in the Jupiter Symphony, would be well advised to consult a doctor. Yet an eminent French critic (and all French critics are eminent) did notice this decadence in *Die Zauberflöte* and seriously pointed out that two bars of the theme of its overture (*not* including

the sforzandos off the beat) were plagiarized from a sonata by
Clementi.

There is a river in Monmouth and a river in Macedon; there is
a B in both; there is in Haydn's 88th symphony a formal introduction that has no mysterious features, and there is the following
opening figure of the allegro—

Ex. 1.

Very clever persons, who take in music by the eye, have pointed
out the extraordinary resemblance between this theme and that of
the finale of Beethoven's Eighth Symphony. The resemblance is
equivalent to the scriptural warrant of the minister who, wishing
to inveigh against a prevalent frivolity in head-gear, preached
upon the text, 'Top-knot, come down!'—which he had found in
Matt. xxiv. 17 ('Let him which is on the housetop not come down').

The Top-knot school of exegesis still flourishes in music. This
theme of Haydn's is as pregnant as that in Beethoven's Eighth
Symphony, but it means something totally different both in
harmony and in rhythm; nor did Beethoven's theme, in all the
transformations it went through in his sketch-books, resemble it
more in the earliest stages than in its final form. But the strangest
thing about Beethoven's originality was that he was quite capable
of amusing himself by noting discoveries in the best Top-knot
manner. There is a coincidence of no less than nine notes between
the theme of the finale of Mozart's G minor Symphony and that of
the scherzo of Beethoven's C minor Symphony, and he noted it in
his sketch-book! The point of noting it is precisely the utter
contrast and absence of any significance common to the two ideas.

A detailed analysis from phrase to phrase would be needed to
show the originality of Haydn's treatment of Ex. 1, or indeed of
any of his themes.

There is a second theme, besides counterpoints and bustling
transitional matter; but the rhythmic figure (a) is never long
absent.

Of the glorious theme of the slow movement—

Ex. 2.

I was told by John Farmer that he once heard Brahms play it with wallowing enthusiasm, exclaiming, 'I want my ninth symphony to to be like this!'

Here is a clear case of a movement that is to be measured by its theme. From that theme Haydn himself tries in vain to stray. He modulates to the dominant. That is treated as an incident in the course of the melody, which promptly repeats itself in full. The modulation is tried again with a new continuation. But the new continuation wistfully returns in four bars through the minor mode. Let us, then, have a variation. But not too varied; only a little decoration in counterpoint to our melody. But perhaps the full orchestra, with trumpets and drums, which were not used in the first movement, can effect a diversion. What it does effect is that a sequel shows enough energy to lead fully into the key of the dominant, instead of merely on to its threshold, so that the whole great tune now follows in that key.

The old sequel then returns to the tonic, and to the tune. Another tutti introduces the minor mode, and leads to a key, F major, related only to the tonic minor. This is definitely a remote modulation, and in F major the tune enters, but has to exert itself with new rhetoric before it can return to its own key. There we hear it yet again, with a short coda in which Brahms's ninth symphony retires into a heaven where Brahms, accompanied by his faithful red hedgehog, can discuss it with Haydn, Beethoven, and Schubert over a dinner cooked by Maître du Clavecin Couperin, and washed down by the best Bach.

(*Der Rote Igel* was Brahms's favourite Vienna restaurant, and when the manager told him, 'Sir, this is the Brahms of wines,' he replied, 'Take it away and bring me some Bach'; scilicet: brook, or water.)

The minuet is cheerful, with a quiet joke on the drums. The trio is one of Haydn's finest pieces of rustic dance music, with hurdy-gurdy drones which shift in disregard of the rule forbidding consecutive fifths. The disregard is justified by the fact that the essential objection to consecutive fifths is that they produce the effect of shifting hurdy-gurdy drones.

Haydn never produced a more exquisitely bred kitten than the main theme of the finale.

Ex. 3.

The first strain (8 bars) ends in B minor, the mediant, instead of the usual dominant, which is prominent in the second strain. There are bustling tutti themes, but the bulk of the movement arises from the main theme. Its initial figure (*a*) is of two notes only, and is thus quite unconnected with the 3–note rhythmic figure (*a*) of Ex. 1. The movement is in rondo form, which is by no means so common as might be expected in Haydn's symphonies and larger quartets. Haydn has a way of beginning an important finale like a big rondo, and then, after one episode, running away into some sort of fugue that gives an impression of spacious development which suffices without further formal sections. The completeness of rondo form in the present finale thus rather reduces its scale in comparison with many finales that are actually shorter. This fact is a melodic quality, not a formal or dramatic defect.

SYMPHONY IN G ('OXFORD').
CHRONOLOGICAL LIST, NO. 92

1 *Adagio, leading to* 2 *Allegro spiritoso.* 3 *Adagio.* 4 *Menuetto, allegretto.* 5 *Presto.*

This typical product of Haydn's hilarious maturity was written for the occasion of his receiving the Doctorate of Music at Oxford. It proved too difficult for the available resources, and so an earlier work was substituted. It would be interesting to know exactly what it was that the players on that occasion found specially difficult. The work still has traps for the unwary, but I doubt whether we should find the one substituted for it much easier. Haydn's freedom and unconventionality will complicate the analysis of any of his mature works. Many of his eccentricities— including his difficult passages—show clear traces of his early practical experience, as distinguished from any theories of his own or of earlier times. For example, his love of long passages for wind-instruments alone has been ascribed (why, I cannot think) by some of our highest authorities to a survival of the groupings of instruments in the old concerto grosso. I am quite unable to remember any concerto grosso where passages like these of Haydn's occur; but they occur in operatic music both before Haydn's maturity and in later times, being an obvious means of effect. The early classical wood-wind group is, on the whole, feeble and shrill (especially when there are no clarinets), and makes a theatrical contrast of airy innocence against the bluster of the full orchestra with its rumbling basses and its kettledrums with their dignified thunder and rousing slam. All this is utterly foreign to the spirit of the concerto grosso; and, like other traits of Haydn's art which have been hastily described as primitive, it is far more characteristic of his later than of his earlier work. But he probably learnt its possibilities during his many years of daily practical experiment as court-composer at Esterhaz.

Another thing which might be deduced from the later works, even if the earlier works were not there to show it, is that the little orchestra at Esterhaz must, at various times and in various proportions, have contained some of the finest virtuoso players in Europe side by side with players whose tracks needed covering. In many of Haydn's later works there is something specially tricky for the horn, something of which a clever player can find the knack, but which practical composers do not write nowadays. In the Oxford Symphony the jumping figure of accompaniment to the theme of the finale (see Ex. 4, where, for convenience, it is given an octave higher) is a characteristic example. When we trace Haydn's art back to the Esterhaz period, we find that he was then in a position to write for a quartet of horns in a style compared with which Bach's horn-writing is almost easy. In the same way he treats his violoncellos with a confidence which you will not find in Beethoven, who never entrusts them with a melody unsupported by violas. Perhaps, however, there are two sides to this question, for I cannot recollect that Haydn ever gives the violas anything prominent; so that the question may be also whether Beethoven did not bring forward the viola, and support it by violoncellos.

On the other hand, one of the chief troubles in Haydn's maturest scoring comes from his unwillingness to let a wind instrument sing a tune above accompanying strings without making the first violins play it too. The publication of Haydn's early and middle works having been arrested by patriotic and pedantic jealousies, it is difficult to trace the course of this tendency; but I believe the explanation to lie in that obvious practical process which has dulled the colouring of many a later composer, by inciting him to make a dangerous passage safe by doubling it on a more trustworthy but less characteristic instrument. None of these things are at all primitive; and just as it is a misconception that refers them to survivals from older traditions, so is it a misconception which ignores their presence in modern music, in forms outwardly different, but easily recognizable by any one who understands their principles.

No one can listen to the Oxford Symphony without being struck by the varieties of orchestral colour that Haydn gets from his resources and habits. Often there is more in the score than any one performance is likely to bring out. In the small orchestra of Esterhaz every orchestral group was transparent to every other; and so Haydn never got rid of the notion that a single flute could make itself heard through a full orchestral forte without troubling to keep up to its highest octave. But I strongly suspect that Haydn asked for double wind in his later works whenever he found the string band at all strong; otherwise what is the origin of his custom of applying the word 'solo' to special passages for single

wind instruments ? It has now come to mean 'lead', irrespective
of the number of instruments in unison.

The forms of the Oxford Symphony are, with every appearance
of sonata style and symmetry, so free that adequate analysis
would involve describing almost every individual phrase. There is
hardly any long passage in the first movement that could be disposed of by a technical term, least of all by such terms as 'second
subject' and 'recapitulation'. The introduction was undoubtedly
in some former incarnation a saintly tabby cat whom Thoth or
Ra (or whatever deity is in charge of cats) has elevated to the
heavens of Haydn's imagination. My first quotation gives its
transition from the fireside to the outer world.

Ex. 1.

The allegro spiritoso, having thus begun as if butter would not
melt in its mouth, promptly goes off with a bang, and works up the
two principal figures (*a*) and (*b*) of its theme into a movement so
spacious and so full of surprises that it might well seem to be
among the longest Haydn ever wrote. As a matter of fact it is
among his shortest. But the so-called recapitulation is designed
exactly like one of Beethoven's biggest codas, while the so-called
second subject (which in the exposition differed in material from
the first only by introducing a single square little dance-tune) gives
rise to all manner of new features in this coda. Thus the prevailing
impression is one of perpetual expansion as regards themes and
phrases and developments, while the perfect balance of keys and
harmonies provides that sense of underlying symmetry which
makes the expansion so exhilarating.

From the slow movement I quote enough of the first melody
to show its breadth and its Haydnesque spirit of gravity and grace.

Ex. 2.

This theme is built up into a complete self-contained form, the repeats of its two sections being varied by fresh scoring. Upon its last bar the full orchestra bursts with a storm in the minor mode. The angry outbreak alternates with a quiet theme in F major.

The design of the whole movement is ostensibly the simple form describable as A B A, where A is the main theme and B the middle episode; but Haydn here lifts it altogether out of the sphere of such things as the minuet and trio (the obvious case of the form at its simplest) by reproducing Ex. 3 in D major, and developing it into a beautiful coda, mainly entrusted to the unaccompanied wood-wind.

The minuet and trio are splendid examples of Haydn's inventiveness and freedom of rhythm. The scoring of the trio is especially rich with its syncopated horns and pizzicato strings. I give no quotations. This movement cannot, like the minuets of Haydn's London Symphonies, be said to anticipate Beethoven's scherzos. It has its own business to mind, as a quick minuet such as Haydn was not yet tired of. He did not often write a slow one, except as a finale in rondo or variation form for small sonata-works; the minuet of the Military Symphony is almost the only minuet and trio of Haydn's (except one in the early Quartet, op. 9, no. 4) that belongs to the 'stately' type, which is, indeed, far less common in classical music than it is generally thought to be.

The finale begins with one of the most delightful of all Haydn's themes.

Nobody can say quite how often this theme recurs; the orchestra itself gets into heated arguments as to how the tune really goes, and the doubts generally arise from the third bar onwards. A daddy-long-legs of a second subject sprawls affably into the discussion under pretence of satisfying orthodox theories.

Ex. 5.

It is impossible to describe Haydn's themes, when he is in his Oxford manner, without feeling irresponsible; but the life his themes live is one that has no room for meanness or triviality. This is great music; and nothing other than great music, whether tragic, majestic, or comic, can stand beside it.

SYMPHONY IN G MAJOR: 'THE SURPRISE' (SALOMON, NO. 5; CHRONOLOGICAL LIST, NO. 94)

1 *Adagio, leading to* 2 *Vivace.* 3 *Andante.* 4 MENUETTO: *Allegro.*
5 FINALE: *Allegro.*

The 'surprise' in this symphony is the most unimportant feature in all Haydn's mature works; being merely a single loud chord in the course of an ostentatiously simple tune in the slow movement, at which, said Haydn, all the ladies would scream. There are many outbursts both louder and more sudden elsewhere in this and in all Haydn's symphonies; he was considered a noisy composer in his day; and if it is not noisy to make abrupt contrasts between the softest and the loudest values of an orchestra with trumpets and drums, we must reconsider our use of the term. At all events, no music expresses high spirits more efficiently than Haydn's. And his forms become the more subtle as his animal spirits rise. In this symphony the first movement and finale are among his most brilliant creations. The introduction begins with a broadly melodious dialogue between wind and strings, which might well be the theme of a developed movement. But romantic Haydnesque shadows pass over it, and it leads to the real first movement, which begins slyly, for a moment, outside the main key.

Ex. 1.

When a main theme begins thus on a foreign chord, two consequences are possible as to its return. The return may be prepared by a great emphasis on or towards the key of the foreign chord, in which case the arrival of the theme will be a surprise, inasmuch as the remote key did not at first remind us of home. This effect Haydn brings off on repeating his exposition. If, on the other hand, emphasis is directed to the dominant of our own tonic, the main theme, beginning there or thereabouts, will glide off in some quite new direction. Haydn is very well aware of all such possibilities; and he always uses the one you did not expect.

His 'second subject', more regular than usual with him, begins with as unrestrained an outbreak of dance-rhythm—

as can be found in symphonic music, and subsides into one of Haydn's inimitable pastoral tunes.

In the recapitulation Haydn interpolates (as usual) one of Beethoven's most brilliant codas between the waltz and this tune.

The theme of the slow movement, when taken as an andante according to Haydn's present instructions, has an anserine solemnity which undoubtedly enhances the indecorum of the famous *Paukenschlag*. Some years afterwards Haydn put it in a different light when in his *Seasons* he took it at a lively pace and gave it to a piccolo, to represent the whistling of the ploughman as he 'tunes his wonted lay'. But in the symphony it waddles through the poultry-yard in several variations, the first being in the minor and inclined to episodic developments. At the return to the major mode the oboe seems to have laid an egg. The subsequent variations show fine contrasts of colour; and the coda, as always in Haydn's mature slow movements, rises to poetry.

The minuet is lively and full-toned, while the trio, in the same key, gives one of Haydn's most original melodies to the first violin, doubled in various ways by solo wind instruments.

The finale works out a rondo-like melody—

into a highly developed sonata form with a well-contrasted 'second subject'.

The returns of these themes show the height of Haydn's power in the unexpected-inevitable.

SYMPHONY IN C MINOR (SALOMON, NO. 9; CHRONOLOGICAL LIST, NO. 95)

1 *Allegro moderato.* 2 *Andante.* 3 MENUETTO. 4 FINALE: *Vivace.*

The inexhaustible Haydn most nearly approaches to regularity in form when he is writing in a minor key. In quick movements (first movements or finales), the minor mode inspires him to a temper too blustering for tragedy, though solemnity is (as in his most comic moments) never far off. Unlike the cynics, he is literal-minded in his serious note, and it is his humour that is all in play. But he is no tragedian; and the minor mode impels him to become formal because formality is outwardly solemn. And then, as he once said, apropos of not wishing to be flattered by embarrassed portrait-painters, 'anybody can see that I'm a good-natured fellow'. He is too great to be compared with Dr. Johnson's friend Edwards, who found that philosophizing would not do because cheerfulness was always breaking in. But he could have put Mr. Edwards into a minuet or a mysterious introduction without waiting to collect the opinions of Bozzy's eminent friends that 'this was an exquisite trait of character'.

Of the twelve great London Symphonies written between 1791 and 1795, this is the only one without an introduction. An experienced musician will see at a glance that the pregnant opening figure is destined for polyphonic development; e.g. as the bass for all manner of modulating sequences: while all Haydn-lovers will know they may expect rhythmic expansion in the continuation.

Ex. 1.

The second subject, reached in a few masterly and masterful strokes, promptly shows that 'I'm a good-natured fellow'. I quote it with the scale-counterpoint which adorns it on repetition.

Ex. 2.

In most published scores this figure disappears in the recapitulation: but the new critical edition shows that Haydn (probably during a rehearsal) added it on a solo violin, a detail which enhances the heavenliness of Haydn's cheerful recapitulation.

The andante is an example of one of Haydn's variation-cum-rondo designs. It is no use offering a prize for guesses as to how Haydn will continue a given lyric melody—the Haydn kitten has more ways of jumping than the great god Whirligig himself (whom, as we learn in *The Water Babies*, mortals call Public Opinion).

EX. 3.

The tune is followed by a normal variation (melody in the violoncellos). A second quasi-variation in the minor turns out to be an episode, shorter than the theme, but with rhetorical pauses and some feeling of action in its way of leading back. Then, after stating the first part of the theme unvaried, a complete variation (in demisemiquavers, forte) runs its course, and the movement ends with a peaceful coda on the first part.

The minuet is on a large scale, as always in Haydn's mature symphonies. Its main body is in C minor, and is not without agitation. The trio is a brilliant and difficult violoncello solo in C major, accompanied by pizzicato strings. All Haydn's scores are remarkable for the confidence he shows in at least the leader of orchestral violoncellos; a point in which Beethoven differs notably from him.

Heavenly as is the opening of the finale—

EX. 4.

the second part of this tune transcends it. The first phrase is destined for polyphony, and is so treated with great brilliance, passages of close canon alternating with occasional dramatic storms and peaceful returns to the main tune, in a free rondo form. The total effect of the symphony is so spacious that you would never guess that it is one of Haydn's tersest works.

SYMPHONY IN B FLAT (SALOMON, NO. 8; CHRONOLOGICAL
LIST, NO. 98)

1 *Adagio, leading to* 2 *Allegro.* 3 *Adagio cantabile.* 4 MENUETTO:
Allegro. 5 FINALE: *Presto, ending with Più moderato.*

The inexhaustible Haydn was no more an academic composer than Verdi, who once avowed 'I am not a learned composer, but I am a very experienced one'. So was Haydn; but he was also a very learned composer, though our academic dogmas have taken this on trust and have carefully avoided facing the facts of his technique and form. His technique, by which I mean his handling of instruments and musical texture generally, shows deep traces of two disturbing causes, often closely allied and much alike in some of their results; the first, a long experience of disappointment gradually turned to success in securing good, or at all events safe, performances under bad conditions; and the second, a confirmed habit of composing at the pianoforte. The orchestral works of Haydn's middle period, the forty-odd symphonies written between 1771 and 1788, are not yet accessible in full score. Meanwhile there is no means of tracing the presumably not abrupt change from the orchestration of the Esterhaz symphonies (the first forty or so), where a crudely primitive treatment of the band as a whole contrasts with appalling displays of virtuoso technique for individual instruments, to the orchestration of the Paris and London Symphonies, in which the general orchestral tone and style are among the infinities of art where comparisons are irrelevant, although painful precautions are taken to save solo passages from disaster. Thus, the theme of the finale of his last symphony is obviously typical of the horn; but Haydn will not risk it on that instrument except once in a tutti. Yet at Esterhaz in 1765 he wrote a symphony with a quartet of horns, all four of which were to execute fireworks compared with which Bach's most elaborate writing would be easy. And nowadays a trumpeter or horn-player who wishes to play Bach must either have a special instrument constructed, or else develop his lip into a condition in which he can play nothing else. What is certain about Haydn's work at Esterhaz is that it was written for performance, that it was practised under conditions which literally enabled Haydn to ring his sitting-room bell for players to come and try experiments, and that it was satisfactorily performed. Such are the possibilities of an orchestra endowed on a living-wage-and-retiring-pension basis, even at a time when the art of orchestration was primitive.

At Esterhaz, then, Haydn learned the utmost capacities of individual instruments, and made more rapid progress with them than with the orchestra as such. Strange to say, the one orchestral player in whom he never lost confidence in his later experiences was the leader of the violoncellos, for whom, in the accessible symphonies of all periods, Haydn writes important and often difficult solos. It is not strange that he should have been interested in the instrument, for it, and a kind of gamba called the baryton, were the instruments of Prince Esterhazy; but Haydn's later experience of orchestras in the cold, hard world must have been different from Beethoven's, for Beethoven invariably doubles his orchestral violoncello melodies by violas and uses the solo leader only once in all his works, the early *Prometheus* ballet.

In saying that Haydn was not only an experienced but a learned composer, I have specially in mind the style and forms of this symphony. The Haydnesque animal spirits are moderated though not suppressed in the first movement by highly intellectual themes developed in ways which, though not actually more thoughtful, seem more learned than usual. Haydn never lost his love of practical joking, from the day when he was expelled from the church choir for cutting off the pig-tail of the boy in front of him (during Divine Service) to the day when, in 1792, he 'made the ladies scream' by an unladylike bang in the andante of the 'Surprise' Symphony (no. 94, the third of these London Symphonies). But in the present symphony all the surprises are in matters of harmonic, melodic, and rhythmic interest; and not even the Great Bassoon Joke has time to intrude. The first two phrases of the severely solemn and dark introduction show at once the kind of surprise we are now to have as a means of educating our sense of what to expect in music. My quotation stops short of the point. Listeners and score-readers are all the better for a chance of guessing right or wrong in such matters.

Ex. 1.

A third phrase leads back to the dominant of our main key, on which dominant the introduction, scored for strings alone, pauses with gestures of imperious expectation.

The allegro turns out to be based on the same theme.

Ex. 2.

The sceptred pall of the introduction has gone sweeping by, and solemn tragedy is now perhaps forgotten, in spite of the theme's remaining the same. But the high spirits are occupied in things of the mind; and Haydn does not even yield to his usual love of a cantabile melody. Late in the course of the second subject the

vigorous tuttis are silenced for an exquisite appeal to finer
sensibilities—

Ex. 3.

the phrase taking a profound turn of harmony before it closes.

The slow movement is one of Haydn's broadest and gravest
utterances. It might almost be called his Requiem for Mozart, the
news of whose death had so deeply shocked him during his London
visit. Nowhere in the latest works of Haydn or the earlier works of
Beethoven can we find such accurate modelling of forms upon
Mozart, as distinguished from mere reminiscences of phrase and
style. Reminiscences are there also, and, as is usual with reminiscences, are looser in style than their originals—but only, in the
present case, to achieve a point of their own by way of compensation. The style is more severe than the kind of Mozart-music that
Haydn is thinking of. The main figure of the first theme is a
devout phrase which Haydn afterwards used in his last great work,
The Seasons, in the prayer 'Sei nur gnädig', which develops into
a positive quotation from Mozart's Requiem (see Vol. V, p. 152).

Ex. 4.

Adagio cantabile.

As for the second subject, the following comparison is emphatically not the kind of thing Brahms meant when he said that
'plagiarism is one of the stupidest topics of the noodles'.

Ex. 5.

Haydn, 1792.

Mozart, 1788.

As I have already hinted, and as the divergence of bars 5–6 shows, Haydn's reminiscence of Mozart's last symphony (mis-called 'Jupiter') is a little looser in structure—at the moment. He has not caught the cross-rhythm which in Mozart compresses the chromatic sequence and leaves room for a broader expanse before the close. On the other hand, Mozart's more highly organized paragraph is intended to be capped by a formal cadence-theme, whereas Haydn's purpose is to plunge dramatically into a strenuous development. The contrast between the two masters is thus seen even where Haydn is most touchingly docile towards his spiritual son, who has left him alone in the world of earthly music with only the awkward and stubborn young Beethoven to fill the void.

With the minuet and finale, Haydn's high spirits return in spate. The minuet needs no quotation, but the finale has some unique features. Its main theme is of a type which Haydn first struck in a string quartet of his middle period (op. 33, no. 2, in E flat). He wagered that the ladies at court never could wait till a piece of music was finished; and he won his wager by making his finale a little rondo on a tune easily broken into two-bar phrases, so that towards the end he need only stretch out the 'pauses between the clauses' until conversation must inevitably intervene.

His present theme is more highly organized—

Ex. 6.

but it and the second subject—

Ex. 7.

lend themselves to a style of quizzical iteration with unexpected, or, more subtly, with flatly obvious conclusions—for example—

Ex. 8.

In spoken language I have seen the contemporary counterpart
of this style in some published and more unpublished letters of
Mozart; and the method is identifiable in English with the old
joke about the piece of church music in which the choir's main
occupation was 'to catch this flee, to catch this flee, to catch this
fleeting breath'. Scholars of Musical Comedy and Revue tell me
that this figure constitutes a well-established art-form in modern
poetry, but I cannot remember its technical name. Of course, its
crude origins were known in ancient Greece as the παρὰ προσδοκίαν
of Aristophanic Comedy—e.g. the sleepless Strepsiades: 'I'm
bitten through the bed-clothes by a b-b-b-b-bailiff.' But, like
Haydn, we digress.

In the development a solo violin emerges with Ex. 8 in a remote
key, and the range of modulation is wider than my widest digression.
But the most special surprise in the whole symphony is the coda,
where Haydn changes the tempo to più moderato. The main beats
of the rhythm remain thus enlarged to the end; and of course all
the energy has, for the moment, dropped out of the main theme,
which becomes very demure when you can count its six quavers.
But perhaps you forgot that they can now divide into semiquavers
faster than anything yet heard in this symphony. And so the coda
rushes away in a torrent—

Ex. 9.

Più moderato.

and when the main theme finally returns, a glorious afterthought, pencilled by Haydn into the completed score and fortunately accessible in the now slowly progressing critical edition of
his works, maintains the new flow to the end. This afterthought
incidentally reveals that even in these ripest works of the veteran
'Father of the Symphony' a harpsichord or pianoforte was still
used, like Bach's and Handel's continuo, to 'fill out' what in fact
was no longer capable of additional fillings. The conductor, indeed,
sat (as the programmes used to say) 'At the Pianoforte', instead of
using a baton. As to any genuine continuo playing, one can, with
Haydn's or Mozart's mature orchestration, only compare the
functions of a pianoforte to those of the Beaver in the *Hunting of
the Snark,* who sat quietly in the bow making lace, and occasionally
studied arithmetic under expert guidance, but who 'had often, the

Bellman said, saved them from wreck, though no one precisely knew how.'

The gentleman at the pianoforte must often have been strongly tempted to 'gag', especially when he was the composer; and on this occasion Haydn's gag becomes a vital part of the composition. I await with impatience the appearance of the rest of his middle and later works in the critical edition which alone throws such lights upon them.

SYMPHONY IN E FLAT (SALOMON, NO. 10; CHRONOLOGICAL LIST, NO. 99)

1 *Adagio, leading to* 2 *Vivace assai.* 3 *Adagio.* 4 MENUETTO: *allegretto.* 5 *Vivace.*

This symphony conforms just closely enough to the orthodox scheme of sonata form to make that scheme a guide that can only divert our attention from its most important points. In the first movement (vivace—excluding the slow introduction) it is easy enough to call Ex. 1 the first subject and Ex. 2 the second.

Ex. 1.

Ex. 2.

And it is true that both are clearly and consecutively recapitulated after a long and varied development. But this way of describing them only blinds us to the meaning or the existence of such facts as that Ex. 2 enters a long time after the firm establishment of the complementary key, and that the so-called 'recapitulation' makes far more of it than it amounted to in the exposition. The fact is that Haydn knew nothing and cared less about first and second subjects and how to balance and distribute them. Balance of keys, balance of sentences, and balance of contrasts, animated by a sense of dramatic movement so powerful and rapid that he gave up opera-writing early in his career because the conditions of theatre-music paralysed him—these, and not the external signs of symmetry, are the principles of Haydn's form. And as to his 'recapitulations', why, the very use of the word has blinded historians to the fact that Haydn says in the place of his 'recapitulation' what Beethoven says in his codas. Again, it has often been noted that Haydn likes to make his 'second subject' out of the same theme as his first. A really clear contrast such as Ex. 2 shows is seldom to be found except at the tail-end of the exposition; and no doubt it is the extremely effective recurrence of such a tail-end as the last sentence of a whole movement (see the adagio of this symphony) which has made theorists talk of Haydn's neat symmetry. But could anybody seriously believe that, with a second subject mainly on the same theme as the first, anything like a regular recapitulation of both would be tolerated by a self-respecting artist?

No; Beethoven's coda was first invented by Haydn. Without spaciousness he could not breathe, and no prose-writer has shown more mastery of the long sentence. Ex. 1 is by no means an outstanding specimen of Haydn's inventiveness (none indeed of the themes in this symphony is that), but it shows at a glance that its inventor could no more help making his phrases and paragraphs lively and shapely than most composers can help making them halting and angular.

In saying that none of the themes in this symphony is a remarkable example of Haydn's inventiveness I am making no criticism, but merely observing that, like many of the greatest things in music, its originality does not come to the surface in the themes. Beethoven's so-called 'Harp' Quartet, op. 74, is perhaps the *locus classicus* for a work of extraordinary romantic power, in which just the most impressive passages are developed from 'tags' which no composer would look at twice. The inference is, neither that the great composer makes wonderful works out of insignificant material, nor that these themes are after all in some mysterious way 'distinguished', but that these themes do not by themselves convey so much of the dominating ideas of the composition as more 'distinguished' themes convey of the compositions to which they belong. The critic who regards 'distinction' as a *sine qua non* in the themes of classical music will be hard put to it to deny that on this showing Spohr was the greatest of the classics. He was undoubtedly the most fastidious in his social tone.

This symphony, on the other hand, is not a work in which the themes are deliberately reduced to formulas in order that the attention may be diverted from 'form' to 'colour', like Beethoven's 'Harp' Quartet and Mozart's greatest works for wind-instruments.

Haydn is simply making one of his greatest symphonies out of his ordinary vein of melody. In the introduction he is impressively romantic and serious; with one of his great surprises in the dramatic modulation to the remote key of E minor after the first pause, and with another fine stroke in the drift therefrom to a key which shows no sign of returning to the tonic at all, until the wood-wind introduces the right chord as an afterthought which leads straight to the vivace assai.

The vivace assai is, we have seen, a first movement in Haydn's own free form, with a 'recapitulation' which is really a typical Beethoven coda.

The adagio, one of Haydn's most majestic things, is also a first movement, in which what orthodoxy would call the 'second subject' comes only as the last eight bars of a very spacious exposition, which had long ago settled into its 'complementary key' with no other material than that of its first subject. If you turn to the end of the movement you will see that, with an interpolated climax that adds two bars, this same theme with its formal cadence-figure has the last word; but before you conclude that orthodoxy is for once right about Haydn's formality, please note that this is a second recapitulation of that theme; that it comes, with its gorgeous new scoring, after a coda which began by expanding the little cadence-figure into the biggest climax of the whole movement; and that the entire coda is actually longer than the very large development section. From the first note, which tells us that, like most of Haydn's later slow movements, this is in a key remote from that of the whole work, to the last note, which rounds the movement off with a touch that is epigrammatic rather than formal, this adagio is typical of that greatness in Haydn which moved Cherubini to tears, and of that freedom which taught Beethoven's inmost soul more than he, the uncouth pupil, could learn from Haydn the tired teacher.

It is well known that Haydn once, when bored by a musical grammarian, said, 'What nonsense this is!—I wish somebody would write a new minuet instead of bothering about pedantries.' Haydn did write many new minuets; and so did Beethoven. But Beethoven began to call his minuets 'scherzos' long before they were bigger or richer than such minuets as this one, with its characteristic capriciousness of rhythm, its freaks of instrumentation, and its trio in a remote key (C major).

The finale is a brilliant specimen of Haydn's comic vein; a sonata-rondo with some of Haydn's best fooling by way of 'second subject'. It has a brilliant fugued development in which the first theme is no more dignified by inversion than it was right-end-upwards; and it shows all that freedom of form that makes it necessary for us to anathematize our text-book knowledge before we can listen to Haydn with ears naïvely tuned to his note.

The scoring of the whole symphony is experimental and imaginative, as always in Haydn. Its eccentricities begin with the first note of the second clarinet, which is the sole support of the strings in the first phrase. This anticipates a famous passage in Weber's *Oberon* Overture, where low clarinets blend with the 'cellos in the introduction. Repeated chords for the wood-wind are usually supposed to have been 'invented' by Beethoven in the allegretto of his Eighth Symphony; but that is a comic passage; and Haydn has used them with glorious solemnity here at the end of his adagio. It would be easy on these lines to prove that Beethoven never 'invented' anything; but the truth is that such great artists always do invent everything, and that it does not in the least matter which of them invented anything first.

SYMPHONY IN G MAJOR ('MILITARY'), (SALOMON, NO. II; CHRONOLOGICAL LIST, NO. 100)

1 *Adagio, leading to* 2 *Allegro.* 3 *Allegretto.* 4 MENUETTO: *Moderato.* 5 FINALE: *Presto.*

The title 'Military' Symphony explains itself when, in the allegretto which does duty for the slow movement, the apparatus known in 1794 as Turkish music crashes in, with an import sometimes tragic, sometimes triumphant. Turkish music consists of the big drum, cymbals, and triangle. As used by Mozart and Haydn, the big drum is played with a big stick and a little stick together, the big stick marking the accents, while the little stick keeps up a trotting rhythm. The cymbals clash in time with the big stick, while the triangle rings an alarum, or trots with the little stick. The 'Turkish music' appears only in the slow movement and finale of the Military Symphony and in no way interrupts the development of Haydn's most characteristic forms. But recent criticism has discovered that Haydn's use of it is in Bad Taste. Turks will be Turks; Tasters will be Tasters; and it is neither in the primitive nor in the sophisticated, but in the mixture of the two that vulgarity lies.

Haydn's introduction begins with a melody which would be quite capable of developing into a complete slow movement. It is not so cat-like as the introduction to the Oxford Symphony, but it is a very exquisite and silky creature and develops a serious mood towards the end, the full orchestra entering in the minor and modulating to E flat; after which dramatic incident it is clear that this is no independent movement, but an introduction to something larger.

The allegro begins with a theme so typical of Haydn that we are apt to forget that in the whole range of classical music no other symphonic first theme has ever been scored in that way.

Ex. 1.
Allegro.

I cannot refrain from transcribing Gevaert's description of this passage: 'Couverts par un timbre velouté, les hautbois perdent leur aigreur, mais non pas leur finesse. Tout le petit édifice harmonique, s'appuyant uniquement sur la sonorité mince du 2° hautbois, est d'une sveltesse extrême.'

A blustering tutti leads to the dominant, in which key Haydn begins by throwing new lights on his first theme instead of proceeding to something new. But there is another personality to be reckoned with in this drama, and after the solemn formula of two bars of preliminary accompaniment, one of the gayest themes in the world enters and carries on the movement with an impetus remarkable even for Haydn.

Ex. 2.

The development starts in a remote key after an impressive pause, and is one of the richest and most dramatic in all Haydn's works. The recapitulation is, as always in Haydn's mature works, very free and more like Beethoven's larger codas than like any more formal procedure; but Ex. 2 is too strong a personality to be suppressed or cut short, and so the final effect of the movement is nearer to orthodox ideas than is usual with Haydn.

The slow movement (allegretto) needs no quotation. Its one theme is made of figures common to Haydn and Mozart, if not indeed to other contemporaries. There is a peculiar solemn brightness in the scoring and the simple phrase-rhythms, which comes from Mozart's *Zauberflöte*, and has the quality of some august ritual, masonic or military. The movement is in the simplest of forms, with one episode in the minor (introducing no new theme) and a dramatic coda. It is in the minor episode that the military instruments first appear. The coda dramatically introduces a trumpet-signal. Research into the bugle-calls of Austria and England at the end of the eighteenth century would doubtless elicit some interesting anecdotage about the origin of the particular fanfare used by Haydn; but for us the dramatic effect and its immediate consequences in a powerful modulation will be quite sufficient.

The minuet stands alone in Haydn's later symphonies and quartets in that it does not anticipate the tempo and mood of Beethoven's scherzos, but is a stately movement of the old type, splendidly vigorous in its first part, with a graceful trio in admirable contrast.

The finale begins with one of those themes which we are apt to take for a kitten until Haydn shows that it is a promising young tiger.

Ex. 3.

It sounds like a rondo theme, but the movement develops into full sonata form. The second subject is introduced by the following whimsical broken figure—

Ex. 4.

and is in itself purposely slight and perfunctory, like the themes Beethoven puts in a similar position.

Ex. 5.

Its consequences are momentous enough in the coda, and it appears in a remote key in the development. Beginning with Ex. 4, this development is one of Haydn's most extraordinary passages, modulating to extreme distances and building up Ex. 4 into the most unexpected sequences, especially by inverting it.

The recapitulation represents Ex. 5 only in a rumbustious fortissimo in which the military instruments suddenly reappear in all their Turkishness. Even after this the first theme (Ex. 3) is given leisure to return in peace and engage the flute, oboes, and horns (not forgetting the drums) in polyphonic discussion, before the full orchestra with its Turkish music brings this military symphony to a brilliant end.

SYMPHONY IN D MAJOR, 'THE CLOCK' (LONDON, NO. 11; CHRONOLOGICAL LIST, NO. 101)

1 *Adagio, leading to* 2 *Presto.* 3 *Andante.* 4 MENUETTO. 5 FINALE: *Vivace.*

Haydn's freedom of form is a topic illustrated differently by each of his mature works, but in this essay I will take the freedom of form for granted.

A solemn and quiet introduction in D minor lays stress on a slow but ominous rising scale. This, perhaps only accidentally, fore-shadows the main theme of the Presto.

Ex. 1.

The five-bar rhythm of this lively theme is an indication that Haydn's ways of moving are going to be as unconventional as ever, in this obviously very experienced work. The tuttis romp in with all the vigour that gave Haydn the contemporary reputation of being a noisy composer; a reputation which is perfectly justified.

There is a definite new theme by way of second subject; a thing far from a matter of course in Haydn's later works.

Ex. 2.

It is full of coaxing and mockery, and leads to a more than usually boisterous climax. It would be a crime to omit repeating the exposition; the downward scale that leads back to Ex. 1 is among the most characteristic points in the movement.

The development is, as usual with Haydn, spacious, but has no great surprises. The recapitulation, on the other hand, is very free, and takes Ex. 2 a long new journey, working up to the biggest climax in the whole movement, and merging imperceptibly into a coda in which Ex. 1 returns to round off the form. (The fact is that Beethoven's codas are Haydn's recapitulations.)

The accompaniment to the exquisitely kittenish theme of the andante shows at once why this symphony is called 'The Clock'.

Ex. 3.

When the whole theme, with its two repeats, is over, its last bar
is trodden upon by a stormy episode in the minor, based on the
fourth bar of Ex. 3.

After this episode the main theme returns, scored with an
audacity and genius that produce something without any parallel
in earlier or later music. The theme is on the first violins, accompanied only by one flute and one bassoon ticking away at the clock-
figure at a distance of two octaves and a third. This scoring, with
a little help from an oboe, persists throughout the whole thirty-four
bars of the theme. Then there is a long pause. The ticking starts
again in the second violins, leading to E flat, from which point the
theme starts a crescendo leading back to G. By the way, whenever
Haydn is returning to the first bar of his theme, the introductory
bar is always present as an extra. Here it comes again, quite quietly,
and so by no means prepares us for a triumphant outburst of the
whole orchestra, turning the theme into a sonorous tutti. It is
given in full with this rich scoring, after which seven bars of quiet
pedal on the tonic bring the movement to an end.

The minuet is in Haydn's triumphant lively manner, mainly
with full orchestra. The trio requires quotation; for Haydn here
plays a practical joke which has, within my own experience,
caused critics (whom I do not blame) to accuse the orchestra of
'raggedness'.

Ex. 4.

The persistence of the tonic chord is not a misprint: in the autograph the bars are numbered, as is usual with repeated groups, to
prevent mistakes. Then the repeat is written out in full, and (here
is the strange thing) with a change of harmony at the question-
able bars. The joke is not inexplicable—but it needs pointing
out as a joke, which is unusual with Haydn. Perhaps it is a
bad one.

The finale is full of interesting features. A big ternary rondo
theme, 8 bars, plus 12+8—

Ex. 5.

is followed by a very spacious transition-passage leading to the dominant. In that key Haydn seems to be making a second subject out of the materials of his first, especially its first three notes; but just before returning to the tonic he gives us a new theme (slightly connected with the second part of his main theme, after Ex. 5).

Ex. 6.

Then, in true rondo style the main theme returns (with a forte repeat of its first eight bars and an ornamental variation of its last); and plunges into a stormy episode in the tonic minor. When this has blustered its way for about forty bars to a pause on the dominant, we expect another return to the main theme. Instead, Haydn runs away with a double fugue—

Ex. 7.

which eventually bursts into a grand tutti.

At last we are allowed to hear the first eight bars again. They have a lovely subdominant colour, like sunset light. The last two bars are reiterated and suddenly turned into a runaway wind-up.

SYMPHONY IN B FLAT (SALOMON, NO. 12; CHRONOLOGICAL LIST, NO. 102)

1 *Largo, leading to* 2 *Allegro vivace.* 3 MENUETTO: *Allegro.* 4 *Adagio.*
5 FINALE: *Presto.*

According to the autograph this is the ninth of what Haydn called the London Symphonies and posterity called the Salomon, after the impresario who arranged for their production in the years from 1791 to 1795. It is the 102nd of the 104 symphonies which the most recent musical scholarship has sifted out from the miscellaneous and doubtful works that have at various times passed as Haydn's symphonies.

Like every mature work of Haydn, it has a form of its own which constantly upsets the orthodoxies of text-books. If comparisons were any use in dealing with classics, I should be inclined to select as Haydn's three greatest instrumental works the String Quartet in F, op. 77, no. 2; the 104th and last Symphony, in D major, known as Salomon No. 2, and the present symphony. It has all Haydn's characteristic freedom of form, and more than Haydn's usual symmetry. He is a composer whose devices are singularly difficult to explain away by rules of symmetry; and there are works as large as this symphony where the orthodox methods of sonata analysis hopelessly break down. The main reason for this is that Haydn is a great master with an eminent love of spaciousness, working on a very small scale. In order to make the most of his small space he tends to write his largest movements on a single theme, and has a wonderful art of building that theme into paragraphs of all manner of shapes and sizes without ever falling into any confusion between the manner of formal exposition, where that is wanted, and a free discursive development elsewhere. But in such circumstances a regular recapitulation is out of the question; and what the orthodox text-books assume to be Haydn's recapitulation is neither more nor less than a true Beethoven coda of the ripest kind. Where then does the symmetry come in? It comes in at the end of the exposition, which Haydn always rounds off very neatly in a phrase quietly reproduced at the end of the movement, just where it is the last thing you would expect.

The possibility of asserting symmetry in greater volume depends for Haydn upon the scale of his work. This is generally so small that an extensive symmetry would run counter to the dramatic force of his style. The master from whom Haydn learned that a perfect maturity could be attained both in opera and instrumental music was, of course, Mozart. But the paradox ensued that Haydn failed conspicuously in opera because his style was too swiftly moving, in other words too dramatic, for the operatic forms at his disposal; whereas Mozart, the supreme master of comic opera, is the very composer whose instrumental music was on a large enough scale to emphasize formal symmetry. If, then, this symphony does show a recognizably orthodox scheme in its first movement and finale, with clearly marked second subjects and identifiable recapitulations, the reason is that Haydn feels that he is writing on a large enough scale to use a variety of contrasted themes such as will not waste his all-important space by being recapitulated. The only way to get the benefit of Haydn's or any great composer's sense of form is to listen naïvely to the music, with expectation directed mainly to its sense of movement. Nothing in Haydn is difficult to follow, but almost everything is unexpected if you listen closely and without preconceptions.

The introduction I leave without quotation. After a solemn initial note it begins, like most of Haydn's introductions, with a calm melody. This soon loses symmetry when the basses take up its main figure and carry it into rather remote keys; but the more the music broadens the more evident is its intention of leading to something quite different. It is developed just far enough to give a very definite feeling of breadth; and then after a pause the allegro sets in with the utmost energy.

The first subject begins with a symmetrical melody—

Ex. 1.

(a)   sf (b)

given out by the full orchestra and repeated by the flute, doubled, as almost always in Haydn's scoring, by the first violins. In this case the colour of the doubling has a definite intention which will appear later on. A rousing tutti on kindred material breaks in upon this repetition, and soon leads to the dominant (F major) where a very vigorous new theme enters, without ending or interrupting the flow of the passage.

Ex. 2.

&c.

It will be seen that the accompaniment of this connects it with the first theme. Before the passage has come to a close, there is something which a too clever analysis might connect with the introduction. As this appeals to the eye rather than to the ear, I have protected the listener from temptation by not quoting the introduction. Haydn is perfectly capable of having intended the allusion, and equally capable of laughing at anybody who taxes him with it. What really matters is the Beethovenish passage that follows the close of this tutti.

Ex. 3.

ff

Its violent rhetorical pauses are impressive enough here; but what would not occur to a lesser composer is to make the passage take a slightly different course each time that it occurs, whether in the development or in the recapitulation. Haydn here concludes his exposition with a new version of Ex. 2, followed by a cadence formed from the third bar of Ex. 1.

The development is inexhaustible; it seems as if everything

happened here. All the above quotations are worked out into quite different themes. Ex. 3 becomes a romantic decrescendo, a cantabile, and a tutti. Ex. 2 becomes a grotesque three-part canon, which stamps its way through three different keys and finally disappears, one voice after another, on to the dominant of C. Here, after a pause, we have in C major (which is of all keys the most contradictory to our tonic) the first theme as a genuine flute solo. There is not the slightest prospect of getting home from here to B flat, but the full orchestra comes storming in with all Haydn's blustering masterfulness, and in its own good time works its way round in the right direction. The recapitulation, when it does arrive, is easily enough recognized in the rough, thanks to the variety of its material. But no doctrine prevents Haydn from combining it with a great deal of further development, such as one would find in a Beethoven coda.

The slow movement sums up an unappreciated chapter in musical history. It is considered correct to say that Carl Philipp Emanuel Bach effected the transition from the style of his father to that of Haydn and Mozart; and it is true that Haydn and Mozart regarded him and more than one other son of the great Sebastian as the elder masters who were contributing to the progress of music at the time. But when it is inferred from this that Haydn's and Mozart's types of form and development are in any way fore-shadowed by Philipp Emanuel Bach, the inference will not bear examination. We have in the slow movement of this symphony a splendid example of what that influence exactly was; and probably we have in it the very latest example. Philipp Emanuel Bach's tendency never was dramatic in the true sense of the word, and it became less and less so as he developed. (It was his more popular brother Johann Christian, the 'London Bach', whose works adumbrate certain dramatic details in the true sonata style; and it was the Bach and Abel Concerts which Salomon continued when he brought Haydn to London.)

Music can make an externally dramatic impression by means not in themselves musical—e.g. the most dramatic feature in Ex. 3 is the fortissimo unison followed by a bar's rest; in other words, a noise and a silence. And so Sir Henry Hadow is able to quote from one of Philipp Emanuel Bach's oratorios a musically very simple passage (dealing with the moment when Moses struck water from the rock) as sounding a new note in music, simply because there is really very little in it to interfere with certain obvious theatrical pro-cedures. But Philipp Emanuel Bach was very fond of music for music's sake, and his whole tendency, even in his oratorios, runs to luxurious lyric sentiment. And in his later sonatas he was so far from developing in the direction of Haydn's and Mozart's dramatic power, that his whole attention was concentrated on a question of ornamentation. Players and singers at that time were allowed great freedom in interpreting and adding to the ornamentation the composer indicated for his melodies; and it seemed to Philipp Emanuel Bach, especially as the art of ornamentation was falling into decadence and chaos, that the time had now come for writing sonatas in which the repetitions were written out in full with variations. These *Reprise-Sonaten*, then, were his latest contribution to the development of music; and it is impossible to conceive anything more calculated to confine music to lyrical and decorative expression and to slacken the sense of movement. The only composer of importance who has preserved this notion of Philipp Emanuel Bach's is Haydn, who in a number of early works showed that he recognized its value for a certain type of melodious slow movement. Unlike Philipp Emanuel Bach, he also saw that to repeat both parts would make the movement too long. He accordingly made a varied repetition only of the first part, and in the recapitulatory portion of the second part devised an ornamentation which would combine both versions. A slow movement of this kind need not be expected to occur in any work of Haydn's later than the date of his acquaintance with Mozart. Only once, in this ripest of symphonies, has he taken a favourite slow movement from a pianoforte trio,[1] an unusually beautiful specimen of Viennese musical rococo, transposed it from F sharp major to F, and written out a full repetition of the first part (which was not repeated in the original trio) in order to add, not fresh airs and graces, but perhaps the most wonderful orchestration to be found before Beethoven. It would be an educative puzzle to guess by ear alone how the last bars of this slow movement are scored. The orchestra happens to consist of one flute, two oboes, two bassoons, two horns, two muted trumpets, muffled drums, and strings. Even in this purely lyric movement there is a certain dramatic element besides the wonderful colouring, but it is notable that it occurs in the second part, which is not repeated.

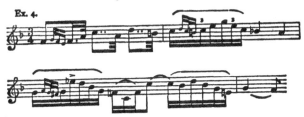

Ex. 4.

---

[1] The trio version is generally supposed to be arranged from the symphony; but the style of the first movement makes this very difficult to believe.

My quotation shows the first theme. If, instead of dismissing it as a familiar piece of Viennese rococo, we face the plain facts, we shall find that very few rhythms in modern music are as complex or as subtle as this. If you take its exceedingly slow main beats you will find of course that they will prove to be uniformly a simple matter of three divided by two; but the modern composer very rarely follows out so slow a uniform rhythm with so much variety of detail. It looks much more complicated to have no underlying uniformity and to change the time signature every two or three bars; and it also may look more subtle to have unusual groups such as 5, 7, or 13, whether uniformly or capriciously. But we may fairly question whether these are always real complexities or real subtleties. Some of the most imposing of them have been known to straighten themselves out into quite commonplace rhythms to the naïve listener who is deprived of the aspect of the printed page. On the other hand, the rhythm of Haydn's adagio is undoubtedly a combination of eighteen triplet semi-quavers in a bar alternating freely and combining with twelve semiquavers, though he uses the simplest possible notation to convey it. Moreover the very next note of the melody after my quotation fills a whole bar by itself. Modern studies in musical rhythm, such as the first movement of Ravel's Trio, closely resemble metrical effects in poetry; and they have no room for such a phenomenon as a note or a syllable that is eighteen times the length of the prevalent rhythmic unit and yet does not check the flow.

The Minuet requires no quotations except for the rhythmic figure ♩ | ♩ ♩ which is treated in the second part with the humour which is often called Beethovenish when Beethoven is most like Haydn. The trio has a broader melody, over and under which various instruments from time to time make an acquiescing cadence of two notes. This, however, they put into different parts of the phrase, so that it never twice means quite the same thing.

The finale begins with one of Haydn's best themes of the kittenish type.

Ex. 5.

Young tigers are also very charming as kittens, and this finale has powerful muscles with which to make its spring. It has a well-defined second subject, almost as original as that in the first movement; beginning with a chromatic theme—

and ending with a rousing dance. The first subject, as might be
expected from its character, returns in the tonic like a rondo theme,
with some lively fresh touches in the scoring. Then it plunges
angrily into the minor as if to start a blustering middle episode.
This speedily turns itself into a lively development with some of
that very efficient fugue-writing which is to be found in almost
all Haydn's larger finales. It is tersely handled, and leads to a
recognizable recapitulation of both the first and the second subjects in the tonic. But before the final dance-tune is allowed to
conclude matters, Haydn's (*sc.* Beethoven's) coda intervenes. It
does everything that even the coda of a Haydn finale can think of,
beginning with the Great Bassoon Joke, and continuing with
Haydn's characteristic insinuation that everybody in the orchestra
has the theme on the tip of his tongue but cannot pronounce it.
Then the rousing dance-tutti is allowed to conclude the matter,
and even the drums assure us that they know the first figure of the
theme, ♫ | ♩

SYMPHONY IN E FLAT, 'WITH THE DRUM-ROLL'
(SALOMON, NO. 1) NO. 103

1 *Sostenuto;* leading to 2 *Allegro con spirito.* 3 *Andante.* 4 MENUETTO.
5 FINALE: *Allegro.*

In the autograph this symphony is entitled 'Londoner Symphonie
No. 8'. No task could be more futile than the attempt to range
Haydn's twelve London Symphonies in order of merit. Their
differences grow upon us with their merits as we emancipate ourselves from the doctrine which regards them as pianoforte duets
with smashed-china climaxes tempered by the inhibitions of two
nice little school-girls with flaxen pigtails. As I have remarked in
analysing other symphonies of Haydn, the orchestration of these
works, though deeply scarred with evidences of primitive conditions
in orchestral performance, is equally wonderful for its power and
its subtlety. Haydn's contemporaries found him noisy; and to-day
our more sensitive disciples of Rimsky-Korsakov blame Beethoven
for a treatment of the trumpets which is demonstrably less violent
than Haydn's. We also ascribe to Beethoven's deafness the fact
that his scores are full of interesting detail which seldom, if ever,
reaches the listener's ear. But in any mature symphony of Haydn

you will find that more detail is thus lost than in Beethoven's Ninth Symphony. And Haydn's detail is often lost beyond the recovering power of double wind and enthusiastic rehearsal; whereas to my own knowledge accident or design has at one time and another brought to my ears every detail that my eye has ever read in Beethoven's scores.

The fact is that neither Haydn nor Beethoven ever thought that aesthetic economy implies that everything in a symphony directly reaches the ear. Their view was in part that of the Greek sculptors, who, arguing that the gods see everywhere, finished the backs of statues which were placed where no mortal eye would see more than the front. But there was also a more human view. Mr. Crummles's leading tragedian could not put himself into Othello's skin until he had blacked himself all over. And the total experience of the players in a symphony is as that of the gods, who see every-where. They play better all the time when their parts are more interesting than the listener realizes.

Although it is futile to compare the merits of Haydn's London Symphonies, it is permissible to compare their features. In this way we may venture to say that the Symphony with the Drum-roll is one of the most original of the twelve. Its forms are those most peculiar to Haydn and most unlike Mozart; and the opening drum-roll is merely the most obvious and the least remarkable of its unique features. The contemporaries of Beethoven must have forgotten the darkness of Haydn's introductory theme—

Ex. 1.

if they thought Beethoven's genius more eccentric than that shown in this opening. Perhaps, however, they had become accustomed to make too much allowance for Haydn's notorious humour when such awe-inspiring tones came to their ears. And indeed it is true that when this introduction has come to its deepest gloom cheer-fulness arises out of its last notes, just as it always broke in upon the philosophy of Dr. Johnson's friend Edwards.

Ex. 2.

Butter does not remain long unmelted in the mouths of Haydn's kittenish themes; and the full orchestra immediately bursts in with a new idea, unquoted here. But Haydn is in no hurry to change his key as yet; nor, when he changes it, does he at once introduce contrasted material. At last, however, a waltz strikes up—

Ex. 3.

and is followed by the solemn theme of the introduction transformed to something livelier than anything Mr. Edwards ever imagined.

Ex. 4.

The exposition as a whole is terse; but the development is unusually rich even for Haydn, who is always ready to expand. A new version of Ex. 1 intervenes dramatically, in quick time but with something like the gloomy colour of the opening, and with chromatic wailings above it. The key is the tonic, but we do not realize that we are at home, and cheerfulness is more present to us when Ex. 3 intervenes in the quite irrelevant key of D flat. After these and other adventures the tonic is again established on really convincing terms, and a more or less regular recapitulation follows. By way of coda the introduction reappears in its original tempo and is dismissed with laughter.

The andante is a set of variations in Haydn's favourite form, with two alternating themes, one in C minor and the other in C major. The minor theme is bleak in its two-part harmony, but full of ironic wit. Note the three turns of meaning given to the figure marked (a).

Ex. 5.

The second theme, allied in melody to the first, bursts out in full sunshine.

Ex. 6.

Haydn usually finds room for two full-sized variations of the first theme and one of the second; but here, as in the wonderful pianoforte Andante in F minor, he has room for two of the second, together with a very spacious coda. And so this movement ends happily in the major.

The Scotch snap which is prominent in the theme (unquoted) of the minuet indicates that into the courtly splendour of the famous minuet of Mozart's E flat Symphony an element has been introduced with which the Hof-Marschall has not been accustomed to deal. It is dealt with by the Great Bassoon Joke, aided by the horns. But this gives rise to graver thoughts; and the modulation, in the second part, to C flat and G flat is no joke. In the graceful trio, Haydn and Mozart meet on the common ground of a raillery in which the rustic is at no disadvantage with his urbane friend.

The finale begins romantically with the characteristic two-part harmony of horns in a phrase which is destined to blaze gloriously in the trumpets before the symphony is over. At present it serves as accompaniment to a melody that has been found, like many other of Haydn's themes, to be a Croatian folk-song—

Ex. 7.

(But perhaps too much has been made of Haydn's Croatian origins, both racial and musical. Dr. Kuhac's famous book on the subject was a by-product of one of the nineteen internecine national propaganda which used to turn the nineteenth-century Austrian Parliament into a bear garden).

Whether this theme has the honour to be Croatian or merely to be Haydn's own, it pretends to be a brand-new second subject when it appears later on in B flat with its phrase-accents turned round—

Ex. 8.

There are other themes, besides inexhaustible other transformations of this one. The end is inspired by the enthusiasm with which the trumpets take up the opening horn theme.

SYMPHONY IN D MAJOR (SALOMON, NO. 2; CHRONOLOGICAL
LIST, NO. 104)

1 *Adagio, leading to* 2 *Allegro.* 3 *Andante.* 4 MENUETTO: *Allegro.*
5 *Allegro spiritoso.*

In almost any edition of Haydn's works you may safely assume
that the work called No. 1 or No. 2 is really the last. Modern
research has sifted out 104 works as genuine symphonies from the
innumerable crowd of symphonies, divertimenti, operatic overtures,
and supposititious works that have passed as Haydn's: and this Symphony in D, arguably the greatest of Haydn's instrumental works
(with the Quartet in F, op. 77, no. 2, as its compeer) is, of course,
No. 104 in the chronological list of the symphonies now in course of
publication in the long overdue edition of Haydn's complete works.

The solemn Introduction in D minor strikes one of those tragic
notes of which Haydn knows the depth as well as or better than the
gloomiest artists. But he generally prefers to use it as prelude to
some such heavenly tune as this.

Ex. 1.

Students who believe that the text-book scheme of sonata form
is anything like as close to classical precedent as a Dutch doll is to
human anatomy, will get into difficulties if they try to prove that
the mature style of Haydn follows the rules. This first theme does
duty for the 'Second Subject' as well; and, of the two themes that
are new in the second subject, the one—

Ex. 2.

is heard again in the course of something far more like a big
Beethoven coda than a recapitulation, while the other I need not
quote, as it never returns. The fact is that Beethoven derived his
regular recapitulations from Mozart and his big codas from Haydn,
and that his form differs from Haydn's and Mozart's mainly in
combining the two procedures in the same work. The two figures
labelled (a) and (b) in my quotations give rise to an unfailing
variety of new phases and developments. The essential character
of Haydn's form is dramatic surprise at the moment, with sym-

metry emerging as the final impression of a series of paragraphs,
no two of which are symmetrical to each other or in themselves.

After all the a-priorities have been accepted as to powdered
wigs and courtly formulas, will the a-priorists kindly predict what
modulation Haydn is going to make at the end of the sixth bar of
the following theme of the slow movement?

Ex. 3.

The peaceful codetta to this theme is another of Haydn's profundities—

Ex. 4.

which reveals its depth fully when, after perhaps the greatest of
all Haydn's ruminative digressions into the remotest of keys, it
returns at the very end of the movement and expands into a quiet
pastoral close.

The minuet and trio I leave without quotation. Both are full of
rhythmic and orchestral surprises. The inquiring first notes of the
trio are ambiguous until the harmony enters in the unexpected key
of B flat. The phrasing is irregular with more than the humour of
the dance in the third act of *Meistersinger*: and, like several of
Haydn's last minuets, the whole movement covers more ground
than any Beethoven scherzo before that of the Eroica Symphony.

I venture to think that Brahms would have thoroughly enjoyed
hearing this symphony at a concert that included his own Symphony in D. Haydn's finale is obviously the grandfather of Brahms's
in certain features to which I draw attention.

The first theme I quote as it occurs in its counter-statement, with
another melody below it.

Ex. 5.

This enables me to refer to derived themes by their 'figures' (*a*), (*b*), (*c*), (*d*).

In the course of the second subject (which begins with Ex. 5 turned inside-out with the lower melody on the top), the following whirlwind—

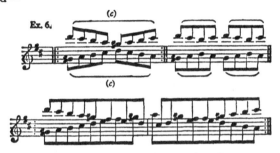

obviously inspired the brilliant passage in the corresponding position in Brahms's finale.

A more sustained figure—

is the only new theme in Haydn's second subject; for the following impudent prophetic plagiarism from Brahms's cadence-theme—

is, as indicated, an ingenious transformation, not to be outdone by Wagner or Liszt, of the figures of the main theme. There is not a line in the movement which could be guessed by rule; and one of the finest surprises is a sudden reversal of accent in the two notes marked (*d*) from which Haydn derives the last chords of the symphony.

GUSTAV HOLST

BALLET FROM 'THE PERFECT FOOL', OP. 39

It is night. The Wizard is commanding the Spirits of Earth, Water, and Fire to bring him the wherewithal for the making of a magic potion. It will look and taste like pure water. If a woman drinks it, it is but water. If a man drinks it, his eye becomes all-powerful, compelling the love of women and slaying the foeman with a blast of fire. With the dawn of to-morrow the Princess is to choose a husband. Concerning her it has been prophesied that she shall marry the man that does the deed no other can do. Surely the Wizard, when he has drunk the potion, will be the man in question! (But his plans did not take account of the Perfect Fool, nor of the Perfect Fool's Mother.)

First the Wizard summons the Spirits of the Earth.

Ex. 1.

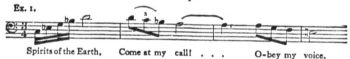

Spirits of the Earth,   Come at my call! . . .   O-bey my voice.

They come from the depths, like Nibelungs, bringing the magic cup which is to hold his potion.

Ex. 2.

Next he summons the Water-Spirits, that they may fill the cup with essence of pure consuming love—

Ex. 3.

(This passage will become a *locus classicus* for limpid orchestral colouring obtained with the simplest materials.)

The Water-Spirits move gently, and eventually subside in the tune the Princess will sing when she comes at early morn to choose her husband (overleaf)—

Ex. 4.

Lastly, the Wizard summons the Spirits of Fire that they may enter into the potion for the blasting of enemies. Their music requires no melodic quotation. Once it has blazed forth, nothing can stop its course as it tramps onward over an ostinato bass

while the lighter rhythms flicker above and sometimes accumulate in big flames—

At last it dies down, and the Salamanders, having fulfilled the Wizard's last command, disappear. The Wizard is weary. He sleeps, until the coming of the Perfect Fool and his astute Mother.

FUGAL OVERTURE FOR ORCHESTRA

Musical terms are nowadays used in such Pickwickian senses that persons may probably be found who, hearing the following opening of Holst's Fugal Overture—

Ex. 1.

will aver that it is the subject of the fugue. That, together with the supposition that the critic's attention wandered never to return after the first four bars, is the only possibly explanation of the statement, by an otherwise laudatory London musical reviewer, that this overture sounds 'oddly unfugal'. No orchestral writing could well be more fugal, though few things are more whimsical, than the conduct of this overture from the first moment when its main theme starts in the basses, in the Lydian mode.

Ex. 2.

Within the memory of very old persons still living it used to be thought that eight was twice four. The first movement of Ravel's pianoforte trio, however, showed us that eight quavers might fall so persistently into the rhythm of 3+2+3 that no ear could feel the common-time rhythm of four crotchets at all. Holst, in a

quicker tempo, here gives us a persistent rhythm of 3+3+2 (or a
⁹⁄₈ minus 1). Being a practical man, he has it conducted by the
ordinary four-in-a-bar, and leaves the result to the ear.

A counter-subject in gurgling semiquavers wriggles its way
down the wind-band at sixes and sevens.

Ex. 3.

Soon a new subject is announced by the brass. Its rhythmic groups
are quite different, and equally removed from those of common time.
I draw no bar-stroke, and if, as is probable, I have got the latter
part of the theme wrongly grouped, I err in the company of some
interlocutors who express divers opinions in its episodic discussion.

Ex. 4.

A dramatic break-off is followed by the 'augmentation' of the
first theme. The rhythm 3+3+2 (unlike plain common time, and
like Beethoven's triple-time fugue-subjects) assumes quite a
different ictus by being taken twice as slow.

Ex. 5.

Extremes meet in the combination of the two original subjects on
piccolo and contra-fagotto.

Ex. 6.

With these resources, together with close stretti (or overlappings of the subject with its answer), this brilliant masterpiece runs its classic course in the finest musical language of the present day. It is used, at the composer's suggestion, as an overture to *The Perfect Fool* when that one-act opera is given without any other piece.

MAHLER

SYMPHONY IN G MAJOR, NO. 4

1 *Bedächtig.* (*Moderato.*) 2 *In gemächlicher Bewegung. Ohne Hast.* (*At a deliberate pace; unhurried.*) 3 *Ruhevoll.* (*Calm.*) 4 *Sehr behaglich.* (*Very comfortably.*)

Mahler was born in 1860, and died in 1911. He earned his reputation as one of the world's greatest conductors. As a composer he fascinated a few musicians, but infuriated almost all the rest. The fury that he aroused was not partisan like that aroused by the compositions of Liszt. Even at the present day people who dislike Liszt are repelled, as Ruskin would have been repelled, by qualities to which they impute a sinister ethical significance. This is not altogether to Liszt's disadvantage. People who believe in the devil are either too much horrified by their belief to tolerate the slightest mention of him, or they find a naughty thrill in playing with their superstition. On the whole, a belief in the devil is a superstition which is likely to survive, and even to flourish when all other capacity for belief is exhausted. It is so very easy to live up to.

And it supplies ready-made every conceivable gradation of contrast, and can give to the most facile pathos the apparent strength
of sardonic humour. In the time of Ruskin and Clara Schumann
it was impossible not to be angry when the devil interfered in
aesthetic questions, as he always did.

The opposition to Mahler is angrier, less serious, and more
damaging. In Holland Mahler has for the last fifteen years or so
been as nearly deified as any composer in history. This is odd,
because there is perhaps no country in which musical criticism is
more *blasé* towards older music. A great artist not long ago ventured to play in Holland Joachim's Hungarian Concerto, which I
personally regard as a work not only of immense historical importance, but a monumental accumulation of beautiful musical thoughts
second only to the greatest classics, and of a quality which none
of the greatest masters could afford to despise. The most eminent
Dutch critics were agreed in wondering that such stuff had ever
been published at all. No great insight is needed to discover a
certain stiffness in Joachim's style as a composer. And as for its
relation to earlier classical music, no listener need be a listener at
all to discover its derivation. We have been told all about that.
Let us hope that the vogue of Mahler in Holland is already a sign
that anti-classical snobbery is becoming out of fashion. For the
infuriating quality of Mahler's music is particularly antiseptic
against snobs, though perhaps it cannot prevent the rise of Mahlerite snobs. There is no class of composer, diabolist or purist,
for whom a first impression of Mahler will not cause pangs of
jealousy. Mahler is no Shakespeare, and few, if any of us, are
Coleridges; but we could all write like that 'if we had the mind'.
He has no inhibitions. The experienced composer, academic,
revolutionary, self-centred in Delian or Debussian circles ever
narrowing, or eclectic in an expanding Straussian universe, encounters the style and achievements of Mahler with something of
the horror which we are told that Dr. 'Froyd' evinced when the
blonde lady revealed to him that she had neither dreams nor
inhibitions, and that she never did not do anything 'vialent' that
she wanted to do, though 'the bullet only went into Mr. Jenning's
lung and came out again'.

My own belief is that a vogue for Mahler has already been of
great benefit to musical culture all over the world, and will continue to be useful for a longer time than I can estimate. There is
a fundamental inaccuracy in saying that an artist has too much
facility, unless we make it quite clear that we mean by 'facility' the
condition in which the artist's thoughts have no chance of maturing.
A tree that needs pruning may be said to have too much facility in
producing leaves, but its trouble is that until it is pruned it has very

little facility for producing fruit. The stream which spreads itself into an unwholesome marsh instead of developing into a mighty river is not suffering from too much facility or too much water. It has simply not been helped by nature or art to dig a proper channel in which its waters can accumulate.

In the last resort, every artist needs all the facility he can get. What we composers find so disconcerting about Mahler is that every aspect of his work shows all the advantages of an unchecked facility and none of the disadvantages. It has us beaten at every point, and leaves us no resource but to sit upright in our dignity as men of taste and say, 'This will never do.' We cannot fall back upon the device of classifying Mahler as one of the conductor-composers who have drifted into composition through the urge to display their vast memories as experienced conductors. Mahler was only twenty when he produced his first important work, *Das Klagende Lied*. We cannot say that his music is reminiscent, for our chief objection to it is that no other composer has had the effrontery to proceed further with the ideas that give Mahler his simple pleasures. The very first note of his First Symphony is a sustained A eight octaves deep. I do not suppose that I was the only eleven-year-old child to whom it occurred to strike, with the aid of two other children, all the eight A's on the pianoforte. Weber thought Beethoven ripe for the madhouse when Beethoven in the coda of the first movement of his Seventh Symphony held a sustained E five octaves deep. But that was in a passage with a long history of highly organized development behind it; and it is curious that Weber did not rather select the five-octave B flat at the very beginning of Beethoven's Fourth Symphony, though he had already cited that introduction with scorn as an instance of the bluff of spreading a dozen notes over a quarter of an hour.

These illustrations will give the devout Mahlerite his cue for claiming that history is repeating itself by displaying exactly the same opposition to Mahler as was shown to Beethoven in his day. We need not trouble to discuss the inference that Mahler is another Beethoven; and, though history repeats itself, its variations are extremely difficult to analyse. But we can say with certainty that Mahler's example has set modern composers free from inhibitions which were for the most part harmful and snobbish. He has been a greater liberator in this way than Richard Strauss, for Strauss indulges his vein of naïve melody under the pretext of caricature. Till Eulenspiegel and Don Quixote are his heroes. The element of caricature is present in Mahler, but he is terrified lest it should be suspected where he is as unconscious of it as Dickens in his most conscientiously pathetic passages. Nothing can lend itself more to caricature than the grotesque folk-pastoral poem from *Des*

Knaben Wunderhorn, but Mahler's direction to the singer is: 'The voice with an expression of childlike cheerfulness without the slightest suspicion of parody.' In the twentieth century it is impossible for an artist to indulge himself with simple forms and simple melodies without feeling conscious of the dangers of affectation or caricature. Mahler is so enormously rich in every technical resource that, as Röntgen used to say, one cannot trust his simplicity. This pastoral style is *à la campagne*, and Marie Antoinette could be *à la campagne* at the Trianons.

On the other hand, the most devout Mahlerite will hardly claim that the master's style is aristocratic, either by nature or by affectation. On the whole, we composers and men of taste will be well advised to abandon our opposition, for if we persist in it there is no point on which we can clear ourselves from the suspicion of being jealous. Mahler did not care two hoots for popularity. He was extremely exacting as a conductor, and was sometimes in bodily peril from the anger roused by his ruthless efforts in raising the standard of the Vienna Opera House to its supreme height. In point of style he might be called a musical Dickens born out of season. In every technical direction—form, counterpoint, and instrumentation—his musical facility is so enormous that we cannot compare him to any of the other *monstr'-inform'-ingent'-horrendi* masters that otherwise resemble him, and who become objects of fanatical worship at the expense of the more orthodox classics. And so the opposition to Mahler deprives him even of the martyr's crown. We do not wish it generally known, but we would all like to write like Mahler if we dared; and we all think that we could. The martyr whom he most nearly resembles is Bruckner, but Mahler is anything but helpless, and rouses none of the sympathy of a naïve artist struggling for self-expression. Far from it. We find his facility deadly. His Third Symphony is a musical phantasmagoria in which all the elements that have ever been put into a symphony before are conglomerated with all the musical equivalents of a picaresque novel and a Christmas pantomime. It was intelligently anticipated by Aristophanes in a word beginning *lepado-temacho* . . . and filling six or seven lines in Liddell and Scott's Lexicon. On internal evidence it was written during a holiday at Llanfairpwllgwyngyllgogerychwyrndrobwll-llantysiliogogogoch. Yet the history of this Third Symphony shows that Mahler could exercise artistic restraint; for he so compressed its plan that he extruded one of its items, which he preserved for a more conspicuous existence as the finale of his Fourth Symphony.

The musical culture of Great Britain will probably be the better for the rise of a vogue for Bruckner and Mahler; and perhaps

Mahler will do us more good than Bruckner, because his mastery will discourage the cult of amateurishness, which keeps us contented with ignorance and ready to believe that ineptitude is noble in itself; and the good taste which is ready to take offence at Mahler's sentimentality will be all the better for being shocked. It will find itself compelled to recognize that the difference between good and bad is not a matter of fashion; though, with all respect to Horace, it can never cease to be a matter of dispute. For my own part, I flatly refuse to class Mahler with either Liszt or Meyerbeer. Liszt is for me a composer whose art has a definite taint which ruins my enjoyment of much that would otherwise fascinate me. Meyerbeer is a very clever, and sometimes very inventive, composer who is such a thorough humbug that I cannot regard him as a real person at all, and cannot be bothered to argue with people who can. There will be reservations with all such matters; and I am entirely in agreement with Wagner, who had the courage to scandalize all his friends by praising in the highest terms the duet at the end of the fourth act of *Les Huguenots*; but one decent moment will not make Meyerbeer into a good artist, and all the bad taste of Dickens, Victor Hugo, Byron, and Berlioz will not make Mahler a bad composer.

Mahler's Fourth Symphony is pastoral throughout. The orchestra pretends to be small, inasmuch as it has no trombones and only four horns. On the other hand, it is very expensive in extra wood-wind, and denies itself nothing in what is known as the 'kitchen department', such as sleighbells and gongs. The first movement begins with farm-yard noises—

on a B minor chord, through which the violins swing into G major with the gallantry of a rustic who has been to town.

I quote scarcely half the large number of themes that Mahler pours out and adorns with instrumentation and counterpoint of infallible mastery and clearness. The counterstatement of Ex. 2

is in free canon, combined in the third bar with a casual counterpoint which afterwards becomes an important theme.

Ex. 2 a.

Another pair of yokels in double counterpoint—

Ex. 3.

leads to the dominant, upon which, with the abruptness of Mozart's
most perfunctory style, the 'second subject' radiates expression
from every pore of its infant complexion.

Ex. 4.

But under this burlesque simplicity the discerning composer may
espy the cloven hoof, indicated by dropped and added beats which
betray that Mahler's phrase-rhythms are as supple and subtle as
his scoring.

I may as well quote one more theme, which brings new elements
and leads to the end of the exposition.

Ex. 5.

Its opening figure eventually dies away into the chord of B minor,
and the initial farm-yard sounds (Ex. 1) are resumed, leading back
to Ex. 2.

The movement now proceeds to shape itself more or less like
a rondo, instead of going into a development section. Ex. 2 (a)
is expanded into a peaceful tonic-and-dominant die-away, coming
to a long-drawn full-close. Then the farm-yard sounds are resumed, and something like a development arises. It develops
what it likes, and settles where it likes. It soon makes up its mind
that A major is a proper key in which the three repeated notes of
Ex. 4 may become a long-drawn 'Cheer, boys, cheer' over ruminations of the figure of Ex. 2 (a). For twenty-three bars this complex, or simplex, refuses to be dislodged from A as its bass-note.

It then strides casually into the middle of next week, which you may call E flat minor if you like; and the other figures of the exposition enter into discussion with each other, modulating rapidly, and sometimes settling to episodic sections in this or that key, always with plenty of variety and quite clear sequence. At last a tremendous climax is reached in C major, with triumphant shouts of the upper theme of Ex. 3. The decline from this leads to the return of the main theme (Ex. 2), but, very cunningly, not to its opening, but to its third bar; as if the theme, after having travelled round the world, were to walk in to breakfast unannounced, remarking, 'As I was saying . . .' It drifts into a recapitulation which is disguised by the fact that much of the matter is now given to the bass with new counterpoint above. The transition theme (Ex. 3) enters in the bass with something of the excitement of the C major climax of the development, and Mahler puts as a mark of expression the word *wild* (ferocious). The 'Cheer-boys-cheer' simplex (Ex. 4) is given with grandiose full tone, which subsides only at the cadence group (Ex. 5). When this has died away the farm-yard sounds are resumed, and the unquoted sequels of Ex. 2 are worked up into a full-sized coda, which eventually settles to a passage of sustained calm developed from Ex. 2 (*a*) and dying away into a very slow allusion to Ex. 2, which quickly hastens its pace and ends the movement in high spirits with a derivative of both members of Ex. 3 compressed like one of Humpty-Dumpty's portmanteau words.

The enemy dare not blaspheme at the themes of the first movement, for to question their originality and distinction is to expose oneself to the charge of not seeing a joke. The themes of the scherzo will hardly give the enemy occasion to blaspheme, whether he likes them or not, for they are unquestionably original; and, if their spice has a smell of garlic, this is at all events a rural smell. The key of the movement is C minor, but it arises from an introduction in an outlying region.

Ex. 6.

A solo violin enters aggressively (*sehr zufahrend*), and wrenches the harmony round to C minor with the following sour theme—

Ex. 7.

You will notice that the tone of the instrument is not exactly that of a Stradivarius played by Joachim. Mahler's direction is *wie ein Fiedel*, which may be rendered 'like a kit', or 'fiddle' if you like; and the long-suffering player has to play upon a violin that has endured the indignity of being tuned a tone higher.

The movement trips its leisurely way through a free rondo form to which the episodes might give the impression of a scherzo with two trios—

but for the fact that they return at once to the main theme before they round themselves off. The form assumes a more important aspect after the second return of the main theme, for then the material of both trios is elaborated in a spacious development, which goes through many keys before finally settling down in C major in a coda in which all the figures of scherzo and trios are discussed in dialogue.

The third movement is in a kind of variation form to which the nearest parallel may be found in the middle movement of Sibelius's Fifth Symphony. The theme is no fixture, either as bass, melody or scheme of harmonies. Its constant element is a type of bass, the course of which follows the convenience of the moment; and over this bass long-drawn melodies and counterpoints ruminate at leisure.

Thus it is impossible to limit the theme or to count the variations. After sixty bars Mahler makes a definite change of key to E minor, where, in a much slower tempo, an oboe sings a dirge over a version of the bass figure which is diminished from crotchets to quavers. The dirge, taken up by other instruments, develops with great passion, and a return is gradually made to the home tonic. The effect of a ritardando followed by a change to a tempo twice as fast makes it impossible to distinguish the diminished version from the original version of the bass. In a footnote, Mahler now admits that he is writing a variation. The new counterpoints are richer, and the pace accelerates. Like the first variation-group, this one dies away, and the dirge complex is resumed, starting in G minor and passing soon into the remote key of C sharp minor. After an impassioned climax in this key, it subsides into a new group of variations passing one into another with absolutely abrupt changes of tempo: first andante 3/4 time, then allegretto 3/8, and then in E major allegro 2/4, quickening to allegro molto and suddenly falling back to andante. Upon this there is a long-drawn coda, which is dying away peacefully in G major when suddenly there is a tremendous burst of glory in E major, a key for which the E minor of the dirge has not prepared us. The glory dies away in a haze of light, passing back into G major and expiring very slowly on its dominant.

The discerning listener may perhaps have heard a figure for four horns before the expiry of the outburst in E major which surprised us so at the end of the slow movement. I have not quoted this figure, because Mahler has taken more trouble to bring out another shrill motive in the trumpets. But from this figure arise the first notes of the soprano song with which the symphony ends.

Ex. 11.

Wie ge-nies - sen die himm - • • • • li-schen Freu - den

The words are a poem from the famous anthology of folk poetry, *Des Knaben Wunderhorn*. The orchestra supplies preludes and interludes and an extremely delicate and highly coloured accompaniment. I forbear to transcribe or translate the poem word by word. No reasonable person will be shocked at its innocent profanity; but until we have all learned to accept Mahler as a classic, we had better not expose him to the blasphemy of the enemy who would cast doubts upon the composer's reverence for sacred subjects. Lewis Carroll, in his *alter ego* as the Rev. C. L. Dodgson, was severe in his condemnation of those who quoted the innocent profanities of children and then pleaded the innocence of the child as if it was their own innocence. He did not consider the possibility that one might quote innocent blasphemies with something like reverence for the innocence. Certainly it is difficult to imagine that anybody would quote them, as Dodgson implied, for the jejune purpose of blaspheming.

I have already remarked on Mahler's emphatic forbidding of any touch of parody in the performance of this finale. The poem describes the pleasures of a simple soul in Heaven, far from the strife of the world, which exists only in order that *Weltgetümmel* may rhyme with *Himmel*, as it does in Bach's most solemn cantatas. We live an angelic life and dance and skip while St. Peter in Heaven looks on.

Ex. 12.

Sankt Pe - ter im Him - mel sieht zu!

The next stanza brings back and develops the farm-yard sounds of the first movement. A certain savagery in the tone is accounted for by the fact that Herod is the accepted Family Butcher in this unorthodox heaven, and that St. John and St. Luke allow him a free hand. St. Luke kills his ox, the wine of the heavenly cellars costs nothing, and the angels bake the bread.

The third stanza describes the heavenly vegetable gardens, with gardeners who, contrary to the severe baronial Scottish tradition, will let you have everything. Game of all sorts runs towards you, and all manner of fish swim into St. Peter's net.

With one more short farm-yard interlude from Ex. 1, the music subsides into E major, thus accounting for the outburst in that key at the end of the slow movement. Mahler's harmony is the most diatonic that has been heard since classical times, though it has no inhibitions whatever. His classical keys and his other ancient and modern modes are always perfectly clear; but he does not feel any obligation to end a symphony or a movement in the key in which it began, and so his Fourth Symphony, after having been as firmly centred round G major as any symphony of Haydn, calmly subsides into E major for the last stanza of its final song, which describes the music of Heaven, with St. Ursula smiling upon her eleven thousand virgin dancers, and St. Cecilia and all her relations as the most excellent of court musicians.

After all, we have the authority of Dante in more than one of the sublimest passages of the *Paradiso* for supposing that, though Heaven is not confined to what any mortal can understand, it includes all that we can understand. Bruckner understood considerably less of most things than Mahler. He would probably have been horrified at the notion of setting this poem. I, for my part, would be horrified at the idea of Meyerbeer setting it. Mahler I suspect of having wept as copiously over it as Dickens over Little Nell or Macaulay over the end of the *Iliad*. Such a temper has its dangers for judges and dictators; but it is much more useful in the present state of music than tastes that are too refined for Beethoven, and it is positively antiseptic against many types of morbid art. For Mahler himself the safeguard lies in his enormous technique; and for students of all kinds of musical technique Mahler will be none the less use to them if they are shocked by him.

MENDELSSOHN

ITALIAN SYMPHONY, IN A MAJOR, OP. 90.

1 *Allegro vivace.*   2 *Andante con moto.*
3 *Con moto moderato.*   4 SALTARELLO. *Presto.*

Although the Italian Symphony is one of Mendelssohn's most perfect works, it was withheld from publication during the composer's lifetime. Before he had finished it, in 1831, he was complaining that it cost him some of the bitterest moments in his life; and in 1847 he died without having accomplished his purpose of revising the finale. As Parry remarks, there are no signs of bitter moments in the work as we know it. Nor can we see where the finale could be improved. But the work may be perfect though Mendelssohn was disappointed in it; and an instinct deeper than his conscious self-criticism may have prevented him from altering it.

The Italian Symphony is the work of a young man with an energy matched only by his technical facility. In relation to Mendelssohn's musical experience, it stands where Mozart's Paris Symphony stands in Mozart's career. Now, how would Mozart have felt towards his Paris Symphony if, instead of being able simply to enjoy his own sense of power and progress, he had become conscious of the existence of a much greater music that had already dealt with similar problems? The only great music before Mozart dealt with matters so entirely different from his symphonic, operatic, and sonata-style affairs that it could inspire him without interfering with his pleasure in new ideas. At first sight, and indeed all the more on further acquaintance, the Italian Symphony seems too unlike any other classical work to give us or its composer cause to fear comparisons. But to Mendelssohn such originality was not enough. The excitement of composing such energetic music was tremendous, and was enhanced by the unique pleasure of scoring it with an orchestration that remains to this day unsurpassed for beauty and accuracy. This being so, the young composer might surely hope that when he had not only finished but perfected his masterpiece, it would continue to excite in him the feelings with which he composed it. While he was composing it he must have felt like a personification of Beethoven's Seventh Symphony. That classic is one of the things which Mendelssohn knew so well that he was in no danger of plagiarizing from it. The Italian Symphony was not meant to resemble it, and does not resemble it in any indiscreet way. But the very idea of an energetic symphony in A major must call up the memory of Beethoven's Seventh. And the last consolation that would satisfy Mendelssohn would be the plain fact that at the age of twenty-two a composer cannot be expected to show the power of movement of a composer of twice his age. It is not a question of technique. Neither Mendelssohn nor Mozart is a good example of slow and late development. The Italian Symphony, published as Mendelssohn's fourth, must really be his sixteenth, since his first published symphony was preceded by twelve unpublished ones; and Mozart was overwhelming the Milanese with operas at the age of fifteen. But there is a kind of easy-going spaciousness which suits a young composer, and no longer satisfies an older one. Worse advice cannot be given than that which would have a composer pretend to be past fifty when he is only just past twenty-one. The Paris Symphony and the Italian Symphony are both—at least in their main movements—young, loose-limbed works. Luckily for Mozart, the devil was not able to produce the Jupiter Symphony before its time in order to wet-blanket the young composer by showing him how he ought to compose when he had become a considerably different person. Mendelssohn had no such luck. He was docile, and had been carefully brought up to think his gifts normal. Competent criticism from others never came his way, and nothing is further from the truth than the idea that he lived in an atmosphere of adulation. He lived and behaved like a gentleman; and while his music, at its best and at its worst, gave abundant pleasure, it was produced in solitude. Nobody could help him.

We may then safely conclude that Mendelssohn's own dissatisfaction with the Italian Symphony is rather an objection to the laws of human growth than the recognition of defects that self-criticism and revision can remedy. Certainly in the first three movements every bar and every note is in the right place, except for one tiny oversight in the slow movement which only a mistaken piety would leave uncorrected. As to the finale, no defect is discoverable; but we can imagine that Mendelssohn could have wished to broaden its design towards the end. On the other hand, it is possible that the revising of it would have proved to be an arbitrary and endless business, leaving the movement neither better nor worse than before. Mendelssohn and Handel often show a merely restless inability to abide by a final settlement of their music. Much is omitted in modern performances of *The Messiah*: and one thing that is always omitted is the air 'Thou art gone up on high'. Yet Handel wrote six versions of this air!

The splendid opening theme of the Italian Symphony is famous for its brilliant scoring with an accompaniment of repeated chords in the wood-wind; a device to which some purists object. The only ground for objection is that few students can calculate how such things will sound, and that no poultry-yard can rival the consequences of miscalculation.

Ex. 1.

In a characteristically rapid tempo, but with the leisurely youthful phrasing that cannot be hurried however fast the motor may go, Mendelssohn works out a broad opening and a masterly transition to the dominant. His second group begins with a theme which is obviously in no hurry.

Ex. 2.

But its rhythm is, like many underrated features in Mendelssohn's works, more subtle than it looks on paper. The first figure has two aspects. As first announced it begins on an accented bar. The unexpected long notes at its sixth and eighth bars prolong the phrase and bring its next clause into a different position, thus—

Ex. 3.

where the first bar is unaccented; so that the phrase is very different from the la-di-da affair made of it by misrepresentative quotation. Hence in the sequel the accent of Ex. 2 becomes reversed, as indicated by the lower group of figures. One of Mendelssohn's great romantic moments is the entry, soon afterwards, of the clarinet with an augmented version of Ex. 1, in C sharp minor. This quickly leads to a brilliant tutti, after which there is a quiet passage, important in its relation to the rest of the movement, leading back to the beginning. As this passage is omitted from the repeat, it is absolutely necessary that the repeat should be played, otherwise an essential part of the material will not be heard at all.

The development begins with a fugato on a new theme.

Ex. 4.

Here again the rhythm has two aspects. The theme is at first given with the accent on its second bar. As its entries become more crowded the accent shifts; and when the whole orchestra is treating the theme in a grandiose marching style, the accent has settled upon the first bar. By this time however the first theme, Ex. 1, has something to say, as it enters into polyphonic and melodic combination with this fugue theme in a most masterly imbroglio. The slow decline from its climax is another great romantic event; and the beginning of the subsequent crescendo leading to the return has left its mark on one of Brahms's most powerful passages, the return in the first movement of his First Symphony. (The cruel sport of snob-snubbing was a temptation Brahms could never resist when he heard sneers at Mendelssohn.)

In the recapitulation Ex. 4 is inserted into the second group; there, accented on the first bar, it replaces the romantic incident of the augmented first theme in the clarinet. The coda drifts into a quicker tempo and makes brilliant use of the passage that was omitted on the repeat before the development.

Parry was puzzled to know why the slow movement was inspired by Naples, and certainly it needs no illustration from the Bay, or from Vesuvius, or from any of the things that we are told it is worth dying to see. But there is no difficulty in tracing the main idea of this movement to a religious procession which we know that Mendelssohn did see in the streets of Naples. He might have seen it in any other Italian town: the weather would have been the same, and the rest of the background would not have made much difference. The wailing introductory figure is just such an intoned litany as Berlioz uses on a larger scale in the 'Domine Jesu' of his *Requiem*; and the rest is eminently processional and picturesque.

Ex. 5.

The combination of violins and flutes at the repetitions of the tune is one of the most delightful *tours de force* in all modern orchestration—modern is the word for it, since it is a paradox on any orchestral hypothesis. Verdi, substituting voices for violins and adding a third flute, gave the device a more literal interpretation in the 'Agnus Dei' of his *Requiem*. But the wonderful thing about Mendelssohn's idea is that it seems quite normal. The effect is so like an organ that the movement has become a favourite with organists who want to make the organ sound like an orchestra.

A second theme in the dominant major—

Ex. 6.

introduces a note of human wistfulness into the austerity of the litany.

The graceful movement that has the function of a minuet is more than pretty. The trio, with its dominant major key and its solemn horns, is beautiful with that depth that can be sounded only by a poet who knows that solemn things must be said with the lightest touch if they are not to become blasphemous. Mendelssohn has here exactly the touch that he misses in later and ostensibly more serious efforts.

The main themes of the finale can be represented by their prevalent saltarello rhythm.

Ex. 7.

W. S. Rockstro, a copious contributor to *Grove's Dictionary*, who knew and used the correct technical term for everything in music, no matter how familiar the thing or how sesquipedalian the term, has told us that, while the two principal themes of this movement are indeed saltarellos, the eel-like legato running theme which is a prominent feature in the development—

Ex. 8.

is a tarantella. The victims of tarantula-bite cannot even stop to jump in their dance.

Be this as it may, the finale of the Italian Symphony is a high-spirited romantic movement, with all the tendency of romance to vanish mysteriously round the corner. Haydn had ended two of his greatest quartets with a finale in the minor mode when the first movement had been major. But he could not bring himself to make the finale end unhappily at last. Mendelssohn, whose finale is here as unlike other things as the rest of the symphony, remains in the minor to the end. It would be an exaggeration to call its humour sardonic, but it is admirably free from either sentimentality or callousness. One detail, very amusing as Mendelssohn puts it, became magnified into a downright offensive feature in the finale of Saint-Saëns's G minor Pianoforte Concerto. The comparison is useful as a touchstone for the difference between an early work of genius and a piece of slick classicism.

OVERTURE, 'MELUSINE'

Mélusine was, as we are told by the *Encyclopædia Britannica*, the tutelary fairy of the house of Lusignan. In consequence of the kind of family quarrel that is to be expected with mixed marriages between fairies and mortals, she suffered on every Saturday from a change into serpent-form from the hips down. The condition was temporary and remediable by suitable bathing. But it was necessary for her to find a husband who would never see her on Saturdays. Raymond of Poitiers fulfilled this condition until he yielded to the fatal curiosity of fairy-tale husbands, whereupon she flew away in serpent-form,—*poussant des cris de Mélusine*, as the proverb still runs. Henceforth her cries have always been heard before the death of a Lusignan. This is the official legend, but there seem to be other versions, in which Mélusine's transformations were more fish-like than serpentine.

Although Mendelssohn had already written his wonderful *Hebrides* Overture, he thought the *Melusine* Overture the best thing he had ever done. He finished it in October 1833, and in April 1834 he writes to his sister, Fanny Hensel, in answer to her questions about its subject: 'Now attend. I'm cross! There you go, asking me which tale you're to read! Well, how many are there? And how many do I know, and don't you know the story of the lovely Melusina? It's enough to make one crawl away and disguise oneself in all manner of instrumental music without titles when one's own sister (unnatural woman!) doesn't even approve of the title. Perhaps you've really never heard of this beauteous fish. However, when I consider how you might growl at me for growling at you in April about a letter you wrote in February, I will give in and be kind. I wrote this overture for an opera by Conradin Kreutzer, which I heard about this time of year in the Königstädter Theatre. The overture, I mean Kreutzer's, was encored, and I disliked it quite particularly, and also the rest of the opera, except Hähnel; but she was very engaging, especially in one scene where she appeared in her fish-form and combed her hair; whereupon I got a wish to make an overture which people wouldn't encore, but would receive more inwardly, so I took what I liked of the subject (and that corresponds exactly with the fairy-tale), and, in short, the overture came into the world, and that's its family history.

In August 1834 he writes from Düsseldorf to his father that he wanted to try his new Pianoforte Rondo in E flat from the proof-copies, and summoned all the local musicians to rehearse it. As they would have been offended at being paid for it, he gave them a supper and made them as drunk as they liked. This, however, was not the chief fun, but the Overture to *Melusine*, which he also played for the first time, and which pleased him much. 'With many pieces I know from the first bar that they'll sound well and have some go in them, and so it was now, as soon as the clarinets curled upwards in the first bar. The thing went badly, and yet I had more pleasure than with many perfect performances and went home in the evening feeling more cheerful than I had for a long time. We played it three times, and after the third time,

directly after the last soft chord, the trumpets burst out in a flourish
with very comical effect. It was also nice when we were at supper,
and someone made a long speech . . . and toasted me, whereupon
the trumpeters and drummer jumped up like mad and ran to their
instruments to make another flourish; and then I made a manly
speech, worthy of Sir Robert Peel, in which I preached unity and
Christian love and keeping time, and concluded with toasting the
progress of Düsseldorf music.'

The proceedings lasted till midnight, not without some quarrel-
someness by way of showing the effect of Mendelssohn's Peel-ine
oration.

Later, on 30 January 1836, Mendelssohn writes from Leipzig
to his sister that 'Many people here think *Melusine* is my best
overture; anyhow, it's the most intimate, but the rigmarole of the
Musikalische Zeitung about red coral and green sea-beasts and
magic castles and deep seas is all rubbish and astonishes me. All
the same, I'm going to take leave of water for some time, and
must look around for other prospects.' This last sentence refers
to his father's advice that he should 'hang upon a nail' the fairy-
tale subjects which had hitherto occupied him, and turn to something more serious. Perhaps the chief tragedy in Mendelssohn's
short career was that he took this advice.

The only weakness in the *Melusine* Overture is shown in the
half-phrase from the fifth to the eighth bar of its main theme—

Ex. 1.

a weakness for which the *locus classicus* is the Duetto in the *Songs
without Words*, where the inefficiency of the second clause shows
up fatally against the Aria 'With verdure clad' in Haydn's *Creation*.
The orthodox Mendelssohn-baiter glances at the first eight bars
of the *Melusine* Overture and inquires no farther. He does not
improve his taste by any so easy and summary a judgement. The
flaccid second clause is the only weakness in a composition very
perfect and distinguished and incomparably more serious than any
of Mendelssohn's later efforts to follow his father's deplorable
advice. The other themes are undistinguished; but weightier
themes would have spoiled the whole. The agitations and sorrows
of this piece are those of a fairy-tale, even if it be one that for some
persons concerned in it may end sadly. They are true and deep

(*innerlich*), as Mendelssohn always is when he is writing what he
wants to write and not what he thinks he ought to write.

The opening clarinet-figure, whether it curls upwards, as in
the theme, or downwards, as in the counterpoints, presumably
represents the Saturday lower half of the lady, whether fish-like
or serpentine or in the compromise of an eel. It may also represent
waves of water, or, for all I know, the waves in which 'die Hähnel'
combed her hair. None of these questions has the interest of good
gossip, and for all they are worth Mendelssohn might just as well
slink away from his *Rabenschwester's* questions and bury himself
in absolute music. Far more interesting are the originality and
freedom of the whole musical form, with its alternation between
the beauty of calm water and fairy-tale terrors and woes. These
more passionate elements are represented by the following pair
of themes; conventional, but in the right conventions.

Ex. 2.

Ex. 3.

The work is undoubtedly not so deep as the *Hebrides* Overture
or the music for *A Midsummer Night's Dream*; but Mendelssohn
was not mistaken in thinking it one of his best. His father was
mistaken in thinking that his son's fairy-tale world was a groove
or in any danger of becoming a groove. Within that kingdom
Mendelssohn was free and able to produce works far more distinct
from each other than his 'more serious things'. You cannot drift
from *Melusine* into the *Hebrides* or the *Midsummer Night's Dream*
any more than you could drift into *Elijah*.

OVERTURE, 'THE HEBRIDES', OP. 26

If those compositions (including single movements from larger works) which have the qualities of the *Hebrides* Overture were set apart and regarded as the only authentic works of Mendelssohn, there would be no disputing his claim to rank among the great composers. Perhaps when the scholars of a thousand years hence decipher European music of the five hundred years between 1450 and 1950, they will conclude that the pseudo-Mendelssohn of early Victorian idolatry was not the same person as the master of the *Midsummer-Night's Dream*, of the *Hebrides*, and many single movements ranging from the tragic scherzo of the F minor Quartet, to those *Songs Without Words* of which the reckless prettiness achieves real beauty. Even to us Mendelssohn is one of the strangest problems in musical history. Perhaps, in the violent reaction against the worship he received during his life and after his early death, it has been too readily assumed that he had expressed all that was in him. Gluck, Handel, Haydn, Wagner, and Verdi—none of these would have been particularly great names to us if we possessed only the works they had written before they reached the age at which Mendelssohn died. The dangers of a Mendelssohnian facility are notorious; but men of genius, including Mendelssohn, need all the facility they can get. Handel was a fluent composer at the age of eleven, and seemed absorbed in fashionable Italian opera at the age of Mendelssohn's death; while only the immense gulf between Wagner's early and his mature art blinds us to the historic importance of the fact that his worst early work, *Rienzi*, was a world-famous success. *Respice finem* is a very good motto if the end is there for you to look at; but surely no one can say what another thirty years' experience of so eventful a period in musical history would have done for a nature like Mendelssohn's.

The *Hebrides* Overture far transcends the typical praises that Mendelssohn's posterity has consented to assign to him. It is indeed a masterpiece of delicate and polished orchestration, and, as Wagner said, an 'aquarelle' by a great landscape-painter. Also it is perfect in form. But none of these praises imply anything really beyond the comprehension of an age of antimacassars; indeed Wagner's word 'aquarelle' was deliberately chosen by him to deprive his anti-Semitic diatribes of any remains of generosity that might lurk in them.

The perfection of form in the *Hebrides* Overture is the perfection of freedom; it has the vital and inevitable unexpectedness of the classics. It is of loose texture, in a way. Mendelssohn at fifty might have grown into a Handel or a Haydn; he would never have become a Bach, nor even a Mozart. His finish and polish would always have remained his manner, when not his mannerism: it never was his method. Form really meant little to his artistic consciousness: he judged of forms as schoolboys judge of 'good form'; and instead of developing classical forms on vital evolutionary lines as Beethoven developed them, he practised each form only to demolish it by easy short cuts to effect. At the same time it is not true to say that he lacked an infinite capacity for taking pains. Both he and Handel had that almost as markedly as Beethoven. But Beethoven took pains in a reasonable, labour-saving way: his numerous preliminary sketches begin so surprisingly badly because he had the common sense to sketch as quickly as possible, and to waste no pains on a detail until he was sure of its surroundings. Thus, from his first sketch to his fifteenth or so, Beethoven could maintain the freshness of an extemporizer, while at the same time he need never make the same mistake twice; until at last he had only to put into full score what had passed through a scrutiny that had rejected everything which he saw to be unnatural or obscure. With Mendelssohn, as with Handel, all the pains were taken with already finished and polished work; and the result is, no doubt, sometimes worth the trouble it cost. But both composers seem to have achieved their greatest without much revision. More often than not, the result of *six complete versions* is an air like 'Thou art gone up on high', which very few people have ever heard, though you will find it in every vocal score of *The Messiah*. But you will also find a footnote which says 'This air is generally omitted'.

The autograph of the *Hebrides* Overture is in the possession of the family of the late Professor Case, who showed it to me at Oxford in the 'nineties. It certainly contains alterations; but my recollection of it, though vague, is that the alterations are of a kind that happen only in works written at high speed when the material has been prepared rather by the general *savoir vivre* of a receptive brain than by special attention. The beauty of the handwriting extends to the trellis-work which deletes one or two passages which had begun to take the wrong turning or to miscalculate the length of a phrase; and if my memory is correct, one of these passages is the gorgeous modulation to F minor in the middle of the development—but I do not think it amounts to any change of idea. From the moment when Mendelssohn, while actually standing in Fingal's Cave, jotted down, in crotchets and quavers, the first bar—

Ex. 1.

to the moment when he wrote the last pizzicato notes below the mysterious sustained trumpets and the flute with its last fleeting allusion to the second subject (Ex. 3), Mendelssohn was surely occupied chiefly with the unconscious digesting of his impressions of Hebridean scenery, the roar of the waves rolling into the cavern, the cries of sea-birds, and perhaps almost more than anything else, the radiant and telescopic clearness of the air when the mist is completely dissolved or not yet formed.

It must be confessed that Mendelssohn never showed any interest, hardly even an 'intelligent' interest, in folk-music. The scherzo of the Scotch Symphony got as far as a partly pentatonic tune with a distant and probably accidental likeness to 'Charlie is my darling'. What really interested Mendelssohn was scenery. There his mind expanded without that sense of duty which appears in his naïve and genuine expressions of reverence for the contents of the Tribuna in Florence; expressions which prompted Samuel Butler to one of the least good-natured passages in all his writings. Yet even in Italy, Mendelssohn confessed that he could not be bothered to look at Roman ruins when he could contemplate the ruins of a rocky shore. Mendelssohn may have created conventions; but the theory that he himself was conventional will not fit the facts of his life and letters. He was far too industrious and public-spirited to do himself justice as an artist before his career was cut short.

The reason why I have quoted only the first bar of the first theme is the fact (almost without parallel except in such rich streams of melody as the finale of Brahms's First Violin Sonata) that the continuation of the theme is different every time it recurs. It is true that this is mainly a case of building up long passages out of repetitions of a single figure; but the constant difference between fine art and machinery is that the machine repeats its action as long as you keep the power on, whereas in the work of art the long passages owe their noble proportions and their beauty to the single figure. Thus our Ex. 1 makes phrases of different and even contrasted type every time that we think we are listening to its symmetrical recurrences.

Ex. 2 shows an important transition theme, in which I mark with letters certain figures that are used in other combinations.

Ex. 2.

Ex. 3 is the second subject—in its first and complete form quite the greatest melody Mendelssohn ever wrote.

Ex. 3.

In the recapitulation this deep melody is given to the clarinets, and its new serene tone has always attracted attention. Yet few commentators have noted that it completely diverges from Ex. 3 at the sixth bar. Shortly afterwards the lively coda breaks in with material that for several lines owes nothing to any of the themes, and so throws the final peroration of Ex. 1 into admirable relief. Perhaps the most surprising stroke of genius comes at the very end. The trumpets have entered pianissimo during the height of the climax, so that their long note is heard only between the crashes, while the figure of Ex. 1 descends into the darkness, and a quick allusion to Ex. 3, in the minor, flies upwards and away.

OVERTURE, 'CALM SEA AND PROSPEROUS VOYAGE', OP. 27

The inspiring cause of Mendelssohn's *Meeresstille und glückliche Fahrt* is a short poem or pair of contrasted poems by Goethe. Neither in English nor in German does the mere title indicate the meaning of the poems to the prosaic modern reader, who naturally thinks of the calm sea as the essential condition of a good channel crossing. But the poet's sea voyage is not by steamship, and his calm sea is an anxious matter. 'Deep silence broods over the waters; the sea rests without movement; and the mariner is troubled at the sight of the smooth levels around him. No breath of air from any quarter; the deathly silence is awful; throughout the enormous distance not a ripple stirs.' Mendelssohn's treatment of this part of Goethe's poem clearly resembles that of a very little known work of which I have only once heard a performance, and which there is no reason to suppose Mendelssohn himself had seen, though it had been in existence for some years; namely, Beethoven's choral setting of the poems, op. 112. It is interesting to see how the two conceptions begin to diverge when the essential condition of the prosperous voyage comes. Both composers are delightfully realistic on quite different lines when they depict the rise of the wind.

Beethoven, who is composing a setting of the actual words for chorus (a medium in which he was never fully in practice), is severely restricted, and the words have not much to gain from choral expression. 'The clouds are torn apart, the sky is clear, and Aeolus takes off the chains of anxiety. The winds rustle, the seaman bestirs himself; hasten, hasten! the waves divide; the distance approaches; already I see land.' Beyond the contrast between a slow and a quick tempo, and the possibility of some *piano* echoes and repetitions by semi-chorus, there is very little chance of building up the vocal setting of the Prosperous Voyage into more than an appendix to the Calm Sea. The opportunity is far greater for a purely instrumental piece; and accordingly, as soon as Mendelssohn has broken into the profundities of the calm by a faint breath of zephyr in the flute, all the conditions are ready for a first-rate piece of broadly impressionistic music. It is unnecessary to quote the themes, though there are several of them; one very familiar figure as old as the hills has been explicitly quoted in a passage of the highest poetic power in the Romance of Elgar's *Enigma* variations.

Speaking generally, it is quite ridiculous to regard Mendelssohn in this work, and in several others among his ripest conceptions, as proceeding on orthodox classical lines. There is no doubt that the work is a classic; but its form is entirely peculiar to itself, and the clue to it is Goethe's little poem of which I have given the prose meaning. An amusing and effective point in the whole scheme is the pompous triumphant finish, not in a quicker tempo but allegro maestoso twice as slow, indicating not only the sight of land but the arrival and the welcome (evidently official) given to the voyagers. But before we allow ourselves to smile a superior smile thereat, we had better wait for the last three chords, which are a poetic surprise of a high order.

OVERTURE TO 'RUY BLAS'

The Mendelssohn of *A Midsummer-Night's Dream* is, both in the overture and in the rest of the music, so wonderfully and classically attentive to his Shakespeare that I could not help forming high hopes that the popular and effective overture to *Ruy Blas* would appear in a new light to a listener who knew 'what it was about'. Alas! Victor Hugo's play, which I have just read with much edification, has not more than enough in common with Mendelssohn to show that though the composer was undoubtedly writing apropos of it (the play was produced in 1838, the overture in 1839), his attention to it was perfunctory. It might have made as good an opera as *Hernani*, or even as *Le Roi s'amuse* (alias *Rigoletto*); and if Mendelssohn, after the failure of his juvenile *Hochzeit des Camacho*, had had the good fortune to be induced to make an opera of *Ruy Blas*, his attention would have been aroused, assuredly with masterly results, to many interesting musical resources which, as fate ruled, escaped him. The wonderful and profound second movement of his F minor Quartet persuades me that he might even have mastered the note of tragedy, which Hugo certainly could sound. But Mendelssohn never, until that latest of his works, distinguished it from the agonies of a lost purse or missed railway-train; and Hugo's conspirators could have kept no secrets if they had been as fussy as the main theme of the *Ruy Blas* overture (Ex. 2, overleaf). I have nothing against that theme as an effective musical expression of irritability; but the kind of person it fits is not to be found in a play where everybody is a conspirator in some sense, and where the outcome is inevitably tragic. Mendelssohn's *Ruy Blas* overture is a piece of vigorous and effective music which has well earned its popularity with audiences that know nothing about its subject. And I can assure the listener that audiences may continue with quiet consciences in that ignorance. Mendelssohn could not abide Hugo's histrionics: he never realized their close affinity to his own, and if he could have had his way, the Overture to *Ruy Blas* would have had no other title than that of the pension fund for the benefit of which it was written. Any story that this overture can suggest to a reasonable music-lover will probably fit the music better than Hugo's play. What do these famous fate-laden opening chords import, with their dramatic later reappearances in changed harmonies?

Ex. 1.

It is true that the first words of the play are an omen which fore-tells fatal developments; the villain, Don Salluste, calls to his lackey:

> 'Ruy Blas, fermez la porte,—ouvrez cette fenêtre.'

And later on, when the lackey is distinguishing himself as a brilliant and masterful cabinet minister, and prospering in his love affairs with the Queen, the villain reappears in secret, and compels Ruy Blas, by mere force of past habit, to shut a window for him. But on neither occasion can Don Salluste have given orders to servants in a tone as loud as the forte of two trumpets, three trombones, four horns, and all the lower wood-wind. In a play fairly well supplied

with stage directions we are not even told that he raised his voice:
indeed at the beginning he himself continues by remarking that
everybody is still asleep. We cannot ascribe to music the power of
telling the listener (without collateral evidence) that it is representing reverberations in the soul instead of the sounds that caused
them. So, if we must think of anything but music, we may just as
well regard these chords as announcing the massacre of St. Bar-
tholomew, or the anarchism of anabaptists, or any similar assets
of the Scribe-Meyerbeer tradition; and let us be thankful to
Mendelssohn for producing his effects in terms of art so clean and
genuine. What he has in common with Hugo is a Byronic *élan* and
a technical virtuosity that are sometimes distractingly amusing.
Irreverence suggests that Mendelssohn's admirable staccato second
theme (Ex. 3, below) is inspired by Hugo's amazing jugglery with
alexandrines, which he can keep in regular movement while
dividing them syllabically between different persons. When the
Queen sends Don Guritan on a distant errand to prevent him
fighting a duel with Ruy Blas, the climax, stage-direction and all,
is deliciously Mendelssohnian. Here is the last of four similarly
divided lines; you and a friend should practise reading it together
in strict time. (G = Guritan; R = the queen.)

(G) Je . . (R) Non. (G) Mais . . (R) Partez! (G) Si . . (R) Je vous
embrasserai! (*Elle lui saute au cou et l'embrasse.*)

The rest of Mendelssohn's themes begin as follows; the main
allegro theme—

Ex. 2.

a violent transition theme which I do not quote; the second
subject, true enough to the play in its first timid staccato and in
the low-pitched cantabile that afterwards holds it together—

Ex. 3.

and an energetic theme which is destined to bring the overture to
a brilliant triumph utterly unlike anything in the play—

Ex. 4.

for Ruy Blas, though he triumphs morally, thwarting the vile conspiracy and saving the Queen's honour, conquers only in the moment of death, leaving the Queen to lifelong remorse. Not so does Beethoven illustrate the salvation that Egmont died for; he keeps it outside the tragedy. It would be amusing to write a new programme for Mendelssohn's overture; it would associate the brazen chords with some formidable and recognizable emblem of power, it would deal with persons not essentially tragic, and it would end with every really nice dog in triumphant possession of his bone.

OVERTURE TO 'A MIDSUMMER-NIGHT'S DREAM'

Just before the war great admiration, stimulated by friendly controversy, was excited by a performance of Shakespeare's *Midsummer-Night's Dream*, in which the setting was neither the realistic illusion theatre of our intellectual nonage, nor the austere endeavour of the Elizabethan Stage Society to get Shakespeare's half-open-air circus under the roof of a modern London playhouse. The setting was entirely modern, and perhaps best classified as 'expressionistic'. There was no nonsense about it, and not even Shakespeare's poetry (to say nothing of his verse) was sacrificed. The fairies, whose representation was the most heterodox feature of this distinguished production, had not only golden clothing but golden faces and hands; and the effect was by no means unfairylike; indeed it was an excellent stimulus to the imagination of an audience that must always be severely strained by the necessity of having to accept as fairies a troupe of actors whose dimensions are reckoned in irreducible feet instead of elastic inches. (Oberon and Titania are, of course, full size; but Master Cobweb is supposed, by Bottom, who knew a thing or two, to be in danger of getting himself soused with honey from the bag of a bee, while the stature of Puck varies from that of a treacherous three-legged stool to something small enough to escape notice in a punch-bowl till his mischief has made the drinker sputter.)

New music was composed for this production, for it was agreed on all hands that in the circumstances Mendelssohn's music would not do. Now for any conceivable production of *A Midsummer-Night's Dream* Mendelssohn's music will 'do' exactly as well as Shakespeare's poetry. Mendelssohn's worst music is out of fashion; but the sifting of good from bad in the voluminous output of a spoilt man of genius is not a task that can be entrusted to snobs; nor can it be simplified by assuming that every turn of phrase which is familiar to us in the bad works is intrinsically bad wherever it occurs. There are three sufficient reasons why, until we possess a musical civilization in Great Britain, Mendelssohn's music will not 'do'; first, because (apart from the rising generation of opera-goers) the British playgoer is trained to treat music and musicians as the dirt beneath his feet; second, because no British non-operatic theatre-orchestra is a third of the size necessary for a decent performance of mature classical orchestration; and last, because, doubtless with exceptions that it would be invidious to name, the British actor-manager is more impenetrably ignorant of music than any reputable musician has ever dared to be ignorant of literature and drama.

As to Mendelssohn's music to *A Midsummer-Night's Dream*, let us take it at its most bedraggled and humiliated moment. Neither the greatest music nor the greatest poetry in the world was ever meant to stand the strain that custom has put upon *The* Wedding March. It has stood the strain remarkably well, and would have suffered no strain at all if performances of it had been restricted by law to the exact full orchestra for which Mendelssohn composed it. It is festive and regal, and, to all appearance, quite unromantic. It precisely suits Duke Theseus and his Hippolyta, who are neither more romantic nor younger than any favourable specimen of an Elizabethan Lord of the Manor with his Lady; and the wit of man has never devised a less banal third term between Fairyland and the efforts of Bottom's troupe. Now, how many people, even among music-lovers, know why the Wedding March, being in C major, begins with a plunge into E minor? The reason is that after Theseus breaks up the Bergomask dance, with the speech beginning, 'The iron tongue of midnight hath told twelve', and continuing, 'Lovers, to bed; 'tis almost fairy time', the march is resumed as the court makes its exit; and the music fades into distance until the E minor opening phrase resolves itself into the fairy theme of the overture when the torchlights are gone and Puck and the fairies appear. Only an experienced opera company can time such things efficiently; and still more hopelessly out of reach of the British stage is the wonderful music scattered through the dialogues in the forest scenes. The trouble is not that our actor-managers do not want music; on the contrary, their custom has often been to demand an almost operatic continuity of musical gutter-scrapings. But until the British Empire has got rid of its tradition that to be musical is to be illiterate, and that the dignity of literature accordingly depends on being unmusical, we shall do well to confine our case against Mendelssohn to works which we are in a position to criticize intelligently.

The composition of the overture to *A Midsummer-Night's Dream* occupied Mendelssohn for a year, during which he attained the age of seventeen. The rest of the incidental music was written four

years before his death, and in that music Mendelssohn has recovered the unperturbed instincts of his boyhood.

The first theme—

obviously represents the fairies; but the overture does not tell us
all about the mysterious opening chords, as we shall find in the
play, when Titania awakens to fall in love with her monster.

Another mysterious chord that occasionally interrupts the
fairies' dance—

is not over-familiar, even in more recent harmonic styles, and
(though easily explained by classical theory)[1] was far beyond the
scope of any of Mendelssohn's contemporaries. (Beethoven was
still writing his last quartets in 1826.)

The world of festive daylight bursts abruptly into the Dream—

and soon the horns of Duke Theseus's hunting party resound.

Through the ensuing triumphant strains may be heard a strange
bellowing tone, bovine rather than brazen. It is the voice of
the ophicleide, literally, as well as Shakespearianly, the Bottom of
the brass instruments as known in 1826. Composers were already
beginning to feel that three trombones could not by themselves
produce a harmony that was essentially more than a group of
middle parts. The first bass instrument used to supply the want

---

[1] A reviewer has pointed out its use by Mozart in *Così fan tutte*.

was the serpent, an S-shaped wooden affair with holes. Presumably this is what Mendelssohn first wrote for here, for he still uses
it in *St. Paul*. But by the time this overture was published (the parts
in 1832, the score in 1835), the serpent had been improved into a
brass instrument with keys, and the pundits of Kneller Hall (after
consultation, no doubt, with the Professors of Greek at the four
Scottish and principal European Universities) had translated the
words 'Keyed Serpent' into 'Ophicleide'. Even in its improved form
the instrument was a ridiculous bass for any sober harmony of trombones, and Berlioz lived long enough to direct that in all later editions
of his works it should be replaced by the bass tuba;[1] a situation
summarized half a century later by the poet Lewis Carroll, who, far
from writing nonsense, obviously referred to Berlioz in saying

'He thought he saw a rattlesnake which questioned him in Greek;
And when he looked again, it was the middle of next week.'

It would accordingly be the height of researcher's folly to hunt
up genuine serpents and ophicleides for performances of *St. Paul*
and *Elijah*. But for *A Midsummer-Night's Dream* the ophicleide is
essential: the tuba can no more replace it than Philostrate, Duke
Theseus himself, or an efficient and conscientious police-sergeant
could replace Bottom. There is no more overwhelming proof of
the boy Mendelssohn's genius than his one perfect use of this
hopeless failure among would-be orchestral instruments.

The ophicleide soon asserts itself in an impudent proleptic
plagiarism from Rachmaninoff's celebrated Prelude in C sharp
minor ('this prophecy shall Merlin make, for I live before his time',
as the Fool said in *King Lear*). The music proceeds in orthodox
sonata form to B major, the dominant, and subsides into a placid
second subject which may safely typify Hermia and Helena.

Ex. 5.

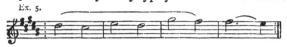

Modern criticism has discovered this to be somewhat school-
girlish; which is precisely true of Hermia and Helena, and is
essential to their charm. The horns of Elfland, not too faintly
blowing, alternate with a suave cadence—

Ex. 6.

[1] Not always: see Mr. Tom Wotton's excellent little book, *Berlioz*
(O.U.P.), for corrections on such points.

which grows in girlish enthusiasm until the climax is overtopped by less elegant strains.

Ex. 7.

Many a talented boy besides Mendelssohn would have enjoyed devising a musical suggestion of Bottom's ass's head; but who else would, seventeen years before writing the rest of the music, have noticed even the existence of his Bergomask Dance and seized the opportunity of incorporating the human aspirations of the whole troupe by combining the two ideas? One of the marks of mature genius is that, within the hypothesis of its art-forms, it is never inattentive. Not all things are relevant to its attention, and it would be useless to urge the authority of Shakespeare in support of any claims Czechoslovakia might urge upon the League of Nations to obtain command of the sea. So we should not find Mendelssohn's accuracy damaged by the discovery that the true Bergomask Dance is not in rhythms of the bourrée type, as Mendelssohn has it, but is really more closely allied to the pavane. This discovery, by the way, is a pure fiction of my own; but plenty of music has been written or compiled for Shakespeare on the lines of such scholarship without the slightest attention to dramatic moods and situations; as if poor Bottom and his colleagues were more likely to know the correct meaning of 'Bergomask' than the correct meaning (than which nothing was farther from their seraphically innocent thoughts) of 'there we may rehearse more obscenely and courageously'.

After the Bergomask Dance the hunting-horns of Theseus make a triumphant end; upon which the fairy themes return suddenly, and a wonderful development takes us deep into the darkening forest, where sudden sounds, at first startling, grow fainter, and more terrifying the fainter they grow; until at last, with the cadence of Ex. 5 in a mournful minor key, poor Hermia, 'never so weary, never so in woe', lies down exhausted to sleep on the ground. (I could have sworn that this passage is used in the incidental music at those words; but the probability of such a use has deceived me, and I find that Mendelssohn has other threads in hand at that point.)

A soft light shines over the last minor chord. It is the first of the four fairy harmonies; and the ensuing recapitulation, very regular in form, is full of wonderful new sounds. Indeed, throughout the whole overture there is not a bar of merely conventional, hardly even of normal, orchestration, though every first principle is beautifully illustrated. The outburst of Ex. 3 is omitted, as it is bound to recur, now in the tonic, at the end of the second subject after the Bergomask Dance. The coda is, of course, devoted to the return of the fairies, with their blessing upon the House of Theseus and Hippolyta. But who would have thought that the brilliant tutti-outburst of Ex. 2 was going to be transformed into a poetic reminiscence of the Mermaid's Chorus in Weber's *Oberon*, which had just been produced when Mendelssohn was finishing this overture? Mendelssohn had no very strong memory for the origin of his melodic ideas; but plagiarism is objectionable only when the plagiarist can neither remember nor rediscover the point of his original: and this final inspiration of the *Midsummer-Night's Dream* Overture is as far above Weber's Mermaids' Chorus as the fairies of Shakespeare are above the fairies of Planché.

The overture ends with its four opening chords. The fact that the final drum-roll is not on the bass-note is one of the most consummate subtleties to be found in any orchestration; and the chords are otherwise more softly scored than those of the opening.

A few years after Mendelssohn had written this overture, he was travelling in Italy, and, at a party where all the talent and fashion were gathered together, was drawn into a lively discussion of a Shakespearian revival—if 'revival' be the term for something that nobody concerned had ever heard of before. The play in question was called *Il Sonno d'una Notte di Mezzastate*, and was 'all about the doings of witches. In it occurred the stale device of a play within the play, and this internal play was full of anachronisms and infantilities': whereupon, writes Mendelssohn, 'all the ladies joined in and advised me not to read it on any account'.

INCIDENTAL MUSIC TO 'A MIDSUMMER-NIGHT'S DREAM'

The first entr'acte is perhaps the most famous and certainly one of the most typical of Mendelssohn's scherzos. Written, like the rest of the *Midsummer-Night's Dream* music, many years after the marvellous overture, it shows in the work of the experienced man no loss of the spontaneity of the adolescent genius. It is always praised as a masterpiece of orchestration. Some day, when current criticism knows a little more about form, we may come to recognize that the best works of Mendelssohn are not more remarkable for their scoring than for the Haydnesque freedom of their form.

There are several themes in this scherzo. The first is a formula professing, like Domenico Scarlatti's openings, to do little more than assert its key.

Ex. 1.

But it proves capable of development and combination with other themes. The main theme of the second group, on the other hand, is a highly organized phrase full of wit and unexpectedness in the ways in which it coils upon itself.

Ex. 2.

It is given to the whole mass of strings in a multitudinous whisper that is as admirable in its 'night-rule about this haunted grove' as the alarming crescendos that mark later stages of the design. The scherzo ends with an astonishing *tour de force* for the flute. Listeners who wish to appreciate what this involves may be recommended to pronounce two hundred and forty intelligible syllables at the uniform rate of nine to a second without taking breath.

At the last chord, the curtain rises, and Shakespeare introduces Mendelssohn to Puck, who cries 'How now, spirit? Whither wander you?' (Two flutes answer with two bars of Ex. 1.)

> FAIRY: Over hill, over dale,
> Thorough bush, thorough brier,
> Over park, over pale,
> Thorough flood, thorough fire,
> I do wander every where,
> Swifter than the moone's sphere.

Fragments of the scherzo accompany the whole dialogue till the Fairy March, that brings in the ill-tempered Fairy King and Queen.

It has been asked why I produce stage music on the concert platform when I express so strong and so evidently conscientious an objection to concert excerpts from Wagner. I have no indiscriminate objection to such excerpts as are intelligible or made intelligible by their method of presentation. My objection is directed against nonsense, whether on the concert platform or on the stage. On some other occasion I shall enter into the details of this matter. Some things in Wagner are reduced to formless nonsense by extraction from their contexts; some are reduced from the sublime to the vulgarly sensational; and some are injured only by a slightly abrupt or perfunctory end. A few pieces really belong to the concert platform, and one, the Paris Venusberg music, is actually out of scale and style with the opera into which Wagner inserted it; a defect which disappears when it is isolated.

My conscience is completely satisfied by performances of dramatic music on the concert platform if the dramatis personae are adequately represented by singers, or, in cases where there is much spoken dialogue, by a narrator who can compress the facts of the action into something not out of proportion to a performance primarily musical. Whole scenes and acts from Wagner's dramas need only the singers themselves, without interruption or explanation, and might reveal to concert audiences much that escapes an attention fatigued by the enormous scale of the whole drama. Brahms, who was by no means the anti-Wagnerian that his friends wished him to be, used often to go to one act of a Wagner opera each day; and I myself found the second act of *Tristan* an experience of new vividness on an occasion when I arrived in town too late for the first act. Some of the greatest dramatic music in existence is almost impossible to produce except in the concert-room. Goethe's *Egmont* is in Germany itself kept on the stage mainly by Beethoven's music, which the German playgoer is musical enough to wish to hear, though the play itself does not attract him. So even in Germany the need is felt of a device for presenting the music in the concert-room with the aid of a narrator.

The *Midsummer-Night's Dream* music of Mendelssohn is in the predicament that while the play is eminently effective in modern British theatres the music is hopelessly beyond the capacity of anything short of a first-rate opera; Mendelssohn having written for a barbarously Early Victorian country in which the subtle distinction between theatre and opera-house was not clearly marked. It was actually supposed in his day, and the superstition lingers in his country yet, that music in the theatre was as good as music anywhere else. Hence the music for the *Midsummer-Night's Dream* is, like that for *Egmont*, written for a full orchestra, needing the utmost care and accuracy in performance. Except for the absence of singing in the dramatic roles, no dramatic company, however distinguished, could possibly cope with it on terms of less equality than those of opera. A whole concert would be needed to present the music completely in an intelligible framework of spoken dialogue and narration. In such a concert the lover of poetry could enjoy as an honest series of quotations a considerable amount of Shakespeare's poetry, and might even learn something

about it from Mendelssohn. No literary conscience can possibly
be offended by such a presentation, which does not mutilate
because it never pretends either to completeness or to dramatic
illusion.

The lover of music will certainly learn some surprising things
about Mendelssohn. He will find that that much-abused Early
Victorian has nothing in common with the Age of Inattention
which was about to begin its enormous task, now almost completed,
of releasing the fine arts from all responsibilities. Berlioz has
told us that parts of his *Romeo and Juliet* are unintelligible to
audiences to whom Shakespeare's play, *avec le dénouement de
Garrick*, is not extremely familiar. Such erudition Mendelssohn
does not demand of his audience. The words of Shakespeare,
as known in current texts, both in English (which Mendelssohn
spoke and wrote almost perfectly) and in excellent German trans-
lations, are enough for him. But how many of us can read poetry
as simply and accurately as Mendelssohn reads it? And of those
who can, how many artists with anything like Mendelssohn's 'fatal
facility' would have the modesty to keep it in check long enough
to notice and act upon the words I underline in the last chorus?

> OBERON: And this ditty *after me*
>   Sing and dance it trippingly.
> TITANIA: First, *rehearse* your song *by rote*,
>   *To each word a warbling note*.

Mendelssohn has grasped two essential points here: first, that both
Oberon and Titania have here taught the fairies their ditty before
they sing it; secondly, that they are to sing trippingly as well as
dance trippingly—that is to say, as Titania explains it, a note to
each word, not a coloratura. Her own stanza is set legato, which
keeps this rule and yet gives ground for her epithet 'warbling'.

You cannot compare this music with the play in any respect
or on any detail without finding Mendelssohn completely in touch
with his text.

Into an hour it is possible to pack all the music except the
scherzo, the Fairies' March, and the accompaniment of the dialogues
in which the quarrel of Oberon and Titania is explained and
shown. There is no music to the first act; and the scherzo does
not make a good contrast immediately after the overture. A larger
selection of poetry would be possible by devoting a whole concert
to the work: this selection would then interpose some readings
from the first act between the overture and the scherzo; would
show how the scherzo is continued in the dialogue between Puck
and another fairy; and would include the Fairies' March, the
quarrel, and the formation of Oberon's nefarious plot with the

magic flower of love-in-idleness. But unless some twenty minutes is available for all this, it is better to summarize it in a short explanation and so obtain the excellent and delicate contrast between the overture and the song, 'You spotted snakes with double tongue', with which the fairies sing Titania to sleep.

At the end of that song you may detect the tragic irony beneath—

> Now all is well.
> One aloof stand sentinel.

The poor little sentinel is no match for Oberon, who steals in and squeezes the juice of love-in-idleness into the sleeping Titania's eyes. She is now doomed to fall in love with whatever 'vile thing' Puck contrives to bring to her first waking glance.

Oberon has also charged Puck to seek out an Athenian, Demetrius, who scorns the love of Helena. Both are wandering in the forest on this midsummer night, he in flight and she in pursuit. Puck is to find them and to contrive that when the Athenian youth sleeps he shall awaken, with the juice of the magic flower in his eyes, when Helena shall be the first living creature he sees. A glorious tangle ensues, for Puck finds the wrong man, Lysander, with his true love Hermia: the father of Hermia intended her to marry Demetrius, who is himself in love with her; and her disobedience is punishable either by death or by consignment to that eminently Athenian institution, a nunnery. She has fled to the woods with her faithful Lysander. In modest separation they lie down to sleep. Puck hastily identifies the discourteous churl whom the poor maiden dares not approach. He squeezes the charm on Lysander's eyes. Enter Helena running in pursuit of Demetrius, who runs faster and leaves her. She sees Lysander, and, seeking his help, awakens him. The charm works; he instantly tears passion to tatters in praise of her. First infuriated at what she takes for mockery she soon flies from him in terror, and he pursues.

Hermia awakens from an ominous dream and finds herself deserted. She wanders away in vain search. And now Mendelssohn, in a movement little known to concert-goers, and less known to theatre-goers, achieves one of his most perfect and subtle character sketches. Perhaps the main tragedy in his artistic development is that he did not understand this achievement himself, and in other works mistook its note for that of tragedy. Elsewhere he has taught us to dread the direction *agitato*, and even made us think that, in accordance with a suggestion of Charles Kingsley's, agitation ought to be assigned especially to aunts. But here, just as the school-girlishness of the second theme of the overture is an exact realization of the special charm of Hermia and Helena, so is the agitation of this intermezzo a perfect realization of the quality and quantity of their troubles. If Mendelssohn had never mistaken such things and such persons for Antigone or supposed that chorales and the thunders of Sinai were their appropriate consolations, all might have been well. And here all is well; besides perfect fitness to the human situation he has realized the midsummer madness in a peculiar orchestration, full of strange echoes and still stranger resonances. Possibly one detail of this was in his mind when in criticizing his sister's orchestration he said, 'Don't you know that you have to take out a licence for writing the low B flat for the oboe, and that it is allowed only in cases of witchery or great grief?'

The intermezzo dies away, and there is a desolate darkness before dawn. The dawn brings a comfort which (though marked *Allegro commodo*) does not at first seem relevant. Puck's comment on it is—

What hempen home-spuns have we swaggering here . . .?

These are the Athenian artisans, assembled in dangerous neighbourhood of Titania's bower, to rehearse the play they hope to be allowed to present to Duke Theseus 'on his wedding-day at night'. Puck soon takes control, changes the head of their star actor into that of an ass and so puts the rest to flight. Bottom the weaver, unconscious of the real enormity of his unshaven appearance, thinks that his companions are trying to frighten him. He sings to keep up his courage, and does not notice that something has gone wrong with his nasal resonances. Something has also gone wrong with the beautiful first four chords of the overture, with which Titania awakens. But her ear is much enamoured of Bottom's note. Oberon's charm has worked. If Bottom is astonished by his exalted surroundings his astonishment is so profound as to leave him no leisure but to adapt himself to them instantly. His manners are worthy of Titania's illusion; he accepts her favours with neither shyness nor arrogance, and converses affably with the fairies appointed to wait upon him, guessing shrewdly at the names of their kinsfolk, to whom he sends polite messages. They hail him with fairy trumpets and drums. (Did you know that two flutes can make a first-rate fairy kettle-drum roll?)

In another part of the wood Oberon learns from Puck of this brilliant success. But Demetrius and Hermia appear, and it becomes evident that Puck has made a strange mistake. Hermia is accusing Demetrius of having made away with Lysander, and his protestations are no more acceptable than his love, to escape from which she had braved her father's wrath and fled to these woods. She leaves Demetrius, and he, exhausted, lies down and sleeps. Oberon charms his sleeping eyes so that when he awakens he may love her who pines for love of him. Puck's task is now to lead Helena to the spot. She comes, but she is pursued by Lysander, and, as Puck joyously foresees, Demetrius will now awaken and find in Lysander a hated rival for Helena's hand. Nor will Helena be any better pleased to find Demetrius joining in a conspiracy to mock her. And so it turns out. Hermia comes in and shows herself an excellent match for Helena in a scolding bout. The two men go off to fight a duel. The ladies do not trust each other's company. Puck, imitating the voices of Demetrius and Lysander, misleads the gallants round and about until he has brought them, exhausted, to lie down and sleep within a few yards of each other. In the orchestra his laughter gradually becomes the panting breath and dragging limbs of Helena and Hermia, who also arrive in utter misery at the same place, and, unconscious of each other's presence, also fall asleep. Puck puts into Lysander's eyes an antidote given him by Oberon. All shall be well.

And now concert-goers can find out the meaning of the famous Nocturne with its beautiful horn solo. It is not fairy music; it is the comfort of rest to tired mortals blest with natural sleep before an awakening to happy normal daylight. These mortals are not Olympian, neither are the impassioned rising phrases that break out in the violins as a contrast to the serene melody of the horn. But their answer in the far-off pianissimo wood-wind is as superhuman as the midsummer moon, and the whole scheme is as Olympian as Mozart or Beethoven. Towards the end the tone becomes fairy-like, for the scene reopens upon Titania's bower.

Dawn is at hand. Oberon, having taken Titania at a disadvantage, has obtained from her the changeling boy who was the object of his quarrel. He now undoes the charm. She awakens. The four mortals sleep on, with the blessing of the fairy king and queen. The day breaks. Hunting-horns announce the approach of Theseus and his court. They find the sleeping lovers, whom the huntsmen awaken with their horns. Theseus overrules the objection of Lord Egeus to the marriage of his daughter Hermia to Lysander, and ordains that both pairs of lovers shall be united on his own imminent wedding-day.

The fifth act is introduced by the gloriously squirearchic Wedding March, the curtain rising at a carefully chosen moment after the second trio. Of all the entertainments submitted for choice by the Master of Ceremonies, Theseus, recognizing sincere loyalty, chooses that of Bottom's troupe. (If Oberon influenced Theseus in this matter, which we are not told, he did no more than pay his debt to Bottom as one gentleman to another.) The play is a great success, in the quiet manner of success at Court where kid-gloves are sordines to applause, and the audience is inclined to make audible contributions to the dialogue. But we may be pretty sure that Bottom got his sixpence a day for the rest of his life. The Funeral March of Pyramus is in the same key as that in the 'Eroica' Symphony, but it is simpler in form, and scored for a smaller band, consisting of a clarinet, a bassoon, and a pair of kettledrums. The Bergomask Dance, which Theseus chooses in preference to an Epilogue, is based on the donkey theme of the overture.

At twelve o'clock Theseus stops the dance, and the royal procession makes its exit to the receding sounds of the Wedding March. These magically become the fairy theme of the Overture as Puck enters upon the now darkened stage. The fairy king and queen enter with all their court. During the first four chords of the overture Oberon and Titania dictate to the fairies what they are to sing. They 'sing and dance it trippingly', pronounce their blessing on the house, and depart. Puck delivers his epilogue through the first (and last) chords of the overture.

SCHERZO IN G MINOR, FOR ORCHESTRA

Mendelssohn's thirteenth symphony was written in 1824, when he was fifteen years of age. It now figures as his First Symphony, and is a clever piece of work, though hardly presenting any striking features that would make a revival interesting now. In the same year he produced his Octet for 4 violins, 2 violas, and 2 violoncellos. There are not many string octets in existence; and where the necessary eight players find themselves together they would be tempted to do even a mediocre work that was decently written for the combination. They would, for instance, gladly attack anything as good as Mendelssohn's First (or thirteenth) Symphony. But it so happens that his Octet is unmistakably a work of genius. Its first movement is an admirable specimen of Mendelssohn's most spirited and energetic style; and if sometimes the inner parts degenerate into orchestral tremolo, Mendelssohn as the first offender has received the whole blame for a vice which is cheerfully condoned when later composers indulge in it far more unscrupulously. The slow movement is rather vague in structure and theme, but extraordinarily beautiful in scoring and colour. I have no reason to doubt that, if produced under the name of a later composer, it would be regarded as notably original and romantic. The finale is very boyish, but so amusing that it wears a good deal better than many a more responsible utterance. As to the scherzo, it is as far beyond praise as any classic can be. It is not quite the first of Mendelssohn's visits to his own fairy kingdom. There are two or three almost uncannily romantic scenes from that country in pianoforte works which he wrote at the age of fourteen, and they are by no means very like each other. The scherzo of the Octet is their archetype, and eight string players might easily practise it for a lifetime without coming to an end of their delight in producing its marvels of tone-colour. But now the humour of the situation begins. On 25 May 1829, Mendelssohn, being then twenty years of age, conducted his thirteenth-first symphony at a concert of the Philharmonic Society in London. He dedicated the work to the Society, but, before producing it, came to the conclusion that its minuet was perhaps not very interesting, and so he swiftly arranged the scherzo of the Octet for orchestra to take its place. This was neither the first nor the last time that this scherzo proved a favourite piece. There is one occasion recorded in Mendelssohn's letters where it was performed, and very well performed too, in a Roman Catholic Church at a service, to Mendelssohn's own scandalized amusement. Be this as it may, the orchestral version is quite as wonderful as the original, and it would be impossible to guess that it had ever existed in another form. Mendelssohn has drastically altered a great deal of the movement and has considerably shortened its by no means long development. We must not hastily jump to the conclusion that all the alterations are in the nature of criticism of the earlier work. The new orchestral medium has inspired Mendelssohn with sharper contrasts and broader effects; and this has had the paradoxical result of compelling him to spend less time over gradual changes of colour and wealth of special detail for eight individual players. Wagner has told us that he found it easier to start our orchestral sight-readers than to stop them. And this state of things he maliciously dubbed 'the Mendelssohn tradition'. The real Mendelssohn tradition consisted in doing precisely what Wagner himself was driven to do: teaching the orchestra to play a quarter of the programme really well, in the hope that thus an improvement might be manifest in those items which there was no time to rehearse. From the very first note the orchestral version of this scherzo is full of practical devices.

The whole piece drifts by in an intense pianissimo and the lightest of staccatos. Its first theme is a mere formula asserting the key after the manner of Scarlatti.

The second subject (the movement is in tiny but highly organized sonata form) is a very definite theme starting in B flat, but gradually shifting to D major.

It ends in a staccato cadence figure, which becomes important in the development and coda.

A great deal might be written about the two versions of this movement, and it would be interesting some day to hear them together. I am not, however, so historical-minded as to think that the orchestral scherzo has anything to gain by being swamped in the rest of the early symphony in which Mendelssohn inserted it. The only reason I can see for its neglect as an item in our orchestral repertories is the singular fact that it was first published in 1911.

* In the orchestral version Mendelssohn facilitates the start by giving the first violin an inaudible bottom G instead of the quaver rest.

MOZART

SERENADE IN D MAJOR (KÖCHEL'S CATALOGUE,
NO. 250), composed for the wedding of Elisabeth Haffner,
July 22, 1776

1 *Allegro maestoso: leading to Allegro molto.* 2 VIOLIN CONCERTO—
Andante—MENUETTO—RONDO (*Allegro*). 3 MENUETTO *galante.* 4 *Andante.* 5 MENUETTO. 6 *Adagio: leading to Allegro assai.*

The Haffner Serenade is the largest of all symphonic serenades,
and something more. Mozart understood by the term a symphonic
work in a festive style, and with licence, or occasion, to extend itself
to a greater number of movements than is usual in symphonies.
The occasion for such a serenade was generally some such wedding
as that of Mozart's friend Elisabeth Haffner to the excellent Herr
Spath of Salzburg. Miss Haffner was the daughter of the mayor
of Salzburg. For her Mozart wrote a serenade of dimensions suited
to the wedding breakfast. This probably lasted from midday till
nightfall; and the serenade concluded the proceedings by moonlight.

The Haffner Serenade resembles four other orchestral serenades
by Mozart in the same key (D major, almost the official key for
festive orchestral music) in containing a group of concerto-move-
ments. In Mozart's own catalogue of his works these groups are
mentioned separately as 'concerto in' such and such a serenade.
The two greatest of these orchestral serenades, the Haffner and
another work (Köchel 320), were for a long time accessible in
full score only as symphonies, the concertante movements being
omitted. It seems that Mozart himself used to produce these two
serenades in this form. Even so, they would still amount to
complete symphonies with an extra movement. But the scores
published in this form have other defects which do not inspire confidence in their texts; and the complete original works are the more
welcome since the concerted movements are not only very beautiful
but are incomplete without the rest. The serenade may be a super-
abundant symphony without the concerto, but the serenade-
concertos are manifestly incomplete. Nevertheless I have the
strongest suspicion that a certain Concertante for flute, oboe, horn,
and bassoon, written in Paris and supposed to have been lost, is
really the Concertante for those instruments in the Serenade,
Köchel 320. The Meiningen Orchestra toured Europe at the
beginning of this century with a concertante for not quite the same
group of instruments, which was supposed to be the lost work
recently discovered. I had to write an analysis in the programme.
Being thus retained as counsel for the defence, I could not say
what I thought, viz. that no pupil of mine would be allowed to get

through the writing of two of those fifty-odd pages of blundering form and inept scoring, to say nothing of ascribing them to Mozart. It is my proud boast that a former Chancellor of the Exchequer, on reading my carefully worded testimonial to the work, immediately asked me 'What's the matter with this?'

[No! That essay is not among my collected works. If I ever deal with that concertante again, I shall not write in testimonialese.]

Authorities will differ about what constitutes a theme within the meaning of the act. I have selected twelve items for illustrating the Haffner Serenade. Those of the first andante (Exs. 3, 4, 5, 6) fall, with the exception of the last, into a single complex paragraph, being parts of a concerto-ritornello. If the whole serenade were illustrated in the same way, the number of quotations would be at least 32, and these would not include formulas and derivatives.

The opening allegro maestoso sounds like a first movement until it proves to be only an introduction to a much livelier allegro in alla breve time. This real first movement uses the second figure (*b*) of the introduction as a transition-theme and makes much of the first figure (*a*) as a feature in an otherwise mainly episodic development—

Ex. 1.

Figure (*a*) also forms the triumphant growl with which the movement ends. From the second group I quote one of Mozart's most Rossinian themes.

Ex. 2.

The slow movement with violin solo is a worthy forerunner of one of Mozart's sublimest adagios, that of the D major Quintet. Its opening ritornello contains in an unbroken flow of melody the following three figures:

Ex. 3.

Ex. 4.

Ex. 5.

Of these, Ex. 4 reappears in the D major Quintet, and reaches the highest circle of the musical paradise in the Kyrie of Beethoven's *Missa Solemnis*.

To these themes the solo violin adds a transition-theme—

Ex. 6.

and a new item (unquoted) to the second group.

A beautiful minuet in G minor follows. The trio, in G major, is scored for winds with the solo violin.

And now the solo violin is allowed to say a few words in rondo form. Few, if any, concertos have larger or livelier rondos. The solemnity of the occasion is well displayed in the main theme, scored with an exquisite bell-like figure in flutes and trumpets—

Ex. 7.

and the three well-contrasted episodes, in the dominant, the submediant (E minor), and the subdominant, with a full recapitulation of the first episode in the tonic, are worthy of their august positions and responsibilities.

The concerto being now over, the full orchestra resumes its splendours, and the trumpets resound in a *Menuetto galante* in D major. The trio is in the minor, and is serious, as befits the majesty of a slow minuet. (In Mozart's later serenades we are almost as likely to find a serious note as anywhere in his works. The second movement of Köchel 320 is definitely tragic; and the only explanation of the title of serenade for so solemn a work as the wind octet in C minor that was afterwards arranged as a string quintet is that the term may have become generic for wind-music.)

Now comes an Encyclopaedia Mozartiana of rondo form. In the andante in A major we have the most luxurious rondo before that of Brahms's Sextet in B flat. Everything happens that can happen in a rondo without disaster, and yet the movement is not inordinately long. The amiable main theme—

Ex. 8.

goes through delightful variations and re-scorings, and good-naturedly gives up its precedence to a more feline sister who always turns up instead, and always makes quite sure that you have heard what she has to say.

Ex. 9.

A third member of the family has a little the manner of an elder person, being at once enthusiastic and conciliatory.

Ex. 10.

He, she, or it is the source of most of the episodes, and always has the last word.

Another minuet follows. It is lively, and has two trios, the first being in G major, with solo wind instruments, while the second is in D, led by the winds with an undertone of military trumpet-calls.

A solemn adagio begins as if to develop at leisure into another meat-course of the wedding breakfastlunchteadinnersuppernight-cap. But it knows its business and leads straight into the perfect finale to this inexhaustible but accurately balanced work. The main theme is one of those affairs that will combine with anything whatever. Drive on, coachman!

Ex. 11.

The other themes work up into sonata form. Here is the beginning of the most serious one.

Ex. 12.

SYMPHONY IN D MAJOR (PARIS SYMPHONY).
(KÖCHEL'S CATALOGUE, NO. 297)

1 *Allegro assai.* 2 *Andantino.* 3 *Allegro.*

Mozart's Paris Symphony is famous as a work of great historical importance. While I am writing this analysis an eminent colleague is stimulating the musical intelligentsia of Harvard by inveighing against reverence for the classics; which in some forms does, indeed, as he says, clutter up the minds of people whose opinions might otherwise become independent and valuable. An apparent reverence for the classics is as likely as any other form of snobbishness to mask an inactive mind which is too vacant to be charged with being cluttered up with anything at all. Accordingly, it cannot be said to do any harm so far as it goes, since it goes nowhere. But I know nothing that can clutter up the mind more ruinously than a preoccupation with the squalid conditions to which all artists, great and small, accommodated themselves with more or less difficulty or complacence in periods that have become classical. Some ingenuity may be wasted in imputing psychological thought to Shakespeare when he is producing inconsistencies which are more completely explained as crass accommodation to inartistic conditions, or even as carelessness. The more we know of such things the better, so long as we realize that a man of genius cannot suppress his real self, however much he may try; unless, indeed, he stops working altogether. Under mundane conditions, art may attain three heavens: one, the highest, which is above all conflicts; the second, where an artist enjoys accommodating himself to his world and is above consciousness of his irony; and the lowest, but still a heaven, in which he writes with his tongue in his cheek. Below this lies hell, into which Mozart did not descend even in his church music. Of purgatory I have no official information. We Protestants have our limitations.

Mozart's trials in Paris may have brought him down to the third heaven, but I see no evidence that he did not enjoy the concessions to Parisian taste which make the features of the Paris Symphony almost amount to a code of etiquette. He took such advantage of these concessions that he enlarged the Parisians' ideas of music almost as extensively and quite as deeply as Gluck had enlarged their ideas of music drama. He writes to his father on 11 September 1778, that his earlier symphonies wouldn't do there: 'Our taste in Germany is for length, but really it is better to be short and sweet.' This was apropos of the advice that the Parisians preferred symphonies to have no 'repeats'; and, accordingly, the Paris Symphony is the first important sonata-work before Beethoven in which there are no long repeats. Yet it is longer than any of Mozart's earlier symphonies. For Parisian audiences needed repetitions of phrases on the spot as much as the audiences of any mob orator. To this day French composers tend, like Couperin and brilliant and colourful Russians like Rimsky-Korsakov, to say each sentence twice over: sometimes in other words, like the parallelism of Hebrew poetry, but more often in the same words.

Another instruction which amused Mozart very much was that every symphony should begin with a *grand coup d'archet*. Mozart obeyed instructions, and, before the symphony was played, was well satisfied that it would please the few French people whose opinion was worth anything. As for stupid people, he saw no great misfortune if it didn't please them; but he had hopes that even donkeys would find something to like in it, and above all, he had not muffed the *premier coup d'archet*. He didn't see why the dolts made such a ridiculous fuss about an orchestra that just begins all together as in other places. A friend told him that an excellent musician, Dal Abaco, was asked whether he had been at Paris and heard a *Concert Spirituel*, and what did he think about the *premier coup d'archet*? 'Did you hear it?' 'Yes,' said Dal Abaco, 'I heard the first stroke and the last; and the last pleased me better.' Well, here is what Mozart made of the *premier coup d'archet* and of the need of mob-orator repetition—

Ex. 1a.

The Coup d'archet.

wind.   1st time.

2nd time.

Ex. 1b.   Further consequences of the *Coup d'archet*.

Ex. 1 c. By diminution.

Ex. 1 d.

Ex. 1 e.

As for the mob-orator repetition, it was as much a need to the twenty-year old Mozart at this stage of his development as it was to any contemporary audience. But you will notice: first, that the *coup d'archet* has found its organic and thematic answer in the rhythm of the wind instruments, whose every note is so significant that the second flute is an individual who prepares for the entry of the first flute. Moreover, the repetition expands. Mozart, at the age of twenty, cannot make a concession to the stupidest Parisian conventions without producing musical forms decidedly more advanced than anything you can find in the phrasing of Schumann's Quintet, with all its wealth of epigram; and so it is through the whole symphony. There is not a note without its permanent value, and Mozart is able to use the stupid Parisian conventions as a means of educating the Parisians out of them. He was instructed that finales ought also to begin with a *coup d'archet* in unison, instead of which he began his finale with eight bars piano for the violins alone. As he expected, he heard an excited 'Hush, hush' from the audience at the beginning. Then came the forte, and at the same moment a burst of applause; whereupon Mozart, who had been in deadly anxiety at the horrors of the rehearsal, went with feelings of great relief to the Palais Royal and ate an excellent ice.

I need not quote many of the twenty or thirty other themes with which the symphony is comfortably packed.

As far as I can see, Ex. 2 must be the theme of which Mozart writes: 'In the middle of the first allegro was a passage which I knew could not fail to please. All the audience were charmed by it, and there was great applause, but as I knew when I wrote it what an effect it would make, I brought it round an extra time at the end of the movement, with the same result, and so got my applause da capo.'

Monsieur Le Gros, the director of the *Concerts Spirituels*, declared that this was the best symphony he had ever heard, which, as Parry remarks, is not be to wondered at, considering that nothing like it had ever been written before; but he did not like the andante, and told Mozart that it modulated too much and was too long. 'This impression', said Mozart ,'arose merely because the audience had forgotten to clap so noisily and so persistently as in the first movement and finale. The andante pleased me and all connoisseurs and amateurs, and most of the audience, best of all. It's the exact opposite of what Le Gros says. It's quite natural—and short; but in order to please him and, as he believes, many others, I have made another andante. Each is right in its way, because each has its own character, but I like the second still better.' The second andante is, accordingly, the one that survives in the Paris Symphony. Mozart took unusual pains over the second andante, revising it so much that he had to clear it up by writing an extra fair copy. Le Gros and his like cannot have had the slightest conception of the meaning of Mozart's alterations; but they were doubtless flattered by the fact that he had written a new movement to please them. Here is its main theme—

and here is the beginning of the finale which surprised the Parisians out of their dependence on the *premier coup d'archet*—

Grateful as the Reid Orchestra is for all evidences of public recognition, we are glad that the music-lovers of Edinburgh are not so immediate in the expression of their opinions as the public of the *Concerts Spirituels* in 1778.

Mozart was afraid of no one; and he took the opportunity of beginning his second group with a fugato which must have impressed the Parisians as very learned. For the orchestra it has a characteristic advantage: like the rhythmic figure of the initial *coup d'archet* (Ex. 1), it gives opportunity for every member of the wind band to assert himself as an individual, the second player answering or anticipating the first.

However much the historian's mind may be cluttered up by his knowledge of the philistinisms with which Mozart dealt so diplomatically in the Paris of 1778, there is no denying that, while these philistinisms may have prevented Mozart at the age of twenty-two from offering the Parisians work that might anticipate the depth of his later thoughts, he thoroughly enjoyed enlarging—or, rather, revolutionizing—their notions of craftsmanship by introducing to them all, and rather more than all, the refinements of orchestral technique developed at Mannheim, such as the crescendo, the diminuendo, and other *coups d'archet* than the first and last.

SYMPHONY IN C MAJOR (KÖCHEL'S CATALOGUE, NO. 338)

1 *Allegro vivace*. 2 *Andante di molto*. 3 FINALE: *Allegro vivace*.

Jahn believes this work to be the symphony of which Mozart writes
to his father that 'it went *magnifique*' with an orchestra of 40 violins,
12 double basses, 6 bassoons, and 'all the wind doubled'. Against
this identification is the fact that apart from the 6 bassoons the
symphony has no wind to double except the oboes and horns, for
nobody could suppose that the trumpets wanted doubling. Mozart
may have been writing of a revival of the Paris Symphony, which
has full wood-wind, including clarinets. It is surely not necessary
to suppose that every time his letters mention a symphony it was
a different work. The question of identity is not important: the
point is that already at the date of this C major Symphony, when
Mozart was 24, his orchestral style was inveterately grand and
suited for performance on a scale larger than that of the Bayreuth
orchestra. The substance of the first movement may have misled
Jahn to overlook the fact that the score contains neither flutes nor
clarinets to account for 'all the wind'. The themes of the first
movement certainly mark a new stage in Mozart's development.
Grandiose he had already been in the Paris Symphony; sometimes,
indeed, with his tongue in his cheek, as when he obeyed advice in
beginning it with a grand *coup d'archet*, and then, having satisfied
Parisian fashions, began his finale pianissimo. But in this C major
Symphony the grandiose note belongs to something deeper. Even
the piano echo and expansion after the fourth bar of the vigorous
opening formula—

Ex. 1.

is more like a serious dramatic question than any echoes in the
Paris Symphony. And the subsequent plunges into minor keys,
frequent throughout the movement, are wholly serious.

The 'second subject' (so called in our beautiful English terminology, because it may be anywhere about the middle of seven or eight
different themes) marks the epoch of Mozart's full maturity of
invention. Not of his full command of form; many subtleties were
to be added to that in his later works. Up to this moment he had

found out many musical tunes, and, especially in the early concertos, had shown himself bristling with epigram. But now he invents a melody, rich as the most brilliant epigram and broader than any he had ever put into instrumental or vocal music before. It attains the level on which comparisons become impossible. Different melodies may be invented, but not finer ones.

Ex. 2.

Following the custom prescribed for his Paris Symphony, Mozart does not repeat the exposition, but proceeds at once to the development. This is entirely episodic. Twelve impressively gloomy bars lead to the dark key of A flat, where a dramatic passage proceeds, in plaintive dialogue between strings and wind, to the dominant of C minor. There it remains in suspense just long enough to determine the right moment for the return of Ex. 1, with a regular recapitulation.

The slow movement is headed *andante molto*; which has led to mistakes as to its tempo, since we have come to consider andante as meaning 'slow'. But Mozart still has some recollection of its proper Italian sense of 'going'. His *andante molto* therefore does not mean 'very slow' but 'decidedly in motion' or 'ambling along'. *Andante assai con moto* would be tolerable musician's Italian for the purpose. In this light the movement is the richest slow movement Mozart had as yet produced, and he did not often surpass it in subtlety. It is eminently witty, and the attention is concentrated on its pure musical sense without any distractions of orchestral colour, for it is scored for strings alone, except for the bassoons, which however merely double the basses. The harmony gains a characteristic Mozartian richness from the constant division of the violas into two parts.

I give the first theme as it occurs in its counter-statement, where it is given to an inner part, with a counterpoint above.

Ex. 3.

Though the movement is short its effect is eminently spacious, the rhythm being expanded by echoes and interpolations with a mastery that anticipates the Mozart of ten years later.

There is a 'second subject'—

Ex. 4.

followed by plenty of accessories. After the exposition a link of four bars leads at once to a regular recapitulation. The link, which was derived from the first theme, is turned into a neatly epigrammatic end.

As in the Paris Symphony, there is no minuet. The finale is a lively dance in presto 6/8 time, like that of the opening of the ball-room scene in *Don Giovanni*. Imagine the Lancers becoming so fast that it would do for a Tarantella. Quotations are not necessary. The movement is thoroughly effective and appropriate; but this adds interest to the fact that in style and technique it is very like the finales of Mozart's earlier symphonies. It thus serves to measure the advance made by the rest of the work. Here it does not jar, yet you could put it on to an earlier symphony without damage. And if you transposed it into E flat few people would detect its substitution for the opening of the ball-room scene in *Don Giovanni*. But it would be unthinkable as a finale for the Linz Symphony; though it has its impressive minor passages and pianissimos.

SYMPHONY IN C MAJOR, NO. 36 ('LINZ SYMPHONY') (KÖCHEL'S CATALOGUE, NO. 425)

1 *Adagio, leading to* 2 *Allegro spiritoso.* 3 *Poco Adagio.*
4 MENUETTO. 5 *Presto.*

The Linz Symphony, composed at that country town in November 1783, ranks with the supreme last triad of symphonies, the great concertos, and the great quartets and quintets, as one of Mozart's most perfect instrumental works. I cannot explain its neglect in recent years. I have only once heard it in my life; but it was evidently very well known in the 'forties, for extracts from it abound in the *Harmonicons* and *Musical Libraries* of that time. Later writers on Mozart trace in it the influence of Haydn. This would not have struck me, for I should expect that influence to enlarge the place of the development-sections in Mozart's sonata forms; whereas in this symphony the developments are even shorter and more episodic than is already usual with Mozart, while the recapitulations (where Haydn usually proceeds to digress) are typically full and regular. We might call the introduction a

Haydnesque feature, since an overwhelming majority of Haydn's later symphonies have it, while it is not easy to recall more than a dozen in all Mozart's works in sonata style. But it is of Mozart's dozen, and not of Haydn's majority, that the present example is typical. It is an architectural portico, not an avenue or a tunnel, like the openings—sometimes tuneful, sometimes mysterious—which make us wonder what Haydn is up to this time.

In the ripening of Mozart's symphonic style the Linz Symphony has much the same position as Beethoven's Fourth Symphony has in Beethoven's style. Both represent the supreme mastery and enjoyment of a sense of movement. Both also represent this as the composer had not so conspicuously or consciously represented it before. Few quotations are needed. The first theme of the allegro stimulates the sense of movement by its irregular phrasing.

This, and its free expansion, may point to the alleged special influence of Haydn on the Linz Symphony; and another Haydnesque technicality might be found in the difficulty of selecting a definite point at which we can say that the 'second subject' begins. But such technicalities are unimportant; and on the whole the Linz Symphony probably influenced Haydn much more than Haydn influenced it. Certainly it influenced brother Michael Haydn and Beethoven, both of whom copied Mozart's use of C trumpets and drums in an F major slow movement.

I quote the E minor outburst of the second subject—

in order to call attention to the spacing of a chord, of which the scoring for oboes, trumpets, horns, and bassoons is one of Mozart's

miracles. There is a fine collection of rumbustious tutti themes after this, interrupted by an undoubtedly Haydnesque *piano* piece of quizzing. A running link-passage for the first violins leads back to the repeat of the exposition, and onwards to the short development, of which it forms the staple, also working up into an excellent short coda after the recapitulation. It is a fundamental error in criticism to regard the shortness of Mozart's developments as a defect. They carry enormous weight in his architecture.

The slow movement, in sonata form, is one of Mozart's most beautiful and characteristic inspirations. I have already mentioned how its solemn trumpets and drums impressed other composers. Here is the first theme.

Ex. 3.

The only other quotation I need give is the remarkable episodic link-figure which arises in the short development, and, with its changes of meaning on its penultimate chord, strikes the mysterious note of romance with a power that no remoteness of date can weaken. The penultimate B(*) is sometimes flat and sometimes natural.

Ex. 4.

The gallant little minuet, with its graceful trio, is on hardly a larger scale, though in freer rhythm, than those hundreds of orchestral dances which Mozart wrote for the public ball-rooms of Vienna.

The finale is a wonderful example of the art of spinning along like a tireless athlete, and *not* like a sleeping passenger in a motor-car. From its six distinct themes I quote four; the opening—

Ex. 5.

the transition-theme, which is worked out vigorously in the rather full development—

Ex. 6.

the opening of the second subject—

Ex. 7.

and the ensuing purposeful fugato theme—

Ex. 8.

without the spaciousness of which the remaining bustling and running themes would miss all that raises their glorious energy above the level of Rossini's volubility.

The Prague Symphony is, except for its finale, on a larger scale; but there is in all Mozart nothing greater than the Linz Symphony until we reach the last three symphonies and the great chamber-music.

NOTE

The three symphonies written in six consecutive weeks of the last years of Mozart's life express the healthiest of reactions on each other, and the very fact that they are all in Mozart's ripest style makes the full range of that style appear more vividly than in any other circumstances. Consequently, they make an ideal programme when played in their chronological order; and for such an occasion this prefatory note was written. The E flat Symphony has always been known as the *locus classicus* for euphony: the G minor accurately defines the range of passion comprehended in the terms of Mozart's art: and the C major ends his symphonic career with the youthful majesty of a Greek god. Within these three types each individual movement is no less distinctive, while, of course, the contrasts within the individual symphony are expressly designed for vividness and coherence. Even in the treatment of the orchestra, where Mozart's material resources would mean starvation to any but the most spiritual of modern composers, each symphony has its own special colouring: and that colouring is none the less vivid in that it is most easily defined by stating what instruments of the normal orchestra are absent.

Thus the E flat Symphony, being without oboes, is eminently the symphony with clarinets. Mozart was the first to appreciate the true importance of the clarinet both in chamber music and in the orchestra. He found it already released from its military duty of replacing the clarino or high trumpet of Bach and Handel; but he could not have found in Gluck's or even Haydn's earlier clarinet-writing anything like his own sense of the value of every part of the instrument's compass: the low 'chalumeau' notes, hollow and ominous in sustained or legato passages, and deliciously 'nutty' in non-legato formulas of accompaniment as in the trio of the minuet in this symphony: the glorious cantabile of the soprano octave before it reaches the high military notes (in the trio of the minuet the first clarinet has this to the low accompaniment of the second): and the four or five notes in the middle register which, rather flabby and dull if brought into the foreground, are an invaluable background for any and every other orchestral tone. It is this last modest use to which the orchestral clarinet was devoted by Gluck, and, for the most part, by Haydn, until Mozart taught him better: and it survives as late as Beethoven's tremendous *Overture for the Consecration of the House*, where the fugue form requires a certain archaic severity of orchestral tone.

In the E flat Symphony Mozart compels himself to use the clarinets in all possible ways, because he does without oboes throughout the work. In the G minor Symphony he at first did without clarinets, and most editions of the score give only his original version; but he afterwards rewrote the oboe-parts, giving all their softer and less rustic utterances to the clarinets, and it is a great mistake not to accept his revision. In the C major Symphony there are no clarinets and no room for them in its scheme. The whole orchestra is affected by these differences of scheme; and an intimate knowledge of these three scores is the foundation of a fine sensibility towards the possibilities of modern orchestration.

SYMPHONY IN E FLAT (KÖCHEL'S CATALOGUE, NO. 543)

1 *Adagio, leading to* 2 *Allegro.* 3 *Andante con moto.* 4 MENUETTO: *Allegro.* 5 FINALE: *Allegro.*

The E flat Symphony begins with a slow introduction, which, like most of Mozart's other not very numerous examples, is in the character of an impressive architectural feature. Haydn, whose mature symphonies have slow introductions in at least nineteen cases out of twenty, often makes the introduction mysterious, and nearly always puts some element of dramatic surprise into it. Mozart here aims only at the dramatic effect of formal impressiveness. Beethoven himself did not write a longer introduction (though he wrote more directly dramatic ones) before his Seventh Symphony; and Mozart in the last bars of his E flat introduction has uttered one of those sublimities that are incomparable with each other and with everything else, except as touchstones for one's own sense of beauty.

Ex. 1.

The graceful theme of the allegro, thus introduced, is a distinguished example of a familiar Mozart type; but familiarity should not blind us to the resourceful economy of its instrumentation, and of its counter-statement in the bass, with new imitations and figures equally rich and convincing in the treble. Then comes a long and brilliant tutti, which, after stating several new themes, brings about the transition. The bars that establish the dominant key of the second subject contain a lively figure which I need not quote, as its position makes it easily identified. We will call it the transition-figure. Of the second subject I quote (with abbreviations) almost the whole of its first sentence. Familiarity is apt to make us think this typical, not only of Mozart, but of his period. As a matter of fact no other eighteenth-century composer was capable of writing anything remotely like it; and Beethoven himself, who attained the same freedom in his Fourth Symphony, contented himself with handling simpler paragraphs in his Third (the Eroica).

Ex. 2.

The violins finish this sentence by adding a gorgeous counterpoint to its last five-bar phrase, the fifth bar being obliterated by another outburst of the brilliant tutti, which now ends the exposition with the transition-figure in tonic position. The development is very short and formal, executing its few and simple processes by means of the transition-figure and the five-bar phrase at the end of Ex. 2. After another rousing tutti the wind-instruments lead in three quiet bars back to the recapitulation, which is perfectly complete and regular. There is no coda beyond an amplification, with plenty of trumpet and drum, of the close of the exposition. All this simplicity and symmetry are essential to the bigness of the scheme. The composer who can produce it is not the man who, having got safely through the exposition, turns with relief to the task of copying it out into the right keys for the recapitulation; but he is the man who conceives the exposition with a vivid idea of what effect it will produce in the recapitulation. This is why he can tell when to let it alone. Even here, in the most regular of all classical movements, you may notice a beautiful little enhancement of Ex. 2 at the repetition of its first phrase.

   If the first movement combines free and varied phrases with a simple big design, the slow movement seems in its first theme to take its stand upon rigid form.

Ex. 3.

But this formal theme, which takes up a considerable time in building itself into a regular 'binary' structure, is the chief member of one of the most highly organized movements in all Mozart. Notice particularly a moment towards the close of the theme where it is clouded over by the minor mode. An obvious general feature is the surprising amount of development concentrated on the figures (a) and (b) of the theme, which pervade every instrument and almost every stage of the movement. The form of the whole is roughly that of a first movement with no repeats (I am not considering the small repeats of the two portions of the 'binary' first theme), and with no development section, but with a full recapitulation and a final return to the first theme by way of coda.

   The transition to the second subject is made through a stormy tutti, beginning in F minor and subsiding into a broad passage of preparation on figures (*a*) and (*b*). This finally settles on a new theme in which instruments take each other up imitatively.

Ex. 4.

&c.

This is stated and counterstated with great breath, and then it leads back to the key of the opening. The recapitulation of the first theme seems to be going to make no changes except merely decorative additions to the scoring, borrowed from the quiet part of the transition; but just towards the close of the theme, where it is clouded over by the minor mode, it modulates to B natural (=C flat) minor, and in this very remote key the stormy transition theme bursts forth with enhanced vigour. It soon reaches the quieter preparations in the right key; and the passage which finally settles down into the recapitulation of Ex. 4 is so subtle and difficult that it has been selected in a volume of 'orchestral studies' for the violin, comprising the outstanding difficulties in Strauss and Wagner.[1] It is worth noting that throughout the movement Mozart's handling of the auxiliary notes in figure (*b*) of Ex. 3 boldly anticipates a feature in the harmonic style of Strauss that has shocked orthodoxy.

The colouring of the later stages of Ex. 4 in the recapitulation is particularly gorgeous and deep; and the crown of the movement is the new turn given to the final shortened summary of the first theme; a passage which looks forward to the close of the slow movement of Beethoven's C minor Symphony, though its beauty is complete in its own right.

I have already called attention to points of scoring in the trio of the most celebrated of all Mozart's minuets. Perhaps, if the minuet were less celebrated in bad pianoforte arrangements, there would be less widespread misconceptions as to its tempo. It is *not* a 'stately' and posturing dance: it is an allegretto, which in Mozart's and Haydn's minuets indicates something fully half-way to the tempo of a scherzo. When Mozart wants the minuet of *Don Giovanni*, he writes *menuetto galante*, or *moderato*.

The finale is in sonata form with repeats, like the first movement. All its themes, throughout the second subject, are derived

[1] The Leipzig edition of the band-parts has, as usual, ruined Mozart's beautiful phrasing, including the main point of his harmony, by editorial bowings. Every well-known orchestral composition of Mozart requires some eight hours' work with a blue pencil to remove the geological deposits of officious stupidity from the band-parts.

from figure (*a*) of its first subject—

Ex. 5.

with the exception of the long and brilliant tutti which effects the transition.

The way in which the second subject pretends to make a new theme by the impudence of a flute and bassoon who cut figure (*b*) off from the rest, almost tempts one to think that Mozart had been reading the *Frogs* of Aristophanes: the manner is so exactly that of some one finishing an interrupted verse with a ridiculous tag. The truth is that Aristophanes (if he had been musical, as presumably he was) would have found himself very much at home in Vienna or even Salzburg ('the fatherland of clowns' says the librettist of Mozart's *Schauspieldirektor*) at the close of the eighteenth century.

One more quotation is desirable: the wonderful and by no means conspicuous passage for wood-wind at the end of the development, leading back to the recapitulation. It is, of course, the background for the all-pervading figure (*a*).

Ex. 6.

The recapitulation is regular, with a completeness that gives the utmost weight of finality to the abrupt end.

SYMPHONY IN G MINOR (KÖCHEL'S CATALOGUE, NO. 550)

1 *Allegro molto.* 2 *Andante.* 3 MENUETTO: *Allegretto.* 4 FINALE: *Allegro assai.*

The Symphony in G minor has been compared with all manner of tragedies; and if the motive of such comparisons be to induce us to take Mozart seriously, they have an excuse. It is quite impossible to exaggerate the depth and power of Mozart's thought; those enthusiasts who may seem to do so, have in fact merely mistranslated the language of music, or of poetry, or of both. The danger of such mistranslations is that they are as likely to misrepresent life as to misrepresent art. We can only belittle and vulgarize our ideas of Mozart by trying to construe him as a tragic artist; neither the literature with which he came into contact, nor the musical forms which he brought to such exquisite perfection could give him scope for any music which by legitimate metaphor could be called tragic. This does not imply that he could not have risen to an opportunity for tragedy; we have no means of knowing the limitations to his powers of expression. He died young, and he touched no problem without solving it to perfection. What is finished of his *Requiem* is of a world beyond tragedy; the *Dies Irae* is in one sense a catastrophe, but a universal catastrophe is not tragic if nobody (or everybody) survives it; for it is in 'the pity and terror' of the spectator that the tragic catastrophe does its purifying work. And in the true tragic sense the *Dies Irae* is not even a catastrophe, it is a universal ordeal that lies in the future; an ordeal for which Mozart prepares himself with solemn rites.

If we are to understand Mozart, we must rid our minds of the presumption that a tragic issue is intrinsically greater than any other. In music this is conspicuously untrue. There is no question that the most tragic of musicians is Beethoven; yet only three of his most powerful works have really tragic finales, while others, sounding fully as tragic a note in their first movements, end in triumph (the Fifth and Ninth Symphonies), or in some pathetic vision as of a happiness secured for the unborn (the F minor and A minor Quartets), or—let us face facts as Beethoven faces them—in a violent temper (the C minor Violin Sonata and E minor Quartet). If we can face the facts of Beethoven's tragic music, we can also face the fact that Mozart's whole musical language is, and remains throughout, the language of comic opera. He has even been blamed for using it in his *Requiem*; and the blame would be deserved if his language meant something he did not intend to say. But the blame should fall on the critic who allows the accidental associations of an artist's idioms to blind him to their true meaning. The word 'awful' does not mean in a modern drawing-room all that it means in Miltonic poetry; but need that prevent a modern poet from using it in a Miltonic way? or from using it properly in a drawing-room?

This is an extreme case for which there is hardly a parallel in Mozart; but the opening of the G minor Symphony, taken together with some of the comments that have been made on it, gives us as delicate a touchstone for the whole question as could well be devised. Sir George Grove in his analysis of this symphony very pertinently remarked that it is difficult to see, in the repeated notes at the end of each step in the theme, those depths of agony ascribed to the opening by some critics. Just so: it is not only difficult to see depths of agony in the rhythms and idioms of comedy, but it is not very intelligent to attempt to see them. Comedy uses the language of real life; and people in real life often find the language of comedy the only dignified expression for their deepest feelings. They do not want the sympathy of sentimentalists who would be hard put to it to tell tragedy from burlesque; and the misconceptions of people who would imagine their situation and language to be merely funny are altogether below their horizon. They rise to the height of human dignity by treating the ordinary language of their fellow mortals as if it were good enough for their troubles; and Mozart and Molière are not fundamentally at variance with Sophocles and Wagner in the different ways in which they immortalize this meaning of the word 'reserve'.

We need not, then, be shocked to find that the language of the opening of the G minor Symphony is much the same as that of the overture Rossini used for the *Barbiere* after writing it for some other purpose. Rossini's overture fits the *Barbiere* admirably; for its feebly shrill and bickering opening can hardly fail to suggest something like the state of mind of poor little Rosina ready for any adventure that may bring escape from her grumpy old guardian. Now, even to those of us who are most fond of the *Barbiere*, this sort of thing hardly bears mentioning in relation to the G minor Symphony. The language, we admit, is common to both: where does the gulf lie?

In the 'forties Liszt published, or at all events played in public, arrangements of Beethoven's nine symphonies, introducing them with a declaration to the effect that it was possible to produce on the pianoforte all the essentials of an orchestral score, except those of sheer mass and varieties of timbre. The arrangements are still in print, and prove conclusively (to any one who can read the originals without their aid) that Liszt was by far the most wonderful interpreter of orchestral scores on the pianoforte that the world is ever likely to see. Yet when Mendelssohn heard of Liszt's declaration, he instantly said, 'Well, if he can play the beginning of Mozart's G minor Symphony as it sounds in the band, I will believe him'. With his usual acumen, Mendelssohn hit upon a passage *scored for strings alone*, which for sheer impossibility of translation to the pianoforte surpasses anything that can be found in Beethoven, or perhaps in any later writer. Yet it is hardly possible to say that its mysterious agitated accompaniment of divided violas makes it much more complicated than the *Barbiere* opening with its coarse little accompaniment in repeated chords.

These two elements of utter simplicity and utter impossibility of translation are among the most obvious signs of the highest poetic power. We do not often find such a bundle of anecdotes and illustrations to demonstrate their presence as we have been able to find for this particular opening, concerning which still more might be said, as the autograph gives some interesting changes of detail, the first bar being an afterthought which changes the rhythmic ictus. But these qualities are equally present in every line and every aspect of the whole.

As has been mentioned above, Mozart first wrote the symphony without clarinets, but availed himself of them at the first opportunity. The Eulenburg score and the Edition Peters give only the original version; but no conductor with a feeling for Mozart's style (and a knowledge of how he sighed for clarinets where they were not forthcoming) would dream of neglecting Mozart's careful revision. The Philharmonia score gives the revised version.

As the Gesammtausgabe is the only one that fully displays both versions, it may be of interest to students of such matters to try and find out during actual performance what the changes are, if only such an exercise is not carried to a point where it rivets instead of stimulating attention to the music. Generally speaking, Mozart has substituted the mellow tone of the clarinets for the acid tone of the oboes everywhere, except in a few places (chiefly sustained discords) where the acid tone has a definitely pathetic effect, and in the trio of the minuet where the use of oboes and horns is in a definitely pastoral style. Where the oboes are not suppressed, they are extensively rewritten, to make room for the fuller harmony the clarinets can help to provide.

Another point in the study of the small orchestra is the ingenious use Mozart makes in this symphony of two horns pitched in two different keys, both of them high; by which means he anticipates Berlioz in a device which doubles the normal number of notes possible in his time on the limited scale of the horn. Much of the surprising fullness of tone in the first movement and finale of this symphony comes from the fact that the horns are able to contribute to the harmony, when in normal circumstances they would have to be silent.

Perhaps the most luminous thing ever said about Mozart was the remark of Edward Fitzgerald, that 'People will not believe that Mozart can be powerful, because he is so beautiful'. If these general observations can help to show his power, they will have proved more useful than any detailed analysis of the symphony from point to point. The contrasts between the four movements will then speak accurately for themselves without my attempting to characterize each with an 'appropriate', and therefore stifling, epithet. We can learn to know them as we know friends whose deepest feelings are not hidden from us because we tacitly agree not to press on them with heavy words.

SYMPHONY IN C MAJOR (KÖCHEL'S CATALOGUE, NO. 551)

1 *Allegro vivace*. 2 *Andante cantabile*. 3 MENUETTO: *Allegretto*. 4 FINALE: *Allegro molto*.

Much may be forgiven to those who, like all sensible people, find 'C major Köchel, No. 551' a not very suggestive name by which to distinguish Mozart's last symphony from the cheerful little work in the same key (Köchel, No. three-hundred-and-something) or the exquisite 'Linz' Symphony in C (Köchel, No. four-hundred-and-something), which ought never to have been allowed to drop out of the concert repertory; to say nothing of more than one interesting juvenile symphony in C among the first three hundreds of Köchel's Catalogue. Nor does symphony 'No. 41' prove much more helpful; especially when the miniature score misprints it 49 on the inside, and calls it No. 5 on the outside.

At the same time, the title 'Jupiter' takes rank with the titles 'Emperor Concerto' and 'Moonlight Sonata' as among the silliest injuries ever inflicted on great works of art. Mozart's musical culture may have been Italian, but his artistic nature was neither Roman nor Graeco-Roman. He was as Greek as Keats. He might have written a Zeus symphony. He never did; and this one is hardly nearer to Zeus than it is to Jupiter. It has pomp—but so has the Messenger of the Gods. Hermes might do for it; he is young enough, and Praxiteles made him reflective enough for Mozart's slow movement. But, after all, nothing is satisfactorily like the music but itself; and even the diverting light which another piece of music sheds on an important theme in the second subject of the first movement would mislead us, if we forgot that the origin of the theme outside the symphony is as unlike its effect inside the symphony as the moon by daylight is unlike moonlight.

One of the most significant differences between Mozart's last three symphonies concerns the character of their themes. In the E flat Symphony the themes are evenly poised between formulas on the one hand and attractive melodies on the other, with euphony always paramount. In the G minor Symphony almost every theme is highly individual and, even when formal in phrasing, quite unexpected in its course. In the last symphony we reach what is really the final subtlety of an immensely experienced artist, such as the god-beloved Mozart of the *Magic Flute* or the octogenarian Verdi of *Falstaff*. Most of the themes are not only formal, but are

actual formulas. There are people who mistake this for a failure to
achieve originality. They, as Mark Twain pointed out, whistle or
hum the melodies during operatic performances, to show their
culture, 'and their funerals do not occur often enough'.

Here is the opening theme, a formula typical of Mozart, and in
common use before him: energetic gestures (*a*), alternating with
gentle pleadings (*b*). The small notes show the radiant new
accessories which adorn the quiet counter-statement which follows
the majestic pageantry of the opening.

Ex. 1.

Analysts and historians make a plausible but unfortunate
mistake when they prove Mozart a 'formalist' by the fact that in
old scores the printer takes advantage of the exactness with which
the first twenty-three bars are reproduced after the development,
and simply makes a da capo sign. (Pages 19 and 20 of the Eulenburg
miniature score.) Similar economies could be practised in the
printing of the most modern music; and if Mozart uses formulas
that are incapable of variation, it is always in alternation with
passages of perfect freedom; indeed his use of the formulas is
a part of his freedom. The recapitulation of the quiet counter-
statement will be found to be a very different story. The second
subject is almost as varied and voluminous as that of the first
movement of Beethoven's Eroica Symphony. Besides its opening
new theme, it produces several novel results from its treatment
of figure (*b*) of Ex. 1, with the same touch of Straussian harmonic
freedom that we may notice in the treatment of a similar figure in
the andante of the E flat Symphony. Quite late in its course we
have the following new theme. I give the text to which Mozart first
wrote the tune in a little air inserted in some one else's opera a year
before this symphony was composed.

Ex. 2.

Voi sie - te un po' ton - do, mio ca - ro Pom-pe - o, le usan - ze del

mon - do an - da - te a stu - diar, an - date, an - da - te, an - da - te a stu - diar

Perhaps it is Mr. Charles Surface (Lamb's appreciation of Joseph takes us too far from the humble regions of *opera buffa*)—anyhow it is some such perfect knight in the Utopia of Gallantry saying to a young Sir Peter, or some such harmless, necessary husband, 'You are—may I say—a square-toes, my dear Pompeo; go and study the way of the world'. The art of Sir George Henschel would raise the naughty little aria to the poetic level it attains in the symphony.

The slow movement, a very finely developed example of first-movement form, can be thoroughly enjoyed without musical illustrations; but listeners need not be deprived of a share in the pleasure Mendelssohn felt when he found that the lovely reappearance of the first theme just before the final cadence-formula (bottom line of p. 43 and top line of p. 44 in the Eulenburg score) was an afterthought added in the autograph on an extra leaf.

Then comes the bright little minuet with its flowing lines, and its trio which so gracefully agrees to everything so long as it gets its own way.

Here is the whole thematic material of the famous finale, except the various continuations by which these ancient 'tags' of counterpoint are turned into sonata-form tunes.

Ex. 3.

The aesthetic discovery that these themes are on the one hand mere 'tags', and on the other hand suggestive of anything rather than the sonata form into which Mozart works them—this discovery marks an epoch in the history of criticism second only to that marked by Jeremy Collier's discovery that Shakespeare's 'genius was chiefly jocular, but when disposed he could be very serious'.

Of these five themes, No. I first appears as the first subject with a tune-like continuation. No. II follows it as pageantry, eventually to round off the whole finale. It is sometimes inverted (i.e. beginning at the bottom of the scale and curling up to the top). No. III brings about the transition to the second subject. Nos. IV and V appear in combination as the beginning of the second subject, No. IV being worked up into very close 'stretto', i.e. answering voices pressing on each other afresh at every note. The tune-like continuation of No. I then works up to a climax.

The development sheds new light on No. I in dialogue with No. II. After the recapitulation a large space is devoted to the exhilarating coda which has, in Germany, earned for this symphony the sub-title 'with the Final Fugue'. In a kind of fugal round all the five themes are combined. At last No. I breaks into its original tune-like continuation, and No. II brings Mozart's last symphony to an end with a flourish of trumpets.

OVERTURE TO 'DER SCHAUSPIELDIREKTOR' (THE THEATRE-MANAGER)

Der Schauspieldirektor is a one-act comedy, in which Herr Buff engages a troupe for his theatre. He hears several actors and actresses in comic and tragic scenes; then the tragedy queen sends for her husband, who is a tenor; the leading gentleman sends for his wife, a soprano; and, another *prima donna* being already there, a fine quarrel ensues as to who is first. This quarrel the tenor assuages, and, according to the librettist, harmony is restored. (But Mozart knows better.)

Of course, the scheme is an excellent framework for inserting any number of good things from the two fat volumes of stray arias and ensemble pieces Mozart wrote at various times for concerts, for other people's operas, and for singers who wanted something special at later performances of his own operas. And, as a concert-platform is quite a plausible scene for a voice-trial, I hope some day to produce a suitable adaptation and amplification of Mozart's 'Theatre-Manager' in its entirety, and with a really wide and interesting selection of his wonderful stray arias.

The overture and four numbers, which constitute the whole work as Mozart presented it, date from two months before *Le Nozze di Figaro*, and are unsurpassed in all his works for richness and delicacy. The overture is actually more polyphonic than that of *The Magic Flute*, and, though not cast in contrapuntal forms, not less polyphonic than the finale of the last symphony (which I refuse to call by its popular English nickname). But, like that finale, it enables me to economize in musical quotations by giving a single illustration that combines both first and second subjects. I quote from the recapitulation, where the complexity is at its height.

OVERTURE TO 'LE NOZZE DI FIGARO'

There are at least six themes in this liveliest of overtures. The first and the beginning of the second are shown in Ex. 1.

It is interesting to compare this opening with that of a contemporary opera which was recently revived with some success in London—Cimarosa's *Il Matrimonio Segreto*. Cimarosa begins with the solemn opening chords of Mozart's *Zauberflöte*, only they are

all on the tonic instead of being three different chords. He then
proceeds as follows—

Ex. 2.

which he repeats a third higher. In about forty bars he arrives at
Mozart's ninth bar, and in another twenty at the crash of the tutti.
Also he instructs us in the powers of two, beginning with the fact
that twice four is eight. Mozart's simple-seeming opening makes
its phrases so overlap that Prout and other seekers after symmetry
have tried to persuade us that it begins a bar before the first note.
If the audience will kindly sneeze or otherwise indicate the real
moment of opening, the conductor will start a bar later and all will
be square. Such is the progress of musical education since the
death of Mozart.

Symmetrical or irregular, the *Figaro* overture allows nothing to
stop it. A repeated figure suggestive of an irreverent allusion to
Handel—

Ex. 3.

leads without modulation to a quizzical 'second subject', which
culminates in a broad melody.

Ex. 4.

&c.

In the autograph Mozart made the returning link-passage lead to
a melancholy andante in D minor, 6/8 time, just as in the *Seraglio*
overture, where the place of a development is occupied by a minor
paraphrase of Belmont's first aria. There is no subsequent trace of
this D minor movement in *Figaro*, and Mozart had written only a
couple of bars before deciding that it was out of character. So also
is anything like a development. The music gaily recapitulates itself.
But though it was not going to be bothered with a development, it
has plenty of energy for a long coda in which Ex. 3 makes a grand
climax.

OVERTURE TO 'DIE ZAUBERFLÖTE'

Professor E. J. Dent's book on the operas of Mozart includes all his
researches into the origins and purposes of *Die Zauberflöte*; and
a remarkable performance that was given of it under his and
Mr. Clive Carey's direction at Cambridge some years ago (before

the war) marked a new epoch in the British appreciation of Mozart in general and of this supreme achievement in particular. It is now well known that the apparently nonsensical pantomime which constitutes its libretto is, in spite of having been begun with more trivial intentions, a masonic manifesto with the loftiest motives. Goethe saw all that it implied, and actually wrote a second part to it, bringing its historical and political allusions up to date, and projecting his prophetic imagination into the future. This second part is by no means a mere scenario, and is well worth study by those who choose to go deeply into the meaning Mozart's opera had for persons of a later generation whose culture was not primarily musical. Mr. Lowes Dickinson's *Magic Flute* is not concerned with any such literary history; it represents the thoughts of a poet-philosopher on the present predicament of human society, and it takes its title from Mozart's opera because the philosopher was deeply susceptible to music and understands the full range of Mozart's ideals. In Mozart's masonic fairyland the ideas of universal brotherhood are realized on no false assumptions of equality, and no oppression of the lower by the higher. Tamino and Pamina pass through the ordeals of fire and water and enter into their kingdom in the light of Isis. The simpleton Papageno, who knows nothing of all this, and cannot hold his tongue, nevertheless finds his Papagena when he is reminded to play upon his glockenspiel instead of hanging himself. In these holy halls revenge is unknown; the enemy is forgiven, and his doom is that he has made himself powerless. This spirit is reflected by Mozart in what is on the whole the greatest of his overtures. He has no opportunity here for the sublime terror of the introduction to the overture to *Don Giovanni*, where he foreshadows the music of the ghostly statue; nor can he produce a dramatic thrill by so diverting the end of his overture as to lead to the rise of a curtain on a scene of adventure at nightfall. His task is simply to produce a formal overture on a grand scale, combining without offence an almost religious solemnity with the lightness of touch required by other features of his pantomime. Mozart's overtures are, with little or no paraphernalia of definite allusions to themes in the operas, so closely fitted each to its individual purpose that it would be quite impossible to interchange them. Here the solemn use of trombones and the all-pervading contrapuntal treatment of the opening subject (itself in fugue) make this by far the most intellectual and, with all its brilliant cheerfulness, the most serious overture hitherto written for the stage. Gluck, in the overtures to *Iphigénie en Aulide* and *Alceste*, had struck a lofty tragic note with primitive means; but it needed all the power of Mozart to strike a lofty intellectual note in the overture to a work the serious aspects of which are so

entirely symbolic that it outwardly presents the appearance of a
nonsensical pantomime. The only definite allusion to the rest of
the opera is in the 'threefold chord' that intervenes between the
exposition and the development. This solemn chord, given out
by the wind-band three times with pauses, is a masonic signal
which is heard at every turning-point in the action.

Among many interesting uncatalogued items in the Reid Library
at Edinburgh is a publication by André (the original publisher of
many of Mozart's works), consisting of the full score of this overture exactly as it stands in Mozart's autograph, with certain parts
printed in red; the red print corresponding to all that in Mozart's
autograph was written later than the rest of the score. It so
happened that Mozart here used a much paler ink for the filling
out than he had for the skeleton score which he drafted first. I here
compress into as few staves as possible a passage from the second
subject which shows an interesting alteration, where a little introductory run for the clarinet has been suppressed. The pale ink
(or red print) I indicate by smaller notes.

OVERTURE TO 'LA CLEMENZA DI TITO'

This admirable example of a festival overture should not be allowed
to fall into neglect. The opera to which it belongs is Mozart's last
dramatic work, the composition of which, undertaken during journeys by coach and at all conceivable odd moments, overlapped with
that of *Die Zauberflöte*. A revival of it is possible only at Mozart-
festivals of which the object is to represent as nearly as may be his

whole work: it is a *pièce d'occasion* rendered all the more infuriating for the amount of good music which it stifles. The drama is supposed to be one of Metastasio's best. This is a pity. Its evident object is to glorify emperors *ex officio*. Titus Vespasian considers that he has lost that day on which he has not made somebody happy. If the day selected by Metastasio is a fair sample, Titus was an inverted Henry VIII or Shah Shahriah, with a quota of three wives a day, whom it was his duty to pardon for determined attempts to assassinate him by the hands of their discarded lovers. Into the mouth of Vitellia, the horridest female that ever disgraced a libretto, Mozart puts his last and almost sublimest aria, *Non più di fiori*, and contrives to get some more good music out of marches and choruses, and one-and-a-half dramatic moments. For the rest he does not exert himself, while Metastasio's machine is grinding its faultless verses; but in the overture he produces a fine piece of musical architecture, in which several festive formulas are put into new shape. The second subject, a very slender affair in airy dialogue for flutes and oboes, set a fashion which Beethoven followed in his *Prometheus* Overture. The carillon scales in the first subject are a picturesque feature, the value of which is enhanced by the fact that the opening does not reappear until after the recapitulation of the second subject, whereupon it forms a noble coda.

OVERTURE TO 'COSÌ FAN TUTTE'

Not only the wit of Da Ponte, but the irony of Mozart's music in *Così fan tutte* baffled their contemporaries and the literal-minded romanticists of the nineteenth century. In my young days the orthodox view of *Così fan tutte* was that it showed a reactionary falling-off into operatic conventionality after the epoch-making advances that Mozart had achieved in *Figaro* and *Don Giovanni*. We had to wait for Richard Strauss to point out to us early in the present century that *Così fan tutte* is a masterpiece of parody and irony. The story is ridiculously improbable, and the improbability becomes infuriating if, as has been averred, it was founded on fact. The cynical old bachelor has persuaded the two heroes to test the fidelity of the two heroines by pretending to go off to the wars, and returning, fantastically disguised, in order to make love to each other's lady. After violent protestations and sham suicides, the disguised lovers are accepted; but the wedding-breakfast is interrupted by their sudden return as themselves. On such altitudes of farce emotions are extremely lofty, but their boiling-point is low, and the wedding-breakfast is quickly redistributed in the right way. The first requirement of the highest order of parody is that it should take its opportunity of being obviously more beautiful than the things parodied. The things parodied are severely limited by irrelevant realities. As Stevenson's young poet of the Cream Tarts discovered, when 'opulent orotunda' is obviously what you want to say, some nonsense about sense interferes. From any such nonsense *Così fan tutte* is free, and takes its opportunity to become a miracle of irresponsible beauty unlike anything else in Mozart. No other opera has such a wealth of ensemble-music, and such a variety of forms. All the emotions are, *ex hypothesi*, either superficial or feigned. Mr. Christie, the Maecenas of Glyndebourne, has hit the mark in describing *Così fan tutte* as a dream.

The Overture is one of the funniest things Mozart ever wrote. Its themes, alternating their whisperings and chatterings with a hilarious kind of Hallelujah Chorus, tell us in Mozart's language that the persons of this dream are, humanly speaking, rubbish, but far too harmless for any limbo less charitable than the eternal laughter of Mozart. The only theme I need quote is the solemn motto of the introduction and of the whole opera: 'That's what all girls do.'

ORCHESTRAL DANCES

Three Minuets from No. 601 *of Köchel's Catalogue, composed*
5 *Feb.* 1791—*A major, C major, and G major.*
Six Waltzes with coda (Köchel No. 567), *composed* 6 *Dec.* 1788—
B flat, E flat, G major, D major, A major, C major.
Any number of other sets and selections.

At the turn of the eighteenth into the nineteenth century the dance music for the public ball-rooms of Vienna (no *Valse des Fleurs* for a Tchaikovsky ballet, but public dance music for the ordinary public to dance by) was, more often than not, supplied by great composers. Schubert's dances are well known; Beethoven's, with some queer things foisted upon his name, are not less well known, and an interesting set dating from his middle period was discovered not long before the war. Weber's are not inaccessible; but Mozart's, which are immeasurably the finest and richest, are unaccountably neglected. It is quite impossible to exaggerate their importance from every point of view. I have cut down my selection to nine. There are some hundred and thirty, most of them written in the last three years of his life, all of them bristling with epigrammatic wit, and orchestrated in a style that puts them absolutely beyond the reach of pianoforte arrangements. Perhaps this is one reason why they are almost unknown. The orchestra is without violas, and there are only two grades of loudness, *forte* and *piano*. On the other hand, the wind-band is extremely varied, and something queer is always turning up; a hurdy-gurdy, a side-drum, a piccolo (really, like all Mozart's piccolo parts, a kind of flageolet), and a set of tuned sleigh-bells are among the items we should need in order to do justice to the whole of Mozart's dance music. With hardly an exception, all the minuets and waltzes are of the same length, viz. eight bars repeated, eight bars repeated; trio the same, and minuet (or waltz) *da capo* without repeats. So the dancers are never put out. But if any one thinks the phrasing is going to be stiff within this tiny square frame, the mistake will soon appear!

Let us not forget that this dance music is no dream of Utopia, but was a bourgeois reality in Vienna a hundred and thirty years ago.

MASONIC DIRGE (KÖCHEL'S CATALOGUE, NO. 477)

Mozart took Freemasonry very seriously, and his Masonic music has a religious depth the expression of which is not interfered with by the language of comedy which permeates even the most serious Church music of his time, and makes some of his Masses far more scandalous than those of Haydn, who apologizes to the Almighty for finding worship irresistibly conducive to cheerfulness. The Masonic parts of the *Zauberflöte* have a strange and ethereal solemnity, which profoundly influenced Beethoven, and which no one but Beethoven could reproduce.

The *Maurerische Trauermusik*, or Masonic Funeral Music, was written in 1785, and was probably used on several occasions during Mozart's lifetime, since we find him altering the scoring according to circumstances, replacing the horns by his favourite corni di bassetto, or alto clarinets, which always contribute to the peculiar colour of his Masonic music, and, next to the strings, are the dominant orchestral colour in his *Requiem*. The corno di bassetto is nowadays difficult to procure. It is an alto clarinet with a few extra notes at the bottom, but otherwise with the same fingering as the ordinary clarinet. A modern alto clarinet is now on the market, but with sublime idiocy its makers have omitted to supply the extra low notes which are essential to all Mozart's music for the corno di bassetto; that is to say, essential to the only extant music for the instrument that is worth playing. Fortunately the original single bassett-horn part of the *Trauermusik* is not noticeably different from that of a bass clarinet.

The *Trauermusik* is a short adagio in C minor, of which the beginning and the end are a structure of slow wailing chords on the wind instruments, to which the strings add a flowing quaver accompaniment. This beginning and ending are a frame for a wonderful figured chorale in E flat, where the strings make an accompaniment, sometimes heroic and sometimes lyric, to a Gregorian tone which neither I nor Otto Jahn can precisely identify, but which is closely allied to that of the *Lamentations*.

SCHUBERT

The tragedy of Beethoven's deafness needs no comment; but the history of the arts is full of tragedies not less pathetic and far less inspiring to the imagination. If Beethoven had died as young as Schubert, he would still have been a very experienced master of the orchestra who had produced a large number of works easily the most important of their day, all of which were performed under his direction without serious hindrance from his as yet incipient deafness. But Schubert, who was not deaf, never heard his own mature orchestral music at all; except for one unfortunate experience in the rehearsal of an opera, which he indignantly withdrew on being asked to make alterations and cuts.

There are surprisingly few discoverable traces of this privation in Schubert's scoring. It shows certain typical habits that usually vanish with practical experience; and where Schubert miscalculates, he does not do so, like Beethoven, in pursuit of a definite new orchestral idea. There is no foundation in fact for the widespread notion that Schubert's orchestration is more 'modern' than Beethoven's: its experimental features, though interesting, are neither numerous nor various; and several things that appear to be experimental, or even successful, are quite possibly due to misconceptions. This is certainly the case with some of the trombone passages, where a careful study of the harmony and structure demonstrates that Schubert thought that trombones would balance nicely with horns. And so they will, if you can guess where that is the composer's intention, and if you explain it to the artists concerned. With this and a few similar precautions, Schubert's orchestration is a very powerful means of expression, and possesses all the essential orchestral qualities in typical simplicity. Brahms noted this as a pronounced tendency even in Schubert's earliest chamber-music; and it goes far to make his pianoforte-writing unplayable. Perhaps the clearest symptom of distress at lack of opportunity for hearing his own orchestral music is the magnificent quality and enormous quantity of his four-hand pianoforte works, one of which, the Grand Duo in C, proved, when orchestrated by Joachim, to be essentially one of the most important symphonies in the classical repertoire.

Few of Schubert's large instrumental works are free from obvious redundancies and inequalities. But musical criticism is apt to lose its sense of proportion, in consequence of the unusual standard of perfection in design and execution set by the great masters of classical music, and by the perfect preservation of most of their works. Critics of literature and the fine arts are better trained to recognize in imperfect examples the qualities which will produce perfection under special conditions: thus they do not so constantly make the mistake of assuming that work which shows the highest qualities can be outweighed by work which does not. Such a mistake is obviously made (*pace* Matthew Arnold) when we say Shakespeare was 'no artist' because he very often neglected his art; and such a mistake is made, less obviously, but more grossly, when we say that Schubert is no master of form because any fool can see where Schubert fails. Brahms at any rate made no such mistake; the ancestry of his forms is pretty evenly divided between Bach, Haydn, Beethoven, and Schubert. The influence of Mozart is probably too subtle to be distinguished in Brahms's work from the overpowering impress of Beethoven's huge forms; but the traces of Schubert amount to an integral part of Brahms's personal style.

I confess to seeing no reason for considering Schubert a less great master of large forms than Shakespeare up to the time of, let us say, *Richard II*. And it is a sure mark of a good judgement of musical style when Schubert is regarded, on the strength of his important works, as a definitely *sublime* composer. It does not matter when, where, and how he lapses therefrom: the quality is there, and nothing in its neighbourhood can make it ridiculous.

SYMPHONY IN B FLAT, NO. 5 [NO. 7]

1 *Allegro.* 2 *Andante con moto.* 3 MENUETTO. 4 *Allegro vivace.*

By the time Schubert was eighteen he had written five symphonies, of which the fifth, in B flat, is a pearl of great price. His First Mass, in F, and the charming one-act opera, *Der vierjährige Posten* (revived by Fritz Busch a few years ago, with a new libretto and additions from other operas), belong to the same period, and have, in common with this symphony, a style quite distinct from that of the later Schubert, and completely capable of justifying its own existence.

In his later and larger instrumental works, Schubert notoriously fails to achieve concentration and terseness. But no theory holds less water than that which imputes his later defects to his lack of sound early education. The criticism which accepts that view cannot, in the first place, tell defects from qualities; and there are unorthodoxies in Schubert which are the signs of new forms of music, and not mere failures to achieve old forms. Every work Schubert left us is an early work; and his gigantic latest works in big forms are in a condition little more diffuse than Mozart's *Entführung* (known in England as *The Seraglio*). As for his earliest successful works, no student of any academic institution has ever produced better models of form. At all events, no academic criticism has yet been framed that can pick holes in this little symphony in B flat. The only possible cavil is that Schubert does not seem fond of long developments, and that he so relishes the prospect of having nothing to do but recapitulate as to make his first subject return in the subdominant, in order that the second subject may come automatically into the tonic without needing an altered transition-passage. In other words, Schubert's early forms are stiff. And as the upholders of musical orthodoxy were in the 'eighties (and are still) painfully puzzled by any forms that were not stiff, they were in no position to criticize Schubert's early education or its early and later results.

Of the first movement of the B flat Symphony I quote the openings of the first subject, omitting the four delicious bars of introduction—

Ex. 1.

and of the second subject—

Ex. 2.

The whole movement is full of Schubert's peculiar delicacy; and its form escapes stiffness like a delightful child overawed into perfect behaviour, not by fear or priggishness but by sheer delight in giving pleasure.

The slow movement reaches a depth of beauty that goes a long way towards the style of the later Schubert; especially in the modulating episodes that follow the main theme. The main theme itself, however, is a Schubertized Mozart, as the following comparison will show.

Ex. 3.

But the rondo of Mozart's Violin Sonata in F (Köchel's Catalogue, No. 377) is a young lady whose delicious simplicity may get more fun out of prigs than they are aware of; while Schubert's theme never thought of making fun of anybody or anything. It is seriously beautiful, and the first change of key—

Ex. 4.

is unmistakably romantic, like those in Schubert's grandest works.

Any minuet for small orchestra in G minor, loud and vigorous, with a quiet trio in G major, must remind us of the minuet of Mozart's G minor Symphony. But Schubert's is much simpler. Its rhythms, though free enough, are square, just where Mozart's are conspicuously irregular; and where the only rustic feeling in Mozart's trio is that given by the tone of the oboes, Schubert's trio is a regular rustic dance with more than a suspicion of a drone-bass.

The finale is in first-movement form, with a binary-form theme on Mozart's models. I quote the two main themes: the first subject—

Ex. 5.

and the second.

Ex. 6.

It runs along merrily, and retains to its last note the early-Schubert flavour of this very perfect little work.

SYMPHONY IN C MAJOR, NO. 7 [NO. 9]

1 *Andante, leading to* 2 *Allegro ma non troppo.* 3 *Andante con moto.*
4 SCHERZO: *Allegro vivace.* 5 FINALE: *Allegro vivace.*

The C major Symphony begins with an introduction which consists of a broad and leisurely working out of the following tune, given out at first in unaccompanied unison by two horns.

Ex. 1.

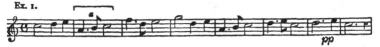

The figure marked (*a*) becomes the basis of many important themes in the ensuing allegro, which starts as follows, after the opening tune of the introduction has been stated in its fourth version and worked up to a great climax.

Ex. 2.

My quotation presents the theme as it stands in the autograph, except that for obvious reasons I substitute cross-strokes for the traces of Schubert's penknife. It is an impressive (though not yet the most impressive) sign of the white heat at which this huge work was written, that the whole first movement was fully scored before Schubert noticed that he really must put more meaning into the all-pervading figure (*b*) that constitutes the first two bars of his main theme. The substitution of D for G at the end of each bar does not spoil the natural way in which the figure arises from the last bass notes of the introduction, and it suffices to make the theme important in itself. But Schubert had to alter this note, or substitute a rest, everywhere from beginning to end of the movement. The figure is ubiquitous, and the alteration is neatly made with a penknife literally hundreds of times.

This opening theme immediately closes into another, which I quote in connexion with the close of Ex. 1, in order to call attention to a figure (*d*[1] and *d*[2]) which becomes prominent near the end of the movement.

The second subject, reached, as usual in Schubert, by a very simple *coup de théâtre*, starts in a minor key in which it is not going to settle.

This glorious theme veers round towards the normal key of the dominant, G major; whence however it wanders away into the most wonderful of all Schubert's unorthodox digressions, a *locus classicus* for the imaginative use of trombones in a pianissimo.

Ex. 5.

This passage, which, as the quotation shows, is derived from (*a*) of the introduction, and leads to a triumphant climax in G major, is so masterly in design as well as in poetic power that it is far more like a new art-form than a failure to execute an old one. Many of Schubert's outwardly similar digressions are weaknesses, but every case must be taken on its individual merits; and nothing will induce me to believe that Beethoven would have tolerated a word against this passage in its present position if he had lived to see it.

The rest of the movement explains itself with all Schubert's fluency, and, long though it necessarily is, with more than Schubert's usual concentration. The development is conspicuously free from redundancy or digression, and the recapitulation, which keeps most of the first subject (Exs. 1 and 2) in an alert pianissimo, shows Schubert's characteristic vitality of form in changing the relations of the keys in the second subject.

The coda is in quicker tempo, and has the energy to make a splendid climax; a marked contrast to most of Schubert's codas, which are apt to collapse with a frank gesture of exhaustion. Here the movement ends with an apotheosis of the introduction (Ex. 1). The scoring, as Schubert finally left it, is notoriously miscalculated; but there is a better remedy for it than the horrible marine-parade custom of giving the tune to the trumpet. All that need be done (beyond the usual precautions with the trombones) is to restore Schubert's first version of the string parts, which happened to be perfectly transparent until he altered them, though not one listener in a hundred could tell the difference in sound or sense, except for the all-important fact that in the first version the theme in the wood-wind can be heard, and in the second it cannot.

The slow movement, in A minor, after establishing its in-
domitable march-rhythm in a few wintry bars of introduction,
sets out bravely with the following heart-breaking show of spirit
in adversity.

The burden of the song goes, with Schubert's characteristic half-
Italian pathos, into the major mode.

There is an energetic sequel, marching along in the same rhythm
and with the same brave figures (a) and (b); and again and again
the procession of themes comes round until at length there is a
change to another key.

The second subject is a broad working-out of a serene melody
of consolation, in F major.

The return from this to A minor is famous as one of the simplest
and most romantic passages ever written for horns. They toll like
a bell haunted by a human soul; and when the first subject returns
there is a new trumpet-part that enlivens and deepens the pathos.
The energetic continuation is worked up to a great climax, from
which the reaction, after a dramatic pause, is intensely tragic; and
then the second subject enters in A major, with radiant new colours
and a flowing accompaniment which continues even through the
returning passage, where clarinets now replace the horns. Then
fragments of the first subject are built up into a mournful coda, even
the burden of the song (Ex. 7) being now in the minor mode.

The scherzo has a far greater number of themes than can be
quoted here; and it yields to nothing in music as regards the
perfection and freedom of their treatment. Like the scherzo of
Beethoven's Ninth Symphony, the main body of the movement
is in miniature but highly organized sonata form. I quote the
beginnings of the first subject.

of the second subject—

and of an important episode in the development which recurs very happily at the end of the movement—

leaving unquoted Schubert's afterthought, the wonderful new cantabile which, shortly after Ex. 11, breaks through all these activities and adds 'the gleam, the light that never was, on sea or land'; leaving also unquoted several other accessory phrases, mostly derived from figure (*b*) of Ex. 10. The variety of rhythm throughout is inexhaustible.

As for the trio, it is a huge single melody (in 'binary' form with repeats, as usual)—one of the greatest and most exhilarating melodies in the world: and it needs no quotation. Unfortunately the scoring, though full of interesting points, does not easily realize Schubert's evident intentions: and until we can afford a double wind-band we are compelled (as in many passages in Beethoven's later works) to damp the accompaniment down till it seriously loses in energy of character. A very eminent conductor once made one of the leading London orchestras play the string-parts pizzicato: a brilliant but thoroughly debased remedy, of which he afterwards had the good grace to be ashamed. Anyhow, the melody must be heard. Towards the end there is one remarkable effect produced by a solitary trombone in the middle of the harmony. This is usually damped down with extreme caution; but I have always had the impression that Schubert was here definitely exerting his imagination, and that the strange red-hot tone should be allowed to show itself. At all events none of these problems can be measured by degree-examination criteria.

The truest lover of Schubert confesses that he would not wish the Unfinished Symphony to have a typical Schubert finale. But Schubert wrote two finales which are typical Schubert without

being his typical finales. These two are the finale of the String
Quintet and the finale of this symphony. Possibly we might add a
third, also in C major—the finale of the Grand Duo that ought to
have been a symphony. And of course there are other finales that
have magnificent themes and passages, notably in the three great
String Quartets. But the two supreme finales are such that nobody
can accuse them of being weaker than the rest of the works. The
finale of the C major Symphony is in fact an example of grotesque
power fully as sublime as the griffin which Ruskin described so
splendidly in *Modern Painters*, part iv, chapter viii.

The two themes of its first subject—

and—

set up a very energetic spin which, like all Schubert's openings,
promises well, but which does not, to people who know their
Schubert, offer any security that it will maintain its energy in the
tropical ease of its composer's mood after he has got through the
three other movements so triumphantly. And indeed Schubert had
a narrow escape here! If ever a powerful piece of music had a
backbone to it, that backbone is the sublimely grotesque main
theme of the second subject, arising so inevitably and so astonishingly out of the four premonitory repeated notes of the horn, and
stretching itself *ad infinitum* while the violins madly turn somer-
saults with the persistent figure (*b*) of Ex. 12. This was the passage
which, when Mendelssohn rehearsed it with the Philharmonic in
London, caused the players to giggle and behave so badly that he had
to withdraw the work; and even within living memory it roused the
pedagogue and blinded the humorist in that great musician Hans
von Bülow. Well, it is to be hoped that we know better now. But
here is what happened in Schubert's autograph.

accompanied by (b) inverted

He had got as far as the four premonitory notes of the horns; and then he dashed off into a schoolmasterly little fugue, from which the only possible reaction would have been a schoolboy's practical jokes. By good luck almost unique in Schubert's short career, he lost interest in this project before he had written nine bars of it— or perhaps the real gigantic inspiration came before he could develop interest in the frivolity he had started. Whatever the mental process was, it cannot have taken three-quarters of a minute; the dingy little fugue-subject was struck out before the answer had well begun; the danger was past, and instead of a weak facility, we have the momentum of a planet in its orbit.

From this weird new inspiration arises a vast variety of ideas. The figure marked (e) produces remote faëry music in the development; and throughout the movement the four repeated notes (d) are as powerful and terrible as anything in Beethoven or Michelangelo. The coda is one of the greatest in all symphonic music. A clever critic, somewhat obsessed with the notion that the only interesting art is morbid, once asserted that this coda expresses Schubert's terror of death. There is nothing to be ashamed of in feeling terror at things which overwhelm us by revealing their vastness; and Schubert can rouse this feeling as one who knows it. But he was not afraid.

UNFINISHED SYMPHONY IN B MINOR [NO. 8]

1 *Allegro moderato.* 2 *Andante con moto.*

This, the most perfect of Schubert's large instrumental works, was written in 1826, and was left unfinished, like the scarcely less great Sonata in C major, simply because the remainder did not drive Schubert to the labour of writing it down. Perhaps it is a pity that Schubert did not finish the scherzo; its theme (of which nine bars were scored) is magnificent, and the sketches for it very promising. But we may be almost certain that the finale would have been like many another of Schubert's—there is a Rondeau Brillante in B minor for pianoforte and violin which would perfectly answer the digressive purposes of the typical Schubert finale. And we should much have enjoyed hearing Noll running on. However, the mood which inspired Schubert in the first two movements here, for once, dominated him like Dr. Johnson, and would not let him enjoy hearing himself run on.

Ex. 1.
Allegro moderato.

The sublime depth and pathos of the opening is not without parallel in Schubert's larger works; indeed it is thoroughly characteristic of them. But it is maintained throughout the two complete movements as Schubert has never even attempted to maintain it elsewhere except in movements purely lyric in form. No doubt there are several themes and long passages which, taken out of their context, show no obvious difference from other picturesque and pretty things in Schubert's more unequal works; and there have been musicians who see the resemblance between Schubert's second subject (Ex. 2) and Viennese bourgeois types of beauty, just as there have been art connoisseurs who see the resemblance between a Madonna and a *contadina*. And if that is all they see, let them continue to enjoy music as a by-product of dancing, and art as a by-product of artists' models. Schubert's Unfinished Symphony is an excellent test for freedom from critical bad habits—a test such as the extraordinary perfection and integrity of classical music seldom offers.

The form of the Unfinished Symphony is on the same high level as the style. This will seem almost a wilful paradox to those who have throughout their lives imbibed the ordinary doctrines of musical form, according to which Schubert had no mastery at all. Though lack of space compels me to dogmatize here, I feel amply justified in saying that the real dogmatism is entirely with the ordinary doctrines. These are supported only by a dead weight of uniform 'masterpieces' which the world is politely letting die, whereas the record of the immortal classics presents a variety of forms which can yield their principles only to an attention concentrated on each individual case. The work stands or falls by itself. What may be irrelevant or crude in ninety-nine works, may be a crowning perfection in the hundredth.

For instance, the transition from first to second subject is always a difficult piece of musical draughtsmanship; and in the rare cases where Schubert accomplishes it with smoothness, the effort exhausts him to the verge of dullness (as in the slow movement of the otherwise great A minor Quartet). Hence, in his most inspired works the transition is accomplished by an abrupt *coup de théâtre*; and of all such *coups*, no doubt the crudest is that in the Unfinished Symphony (Ex. 2). Very well then; here is a new thing in the history of the symphony, not more new, nor more simple than the new things which turned up in each of Beethoven's nine. Never mind its historic origin; take it on its merits. Is it not a most impressive moment?

Ex. 2.

Take, again, the continuation of the second subject, generally a weak point with Schubert, who did not grasp that the time for exposition of themes is not the time for discursive development of them. In this symphony Schubert seems indeed to stray into his usual by-paths, inasmuch as the main theme of the second subject contains figures that are used in two different derivatives before the close of the exposition. But if we forget that Schubert wrote other works, and confine our attention to the matter in hand, we shall find that these derivatives are masterly in their terseness, variety, and breadth; and even if we take the risk of comparing what Schubert has done here with what Mozart and Beethoven would do, we shall see every reason to believe that they would have done exactly the same. The exposition is, in short, masterly; and it in no way undermines the strength of the development. The development is powerfully dramatic, and Sir George Grove never made a better point than when he called attention to its pathetic use of the syncopated accompaniment of Ex. 2 *without the melody*. The recapitulation shows every quality of freedom and life which only the greatest masterpieces can show. In choice of key, method of return to the tonic, et cetera, every technicality is individual and true. The short coda, beginning like the development, and blazing up only to die of exhaustion, is very typical of Schubert; but the exhaustion is here a realized poetic fact, not a mere convenience to the composer.

The loose structure of the slow movement[1] is, again, a thing not
to be confused with the mere digressiveness of Schubert's weaker
examples: the weaker examples themselves should rather be taken
as tending towards the definite and convincing breadth of design
accomplished here. Nor should the pastoral and picturesque types
of theme and style blind us to 'the gleam, the light that never was,
on sea or land'. Two quotations are necessary, one for the first
theme—

Ex. 3.

and the other, not so much for the wonderful clarinet theme with
its answers in oboe and flute, as for the long notes that lead to it.

Ex. 4.

These four notes (a) are turned to such account in the coda that they
produce as subtle a stroke of genius as can be found anywhere in
music.

Ex. 5.

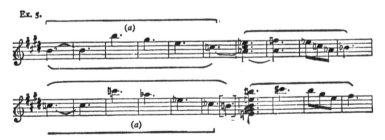

[1] It is a mystery why a movement marked *andante con moto* should be
traditionally played *adagio sostenuto* by the very people who are severest
in their criticism of Schubert's loose length. I remain unrepentant after
stern rebuke for assuming that *andante con moto* means what it says.

Every one who knows a good theme when he sees it will be
pleased and tantalized by the following. It is the beginning of the
scherzo.

ENTR'ACTE IN B MINOR AND BALLET IN G MAJOR, FROM 'ROSAMUNDE'.

Rosamunde is not an opera, but a play to which Schubert wrote
incidental music consisting of an overture, three entr'actes, two
ballets, a song, a chorus of ghosts or spirits, a chorus of shepherds,
a chorus of huntsmen, and a pastoral melody. The heroine was
not Fair Rosamond, but the Queen of Cyprus. Further checks
to our curiosity are that the authoress was the gifted Helmine
von Chezy who made such an unholy mess of Weber's *Euryanthe*,
and that this particular play is lost. Which is just as well. If
anything she wrote could have had an illuminating relation to
such grand tragic music as Schubert's B minor Entr'acte, she
would have been a great poet. And we know that she was not.

To my surprise I had some difficulty in obtaining parts of the
B minor Entr'acte. It seems to have dropped out of recent
orchestral repertoires. *Rosamunde* is now represented mainly by
the Overture to *Die Zauberharfe*, while its real overture, a much
slighter effort, has been assigned to the opera *Alphonso und Estrella*;
and the rest of the music is represented only by the lighter ballets.
And even these have been re-orchestrated by Reger, whose untimely
death makes it impossible to ask him why.

The B minor Entr'acte, with its rhythms which at first seem
stiff, but which accumulate to massiveness, was at one time a
hackneyed piece. Its opening theme—

soon develops the characteristic Schubert-Rossini pathos of a soft change to the major mode. Later, a lamenting theme appears in the dominant—

Ex. 2.

and is followed by a solemn passage which every British musician among my contemporaries will remember to have been quoted with due reverence in Prout's treatises on instrumentation.

Ex. 3.

The delicious Ballet in G requires neither quotation nor comment.

SCHUMANN

SYMPHONY IN B FLAT MAJOR, NO. 1, OP. 38

1 *Andante un poco maestoso, leading to* 2 *Allegro molto vivace.*
3 LARGHETTO: *leading to* 4 SCHERZO: *Molto vivace.* 5 *Allegro animato e grazioso.*

Schumann's first symphony is intended by him to express the emotions of springtime, and does in fact express those of the springtide of the happiest years of his life—his year of song, 1840, when he triumphed over all the obstacles which old Wieck opposed to his marriage to his Clara, and poured out the first and greatest two volumes of his four volumes of songs; and 1841, when, with his powers as yet undiminished by illness, he devoted his attention to the larger forms of music. His adventures in these forms were to him a source of happiness akin to his marriage: and for at least five years the works that resulted were beautiful enough to justify his turning aside from the lyric forms in which his mastery was indisputable. But there are some things which you cannot have both ways. Schumann is a master of epigram. His ideas normally take the shape of gnomic sayings; and no writer is fuller of memorable *Einfälle*; of such 'good things' as, according to Mr. Puff, form the sole *raison d'être* of a plot. It has been observed by more than one eminent critic that the creators of such *Einfälle* seldom show high constructive genius on a larger scale. But what else can we expect? Large forms imply the expansion of initial ideas by development; and development is the very thing that an epigram will not bear. At the same time, it is a harsh judgement that forbids the epigrammatic artist to pile up his ideas into large edifices: his mind may be full of things that cannot be expressed except in works on a large scale. And if the artist cannot give such works an organic structure, why should he be forbidden to create artificial forms which enshrine his ideas as the coral-reef houses its millions of polypi? At all events, Schumann has abundantly proved that it is better for a symphony to be like a nobly rough mosaic with crude schematic forms than like a bad, sleek oil-painting. Indecently soon after Schumann's death, Joseph Rubinstein, no relation to the great Anton, wrote a famous article, in which Schumann's first symphony was thoroughly analysed with the systematic purpose of proving that Schumann could not compose at all. Every point that Rubinstein made is true; Schumann cannot develop an idea, he can only make sequences on it. He cannot even state an idea that is capable of development: the main theme of his finale (Ex. 13) shows that he does not know the difference between a symphonic theme and a lyric arabesque. The sequences are such as every competent teacher promptly weeds out of his pupils' first exercises. And so on, and so on. The Rubinstein tradition has never been favourable to Schumann's larger works; but Joseph's criticism is an affair of the pot and the kettle. When Nicholas Rubinstein died, Tchaikovsky dedicated to his memory a huge trio, in which every one of these faults is enormously magnified, and there is no epigrammatic vein at all. The trio ought to have been dedicated to Joseph.

It is quite true that Schumann's treatment of large forms is no model for students. It presupposes a style like Macaulay's, in which 'it is impossible to tell the truth'. Macaulay thought his own style a very bad model for students. But a style in which it is impossible to tell the truth may be a great advance on a style in which it is impossible to express an opinion; and in any case the composer is not speaking on oath, as even the most partisan historian must be.

Schumann's antithetic sententiousness is so honestly exhibited as the rules of his game that no reasonable person ought ever to have misunderstood it. His orchestration is another matter; tragedy was latent in it from the outset, and became manifest in his pitiful failure as a conductor. The first two symphonies had the advantage of being conducted by Mendelssohn, who showed his unselfish care and consummate mastery by making a success of each performance, and his profound and instinctive respect for another artist's personality by not interfering with what must have seemed to him the incredible clumsiness of Schumann's scoring. Mendelssohn early learned the unwisdom (if he ever needed to learn it) of trying to change a grown man's habits. Perhaps he helped Schumann with more detailed advice than we know of; for the scoring of the First Symphony is not nearly as opaque as that of later works, and so perhaps it profited by as much of Mendelssohn's advice as Schumann could digest in one work. The few outstanding defects in the published score are ridiculously easy to correct, and it is a mistaken piety to leave them uncorrected. One thing must be made clear; whatever need Mendelssohn or later conductors may have found for correction, there is no room for really different orchestral ideas. When a redistribution of the mass of wood-wind is advisable in order to bring the main theme out, we need not worry about the changes in tone-colour that may result. Unlike Beethoven, Schumann has not in such cases clearly imagined a definite tone-colour that would be spoilt by any change. When obstacles to clearness have been removed, the resulting purity of tone is indeed rather new to listeners who have hitherto tried to hear Schumann's orchestra in its native fog; but the revelation is nevertheless that of Schumann's real intention. What is wholly inadmissible is the introduction of new 'beauties', which have even been known, within living memory, to include a *forte* end to the scherzo.

The need for some revision in modern performances of Schumann's works is forcibly shown by an incident in the history of the Meiningen Orchestra. When that wonderful band, with its wonderful conductor, Steinbach, visited London in 1902, the English committee begged for a Schumann symphony. In those days it was supposed that Brahms could not orchestrate much, if at all, better than Schumann; and Steinbach was, next to Joachim, the most authoritative interpreter of Brahms. Steinbach's reply to the Committee was 'Schumann we cannot and will not play'. Under further pressure he consented to play the overture to *Manfred*.

It may safely be said that no orchestra ever earned its reputation by its interpretation of Schumann. It is possible, with a minimum of re-touching, to make a Schumann symphony sound normally clear and euphonious. But it is difficult; and the difficulty is not evident. As for a brilliant performance, that would be an outrage on Schumann's holiest intimacy. To perform Schumann faithfully and with a modest helpfulness in certain technical matters is a task in which every thoughtful musician will rejoice. The inner content of this music is a perpetual springtime of young enthusiasm; the externals are robed in an old dressing-gown and carpet-slippers amid thick clouds of tobacco smoke. But in this atmosphere humbug can no more survive than in the presence of Bach or of Beethoven. Schumann's dreams do not come from opium. His mind at its full vigour has more kinship with Browning's than with any other artist, whether in music or verse; and even when his health gave way, the failure of his mind appeared in his music merely as loss of power and coherence, not as any change of direction from its original impulse.

The opening of the First Symphony was intended to sound like a summons from heaven, evoking the vital forces of springtime.

Ex. 1.

It originally began a third lower, like the theme of the following allegro, and was given to the horns. But the valve horn was not yet in use, and on the old natural instruments the notes G A, in the key chosen by Schumann, were 'stopped' notes tolerable only in a soft passage, and comically shocking in a forte. As far as this symphony is concerned, the accident was lucky, for the opening is much finer with trumpets, and a third higher, as it now stands. But for a man so easily discouraged as Schumann, nothing can have been more unlucky than that he should receive a shock at the very beginning of the first rehearsal of his first finished orchestral work. And it is not as if the misfortune concerned a general principle of orchestration: within a year or two a pair of ventil horns was to be found in every orchestra, besides a pair of natural ones I am inclined to ascribe much of the deterioration of Schumann's scoring to precisely this accident. He soon followed his First Symphony by the powerful work in D minor, which was kept back for revision and eventually published as his Fourth Symphony, after a re-scoring which is hardly better than a heavy process of doubling in order to avoid risks from the composer's incapacity to conduct. It is a pious duty to use the original score of the D minor Symphony as a model for reducing all Schumann's later orchestration to its essentials. The First Symphony does not need much work of this kind; the ossification of its tissues has not gone far.

The introduction continues with a suggestion of the first stirrings of sap in the trees and awakenings of woodland life; and at last the Spring enters in full vigour.

Ex. 2.

A quieter second group begins with an admirably contrasted theme in a subtle blend of keys—

Ex. 3.

and ends with a vigorous cadential epigram difficult to bring out as Schumann scores it.

Ex. 4.

The development picks up its sequences in Schumann's way, which somewhat resembles the way of Schubert and of all young composers who have not been trained under the eye of a Rubinstein; but most especially of those who have. It combines the initial figure of the main theme with a fine episodic counterpoint.

Ex. 5.

When Shakespeare called springtime 'the only pretty ring-time', he obviously referred to Schumann's happy use of the triangle in the lighter passages of this development.

The recapitulation arrives at the top of a grand climax in which the opening phrases of the introduction blaze forth in the full

* The light syncopated echo turns the crass fifths from a blunder to a very accurate paradox.

orchestra, to be followed by the continuation of the allegro theme
instead of the theme itself (Ex. 2), which, admirable in its original
place, would have been prosaic here. (This is the kind of lesson the
school of Rubinstein never learnt.)

The coda introduces, with the happiest effect, an entirely new
spring song—

Ex. 6.

whose rhythm ousts the otherwise ubiquitous Walrus-and-Car-
penter metre of the movement. Then that metre is resumed in
quicker tempo, until at last the original trumpet-call to spring
concludes the design.

The slow movement, unlike the short *intermezzi* that occupy its
place in Schumann's later symphonies, is a spacious lyric with
sustained development. Its orchestration is rich, and so successful
as to indicate that Schumann had a decided talent in that category,
though he afterwards stifled it. The main theme is a broad
cantabile—

Ex. 7.

which alternates with a modulating theme introduced by the
auxiliary inner figure (*a*) of Ex. 7.

Ex. 8.

The whole is scored for small orchestra, until in the coda the
trombones enter softly with a very solemn modulating sequence.
This, at first seeming to arise from Ex. 7, proves to be an anticipation of the theme of the scherzo, which follows without break.

The scherzo is in D minor, a key which it enters by the subdominant.

Ex. 9.

The first trio is a highly imaginative and picturesque design in D major, in chords distributed between wind and strings in a constant rhythmic figure (amphibrachic, if you prefer nice long Greek words to simple musical ideas).

Ex. 10.

The first return of the scherzo is immediately followed by a second trio in B flat.

Ex. 11.

The style of this is of course epigrammatic; but the theme is rather too—shall we say—normal for an epigram: and that, perhaps, is why Weingartner regards this second trio as 'an awful example'. I cannot help suspecting that his point of view is slightly Rubinsteinian. The mood of the second trio shows a bustling energy which sets off the abbreviated da capo very well, while the sequences do not last long enough to make us feel the substance to be too dry. Certainly it is not a good model for students; but to adopt Dr. Johnson's criticism in its two forms, the colloquial and the lexicographical, it has wit enough to keep it sweet, while a student's imitation would doubtless not have sufficient vitality to preserve it from putrefaction. The coda, with its mysterious fleeting vision of the first trio, is really wonderful.

The finale begins with a scale in a striking rhythm—

Ex. 12.

and proceeds to a main theme as slight as a daisy-chain (and why not?)—

Ex. 13.

A transition-theme alternates the canzonetta of Mendelssohn's Quartet, op. 12, or the theme of the finale of *Kreisleriana*, with Ex. 12.

Ex. 14.

A second group turns the rhythm of Ex. 12 to girlish purposes—

Ex. 15.

and a single tonic-and-dominant cadence theme brings the exposition to a normal close, the whole being repeated from Ex. 13.

The development is a very different matter. Beginning dramatically—

Ex. 16.

it first deals gently with Ex. 15, but then, at the summons of trombones, takes that rhythm back to the original scale-figure (Ex. 12), which it builds up into an enormous and impressive sequence on the following lines—

Ex. 17.

developing into a surging new figure.

Ex. 18.

The sequence rises to an ominous forte, but never to a fortissimo; and the climax is actually a decrescendo. The home dominant being at last reached, the recapitulation is ushered in by that most dangerous of unorthodoxies, something that is thoroughly old-fashioned: that is to say, an unbarred cadenza for the flute. As Wagner's Hans Sachs says, 'in springtime it must be so'.

The full energy of the finale appears in its coda, which grandly works up the thread of the development to a triumphant end.

SYMPHONY IN E FLAT MAJOR, NO. 3, OP. 97

1 *Lebhaft.* 2 SCHERZO: *Sehr mässig.* 3 *Nicht schnell.* 4 *Feierlich.*
5 *Lebhaft.*

The 'Rhenish Symphony' has suffered a neglect which is probably
due mainly to the fact that Schumann's orchestration grew worse
with the growth of his experience as conductor at Düsseldorf.
Written in 1850, it shows no signs of the illness which a few years
later invaded his mind and body; and there is no foundation for the
notion, sometimes expressed, that it belongs to the sad and voluminous number of the works of his declining health, though it happens to be, in conception, the last of his symphonies.

As the Fourth Symphony shows in many points the influence of
Beethoven's C minor Symphony, so does its successor, this third or
'Rhenish' Symphony, show in its first movement some kinship with
the *Sinfonia Eroica.* The main theme is a grand paragraph that any
pupil of Parry will recognize as a source of inspiration to his own
school of British music.

Ex. 1.

A terse auxiliary theme—

Ex. 2.

effects many of the important transitions in the movement.

The second subject begins in G minor, with a wistful cantabile—

Ex. 3.

which soon gives way to more strenuous jubilation in the orthodox
dominant, resuming the material of Exs. 1 and 2. The development
moves on long sequential lines (distinctly like a stiffened version of
those laid down in Beethoven's Eroica), making prominent use of
Ex. 3 and introducing at intervals an episode, urgent in expression.

Ex. 4.

Again the influence of Beethoven's Eroica is seen (though in a way that only strengthens the evidence of Schumann's independence) in the long and exciting preparations for the return to the tonic—one of the most genuinely dramatic things Schumann ever achieved.

The recapitulation is regular, until Schumann substitutes for the short formal cadence theme of his second subject a new and broader cantabile. He is always peculiarly happy in his art of introducing new ideas at the last stage of his design, and the continuation of this cantabile—

Ex. 5.

adds greatly to the energy of the coda.

The scherzo is a slow *Ländler* with a comfortable Rhenish rusticity in its lilt.

Ex. 6.

One's first impression of the sequel is that it is trying to make a free variation of the theme—

Ex. 7.

but its bustling semiquaver figure does not conform to that harmonic plan, and subsides eventually into an accompaniment to the mysterious theme of the trio, which is in A minor, while the bass quivers throughout on C; a *locus classicus* for that elusive phenomenon a 'mediant pedal'.

Ex. 8.

After the resumption of the main theme Schumann finds occasion for a new idea in his coda. Quotation is unnecessary.

The tiny slow movement is of a type invented by Schumann in his symphonies; the suggestion for its form, though not for its mood, coming from the allegretto of Beethoven's Eighth Symphony, via the andante of Mendelssohn's Italian Symphony.

Two gentle melodies, a main theme with a transition-theme, alternate with a more warmly full-toned second subject, so as to produce an *arioso* form without development.

First theme—

Transition-theme—

Second subject—

If the impressive fourth movement is regarded as part of the finale, not merely as introductory, then the final quick movement will become intelligible as the natural and almost lyric reaction from the awe inspired by the Cathedral of Cologne as described in one of the finest pieces of ecclesiastical polyphony since Bach.

At the end of this solemn movement Schumann again introduces a new idea, which I do not quote.

The fifth movement, if regarded as complete in itself, would seem to have no action at all. After a broad cantabile theme—

a transition (suggested by Ex. 12) seems to lead to the following second subject.

But this theme behaves merely like an incident in the main stream of melody, and the subsequent developments have a merely decorative or pattern-making effect. Even when a new idea—

leads back to a recapitulation from Ex. 13, the effect is not dramatic. But the purport of the whole, as in itself the dramatic contrast and consummation to the fourth movement, becomes manifest when the orchestra gathers itself up to a solemn climax in which a new idea is combined with a diminution of Ex. 14—

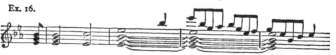

and the Cathedral-polyphony returns in triumph, to culminate in an unmistakable allusion to the theme of the first movement, Ex. 1.

SYMPHONY IN D MINOR, NO. 4, OP. 120

INTRODUCTION (*Ziemlich langsam*), *leading to* I *Lebhaft, leading to* II ROMANZE, *leading to* III SCHERZO, *leading to* IV *Lebhaft.*

This first version of what was afterwards known as Schumann's Fourth Symphony was published in 1891, fifty years after it was written. Schumann himself withheld it for ten years and then in 1851 produced it in the revised version now known as his Fourth Symphony. The revision effected many improvements in form, and included some remarkable changes in notation which indicate that Schumann thought his original notation likely to mislead conductors. Now whenever this happens it will generally be found that the new notation misleads the conductor in the opposite direction, for it is the nature of all such cases to be on the border-line. Hence, if a composer has found that his old indication of tempo produced a tendency to drag, his new indication will certainly produce a tendency to hurry on the part of any one who does not know the history and motive for the change. The other alterations in this symphony concern the scoring; and herein lies a tragedy. The revised version is undoubtedly at all points easier to play—after a fashion. It has profited by experience and profited in the wrong way. In 1851 the symphony appeared as Schumann's fourth, but the original edition of the score explains that it was 'sketched' shortly after the First Symphony; so that the symphonies known as the second and third were really the third and fourth. Brahms discovered the original version of the Fourth Symphony, and caused it (not without some demur from Frau Schumann) to be published. The fact was revealed that Schumann's original and inexperienced talent for orchestration was by no means contemptible, though he evidently had had little liking for display. Professor Niecks, in his posthumous biographical notes on Schumann, gives abundance of interesting information as to Schumann's difficulties in orchestral conducting; how, for instance, when the horns were completely helpless over an important entry in a new overture by Joachim, Schumann could give them no better help than to whisper sadly over his shoulder to Joachim, 'They've missed it again'. The progress in Schumann's own orchestration is set steadily in the direction of making all entries 'fool-proof' by doubling them in other parts and filling up the rests. That way safety lies, and the same may be said of proclaiming Martial Law. Fortunately the recovered early version of the Fourth Symphony can show us what was likely to be in Schumann's mind in all types of theme and contrast: so we have excellent guidance in the use of the billhook on the strangling undergrowth of his wood-wind.

Schumann had in his First Symphony made some disconcerting discoveries as to the ways in which orchestral balance may go wrong; but the material of that triumphantly melodious work had not presented him with many difficult problems of orchestration, and though the final result is not without its difficulties and risky passages, the First Symphony was probably on the whole an encouraging experience to him. In 1912 I was privileged to see two movements of a yet earlier unpublished symphony which had cost Schumann an immense amount of trouble before he left it unfinished after making nearly two complete full scores and innumerable sketches. If he had finished this earlier symphony he would almost certainly have been much happier in his experience of the orchestra; it gives every evidence that he was on the right track; it would have proved effective and not difficult for the orchestra, and the discouragement of his failure to finish it may have been greater than he himself realized.

The success of what we now know as the First Symphony would of course retrieve this set-back. But then followed a greater discouragement, and one that involved perhaps the noblest and most ambitious inspiration that Schumann ever experienced. The D

minor Symphony is perhaps Schumann's highest achievement for
originality of form and concentration of material. In revising it he
increased the concentration in certain matters of detail; thus, for
instance, the all-pervading restless theme of the first allegro became
an accompaniment to the triumphant opening of the finale; and
again, it is only in the revised version that we are expressly told to
play the whole symphony straight through as a single movement.
But the essential differences in structure are quite inappreciable.
The whole work was from the outset fully as advanced an example
of free form and concentrated thematic continuity as any symphonic
poem that ever professed to be revolutionary. So novel a work
could not fail to be more risky in performance than its predecessor;
and when anything went wrong with a performance under Schumann's direction, all he could do was to look distressed, or try not
to look distressed, and ask the band to play it over again. Eventually he would make things safe by doubling the difficult or weak
points, and so his score would become playable but opaque. In
later works his orchestration took this final state of petrification as
its starting-point; but here in the D minor Symphony we have been
privileged to rediscover what Schumann's imagination could create
before an imperfect kind of practical experience disappointed him.
The later version contains some undoubted improvements, some of
which ought to be introduced into the original. And the ideal
version of the symphony would undoubtedly be arrived at by
taking the later version as the text and striking out all superfluous
doublings until we reach the clarity of the original. This is a very
elaborate process; but it has been executed recently in Germany.
Weingartner applies a similar process to all Schumann's scores;
and whatever qualms one may feel about it on principle, there
is no question that this original version of the D minor symphony
presents a justification perhaps not elsewhere to be found in the
fine arts.

Original as Schumann's D minor Symphony is, there is one work
which has inspired three of its most salient features, namely, the
C minor Symphony of Beethoven. Schumann's introduction, with
its broad melody—

Ex. 1.

is a new type of symphonic opening; the purely rhythmic transition
to the allegro is a simple device which in the later version is filled
out by foreshadowings of the main theme. The allegro itself—

Ex. 2.

(a)

shows unmistakably in the original notation that Schumann was
here inspired by the first movement of the Beethoven C minor
Symphony, with its exceptionally short exposition and its tendency
to broaden *ad infinitum* as it proceeds. The comparison is worth
making from Beethoven's point of view as well as from Schumann's;
it so completely proves that Beethoven, though popularly supposed
to have founded the whole movement on a single figure of four
notes, deals from the outset in huge paragraphs, whereas Schumann
never attempts to advance beyond square couplets. With these he
conveys a very pleasant impression of sonata form; nor, so long as
we do not expect anything dramatic, is there cause for cavil that his
second subject is not only (like many of the greatest in Haydn and
Beethoven) made of the same material as his first, but moves in
couplets of exactly the same type.

Ex. 3.

(a)

By degrees Schumann shows us, in his own boyish vein of slow
thought and quick expression, that he is full enough of drama after
all; but it will hardly develop on the lines of sonata form, and this
symphony is one of the few works in which Schumann has contrived to set himself free. He brings what has sounded like his
exposition to an abrupt and formal end; and then starts an
apparently orthodox line of development which goes through
enormous sequences in various keys, building up in the process a
pair of new contrasted themes, of which I reduce the first to
a generalized version.

Ex. 4.

&c.

Ex. 5.

&c.

&c.

(a)   N.B. The later version has no such thematic accompaniment.

These, though the rhythm remains rigidly square, really do make
very much longer paragraphs than anything in the exposition. The

process is repeated wholesale in another cycle of keys. There is no
sign of a return to D minor for purposes of recapitulation; not
would such a form be effective in the circumstances. What happens
is that eventually the cycle of keys comes round to D major, and
the episodic cantabile (Ex. 5) bursts out in the full orchestra and
brings the movement to a triumphant and abrupt end.

Whereupon (according to the indications of the revised version)
we proceed straight to the next movement; a delicious little romance
in which a plaintive lyric melody in tiny couplets—

Ex. 6.

&c.

is brought into unexpected alternation with the broad melody of
the introduction (Ex. 1). By way of central episode a solo violin
embroiders the framework of this introduction with a beautiful
arabesque in D major.

Ex. 7.

&c.

This is worked out in binary form with repeats, after which a few
bars of the tiny opening couplets bring the movement to an end
which it is hard to call A minor rather than the dominant of D.

And now the scherzo bursts in; making a spirited tune play bass
to rhythms in the wood-wind which reveal themselves as the first
triumphant episodic theme (Ex. 4) in the middle of the first movement.

Ex. 8.

&c.

The trio is a transformation of the arabesques (Ex. 7) in the slow
movement.

Ex. 9.

The scherzo returns in due course and, under the influence of
Beethoven, so does the trio. It dies away; and then comes a darkness
before dawn which just avoids provoking comparison with that of
the same point in Beethoven's C minor Symphony, inasmuch as it
is a quite definite series of developments of the main allegro figure
(Ex. 2) with hints of Ex. 4. It leads majestically into a finale which
represents delightfully the effect of the enormous triumph of
Beethoven's C minor Symphony upon this intensely thoughtful
composer, who has never lost a certain boyish impulsiveness of
expression. The theme is that of the scherzo and of the middle of
the first movement (Ex. 4), with no allusions to other figures
though in the final version Schumann added the main allegro
figure in the bass, thus securing its survival in the finale.

Ex. 10.

In his simple sectional way, Schumann builds up a very effective
sonata movement with an important transition-theme—

Ex. 11.

and a second subject in which that of the slow movement of Beethoven's Second Symphony sets its cap at a rakish angle.

Ex. 12.

Nothing is more characteristic in the difference between the two
scores than the natural dialogue of single wood-wind instruments
which Schumann wrote here, and which he afterwards turned into
a thick plaster for full wind-band.

The development is broad, and, discreetly avoiding the first
subject, leads straight to a recapitulation of the second; and then
the movement expands with a fresh melody—

Ex. 13.

into a coda, which forms a fitting climax to the whole symphony as
a single design. The pace quickens to a presto without the slightest
loss of dignity or balance. In this finale, as in the first movement,

there has been a change of notation, from the 2/4 of this original version to the common time of the later. As with the first movement, so here: information as to the change is valuable as giving the real tempo and showing that we are much more likely to take the final version too fast than, with it in our minds, to take this version too slow.

OVERTURE, SCHERZO, AND FINALE, OP. 52

1 *Andante con moto: leading to Allegro.* 2 SCHERZO: *Vivo.* 3 FINALE: *Allegro molto vivace.*

This work was written at the same time as Schumann's First, Second, and Fourth Symphonies—that is to say, it was written in 1841 and revised, especially as to the finale, in 1845. Schumann is said to have thought of calling it a Sinfonietta. It is a pity that he did not finally decide on that title, for it precisely describes both the character and range of the work; whereas its present title implies something much less coherent, besides bringing in the quite irrelevant idea of an overture. There is, however, some colour for the title of 'overture' for the first movement, inasmuch as that movement is clearly influenced by a classic which we might as well revive, Cherubini's Overture to *Les Deux Journées*. Professor Niecks points out that that overture and other works of Cherubini impressed contemporaries as eminently romantic. What Berlioz says about Cherubini is not evidence; or, at all events, it is more evidential of Berlioz than of Cherubini. The *sprechender Bass*, the dramatic utterances of unaccompanied violoncellos and basses descending into the depths in impassioned recitative, is not the exclusive property of Berlioz and Liszt; nor are the sublime instrumental recitatives in Beethoven's Ninth Symphony its prototype. It was discovered by the earliest pioneers of instrumental and dramatic music in the seventeeth century; and in the Overture to *Les Deux Journées* Cherubini used it with a power which Beethoven could surpass only on the condition of seeing exactly what Cherubini meant by it.

The trouble with Cherubini is not that his style in opera is pedantic, but that his excellent histrionic devices are executed with an irreducible minimum of music. His style is theatrical in no vulgar sense. On the contrary, it is meticulously noble, if that is not a contradiction in terms; and so his romantic rhetoric impresses us now like stage scenery lying on the ground exposed to daylight. Schumann under the influence of Cherubini is more fortunate. Four bars of the introduction to his Sinfonietta, as I prefer to call

it, compress into an epigram the whole romance of Cherubini's
Overture to *Les Deux Journées*.

Ex. 1.

The allegro of the overture dances its way in Schumann's happiest vein of homage to Mendelssohn.

Ex. 2.

It drifts easily towards a second group in which the rhythms become broader and broader.

Ex. 3.

The intervention of material from the introduction, developing
figures (*a*) and (*b*) at full speed, shows that Schumann intends to
strike a dramatic note; but the continuation, after an abrupt
pause—

Ex. 4.

proves that the movement of drama is precisely what his music
cannot achieve, and is not really attempting. More clearly than in
his larger symphonies, Schumann is building quasi-lyric epigrams
into the musical equivalent of narrative or descriptive poetry that
does not attempt the movement of either epic or drama. His
Pegasus does not fly, but it ambles very comfortably and becomes
more lyric than ever when the tempo becomes faster in the coda.

Ex. 5.

Our recovery from the anti-romantic reaction ought by now to
allow us to treat this music as its boyish enthusiasm deserves.
When Schumann was in fashion, every sentimental person proclaimed him as essentially manly, and therefore a composer in

whose sentiment we could wallow without risk. But the truth is that Schumann is essentially boyish; and one paradoxical result is that he can afford to be crassly Mendelssohnian and to echo precisely Mendelssohn's weakest turns of phrase, because he is a naïve hero-worshipper. We must not sentimentalize Schumann. He has all the manly schoolboy's horror of any such tendency. On the other hand, nothing could be more detestably inartistic than to treat him with a schoolmasterly patronage or irony.

In the compact little scherzo—

Ex. 6.

and trio—

Ex. 7.

we have Schumann in his normal lyric element, with the normal sectional forms of his *Phantasiestücke*. The coda alludes very prettily to Ex. 2 from the first movement.

The finale moves imperturbably like the Red Queen crying, 'Faster, faster!' as she rushes with Alice ever onward under the same tree in Looking-Glass Land. The first theme starts as a kind of double fugue—

Ex. 8. Upper theme.

which after three entries continues in lyric couplets or quatrains.

Ex. 9.

It drifts into the dominant, and there proceeds with new themes which constitute a second group, the result being a sonata exposition in the sense in which Berlioz purports to have achieved such a thing in the *Symphonie Fantastique* and the *Harold* Symphony; but, as we shall see, Schumann shows that he is aware that he has not achieved a classic example of the form. He directs that his exposition should be repeated, and he proceeds to extract from its last notes material for a discursive, but episodic, development—

Ex. 10.

Alice is decidedly short of breath; but she clings to the hand of the
flying Red Queen, while the four-bar phrases pursue their inex-
orable course. When Alice's second wind makes a quiet legato
possible, the second violin and viola convey fierce hints of an imminent return—

Ex. 11.

In due time the opening fugato (Ex. 8) returns in the home
tonic, and is cunningly expanded before proceeding with its lyric
continuation; and now Schumann proves that he knows that his
exposition had not the key-perspective of the sonata style, for he
gives his whole second group unaltered in the dominant, reserving
the home tonic for a coda which consists of a boyishly pompous
augmentation of the whole main theme of its sequel (Exx. 8 and 9),
and so brings one of his most delightful works to a punctual close.
The boldness of keeping his whole second group in its original
dominant shows a recovered mental energy far in advance of the
convalescence which had proved manifestly not equal to carrying
him through the finale of his Second Symphony.

OVERTURE TO BYRON'S 'MANFRED', OP. 115

Like all the most un-Byronic persons of his day Schumann was
profoundly impressed by Byron; and *Manfred*, perhaps one of the
noblest of Byron's works, inspired Schumann to the noblest of his
orchestral music. It really matters very little that Schumann himself was so un-Byronic. The particular Byronic trait that he lacked
was nothing but the bluff of a mysterious and mythological wickedness. Schumann had a reverence for sorrow of all kinds, as the
root of his keen appreciation of romantic poetry; and romantic
poetry attains great heights in *Manfred*. Schumann wrote incidental music to the whole of the play—not quite so much music
as was performed in Sir Thomas Beecham's production, and
especially not quite so much soft music from the *Kinderscenen*
and *Albumblätter*. On the whole it is permissible to say that
Schumann's interpretation of *Manfred* in music has a strength
and impressiveness nearer to Byron's intentions than the effect of
any possible performance of a play in which, as a matter of fact, the

hero almost always appears in a state of complete nervous break-down. At last he does indeed confront the abbot with:

'Old man, 'tis not so difficult to die.'

Schumann has gone beyond Byron's text in accompanying the death-scene of Manfred with the sounds of a requiem sung from the neighbouring monastery, but I see no reason to believe that there is any substantial contradiction to Byron in thus heightening the effect of the close. Schumann's reasons are not sentimental. The monastery is in the neighbourhood of the scene; and it is the essence of Byronism to admit the existence of what it so ostenta-tiously defies. The study of the play, with its incidental music, throws into high relief the power and depth of its overture.

The overture begins hastily with three loud syncopated chords, which, though standing alone at the beginning, so that the ear can-not grasp the syncopation, would sound entirely different if they were on the beat, since the players would not so attack them as to give them their present peculiar breathless expression.

Ex. 1.

From a slowly moving cloudy sequence of harmonies the following theme emerges—

Ex. 2.

and after a while the time quickens slightly, with a sudden forte in which figure (a) of Ex. 1 reappears. The time continues to quicken until it becomes an allegro ('In a passionate tempo') and Ex. 2 is stated with other figures as an impassioned first subject.

The second subject, in F sharp minor and major (=G flat), contains the following themes—

Ex. 3.

of which (e) is used in the Requiem at the close of the incidental music.

IV

Ex. 4.

The second subject, coming to a climax of pride and indignation, merges into the development, which is founded entirely on its materials, especially at first (g) and (h). The impressive pause on a sustained chord for trumpets will not fail to arrest attention. The dramatic outburst, in the very key of the second subject itself, of an impassioned transformation of (g) and (f), is the only quotation needed for this section.

Ex. 5.

This leads in broad sequences back to the tonic, preparing for the return at great length and with fine climax. The recapitulation of first and second subject is complete and regular, but the second subject comes to a somewhat greater climax as it merges into the coda. This consists mainly of an impressive diminuendo on figure (f) with a new theme on three trumpets.

Ex. 6.   Trumpets. (Wood-wind in 8ves.)

The tempo slackens till it reaches the slow pace of the cloudy opening, and the overture ends quietly with fragments of second and first subjects (*e*) and (*c*) in the same mysterious darkness in which it began.

SIBELIUS

SYMPHONY IN C MAJOR, NO. 3, OP. 52

1 *Allegro moderato*. 2 *Andantino con moto quasi allegretto.*
3 *Moderato, leading to* 4 *Allegro.*

The symphonies and other large orchestral works of Sibelius would, if they had no other merits, command the attention of every lover of music who is interested in the problem which baffled Bruckner and eluded Liszt: the problem of achieving the vast movement of Wagnerian music-drama in purely instrumental music. Liszt achieved at best, as in *Orpheus*, a large orchestral lyric, or, as in *Mazeppa*, an enlarged *Étude d'exécution transcendante*: at worst, as in *Ce qu'on entend sur la montagne*, forty minutes of impressive introductions to introductions. Bruckner conceived magnificent openings and Götterdämmerung climaxes, but dragged along with him throughout his life an apparatus of classical sonata forms as understood by a village organist. His was the fallacy of the popular natural-history writer who tells us that a flea magnified to the size of a dog could jump over Mount Everest, whereas the poor creature could not support its own weight without a vertebrate anatomy. Your pocket working model has—I forget what inverse-geometrically greater power than the full-sized machine.

Most of the later solutions of the problem of instrumental music on the Wagnerian scale of movement have continued to use and to extend the Wagnerian apparatus, especially in harmonic range and polyphony. Much of the resulting complexity is apparent rather than real, for the problem is subtle rather than complex, and modern composers have more common sense than is indicated by modern methods of high-art advertising. False simplification is a more menacing danger to the arts nowadays than over-elaboration; as we can easily discover when our analysis has distinguished the apparatus from the work. The simplicity of Sibelius is not a simplification, and his art is neither revolutionary nor negative. His latest symphonies retain something like the classical division into three or four movements, for the true classical reason that his designs complete themselves sooner than the emotional reactions they demand, so that these reactions must be expressed in separate designs. He does not share the superstition of many modern composers that a work in sonata form *must* have four movements, including an adagio and a scherzo:

a superstition only apparently originating in the classics. They arrived at the custom of writing in four movements whenever they used more than three players, because it seemed expensive to collect more players for a work of less than full size. No modern composer, whether on classical or revolutionary lines, has achieved anything like the variety of forms shown in the sonatas, duets, and trios of Haydn, Mozart, and Beethoven. Those three masters worked out their own salvation, and in due time learnt from each other in spite of differences of age. They learnt by experiencing the necessities of each individual work; and the accumulation of such experience leads to a knowledge of universals, and has no concern with averages. Beethoven produces his C sharp minor Quartet, with its apparently improvised form, by the same creative process as that of his Sonata in B flat, op. 22, the most diplomatically regular of all his works. The diplomatic regularity was not imposed on him by precedent, and the free form was not troubled by any wish to 'get away from' old formulas and restraints. Beethoven's movement was equally unhampered in both.

By its movement you may know when music is free. Pioneers may be free from human tyranny, but it is idle to call men free when their minds have never had leisure for other interests than the bare necessaries of life. The enjoyment of 'roughing it' begins after the technique of desert life or polar exploration has been mastered. Sibelius, standing on the shoulders of the late nineteenth-century masters of 'symphonic poems', moves with perfect ease in his least convincing works, and the ease is strengthened into freedom in his masterpieces. Although his designs complete themselves so quickly that his symphonies (except the Seventh) break up into three or four movements, they have little real analogy with the sonata forms. In his First Symphony the sonata forms are easily traced, but even there they are neither a necessity nor a convention, but a convenience which may not be convenient another time. With the Fifth Symphony nothing whatever is gained by thinking of them at all; and, even without thinking of them, much criticism has been directed to Sibelius for his neglect of qualities which those forms imply. His intention and achievement are entirely different: instead of working out groups of complete themes on various principles of alternate exposition, development, and recapitulation, with essentially dramatic and narrative effects throughout, he makes his scheme build itself up out of fragments until a full-sized theme arrives as a supreme climax. Two such processes will cover the ground of one of his largest movements, and sometimes, as in the finale of his Third Symphony, one will suffice. The result is that, in works of no inordinate length, Sibelius achieves climaxes on the biggest Wagnerian scale without any redundancies, hesitations, or confusions from the habits

of older art-forms. A Bach toccata is perhaps the most recent
precedent for this order of musical architecture.

Sibelius's Third Symphony is dedicated to his friend Bantock. The
long passages that arise out of Ex. 5 are said to represent the composer's impression of fog-banks drifting along the English coast.
The quality of the themes, especially of Ex. 1, is such as we would
be glad to think distinctly English. If this work should come to be
known as Sibelius's English Symphony, we might come to consider
ourselves not so anti-musical after all.

The first movement is more like a normal classic than any other
in Sibelius's symphonies. The splendid opening theme—

Ex. 1.

Allegro moderato.

swings into a crowd of accessories, such as—

Ex. 2.

and as the transition-theme—

Ex. 3.

with a power of movement that takes us into the heart of the
classical symphonic style. Three slow rising notes on trumpets
and trombones lead, like the abrupt attitudinizing transitions of
Schubert, to a 'second subject'.

Ex. 4.

A very typical feature of Sibelius's style is the emergence of a
long-drawn melody from a sustained note that began no one can say
exactly when. Another characteristic point is the way in which one
theme gradually shows a kinship with another. The continuation
of Ex. 4 thus tends to resemble the opening of Ex. 1 reduced to
sustained instead of repeated notes. At present, however, this is
not shown, but the theme passes naturally into the rolling figure of
Ex. 5—

Ex. 5.

which from this point pervades the movement as fog-banks pervade our shores.

The development is indeed almost one single extended passage arising out of Ex. 5. Fragments of other themes, notably from the second bar of Ex. 3, together with the 'conflation' of Ex. 4 and Ex. 1, loom through the fog and grow to a climax, on the top of which the recapitulation sails in with glorious vigour. The second subject is brilliantly re-scored.

The coda is of a kind peculiar to Sibelius. The music suddenly becomes almost ecclesiastical in tone. A new hymn-like theme appears—

Ex. 6.

and the movement ends in solemn calm.

The second movement is an intermezzo combining the functions of slow movement and scherzo: the lyric function of a slow movement with a gentle dance-rhythm for a quiet and slightly pathetic scherzo.

The key is remote: G sharp minor stands to C, as Beethoven's F sharp minor stands to B flat in his Sonata, op. 106. The rhythm revives an ancient ambiguity of triple time. In ancient days the notion of triple time was by no means so rigid as it is in modern music. To the modern musician twice three is not only different from thrice two but hard to reconcile with it. Once you have established the system ONE-two-three-FOUR-five-six, you will find it hard to change casually into ONE-two-THREE-four-FIVE-six. A poetic ear has no such difficulty; for poetic stresses are much lighter and less rigid than the powerful muscular energies of musical rhythm. Nevertheless, in the sixteenth century the musical triple times were as vague as the poetic. In all Palestrina you will find no sustained passage on a six-beat basis that does not shift from twice three to thrice two. In the eighteenth century the shift from thrice two to twice three is a regular characteristic of the French courante; and in every cadence in triple time in Handel's works you will see the opposite shift, the majestic broadening from twice three to thrice two. 'The glory of the Lord shall be re-veal-ed.'

I   2 3   I   2   3 4 5 6   I

Prout quotes a whole series of such cases as examples of Handel's faulty declamation.

Sibelius has erected 'Handel's faulty declamation' into a system throughout the charming intermezzo of his Third Symphony; and, as Bantock tells me, he requires the conductor to beat the time in such a way as to emphasize these shifting accents.

Ex. 7.

Ex. 8.

Towards the end of the movement a ruminating passage introduces other figures of curling runs; but no further quotations are needed.

The finale is in a form invented by Sibelius. At first only fragments of themes are heard; of which I quote two.

Ex. 9.

Moderato.

Ex. 10.

Several others might be added, but their bustling movement in a crescendo will suffice to mark them. The essence of the whole is just this, that nothing takes shape until the end. Then comes the one and all-sufficing climax. All threads are gathered up in one tune that pounds its way to the end with the strokes of Thor's hammer.

Ex. 11.

SYMPHONY IN E FLAT MAJOR, NO. 5, OP. 82

1 *Tempo molto moderato, leading to* 2 *Allegro moderato.*
3 *Andante mosso, quasi allegretto.* 4 *Allegro molto.*

This symphony is easily followed with the aid of enough quotations to show how one element of a theme leads to another. Here are the six main elements with which the opening section (almost a slow movement) builds itself up from its dawn-like beginning. They show several features of Sibelius's style; most obviously his love of letting the first note of a phrase begin at the obscurest point of the measure and swell out; also his austerely diatonic or modal harmony, varied, as in Ex. 4, by collisions severely logical in origin and consequence.

Ex. 1.

Tempo molto moderato.

(a)

Ex. 2.

Ex. 3.

Ex. 4.

fz

Ex. 5.

Ex. 6.

&c.

fz   *fz*   *fz*

&c.

The climax attained with Ex. 6 is followed by a resumption of the whole process, beginning with figure (*a*) of Ex. 1, which leads to the continuation of Ex. 2, and thence to Ex. 3; the key having returned from the bright region of G major to the environs of E flat. Ex. 4 does not follow on here, but the pair of themes, Exs. 5 and 6, are recapitulated in E flat, the tonic. Symmetry being thus established, Ex. 4 is worked up into a wonderful mysterious kind of fugue which quickens (by 'diminution') into a cloudy chromatic trembling, through which its original figure moans in the clarinet and bassoon. An impassioned development of Ex. 5 (largamente) intervenes, and, with a new version of Ex. 2, moves to B major, then, without real change of tempo, breaks into a dance-measure (allegro moderato). This might be regarded as the real first movement, to which the rest was introduction, if the classical terminology had any real application here. But the very fact that there is no change of tempo (the crotchets of the allegro being equal to the quavers of the moderato, so that four 3/4 bars are equal to one 12/8) shows that we ought not to expect the remotest connexion with sonata ways of moving. In the sonata style the composition moves like an athlete; its movements are voluntary muscular actions, and its changes of key are not merely architectural but dramatic events. This is all quite compatible with a sublime sense of cosmic movement, controlling the whole, and making the persons of the drama automatic contrivers of their own fate in all that they think to be their free action: but it depends on keeping the cosmic movement in the background until the actors' movement is finished. Here we are not dealing with the actors' movement at all; nor has any music dubbed 'modern' attempted either to recover that classical sense of movement last recovered by Brahms, or to make a synthesis of it with the purely cosmic movement which is almost the only modern escape from stagnation.

Beginning in B major with a dance-tune in which figure (a) is embodied with other figures—

Ex. 7.

this allegro moderato moves back to E flat, where a trumpet joins the dance with a tune of its own.

Ex. 8.

This returns to B major, and, after developments in a more plaintive mood, Ex. 8 extends itself in a mysterious staccato labyrinth, beginning thus—

Ex. 9.

In due course the trumpets point to the key of E flat with figure
(*a*), followed by hints of Ex. 6. This (which, you will remember,
was recapitulated with a symmetrical effect in the moderato) now
unifies the whole design by bursting out in full force, and leads to a
presto final climax, pervaded by the notes of figure (*a*) chimed
simultaneously as a chord.

The little middle movement (*Andante mosso quasi allegretto*)
produces the effect of a primitive set of variations, such as those in
the allegretto of Beethoven's Seventh Symphony, where the theme
is not varied at all, but merely scored in a progressive series of
different ways with a counterpoint. But it produces this effect in
a paradoxical way, inasmuch as it is not a theme preserving its
identity (melodic, harmonic, or structural) through variations, but
a rhythm—

built up into a number of by no means identical tunes; e.g.—

Ex. 10.

As the tunes proceed, quaver motion confirms the sense of progressive variation. After this sense has been established, an unquestionably independent episode (più tranquillo, around E flat)
sounds a more sonorous note, and thus makes a return to the
G major material dramatically welcome. Towards the end there
are mysterious gestures and modulations, but the little movement
resolves them with its own childlike calm.

Huge as is the effect of the finale, it can all be summed up with
the help of two quotations. The bustling introduction—

Ex. 11.

provides a rushing wind, through which Thor can enjoy swinging
his hammer.

Ex. 12.

While he swings it there are sounds of a cantabile trying to take form. Thor's hammer swings us into C, in the minor of which key Ex. 11 develops itself.

In due course we reach the key of G flat. In this dark region the whole process represented by Exs. 11–12 is resumed, but pianissimo. And so we eventually come to E flat, where, without change of tempo, Thor swings his hammer in 3/2 time, the cantabile attains full form and glory, and the symphony ends with the finality of a work that knew from the outset exactly when its last note was due.

SYMPHONY IN C MAJOR, NO. 7, OP. 105

In spite of the violent objection which every self-respecting musician must feel towards the use of good music as a background to talking and eating, I confess that I was thrilled when, in its New-Year's-Eve review of 1933, the British Broadcasting Corporation used a gramophone record of parts of Sibelius's Seventh Symphony as 'slow music' during the recital of the flight over Mount Everest. Let this sentence do duty for all further efforts to describe in words the austere beauty and rare atmosphere of Sibelius's mature style. Unlike mountain atmospheres, however, that of Sibelius is by no means lacking in oxygen.

It is well that this symphony has met with something like proper appreciation while it is still new. That appreciation has not exaggerated its merits; but it has exaggerated one or two aspects, the report of which may alarm the naïve listener. That versatile if Conservative critic, Mr. Punch, has already remarked that the word 'bleak' has been overworked by the exponents of Sibelius. That word might easily be overworked by admirers of Mount Everest or of the moon. For such things it is a jejune epithet, but we need not trouble to find a better. Only a real poet can afford to tell us that the sky is blue, and he probably will not need to call it azure. If the listener can put up with a good description of the flight over Mount Everest he need not be afraid of the bleakness of Sibelius.

Reports of the length and difficulty of this one-movement symphony are more definitely alarming: it has been described as the longest single and continuous design as yet achieved in absolute music; and experts who have discovered the main theme, as given three times by the first trombone (near the beginning, towards the middle, and at the end), have announced that discovery as the result of a closer familiarity with a complex work. As to its length as a single design, it is not much longer than Leonora No. 3, or the first movement of Schubert's G major Quartet, and not as long as Beethoven's *Grosse Fuge*, which was intended to be the finale of a quartet in six movements, but which makes no allusion to the themes of the other five. As to its difficulty, far be it from me to underrate the technical difficulties of any work for which the rare (and, in this category, unoxygenated) musical-economic atmosphere of Modern Athens gives its orchestral players only six hours' practice a week. Nothing is easy in such conditions; but Sibelius was a very experienced composer many years ago, and this is his opus 105. But the work has a reputation for complexity as well; and this is misleading. Subtlety is quite a different thing, and easily misunderstood; but nobody ever began to understand subtleties by suspecting complexities that do not exist.

In any tolerably competent performance of a typical work of Sibelius, the listener may rest assured that if he finds that an important melodic note has been in existence some time before he was aware of it, the composer has taken special trouble to conceal the beginning of that note. If the listener feels that unformed fragments of melody loom out of a severely discordant fog of sound, that is what he is meant to feel. If he cannot tell when or where the tempo changes, that is because Sibelius has achieved the power of moving like aircraft, with the wind or against it. An aeronaut carried with the wind has no sense of movement at all; but Sibelius's airships are roomy enough for the passengers to dance if they like: and the landscape, to say nothing of the sky-scape, is not always too remote for them to judge of the movement of the ship by external evidences. Sibelius has not only mastered but made a system of that kind of movement which Wagner established for music-drama, and which the composers of symphonic poems before Strauss have often failed to achieve and have not always realized as essential to their problem. Moreover, he achieves it in absolute music without appealing to any external programme. He moves in the air and can change his pace without breaking his movement. The tempi of this Seventh Symphony range from a genuine adagio to a genuine prestissimo. Time really moves slowly in the adagio, and the prestissimo arouses the listener's feeling of muscular movement instead of remaining a slow affair written in the notation of a quick one. But nobody can tell how or when the pace, whether muscular or vehicular, has changed.

An adequate analysis of this noble work would be too subtle to be readable; and the listener would probably find its points more evident in the music than in any words. The following five quotations will, I believe, serve the reader's purpose, though there should be at least ten themes to make a complete list.

The beginning is in darkness, with adumbrations of more than

one future theme. Dawn grows into daylight with a long-drawn
passage beginning with violas and 'cellos and pervading the whole
string-band in a kind of Mixolydian harmony, differing, like all
Sibelius's modal harmony, from Palestrina's only in the boldness
of its dissonances. The winds join towards the climax; and then
the main theme is given out by the first trombone—

Ex. 1.

Fragments of other themes, including figures of the introduction,
follow; and the time quickens gradually, while one of the new
figures gains ascendancy and eventually takes shape as a dance—

Ex. 2.

The pace becomes wild and the modulations far-flung with a new
sequential figure alternating with the second figure of Ex. 2.

Ex. 3.

Yet this muscular energy becomes absorbed quite imperceptibly
into the vast cloud-laden air-currents through and over which
Ex. 1 returns in solemn adagio with C minor harmony. Again the
pace increases; Ex. 3 returns at full speed and leads to new figures,
scudding through the air. (Perhaps you may catch the rhythm of
the trombones—

but the composer marks it pianissimo.) Sunshine emerges upon a
song that would add naïveté to the most innocent shanties of the
human sailors in Wagner's *Flying Dutchman*.

Ex. 4.

This develops, like the earlier themes, with increasing energy and
with several accessories. The climax of its development is cut off
by a momentary allusion to Ex. 3; after which the last phase of the
symphony begins with an accumulation of sequences on the following figures—

Ex. 5.

The presto on the home dominant to which this accumulation
leads proves to be the accompaniment of the final return of Ex. 1
in its proper solemn adagio. With this, and with some of the unquoted introductory figures, the symphony ends in tones of noble
pathos.

'TAPIOLA', SYMPHONIC POEM
FOR FULL ORCHESTRA, OP. 112

Tapiola is the god of the northern forests, and the following verses
represent the 'programme' of this tone-poem—

> Wide-spread they stand, the Northland's dusky forests,
> Ancient, mysterious, brooding savage dreams;
> Within them dwells the forest's mighty God,
> And wood-sprites in the gloom weave magic secrets.

The music is quintessential Sibelius, and is, perhaps, even more
typically than most of his works, describable as a vast and slow
crescendo to a climax, after which the descent into silence is short
and solemn.

I have attempted on other occasions to write of Sibelius's
peculiar methods and art forms, which have always struck me as

triumphantly achieving what Bruckner might have achieved in a
purely instrumental music on the Wagnerian time-scale, if only
he had not encumbered himself with misconceived survivals of
sonata form. Sibelius's emancipation from such things is complete,
and he is no less independent of the sense of duty which forces the
construction of brand-new systems of harmony upon ninety-nine
out of a hundred of the composers whose names strike terror into
the hearts of simple souls who 'do not like this modern music'.
There is plenty of unorthodoxy in Sibelius's harmony, and it has
many strange modes, most of them ruthlessly diatonic. But there
is no concession to fashion.

Tapiola is a god who pervades a mighty forest; and a detailed
analysis of his music will make it impossible for us to see the wood
for trees. On the other hand, there is such a thing as having so
nobly generalized an idea of the wood as not to be able to know a
tree when you see it. Music, after all, must be heard from one
moment to the next; and, while there is a strong family resemblance
between Sibelius's many short themes which reiterate themselves
in emotional outbursts, the listener may find some help in a series
of quotations showing roughly how one thing leads to another.
The ingenious analysis of the connexion between one theme and
another, either by transformation or by figures common to both,
is quite beside the mark. More illumination might be obtained by
a description of the orchestration, but this again is of use mainly
for students who wish to know how to orchestrate, and for conductors who have to realize the composer's intentions. For the
listener, a much shorter way to appreciate Sibelius's orchestration is to listen to it. This is particularly easy in *Tapiola*, inasmuch
as the orchestral colours not only do not change rapidly, but
often show their changes against a background of extraordinary
tone-colour which persists for an amazingly long time, as in the case
of the vast passage which contains Exx. 2, 3, and 4. Here, then, is
an incomplete, but fairly representative, series of the themes, or
phases of themes, which will meet the listener as he wanders
through this dark forest with due reverence for its presiding deity.

With Ex. 5, a lighter tone seems to indicate the 'wood-sprites in the gloom weaving magic secrets'.

A darker theme emerges in Sibelius's characteristic way at an unexpected rhythmic point in a long note.

In the course of an ominous crescendo it becomes associated with another new figure.

The crescendo does not fulfil its threat, but passes again into darkness and mystery. Mysterious bright light then appears, with pathetic harmony, high above the gloom.

After some time, this unexpectedly gives rise to a formidable crescendo—

Ex. 9.

and a great storm ensues, in which several new figures are heard which I need not quote. The last theme which I shall quote arises from the storm—

Ex. 10.

and soon afterwards the tone-poem takes shape as a purely musical form by means of a definite recapitulation of the group of themes comprised between Exx. 2 and 3 with their strange background.

At last a hurricane rises, which bends the tree-tops and threatens the giants of the forest. The last themes that are heard are a combination of Exx. 8 and 7. The tone-poem then closes with an Amen of slow, bright, major chords, which I give, to save space, in their ancient values of dotted breves and longs.

Ex. 11.

SMETANA

OVERTURE TO 'THE BARTERED BRIDE'

This brilliant overture is the prelude to a charming opera which is prominent among the artistic assets of Czechoslovakia. The opera is on lines of lyric comedy, and no great new light is shed on the overture by discussing the play. The object of the overture is to create the liveliest possible comic atmosphere—such as no overture since *Figaro* has attempted; and also to sound a bucolic note conspicuously absent from *Figaro*. The liveliness starts headlong with the running theme which, arising out of the syncopated opening—

Ex. 1.

runs round like a squirrel in a cage, trying to behave like a fugue but never getting off its tonic.

Ex. 2.

The bucolic element is supplied by this tune—

Ex. 3.

After it has been worked up as a rumbustious second subject, the development begins with a quiet reflective passage for wood-wind, on a slow theme which I cannot trace elsewhere. This throws the bustle and jollification of the rest into higher relief. Towards the end also, Ex. 3 goes through quiet romantic modulations. But the underlying tempo never changes, and the total effect is of extreme brilliance and speed.

RICHARD STRAUSS

TONE-POEM (AFTER NICOLAUS LENAU). 'DON JUAN', OP. 20

The three early symphonic poems of Strauss—*Don Juan* (op. 20), *Macbeth* (op. 23), and *Death and Transfiguration* (op. 24)—are of a maturity which is perhaps more astonishing in *Don Juan* than in the other two. *Tod und Verklärung* has a greater reputation with concert-goers, mainly because its intention is obviously sublime and the sentiment of the subject-poem is popular. But it is, both in poem and in music, not without the boyish facilities which the sentimental public loves. The hero, dying in a garret, remembering his childhood, his ideals, the cruel, censorious world that forbade him to follow them, the glorious transfiguration itself, are none of them ideas that have cost an amiable burgess a moment's anxiety, or the author of the poem as much thought as Strauss, even in his youth, put into orchestrating a common chord. But the *Don Juan* of Lenau is a poem with ideas beyond echoes of Byron, and beyond ambition to shock the reader. And their spirit, with its health, its egotism, and its un-Byronic acceptance of the consequences, is realized by Strauss in a music which seems incredibly remote from that of the Good Boy of the Conservatoire displayed in the opus numbers before this opus 20. The form is entirely admirable; the invention of themes is vigorous and by no means easy to trace to its intellectual antecedents; and the orchestration remains unsurpassed by Strauss himself in later works, except in so far as his whole musical language has changed to something he would not have accepted in his youth. And there is not so much of this change as one is inclined to think. The orchestration of *Don Juan* shows in every particular the ripest results of experience. It is by no means without its difficulties, though they are never of the kind which, in later works designed for double-sized orchestras, relies on the safety of numbers and gives the players passages which are merely 'wild-cat' for the individual, but which Strauss explains as the 'al fresco' technique of the modern orchestra. Yet the technique of *Don Juan*, though not al fresco, is thoroughly modern: it shows no 'conservative' tendencies in relation to its materials.

The first theme might conceivably have derived its inspiration from Berlioz, and the erotic passages theirs from Wagner; but only as one statement of the truth is inspired by another. Rebecca West, protesting against the laudation of Byron, accuses him of 'that quality of vulgarity which is like an iron wall between those who possess it and any kind of experience; since they are preoccupied with the value which experiences fetch in the eyes of the world, they never get in touch with the essential qualities of their experiences, and hence never develop any qualities of their own'. That iron wall comes between the verbal poet of *Tod und Verklärung* and the possibilities of basing really first-hand music on his poem. There is no such barrier between Lenau and the young Strauss. Whatever room this or that work may allow for difference of opinion as to the firmness of the artist's purpose, mastery is mastery wherever it is to be found; and at twenty-five years of age Strauss has mastered the potentialities of Lenau's *Don Juan* with a vigour that makes one puzzled by the amiable personal loyalty which could blind him to the second-hand quality of Ritter's *Tod und Verklärung*.

With 'programme music', even when it is so naïve as Berlioz's, it is a mistake to attempt to refer the music to details. Either it coheres as music, or it does not. Descriptive sounds may be realistic enough to explain the incoherence on a lower plane than that of the music. More often, they may completely fail to do so, or may seem to explain something not intended, as when the old lady complimented Berlioz on the vividness with which his music represented 'Roméo arrivant dans son cabriolet'. It is not necessary to master the details of Lenau's poem, though if Strauss's music had been written for the stage it would (like Mozart's, Wagner's, or Puccini's) have had its counterpart for every gesture of the action, and every material object and colour seen or described. But Strauss's *Don Juan* is not stage music, and the three extracts he quotes from Lenau's poem are all that he wishes to lay before the public as a guide to the music. Study of the whole poem will be much more illuminating in the light of the music than study of the music in the light of the poem.

Don Juan says (in German hendecasyllables with double rhymes):

'Fain would I run the circle, immeasurably wide, of beautiful women's manifold charms, in full tempest of enjoyment, to die of a kiss at the mouth of the last one. O my friend, would that I could fly through every place where beauty blossoms, fall on my knees before each one, and, were it but for a moment, conquer. . . .'

'I shun satiety and the exhaustion of pleasure; I keep myself fresh in the service of beauty: and in offending the individual I rave for my devotion to her kind. The breath of a woman that is as the odour of spring to-day, may perhaps to-morrow oppress me like the air of a dungeon. When I in my changes travel with my love in the wide circle of beautiful women, my love is a different thing for each one: I build no temple out of ruins. Indeed, passion is always and only the new passion; it cannot be carried from this one to that; it must die here and spring anew there; and, when it knows itself, then it knows nothing of repentance. As each beauty stands alone in the world, so stands the love which it prefers. Forth and away, then, to triumphs ever new, so long as youth's fiery pulses race!

. . . .

'Beautiful was the storm that urged me on; it has spent its rage, and silence now remains. A trance is upon every wish, every hope. Perhaps a thunderbolt from the heights which I contemned, struck fatally at my power of love, and suddenly my world became a desert and darkened. And perhaps not,—the fuel is all consumed and the hearth is cold and dark.'

The philosophy of these sentiments is not good citizenship, but it is neither insincere nor weak. It is selfish, but not parasitic; and it cares nothing for support from other people's opinions. It doubts, without any interest in the doubt, whether the heights it has scorned really exist or, if existing, would concern themselves to censure it with a thunderbolt. The wrath of heaven and the natural burning out of the allotted stock of fuel are ends equally trivial and equally inevitable to a career urged onward by the tempest of its passion for beauty.

Lenau's Don Juan is slain in a duel by the avenger of one of his victims. Strauss's music unmistakably represents, amongst other things, Don Juan's actual death, and the themes could no doubt be identified with various characters in the poem. The Berliozian opening themes unquestionably represent Don Juan himself, in all his youthful manly vigour.

The three themes here quoted culminate in a superb gesture as of welcome to Love wheresoever it may be found.

The plaintive accents (*flebile*) which answer the gesture are met with mockery; but soon the expected miracle happens. If Strauss had been intending to write in classical sonata form, he could not establish more clearly the orthodox dominant for a second subject than he does in the glittering passage which (with the entry of a solo violin) leads to a long love-scene in B major developed from the opening of Ex. 4. Nor, if Berlioz had intended to convince his admirer of the realism of his representation of 'Roméo arrivant dans son cabriolet', could he have achieved anything more unmistakable than the way in which the 'cellos follow the climax of the passion by a dryly questioning entry of Ex. 1, in the mood of our superman *'fliehend Ueberdruss und Lustermattung'*.

The love-theme makes one wistful attempt to claim him, but soon he is storming away *'hinaus und fort nach immer neuen Siegen'*. The next episode begins with a theme full of bitter pathos—

answered by a wailing figure (again marked *flebile*) in the flute. The second figure of Ex. 1 (bars 3 and 4) has something to say in the matter, and soon the trouble is soothed, and the first figure of Ex. 5 becomes a subdued accompaniment to a melody of intense repose, given to the oboe (an outstanding revelation of the character of that instrument) over a very dark and soft background, the double-basses being divided in chords of four notes.

Ex. 6.

From this we are roused by a very noble theme.

Ex. 7.

It causes the utmost distress to the calm melody of Ex. 6, and soon leads to fierce conflicts. Mockery is expressed by a new jingling theme which I do not quote; and another figure—

Ex. 8.

rises into importance. Don Juan's other themes bring matters to a fatal issue. His death in a duel is easily recognized in the music, and wailing fragments from the developments of Ex. 4 are heard over the reverberations of his fall. But—

Es war ein schöner Sturm, der mich getrieben.

The orchestra revives the memories of his power and of what it is not unjustifiable to dignify with the title of his ideals. The manly themes, including Ex. 7 and Ex. 8, blaze up to an exalted climax on a grand scale. Suddenly the light fails—

der Brennstoff ist verzehrt
Und kalt und dunkel ward es auf dem Herd.

TCHAIKOVSKY

SYMPHONY IN E MINOR, NO. 5, OP. 64

1 *Andante, leading to Allegro con anima.* 2 *Andante cantabile, con alcuna licenza.* 3 *Valse. Allegro moderato.* 4 *Finale. Andante maestoso, leading to Allegro vivace.*

It cannot be too often pointed out that the duty of the writer of programme notes is that of counsel for the defence. Whatever the discerning critic may find to say against a composition, the programme writer has no business to say anything that interferes with the listener's enjoyment of the music; but he may be guided by times and seasons. When the work is so new and strange that responsible opinions may differ as to its strong and weak points, the analyst is justified in taking the strongest defensive line, limited only by carefully avoiding any attack upon music of other tendencies.

At the time of Brahms's death in 1897, Tchaikovsky was at the height of his popularity, and his own recent death was shrouded in tragic mystery. Even the 'Brahminen' were remarkably timid in their obituary estimate of Brahms, and it was the correct thing to say that his symphonies were eclipsed by Tchaikovsky's. Of course they were, for they were not light music; and with this awful statement I have perhaps more than redressed the balance that I find myself to have disturbed by my high and sincere praise of Tchaikovsky's Pathetic Symphony. Now that my analyses have been collected in book form, the limitations of a counsel for the defence become manifest. The reader, no longer so conscious of the needs of the concert-goer, is apt to assume that I am still talking of the highest classical values, when I am merely stating the legitimate case for other music which is conspicuously the best of its kind. I have said nothing in praise of the Pathetic Symphony which I wish to retract. Nor have I given any grounds for supposing that I think its forms more than successful according to their lights. But I should not have helped the listener by introducing what I take to be Tchaikovsky's best work with an air of damaging patronage. If in 1907 a programme writer had dared to insinuate that Tchaikovsky was primarily a writer of light music and that his tragedy was melodrama, the only effect would have been to excite the exultant fury of the 'Brahminen' against the numerically overwhelming opposition of all more persuasive and popular critics. The controversy would have soared to the Empyrean of that region which the Germans have somehow failed to designate by the name of *Heibrau*, and everybody would have been made uncomfortable; though not nearly so uncomfortable as Brahms and Tchaikovsky would have been in the presence of each other.

To-day the situation is different. The *Heibrauen* do not seem clear as to the distinction between a writer of deservedly popular music and a humbug. At all events, the distinction becomes easier to appreciate when the music is at least a hundred years old. No sensible person is nowadays distressed at seeing a case made out for Weber; and no responsible person at this time of day wants to make out a case for Meyerbeer, though his arch-enemy, Wagner, qualified his fiercest denunciations by a most generous praise of the end of the fourth act of *Les Huguenots*. A clear distinction between good music and bad ought to be absolute for responsible persons. The distinction between bad good music and good bad music is an excellent conversational topic for talkers who can keep their tempers, but I have never ventured to prescribe it as a subject for students' essays. Nor do my duties as counsel for defence compel me to say anything further that can interfere with the listener's enjoyment of Tchaikovsky's Fifth Symphony. I hope all listeners will be able to enjoy the whole of it. Confession and avoidance, however, can remove a serious obstacle to their enjoyment of the finale. I have said of the Pathetic Symphony that its slow finale 'is a stroke of genius which solves all the artistic problems that have proved most baffling to symphonic writers since Beethoven'. The statement has shocked some people almost as much as if I had said that it was the greatest finale since Beethoven; but the problems I refer to are simply the problems of getting up any sense of movement in a finale at all; and I am afraid that my *locus classicus* for impotence in that matter is the finale of Tchaikovsky's Fifth Symphony. If the composer had intended to produce the nightmare sensation, or the Alice-and-Red-Queen sensation, of running faster and faster while remaining rooted to the spot, he might have been said to have achieved his aim here; but the melancholy fact remains that this finale resembles all other compositions in which the vitally necessary problem of movement has simply not occurred to the composer at all. I have been generously praised for my defence of Bruckner, whose popularity, now at best-seller height in Germany and Austria, has not yet begun in England; and, that being so, nobody has objected to my saying frankly that you must not expect Bruckner to make a finale 'go'. But the popular Tchaikovsky is in worse case than Bruckner, for he evidently expects his finales to 'go', and neither the naïve listener, nor the still more naïve *Heibrau*, can at this time of day be helped by an analysis that leaves it to him to discover the fact that Tchaikovsky's finale wants to go and cannot.

One sometimes encounters the view that Tchaikovsky's Fifth Symphony is finer than the *Pathétique*, on the ground that it has fewer 'tricks'. Tchaikovsky's orchestration is undoubtedly vivid, and the salient features of the Pathetic Symphony are specially ingenious. I don't know if anything else in the Pathetic Symphony is to be called 'tricks'; but if tricks are good tricks, I prefer to have as many of them as possible, and I am not disinclined to call them ideas. So now let us see how many ideas we can find in this Fifth Symphony, and let no *Heibrau* persuade us to throw the baby out with the bath-water.

The introduction sets forth a dour melody which I leave to musical folk-lorists to put into the right pigeon-hole among their Russian folk-songs, premising only that Tchaikovsky was abundantly capable of inventing it himself.

Ex. 1.

It appears at dramatic points in later movements of the Symphony, and may be regarded as its motto.

The allegro begins with an equally lyric theme—

Ex. 2.

which builds up by a crescendo of repetitions to a big tutti which eventually effects a transition to dramatic action. Great harmonic distinction is given to this theme by its first note. Those who misremember it as B will learn a useful lesson in style when they come to notice that this note is C and not B.

From this tune the music rouses itself to fluent dramatic action, in the course of which a new incident—

Ex. 3.

seems to be about to make a transition; but this is eventually effected by Ex. 2.

From this the transition is prompt, and a new theme appears in the dominant minor.

Ex. 4.

This shapes itself as the first member of a second group, which soon changes its key to the unusual region of D major, the flat seventh, where a new pair of themes is given, of which the first—

Ex. 5.

is remarkable for the colour of the wind chords, while the second—

Ex. 6.

introduces a melting cantabile in a Brahmsish cross-rhythm. The direction 'molto più tranquillo' has led to a tradition that pulls this passage entirely out of relation to the main tempo, but Tchaikovsky adds a metronome mark ($\downarrow$. = 92) which leaves it well in touch with the rest. His exaggerated markings indicate nerves rasped by the inattention of conductors and players to ordinary nuances. Like most of such nervous reactions they defeat their object; and later editors make matters worse by adding more marks. Ex. 6 leads to a passionate climax in which the figure of Ex. 2 appears, after which Ex. 5 brings the exposition to a triumphant end.

The sounds of triumph fade away and pass into a contrapuntal development of the figures of Exx. 1 and 5, modulating through dark keys. Suddenly a storm bursts out on the transition theme

(Ex. 3). Then Ex. 4 is developed in combination with other figures. At no immoderate length another climax is reached, and a return is made, through an outlying region of G minor, into the home tonic with a very impressive sudden diminuendo. The bassoon, an instrument much honoured and sometimes sorely tried in this symphony, brings back the main theme (Ex. 2) at exactly the right moment.

The recapitulation is quite regular, B minor being replaced by C sharp minor, which leads to the home tonic.

The coda works up Ex. 2 in a lively crescendo, the climax of which initiates a basso ostinato on the notes E, D, C, B, which persists for 28 repetitions to within 8 bars of the end, while Ex. 2 is almost as obstinate in the treble. The diminuendo reaches a darkness almost as Cimmerian as those in the Pathetic Symphony. But it would be a mistake to impute any deep psychic gloom to this excellent and pleasantly sardonic first movement, or indeed to any part of this symphony.

The andante begins with 8 bars of hymn-like chords which, starting as if in B minor, swing round to D major, the key of the second group in the first movement. These chords might well have become an important theme, or at least a canto fermo; but they are not heard again, their sole function being this swing from B minor to D. They drift into an accompaniment to a broad melody given out by the first horn.

Ex. 7.

From this arises an auxiliary theme in the bright key of F sharp major.

Ex. 8.

This is the chief topic of the most impassioned climaxes in this movement.

A middle episode, 'moderato con anima', modulating widely, begins in F sharp minor with the following theme—

Ex. 9.

At its climax the home dominant is reached, and the motto theme (Ex. 1) appears with great emphasis in a significant new position.

One of the most famous of all Tchaikovsky's rhetorical strokes is the short pause and swinging pizzicato chords which follow this by way of return to the main theme (Ex. 7), which is now adorned by rhythmic imitations in the oboe and other wind instruments.

The final climax of the movement concerns itself chiefly with Ex. 8. Towards the end the fateful motto theme intervenes thunderously in a new position. After this the rest of the movement is an impressive dying away on the topic of Ex. 7.

The graceful valse which does duty for scherzo can be enjoyed without the aid of quotations. A notorious passage for the bassoon owes most of its atrocious difficulty to the assumption that Tchaikovsky intends it to be brilliant. I see no reason to doubt that his intention is rather that it should be the one note of passion in an otherwise indolently graceful movement; and, in particular, that it should thus enhance the contrast afforded by the lively trio with its spiccato runs. In the coda the ghost of Ex. 1 appears dimly.

By way of introduction to the finale, Ex. 1 presents itself very much in the flesh and in majestic tonic major. It alternates with a new chord theme—

which introduces darker keys (G major in relation to E minor), and eventually causes the bass to settle upon G, and to remain there not only while the introduction dies away, but also while the following self-repeating theme of an allegro vivace breaks through—

I have already expressed my doubt as to whether Tchaikovsky intends his finale to give an impression of struggling vainly to achieve flight, but perhaps the listener will enjoy it best if he

assumes that to be the composer's intention. New figures, such
as—

Ex. 12.

do not release us from the rhythmic bondage of the old themes
with which they combine, and their presence in the bass does not
long prevent the bass from subsiding into vast pedal points.

Ex. 13.

When at last a new cantabile appears as the chief member of the
second group, it enters over an ostinato that has already persisted
for a long time, and is going to persist much longer. Again we find
ourselves in the D major characteristic of the work.

Ex. 14.

By way of change of movement, the motto theme (Ex. 1) bursts
out in full majesty without slackening the tempo, and its second
figure is ingeniously paraphrased in terms of Ex. 11, thus initiating
a development in which Ex. 13 stalks on its way, sometimes below,
and sometimes above, the ostinato figure derived from the first
notes of Ex. 11.

At last an impressive diminuendo with fine modulations reduces
fig. (b) to repeated chords, while the other ostinato, fig. (a), discovers that it has been representing the home tonic for a long
time. Then a recapitulation begins, Ex. 11 bursting out suddenly
as bass to a new theme. The other materials follow in more or
less their original sequence, the second group answering its former
D major by the new and bold colour of F sharp major. This is
brought round to the home dominant, on which the rhythm, but
not at first the actual theme, of Ex. 1 asserts itself. Its actual
appearance as a theme is carefully deferred until a grand climax

of themeless chords has duly prepared us for a triumphal march ('moderato assai e molto maestoso') in the major. As such, with new counter-points, Ex. 1 now displays itself at leisure, with accompaniments of increasing brilliancy. Then there is a return to presto, where a further coda deals with Exx. 12 and 13.

But the last word of the symphony is concerned with neither the issues of the finale nor the motto theme, but with the main theme of the first movement (Ex. 2) in grandiose major and unqualified cheerfulness.

My own conclusion about Tchaikovsky's Fifth Symphony is that great injustice to its intentions results from regarding it as in any way foreshadowing the Pathetic Symphony. Like all Tchaikovsky's works, it is highly coloured; and a critic who should call it restrained would be in evident medical need of restraint himself; but the first three movements are in well-proportioned orthodox form, and my general impression of this symphony is that from first to last Tchaikovsky, though I have never been able to impute to him a sense of humour, is thoroughly enjoying himself. And I don't see why we shouldn't enjoy him too.

PATHETIC SYMPHONY IN B MINOR, NO. 6, OP. 74

1 *Adagio, leading to Allegro non troppo (alternating with Andante and other changes of tempo)*. 2 *Allegro con grazia*. 3 *Allegro molto vivace*. 4 FINALE: *Adagio lamentoso*.

It is not for merely sentimental or biographical reasons that Tchaikovsky's sixth and last symphony has become the most famous of all his works. Nowhere else has he concentrated so great a variety of music within so effective a scheme; and the slow finale, with its complete simplicity of despair, is a stroke of genius which solves all the artistic problems that have proved most baffling to symphonic writers since Beethoven. The whole work carries conviction without the slightest sense of effort; and its most celebrated features, such as the second subject of the first movement, are thrown into their right relief by developments far more powerful, terse, and highly organized than Tchaikovsky has achieved in any other work. The extreme squareness and simplicity of the phrasing throughout the whole symphony are almost a source of power in themselves: like the cognate limitations in Russian and French music, they indicate the deep impression made by Schumann on artists of widely different temperaments. Anything less like Schumann in emotional tone it would be impossible to conceive; and as for orchestration, Tchaikovsky is as remote from the Handel of the Crystal Palace as from Schumann. But there is no doubt about the Schumann element in his form and style. Schumann, of course, has different things to say, and has more leisure to say them; consequently he speaks mainly in epigrams, and shows more relish in making them witty. The Russian has no use for epigrams; but the square-cut style which suits them—the cult of antithesis, of the heroic couplet, of verse in which the sense never runs across from line to line, of sentences which have nothing to gain by being grouped into big paragraphs—such things suit Tchaikovsky's methods, and are compatible with a dramatic power to which even his operas (successful though they were) did not rise. All Tchaikovsky's music is dramatic; and the Pathetic Symphony is the most dramatic of all his works. Little or nothing is to be gained by investigating it from a biographical point of view: there are no obscurities either in the musical forms or in the emotional contrasts; and there is not the slightest difficulty in understanding why Tchaikovsky attached special importance to the work.

One of the most original features is the opening in a key which turns out not to be that of the piece, but a dark outlying region (the subdominant). Through ghost-like chords on double-basses a bassoon foreshadows the main theme. The key shifts from E minor to the real key of the symphony, B minor; and the allegro begins with the first subject. I have marked (as usual) with letters those groups of notes which are developed into other combinations.

Ex. 1.

Stated by violas, and counterstated by flutes, this theme soon reaches a climax; and a considerable number of lively subordinate themes follow in a long crescendo of square, Schumannesque, antithetic dialogue. This dialogue, though excited, is by no means tragic, but its climax, with the subsequent solemn dying-away, indicates the advent of something important; and when, after a pause, the second subject enters in a slow tempo, there is no doubt that its beauty has destiny behind it. My quotation gives the theme and the beginning of the dialogue which follows it (Ex. 2). After the dialogue reaches its climax, the theme (Ex. 2) returns in full harmony, and is followed by an 'envoy'—a strain with a 'dying fall'. Once more the theme returns on a clarinet, and dies away finally.

Ex. 2.

Dialogue.

The development opens with a crash, and works up the first theme (Ex. 1) in a stormy fugato, figure (*b*) settling down into a persistent figure of accompaniment to various new themes solemnly given forth by trumpets and trombones. The course of the music is easy to follow; and its finest feature, perhaps the finest passage Tchaikovsky ever wrote, is the return of the first subject, worked up in a slow crescendo starting in the extremely remote key of B flat minor, and rising step by step until, in the tonic (B minor), the whole theme (Ex. 1) is given fortissimo in dialogue between strings and wind. The tragic passage which then follows is undoubtedly the climax of Tchaikovsky's artistic career, as well as of this work: and its natural reaction, the return (in the tonic major) of the second subject, is the feature that fully reveals (perhaps even more than the despairing finale of the whole symphony) the pathetic character of the music. The dialogue, of which Ex. 2 quoted the beginning, is now omitted; and the severely simple coda, consisting of a solemn cadence for trumpets and trombones over a pizzicato descending scale, is a crowning beauty that greatly strengthens the pathos.

The second movement, an extremely simple kind of scherzo and trio, has this peculiar effect, that while it is in five-four time, which is an unsymmetrical rhythm, the bars themselves are grouped in the stiffest series of multiples of eight that have ever found room in a symphony. It is a delightful and childlike reaction from the drama of the first movement, and except for a certain wistfulness in the tone of the trio (Ex. 4), with its obstinate pedal-point in the drums, it successfully hides whatever cares it may have. My figures show how the five beats throughout the movement are really a juxtaposition of a two-four and a three-four bar. Ex. 3 gives the main theme—

and Ex. 4 the trio, which is an even more persistent mediant pedal than its prototype in the scherzo of Schumann's 'Rhenish' Symphony.

There is a short and wittily simple coda beginning with a descending scale in this rhythm $\quad\quad\quad\quad$, in the treble, with an ascending scale of crotchets (the first bar of Ex. 3 without the triplet quavers) rising in the bass to meet it; and ending with a plaintive dialogue on the figure of Ex. 4.

The gigantic march which constitutes the third movement begins with a quiet but busy theme, the triplet motion of which lasts almost incessantly until the final stage, where the second subject stiffens the whole orchestra into march-rhythm. In Ex. 5 I give, below the first theme, the counterpoint which accompanies its second statement.

The second subject (the main figure of which was already anticipated soon after the statement of Ex. 5) consists of a ten-bar tune beginning as follows—

Ex. 6.

and alternating with a second clause of eight bars which I need not quote.

There is no development: the first subject returns without any elaborate process; but its continuation becomes highly dramatic and is worked up to a tremendous climax crowned by the entry of Ex. 6 in G major as a rousing march for the full orchestra. The triumph is brilliant but, perhaps in consequence of the way in which it was approached, not without a certain fierceness in its tone. At all events it would, if translated into literature, be the triumph of the real hero not the story. He might share in it at the time; but his heart will be in the mood of Tchaikovsky's finale.

This experiment, unique in form and unique in success, is carried through on two themes: the desperate first subject, with its curious arrangement of crossing parts in the first four bars (the individual violin parts are quite unintelligible, but their combination gives a plain melody, as shown here in bars 3 and 4)—

Ex. 7.

and the consolatory second subject.

Ex. 8.

This second subject is worked up to a great climax, which leads, after some dramatic pauses, but without development, to the recapitulation. In this the first subject reaches a still greater climax, which dies down until a distant stroke of a gong (the most ominous sound in the orchestra, if discreetly used) brings back the second subject (Ex. 8), now in B minor and in a mood of utter despair. And so the music of the whole symphony dies away in the darkness with which it began.

VAUGHAN WILLIAMS

PASTORAL SYMPHONY

1 *Molto moderato.* 2 *Lento moderato.* 3 *Moderato pesante.*
4 *Lento, leading to* 5 *Moderato maestoso.*

In his Pastoral Symphony Vaughan Williams has set his imagination at work on lines which at no point traverse the ground covered by Beethoven. The very title of Beethoven's first movement shows that Beethoven is a town-dweller who is glad of a holiday in the country; and the other scenes, by the brook, at the country-dance, and during and after the thunder-storm, are all conceived as interesting to the visitor who has left town for the sake of the experience. The experience is deep and poetic; but Beethoven never thought of describing any of his compositions as a 'town' sonata or symphony. One does not describe what has never been conceived otherwise. Now Vaughan Williams's Pastoral Symphony is born and bred in the English countryside as thoroughly as the paintings of Constable. If he had not given us his London Symphony we should have no artistic evidence that this composer had ever thought of town in his life. But whether in town or in the country, this music is contemplative in a way that was not possible a century ago. Beethoven's nature-worship has much in common with Wordsworth's; but since that time pantheism and mysticism have gone a long way further towards Nirvana.

Beethoven's touch, in his Pastoral Symphony, is so light that, as with Mozart *passim*, the listener forgets the power. In Vaughan Williams's Pastoral Symphony the listener cannot miss the sense of power behind all this massive quietness; it is as manifest in the music as in a bright sky with towering, sunlit, cumulus clouds—and as little likely to rouse us to action. Across this landscape of saturated colours there float the sounds of melodies older than any folk-song. These melodies are harmonized on the plan first reduced to formula by Debussy: whatever chord the melody begins with is treated as a mere sensation, and the chord follows the

melody up and down the scale, instead of dissolving into threads
of independent melodic line. But Vaughan Williams adds to this
principle another, which is that two or even three melodic threads
may run simultaneously, each loaded with its own chord, utterly
regardless of how their chords collide. The collisions will not
offend the naïve listener if they occur only between sounds on
planes of tone so different that they do not blend. As applied to
classical counterpoint this principle is as old as Bach; but the
systematic application of it to the anti-contrapuntal method of
Debussy is new. Bi-planar or tri-planar harmony is what the
theorists call it; and it is both more schematic and more free in
this work than in most of the examples that have been discussed
and quoted during the last twenty years. Earlier examples have
generally had one of the parts standing comparatively still, like an
ornamented organ-point; but such a passage as Ex. 3 shows rigid
chords moving quite freely in three planes of harmony.

The symphony begins with a soft, waving figure below which
a theme appears in the bass:

Ex. 1.

The harp supplies a full chord to each note. A solo violin, imitated
by an oboe, answers with another figure.

Ex. 2.

The first theme is then given in imitation between treble and bass.
I quote in order to show the 'tri-planar' harmony.

Ex. 3.

Other themes, some less serene, follow; of which it will suffice to quote two: the one a mysterious pair of chords, to which a cor anglais adds a plaintive question—

Ex. 4.

&c.

and the other a salient example of the pentatonic melodies with which the whole symphony abounds.

Ex. 5.

These and similar materials are worked up quietly and combined, coming at last to a climax from which the movement descends to a pianissimo end on the first notes of Ex. 1.

The second movement is built from two pentatonic melodies—

Ex. 6.

and—

Ex. 7.

both of which stand out against the dark background of a chord of F minor.

Later on a trumpet is heard, playing in the natural harmonic series of E flat. This natural series, which is that of the overtones of a pipe, extends of course *ad infinitum*, but before it has reached its tenth note it has already included one note which has never been absorbed in the classical system of harmony.

Ex. 8

1 2 3 4 5 6 7 8 9 10

The seventh note of this series is flatter than any B flat recognizable either in mathematically pure classical harmony or in the mechanical average embodied in our tempered scale. But to call it unnatural would be like calling a Frenchman a foreigner in Paris because he did not speak English.

The ninth note of the natural series is, again, not the same as the corresponding tempered note; but its exact intonation is thoroughly realized in the classical system, as Helmholtz found when he tested Joachim's intonation on the violin. Obviously the pianoforte, which is obliged to make the interval from C to D equal to that from D to E cannot distinguish the ratio 8:9 from the ratio 9 : 10. A trumpet, however, that renounces the use of modern valves and relies entirely on lip-pressure, is not only able to distinguish these ratios and to add to them the musically unknown ratio 7 : 8, but it cannot possibly get them wrong. Accordingly in this passage the trumpet declaims in free rhythm on these natural sounds. This is the central feature of the movement. At the end a natural horn in F repeats this trumpet-passage in combination with Ex. 6.

In the scherzo a rustic human element seems present, rather at work than at play. (The composer tells me that the element is not human: the music was sketched for a ballet of oafs and fairies.)

This alternates with another theme in livelier time.

A warbling figure, given out by the flute, follows and combines with these. Later a spirited tune in a Mixolydian scale dances its way in the brass and the full orchestra, constituting the trio of the scherzo.

The scherzo returns, rescored; and likewise, for a few lines, the theme of the trio. Patient beasts of burden are manifest as well as human (or oafish) labourers. But the movement unexpectedly subsides in a mysterious fugue—

which explains itself by combining first with a variant of the (unquoted) warbling theme, and then with it and Ex. 10. And so the gnats (or the fairies) have it all their own way.

The finale is a slow movement. It begins with a deep soft roll of the drum, over which a distant human voice (or, if necessary, a clarinet) sings a wordless rhapsody in a pentatonic scale.

Then, after some introductory bars, the following tune is announced:

Ex. 13.

An agitated utterance of the cor anglais, taken up by the solo violin, gives rise eventually to one of the serenest passages in the whole work. It is the shape towards which the phrases of the distant voice were tending at the outset.

Ex. 14

The solo violin intervenes passionately, and leads to a climax in which all the strings declaim the vocal opening. They die away into a figure of accompaniment below which Ex. 13 returns in all its solemnity. Eventually, the symphony ends with the distant voice no longer over a drum-roll, but under a high note sustained like the clear sky.

OVERTURE TO 'THE WASPS'

The plays of Aristophanes give the composer abundant opportunities for music; and Vaughan Williams has made brilliant use of those afforded by *The Wasps*. Besides the choruses, which are restricted and inspired by the elaborate precision of Greek metrical forms, there is material in the incidental music for an effective orchestral suite. Of this the overture, to be performed on the present occasion, is the largest and most developed movement. I have not at hand the means of assigning its various themes to precise functions in the Aristophanic drama, nor is this aspect a matter of Wagnerian importance. The Athenians, according to the play, were going through a phase of litigious mania, for which the demagogue Cleon was largely to blame. Law-suits have bereft poor old Philocleon of whatever wits he once had, and he makes his entry up through the chimney, explaining that he is the smoke. His son Bdelycleon can keep him quiet only by occupying him with the trial of a dog, with counsel for prosecution and defence, pathetic exhibition of the wailing about-to-be dispossessed or orphaned puppies, &c., all complete. The chorus, appropriate to the Athenian temper, is a chorus of wasps.

The overture accordingly presents a compendium of Aristophanic matters, of which the main sentiment is that the Athenians are good-natured healthy enough people, if only they would not allow demagogues to lead them by the nose. Accordingly, apart from the normal Gregorian tones of a wasps' nest, the music consists of a brilliant scheme of tunes galore, in the style of folk-songs, diatonic by nature, but occasionally inveigled by Cleon into a whole-toned scale. I am not interested to know which, if any, of these tunes are actual folk-melodies. Vaughan Williams ranks with Marjorie Kennedy-Fraser among the supreme discoverers and recorders of genuine folk-music; but he can invent better tunes than any that will ever be discovered by research. And if he himself were to tell me that there were pantomimic topical allusions to Aristophanes in the original folk-poems of his tunes, I fear I should be strongly tempted to extemporize additions to such details until my whole analysis became a 'leg-pull'. The listener may be further reassured on another point. The music owes nothing to researches for ancient Greek musical fragments; its archaisms are the latest (or nearly the latest) modernisms of a lover of British folk-music, and it has no tendency to base 'We won't go home till morning' on the supertonic of a minor key, and sing it in five-eight time, thus—

as is the way of composers too learned in ancient Greek music.[1]
Here, then, are the main themes of this overture. First a rowdy
couple of dance-measures, with a tendency to combine in primitive
counterpoint.

Ex. 1.

Ex. 2.

Lastly, a gentle, broad melody first stated by itself in E flat and,
in the final stage of the movement, combined as follows with Ex. 1.

Ex. 3.

[1] This diatribe is emphatically not directed against the wonderful
ancient Greek melody so beautifully used in Ethel Smyth's *The Prison*.
I will not stir up wasps' nests by explaining what it is directed against.

WAGNER

OVERTURE TO 'DER FLIEGENDE HOLLÄNDER'

Der Fliegende Holländer is in many ways the most astonishing of Wagner's earlier operas. We are apt to forget that his *Rienzi* had been an enormous success. *Rienzi* was an opera on Spontini's lines, massive, spectacular, and musically of a coarser fibre than Spontini's. It brought its composer into such prominence that his next work was awaited with widespread curiosity. Would he follow up his great success with a greater, or would he only show signs of repeating himself? The event was utterly without precedent. Wagner followed *Rienzi* with a work that nobody could even pretend to understand. Encouragement came to Wagner from the last quarter that could be expected. Spohr, to whom Beethoven's style was a book sealed with the seven seals of Spohr's own classical prejudices, found matter more to his liking in this new world of which he did not know the manners and customs. He produced both *Der Fliegende Holländer* and *Tannhäuser* with the utmost care at Cassel; and his chief criticism was that Wagner wrote too few rounded periods. In other words, Spohr saw from the reverse side what is the main defect of Wagner's early style. The style has broken away from the classical rate of movement without yet establishing a movement of its own. We take Wagner's mature style as its criterion, and we find that his early style relapses into classical cadences just when it has begun to move on the great Wagnerian scale. To Spohr these lapses, when not accompanied by worse lapses of taste, were the main evidences of Wagner's musical talent. The lapses of taste were not worse than those of Meyerbeer, if as bad. In *Tannhäuser* Spohr found a decided improvement in technical matters. This is rather hard for us to discern nowadays; and Wagner's musical taste certainly did not improve between the *Holländer* and even *Lohengrin*. The occasional vulgarities in the *Holländer* happen both to be associated with a vulgar person, Daland, the mercenary-minded father of the romantic Senta, and also to be unpretentious; whereas the worst things in *Tannhäuser* and *Lohengrin* are supposed to be noble and grand. In order to appreciate the extraordinary maturity of the *Holländer*, it is necessary to hear it as Wagner first intended it, as a one-act opera with the music continuing without break during the changes of scene. No butcher's job has ever been more clumsily done than the process by which this opera has been chopped into three acts. Wagner himself is responsible for the butchery, and it is grim evidence of the iron that had entered his soul before his *Wahn* found its *Frieden* in Bayreuth.

The story of the Phantom Ship is worthy of Wagner's unsurpassable powers of pathos and romantic beauty; and his dramatic treatment of it is in advance of his purely musical powers. This is not evident in the overture, a far riper piece of music than the overture to *Tannhäuser*. There is nothing clumsy in the form, which is free and magnificently fluent. To the listener who is not encumbered by a distracting modicum of technical knowledge, Wagner's design will probably display itself straightforwardly. Listeners who wish to call the features of the design by their right names will be glad to know that the vast opening statement, comprising the following two quotations, is an introduction, and that the main body of the overture begins, at the resumption of the original tempo, with Ex. 4. The Phantom Ship appears in Ex. 1, riding through the storm.

Ex. 1.

The Captain of the Phantom Ship has brought upon himself the curse that he cannot die nor rest from his wanderings until he finds a maid who will be true to him. Senta, the daughter of Daland, a Norwegian skipper has brooded over the story of this 'Flying Dutchman', until she can think of nothing else, and cannot feel that her faithful lover Erik has any claim on her. She is always singing the ballad that tells the weird story that enthralls her; and she especially loves to dwell on the phrase that tells of his one hope of salvation.

Ex. 2.

A wailing echo of its last notes—

Ex. 3.

associates itself, in quicker tempi, with the cries of the sailors at their work in stormy weather.

The main body of the overture begins with a theme suggestive of waves.

Ex. 4.

Clearly heard at the outset, it is afterwards seen by the reader of the score more often than it is heard in performance; for the powerful blasts of wind and brass are often too strong for it. The overture now proceeds like a very broad sonata exposition, and introduces a light and lively second group in F with the following Wagnerian sea-shanty.

Ex. 5.

After this, however, the form becomes unorthodox. I believe it to have had a great influence on Schumann in the first movement of his Fourth Symphony. The whole set of themes, from Ex. 1 onwards, with others unquoted, proceeds to develop in broad sequences. These are piled up with magnificent energy, till they reach a climax in the home tonic major, in which we have no recapitulation but a triumphant apotheosis of Ex. 2. In the opera it is only at the last moment, when the Dutchman has already departed in despair, that Senta flings herself over the cliff into the sea and brings him deliverance; but here in the overture we are shown her long-determined resolution, and the force with which she urged herself beyond all mortal scruples. To my mind the most touching thing in all Wagner's earlier works is the sudden calm cadence, when a light shines through the storm and reveals Senta and her phantom lover united on the deck of the Phantom Ship.

A 'FAUST' OVERTURE

This work is of peculiar interest both for its purely musical qualities and for its historical position in Wagner's many-sided and complex artistic development. It was first composed in Paris in 1840 by the Wagner of *The Flying Dutchman*. In 1855 the Wagner of *The Rheingold* re-wrote it. There is something almost miraculous in the fact that this work achieved its present firm consistency of style, although its creation covered the most unsettled part of Wagner's career. External disturbances were as nothing compared with the conflict not only of style but of aims in the

three romantic operas which Wagnerians still insist on treating as if
they were the normal antecedents of Wagner's maturity. They were
nothing of the kind: they were, on their musical side, the works of
a composer who was continually mistaking bad art for good. The
history of opera is not primarily, or even largely, the history of
good music; and while every word of Wagner's later denunciation
of Meyerbeer is not only true but almost temperate from the standpoint of any pure ideal, much of its bitterness arises from the
unavowed fact that Wagner himself at the age of thirty-five had
still written with most spontaneity and success when he had
written most like Meyerbeer. He never imitated Meyerbeer; but
in his romantic operas he did undoubtedly enjoy and make the
public enjoy just the typical bad things in music that Meyerbeer
exploited; and to-day no one with pretensions to musical taste
will claim that such things as the end of the overture to *Tannhäuser*,
or the brilliant prelude to the third act of *Lohengrin*, can be
explained as the innocent lapses of a great artist's early style. They
are successful bad music; and their success confused the issue in
all the controversies which grew in bitterness as Wagner purified
his music and envenomed his prose. By the time he had purified
his melody and set it free from symmetrical shackles, the cry was
that he had no melody; and there is no denying that the facility of
his early melodic invention had been a facility that ran downhill.

It is a wonderful thing that a man no longer young should not
only produce the seven most voluminous, highly-organized, and
in all respects revolutionary works of art extant, but produce
them under the necessity of constantly inhibiting the impulse to
write the sort of melody that came naturally to him. Before one
can venture to criticize the result, one must learn first to take it
as it comes, then to understand how far there is a historic explanation for what fails to explain itself, and lastly to ignore that history
where it interferes with our direct view of the result. The
problem of Wagner's later melody will then assume something
like the shape of Beethoven's later counterpoint, or Browning's
diction. No amount of hero-worship will make the Wagner of
The Ring a facile melodist, Beethoven a facile contrapuntist, or
Browning a patient seeker of the fit word in the perfect rhythm;
but a reasonably receptive mind will soon be satisfied that at the
worst these artists have succeeded in treating these questions as
all true art treats the imperfections of an instrument. The imperfections all tend to become useful and expressive qualities. The
rough counterpoint strikes fire where smooth counterpoint would
glide past unperceived; the melody, shy in repose, violent in
movement, and always more at home with instruments than with
voices, becomes most human where it is most intractable; and

the wrong word in the wrong rhythm marks a stage in the growth
of the language when the right man utters it.

There is just enough internal evidence in Wagner's *Faust*
Overture to show that it actually was brought into shape during
a period when he was being pulled in different directions by
incompatible ideals. Only a minute examination and a careful
comparison with other works of the period can show this. When
we have traced its different origins we shall have accomplished an
analysis, which, like all analytical processes, is useless to art or
life until we have put things together again. The opening is recognizably by the Wagner of Ortrud and Telramund in the second
act of *Lohengrin*; but it is incomparably more powerful, mainly
because it is musically terse. Also the weird harmonies of its
second figure (Ex. 1 (*c*)) are specifically Wagnerian, whereas
Ortrud and Telramund had little beyond fine orchestration to
give power to their curses.

Ex. 1.

The beautiful gleam of light that comes in the major mode and
seems to suggest the salvation either of Faust or of Gretchen, or
at least the hope of salvation, might have had its context anywhere
in Wagner's three romantic operas; but here again in this *Faust*
Overture it is handled with a terseness and a mastery of form that
lifts it far above the sphere of Wagner's early style.

Ex. 2.

Interrupted by a demoniacal yell, it subsides mournfully into an
unharmonized and desolate phrase for the violins, in which the
main theme (derived from (*a*) in Ex. 1) takes definite shape: there
is a crash, and a pause; and then the quick movement begins as
follows:

Ex. 3.

This first subject soon rises to a climax, and introduces a vigorous diatonic theme in 'dotted' rhythm—

which may be traced to figure (*c*), but which well bears out the statement that Wagner began to plan this overture after hearing a performance of Beethoven's Ninth Symphony. After this there is a powerful wailing theme given by the oboe in its bitter low register. Through rich modulations this leads to an impassioned close in F, in which key the second subject begins, with a soft melody, exquisitely scored.

Ex. 4.

&c.

Here again terse presentation and masterly continuation disguise from us the historically interesting fact that this melody begins more or less in Elsa's vein. The continuation, with its glorious long-drawn close for the strings alone, can only have been written when Wagner's style was ripe for *The Ring*. Then Ex. 2 reappears in a notation of semibreves and minims suitable to the quick tempo, but really amounting (like the end of the *Tannhäuser* overture) to a return to its original slow tempo. This, by the way, is one of the principal points in which music during and since the 'romantic period' (whatever that may mean) has most radically broken with classical methods. To the classical composer this kind of obliteration of the sense of tempo seemed vulgar; and in the *Tannhäuser* overture we may as well admit that it *is* vulgar, all the more because it is evidently meant to be extremely grand. Why is it not vulgar here in the *Faust* Overture? Just because the quiet string passage, which I believe to be the latest feature in the overture, has already relaxed the tempo; so that the relaxation is not associated with the crescendo at all. This development of Ex. 2 works up to a climax of solemn tragic power, where its slow steps acquire a majesty of their own, which borrows nothing either from the quick or from the original slow movement. When the note of salvation (if that is the right word for it) has become a thundering note of judgement, and its echoes have died away under another demoniacal yell, once more, as in the introduction, it is softly reasserted. One cannot but think of the last line but one of the first part of *Faust*:

Mephistopheles.   Sie ist gerichtet!
Voice from above.   Ist gerettet!

Then after a few broken chords the first theme (a) is developed with admirable terseness in a passage strongly suggestive of the Witches' Sabbath; and this leads back to the tonic in a powerful crescendo, returning to a clearly-marked recapitulation with a climax that can easily be traced to its mighty original, the return in Beethoven's Ninth Symphony.

The second subject (Ex. 4) sails in, a quiet angelic figure floating above a storm-wrack that now and again eclipses it. At last it vanishes; and the wailing transition theme (unquoted), that had originally appeared in the lower octave of the oboe, now enters, for the second and last time, in the full wind-band. The hopeful theme of Ex. 2 becomes a final cry of despair. At last nothing is left but the violins, with a lingering sigh from the first subject (a). On the prolonged last note of that figure (C sharp) a shining chord from an immensely distant key poises itself. This wonderful harmony moves calmly towards the tonic major; the violins wing their flight upwards with the rapid figure (d) from Ex. 2; and the great work ends in the light of dawn.

According to Wagner's own account, and according to the quotation which he puts at the head of his score, this magnificent movement with all its contrasts was intended to describe the soul of Faust at the culmination of his weariness of life. Gretchen was to be treated, as in Liszt's *Faust* Symphony, in some other and independent movement. But it is impossible to believe that Wagner really confined himself to this programme. The wish to deal with Gretchen separately may have been either cause or result of the conviction that the Elsa-like theme of Ex. 4[1] was not naïve enough for her; but it is very difficult to suppose that that theme has not more to do with *das ewig Weibliche* than it has to do with Faust's own soul. Of course, it is always possible to say that this and the unmistakable representation of the Witches' Sabbath are seen through the medium of Faust's soul. But still, the quotation which Wagner uses as his headline will never cover much more than the opening theme of the whole. Let the reader judge for himself.

Der Gott, der mir im Busen wohnt	The God that dwells within my breast
Kann tief mein Innerstes erregen;	
Der über allen meinen Kräften thront,	Can stir the inmost of my being, Holds all my power at his behest,

---

[1] Dannreuther refers it 'presumably' to some famous lines in which Faust describes the impulse to get into touch with Nature by walking in the woods and meadows. I think it is more respectful to Wagner to doubt his own merely verbal account of this far from simple music, than to suppose that even in his earliest efforts a deliberate intention to get into touch with Nature could result in anything so wide of that purpose.

Er kann nach aussen nichts be- wegen;	Yet nought without marks His decreeing;
Und so ist mir das Dasein eine Last,	And so my whole existence is awry,
Der Tod erwünscht, das Leben mir verhasst.	Life hateful, and my one desire to die.

This essay will have missed its mark if it leaves the reader with the impression that it discovers in Wagner's *Faust* Overture an odd mixture of styles. On the contrary, it aims at showing how an artist of Homeric genius can make a single style, peculiar to a single and perfect work, out of materials and habits which a little investigation shows to be such as a weaker artist could not reconcile with each other at all. Many a Homeric question, many a problem of Higher Criticism, has led to loud assertions about divided author-ship, or loud denials of the very existence of the reputed author, on far less evidence than will in a few centuries suffice to prove that Wagner's *Faust* Overture was compiled by a committee of university dons from fragments of the lost works of Bœthoven, Marschner, Weber, Meyerbeer, and Spontini.

PRELUDE TO ACT III OF 'TANNHÄUSER' (TANNHÄUSER'S PILGRIMAGE), IN THE ORIGINAL VERSION

By far the maturest part of *Tannhäuser*, indeed the only part of which the music reveals a true Wagnerian power, is the prelude to the third act and the narrative of Tannhäuser's pilgrimage. The prelude, as produced in a performance of the opera, is deeply impressive and fully adequate to its purpose; nor is there any reason why we should dispute Wagner's stage-craft in his reduc-tion of it to its final form in the opera. But a concert piece is a different matter, and we may be allowed to rejoice in the fact that its original form has been preserved. For the final version is the merest summary of the great symphonic adagio which Wagner originally wrote; and in the concert-room such a summary barely escapes producing a patchy effect. In one particular only does the original version seem less clear than the later; and that is in its treatment of the well-known peals of descending scales, which in the final version are much more prominent and seem more clearly to represent the surging up of forces, demonic or natural, and neither good nor evil except as they are mastered and directed. In all other points the original version (published by Novello & Co. in the present century) is far more complete both as a purely musical design and as a piece of musical illustration.

It begins (as in the final version) with one of the songs of the Pilgrims—

alternating with a theme belonging to the saintly Elizabeth, whose
pure love for Tannhäuser redeems him when she dies.

The groans of the penitent Tannhäuser are heard in the following figures—

and the burden of sin which he shares with his fellow-pilgrims is
alluded to by these well-known harmonies, which are the first
manifestation of the real Wagner in the overture—

The saving power of Divine Grace is proclaimed in this severe
scale theme—

and at this point the original version begins to differ from the final
epitome to which Wagner reduced it. A phrase, belonging to the
saintly Elizabeth, appears softly in high wind instruments. I will
quote it later when it takes more definite shape. The pilgrims'
chorus continues for one more phrase, as in the final version. Then,
in the final version, the uprush of demonic powers was typified by
four bars on the famous figure—

which is so prominent in the overture. Here, in the original
version, there is a much more voluminous uprush with no theme
at all. It takes nine bars to grow and die away, and then there is
a long development of St. Elizabeth's theme.

Ex. 6.

Its extreme simplicity is not quite that of the immense style of
Parsifal, but it contributes to a total impression of this prelude
which is decidedly nearer to that of Wagner's last work than even
the final version of this part of *Tannhäuser*.

Another uprush of demonic forces brings us to a solemn entry
of Ex. 6 in the full majesty of the brass. Here, after 36 bars, we
rejoin the final version. But, after the second outburst of the brass,
the final version continues with eight bars of demonic uprush on
the famous demisemiquaver figure, and then concludes with a
solitary allusion to Elizabeth in heaven and her prayer before the
throne—in fact, with the last twenty-three bars as they stand in
the original version. But this original version has another thirty-
five bars instead of those eight demisemiquaver bars; and the
design is unquestionably broader and clearer both as music and as
illustration. Its merits as illustration constitute, in fact, the very
reason for Wagner's abridgement: the penitent Tannhäuser's
confession, including the awful avowal of his sojourn in the
Venusberg—

Ex. 7.

and the Pope's horrified anathema, are so clearly represented that
they prepare the ground for Tannhäuser's *viva-voce* narrative only
too effectively, and Wagner realized that he could not afford so to
delay and forestall his action. But there is no doubt of the right-
ness of his original scheme as a piece of music; and the pathos of
the saint's dying prayers at the end is here, and here only, given its
full intended effect.

INTRODUCTION TO 'TRISTAN AND ISOLDE'

Of all excerpts from Wagner's later operas this suffers least from
adaptation to the concert-room; except indeed when it is welded
together with the arrangement of Isolde's Liebestod, which is in a
totally different group of keys and only destroys the impression of
the Vorspiel, which, in its turn, is not the most effective preparation

for the Liebestod, or, indeed, for anything but what it was meant for—the whole opera, beginning at the beginning.

But Wagner has furnished three most convincing pages of exquisite scoring and subtle rhythm to round off this Vorspiel in its own proper key; which makes it all the more surprising and regrettable that it is so seldom heard alone with this finish. The *Tristan* Vorspiel, viewed in its own chromatic and subtle light, is almost as continuous and single a process of unfolding the resources of harmony as is one of Bach's simplest arpeggio preludes. The tonic around which all the incessant modulation centres is A, at first minor, and then, in the middle and at the close (as added for concert performance), major. The scheme is simply the growing tension towards, and relaxation from, a climax of passion; and the passion is the love of Tristan and Isolde. All the themes are, in the opera, associated directly with that love, or with the fatal magic potion which caused it—except one figure heard in the bass and here marked (*e*), Ex. 4, which belongs to that dramatic motive of honour betrayed, whereby Tristan and Isolde were impelled by their tragic past to drink what they thought to be Death, but which proved to be the far more terrible Love that was to betray them again.

The principal figures, which arise one by one till they gradually combine and pervade the whole orchestra, are as follows. Most of them, it will be seen, are very closely allied.

Ex. 6.

The climax brings in the trumpets with (*b*) of Ex. 1. The sudden dying down of the music led originally to another key (C minor), on which the curtain rose to the song of a sailor in the shrouds of the ship that takes Isolde to Cornwall as a captive bride for the king. In the concert version this key is evaded, and the Vorspiel is most beautifully rounded off by a change to slow common time with the theme of Isolde's Liebestod in A major.

Ex. 7.

&c.

Among the many subtle beauties of this most successful of all Wagner's concessions to concert orchestras, the new tonic position given to figure (*b*) at the end is especially happy; it is, of course, transposed from the end of the Liebestod.

Ex. 8.

PRELUDE TO 'THE MASTER-SINGERS'

The prelude to *The Master-Singers* loses less than most excerpts from Wagner by performance in the concert-room. Its climax is not so perfectly balanced when it can lead only to a final chord as when it leads to the rise of the curtain and the lifting of our attention to a wider world of art; but it is a very complete and highly organized masterpiece of form and texture. Its famous combination of themes I quote—

Ex. 1.

The Song.

The Guild Banner.

The Master-Singers.

for the double purpose of saving space by putting three examples in one, and pointing out that its merit as counterpoint lies not in the combination of themes (which, unlike classical counterpoint, really do not of themselves combine into complete or euphonious harmony), but in the modest accessory parts (here printed in small notes) which so beautifully smooth away what would otherwise be grievous to Beckmesser.

The prelude opens with the Master-Singers' theme (contained in the bass of Ex. 1) pompously delivered by the full orchestra.

A gentle reflective note is struck by Ex. 2, the figures of which are associated with Walter's love-songs.

Ex. 2.

The dignity of the Master-Singers is resumed in a march, the theme of which will be found at doubled speed in the middle stave of Ex. 1. It leads to another broad cantabile of which an irreverent diminution occurs later on in the treble of Ex. 3. In that form I quote it to save space.

Ex. 3.

Surely she'll re-fuse him! Surely she'll re-fuse him!

In the maiden's place I would not choose him!

The whole exordium comes to a grand close, and is followed by
the substance of an eager conversation between Walter and Eva—

Ex. 4.

which leads, in lovely modulations, to E major. In this key the
Abgesang (or envoy) of Walter's prize-song (seen in the top stave
of Ex. 1) alternates with other love-themes from the song that the
Masters rejected, such as—

Ex. 5.

Excited modulations carry us to the opposite end of the tonal
range, E flat, in which key the Master-Singers' theme is irreverently
diminished by the apprentices, whose rude comments on Master
Beckmesser occupy the bass of Ex. 3. A climax is reached; C major
returns in all its glory, and with it the simultaneous combination
of more than half the themes in the opera, beginning as in Ex. 1,
and developing until, as if by sheer weight, the counterpoint
coalesces into the simple processional version of the middle stave
quoted, and so leads in triumph to the rise of the curtain.

'SIEGFRIED IDYLL'

This *Idyll* was written as a serenade for Frau Wagner after the birth
of Siegfried Wagner. (It is said that Frau Wagner very nearly
spoilt the surprise intended for her by becoming anxious about
young Hans Richter, Wagner's amanuensis, who lived in the house,
and who, she thought, was up to no good when he disappeared
every evening—to rehearse this piece.)

The connexion between the *Siegfried Idyll* and the great duet at
the close of the opera *Siegfried* is perhaps more likely to mislead
than to help to an understanding of this unique and purely instrumental work. In scope, in purpose, and above all in movement,
the two things are so entirely different that the allusions made by
the *Idyll* to the opera will not carry us much farther than Virgil's
Fourth Eclogue will carry us in New Testament criticism. Wagner
named his son Siegfried after the hero of his national tetralogy.
The melodies in which Brünnhilde the Valkyrie gave up the
memory of her immortality for the love of Siegfried who had
passed through the fire to awaken her—these themes are woven
with an old German cradle-song into a serenade for the mother of

an infant Siegfried; and what message they have for the public at large is not to be found in the words Brünnhilde sang.

The supreme things in life, the stuff of which tragedies and comedies are made, the *Hort der Welt* which is born wherever old cradle-songs are sung—all these things are within the grasp of great music and great art; but you must leave it to the music, or whatever art it is, to tell you about them; and then you must take the art on its own terms, without attempting to exalt them or debase them by comparison with any other terms. Try to explain the music by other things, and you will achieve nothing but an impertinent intrusion on private affairs, the whole poetic value of which consists in what is sacred because it is universal. Listen to the music as music, and you may have some chance of feeling as Wagner felt when he wrote it.

If one has luck in making one's first acquaintance with Wagner's later style after a familiar acquaintance with the classical types of movement in music, one's first impression will be, quite correctly, that the music is enormously slower and larger in every step it takes. Much of the opposition Wagner met with arose from the difficulty contemporaries had in seeing that his music moved at all. His earlier and most popular works were, in fact, poor and commonplace in composition where they were on old lines, and often vague and lame where they were revolutionary; and the presumption was that his later works, being altogether revolutionary, had no composition in them at all. Nowadays we all know better; and it is almost an arithmetical axiom to us that Wagnerian music moves no faster than the development of a drama, whereas earlier classics, whether instrumental or operatic, had an irresistible tendency to make completely finished and often highly dramatic designs within a space of ten minutes or, at the utmost, a quarter of an hour.

This being so, it may surprise us to find that Wagner's purely instrumental *Idyll* moves almost incomparably slower than the passages in the opera from which its main themes are taken. Eight times as slow is a very moderate estimate. If you know the *Idyll* before you know *Siegfried*, the passages in *Siegfried* will seem to you mere shreds and patches in comparison. The explanation lies in two directions. In the first place, the opera is so enormously larger than the *Idyll* that even a good-sized detached portion will be much more likely to fail to show any definite symmetry or drift; just as a square foot of a fresco may fail to show as much as a square inch of an easel picture. In the second place, in mastering the huge scale of composition he needs for his music-dramas, Wagner has acquired a permanent habit of thinking in that scale and is successful in applying it to 'absolute' music. In short, the

Siegfried Idyll succeeds where practically every 'Symphonic Poem', from those of Liszt onwards, fails. It is a piece of purely instrumental music, quite twice the size of any possible well-constructed movement of a classical symphony, and yet forming a perfectly coherent and self-explaining musical scheme. Its length, its manner of slowly building up broad melodies out of constantly repeated single phrases, and the extreme deliberation with which it displays them stage by stage in combination, are features of style that have nothing to do with diffuseness; they are as purely legitimate and natural terms of movement as the terms on which the earth goes round the sun—many times swifter than a cannon ball, yet it takes several minutes to pass its own length. Whatever difficulty has been felt with the *Siegfried Idyll* would be felt with a classical symphony if our scale of time were but slightly altered; and indeed all Beethoven's broadest passages were bitterly resented by those of his contemporaries who thought him worthy to be judged by Mozart's standards.

The *Siegfried Idyll*, then, is a gigantic though intensely quiet piece of purely instrumental music, connected with the opera only by a private undercurrent of poetic allusion. It begins with an introductory building-up of its first theme out of a single phrase. The theme itself is Brünnhilde's yielding to Siegfried: '*Ewig ward ich, ewig bin ich*'; but it does not move at all on the lines Brünnhilde laid for it. It goes its own way in ample leisure and peace, in combination with a figure (*b*) associated with Brünnhilde's sleep in her slumber, magic, fire-guarded chamber.

Ex. 1.

It gradually moves like a very indolent sonata movement towards a foreign key (the dominant), where a group of several new themes (not in the opera) constitute quite a rich 'second subject'—

Ex. 2.

ending deliberately with an old popular cradle-song—

Ex. 3.

which the listener cannot fail to identify when he hears it in its bare
simplicity on the oboe, with a tiny accompaniment in slow staccato
descending scales. This accompaniment is undoubtedly suggested
by the myth of the Little Sandman who strews sand into children's
eyes at bedtime to make them sleep.

Then the first theme returns, but is interrupted by mysterious
mutterings from the horns. The violins put on sordines and lisp the
close of the cradle-song; clouds come and go from a land of dreams,
a new and strange light appears, and in a distant key and changed
and quickened rhythm the wind instruments give the theme of
'Siegfried, Hope of the World'.

Ex. 4.

In a passage distinguished, even for Wagner, by its rainbow-
coloured orchestration, this theme is built up in countless short
steps which our memory sees in a long perspective. After some
time the first theme appears above it, as indicated in another position by the lower stave of Ex. 4, and at last a climax is reached; the
violins dash down in a torrent, and then, suddenly, a solitary horn is
heard over a long holding note, with an energetic new theme quietly
played, while a clarinet and a flute break in now and then with the
cries of birds—

Ex. 5.

A rustling theme in triplets is added—

Ex. 6.

These new themes belong to the triumphant finale of the duet in
Siegfried, but the opera text will not help us—nor do they give us
any musical difficulty that needs such help. With them the other
themes very soon combine, the first theme, and Brünnhilde's slumber, and 'Siegfried, Hope of the World,' until a trumpet is heard

rising in triumph to the songs of the *Waldvöglein*. This is not the nondescript birds that interrupted the new horn-theme, but the bird whose language Siegfried understood—the bird that guided him to the Valkyries' rock. The trumpet is silent, and the music subsides in a glowingly poetic recapitulation (with various enrichments of detail) of the material which we designated as 'second subject'. The horns croon the old cradle-song until the Hope of the World is safe in sleep.

THE VENUSBERG MUSIC ('TANNHÄUSER')

Wagner himself is responsible for the bad effect of welding his magnificent and mature Venusberg music on to his crude *Tannhäuser* Overture. His temptation was overwhelming, for he was at the height of his fame, and the occasion was his opportunity for generously allowing Paris to rehabilitate its reputation after the riot with which its Jockey Club had ruined the production of *Tannhäuser* years before. And perhaps he did not himself realize how effectively his own mature style ruins the rest of *Tannhäuser*. The only position for a single ballet in that drama is at the opening, before the action has begun: the work is already dangerously long and quite incapable of digesting two ballets; and to have dancers in the decorum of the Landgrave's Hall of Song would be absurdly incongruous with any restriction of their share in the orgies of the Venusberg. The result is that the Venusberg ballet has no dramatic significance at all. Neither, for that matter, has 70 per cent. of the ballet-music of Gluck; most of it has to be explained into the dramas by the choreographers.

The Paris bacchanale replaces a cruder affair that serves to set the scene and pose the actors in the original version of *Tannhäuser*. In the immense grottoes of the Hörselberg Tannhäuser is lying at the feet of Venus, who, knowing that his longing for a return to earthly daylight will soon transcend her power to retain him, is watching with some anxiety the growing frenzy of other denizens of her realm. Both in the perfunctory original ballet and in the mature Paris version, the frenzy of the dancers shocks the goddess's sense of decorum; and at her command a posse of her winged archers discharge narcotic arrows at the dancers, who subside into languorous slumbers.

The original *Tannhäuser* ballet followed the overture, and made an excellent contrast to its Moody-and-Sankey end. The Paris ballet was tacked on by Wagner himself to the overture just after the recapitulation of its crudest passage, Tannhäuser's song, with the result that three passages of Venusberg naughtiness in the overture forestall and destroy all appetite for the perfectly balanced scheme of the new ballet, which I myself am now hearing for the first time in its musical integrity. Its only discoverable defect as a detached piece is that, as printed, it begins nowhere; but either some authentic tradition or the inspiration of a conductor who understands composition has removed this defect by the addition of two bars of Ex. 1 in a manuscript slip inserted in the hired orchestral material.

Exx. 1 and 2 are common to the original and the Parisian ballet.

Ex. 3 is Parisian and is developed in Wagner's ripest style.

Exx. 4 and 5 are ripened from the original *Tannhäuser*, and show the goddess herself, here arising in annoyance at the riot and giving orders for it to be allayed.

Ex. 6 is a song of the sirens, which is the most thrilling feature both of the original and of the Parisian ballets.

Voices are needed to give it its full effect; but to bring these into the concert-room would commit us to the whole scene in which, while Wagner has rewritten his *Kulissen-Venus* into the divinest style of Isolde, he has left poor Tannhäuser's song in its original ragged bumptiousness.

Although the defects of Wagner's early style are sufficiently Meyerbeerish to account for his aversion to that master in particular, it would be fairer to compare them with the style of a more disappointed master, Spontini. The mixture of styles is distressing in any version of *Tannhäuser* as a whole. Might we be forgiven for claiming that the original unadulterated opera has at all events the virtue of 'Spontineity'?

According to the Paris ballet, in the magnificent slow movement that follows upon Venus's orders the song of the sirens introduces two tableaux, representing two of Jupiter's adventures: as the bull that carries off Europa, and as the swan with Leda. Both as music and as drama, these matters are neither here nor there; though the text informs us that both were classical examples of the power of love. What concerns the listener is the exquisite development of another new theme in Wagner's ripest style, 'conflated' with Ex. 3—

which brings the movement to its musically appointed close. The last appearance of Ex. 1 indicates, as in the original ballet, how the troop of archers bow to Venus, signifying that they have succeeded in quelling the riot. The faint suggestion of church bells that haunts Tannhäuser's dreams of earthlight is accompanied by Wagner's new theme (Ex. 7) as the music dies away in its appointed time.

WEBER

OVERTURE, 'THE RULER OF THE SPIRITS'

Rübezahl is an early unfinished opera which Weber began in 1808. The fairy tale on which the libretto is based was never a very promising subject for an opera, and ought in any case to have produced nothing more powerful than a Christmas pantomime. In the deplorable absence of any standard edition of Weber's works it is impossible to give a first-hand account of what exists of the opera, though there is little doubt that, as in the later operas, Weber must have intended almost every bar of his overture to have some reference to the music of the drama. The extant fragments of the opera are said to be immature and not very characteristic of Weber. In 1811 the opportunity of a concert in Munich inspired him to remodel the overture with such success that he declared it to be the most powerful piece of work he had yet done. In this form it remains one of his finest compositions; and it is incomparably greater in conception than any possible musical illustration of the story of the poor wizard whose captive princess cheated him into counting the turnips in his garden while she escaped with the aid of a friendly griffin. So we may profitably refrain from all further speculation about the meaning of this piece as programme music. It would be very difficult to guess that this work had not been composed some fourteen or fifteen years later, when Weber was at the height of his power. Although it is comparatively neglected, it is as effective as any concert overture in existence. It is certainly of some consequence in the history of music, for Wagner did not entirely escape its influence in his overture to *The Flying Dutchman*. It has a great wealth of themes, always, as in all Weber's instrumental music, put side by side in sharp contrast, with transitions executed by a *coup de théâtre*. The number of different themes is surprising, and it may save words boldly to quote six of them.

Exx. 5 and 6 represent the second subject; and it will be seen how the calm cantabile of Ex. 6 is ominously disturbed by the 'cello with its agitated interpolation of Exx. 4 and 1. The return of Ex. 5 in the tonic major on the brass instruments is one of the most successful pieces of pioneer work in the history of orchestration. It would be impossible to guess by the sound of it that this glorious mass of soft harmony for brass instruments was written with the imperfect resources available in the year in which Beethoven was writing the *Ruins of Athens*.

OVERTURE, 'DER FREISCHÜTZ'

The overture to the most famous of Weber's operas is especially remarkable for the completeness with which it sums up all that music can tell of the story to be enacted. Weber, as usual, wrote it after the opera was finished. At the first performance it aroused such a storm of applause that the opera could not proceed until the overture was repeated. Yet the rest of the opera proved still more convincing, and revealed the real poetic power of the overture. The opera has had its ups and downs in respect of fashion; and we shall never quite recover that part of its romantic thrill that depends on genuine vestiges of superstitious horror, such as Weber's contemporaries felt. But we have by this time also got over the period of contemptuous reaction from such sentiments of horror; and we can therefore appreciate the art with which Weber treats the whole apparatus of his libretto. Edinburgh audiences, moreover, are in the fortunate position of having recent memories of a local revival of the work. It is interesting also to note that it has aroused a refreshing enthusiasm in Berlin, contrary to the fears of critics who prophesied that no *blasé* modern audience could listen to it without hostile merriment. But the truth is that, as Dr. M. R. James has proved, the old-fashioned ghost-story, without any psychological jargon or up-to-dateness, is the most thrilling kind of all. It is the old traditional kinds of spook that are really gruesome; and Weber and his librettist knew the old traditions too well to make any mistake about them.

Max (or, for purposes of English singing, Rodolph), once the finest marksman in the forest, has mysteriously lost his skill, and is in despair. Caspar, his treacherous friend, tells him that on the night of a total eclipse of the moon it is possible to cast seven 'free-bullets' in that accursed spot, the Wolf's Glen. These bullets never miss their mark. What Caspar does not say is that the seventh bullet is guided by the fiend-huntsman Samiel, and that Caspar is gaining respite for himself by delivering Max into Samiel's hands. Samiel will direct the seventh bullet to the heart of Max's bride, Agathe; and Max's despair will deliver his soul to Samiel. But Agathe is under the protection of a saintly hermit who stands by her at the fatal moment. The seventh bullet, baulked of its mark, claims Caspar, who dies with a curse. Max confesses his guilt, and is promised pardon when he shall have redeemed himself in a year of probation.

The overture begins with a sound-picture of the depths of a forest. A lyric melody for four horns drifts in slow regularity, and dies away into a dark chord—

Ex. 1.

which indicates the fiend Samiel. The despair of Max (*Doch mich umgarnen finstre Mächte*) underlies the main theme of the allegro—

Ex. 2.

and the first tutti foreshadows the storm that closes the scene in the Wolf's Glen.

Ex. 3.

Ex. 4.

A summons from the horns and a passionate slow melody on a clarinet tell, in one of the most famous passages in romantic opera, how Max first looks down into the awful depth of the Wolf's Glen by the light of the full moon, as yet uneclipsed. Then we hear the main theme of Agathe—

Ex. 5.

In the development, which is, for Weber, very fine and concentrated, Ex. 4 is worked up in an excellent imbroglio. Agathe's theme penetrates the gloom and is mocked by a horrid echo from low trombones. This should be gruesome, and not, as Mr. Cecil Forsyth calls it, a 'circus effect'.

At last, after the darkest hour, virtue triumphs and the overture ends brilliantly.

OVERTURE TO 'EURYANTHE'

Weber was consumptive from his birth: he had no time to lose, and no desire to waste it. Throughout his thirty-nine years of life, his time was lost for him by fools and humbugs. His master, Abt Vogler, to whom he always remained loyal, was one of the most devastating of musical humbugs. He has been described for all time, not by Browning's poem (to which Browning gave the wrong name on purpose), but by that great classical scholar, Otto Jahn, who in his life of Mozart characterizes Vogler as one of those musical philosophers who disguise their lack of solid musical schooling in a vast ostentation of general culture. Vogler's other great pupil was Meyerbeer. It is a pity the two pupils did not exchange their physical constitutions.[1]

Euryanthe is both a more mature work of art and a more advanced development of Wagnerian music-drama than *Lohengrin*, though it is a generation earlier. No one who knows *Euryanthe* thoroughly will consider this an extravagant statement. There are fully a dozen well-developed leitmotivs waiting for the Wagnerian label-sticker; and the division into set numbers (arias, quartets, &c.) is an illusory survival which could just as easily be foisted upon *Lohengrin*, or even upon *Meistersinger*. While there is nothing quite so sublime in *Euryanthe* as the Prelude and the Grail-themes of *Lohengrin*, Weber remains throughout *Euryanthe* on a level from which he is both morally and technically incapable of sinking as

---

[1] I have been reproached for the 'savagery' of this wish. It does not seem savage to Weber; and Meyerbeer can afford to put up with it ever since the gentle Rossini said to the composer of a funeral march for that master, 'Would it not have been better if you had died and Meyerbeer had written your funeral march?'

Wagner often sinks in *Lohengrin*. The whole work is of such a quality that a single glance at an unknown fragment of it would convince you that here is the style of a great man; and there is no form of dramatic music—not even the finale, where *Freischütz* itself shows weakness—which is not here handled with freedom and power.

Why then is this tremendous work so seldom heard? Has Lohengrin, in pique at Elsa's want of faith, meanly revenged himself by stealing Euryanthe's birthright? Ask poor Weber what he thought of Frau von Chezy after he had got 'das Chez' to remodel her libretto for the ninth time. Ask him how he came to call his beautiful and virtuous heroine Ennuyante.

He was not the only composer whom 'das Chez' took in. Schubert was another victim. But his *Rosamunde* was only incidental music to a play; and the play being lost, we do not know what it was about, except that she was Queen of Cyprus. It is, however, pretty clear to a musician where the poetasteress's power lay. She had fluent and typical words and images for all moods, and a good sense of contrast. These assets might readily induce a composer to commit himself long before he had time to grumble that her style consisted mainly of indications of the places where style ought to be. This does not often worry a composer whose own style is enough for him. The trouble comes when a great composer like Weber discovers too late that he is devoting the magnificent common sense of his highest structural power to a drama in which the emotions and contrasts, admirably adapted for music in themselves, are associated with events as crazy as the logic of dreams. The beautiful and virtuous Euryanthe is made to appear faithless to her Adolar by means of the treachery of her confidante Eglantine and the villain Lysiart. It is not injured innocence, nor any lofty scruple, nor tragic ignorance, that prevents her from saying the very first thing a rational being would naturally say when first put into her position; it is simply that if she said it the whole story would collapse, and all poor old Chez's verses and all her puppets could not put it together again. For three whole acts all the situations are topsy-turvy: there are no other Gilbertian qualities. Among the most troublesome features of the whole affair are the ghosts of Emma and Udo, who never appear, but who, like the sociable and explanatory ghost in Andrew Lang's *Castle Perilous*, have to bring about the family prophecies, whether the public can follow the rigmarole or not. Well, anyhow, long ago they committed suicide; and Euryanthe, who had to live in a garden adjoining Adolar's family vault, told the dread secret to Eglantine, who told Lysiart, who told Adolar, who saw at once that this proved that Lysiart had won his wager against Euryanthe's truth. Weber did his best for these poor ghosts, and very shrewdly drew public attention to them by bringing the music of their story into the overture, and demanding that the curtain should be raised for a few moments at that point to show Adolar's family tomb.

Such then is the stuff to which Weber devoted the greatest of all his works. In 1922 a distinguished dramatist, Rolf Lauckner, who had the year before collaborated with me and Fritz Busch in the restoration of two Schubert operas, undertook a thorough re-writing of the libretto. Previous attempts have failed through lack of appreciation of Weber's sense of form. It is no use improving the play on lines which imply that Weber's huge musical design matters less than Wagner's. Lauckner's new text alters not a single mood or contrast in the story, and by a constant process of translation from the jargon of 'das Chez' into the language of poetry, achieves a straightforward and impressive drama which perfectly follows and supports Weber's music. In the whole opera no musical addition is required beyond about forty bars, distributed in three separate scenes, the longest interpolation being in one of the recitatives, and the others being in places where the music was patchy as Weber left it. The patchiness was mainly due to the nonsensical dramatic situations, and it vanishes with their removal.

Only one whole number, and two passages (both of them weak) are sacrificed, and only one number transplanted. The rest, or rather the central principle of Lauckner's drama-therapy, consists in his radical reform of the stage-management, so that the eye can understand the situation before a word has been sung. I own that, with all my admiration for the music of Weber's *Euryanthe*, I was astonished at the effect the new text has upon the many tragic and complex passages which suffered from their absurd original background. Correct theories had not sufficed to show that tragic music can be beautiful while the situation on the stage offends the spectator's common sense. It is not necessary that opera should be great literature. It may be as nonsensical as Mozart's *Magic Flute*. But such pantomimes have in a high degree the common sense of stagecraft; and few authors of nonsense can attain the disciplined aesthetic coherence of Edward Lear or Lewis Carroll. The subject and style of *Euryanthe* admits of no nonsense; and it came as a revelation to me to find that Weber's tragic music was worthiest of Beethoven or Wagner just in those passages where the original libretto was incredible. With a truthful text the music reveals its truth. I hope it may not be long before Weber's greatest work is universally recognized in this new light.

The overture begins with one of Weber's brilliant tonic-and-dominant formulas, and then proceeds with Adolar's act of faith.

Ex. 1.

I trust in God and Eu - ry - an - the's love

The whole first subject is in the highest spirits of a brilliant and triumphant court in the age of chivalry. At length the second subject is heralded by a peal of drums and an amorous phrase from the violoncellos. Thereupon enters another of Adolar's themes—his joy at the prospect of meeting Euryanthe.

Ex. 2.

O hap - pi - ness be - yond be - lief

After more passages of heraldic pomp the exposition comes to a climax with a new theme.

Ex. 3.

The development is preceded by the music of the ghosts in an extremely remote key.

Ex. 4.
Largo.

Then the lively tempo, somewhat subdued, is resumed with an excellent contrapuntal development of Ex. 3, inverted as follows—

Ex. 5.

With admirable clearness this works out its course and leads to a recapitulation, in which the second subject (Ex. 2) is triumphant throughout. And so to the brilliant end.

OVERTURE TO 'OBERON'

The history of music in England is full of disasters, being mainly the history of an art that in one phase after another becomes fashionable without achieving much progress towards being understood. Fashion is always delighted with mystery, and suspects common sense of being ill-bred. We are eminently a literary nation, and fashion has found the common sense of our literature too strong for it to outvote; but British men of letters have sometimes been unmusical, and have pardonably judged of music by the fools fashion makes of musicians, whether in its choice or its treatment of them. The fate of English opera during the greatest periods of classical music is a melancholy example. The trouble began when Dryden, utterly disgusted with the type of mind represented by a certain Monsieur Grabu, whose music was the fashion, carefully arranged his 'opera' *King Arthur* so that Mr. Purcell's music should have no connexion with the action or even the characters of the play. Our first and greatest man of genius in dramatic music was therefore condemned to inaugurate a tradition whereby English opera consisted of music that merely added a series of lyric and spectacular digressions to a play which, if good at all, would be better without the digressions. Planché's libretto of *Oberon* represents an advance on this, inasmuch as the play would not be better without the digressions. It could not by any process become worse, except in its taste and moral tone, which are unimpeachably refined. Planché explained to Weber his excellent reasons for conciliating English operatic tastes, and exclaimed after the first performance, 'Next time we will show them what we really can do'. He should not have wasted a whole work in preliminaries. There was no 'next time'.

The librettist has earned a quite respectful mention from literary critics, who are probably surprised (in spite of the example of Metastasio) to find that a man who writes for music can write at all; and no doubt Planché has done better poems or plays than *Oberon*. At present it is only relevant to say that this libretto has murdered the third and last mature opera of Weber, who devoted his dying energies to learning the English language in order to set it. Again and again he implored Planché to send him the whole text, or at all events to give some explanation of the position in the plot of the single pieces, instead of sending mere unexplained airs for the 'tenor' or 'soprano', or ensemble pieces. It was bad enough to have to work thus in the dark; but Weber eventually discovered something worse. He discovered that it did not matter. So he poured his last and finest music into this pig-trough, and shared the applause with the magnificent scenery. Then a Grand Benefit Concert was arranged for a date which the organizers had not noticed to be the Derby day or some such solemnity. Much sympathy was expressed for Weber when on this occasion the public had to be elsewhere. His illness was becoming alarming, and though his leave of absence was at an end, there was no doubt that he was quite unfit for the return voyage. Some friends called on him the morning before his projected departure, hoping to persuade him to postpone it. They found that he had died in the night. He was thirty-nine years old.

Early English editions of *Oberon* are well provided with accounts of the deep feeling which this pathetic event aroused throughout the country, and with the beautiful poems that appeared in the papers. We evidently enjoyed ourselves over this chapter of our musical history.

Like most classical opera-writers, Weber generally wrote the overture after he had finished the opera. He was thus, even in the case of *Oberon*, able to make the most of the opportunity for defining the moods and foreshadowing the incidents of the drama. In his greatest work, *Euryanthe*, where the libretto was helplessly dependent on an ancestral ghost who never even appears on the scene, Weber actually contrived to make the story clear and effective by raising the curtain to show a tableau in the middle of the overture. And he had developed the system of leitmotivs fully as far as the point attained by Wagner some twenty years after in *Lohengrin*.

The overture to *Oberon* is, accordingly, full of allusions to the opera. But these allusions are peculiar, because the libretto is not even a bad drama (like *Euryanthe*), but the merest twaddle for regulating the operations of scene-shifters. Weber's fairy-music has been compared with that of Mendelssohn's music to *A Midsummer-Night's Dream*, to Weber's disadvantage. What is the use of comparing Planché's fairies to Shakespeare's? Planché's Oberon has taken a 'fatal vow' to hold aloof from Titania until he has found a perfectly faithful pair of human lovers. Everybody knows that he only wants an excuse for waving his wand in order to waft Sir Huon the Bold from Bordeaux to Bagdad in the twinkling of a scene-shift, and, when Braham the Tenor (I mean, Sir Huon the Bold) has rescued Rezia the Fair from the unspeakable Turk, to waft them on to a desert island, bring a pirate-ship to rescue them, get them sold separately into slavery, and by these and the like tomfooleries keep them deprived of all human motives and opportunities for three hours, or until the resources of the scene-shifters are exhausted. This done, he applauds their constancy, and tells them that, thanks to them, he now rejoins his Fairy Queen.

In all this pantomime Weber found three good ideas, which he promptly turned into traits of genius. I see no evidence that Planché himself appreciated the importance of these ideas. He must have expected that Oberon's magic horn would come in prettily; and no doubt he set great store by the opportunity he gave Weber for 'Turkish music' as that inspiring Oriental study was conceived in 1826. It meant simply the use of the big drum, cymbals, and triangle all together in the rhythm of the left hand of the major theme in Mozart's *Rondo alla Turca*. The Turkish music Weber exploited (not for the first time in his life) very cleverly in its place in the opera; but he did not build anything important on it. Oberon's horn was different: it was capable of real poetic power. It can summon Oberon from the ends of the earth, or herald his approach therefrom. When it sounds, we see and hear as if space were annihilated; and everything becomes exquisitely clear and tiny, because its immense remoteness is that of our own inmost soul. Thus, at the end of the opera there is a grand triumphal march at the court of Charlemagne. It is this, and not 'the horns of Elfland faintly blowing', that we hear in *il tutto pianissimo possibile* after Oberon's horn has twice sounded at the beginning of the overture. Through the ignoring of this point, the passage has often been deprived of all its romance by being taken as fairy music instead of very mortal music brought under a fairy spell. Then Weber sounds, in the violoncellos, the note of human love awakening. This, the revelation to Sir Huon the Bold of something better in life than boldness, is the second of the three valuable ideas which Weber extracted from his libretto. The third idea is one which even in its crudest manifestations is a sure mark of greatness in the artist who ventures to use it. It is the conviction that 'the light of common day' is not a thing to be blasphemed. The visions evoked by Oberon's horn vanish with a bang; and all is bustle and pageantry, which the aristocratic composer, thoroughly at home in court-circles, is poet enough to laugh at, but far too well-bred to waste energy in discountenancing.

Again Oberon's horn sounds, and then the clarinet tells how 'A gentle ray, a milder beam Broke sweetly on life's broader stream.' Text-books on instrumentation quote this famous passage either without comment as a piece of orthodox scoring, or with the criticism that a beautiful melody is wasted on a dull region of the clarinet. Both views are misleading. The critical view has the advantage of pointing towards the truth, that whatever Oberon's horn summons comes from the ends of the earth and the depths of the soul. The pianissimo of an immense distance is what should be aimed at here.

The fairy-like and brilliant theme which follows has again no direct connexion with fairies. It is a distant vision of Rezia the Fair on a desert island when she sees the sail of the approaching ship and hails it with her scarf. These then are the principal threads which Weber weaves rapidly and loosely into a gorgeous masterpiece of operatic orchestration. It is more than that. Though the distant visions are, throughout the latter half of the overture, gathered up into a climax of most unfairylike and unsentimental brilliance, yet the last word must be, as I remember Joachim said to me after a performance of the *Oberon* overture at a country musical festival, 'Not a learned composer, but what a poet!'